The
Hunter's
Field Guide

The
Hunter's
Field Guide

to the
Game Birds and Animals
of North America
by
Robert Elman
Wildlife drawings by Ned Smith

A Ridge Press Book

Alfred A. Knopf,
New York, 1974

Editor-in-Chief: Jerry Mason
Editor: Adolph Suehsdorf
Art Director: Albert Squillace
Project Art Director: Harry Brocke
Managing Editor: Moira Duggan
Associate Editor: Barbara Hoffbeck
Associate Editor: Jean Walker
Art Associate: Mark Liebergall
Art Associate: David Namias
Art Production: Doris Mullane

Published in the United States of America
by Alfred A. Knopf, Inc., New York, and
simultaneously in Canada by
Random House of Canada Limited, Toronto.
Prepared and produced by The Ridge Press, Inc.
Distributed by Random House, Inc., New York.
ISBN: 0-394-47887-8
Library of Congress Catalog Card Number: 73-7289
Printed in Italy by Mondadori Editore, Verona.

To Loris

Picture Credits

All wildlife drawings are by Ned Smith.
Boone and Crockett Club score charts and instructions
reprinted by courtesy of the Boone and Crockett Club.
Maps of the North American flyways reprinted
by courtesy of the U.S. Fish & Wildlife Service.

Jacket photographs: Erwin A. Bauer (whitetail deer),
Bill Browning (elk hunter), Hanson Carroll (hunter with dog),
Harry Engels (sheep, bull moose), Walter D. Osborne (geese),
Leonard Lee Rue III (ring-necked pheasant),
Joe Van Wormer (bobcat).

KEY: Where several pictures appear on a page or double page,
credits read from left to right, beginning at the top of the page(s).
Initials refer to the following photographers:

BB   Bill Browning   HE   Harry Engels
EAB   Erwin A. Bauer   JVW   Joe Van Wormer
HC   Hanson Carroll   LLR   Leonard Lee Rue III
                            WO   Walter D. Osborne

Upland Birds
14: EAB. 17: LLR. 20: (all) LLR. 23: LLR
25: LLR, HE. 29: R. J. Robel, Kansas State
University, HE. 30: Nebraska Game Com
mission. 31: LLR. 32: BB. 33: Tim Britt.
38: (both) David Costello. 42: Tim Britt.
44: BB. 45: BB. 49: LLR. 50: LLR. 53:
BB. 58: LLR. 60: LLR. 61: David Costello
65: LLR, BB, David Dale Dickey. 66: Tim
Britt, HE. 67: BB, HE. 68: LLR, EAB, EAB,
BB, BB. 69: LLR, LLR, LLR, HE, JVW.
70 71: David Dale Dickey, Thase Daniel,
LLR, BB. 72: Byron W. Dalrymple, EAB,
FAB, HC. 74: Doug Wilson. 75: (both)
JVW. 76: Thase Daniel. 77: John Wootters.
79: LLR. 80: Jerry L. Hout, BB. 82: Jerry
L. Hout. 85: Buddy Mays. 86: Frederick
C. Baldwin. 87: Frederick C. Baldwin. 93:
Doug Wilson, Arizona Fish & Game Dept.
94: (all) BB. 96: JVW. 101: Arizona Fish
& Game Dept. 104 105: Tim Britt. 113:

LLR. 119: (both) LLR. 120 121: LLR

Ducks
124: EAB. 138 139: JVW. 142: HC. 146:
WO. 148: David Dale Dickey. 149: LLR.
152: JVW. 153: JVW. 155: C. H. Dickey.
157: WO. 159: WO. LLR. 161: JVW. 162:
WO. 165: WO. 166: HC. 168: State of Utah
Division of Wildlife Resources. 169: WO,
WO, David Dale Dickey, WO. 170 171:
Kaiser Products, EAB, Tony Florio, Rus
sell Tinsley, WO. 172: JVW, HE. 173: HC,
WO, BB, JVW. 174: Tony Florio, WO, WO,
C. H. Dickey, EAB, EAB. 176: HC, Tony
Florio. 179: LLR. 180: WO. 183: EAB. 185:
HC. 187: WO. 189: WO. 190: HC. 193:
WO. 196-197: WO. 200: LLR. 203: JVW.
206: LLR. 210: Stephen Collins. 212: HC.
213: WO. 215: EAB. 217: Jen & Des Bart
lett/Bruce Coleman Inc. 219: HC. 222
EAB. 225: HC. 227: Tony Florio. 229:

Harry N. Darrow/Bruce Coleman Inc. 231: D. Zingel/Bruce Coleman Inc. 233: (both) Jen & Des Bartlett/Bruce Coleman Inc. 234: HC. 237: Tony Florio. 240: Jen & Des Bartlett/Bruce Coleman Inc. 241: Thase Daniel, WO, Paul D. McLain, Jerry L. Hout. 242-243: Russell Tinsley, HC, Robert Elman, BB. 244: EAB, EAB, WO, WO. 245: Jerry L. Hout, BB, EAB, Jerry L. Hout. 246-247: BB, EAB, WO, JVW. 248: WO, BB. 252: Tom Schoener/Bruce Coleman Inc.

Geese

255: JVW. 259: JVW. 262-263: WO. 267: Jerry L. Hout. 272-273: WO. 275: LLR. 276: LLR. 277: David Dale Dickey. 279: WO, JVW. 282: EAB. 283: BB. 285: JVW. 289: JVW. 290: (both) JVW. 293: JVW. 297: C.H. Dickey.

Swans

300: Tim Britt. 302: Tim Britt, HE. 304-305: JVW. 306: LLR.

Shore & Marsh Birds

308: JVW. 311: Byron W. Dalrymple. 313: Byron W. Dalrymple. 315: LLR. 318: Thase Daniel. 325: Jeff Foott/Bruce Coleman Inc., Paul D. McLain. 327: Thase Daniel. 330: JVW.

Small Game

332: JVW. 337: Jack Dermid/N. Carolina Wildlife Resources Commission. 338-339: JVW. 342: LLR. 345: Leonard Lee Rue IV. 346: Russell Tinsley. 349: JVW. 353: LLR. 354: LLR. 361: LLR. 362: LLR. 364: LLR. 367: LLR. 370: Russell Tinsley. 373: LLR, LLR, Tennessee Fish & Game Commission. 374: LLR. 375: LLR. 376-377: LLR. 378: LLR. 380: David Costello. 384: (both) LLR.

386: LLR. 390: LLR. 391: LLR. 394: David Costello. 397: (both) LLR. 398: LLR. 401: LLR. 402: LLR. 405: LLR. 409: EAB, LLR. 410: Thase Daniel, Jeff Foott. 411: Thase Daniel, JVW, A.J. Dignan/Bruce Coleman Inc. 412: JVW, WO. 413: (both) JVW. 414: JVW, HE, Mason Williams, Mason Williams. 415: HE, EAB. 416: LLR, HC, HC, LLR. 417: LLR. 418: Camera Association. 419: EAB. 420: LLR. 423: HE. 429: LLR. 430: (both) LLR. 434-435: JVW. 436: Russell Tinsley. 441: Robert Elman. 446-447: LLR. 449: LLR. 450: LLR. 453: LLR. 455: L.J. Prater/U.S. Forest Service. 457: LLR.

Deer

460: EAB. 462: LLR. 464: (all) LLR. 468: LLR. 472: EAB. 481: EAB, Russell Tinsley. 482-483: Paul D. McLain, HE, BB, Russell Tinsley, LLR. 484: Byron W. Dalrymple, BB. 485: (both) EAB. 486: EAB, BB, BB. 487: (both) BB. 488: LLR, HE. 491: JVW. 493: JVW. 494: LLR. 496: LLR.

Medium Game

500: HE. 502: JVW. 506: LLR. 507: Montana Chamber of Commerce. 512: BB. 515: LLR. 516: LLR. 517: Charles F. Waterman. 522: HE. 531: LLR. 533: JVW. 541, 547, 549: EAB. 552: Don Wilson.

Big Game

556: LLR. 562: JVW. 572: EAB. 574: LLR. 578: (all) LLR. 585: Stephen Collins, Bob Hagel. 586: EAB, BB. 587: Frederick C. Baldwin. 588: BB, LLR. 589: LLR, HC. 590-591: BB, BB, Bob Hagel, BB. 592: LLR, BB. 593: Frederick C. Baldwin. 595: LLR. 600: Sid Latham. 604-605: LLR. 610-611: Frederick C. Baldwin. 617: HC. 620: HC. 632-633: LLR. 641: JVW. 644: LLR.

Contents

Introduction

Now and then—certainly not often—I have hunted with men whose chief wish was no more than to bring home a trophy to boast about, men whose motivation was greed or an insecure search for a kind of machismo. Such hunters are seldom very skillful, seldom very successful.

Most men hunt for far better reasons. They, too, are motivated by an insatiable drive, but it is a drive to learn all they can about the game and its habitat. What they want is to know the birds and animals so well that they begin to understand a world once natural to man, now increasingly alien. They want, that is, to go home again. They want to renew the primal bond with the wilderness and its inhabitants. And they become better hunters as the kinship is strengthened. Success in the form of a full bag or a fine trophy remains important. It has to, because hunting is not usually so easy as might be imagined by the uninitiated. More important, though, is an appreciation, an understanding and love, of the wild world. Success comes with that. My hope is that this book will add substantially to the knowledge of hunters regarding game, its behavior, and the marvelously diverse ecosystems in which that game can be found by anyone who comprehends the often silent language of the wilds.

Within these covers I've tried to record the general way of life and a great many details regarding every North American game species; the information herein can help to guide a hunter in his pursuit of any game on this continent. If I've done my work well, it will also help to make any conscientious sportsman a participant, rather than a spectator, in the wild world. As the public awakens (however belatedly) to the need for conservation and to the joys found only in nature, more and more of us are striving to advance from the status of casual hunter, sometimes lucky, to that of hunter-naturalist.

There was a time when I cherished a quixotic ambition to hunt every species of North American game. At first the desire was grounded in a natural curiosity about the lives and ways of animals, and the manner of hunting them. Later it began to involve ego. But perhaps every hunter who can truly claim to love the game he pursues comes to a point at which he realizes he has hunted poorly for many birds and mammals, passably for some, well for a few. His ambition mellows into a desire to hunt well—still for as many species as possible, still in quest of diversity and experience in the wilderness, but first to hunt well. I've seen the habitats of all the American species, explored most of their ecosystems, and successfully hunted many, but not all. It feels good to look forward to new acquaintances in the wilds. When an outdoorsman has done with any need to prove himself to himself, has grown comfortable with his limitations as well as abilities, he does not stop learning—no one who loves the natural world stops learning from it—but he is happiest returning again and again to favorite haunts, favorite game, while grasping every opportunity to become familiar with new species and their habitats.

Perhaps a few readers will wonder how far they can trust a writer who has not had extensive personal experience with every single species he describes. Yet I do not know of an even moderately comprehensive field guide whose author could claim such experience. Most rely to some extent on the work of collaborators, contributors, field workers, or earlier writers. I, too, have made use of writings by experts in the ways of certain species. Some of these men put away their big-game rifles, upland doubles, or duck guns for the last time before this book was written, and I've tried very hard to serve their memories well in my use of their works. For all the geese and grouse and bobwhites I've bagged, I cannot write of them without acknowledging the guidance of such authors as Nash Buckingham,

Havilah Babcock, Ray Holland, William Harnden Foster, and my friend Larry Koller. I have appropriated the knowledge not only of fellow hunters, but of professional ecologists and game biologists. For example, though I've tracked wolves I've never killed one, never dwelt long in their environs, never observed them closely for extended periods. I'm indebted to Adolph Murie's unsurpassed pioneering studies of Alaskan wolves and David Mech's superb recent monograph on the ecology of timber wolves in northern Minnesota. I've never shot a glacier bear—*very* few men have—but I've listened attentively to Warren Page's meticulous account of his hunts for this strange northwestern color phase of the black bear. And I've carefully read the notes of a most successful guide in the coastal locale where the glacier bear is known familiarly as the blue bear.

There is no way to mention, much less to repay my indebtedness to, all the hunting guides, hunting partners, writers, and other colleagues of whom some have been my constant mentors in the hunting life and all of whom have contributed to this book. I would, however, like to mention a few who have helped me solve problems or resolve questions and controversies: James Carroll of the U.S. Fish and Wildlife Service; Anthony J. Florio of the Patuxent Wildlife Research Center; Dr. R. J. Robel of the Biology Division of Kansas State University; John Madson of the Olin Conservation Department in East Alton, Illinois; Dr. Dean Amadon, chairman of the Department of Ornithology at the American Museum of Natural History; Richard F. Dietz and the team of game-management experts at Remington Farms, near Chestertown, Maryland; Laurence R. Jahn of the Wildlife Management Institute; the noted wildlife artist Ned Smith, who contributed the drawings for this book; and my frequent hunting partner, the wildlife photographer Leonard Lee Rue III. He and I have tramped many miles over fields and along the wooded fringes of the Delaware, through friendly green but implacable briers, drab but life-giving lespedeza, green-black cedars, buck-rubbed saplings, the alder runs of the woodcock, the deer-browsed red-maple sprouts, the hemlock edge where a grouse always went up if no one was ready.

On other occasions, alone in the field or with friends, I observed the ways of the species—of the wise and foolish, yet graceful and clumsy mountain goat in British Columbia, of the self-assured, yet cautious bighorn king of Rocky Mountain alpinists—in a much more immediate way than I ever could by the sole guidance of biological tomes or armchair adventure. I hope I can convey to other hunters the delight I've taken in doing my field work, as well as in reading of that done by others.

Most of America's eminent natural historians and conservationists—men like Aldo Leopold and Paul Errington—have been hunters. For the hunter to succeed in his pursuit he must recant the absurd modern belief in conquering nature and begin instead to be guided by it. The hunter has a special incentive to investigate its mysteries—which are, after all, governed by a wild, indomitable logic and are more beautiful as they become less mysterious.

In writing from my own hunting experiences (though all the facts have been scientifically verified), I have included a few passages that may strike readers in some nontypical regions as quirky or surprising. Most kinds of game can be hunted in several effective ways. What is best in one reader's locale, dominated by one peculiar type of habitat or ruled by local seasonal restrictions, may not be the best in the majority of areas, and I've addressed myself to the majority. I have not listed every variation on every hunting method, nor have I dwelt on regional traditions or practices except for those of importance to the hunter—such as rattling for bucks in the Southwest or the refinements of calling moose in the Canadian Northeast. I think, exceptions notwithstanding, that a hunter in any region can follow this book's recommendations with confidence.

I hope, too, that hunters will find much more here than instruction on how to identify wildfowl on the wing or where to look for cottontails or bull elk on a sunny morning. The kill, in fact, is sometimes passed up for one reason or another without in the least spoiling the hunt. What the true hunter wishes to conquer—to kill—is his ignorance of the ways and the world of game. He yearns to know the hare as intimately as the bobcat knows it, and he yearns to know the bobcat equally well. The track, the browsed leaf, the game bed may tell a woodsman not only what the game has been doing and where it is likely to be, but also how it lives. Each revelation strengthens his bond with wildlife and the unpaved realm of nature. I hope this book will help guide readers toward many such revelations.

July 19, 1973   *Robert Elman*

Upland Birds/1

Ruffed Grouse *(Bonasa umbellus)*
& Related Timber Grouse
COMMON & REGIONAL NAMES: *partridge, pa'tridge, pat, mountain pheasant, drummer, willow grouse, pine hen, wood partridge.*

DESCRIPTION & DISTRIBUTION: A road winds west of New York's Hudson Valley past a hollow that almost hides an abandoned orchard. On the orchard's far side, alders hem the bottom of a south slope. Above are scattered berry bushes, then thick aspens and a few maples; over the top there is a narrow beech flat, and on the other side are spruces and a corridor of hemlock. There are four hunters who like to meet at the orchard on cool October mornings. Last time, as we crossed the hollow, a big gray-brown partridge burst with a thunderous whirr from the crown of an apple tree. Two shots reverberated and the tilting bird tumbled to earth. We could not have sworn who hit the grouse—both of us, perhaps. The first flush rarely comes so soon, but it is always startling.

We share a black-speckled setter bitch that quarters wide as we spread out, yet seldom ranges too far ahead. We talk of the scarcity of good grouse and woodcock dogs, of the way grouse refuse to hold for a too-close point, of our exasperation with a dog that used to bump birds far out of range. None of us can see the setter as we shoulder through the alders. When her bell stops tinkling the nearest man tries to get there. Often we take a woodcock before reaching the aspens. Just as often we lose one, hearing the twitter of its primaries but unable to see it or to swing a gun well through the laced whips. Sometimes grouse are in the alders, too, but we find more of them feeding in the aspens, under the beeches, picking among berry bushes

Ruffed grouse rising with blurring roar of wings.

or in laurel, dusting beneath the hemlocks or hiding up in the boughs. As a rule, it is when we surprise them on the ground that they thunder up. They can fly with the stealth of owls.

A hunter in the New England uplands or on the Allegheny ridges or the tote roads in Michigan's woods knows the ruffed grouse as the wittiest, most elusive of game birds. A typical Michigan hunter settles for luck and practiced reflexes; he walks the slash without a dog, convinced no pointing breed can catch scent and freeze before a grouse rises and fades. It is hard to believe that this is the same bird as the willow grouse of British Columbia. There another name, "fool hen," is used almost as often for the ruffed as for the stolid blue and spruce grouse. The author has walked up to a ruffed grouse dusting itself on a Canadian logging road, and watched a hunter flush one from a tree by chucking pebbles at it. In the farmed and settled East and Midwest, centuries of wingshooting have abetted natural selection; the reclusive and the quick-to-fly have survived.

Were the hunted grouse not a nervous, quick-flushing bird and an abruptly veering dodger in flight, it would be an easy target. It is a plump species, of a size midway between quail and pheasant. An average mature male weighs about 1¼ pounds and measures from 17 to 20 inches in length, including a wide, blunt tail 5¼ to 7½ inches long. A female is slightly smaller and has a slightly shorter, narrower tail. The short, wide, cupped wings, spanning about 2 feet, facilitate a darting takeoff and bursts of speed but not sustained flight. (The savory, light-colored breast meat of a grouse characterizes such birds; the darker flesh of ducks, doves, and other long-distance travelers signifies the need of a rich blood supply for the flight muscles.) Across open fields a grouse may fly a quarter of a mile, but any tall cover will generally draw it in before it goes 250 yards. A grouse that is flushed and missed can often be marked down for another try. Unlike woodcock, it will hold tighter for a second point. In thick cover it seldom flies faster than 25 miles an hour. In relatively open spots, however, it flies at least 40 miles an hour; the timed record speed is 51 miles an hour.

It is a wood-brown or gray-brown bird, mottled on the head and upper body with dark bars and darts. The underparts are pale; pale, black-edged eye spots are on the lower back and rump. A loose crest, more pronounced on male than female,

curves back over the head. Both sexes also have a neck ruff, but it is dull and inconspicuous or sometimes unnoticeable on a female. The male's is usually black with green and purple reflections, though reddish brown is more common in some regions. He erects it while strutting or drumming in spring and again in fall while proclaiming territory.

Grouse have a narrow comb of featherless skin over the eye, orange or salmon-colored on most ruffed males, bluish gray on most females. The male's belly and flanks tend to be beige or buff with irregular brownish bars, the female's whitish with

Ruffed grouse, well camouflaged on coniferous perch.

blacker bars. Most hunters examine the tail of each bird bagged in order to verify sex. A tail that can be fanned out 180 degrees is most often a male, whereas gaps usually open between feathers of a fully fanned hen's tail. The tail provides another, somewhat more reliable, indicator: It varies from reddish brown to dark gray and is crossed by six to eleven dark, narrow, pale-edged bars, a much broader, dark or black subterminal bar, and gray tipping; among females, the subterminal bar almost always is broken by brown on the two central feathers, while the male's bar is uniform or nearly so. Birds of the year resemble hens, but show a narrower subterminal tail band, whitish chin patch, mottled primaries, and pointed, unworn tips on the two outermost primaries. Other physical characteristics are adaptations for survival in snow and cold. Grouse legs are feathered almost to the toes, and in winter the toes are fringed with horny rods of cuticle, called pectinations, that give support on snow and are shed in the spring.

The ruffed grouse is the most widespread of America's nonmigratory game birds. It can be hunted from central Alaska east across the lower parts of the Canadian territories and through all the provinces to the Atlantic; on the West Coast it ranges into northern California, on the East Coast down to Tennessee and northern Georgia. Its range generally approximates that of aspens, a primary food source. The best hunting regions are in the New England blanket of woods and farmland, the Appalachians, the forests of the Lake states, the middle and upper Rockies, and the forested Pacific mountains.

There appear to be at least eleven distinct subspecies. The eastern ruffed grouse *(B. u. umbellus)* is the brownish bird most familiar to eastern and midwestern hunters, but the widest-ranging is the gray ruffed grouse *(B. u. umbelloides),* a paler race distributed across Canada and down through the Rockies. Reddish-brown birds, called the red phase, are most common at low elevations, in dry regions, and in the southern part of the range. The gray phase is bagged in higher, wetter, more northerly habitat where conifers outnumber deciduous trees and plumage blends with a gray carpet of dead needles rather than brown leaves. The northern "silvertails" tend to be slightly larger than red-phase grouse, but occasionally both color phases appear in a single brood.

Two crestless, ruffless, but closely related northern and western "timber partridges" add to the profusion. They are the blue grouse *(Dendragapus obscurus)* and spruce grouse *(Canachites canadensis).* Some field guides and hunting manuals list still other species, but zoologist Paul Johnsgard's definitive work, *Grouse and Quails of North America,* ranks them as geographical races of the blue and spruce. The dusky grouse of the Rockies is a blue, as are the sooty grouse of the Pacific mountains and the Richardson grouse of the far Northwest and the Rockies. The Franklin grouse, also of the Northwest and the Rockies, is a spruce grouse, though it has a narrow, grayish-white terminal band on its tail rather than the wide orange-brown bar common to other subspecies.

There are eight races of blue grouse, four of spruce grouse. Blues are found from the West Coast to Alberta and the American Rockies, while spruce grouse range through the same areas and across Canada, the upper woods of the Lake states, and northern-most New England. The blue is the largest of timber grouse; a male is often more than 22 inches long. Both sexes have a long, squared, dusky, occasionally marbled tail with a pale-gray terminal bar. The male is gray or slate with brown and black mottling and wavy bluish-gray lines. His throat and shoulders are whitely streaked or mottled. Over his eye is a pronounced yellow or yellow-orange comb. On the sides of his neck are featherless air sacs, sometimes hardly noticeable when relaxed but extremely conspicuous when inflated. The sacs range from deep yellow and wrinkled on some races to purple and smooth on others. The hen has no comb or air sacs; she is browner, darkly barred and mottled, and has bars of yellowish brown down her breast.

The spruce grouse is smallest—about 15 to 17 inches long. The male's upper parts are gray with wavy black markings. He has a narrow scarlet comb, a black throat edged with white, and a black breast patch with a broken white border. The belly is blackish with tawny or white checkering. When strutting in the breeding season or to claim fall territory, he puffs out his neck feathers almost in the manner of a ruffed grouse. Most races of spruce grouse, regardless of sex, have a brown or blackish tail with a broad orange-brown edge. Both sexes also have little beards of chin feathers like tiny wattles. The hen is brownish,

barred and flecked with ocher, buff, and black. Her underparts are dull white, barred across with brown. When flying in dim light, she is the bird most likely to be taken for a ruffed grouse.

Blues and spruce grouse rely heavily on conifer needles for food, though they also eat the berries, buds, and broad leaves that attract ruffed grouse. Most often found in high country, they are traditional camp meat for mountain hunters. Although they are occasionally taken with shotguns, they perch in the open, flush reluctantly, and almost invariably merit the name "fool hen."

GAME BEHAVIOR & HUNTING HABITAT: The adage that grouse are where you find them has some truth, but they tend to flush from some coverts year after year except during cyclic declines. Like whitetail deer, they have benefited from the spread of small farms, from the subsequent abandonment of many of those farms, from lumbering, and from fire. A climax forest supports very few grouse. They need edges, openings, second growth— a mix of shrubs, brush, and young pioneer trees (aspen, alder, and birch) for food and the taller hardwoods and conifers for roosting and cover. Farming provides edges, fields, and orchards (all the better if deserted and overgrown); fires encourage new growth; logging provides roads, slashings, and clear-cuts.

Aspen buds are the most important of all foods, yet at certain times the aspens yield not a flush while other vegetation holds grouse. In the Midwest, clover patches are good hunting spots early in the season. In the East, wild-grape tangles, blueberry and cranberry patches, rhododendron thickets, or sumac sometimes hold more birds than aspens. In the spring grouse feast on apple buds. In summer they eat fruits and berries, and in fall they return to the orchards for seeds. The hunting season is also a time when they seek beechnuts, acorns, dogwood, serviceberry, bunchberry, willow, maple, hop hornbeam, thornapple, and mountain laurel. The old countryman's myth that laurel (or any other poisonous plant) toxifies grouse meat is disproved at dinner by thousands of hunters each year. Aspen and most other autumn foods remain important through the winter, when hawthorn, greenbrier, and wintergreen also provide sustenance. In the Hudson Valley woods, preferred foods include birch, hazelnut, and blackberry. No list is complete or invariable. When we fail to move grouse in familiar coverts, we open the

Wingprints in snow where grouse flushed (top),
grouse dusting spot (bottom l.), and nest (bottom r.).

crop of the first bird shot; its content may tell us where to hunt.

Often it directs us into thickets where shots must be made fast. All four of us like short-barreled 20-gauge doubles that are equally efficient in woodcock alders. For the same reason we use No. 8 field loads; some hunters use a light charge of 8's in the first barrel and a heavier 7½ load in the second. Three of our guns are bored improved-cylinder and modified, the fourth is custom-bored with a true cylinder and a skeet choke. They all produce wide, uniform patterns.

Though cycles differ considerably from one locale to another, in most regions the second or third year of each decade brings good hunting and the seventh poor. Many species are subject to cycles, but the fluctuations are perhaps most pronounced among ruffed grouse and varying hares. In some places the grouse cycle spans only seven years, in others up to eleven, but the average is ten. A decline continues for two or three years, then a recovery requires three or four and is followed by several fine years. The fluctuations are most pronounced in the North. An area of ideal habitat in one of the Great Lakes states may hold 300 grouse per square mile during a peak, but an eighth as many after the population plummets. A healthy density is probably a bird for every fifteen or twenty acres, but cycles persist without the impetus of severe crowding. They are probably caused by a combination of crowding, climatic cycles, and plant succession.

No single disease or calamity suddenly thins the population. Mortality is always high; 60 percent of an average year's grouse crop dies before the first hunter goes afield. The amount of hunting has no discernible effect on the following summer's census. Cold, wet spring weather can chill grouse chicks and deprive them of essential protein-rich insects. Freezing rain can sheath buds in ice, weakening adult birds with hunger. If the goshawk is no longer abundant enough to be classed as the most efficient predator, there is still a thinning of the surplus crop by foxes, weasels, skunks, owls, snakes, and raccoons. There are feather lice, mites, ticks, blood protozoa, intestinal worms, and other parasites. Diseases include aspergillosis and tularemia. The birds have a potential life span of about six years, yet the bulk of the population dies each year.

Renewal is signaled by a drumming in the woods from

early March until May, likened by the romantic to a ghostly tom-tom beat that quickens until it becomes a drumroll; the less romantic are reminded of an antiquated, sputtering gasoline engine. Ruff out, very erect, the male grouse stands on his drumming log, or sometimes on a hummock, supported and balanced by his fanned tail while his wings beat the air. They strike nothing; the drumbeat is an implosion of air filling a vacuum created by each powerful stroke. Thus he proclaims his territory, and will battle any male that violates it. When a hen appears the drumming soon ends and courtship displays begin. Like quail, grouse are seasonally monogamous, the mates remaining together through spring. Laying takes more than two weeks and incubation at least another three. An average clutch of eleven

Ruffed grouse brought to hand.

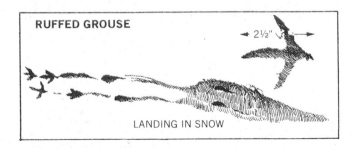

RUFFED GROUSE

2½"

LANDING IN SNOW

eggs begins to hatch about the first of June. If the simple ground nest is destroyed early during incubation, renesting usually results in at least a few fertile eggs.

The young are extremely precocial. The hen almost immediately begins to herd them about in a search for insects. After a couple of weeks they can fly a little, though the hen continues to brood and protect them, luring predators away with a broken-wing ruse or fighting them when necessary.

Dispersal begins in early autumn, the time of the "crazy flight," the Mad Moon. There have been theories about grouse becoming drunk on fermented berries, and other theories equally irrelevant. The grouse that collide with obstacles or crash through windows at this time are the confused and inexperienced young dispersing under pressure from their elders.

Occasionally a hunter flushes a covey from a thicket and is bewildered by a gregariousness associated with quail and true partridges but never with grouse. The dispersal has not yet taken place. Later the grouse will seek solitude. The hunter hopes there will be snow for them. Cold without snow is lethal. Grouse can walk on snow, and would rather walk than fly. They burrow under it, warmed by its insulation and hidden from predators. Sometimes, if the hunter marks a bird down in snow but his dog fails to locate it, or if he hunts without a dog, he can follow the wide, three-pronged tracks, each print placed precisely in front of the last. Having found the snowy crater where the bird landed, perhaps he follows the trail to sheltering rhododendron and flushes the partridge again. Or perhaps, following it to a dead end of flurried wing marks where the bird took off unseen, he wishes it well and turns toward other thickets.

Spruce grouse roosting (top),
and blue grouse displaying and calling.

VOICE: The songs of a northern spring include a series of five to seven low hoots, the territorial call of a male blue grouse. Spruce grouse also hoot, but not very volubly. Ruffed grouse can chirp, coo, cluck, peep, and hiss, but usually reserve vocalization for courtship or for communication between hen and chicks. The fall sounds of the ruffed grouse are an occasional drumming and the startling whirr of a flush.

Pinnated Grouse *(Tympanuchus cupido)*

Sage Grouse *(Centrocercus urophasianus)*

& Sharp-tailed Grouse *(Pedioecetes phasianellus)*

COMMON & REGIONAL NAMES: For pinnated grouse—*prairie chicken, prairie grouse, prairie hen, yellowlegs, squaretail, broadtail, bar-breasted grouse.* For sage grouse—*sage hen, sage chicken, sage turkey, sage buzzard.* For sharp-tailed grouse— *sharptail, pintail grouse, white-bellied grouse.*

DESCRIPTION & DISTRIBUTION: After the first hard frosts strike the Great Plains, all three grouse of the open country make short migrations to areas of easy foraging and slight protection from the weather. Soon the local grouse populations congregate in loose flocks. In some states the season for sage grouse has ended by then, since these birds traditionally provide the year's first upland shooting. But a hunter in eastern Montana can walk the brushy coulees for sharptails and on the same day scout water holes for sage grouse. Both are usually hunted there throughout the fall, as are sharptails and the pinnated grouse (the birds we call prairie chickens) in lower South Dakota. West of the Missouri River and not far above the Nebraska line, as dawn uncloaks a wheatfield, several hunters may be waiting to begin a classic stand-shoot for prairie chickens. Afterward they can walk up sharptails in wheat or corn, or work a pair of dogs through scattered woods on the grasslands.

Chickens develop habitual flight routes to good feeding spots, providing a kind of pass-shooting that would please a duck hunter. The shooters crouch low at strategic spots along fence rows, in shocks or clumps of vegetation, or in ditches. At first light they see loose prairie-chicken flocks coming in low—big, blocky grouse with square tails, their cupped wings beating the air in a series of fast, powerful strokes followed by a long glide. The glide of the huge sage grouse is shorter, but the same basic manner of flight is common to all the heavy-bodied grouse of the plains. They often travel faster than appearances indicate; the pinnated grouse coming in over the wheat are flying 40 miles an hour. A man rises and swings his gun. The first bird tumbles, but another hunter misses a wide-angling bird twice.

There are three subspecies of pinnated grouse: Attwater's prairie chicken *(T. c. attwateri),* a relatively small race now limited to the Texas coast, endangered and fully protected; the lesser prairie chicken *(T. c. pallidicinctus)* of the lower plains; and the greater prairie chicken *(T. c. pinnatus)* of the upper plains. The extinct eastern heath hen was another pinnated grouse, obliterated together with its habitat. The range and numbers of prairie chickens have been severely reduced by the pasturing and plowing of the grasslands, changes less detrimental to sharptails. At present only six states have sufficient pinnated grouse to allow hunting, though several more have begun long-term programs to re-establish the species. The lesser prairie chicken now inhabits the arid short-grass prairies of southwestern Kansas, the Oklahoma panhandle, northwestern Texas, and eastern New Mexico. Hunting for the lesser chicken is probably best in Oklahoma. In huntable numbers, the greater prairie chicken presently inhabits the taller grass of lower South Dakota, north-central Nebraska's Sandhills region, eastern Kansas, and north-eastern Oklahoma. Though South Dakota has the longest season, Kansas has the best hunting; the birds are shot there only in November, when frosts usually bring flocks to the grainfields, and a harvest of more than 30,000 is common. In most years hunting is permitted only in the eastern part of the state because the lesser prairie chicken, occupying the southwestern area, remains scarce.

Both of these pinnated grouse are yellowish-brown or buff-brown birds with heavy, extensive barring of deep brown and black on body and scapulars. The underparts are paler but are also darkly barred. The blunt tail and the primaries are deep brown. The wings usually have white spots on the outer webs, and the tail usually has very narrow white tipping. The yellow

legs are thinly covered with pale feathering. On the sides of the neck are long, stiff, dark quills, or *pinnae* (hence the name pinnated grouse), much more pronounced on males than females. They lift above the rooster's head like short horns when he puffs out his air sacs. When lowered, they cover a bare orange patch on each side of the neck—the air sacs, which inflate to the size of large lemons. Both sexes have a slight crest, and the male also has a pronounced orange comb over the eye. The comb and air sacs of a lesser prairie chicken are brighter orange than those of the larger, tall-grass bird, and the lesser also has lighter barring on the back, more extensive barring on the underparts. A lesser prairie chicken is apt to be 15 or 16 inches long, a greater may be almost 19 inches long. The length is comparable to that of a ruffed grouse, but the prairie chicken is a heavier, shorter-tailed bird. A rooster bagged on the upper prairies may easily weigh 2 pounds.

A sharptail grouse is equally heavy and has an average length of about 16½ to 18½ inches. This, too, is a brown bird but not so dark as the prairie chicken. The upper parts are tan or yellowish buff, flecked with darker brown and black. The wings are brown with conspicuous white spotting. The breast, paler than the prairie chicken's, fades to white on the belly, and instead of barring it has dark lateral lines of V's. The tapered tail is white except for two long, spiky central feathers. Both sexes have a very slight crest and feathered legs. The rooster has a yellow or orange comb and on each side of the neck an air sac, sometimes hardly noticeable when relaxed, that varies from orange or pink to pale violet.

There are half a dozen subspecies, some of the northern sharptails being paler in color and some a bit more migratory than others. Few hunters on the Great Plains realize that the birds range all the way from northern Alaska across the Canadian territories and provinces to Quebec, and from eastern Washington to northern Michigan. Sharptail gunning is superb on the prairies of eastern Alberta and western Saskatchewan. The birds are now hunted in all or parts of eleven states, from eastern Washington to the upper Michigan Peninsula and as far south as upper-central Colorado. Unlike prairie chickens—which require vast tall-grass tracts for survival even though they feed heavily in grainfields—sharptails are relatively adaptable to changes in food and cover.

Greater prairie chicken on booming ground (top),
and sage grouse dancing for hens.

They remain abundant on the north-central plains.

The sage grouse has been similarly fortunate in some regions, although, like the pronghorn, it has been severely threatened where cattlemen have replaced the sage with grass. Two subspecies, much alike in appearance and behavior, range from central Washington down into California and east across the lower parts of the Prairie Provinces and through the plains states (as far down as Nevada, Utah, and Colorado). At this writing, ten states have open seasons. The shooting is usually best in eastern Montana, where it continues throughout the fall. It is also fine in southwestern Wyoming, though it generally lasts only a couple of weeks at the end of August and beginning of September, and in northern Nevada, where the average season consists of a week or so in late September or early October.

The sage dweller is the largest of grouse, larger than any of America's gallinaceous birds except the wild turkey. A hen is likely to weigh 3 or 4 pounds, and a 6-pound rooster is about average; many weigh close to 8. Females are generally a little under 2 feet long, males up to 2½. Both sexes are grayish brown, mottled on the upper parts, pale on breast and flanks, with black bellies and feathered legs. The rooster has a black chin and

Male sharp-tailed grouse engaging in ritual battle (above), and retriever bringing in sharptail.

neck with a white V across the throat. His white breast feathers conceal two large, frontal air sacs, which vary from dull yellow to reddish brown or olive. In spring, when he struts about, the sacs are remarkably distended and the entire white breast and neck area puffs up so hugely that it often lifts above the head. Behind the sacs and the white expanse are black, hairy feathers that lift up behind the head during courtship. The male also has a fairly pronounced yellow comb. Both sexes have long, pointed brown tails marbled and barred with black and white. The feathers taper to thin points, and the rooster cocks and fans them into a sunburst rosette when he struts.

He is less impressive in flight. His great size makes him seem slower than he is. All three grouse of the plains often fly at only 25 to 30 miles an hour and the sage grouse is the slowest, yet even a large sage rooster can easily go 40 miles an hour without a tail wind. Sage grouse are frequently missed by gunners who first give them too long a lead—being more accustomed to the swifter prairie chicken and sharptail—and then, overcompensating for a quickly perceived error, shoot behind them.

GAME BEHAVIOR & HUNTING HABITAT: After the prolonged

droughts of the 1920s and 1930s the recovery of plainsland grouse was impeded by a renewed spread of agriculture, and the birds have always been subject to mysterious cyclic declines. Many years ago, when market wagons clattered over the prairies, the horses used to flush enough birds to fill a buckboard before sundown. Such numbers will never be seen again, but in good habitat the grouse offset natural calamities and attrition by fecundity.

All three species gather for breeding on *leks*—relatively flat, open spaces, sometimes with spots beaten almost bare of

Plains hunter, and sage grouse (opposite).

vegetation. Sharptail and pinnated males come to these spots and assert their territorial rights in the early fall and then return in spring. Sage grouse, though they form the largest gatherings, do so only in the spring. In other respects the performances are remarkably similar. They may begin as soon as the ground is clear of snow, usually reach a peak in March or April, and dwindle in May. As each rooster arrives, he claims his few yards of territory. Numbers vary from perhaps half a dozen to scores.

Each species has its unique display, but in general the displays begin with a rapid stamping and strutting (inspiration for some of the dances by the Plains Indians). Soon the roosters are leaping and fluttering—and doing battle when one oversteps an invisible border—and fanning, cocking, vibrating, and snapping their stiff tail feathers open and shut. The combs engorge, and the air sacs balloon. The sage grouse stands very erect with his folded wings lifted upward as he puffs out his air sacs and breast enormously. The prairie chicken bows low as he inflates his, and the sharptail spreads his wings wide. The displays are accompanied by squawking, croaking, gobbling, bubbling. Well known is the three-noted *whoom-ah-whoom* of the prairie chicken, produced by forceful expulsion of air from the neck sacs and accompanied by violent head-jerking. The booming of a large gathering can be heard across a mile of prairie.

Hens walk about the area noncommitally, but each one

eventually selects a dominant rooster, and mating takes place on the dancing grounds. The hens then wander off to lay their eggs in simple ground nests, returning only if the destruction of a clutch necessitates renesting. Laying requires a couple of weeks, incubation takes about twenty-three to twenty-six days, and most hatching occurs in May and early June. A typical sage-grouse clutch numbers seven or eight, while the other species average about a dozen. Though the young are precocial the mortality rate is high. Predators of eggs or young include badgers, ground squirrels, coyotes, magpies, ravens, owls, hawks, and eagles. In addition, grouse are sensitive to poultry diseases and parasites, herbicides, pesticides, droughts, cold snaps, and storms. Theoretically they might live for about six years but average longevity is only a little more than a year among both hunted and fully protected populations. The chicks, able to fly when just a few weeks old, scatter before summer is over and soon join flocks or form new ones.

By hunting time they are foraging in "packs"—a term as common as "flock" or "covey" in some areas. They feed actively from dawn through the early morning, rest and sometimes go to water during the warm part of the day, and feed again in late afternoon. But the sage grouse differs from the others in habitat and food.

In parts of the West an old prejudice inveighs against eating "sage buzzard" but it is as tasty as the other species. Primarily an eater of leaves and shoots, its chief food is sage, supplemented by grasses and other soft plants (particularly dandelions and clover) and a few grasshoppers. But it also loves alfalfa. Whoever hunts sage grouse on farms or ranches should check the edges of alfalfa fields, as well as irrigation ditches, stock tanks, ponds, and creeks.

Sagebrush flats and basins are the other places to hunt, and here, too, water concentrates the birds, particularly at midday. Coulees are promising, as are wide basins cut by gullies. Sage grouse feed in typical pronghorn country and can be hunted like pronghorns—with binoculars from a high spot. The cover often is thin and low enough to show the birds at long distance. There are times when loose flocks dot a mile of sage flat. A hunter can also look for sign, especially around muddy water holes where he may well find mazes of large bird tracks and heaped accumulations of large, mottled droppings. He cannot be sure how fresh such droppings are because they weather slowly, but he also looks for a second, less durable type, darker and softer. If he finds very dark blobs, the area is probably in current use. He may wait there for birds to fly in or feed toward him, or he can walk to put them up.

It is also possible to stalk them. The birds have good vision and hearing, and they may flush wild when they see movement or hear the scratch of brush plants, but they are not as alert as prairie chickens and sharptails. They try to rise into the wind, and sometimes can be approached crosswind, so that they will not stretch the range by the time they get well up. Their flush is a ponderous lumbering upward before they level off and gain speed. After that they can be difficult targets, and they fly higher than other grouse. Since a flock usually takes off raggedly, a few birds at a time, a hunter can get shots at late-flushing birds by rushing toward them. An alternate method is for a hunting party to form a skirmish line and drive the birds through a sage flat. A second line of standers can take birds that flush too far ahead of the drivers.

Many hunters use full-choked duck guns. Perhaps the ideal is a double with modified and full borings. High-brass No. 6's are the best loads, either in a 12- or Magnum 20-gauge gun. Roosters fly straight; hens twist and dip, but not far enough to escape a good pattern. The way to bag one is to ignore the twisting and give all but the high targets only a little lead.

There are strong differences of opinion as to the value of a pointing dog for game characterized by wild flushes and by ground runs through thin grass or sage. Flushing dogs seem to have no special advantage at putting sage grouse up within gunshot, but a pointer accustomed to working pheasants or Hungarian partridge may circle and pin them until the hunter arrives. Even without any circling, if the dog remains stanch during the first couple of rises a few birds will probably hold just long enough.

With prairie chickens, the best early morning method is pass-shooting at a heavily used feeding field. Sorghum is their favorite crop, followed by corn, wheat, and oats. After leaving the fields they head into the tall cover grasses and usually congregate near or amid food plants such as knotweed, wild rose, clover, bristlegrass, blackberry, buttonweed, ragweed, oak, bluestem, goldenrod, and flowering spurge. A hunter can walk them up there without a dog, and the big late-fall flocks will not always wait out a point. Still, the smaller groups hold fairly well in tall, dense cover for a dog that works carefully.

Several of us once shot over a Brittany spaniel that surprised us by ranging too wide and fast, putting up birds out of gunshot, then vindicated himself by watching them down and moving in on the few singles that did not fly out of sight. Now he stayed fairly close to the guns, and all but two of the birds held. Those two were runners. He circled and pinned them. One made a short dash and rose within range. The other sat until one of us could almost have put him up with a flushing whip, then lined out low with a loud cackle and swerved past two waiting guns. For that kind of early-fall hunting a modified choke and field loads of 7½'s are fine. The shots lengthen as hunting turns the birds "hawky" and then full-choke pass-shooting guns and high-brass No. 6's are best for all of the open-country grouse.

Often sharptails and prairie chickens jump from the same grass, but a dog that handles one species usually succeeds with the other. In corn- or wheatfields sharptails can be shot over a dog or walked up without one. Or several hunters can work birds for one another across a big stubble field.

If they are not in the grainfields, they are probably in or near tall vegetation that provides both feed and cover. A rosebush thicket will hold sharptails, as will the poplar groves and other clumps of trees and brush around prairie potholes or creeks. A flock can roost and water as well as feed there, and sharptails hold well in the groves. Early in the season they are attracted to the same foods as pinnated grouse, but they also rely heavily on buds. They can be flushed out of birch, mountain ash, alder, willow, and chokecherry. Like ruffed grouse, they often roost high; a hunter who watches only the ground and his dog may be too slow to swing on sharptails that go out overhead. Watching the middle distances can be as rewarding in the uplands as in the deer woods.

VOICE: Open-country grouse often cackle or cluck loudly when flushed and are capable of an array of vocalizations, but they are not very noisy except on the dancing ground.

Chukar Partridge *(Alectoris chukar)*

COMMON & REGIONAL NAMES: *red-legged partridge, redleg, Indian hill partridge, rock partridge, gray partridge, chukor.*

DESCRIPTION & DISTRIBUTION: On a hot September morning a hunter walks the canyon rims and slopes near the Snake River in southeastern Washington. His dog works just a little ahead, keeping above because chukars would rather run uphill than fly. The hunter watches and listens, but he sees no black and white head patterns or barred plumage in the scrub, hears no foraging or rallying calls. At the head of an arroyo he brings his dog to heel and eases up to the crest, which rims a canyon with a creek shimmering at the bottom. He sits for a few minutes, using a binocular to study the grass and brush near the creek and a talus slope on the far side. Up near an outcropping he finds what he is looking for: small gray shadows flicking about in sage and cheatgrass. He retreats to where he can cross without being seen, and after a long climb stands on the rim above the covey. He starts down, with the dog to one side in a maneuver that may head off birds. When the pointer stiffens, the hunter walks in fast, to force-flush the chukars before they can scurry past. Soft, sleek, blue-gray forms—a score of them—burst into the air. Though larger than quail, they are as speedy, most of them going at least 35 miles an hour after they level off at 10 or 12 feet. They swing downhill, gaining momentum, reaching almost 50 miles an hour.

Knowing that chukars fly downhill almost as invariably as they run uphill, the hunter picks a target fast and swings with it, but shoots high. A second shot sends the bird wheeling. The dog scrambles down to retrieve it. As the hunter reloads, a last bird bounces out from the rim. All that registers in the shooter's mind is a buff missile with thin red legs sailing down over his head. He fires instinctively. The bird falls, leaving a puff of smoky feathers in the air.

The hunter examines his first bird. Its legs have slight, blunted spurs, marking it as a male. The second one is spurless, and he cannot determine its sex but notices that its outer primaries are rounded enough to indicate maturity. If the distance from the tip of the third primary to the wrist joint is less than 5¼ inches, it is probably a female; the only other way to know

Chukar falling to quick shot (top), and
limit of plump Washington chukars.

is to examine its internal organs. It is a beautiful bird, probably between 13 and 15 inches or so, weighing 15 to 20 ounces, a bit smaller than a ruffed grouse.

Its upper body, wings, and breast are blue-gray, with a brownish-gray or olive wash on crown and back, chestnut brown on the outer tail feathers. Legs, bill, and thin eye rings are red. Lower face and throat are whitish. Just above the nostrils a sharply contrasting black band crosses the face and eyes, almost to the rear of the head, and curves down along the neck and over the upper breast. Below this dark necklace, the breast is blue-gray, fading to light tannish buff on the belly. Its paler buff flanks are sharply marked with eight to thirteen vertical black and chestnut bars.

Chukar partridges are native to southern Europe and large portions of Asia. During the last forty years, at least forty-two states and six Canadian provinces have introduced chukars, originally to supplement dwindling native game birds. Until the 1950s most game departments considered the experiments a failure. Many of the birds had been released in lush, flatland farmbelts where gallinaceous species often thrive, but chukars require far more arid, steep, rocky terrain and cannot survive where winter snows are heavy. As game departments began to release birds in seemingly less hospitable ecosystems, chukars prospered. Largely confined to a canyon-land existence, they have not become detrimental competitors with native birds, yet their range has spread considerably since the mid-1950s. Their population plummets after an excessively dry breeding season, but in regions of abundance they are underharvested.

Apart from Hawaii, where chukars were added to the game list in 1952, nine states and the province of British Columbia have seasons at this writing. Hunting usually begins in September or October in most regions and may last only a few weeks or into winter, depending on the previous summer's nesting success. Chukar hunting is best by far in eastern Washington and Oregon and western Idaho, near the Snake River.

Most books incorrectly list America's chukars as the subspecies *A. graeca,* the European chukar whose call is a ringing whistle. Chukars on this continent are descendants of Indian stock from the Himalayas, bolstered by a few Turkish birds, all of the subspecies *A. chukar,* whose clucks and cackles—with never a whistle—often lead hunters to a covey. They now range chiefly from south-central British Columbia down to Baja California, eastward through the Great Basin and Rocky Mountain states to the edges of the plains.

GAME BEHAVIOR & HUNTING HABITAT: A chukar hunter can recognize the kind of land where he wants to control his dog closely and carry his gun ready to mount. At least a quarter of what he sees will be talus slopes, rock outcroppings, cliffs, or bluffs, and it will be blanketed or liberally sprinkled with sagebrush and cheatgrass, preferably mixed with bunchgrass, ricegrass, and bluegrass, still better if it also supports a few additional herbs or weedy forbs like Russian thistle, filaree, or fiddleneck.

Any nearby wheat or alfalfa fields make such a place ideal; chukars need no cultivated land, but they visit fields close to the escape and roosting cover of canyons. Grasses, forbs, and grains are food, while brush is for nesting cover and shade; sage need not be dominant if there are other shrubby plants—rabbitbrush, saltbush, or greasewood, perhaps. Some of the slopes should be rocky, and some should be at least moderately steep and over 200 feet high. Finally, there must be a few brushy creek bottoms in the area; most coveys stay within half a mile or so of water.

The birds roost on talus slopes or other steep, rocky places, sometimes under shrubs or low trees. Cool weather often makes them roost in a circle, facing out, like quail. In colder or windy weather they also roost in rocky niches or caves, but still remain in a loose covey. A group may number five or forty, or may clump around a water hole in larger congregations, but the average number is about twenty.

A hunter can begin in the early morning by checking south slopes that furnish warm roosts. The height of feeding activity comes at midmorning. On a comfortably cool day the coveys move and forage through most of the afternoon, so they may be flushed out of any grassy area. But in hot weather the midday hunting places are in shady draws, at or near water, and in cool dusting spots where chukars leave sign—tracks, droppings, feathers, hollows scratched in the dirt. A thorough hunter scours the area, checks nearby water holes, then walks the grassy slopes, and before quitting at sundown checks the water holes again.

Grassy hollows high on canyon slopes are favorite foraging pockets. Late in the afternoon the birds usually go to water as they feed their way back up to the rocky roosts. Since they do not burrow down into grass like bobwhites, they are sometimes seen far off.

Chukars have been clocked scuttling up a slope at 17 miles an hour. Running uphill is no way to overtake them, so most hunters work down toward them. Even then, birds often run out of range without flying. A young, wiry man can force-flush many coveys by running down at them. Some of us who are no longer quite so wiry or have studied running tactics with blue quail in the Southwest will admit to putting up coveys by shooting over them. Gunfire gets them airborne, and scattered singles and doubles hold tighter for a dog or man. Intent on regrouping when scattered, most covey birds become reluctant to run aimlessly or lose contact by flying until a pursuer is close. Scattered chukars are also easier to locate because of their rallying calls.

But the cover is thin and they can see a man at a quarter mile. Except for singles in high cover, there is no easy way to halt a run. Wild flushes are less frequent than ground escapes, and, if birds are headed off, some of them may buzz out from underfoot. For fast shooters, an improved cylinder is choke enough; the rest of us may need a modified boring. A western friend who is devoted to chukars uses a European double with an improved cylinder for close birds, a full choke for long shots, and two triggers for instant choice. It is a light 20-gauge gun, ideal with No. 7½ loads.

He also uses a pointing dog. Some hunters, convinced that a dog is more hindrance than help except for retrieving, find chukars purely by sight and sound. They put great reliance on hunting streambeds in dry weather, glassing canyon slopes, driving along back roads to scout. But much can be claimed for a dog that responds to signals and has learned to circle below birds, pinning them or pushing them toward the hunter.

Most of the chukars survive the hunting season, and they can also survive winter temperatures of 30 below zero if they are not kept from feed by more than a few inches of snow. In February and March the males begin to engage in aggressive displays, and may initially recognize females by their passive responses. Pairs form and leave the covey to scrape out nests

in clumps of vegetation. Most males desert the females during the 24-day incubation, but a few linger until the eggs hatch. Clutches average about fifteen eggs. The hen almost immediately leads her precocial brood over the slopes to forage, and within a few weeks they mix with other coveys, then part again by fall to form new coveys. Partridges and quail are less sensitive than grouse to disease and parasites. They are sought by all the common winged and furred predators, and show a particular fear of hawks. Some banded chukars have lived several years; most probably survive a year or two. In semi-arid country an inch of rainfall can be the difference between a paucity of game and a rich hunting harvest.

VOICE: Breeding chukars employ a fairly wide repertoire of calls but in the fall the assortment is reduced. A clucking *whitoo* sound is an alarm that sometimes brings a gun up since it may signal a flush. A foraging covey can occasionally be heard clucking a feeding call—*took, tu-tu-tu-tu.* But the name chukar is onomatopoeic and the characteristic call is a cackle: *chuh! chuh! chuh! chu-kar, chu-karr, chu-kar-a!,* a signal that keeps a covey together. It can lead a hunter to a covey or show him where to cast his dog, and after a rise it may locate scattered singles for him. Imitation usually stimulates chukars to reply. Commercial calls are sold in chukar country, though many hunters produce a convincing vocal imitation without mechanical aid.

Chukar partridge covey flushing from canyon rim.

Hungarian Partridge *(Perdix perdix)*
COMMON & REGIONAL NAMES: *Hun, gray partridge, European gray partridge, Bohemian partridge, English partridge.*

DESCRIPTION & DISTRIBUTION: At first nothing is seen in the yellow wheat stubble where the pointer stiffens uncertainly, tail flagging, then inches forward and stiffens again. A spatter of birds whisks up at least 20 yards ahead. The impression is of a dozen wide russet tails, plump, fluffy bodies, brown wings rounded and blurred. By the time the gun comes up, the nearest target is 30 yards out, only 10 or 15 feet high but wheeling with the covey in an abrupt switch of direction toward a hayfield 300 yards off. Huns seldom burst out as explosively as bobwhites or with quite their speed, but almost always flush farther away, going 30 miles an hour, sometimes unexpectedly surging faster. They are round as Christmas-card partridges, shaped like bobwhites but twice as large. Most of them are 12 or 13 inches long and weigh about an ounce per inch. As the hunter fires at a trailing bird, those in the lead are ceasing their rapid wing-beats and gliding.

The dog brings him a bird that looked pastel brown on the wing, yet typifies a species widely known as the gray partridge. As he accepts the bird he can see the soft, finely vermiculated gray covering its breast and belly. Across the breast and running back on the flanks is a horseshoe marking of dark chestnut. The flanks are gray, too, with vertical chestnut barring. He spreads one of the brown wings, admiring the bright white shafts of the scapulars; pointed outer primaries identify the bird as a young one, but it probably hatched early in the spring since its legs have turned from yellow to adult blue-gray.

Its forehead and cheeks are cinnamon, its crown buffy brown. Sometimes a partridge's back is quite grayish, but this one is the more usual grayish brown, buffily streaked on the sides, mottled near the wings. The central feathers and upper coverts of the squarish, rusty tail are barred and vermiculated. From the horseshoe on the underparts, the hunter guesses his bird to be a cock; the marking is apt to be smaller, indistinct, or absent on a hen, or sometimes whitish rather than chestnut. A closer inspection verifies the sex. The scapular feathers are yellowish brown with fine, wavy black lines; they turn chestnut

near the outside edges. A hen's would be blackish at the base, with light yellow crossbarring, no chestnut, and vermiculation only on the outer parts. Most females also have two to four buff crossbars on the scapulars and middle wing coverts, and a wide buff stripe along the shafts of these feathers.

Gray partridges of five subspecies are native to most of Europe and three more range eastward to central Siberia. Since most of America's early importations came from the plains of Hungary, the species acquired the name Hungarian partridge, or "Hun," on this continent. The first releases, in California and Washington shortly before 1900, were less than successful, but efforts during the next few decades succeeded spectacularly in the same regions and others.

The birds were wanted to replace native upland game diminished by the rape of forests and flaying of grasslands. Having adapted to Europe's tilled plains, they thrive in open terrain—fertile flatlands or gently rolling prairies where small-grain crops quilt grassy expanses. They can live in sage and bunchgrass near streams in the Great Basin but tend to move or spread to the nearest wheat and hay. There are three separate American

Hungarian, or gray, partridge (above), and
small Hun covey, whirring away low over field.

ranges. The westernmost covers eastern Washington and Oregon, northeastern California, Idaho, northern Nevada, and northwestern Utah. Traditionally, the region's greatest partridge harvest is in Oregon and Idaho, although in 1972 the hunting was better in Washington and Montana than anywhere in the country. The midcontinent range on the upper Great Plains is largest, sprawling over the central and lower portions of the Prairie Provinces, Montana, North Dakota, upper Wyoming and South Dakota, western Minnesota, and northwestern Iowa. Hunting is excellent in Montana, Alberta, Saskatchewan, and North Dakota. The third range is in the Great Lakes region: eastern Wisconsin, southern Michigan, eastern Indiana, western Ohio and southern Ontario. The hunting is best in Wisconsin and Ontario. Smaller numbers of the birds are also found in Quebec, Nova Scotia, and upper New York and Vermont.

GAME BEHAVIOR & HUNTING HABITAT: In 1965 the author and two friends kept a log of a week's partridge hunt on farmlands between Williamsburg and Crysler, Ontario. We hunted over Danny, an eight-year-old setter that had won twenty-three field trials but, being a quail dog, needed a few days to learn that Huns in stubble would not wait to fly if he failed to lock on their scent at about 20 yards. Still, our log shows they held reasonably well until the weather turned wet and windy. When the wind was up they were nervous and rose at 50 or 60 yards, out of scenting range. We seldom saw them before they got up, but they saw us. When the wind was down we saw them from far off, gathered on well-drained knolls of cut-over timothy. They watched our approach and left in good time. Now and then a stray whirred out close by.

During the worst period, with scenting conditions poor, we left the dog in the car while we strode the fields briskly, putting up an occasional single or small covey within range. They rarely flew farther than a few hundred yards. They flushed wilder at each subsequent approach, finally disappearing over a hill. When we failed to find them our guide, John Ouderkirk, suggested that we retrace our steps. He felt they might have circled back to where we had first put them up. They had and we took several, though no one bagged his eight-bird limit on any day.

Coveys tend to return after being flushed from a roost or choice feeding spot. They use the same small areas year after year—not the same birds, of course, but their descendants, the same coveys—like bobwhite coveys. Hunters become familiar with old farm buildings or brushy edges or dips where there is feed, grit, and not too much wind.

After the winds eased and the land had begun to dry out, we hunted over Danny again, casting him in wide circles to hold coveys between him and the guns. We accepted his judgment when he acted birdy, even if he seemed to be sniffing ground-runners that had already fled or the lingering scent of birds flushed earlier. Sometimes, having returned to such places, the birds—often a pair—would hold.

Usually a covey stayed together after the flush, but once, when a dozen birds wheeled and teetered right over us and we bagged the two that were in the lead, the others scattered and came down in the field where we stood. Ouderkirk remarked that they were mature. "The mates," he said. "The younger ones are still used to following the leaders. That's why they broke up and came down so close. They'll hold for the dog, too." They did, indeed. Perhaps no scientific study has confirmed this experienced guide's pronouncement, but the same thing has happened on subsequent hunts.

Because so many shots are long, many wingshooters use full-choked 12-gauge guns and No. 6 loads. A 20 gauge serves as well if chambered for 3-inch shells, and many of us prefer a modified boring or a double with one barrel modified and the other full-choked. The combination reduces somewhat the problem of birds typically rising at 15 or 20 yards, offering a first shot at 25 to 35 yards and a second at 50 or more. Until a partridge is well away No. 6 shot is a bit large, but high-velocity 7½ loads are fine.

In January or February fighting and courting displays begin to disrupt a covey. Unusually large coveys—eighteen or twenty birds—are flushed most often by hunters who go afield late in the season; they are apt to split into two groups, to be marked and hunted separately, because they consist of two families. Hens seem to refuse siblings or parents as mates, and many of the cocks leave to seek hens in other coveys.

While the male stands guard, the female scrapes a shallow nest in a clump of vegetation and lines it with dead grass. There are fifteen to seventeen eggs in an average clutch and the hen incubates them alone, but the cock stays and helps to tend the chicks. Nesting failure is high—escalated by the mowing of hayfields—and renesting produces hatches well into the summer. Chick mortality is also high, the chief danger being inclement weather that chills the young. Huns are fairly resistant to avian diseases and parasites but are, of course, subject to predation by a host of carnivores and to poisoning by pesticides, herbicides, and fungicides. About 80 percent of the partridges in a normal area can be expected to die each year. The average longevity is about a year, and by fall a typical covey consists of one or both parents and eight surviving offspring.

The birds can withstand a severe winter if the snow is not too deep. Like grouse, they burrow into it for insulation and concealment; they also tunnel under foot-deep snow to feed. There is no seasonal shift of habitat, so hunters in partridge country soon notice the grain lands where the birds feed, the hayfields or grass or brushy edges where they roost, the buildings or lee hillsides and draws where they shelter from blustery winds, and the bare spots, trails, and back roads where they pick grit.

They are less dependent on water than most birds but must have some in the area.

A Washington hunter may be surprised that in Michigan it is corn rather than wheat that most attracts Huns. Wheat, oats, and barley make up about 70 percent of the fall and winter partridge diet on the Canadian plains and probably throughout much of the range. When birds cannot be flushed by combing the small-grain stubble, they are most likely roosting in hay—alfalfa being the favorite type—or seeking grit along dusty edges. Yet in some dry western habitats they subsist in wild terrain on forb and weed seeds.

VOICE: A familiar springtime sound in northern farm country is a metallic, rusty-gate croak of the cock partridge in need of a mate. But during hunting season the only sounds a gunner is apt to hear are mellow little feeding clucks or soft, conversational chirrings if the birds break their silence before becoming alarmed. When flushed they sometimes cackle but more often chirp or remain silent. The combined chirps and whirring of wings can be startling if a sizable covey flushes close. Once in a while, if the birds scatter, a hunter hears a reedy, plaintive call that has been compared to the sound of wind fiddling a fence wire.

Ring-necked Pheasant (Phasianus colchicus)

COMMON & REGIONAL NAMES: *ringneck, Chinese pheasant, Mongolian pheasant, cackle-bird.*

DESCRIPTION & DISTRIBUTION: With head down and tail stub vibrating, a springer spaniel plunges about an overgrown weed field, circling and making long S-curves. A hunter trots after him, trying hard to stay close. He glimpses a big coppery cock pheasant skulking like a fox across a small opening, head and tail stretched low. The dog pushes harder and the ringneck crosses another gap, this time with head and tail angled high, body up, sprinting for a bramble patch. The hunter slows to a walk and plants his feet for good balance. He is betting the bird will hold until flushed from the island of thick cover. As the dog bellies in, the bird clatters into the air with a cackle

Field where edges or shocks may hold birds.

and a great flapping of rounded wings. The rise is moderately steep and probably faster than it looks, but the hunter is set. He lets the ringneck tower to 25 feet or so, level off, and start away, alternating rapid wingbeats with short glides, accelerating. With the long tail streaming behind, it is a seemingly large target. But pheasant shooters miss enough easy-looking birds to know that a ringneck can better 35 miles an hour after leveling, and sometimes 50 on a long, high flight with the wind at its tail. Except for straightaway shots, the experienced ringneck hunter disregards the bird's body, deceptively lengthened by the tail; he swings on the head or at least the fore part of the target and takes his lead from that.

At least half of a mature cock pheasant's 2½- to 3-foot length consists of its smoothly tapering, buff-brown, black-barred tail plumes. The bird is built like a fighting cock; large as it seems, it usually weighs less than 3 pounds. A 2½-pound rooster may be a bird of the year, but a heavier one is almost certainly an adult, at least eighteen months old. Hens are shorter-tailed,

generally have a total length of about 20 or 21 inches, and weigh about a pound less. Where they are legal game they can be difficult targets, though as a rule not quite so wary as cocks.

There is no handsomer bird than a male ringneck. The black of his head and neck is glossed with iridescent green and violet and topped by long, low ear tufts. Around his yellow eye and on the cheek is a bright-red naked patch, combining comb and wattle. A narrow, immaculate white collar usually rings the base of the neck but is sometimes absent on the Americanized pheasant. It is not seen on the Japanese pheasant, which has recently been released in New Jersey and probably elsewhere. A slightly smaller, faster, shyer, greener, and very hardy bird, it is inclined to roost among conifers and feed on acorns and other wild foods in hilly woods. There are more than forty different pheasants in Asia and Asia Minor, and several European types. The common American pheasant, though predominantly Chi-

Ringneck towering.

nese in heritage, is a unique mongrel, a successful experimental blending of Chinese, Korean, and Manchurian ringnecks, with a small infusion of Japanese green and Caucasian blackneck genes.

The rooster's body is a blend of brown, copper, and russet tones, scaled with black and white. Near the rump is a vague saddle wash of sky-blue. The brown pales on the wing coverts, and the brown primaries are palely barred. The hen is a more subdued brown, with no contrasting colors in the head plumage; she is delicately scaled and mottled with black and some white, and her underparts fade to soft, light buff.

Owing largely to mixed bloodlines, black pheasants are seen occasionally. Albinos are rare, but hunters in the Dakotas sometimes bag "mottled pheasants"—partially white birds. Experiments continue with various fast, adaptable subspecies, while natural selection slowly forges subtle changes in the common type.

Pheasant hunting was a popular European sport in the eighteenth century, while in America the birds were stocked by such eminent wingshooters as George Washington, Governor James Montgomery of New York, and Benjamin Franklin's son-in-law, Richard Bache. Importations were unsuccessful, however, until 1881, when Owen H. Denny, consul-general at Shanghai, shipped Chinese ringnecks to his brother's farm near Corvallis, Oregon. In ten years the progeny of the original twenty-one birds spread through the Willamette Valley. Ringnecks were released during the next few decades in at least ten states. (Pheasants, being large, strong, and aggressive, are sometimes charged with driving quail out, but bobwhite coveys are diminished by hard weather or changing agricultural practices, not by the introduction of ringnecks.)

Midwestern farming methods benefited pheasants until the 1940s, when the birds reached their highest numbers. However, ringnecks must have their fields of corn and other grain seamed and speckled with cover and water sources: hedges, fence rows, windbreaks, groves, grass- and brush-rimmed potholes. A decline began in the 1950s, resulting from the disappearance of diversified family farms and the trend toward huge single-crop corporations. The decline has been exacerbated by Government policies encouraging farmers to retire fields and leave them plowed and bare. As this is written, however, minor changes in the farm program are being considered to encourage the planting of retired fields with food and cover for wildlife.

At present thirty-seven states have pheasant seasons and the birds range across lower Canada, as far north as 400 miles from the United States border in Alberta and Saskatchewan, where the hunting is excellent on the prairie farms. In the East the lower limit of distribution (apart from artificially maintained preserve stock) is an indistinct line stretching from the upper tip of Chesapeake Bay to central Illinois. To the west the line dips through upper Missouri into Kansas and southern Colorado, then almost straight across to central California. Though there are small, scattered populations below the line, pheasants fare poorly in the South. In the 1920s the naturalist and game manager Aldo Leopold first advanced the theory that calcium requirements limit the range; laying hen pheasants need more calcium than birds that evolved on this continent, and they thrive only as far south as glaciers carried heavy lime deposits or in unglaciated pockets of habitat that are rich in the proper type of lime. Hatching success may also be reduced by high ground temperatures.

Hunting is probably best in Iowa, where the 1971 harvest was 1,800,000 ringnecks, and in Illinois. It is good in most midwestern states, in California, and in a number of eastern states that have extensive stocking programs.

GAME BEHAVIOR & HUNTING HABITAT: Most of the cock pheasants bagged in fall were hatched in the previous May or June. In the wild, ringnecks never attain the age of eight years that is common in captivity. Hens, being more resistant than cocks to inclement weather and starvation, live an average of twenty months. Most cocks live only half as long, an even briefer span than that of the fragile dove. Hunters who tell about wise old cock birds seldom examine the spurs. A juvenile cock has a blunt, rough, conical projection, less than ¾ inch long, on the rear of each leg. By the bird's second autumn the spurs are nearly an inch long, harder, darker, glossy, pointed. A cock uses his spurs in April when, strutting and crowing, he claims dominion over a small territory in any good wintering area. Although he has been feeding peaceably with other males, chance meetings

in spring are apt to become savage fights. Hens, singly and in groups, are welcomed with courtly bowing, bobbing, wingspreading, hissing, and tailspreading. The length and spread of a rooster's tail are important sexual attractants. Soon six or eight hens settle in his territory, and in April and May they build shallow nests in dry grasses, sedge, hay, or even grain stubble where there is cover and a copious insect supply for the young. A hen incubates her clutch of eleven or twelve eggs for about twenty-three days. Hatching in most regions begins early in May, and

Hunter accepting cock from Brittany.

the chicks spill from the nest as soon as they are dry. In a couple of weeks they fly fairly well, and the broods disperse in late summer.

The surviving birds in October represent about a quarter of all the eggs laid. Game-farm ringnecks are susceptible to devastating poultry diseases—pullorum, Newcastle disease, and a form of encephalomyelitis—but in the wild they are more resistant to ailments and parasites than any other American game. A more serious limiting factor is predation, and in most areas house cats and farm dogs are among the chief culprits. The constantly villified fox has proved in studies to be responsible for surprisingly few pheasant kills. Other predators include the great horned owl, skunks, hawks, magpies, crows, squirrels, coyotes, and weasels.

Freezing and accidents account for greater numbers. Where potholes are filled and hedgerows bulldozed, there is little cover from fierce prairie winds. During blizzards, snow is beaten under the plumage, where it melts and is frozen again by the winds, killing countless birds. The survivors are weakened, and although winter starvation is low among pheasants some eventually succumb. Where drainage ditches or brush strips parallel highways, road kills are another severe problem. Alfalfa fields and other hay meadows furnish ideal nesting sites, but high-speed mowers destroy countless nests. Hidden under the tall hay, as many as a third of the incubating hens may be destroyed with the nests as they defy the mowers in a futile attempt to shield their eggs.

Yet, somehow, tens of millions of pheasants appear in the cornfields for the autumn harvest. They eat protein-rich insects and calcium-rich snails, and even an occasional mouse or snake, but they are primarily, voraciously, seed-eaters. Corn in some regions makes up four-fifths of their diet. Wheat, oats, barley, soybeans, and weed seeds are other important foods. On some of the brushy northeastern farmlands we often flush ringnecks out of grape tangles, sumac clumps, blackberry patches, old orchards—coverts that seem more natural for grouse than pheasants. Over most of the range the favorite wild foods are foxtail and ragweed.

Along the brushy edges of farm lots, in standing corn, and in wild tangles early in the season when the cover is thick, many of us abide heretically by our 20-gauge Magnums, with chokes no tighter than modified, and sometimes we use shot as small as 7½. A midwestern wingshooter, accustomed to wide open fields, might puzzle at the use of anything but a full-choked 12-gauge duck gun with high-brass No. 6 loads. A good marksman who has had years of gunning in the Iowa fields can wait out a ringneck to 50 yards and count on bagging it with a tight pattern. Much can be claimed for a full choke and large pellets at long range and with birds succinctly described by the writer John Madson as "shingled with galvanized feathers." But another old hunting companion and estimable writer, the late Larry Koller, felt that the use of tight chokes by merely average shooters resulted in a disgraceful number of wing-tipped birds.

Another persistent argument concerns the best kind of pheasant dog. An English pointer, a setter, a Brit—any pointing breed—may perform admirably. Some hunters object that pheasants skulk or run instead of holding, thus inducing bad habits in a quail dog while consistently rising beyond range. Undeniably, there are fine quail dogs that should be used infrequently (if at all) for ringneck hunting, but a good pointing dog can be trained to hunt pheasants very effectively by quartering wide and coming around on the far side to block runs. The only thing a pheasant pointer cannot do is outperform a good flushing dog. A well-trained springer spaniel with a good nose and plenty of stamina will force-flush birds that elude lesser animals. The strain of chasing an eager springer chasing a ground-running pheasant has an excitement as rewarding as a stanch point. Some hunters prefer to work with a slower-going, tightly controlled retriever. A good Lab will flush game and has no superiors in the art of finding downed birds, including lightly hit ringnecks, which can sail a long way, come down running, and hide brilliantly.

During the early part of the season pheasants are sprinkled through the grainfields, along the edges, in stubble, high grass, brush, and sometimes in thin neighboring woods. They feed heavily in the morning and again late in the afternoon, though some are apt to be in the fields at almost any time. Morning is an excellent time for the dogless pheasant drives traditional to many midwestern regions. Depending on the size of the field to be driven, up to a dozen men may serve as drivers, and as many more "blockers" may be stationed at the field's end. It is usually best to drive toward hedgerows, fences, corners, or brush-edged sloughs. A drive can also be productive when it moves toward the small end of tapering cover; to a pheasant, running out of cover is like running into an obstacle that dictates flight. The line of drivers should be somewhat cupped so that birds cannot run out to the field's sides. And the drivers should be in position before the blockers are stationed or the birds will become aware of the blocking line too soon and, again, skulk away to the sides. Because pheasants have keen vision and hearing, the blockers should move quietly. If the cover is very dry it is best to drive against the wind. The birds will rise away, into the wind, but some will be close enough and others will furnish pass-shooting for the blockers. The most common mistakes are to space the drivers too far apart and to move too directly and quickly. Pheasants easily slip through a space of more than 15 or 20 yards between drivers, and even when the men are that close they should waver or zigzag slightly as they move forward.

The same procedure can be used by a lone hunter walking up pheasants without a dog. He is bound to pass many birds that hide rock-still, but fewer will evade him if he zigzags, walks slowly, stops frequently, and occasionally doubles back a short distance. Such maneuvers shatter the resolve of a hiding bird, producing a sudden, steep, air-pounding flush. When walking alone rather than driving, some shooters prefer to hunt downwind in the hope of reasonably easy shots as birds rise into the breeze. Lone hunting is often best after a rain or in heavy dew, because pheasants dislike getting wet and are reluctant to move about in dripping cover until forced to.

At midday it is worthwhile to hunt fence rows, swales, field edges, and grassy hillsides. Resting birds sun themselves on slopes—lee slopes if there is wind. A strong-enough wind can move them into valleys or weedy bottoms, the sort of cover they seek late in the season. Midday is also a time to hunt dusting and grit-pecking spots—old, overgrown gravel pits and the like. In the afternoon the birds drift into high corn, small thickets, meadow edges, hedgerows, and brushy farmyards, but toward evening they head for roosting cover such as high clover, hay, or stubble.

As winter comes on they take shelter in clumps of willow, Russian olive, weedy ditches, windbreaks, sumac and wild-plum

PHEASANT

LANDING IN SNOW

3"

TAIL MARKS

thickets, cattail stands, high brush along sloughs and marsh edges. Large numbers of birds are drawn to limited shelter areas, forming flocks that are often segregated by sex. A flock of hens is likely to be larger than a flock of roosters, but it is sometimes possible to flush twenty or thirty cock birds out of a willow-choked ditch.

Thinning cover and snow combine to increase visibility and the distance at which birds flush. Walking them up is difficult when they are not huddled in shelterbelts, but an inch or so of fresh snow can enable a man to track and flush them. They make big, thin-toed tracks. The three printing toes are widely separated, as with other birds, and the tracks are often more than 3 inches long. Those of cocks are larger than hen tracks. Sometimes a whole flock can be trailed a little way before the prints become a maze. The birds tend to move over a field in a rather direct line—between rows of corn, for example—and then mill about to feed or snuggle down for shelter on the lee sides of stalks, hummocks, clods—any little windbreak. Approaching with the wind at his back, a hunter may walk past several birds without seeing them, but if he stops and turns frequently, ringnecks are apt to rise in a panic-stricken flurry.

VOICE: The pheasant is a wild chicken, capable of all the clucks, croaks, and cackles that typify domestic fowl. Cocks are generally noisier than hens, and what a hunter hears most often is a loud, hoarse cackle as a rooster goes up. Sometimes the strident *ca-a-a-k, ca-ak!*—accompanied by rustling, clattering wings—comes from an unexpected direction and the hunter turns fast, off balance but mounting the gun instinctively.

Dove *(Zenaidura macroura and Zenaida asiatica)*

COMMON & REGIONAL NAMES: For mourning dove—*Carolina dove, turtle dove.* For white-winged dove—*whitewing, Sonora dove, Sonora pigeon, singing dove.*

DESCRIPTION & DISTRIBUTION: Several dove-shooting acquaintances in eastern Tennessee speak wryly of a 12-bird limit as a "box of shells," meaning that at least a couple of shots have been fired for every dove bagged. What sounds like a tribute to the twisting, evasive flight of the birds is a sly boast; after the season has been open for a few weeks, only the good shooters average better than one dove for every four or five shells.

The mourning doves *(Zenaidura macroura)* come in high over the grainfields, loose, skittering sprays of them flying 35 or 40 miles an hour but capable of abrupt accelerations up to 60 with a strong-enough tail wind. A mourning dove is slim and streamlined and has narrow, sharply raked wings and a long, tapered tail. The body is grayish brown—almost mauve in soft light—with dark wings, a black cheek spot, and a pinkish-beige breast and belly. When a dove goes past on a relatively slow, straight course, white spots show on its pointed blue-gray tail, edged with black and white. The sexes look much alike but the female is slightly smaller and duller than the male, has a shorter tail, and lacks the iridescent sheen that stipples a male's neck.

A typical dove has a 19- or 20-inch wingspread and measures only about a foot from bill tip to the point of the long tail. With frustrating regularity, the leading edge of a shot pattern trails the small body and sprinkles ineffectually through the deceptive tail feathers. Early in the season, when the birds have not yet become gun-shy and most of them are not indecisive migrants but local breeders with established flight paths, the shooting sometimes is easy. But a skittish dove can twist right out of a well-placed shot string, and four wingbeats will take it out of range.

Because doves and wild pigeons are migratory, states must set bag limits, shooting hours, and seasons within Federally regulated maximums. In a typical year, seventy shooting days might be permitted between early September and mid-January. The maximum Federal bag limit might be twelve per day in the East, ten in the West, but shooting hours in eastern states generally last only from noon until sunset, while in the West shooting may begin half an hour before sunrise. Most states split their seasons, sometimes three ways (e.g., September, the last half of October, and three winter weeks ending in mid-January). The rest periods benefit hunters as well as birds, for doves grow excessively wary after a month or so of shooting.

The migration of mourning doves is almost as erratic as their flight; some of them appear to remain in one area all year while others travel long distances. They breed somewhere on the continent in every month, nesting in every state except Alaska. A fitful southward movement begins very early in the fall. Most of the September birds in a good hunting locale have bred there; a little later the resident flocks are joined by migrants from farther north, just as "native" woodcock are joined by "flight birds." Still later, most of an area's doves may be transients or birds settling there only for the winter.

Mourning doves are most populous in the Southeast during the hunting season, but there is a western subspecies and so a dove limit can be bagged in at least twenty-five states in a good year. There are also a couple of American subspecies of the closely related white-winged dove *(Zenaida asiatica),* which breeds in Texas, New Mexico, Arizona, lower Nevada, and California. A few whitewings are taken as far east as Florida. Though the population tends to fluctuate sharply, it is high enough to

Mourning dove.

cause occasional crop damage. Southwestern dove hunting is apt to be excellent early in the season; a little later there are big shoots below the Mexican border, since many whitewings winter in South America. A whitewing is stockier than a mourning dove and easily recognized in flight by big white patches on the wing coverts, contrasting sharply with dark brownish-gray primaries and secondaries. Its tail is blunt and broadly tipped with white at the rear corners. Whereas a mourning dove's wings whistle softly as its primaries cut the breeze, a whitewing makes no flight sound. Neither does it twist and turn and dip so disconcertingly, but anyone who has opened a second box of shells during a California whitewing shoot will testify to the difficulty of the target.

GAME BEHAVIOR & HUNTING HABITAT: Doves are fragile birds.

White-winged dove (above), and
Oregon hunter bagging dove over grainfield.

A Pennsylvania study showed that only about half the hatchlings survive the two weeks before they can fly. The mortality rate is 70 or 80 percent in the first year, about 50 percent in the second, and not very many live beyond another breeding season. For every mature dove a hunter bags, he probably takes four or five birds of the year. Yet only a fraction of the doomed surplus is harvested. In 1972 one small southeastern farming area produced about 120,000 doves; in September 40,000 were killed over the local millet and sunflower fields, and some of those were transients. The breeding population was unchanged in the spring. A hard winter, a cold, wet spring, or a summer drought can take a high toll, and the surplus is thinned by the same predators—from owls and hawks to stray cats—that attack most upland birds. Intestinal worms can weaken them, viral diseases can kill them, and cowbirds sometimes steal dove eggs and substitute their own. Like a number of other birds, doves and pigeons may occasionally carry psittacosis or other diseases, including a form of meningitis, but they are perfectly safe to eat—and their dark, rich meat is delicious—when properly cooked.

In a breeding area, spring is marked by a surge of courtship flights and displays. Rival males occasionally engage in pecking contests hardly appropriate for a symbolic bird of peace. Rather primitive twig nests are built in brushy trees, and two eggs are laid. Male and female share in the 2-week incubation of eggs and in feeding the hatchlings "pigeon milk" (regurgitated, liquified food) as well as insects and seeds. Unlike most game birds, dove and pigeon hatchlings are altricial—naked and helpless. But they develop so rapidly that after a fortnight the parents abandon them and nest again. Depending on region and climate, a breeding pair may hatch a couple of broods or half a dozen before stopping, but an average pair produces four to six young.

Where there are no convenient grain crops, doves thrive on bristlegrass, doveweed, ragweed, pokeweed, pigweed, crabgrass, and a variety of other weeds and seeds. But a farmer who has "planted a dove field" (for lease to hunters) is probably raising browntop millet. Newly planted barley and wheatfields will draw doves, too, and another fine place to sit out a warm fall afternoon is a sunflower patch or a machine-picked cornfield. Cane, sorghum, rye, buckwheat, peanuts, or peas will also attract the birds. Whitewings seek the same grains as mourning doves but are often shot over uncultivated, brushy land where they rely on doveweed and other wild plants.

They feed hard during the morning, rest at midday, generally visit the fields again between about two-thirty and four o'clock, go to water, and then to roost. A southern gentleman likes to leave his office early in the afternoon, carrying a folding chair, shell pouch, and shotgun. He makes himself comfortable and inconspicuous in a dry irrigation ditch or the shade of a hedgerow. The gun across his lap is 12 or 20 gauge, bored improved or modified, and the shells are usually field loads of 7½'s or 8's, perhaps high-velocity loads if the birds have been flying high and flaring. Since a southern dove shoot sometimes is a social event, he may have friends with him. They can separate and more or less surround a large field.

Shots at arriving birds are probably least demanding from

a stand among scattered trees near the grain, or later in the day near a water hole. Whenever possible, doves reconnoiter from trees before fluttering down to feed. Sometimes as they come within range of the trees they slow up so noticeably that they almost seem to hover, and they tend to glide toward watering spots. The shooting near water may come in gleefully flustering spurts but it seldom lasts long.

Some hunters wear camouflage. It helps but is not essential for a gunner who stands or sits in partial concealment, or breaks his outline against a tree or bush. Where birds have learned to be cautious, a few rough decoys can be propped in a tree or on a fence, or stick-ups can be placed in a field or, in late afternoon, at the edge of a ditch or pond. In neither case will they bring doves pitching in like ducks, but they will pull some of the birds just close enough.

It is possible to walk doves up in a field with a standing crop or in brushy areas near the wooded night roosts. Where they have high ground cover they are not so quick to take off, though they may still flush out of range or skim close to the ground for quite a way. They will not hold for a dog, but a retriever is an asset, especially in brush where finding fallen doves is as hard as hitting them. A hunter may have at heel any dog he uses for other upland shooting if the animal fetches well.

VOICE: The mournful coo of doves is most insistent when males are courting mates but is also heard where birds congregate in hunting season. Whitewings have more abrasive voices than eastern doves, with a broken tone almost like a rooster's. A few hunters try to encourage doves to swing in close by calling them. A characteristic series of several hollow coos is neither particularly hard to imitate nor startlingly effective.

Band-tailed Pigeon *(Columba fasciata)*

& Common Pigeon *(Columba livia)*

COMMON & REGIONAL NAMES: For band-tailed pigeon—*band-tail, wild pigeon, white-collared pigeon.* For common pigeon—*rock pigeon, blue rock pigeon, rock dove, domestic pigeon, feral pigeon, squab dove.*

DESCRIPTION & DISTRIBUTION: The first clusters of bandtails sweep down fast in September, rising and dipping to follow the contours of slopes as they look for low spots with roosting and foraging trees and water nearby. A good place for a pigeon hunter to be then is behind a boulder, in brush, or against a tree near the crest of a California ridge dotted with piñon and scrub oak. The plump birds are about 14 to 16 inches long, with a wingspan averaging about 2 feet. They are larger than domestic pigeons, yet easily fly 45 miles an hour—faster, straighter, higher than any other American pigeons. Fortunately they are only a little above the trees as they look for feeding and resting places. Their vision is keen, but if the wingshooter hides they will slow up as they climb to the ridge. Giving his target twice the lead a novice might expect, he will shoot before the bird dips and gains momentum.

Bandtails migrate in sporadic waves and not always along the same flyways. But big, loose flocks can be expected where there are piñon nuts and acorns, especially if grain crops are cultivated nearby. (Nothing tastes better than squab fattened on piñon.) For at least a couple of weeks the pass-shooting should be good, and until the pigeons become wary there will be some jump-shooting at fields, water holes, or roosts.

Their grace of flight is accentuated by a muted grace of plumage. A typical bandtail has dense, smooth gray feathering with brownish and bluish overtones on its back and wing coverts. Its flight feathers are a darker gray-brown. Across its fanned gray tail, wider than a common pigeon's, is a dark gray-brown subterminal band and behind that a broad, pale gray terminal band. The feet are yellow, the bill yellow but darkly tipped and softly cered. The head and breast are a smoky mauve that fades out on the belly. The sides of the neck gleam with greenish iridescence, separated from the lilac head by a narrow white crescented bar that crosses the nape but ends above the throat, making the common name "white-collared pigeon" not quite accurate. Females are slightly duller than males but a bandtail that lacks the bar is a juvenile.

Band-tailed pigeons breed from southwestern British Columbia down the Pacific Coast to Baja California, eastward into New Mexico, and up into the lower Rockies. They winter from Puget Sound southward, with the greatest concentrations

(text continued on page 73)

▲ Unusually pale mourning dove.   ▼ Whitewing.   ▼ Typical mourning dove in flight.

▲ Sharptail. ▼ Sage grouse on dancing ground.

▲ Hunter in sage-grouse country.　▼ Courtship display of blue grouse.

▲ Cock pheasant flushing. ▼ Chukars. ▼ Hen pheasant skulking.

▼ Hungarian partridge landing. ▼ Hun's cinnamon facial pattern.

▲ White-tailed ptarmigan.   ▼ Rock ptarmigan in summer.   ▼ Rock ptarmigan in winter.

▼ Willow ptarmigan.

▼ Retriever delivering band-tailed pigeon.

▲ Bobwhite covey flushing.   ▼ Bobwhite male (l.) and female.

▼ Scaled quail.

▼ Desert, or Gambel's, quail.

▲ Rio Grande gobbler.   ▼ Florida turkey.   ▼ Eastern turkey.

▼ Woodcock.

usually in California, Arizona, New Mexico, and below the Mexican border. Migration begins very early in September and dwindles in October. The return takes place chiefly in April and May. Birds from the north often mingle with southern bandtails that shift very little in autumn.

Bandtails once clouded the western skies just as passenger pigeons did in the East. Game marketers sometimes dispensed with guns and used nets. When the Government closed the season for five years beginning in 1914, sizable flocks still wintered in the oak forests around Santa Barbara, but they had become scarce in many regions. Their recovery has been slow; as migratory birds they have benefited from Federal game regulations. They are now hunted in Arizona, California, Colorado, New Mexico, Oregon, Utah, and Washington. The current bag limit is eight daily in California, Oregon, and Washington, five elsewhere. The season generally lasts a month or less, beginning in early September, though some states vary the regulations by county; there is an October season in regions where the birds arrive late.

Of the many other species of pigeons, few hold any interest for American hunters. The white-crowned pigeon *(C. leucocephala)* inhabits the Florida Keys, where it is protected, and the Bahamas, where it is hunted near the poisonwood thickets. Its white crown is a sure mark of identification. The red-billed pigeon *(C. flavirostris)* ranges from above the Rio Grande to Costa Rica; it is protected in Texas but ardently hunted among the stands of Mexican thorn trees. Apart from its small red bill and a deep maroon that often tinges its breast and wing coverts, it looks like a dark common pigeon. Indeed, like the common variety, it is often called a blue rock pigeon.

Undoubtedly, some interbreeding must occur where ranges overlap, and the common pigeon's range is global. America's flocks are feral, descended from domesticated strains of the rock pigeon common to Asia and Europe. In cities they deface buildings and monuments, occasionally spread disease (though the meat when properly cooked is safe to eat), and furnish supplementary food for rats and other vermin. New York City alone has more than 5 million of the birds. In rural areas they can be a severe agricultural nuisance and can compete with doves and other seed-eating wildlife. Where there is no human habitation they roost and nest among cliffs, but can just as well

use building ledges and bridge supports.

As nonmigratory birds, rock pigeons receive no Federal protection and need none. Many states set no closed season or bag limit, for a substantial thinning would benefit wildlife and man. Most of us enjoyed boyhood pigeon shooting and some of us still relish its excitement—not the excitement of numbers but of speed when the birds become aware of danger. The common rock pigeon is, after all, the species used in live-pigeon shoots, among the most exacting of shotgunning competitions.

In its classic form the rock pigeon is a one-pound bird, 12 or 13 inches long, gray with a whitish rump, a broad black terminal band on its tail, two black bars across the secondaries, an iridescent sheen on neck or breast, reddish feet, and a gray bill with a large, pale cere. Wild hybridizing and domestic breeding have produced infinite variations, the most common being black, brown, white, or white patched with another hue.

GAME BEHAVIOR & HUNTING HABITAT: Rock pigeons in wild areas use cracks and holes in cliffs as roosts, but bandtails roost in trees—often tall ones with high dead limbs so that no foliage blocks vision or slows escape if they spot a prairie falcon, Cooper's

Band-tailed pigeon (opposite), a fast
shot on bandtail (top), and water retrieve of bandtail.

hawk, or other winged predator. Only a few birds may live through a second or third breeding season. Though raptors are no longer abundant, pigeons are sought by the various predators that kill doves and other birds, and are subject to the same diseases and parasitic infestations. Nematode parasites in particular can be lethal.

Breeding intensifies in spring but in warm southern regions it may continue through every month except November and December. As the males perform courtship displays and nuptial flights, monogamous pairs form and flocks disintegrate. The male helps to build a flimsy twig nest—usually in a tree in the case of bandtails, on a ledge in the case of rock pigeons. Incubation is shared by the mates. Bandtails hatch in about eighteen to twenty days, rock pigeons hatch a little faster. Two or three broods may be produced where nesting seasons are long. A bandtail hen generally lays only one egg, sometimes two, while a rock pigeon may have a clutch as large as four. It seems doubtful that more than a single chick often survives, because it is not fledged for about a month. By that time a squab may be larger than its parents and there is no room for more than one on the slovenly twig platform. The young are fed on the regurgitated liquid substance called pigeon milk and on seeds and insects.

Band-tailed pigeon, with white neck crescent evident (above), and shooting blue rock pigeons.

After fledging, they continue to consume grasshoppers and a few other insects, but they are primarily seed-eaters.

One reason rock pigeons are so widely distributed is that almost any grain or similar food will keep them healthy. The bandtail hunter knows that his quarry's narrower requirements determine the places where the birds are most often bagged. In most good bandtail habitat acorns, piñon nuts, and hazels are the most important foods, followed by wild cherries, elderberries, wheat, oats, and barley. Pigeons also like dogwood, waste corn in stubble fields, grain sprouts, wild grapes, blueberries, blackberries, mulberries, and manzanita berries.

Since they are in migration during hunting season, most bandtails are bagged by pass-shooting from concealment, and the best spots are on ridges or hillsides near food that draws the birds down. As soon as they begin to settle in, they can also be waylaid or walked up at water holes and grainfields. When flushed they rise a few at a time like mourning doves rather than in a cloud like white-winged doves and rock pigeons. Early in the season they are not very wary, but they quickly learn to avoid danger. A noisy, wing-flapping rise characterizes pigeons surprised while feeding, yet they can alight soundlessly in a tree and perch in silence, often unnoticed by hunters intent on searching the ground. They do not hold for dogs, and—as with doves and woodcock—some dogs seem to have an aversion to fetching pigeons. Nonetheless, a willing retriever is a great help, especially in oak canyons, chaparral, or bush.

Bandtails begin feeding shortly after dawn and keep at it until eight or nine in the morning, then seek grit, dust themselves, go to water, and perch in trees until the afternoon cools. They feed again heavily from about four o'clock until dusk brings them back to the trees for roosting. Because so much bandtail shooting is pass-shooting, western hunters often use 12-gauge full-choke repeaters or double guns bored modified and full, usually loaded with No. 6 high-brass shells. However, early in the season and especially at grainfields or water holes, a modified 20 gauge with No. 7½ loads can be just as effective.

Rock pigeons are generally bagged at closer range. Where they have spread into mountainous terrain, a modified choke is a logical choice, but for grainfield and barnyard shooting an improved cylinder is fine with No. 6 or 7½ field loads.

City pigeons in farming regions usually make morning and late afternoon flights to grain elevators, hog lots, seed and feed warehouses, or grainfields. Large farm flocks roost close to feeding fields, in barns, sheds, and abandoned buildings, under bridges, on rocky bluffs. Farmers usually welcome shooters who reduce the flocks. A common method is to stand in a barn door, thump the wall hard, and shoot at the pigeons that dive out of the loft and from under the roof. The portly birds that look so easy swoop down with startling speed. Many shooters wait until a pigeon has dived close to the ground and has begun to swerve upward, slowing on the rise. A good alternative is to hide in a grainfield and wait for morning or evening flights. Hiding can be essential; pigeons pay little attention to noise other than gunfire, but after the first few shots they flare if they see a gunner in the grain. Decoys work well in stubble. Rock pigeons are fooled by the crudest wooden, cardboard, or plastic-foam cut outs, and will also come to commercial dove decoys.

VOICE: Bandtails make a strange wheezing sound during nuptial flights, but in the hunting season pigeons have a repertoire of owlish cooing and trilling notes. Though quiet on the wing, they can be talkative when feeding and sometimes at roosts.

Willow Ptarmigan *(Lagopus lagopus)*
Rock Ptarmigan *(L. mutus)*
& White-tailed Ptarmigan *(L. leucurus)*

COMMON & REGIONAL NAMES: For willow ptarmigan—*snow grouse, arctic grouse, white grouse, Alaska partridge, willow partridge, willow grouse.* For rock ptarmigan—*snow grouse, arctic grouse, white grouse, rocker, barren-ground bird.* For white-tailed ptarmigan—*snow grouse, snow partridge, Rocky Mountain snow grouse, mountain quail, white quail, whitetail.*

DESCRIPTION & DISTRIBUTION: On tundra or the slopes above timber line, dwarf willow and birch rise from a shrub mat studded with lichen-daubed rock slabs and saucers of old snow. Suddenly a patch of lichen-and-snow-specked rubble breaks into a dozen winged fragments that bluster upward a few feet, cackling and beating the air, then sail down the slope as most high-country grouse will when flushed. Ptarmigan can roost invisibly in the open, their white or spattered brown-and-white plumage camouflaging them completely. They leave the ground about as fast as pigeons and probably have a speed close to 40 miles an hour once up. In country penetrated by only a very few big-game hunters they sometimes seem as stupid as northern spruce grouse,

White-tailed ptarmigan.

Pair of ptarmigan about to flush (top), and
rock ptarmigan in autumn plumage.

but where they have been pressed by shotgunners they can dodge along the ground or flush far out. Though lightly hunted in their remote abode, they are the major upland game of the North.

All three American species are small, plump (and very tasty) grouse that turn white in winter and have fully feathered legs. The males are slightly larger than the females. Willow and rock ptarmigan are circumpolar in distribution; few sportsmen realize that Scottish red grouse are a race of willow ptarmigan, the species of widest American range. On this continent seven subspecies of willow ptarmigan are found from northern Alaska down to central British Columbia and across all of Canada. They also inhabit Greenland, Baffin, and the smaller arctic islands. Both willow and rock ptarmigan migrate to lower, somewhat more sheltered habitat for the winter. As the days become stormy and cold, all species gather into loose flocks. In some regions the groups are sexually segregated, evidently because hens require more forested winter habitat than cocks. Their travel intensifies in October and ends by December; a gradual, sporadic return begins in January. Willow ptarmigan in the lower part of their range wander to the United States border and a few appear in northern Minnesota.

The male is about 14 to 17 inches long and weighs 20 to 24 ounces. His eye is browed with a scarlet comb. His primaries and secondaries remain white all year, while his white-tipped tail remains dark brown except for white central feathers. The rest of his plumage turns white in winter, and his unusually long upper tail coverts often conceal the dark splotch. A spring molt turns the bird predominantly chestnut or rusty hazel, darkly barred on back and sides, fading out on the underparts.

The female is combless and in summer is heavily barred with dark brown and ocher. Both sexes have begun to acquire white feathering in autumn. They look as if flecked with snow, but a male's back tends to remain brownly barred, while a female is more grayish above and white below. The feet of winter-white birds are covered with long, coarse, hairy feathers that help support them on snow.

The eleven American subspecies of rock ptarmigan are not encountered quite as far south as willow ptarmigan except along the Pacific Coast, but they occupy the same general range. They are slightly smaller, males averaging 12½ to 15½ inches,

15 to 19 ounces. Both sexes retain blackish tails throughout the year. The summer plumage of the scarlet-combed male is browner—less rusty—than a willow ptarmigan's and has thin brownish-black markings rather than bars. The female is lighter and more coarsely barred. In early autumn a cock is mostly ash-gray, a hen browner with sprinklings of white. A little later, when they are most likely to be flushed in willow habitat, both sexes turn white. The male has a black streak from the bill through the eye, but the female sometimes has an all-white head and is distinguished from a willow ptarmigan only by her smaller, blacker bill.

The white-tailed ptarmigan's primary range extends from central Alaska down through the western Yukon and British Columbia to Vancouver Island, with a few birds scattered into Washington. Separate populations salt the Yukon-Mackenzie border and the Rockies in Alberta, Montana, Wyoming, Colorado, and New Mexico. There are five subspecies. Below the Canadian border, Colorado is the only state that has ptarmigan hunting—a 2- to 4-week season, usually in September. Whitetails thrive only

Willow ptarmigan before autumn molt is complete.

on alpine tundra. Colorado has fair hunting; the harvest is generally under 5,000. In contrast, 30,000 rock and willow ptarmigan may be bagged in the Northwest Territories and 50,000 in Newfoundland.

The white-tailed species is the smallest of the three. A male is about 12 to 13½ inches long and seldom weighs more than 12 ounces. His summer plumage is mostly brownish, barred, vermiculated, and mottled with black, buff, and white. The rump is tawny or pale yellowish brown, the underparts white. The female is more yellowish and spotty. She is the only hen ptarmigan with a comb; it is not as large or red as the male's, and his is not conspicuous. Both sexes retain white tails and wings throughout the year. In autumn the birds are pale cinnamon on their upper parts, finely spotted and lined with brownish black, speckled white on the breast, and by winter they are pure white except for black bill, eyes, and claws.

GAME BEHAVIOR & HUNTING HABITAT: Willow ptarmigan are bagged at relatively low elevations—on moist tundra with moderately tall shrub growth, along the timber line, in tundralike openings of the boreal forest, in streamside willows, on muskegs and burns. Rock ptarmigan are more often flushed from shorter, sparser vegetation on higher, rocky slopes around timber line or above. White-tailed ptarmigan are more likely to burst off steep slopes and ridges farther above timber line.

The three species are fairly similar as to foraging and breeding. Willow ptarmigan rely chiefly on willow buds and twigs for food, rock ptarmigan or dwarf birch buds and catkins, whitetailed ptarmigan on alpine willow, heath, and mosses. All feed on the buds, berries, seeds, etc. of their alpine home.

Breeding reaches a peak in April and May. The males strut and call from rocks, trees, or hummocks, proclaiming territories as small as 150 yards in diameter for a willow ptarmigan, larger for a whitetail, sometimes a square mile for a rock ptarmigan on open tundra. They soar on song flights and scream flights, and fight squawking battles with rivals. Females wander into a territory, exchange displays with the male, and soon mate. The monogamous male willow ptarmigan helps defend the young. Males of the other species take no part in brooding. The nests are sparsely lined scrapes in screening vegetation. Clutches average five to eight eggs and incubation lasts three weeks or so.

Though the birds are subject to no more than normal predation and are relatively free of diseases and parasites, they exhibit sharp fluctuations of abundance. The longest migrations and sharpest dips in population may follow crowding. Even where density is low and food plentiful, willow ptarmigan have a life span of only about fifteen months and rock ptarmigan are probably comparable. But the hardy little white-tailed birds on the alpine slopes more often live four years.

At first, hunters put up singles and little coveys—probably family groups. As winter approaches the birds "pack" in good feeding spots that are relatively sheltered. Before Colorado's September season closes a hunter may flush twenty birds from heath or willow, and larger flocks sprinkle the arctic tundra.

Whitetails tend to flush farther out and fly greater distances than the others, but all ptarmigan hold fairly well in thick ground cover. If caught in the open, they usually run before they fly. No. 6 loads are recommended in a 12- or 20-gauge shotgun with a modified choke. In Canada, where upland regulations limit gun capacity to two shells, the ideal is a light improved-cylinder and modified double.

A retriever helps where birds fall into cover. Pointing dogs may perform well in brush or willows but can develop the habit of chasing birds in the open. A flushing breed is less help in the open, yet spaniels are becoming popular because they serve so well when the birds begin to cluster in willow runs, birch thickets, and the like.

VOICE: Rock ptarmigan sometimes utter a belching sound or a rapid clicking note, especially in breeding season, and whitetails can scream or hoot. Typical autumn calls are clucks and crowing, but the birds are seldom noisy until flushed.

Bobwhite Quail *(Colinus virginianus)*
COMMON & REGIONAL NAMES: *quail, bobwhite, bob, Virginia partridge.*

DESCRIPTION & DISTRIBUTION: Where a quail hunter does not know of traditional covey locations, he searches for land that

has the look of bobwhite habitation. It may be in Florida's palmetto scrub, Oklahoma's plum-thicket bottoms, Georgia's piney edges, or the Pine Barrens and scrub-oak hills in New Jersey. At one end of a certain ramshackle soybean field in Delaware is a big fallow strip choked with wands of lespedeza and tufted with ragweed. Beyond is a multiflora hedge, brush, honeysuckle and devil's-club, woods. We walk into that strip expecting to see the farmer's wiry little pointer stiffen, tail up, nose to a ragweed clump. A friend's setter comes in tensely to back the pointer, keeping her distance when she honors. The three of us go in quickly, decisively, knowing the covey will bore for the woods. The birds are lying close, as usual, and nothing happens as we pass the pointer; he trembles but does not break point. As we kick through the ragweed, wondering if the dogs are making ground scent left by flown birds, a dozen bobwhites hurtle out, stubby wings thrumming. They seem to spray in all directions, but when they are little more than head high most of them swing for the woods and we have time to swing our guns behind them for a couple of almost straightaway shots. One man has plucked a crossing bird out of the chaos, and the pointer finds it 20 yards away. The straightaways have been dropped farther out.

The facial markings and chunky brown body of a meadowlark can look like a bobwhite flitting out of tall grass, flushing far ahead as a nervous quail might if its calls were unanswered by others in the covey. The lark's tail, however, shows wide white siding. On a close flush bobwhites look rounder than bumblebees; their ability to whiz about at 30 miles an hour and spurt from

Covey of bobwhite quail.

brush at 50 is astonishing.

More than twenty subspecies are distributed across the eastern half of the United States and down through Mexico and Central America. The plains bobwhite*(C. v. taylori),* most plentiful in the Midwest and in Oklahoma and Texas, has been introduced in Washington, Oregon, and Idaho, but has not yet become truly established in the Far West. However, since the bobwhite is a very popular shooting-preserve bird, relatively easy to propagate and inclined to retain fairly wild characteristics when pen-raised, it is bagged in many regions outside its native range.

A few of the races have distinctive markings that would puzzle most upland shooters; the scarce and protected masked bobwhite *(C. v. ridgwayi)* of the Sonoran region has a black face, for example. Most varieties are quite alike, although some southern strains such as the Florida bobwhite *(C. v. floridanus)* are rather small and dark, while some arid-country types such as the Texas bobwhite *(C. v. tefanus)* are pale. The eastern race *(C. v. virginianus)* and New England bobwhite *(C. v. marilandicus)*

are widespread and more typical: mottled brown birds, usually ruddy, sometimes grayish brown, with short, dark bills, naked yellowish legs, and short, rounded, outwardly gray tails that fan wide in flight. An average bobwhite weighs only 6 or 7 ounces, is 9 to 10½ inches long, and has rounded wings spanning 14 or 15 inches.

The male has a white chin and throat and a white stripe from the bill through or just above the eye to the base of the neck. The white areas are separated by a black or blackish-brown irregular streak from the bill through or under the eye to the neck, where it blends into white-spotted dark hazel and widens into a brown, irregular bib on the upper breast. The dark hazel crown has a very short, loose, barely noticeable crest. The back is scaled and mottled brown, the sides and flanks chestnut with ragged black-and-white barring and white spots. The wings are brown and grayish, the belly white or whitish with brown and black V's and specks. A hen has creamy yellow or buff face markings instead of white, and the surrounding feathers are

Sudden point over tight-holding bobwhites (opposite), and wild flush at edge of Georgia woods.

browner than the cock's, with less blackish contrast or none. Her underparts are also buffier, with less white than the male's. The lack of facial white makes a hen easy to recognize as a rule.

Quail are fragile creatures. Sometimes they can be kept in captivity for eight years but their average life span in the wild is less than a year, whether or not they are hunted, and few of them breed more than once. Juveniles—70 or 80 percent of the fall bag—are identified by pointed outer primaries and much buffy tipping on the upper coverts of the first seven primaries.

At present the bobwhite is hunted in thirty-five states. Diminished habitat—the result of land clearing, reforestation, and manicured farms—has robbed the Southeast of its old status as unrivaled bobwhite country. During the 1972-73 season the hunting was best in Oklahoma, Texas, Iowa, Indiana, Florida, South Carolina, Delaware, and New Jersey.

GAME BEHAVIOR & HUNTING HABITAT: Bobwhites in the Smokies move down from "grass balds" to lowlands for autumn and winter, and quail in northwestern Oklahoma shift as far as ten miles from an upland summer range of sage and grass to the dunes and canyons. But in most regions they are sedentary, seldom moving a mile even to find nesting cover. A covey of sixteen or seventeen is not unusual in November; after a hard winter or when breeding dispersal has begun, seven or eight survivors linger stubbornly in the same area. The average home range for a typical covey of ten to fifteen birds is only about twenty-four acres. A southern shooting acquaintance has hunted a large, annually resurrected covey in the same brush patch for almost forty years. He and his friends take care to leave at least half a dozen birds "for seed."

Bobwhites need grasses for nesting cover and, to a limited degree, for spring and summer feeding and roosting. Except where wild foods abound, they need croplands for summer and fall feeding, as well as midday resting and dusting. They need surface water or dew, and arid-country quail are invariably bagged on irrigated land, along river valleys, or in other oases. Finally, they need brush or woods in winter for feeding and all year long for escape cover and roosting. As long as winters are relatively mild and there are no severe floods or prolonged droughts, quail remain plentiful in tracts that mix these components.

Though bobwhites eat insects, seeds make up more than nine-tenths of their fall diet. Weedy herbs and legumes are the principal food plants. Almost everywhere, ragweed and lespedeza attract bobwhites. Other preferred foods are soybeans, sorghum, corn, partridgepea, cowpea, trailing wild bean, wheat, sunflower, smartweed, and beggarweed.

In some southern regions where the foods are plentiful and the weather mild, breeding may begin in January or February; elsewhere it usually begins in March. Males turn their heads to show their white markings, touch the ground with spread wings, rush at others in the covey. A female reveals her sex and stimulates courtship by failing to respond. Together the mates scrape a small ground nest; arched with concealing grasses, lined with dead leaves and grass. Some males help with incubation but most stay off a little way, perhaps to decoy predators. Enemies include cats, dogs, and all the wild carnivores. Incubation takes about twenty-three days, lengthening the breeding cycle to a 50-day period of danger before the eggs hatch, usually in June.

A typical clutch numbers thirteen or fourteen eggs. If they are destroyed early during incubation a female renests at least once but not always with the same male, monogamy being limited by a male's decreasing fertility. A hen is apt to quit breeding during a drought. The repeated spring calls—the familiar *ah-bob-white!* whistles—are mostly uttered by unpaired cocks announcing their availability. Quail are more resistant than grouse to disease and parasites; still, they can contract coccidiosis, enteritis, caecal-worm infestations, or other maladies. Many birds that survive the summer die if winter brings heavy or crusted snow. Where gullies and fence rows are cleared, even a rain can beat down the thin cover and leave them perilously exposed. Birds can also be killed by grain treated with organic mercury fungicides, and reproduction can be disrupted by the effects of persistent pesticides.

The precocial broods drift apart by late summer and form large temporary groups, then form smaller coveys in a final dispersal known as the fall shuffle. Though coveys are attracted to the same little havens of previous years, ages and families are mixed. A covey settles into a roosting headquarters, typically in brush, tangled grass, woodland edges, often on an unshaded, well-drained, south-facing slope where the ground stays warm in the late afternoon. Patches of 2-foot-high weedy herbs can hide roosts, and sometimes wheat stubble is used. If the vegetation is wet, a hunter may be more successful at roosts than in foraging fields, because then quail hardly feed at all. Even in dry weather they move from roosting cover only far enough to feed.

A man without a dog can sometimes walk up bobwhites around roosts or loafing spots. He may find a promising area by sign: a circular accumulation of bird droppings. Quail retain body heat and watch for predators by roosting in a disk formation, sometimes called a "pie" or "roosting ring," with bodies touching, facing out. Ordinarily quail head for fields early in the morning to feed, but in wet weather or on raw, windy days they may delay feeding until late in the morning. Some states extend the fall season far beyond Christmas, a time when field hunting is better at noon than at sunrise. In hot weather, a dogless hunter sometimes finds birds resting at midday in cool retreats, and in cool weather sunning on lee rises or in thin brush; toward dusk he can try the roosting brush or thickets near field edges.

However, the greatest pleasure of bobwhite hunting lies in watching good dogs work: quartering fields, combing edges, checking corners, turning off to investigate brush piles that might have escaped the notice of human hunters. On some southern plantations the dogs are still followed by horse- or mule-drawn wagon. There and in parts of the lower Midwest, four-wheel-drive vehicles are also used.

In any case, bobwhites are likely to lie tight and break suddenly at a distance that probably averages no more than 5 yards. A peerless quail gun is a light 20 gauge with improved-cylinder or skeet boring. A light enough 12 gauge is good if it has a true cylinder or skeet choke, and a 28 gauge, bored improved or modified, is excellent for a skilled shooter. Express loads are probably best in the 28, but field loads are recommended in the larger gauges. A dense, wide pattern of small pellets—No. 8's or 9's—is needed for quail, and scatter loads can be useful in heavy brush.

Occasionally quail run if they are close to heavy cover,

but they lie tighter than most upland game and tighter still if they have been hunted. It is usually possible to cast the dogs so that they can work gradually toward obvious escape cover. Dogs perform best and quail are most active on chilly, sunny days, neither so dry that scenting is difficult nor so damp that birds stay roosted. On such a day or when moving against the wind, dogs catch scent in plenty of time to avoid "bumping" a covey—overrunning birds and flushing them before the hunter can get within range. The hunter has a fair idea of which way most birds will fly once they spray out of the ground cover, and he can improve the chance if the covey is between the dogs and the nearest thickets or tangles. He walks in over the dogs so that the birds perceive danger concentrated at one point, with their accustomed curtain of safety in the opposite direction. A couple of targets at the very least should then offer fairly straight shots, and there is no time for more than a couple even with a repeater. There is, however, time for a deliberate gun swing; the most common error is shooting too soon, forgetting or doubting that the birds will straighten out.

Encouraging straightaway covey flight also has the effect of making birds alight in a small area where the dog can most easily find scattered singles. However, singles can escape detection even then. When a bobwhite comes down after separating from the covey it stays very still for a while, instinctively reluctant to move and spread body scent until the danger seems to be gone. Unless a single has been precisely marked down, a good tactic is to wait a while, then move in with the dog against the breeze. Left alone, singles begin to whistle to one another and move about after no more—usually less—than half an hour. In an hour or so they will be coveyed again.

VOICE: A few hunters use hawk calls to hold quail tight in low cover; the stratagem rarely seems necessary. However, the author admits to having once used a commercial whistle that imitated bobwhites more closely than most of us can by unaided whistling. It did not draw scattered birds but it brought a couple of answering whistles, making them easier to find. There is more pleasure in relying on a dog and one's wits. Occasionally a feeding call is heard: *tu-tu-tu-tu-tu*. More often the birds are unheard until scattered. The rallying call is not so piercing as the double- or triple-noted whistle—most common in spring—for which the bob-white is named. It sounds like *hoy, hoy-eee!* Repeated calls become a series, increasingly loud. There are quail dogs that recognize the sound as surely as their masters and move toward it as eagerly.

Desert Quail *(Lophortyx gambelii;* also classified as *Callipepla gambelii)*

Mountain Quail *(Oreortyx pictus)*

& Valley Quail *(Lophortyx californicus;* also classified as *Callipepla californica)*

COMMON & REGIONAL NAMES: For desert quail—*Gambel's quail, Arizona quail, Olanthe quail.* For mountain quail—*plumed quail, painted quail, San Pedro quail, mountain partridge.* For valley quail—*California quail, Catalina quail, crested quail, helmet quail, topknot quail.*

DESCRIPTION & DISTRIBUTION: All plumed quail—desert, mountain, and valley species—prefer running to flying. And they can run fast—more than 15 miles an hour without much effort. What the hunter sees first is a loose covey of sleek gray and chestnut forms, streaked on the sides with white, their black head plumes bobbing as they skitter through openings in sage, cat's-claw, thornbush, cactus, manzanita, under scrub oak or piñon, into thick chaparral, over bunchgrass and bare ground. Desert and valley quail often skim low, a few occasionally whizzing right through sparse brush. Now and then a valley quail flushes from the ground and alights on a tree branch not 40 feet away. The hunter is bound to chase after the bird and it flushes again, but makes an even shorter flight and is back in a tree before the gun is up. Mountain quail rise much higher; they are the largest of the country's quail and seem the slowest. But they can be equally difficult targets when they take off after running uphill faster than a panting hunter can climb.

Valley quail may be the fastest. Sometimes they seem to rival bobwhites when they spurt across wide openings. But all three species usually go about 30 miles an hour. Though

Male valley quail roosting (top), and hen (l.) and cock desert quail (bottom).

some scattered singles bewilder a wingshooter by lying like wood-cock, most of the shots are long.

The seven subspecies of desert quail, just as often called Gambel's quail, occupy arid and semi-arid lands in lower California, Nevada, Arizona, New Mexico, western Texas, Mexico, and isolated areas in Idaho, Utah, and Colorado. Hawaii has introduced the birds on the island of Lanai. All of these states have late fall or fall-to-winter seasons. The hunting, excellent until a few years ago, has declined because of droughts, which reduced breeding, and escalating land use. Habitat reduction threatens wildlife even in the desert.

A Gambel's quail is apt to weigh 5 or 6 ounces and have a length of 9½ to 11 inches. Both sexes have a blackish, forward-curling head plume and gray or grayish-brown back, tail, wings, and upper breast. The underparts are buffy, the sides chestnut with thin white streaks. The male's forehead is black, separated from a chestnut crown by a white stripe above the eye; his throat is also black and bordered by a white stripe that reaches to the eye, and his belly has a black patch with an irregular pale border. The hen has a shorter plume, sooty crown, and paler face with no black patches or sharply delineated white stripes, and her belly is buff streaked with brown. The juveniles of all western quail have shorter plumes than adults, pointed outer primaries, and buff-tipped primary coverts.

The valley quail, known over much of its range as the California quail, is very closely related to the desert variety and looks almost like the same species. It tends to be a trifle heavier but not distinctly so. The only striking difference is that its lower breast and belly are light buff with dark, distinct scaling like the pattern on a scaled quail. On the male, the buff is strongly tinged with chestnut. The hen's plume is brown rather than black-ish. Like the desert hen, she has a drab facial pattern with no distinct striping or black throat patch.

There are eight subspecies of valley quail, and they have always ranged from southern Oregon and western Nevada down through California to the tip of the Baja peninsula. In addition, they have been introduced in lower British Columbia, Washington, northern Oregon, Idaho, Utah, and the island of Hawaii. These birds, too, are being hurt by habitat reduction. The hunting is still good in much of the original range but is currently best

Hunting desert quail with pointing dog (top), running desert quail (bottom l.), and dusting and gritting spot.

in Washington—along the Columbia, the Snake, and their tributaries.

The range of the five subspecies of mountain quail covers part of the same region, from Washington, Oregon, and southwestern Idaho down through California to the upper Baja. The birds have now been introduced in British Columbia with some success, and in Colorado where their status is still uncertain. At present the hunting is best in California.

A typical mountain quail weighs more than 8 ounces and is about 10 to 12 inches long—unusually large for a quail. Its plume is also unusual; it is composed of two straight, narrow blackish feathers that stand up when the bird is on the ground, though they sweep back in flight. The female's is almost as large and black as the male's. On both sexes the throat is dark chestnut, blackening at the sides and set off by a white line that curves up to the eye. There is also a whitish patch between eye and bill. The breast, head, and neck are slate-gray or gray-blue, dulling to brownish or olive gray on the back, wings, and tail. The belly and lower flanks are dark brown, with wide white bars, edged in black, running up the sides. Sexual identification can be difficult, but the brown of a hen's back usually extends to the top of her head, whereas a male's neck is gray.

Mountain quail, largest of American quail species.

GAME BEHAVIOR & HUNTING HABITAT: All the western quail are covey birds that begin to disperse in late winter or early spring as males whistle or crow from stumps, rocks, or branches, chase other birds, perform aggressive and courting displays, and in some cases change coveys to find mates. Except for hens that renest, they are monogamous birds. The male defends a shallow ground nest and his brood, and in some cases helps with incubation. Among mountain quail, ten eggs make up an average clutch, while desert quail average twelve or fourteen and valley quail average fourteen. Incubation requires about twenty-five days, and hatching reaches a peak in May or June. Though they are hardy, their population declines sharply with drought or habitat reduction. The average life span is about a year, but some live three or four.

Mountain quail migrate seasonally, sometimes moving more than twenty miles. They nest in the highlands, descending in August or early September. By October a hunter has no reason to climb more than 5,000 feet, and he will begin to find them in habitat where he shoots valley quail. In the Sierra Nevada a typical covey of mountain quail consists of five birds, but coveys in some regions are twice as large. Coveys of desert quail are often two or more family groups, twelve or thirteen birds in some areas, as many as fifty in others. Valley quail are the most gregarious; most groups number between twenty-five and sixty, but it is not unusual to find them in the hundreds. Upland traditionalists, hesitating to use the word "covey" for such an astonishing gathering, speak of bands or droves.

Western quail have normal morning and late-afternoon feeding periods and midday periods of resting, dusting, gritting, going to water if it can be found nearby. But each species has food and shelter preferences that can guide a hunter. Mountain quail often come to roadsides to dust or find grit, but in hunting country they are difficult to get near with a gun. Sometimes a chukar hunter puts up valley quail on canyon rims near grainfields, and mountain quail occasionally flush from the same spots. But valley quail prefer the oaks patching foothills and valleys, brushy stretches along stream banks, high sage, brushpiles, river-bottom tangles, vineyards, weedy fields, and grasslands. They roost off the ground in thickets of low trees or tall bushes, yet they feed in fairly open spots, usually near water, and not in dense forest or chaparral. The edges and openings of heavy cover are worth combing, however, and a dry spell brings large groups to water holes or springs. Early in the morning and toward dusk, as well as at midday, valley quail appear along roads looking for grit. Sometimes, when our efforts in the foothills are frustrated, we find compensation on the way back to the car.

Those of us who want only aerial targets can use the help of a good dog—the sort of pointer that has been weaned on pheasant or, for very brushy areas, a flushing dog. We try to cast our dogs where the right seed plants attract valley quail—foods like filaree, mullein, barley, clover, lupine, sage, deervetch, wild oats. When a dog goes into a food patch or the escape cover of shrubs and brush, we are resigned to the probability that he will put birds up out of range, but we take comfort from the scattered singles, which hold more tightly. In fact, most of us are sufficiently confident of close shots to carry a 12- or 20-gauge gun with a skeet or improved-cylinder boring—or modified if we hope for mountain quail in the same area. No. 7½ shot makes a good load for any of these birds. When all else fails, a man and his dog can drive birds over another man, stationed downhill or in a gully, for some fast pass-shooting. The problem is to conquer a tendency to shoot high as birds dip and skim or come right down after rising.

Mountain quail are apt to feed a little higher in the same kind of country. They like to roost or loaf under scrub oaks or other hardwoods and in brush. They, too, are often found near chukars, on rocky inclines, among rosebushes or bunchgrass on mountainsides, in the oaks, along willowed creeks and brushy draws. They have the chukar habit of running to the rim before they fly. Scratching like farmyard chickens, they feed early and again just before dark. Flushing dogs are probably best in the thick canyon cover that attracts them in autumn, but, as with valley quail, a pheasant pointer can often head off birds on a ridge or pin them on a flat. Foods that particularly attract coveys are sumac, hackberry, grape, serviceberry, gooseberry, mullein, barley, manzanita, elder, snowberry, mountain rye, timothy, sage, clover, wild oats, acorns, and conifer and locust seeds.

Deervetch and filaree are like magnets to the plumed birds, including desert quail. Additional foods important to the Gambel's species are bur clover, lupine, mimosa, other legumes, and the seeds of weeds and grasses. They eat cat's-claw and paloverde beans but are probably fonder of mesquite beans than almost any other kind. Being unusually adaptable, desert quail have different preferences in some regions: alfalfa where they can get it, desert hackberry, prickly pear and ocotillo seeds.

Even in late fall or winter the desert may be so hot that hunting is pleasantest—and the quail actively feeding—only before about 9:30 A.M. and after 3:30 P.M. But birds lace the desert with tracks, sometimes leading a hunter to their cool, shady resting spot. If trees are nearby they will roost off the ground in the evening, marking the area with droppings. Only one good thing can be said for hunting in midday heat: Bedded desert quail tend to fly rather than run. Later in the day a hunter can wait where a profusion of tracks marks a run from loafing to feeding spot. The ground cover is apt to be so sparse that he will see birds coming; if he rushes them when they come close, they often flush.

Desert quail run hard and flush wild, yet some hunters use pointing dogs. The environment is as hostile to dog as to man, and not all pointers can adapt to the dangers of cactus needles, thorns, sidewinders, scorpions, and heat. A few hunt happily and well in the desert. Dogs almost always bump a covey too far out on the first flush but do better on subsequent rises or on singles if the birds scatter. Desert quail hold a little tighter after being pushed out once or twice. An experienced dog will check brushy washes, mesquite clumps, ravines, willows along the infrequent watercourses, but may find desert quail almost anywhere. The same spot may hold scaled quail, greater runners than any of the plumed varieties but inclined to fly if pressed hard enough. Early in the season an improved or modified choke may be adequate. A modified or modified-and-full 12 gauge is generally most productive, with No. 7½ high-brass loads. The same gun and shells can serve for scaled quail in the same areas.

VOICE: Foraging desert quail are sometimes located by their soft clucking and growling. Even when bedded they often chatter. Singles crow to rally—*ka-kaa-ka-ka!* In October, mountain quail often utter the same loud whistles they use during the mating season—*queee-ark!* They may cackle when alarmed, but a hunter trying to locate them as they skulk through cover should listen for a whistle—*whew-whew-whew.* Later, the rallying call will sound like *cle-cle-cle* or *cow-cow-cow.* Valley quail cluck softly as they feed. The rallying call is *cu-ca-cow,* or something that sounds like *chi-ca-go.* There is no need to imitate the birds, although a few hunters do. The essential tactic is to follow any sounds and walk in fast with the gun ready.

Scaled Quail *(Callipepla squamata)*
COMMON & REGIONAL NAMES: *blue quail, cottontop, scaly, Mexican quail, blue racer.*

DESCRIPTION & DISTRIBUTION: No one sneaks up on blue quail, but the author and a friend almost managed it one morning in South Texas. We were hunting rabbits as well as scalies, yet we were unprepared when a jack bounced from behind a clump of Spanish bayonet as we stepped within range of the covey and got set to rush the birds into flight. The rabbit's action alerted them. They started to gallop like roadrunners. The shot that potted the rabbit sent a few into the air, resulting in an odd double—one jack, one quail. Meantime, the other man, who was off to one side and had no shot at the fliers, killed one running. Since "blue racers" skitter almost as fast as rabbits, most southwesterners rightly consider it sporting to force a covey up by shooting one on the run. Some that were still on the ground took off at the third shot—that much gunfire and the crackle of pellets in the thorn bushes being too much for them—and each of us brought down one more bird before they flew out of range over a low rise.

We followed them but never again got close after those two or three seconds of chaos. Blues are like that. Whether feeding, dusting, or just loafing in the shade of a cactus or creosote bush, they make little effort to hide until disturbed. They simply run from danger, heading into the nearest brush. A hunter sees twenty or thirty blue-gray shadows scuttling about, then loses sight of them. He gives chase, knowing that if he gets closer they will rise. They do, but sometimes at 60 yards. They can be up and away at 30 or 35 miles an hour, and out of range

before they leave the ground. Sometimes they fly low and come right down again after 20 more yards; sometimes they fly higher than quail are supposed to—50 yards up, perhaps—descend behind a knoll a hundred yards away, and come down walking. Then one's choice is to make a wide circle, hoping to push up the blue-gray blurs from the far side, or look for another covey.

A scaled quail is a 10- to 12-inch bird, usually weighing 6 or 7 ounces. Its head is light grayish brown and has a somewhat bushy, cottony-looking crest, buff on females, whitish and more pronounced on males. Females also have brownish shaft streaks on their cheeks and throat; the comparable feathering on cocks is unstreaked white or pearly. On either sex, the back, wings, and tail are gray or brownish gray, with narrow white streaking

Scaled quail in Arizona.

on the wings. The bluish tone is most pronounced on the upper breast, neck, and upper back. The lightly streaked flanks vary from grayish to brownish. The lower breast and belly are pale or whitish, but males belonging to a subspecies common in southern Texas and neighboring Mexican regions have a light chestnut belly like a male valley quail's. Black feather edging produces a conspicuously scaled effect on the light underparts, breast, and neck of both sexes and all three of the geographic races. Juveniles have underdeveloped crests, buff-tipped upper primary coverts, and considerable barring on their central tail feathers. The average longevity of quail in a harsh desert environment can hardly be much more than a year.

Scaled quail range from eastern Colorado and southwestern Kansas down through the Oklahoma panhandle, the western half of Texas, most of New Mexico, lower Arizona, and southward into central Mexico. They have also been introduced in Washington and eastern Nevada. In some areas their welfare is threatened by heavy grazing, which strips them of nesting and escape cover. However, brush shelters and watering devices are now being used in arid-country game management, and scaled quail are extending their range. The hunting is especially good in New Mexico and Texas.

GAME BEHAVIOR & HUNTING HABITAT: There are regions where scaled and Gambel's quail occupy the same desert habitat or semi-arid brush and grass. Both species are runners, but both can be surprised, headed off, or force-flushed by rushing. In southeastern Arizona the desert blends into high, grassy country where yet a third quail species may go into a mixed bag. It is the harlequin, or Mearns, quail *(Cyrtonyx montezumae)*, also called Montezuma quail, Massena quail, crazy quail, black quail, or painted quail. It has a small range, chiefly in Mexico, and is not abundant. But since it is legal game in Arizona and is flushed from grassy hills and live-oak scatterings, the harlequin merits description.

Smaller than a scaled quail, it is the size of a southern bobwhite. The female, in fact, looks much like a bobwhite hen. The male has a handsome black or bluish-black and white facial pattern and a soft brown crest curving back and down over the nape. His upper parts are mottled brown, with a grayish or olive cast. The central breast is plain brown, but the sides, flanks, and part of the lower breast and belly are dark slaty gray, sometimes almost black, with numerous round spots of white, buff, and cinnamon. The bird lies as closely as any bobwhite and is hunted in the same way. In the tall grass of highlands bordering desert regions, even the scaled and desert quail sometimes hold, and a hunter may do well with a pointer and bobwhite gun.

Where ground cover is sparse and the thorns and cactus needles murderous, most hunters use no dogs. A good gun for such hunting is a modified or modified-and-full 12 gauge, loaded with No. 7½ high-brass shells.

In Nevada or Arizona, where the season opens rather early in the fall, coveys of blues may at first number fewer than twenty birds. Scaled quail tend to congregate in progressively larger flocks as winter comes on; usually they number between twenty and forty, but once in a while a group of more than a hundred gallops about before a desert hunter.

The covey begins to break up in March, as males begin squawking and displaying. Pairing continues into April, and nests are scraped under bushes or brush, sometimes in tall grass, sometimes in haystacks. Pipping comes in May or June. The males help with the incubation, which requires twenty-two or twenty-three days, yet hatching success is often low. In very dry years in desert country, there is little or no breeding. In a good year, when all or most of the twelve to fourteen eggs hatch, five or six young may survive. During the summer, broods begin to form coveys.

Like other quail, blues are seed-eaters. They subsist on plants like elbowbrush, cat's-claw, mesquite, hackberry, sorghum, snakeweed, deervetch, wild privet, lupine, and weedy forbs. Good hunting spots are in weedy washes, canyon mouths, and river valleys. The birds like spiny ground cover and may be found amid cactus, Spanish bayonet, yucca, and the like, or under mesquite or juniper. Sandy ground provides grit and dusting places. Scaled quail can survive for long periods without surface water, but they gather at cattle tanks, springs, and creeks.

Many hunters scout from a vehicle, jumping out and loading on the run when scalies are sighted. Another method is to drive on, around the nearest rise, then walk back, surprising the birds into flight.

VOICE: The squawking of scaled quail is pretty much a springtime phenomenon, but autumnal notes often locate coveys. Some Texans describe the rallying calls as sounding like the name of the Pecos River—*pey-cos*—but when spooked birds are rallying they often utter a two-syllable clinking call.

Wild Turkey *(Meleagris gallopavo)*
COMMON & REGIONAL NAMES: *American turkey, bronze turkey, wood turkey.*

DESCRIPTION & DISTRIBUTION: The sound comes first. About half an hour before sunrise a hunter may hear a distant gobbling and realize that already he has been fooled. He lies hidden behind a log on high, mast-covered ground shaded by a canopy of oaks. He is almost within gunshot of some tall pines marked as a roost by a litter of droppings and feathers. But the gobbling comes from the far side of a narrow valley; the birds have shifted. The hunter moves quickly toward the sound, then slows, still-hunting

as he tops a knoll within calling distance. He hunches behind a blowdown and after a few minutes hears the throaty bubbling again. He scrapes the lid of his cedar box call over the lips of its cavity to produce the high yelp of a receptive hen. The gobble sounds again, but this time he does not reply. For the next half hour he uses the call sparingly, answering perhaps every third yodel. The silent intervals lengthen to five minutes or more, though the gobbling seems to come closer. Finally the tom's calls cease, but the hunter has no notion of moving on. He knows very well that the mating urge of a mature tom turkey is tempered with suspicion and sometimes with male arrogance. Somewhere nearby the tom is scratching about, expecting the approach of an eager hen.

At last growing impatient, the tom comes forward. The hunter hears a rustling patter, but he knows better than to move. The tom moves out a few steps, scratches at the mast, and utters a short gobble. Then he pulls his head back, arching it almost against his back, and puffs out his body feathers until he seems to open like a huge bronze and black flower. His pale

Wild turkeys flocking in winter.

pink head and neck flush red. His tail cocks up and spreads in a wide fan. He jerks his head forward, emitting a long, loud gobble, then pulls it back again. Getting no answer, he relaxes slightly, as if only practicing.

He is just close enough for a shot when his neck tenses and his head turns to focus one eye on the hunter's makeshift blind. He begins to scurry away, taking high, long steps toward the brush. The bird that looked black in its approach looks silver-gray in retreat. He can run at least 20 miles an hour, and the brush will end all hope. The hunter swings his shotgun. The turkey lifts into the air as swiftly as a grouse. A gobbler's flight has been clocked at 50 miles an hour; this one is escaping through the trees at a more typical 40 miles an hour when the shot brings him crashing down.

The bird weighs nearly 17 pounds, no more than average for a full-grown male of the eastern subspecies. About 40 inches long from bill to tail, it has a wingspread of more than 4 feet. The eastern turkey, ranging from lower New England into the South and Midwest, is one of half a dozen races; the Florida turkey sometimes resides far enough north to interbreed with the eastern strain; the Rio Grande turkey, native to the Southwest and Mexico, has been introduced in states as far away as North Dakota and California; the Merriam turkey of the Southwest and lower Rockies has also been introduced in a number of other western states; the Gould's turkey inhabits Mexico and bits of the lower Southwest; and the Mexican turkey is found far below the border.

The eastern and Merriam turkeys are the largest. A mature gobbler of either variety weighs between 15 and 20 pounds, a hen between 9 and 12. The Florida turkey is relatively small and dark, the Rio Grande type leggy and pale, but geographic differences in size and color are minor.

Indians in Mexico and elsewhere had domesticated turkeys long before the Europeans came. Today's farm turkeys, chiefly descended from ancient Mexican stock and bred for size, are much larger and slower than wild ones. Near disaster resulted from early efforts to replenish wild populations by releasing domestic and hybrid birds. Game biologists had not yet learned that wildness—a combination of survival traits—is in large degree genetically determined, and that interbreeding with domestic turkeys would further weaken the wild populations. By the second or third decade of this century, turkeys had become rare or nonexistent in many regions of former abundance. Their dominant need is for relatively mature, open forest—the woods that were swept away by settlement. The birds were killed off by farming, lumbering, fires, and market hunting. Their salvation came with new techniques of habitat improvement and transplanting—capturing birds with drop-nets and rocket-nets over baited clearings, then releasing them like sown seed in new or depopulated areas.

They have shown a dramatic revival. Population estimates run to more than 1,250,000 birds. They are hunted in thirty-five states, some with fall seasons during which either sex can be bagged, some with spring seasons on gobblers only, some with both. Hunting has been particularly good in Oklahoma, Missouri, Arkansas, Mississippi, West Virginia, Maryland, and Florida.

In strong light a wild turkey is not nearly so black as it looks in shaded woods. The dominant color is usually bronze or dark copper, darkening to blackish on the lower back. The body, particularly the breast, glows with iridescent washes of purple, reddish bronze, and dark traces of green. The primaries are barred with white and dark grayish-brown, the tail with chestnut or buff and black. The wide, square-ended, copper, black-margined feathering on much of the body makes a softly scaled effect. The legs are usually reddish gray, and a male's have black spurs that average an inch long at maturity; they are so hard and sharp that Indians used them as arrowheads.

An adult male also has a breast adornment known as a beard. It looks like a stiff, miniature black horsetail, usually 8 or 9 inches long, occasionally longer. A bird of the year has only a small beard, a few inches long. It grows throughout a gobbler's life but is no sure sign of age since the ends may wear away or break. Occasionally a hen sprouts a beard, and bearded hens are usually legal game during gobblers-only seasons because sexual identification is too difficult. A bearded hen may also have spurs, and usually her head shows subdued male characteristics. Normally a female's head is thinly covered with very fine, short, dark, whiskery feathers that shadow the skin and make it appear darker, more bluish gray, than a tom's. Her neck has fleshy folds and protuberances, but they are insignificant by comparison with a male's.

At maturity, an adult gobbler's naked head has wattles hanging from chin and throat, while the lower throat and neck are lumpy with fatty growths called caruncles. He also has a fleshy lobe—called a frontal caruncle, leader, or snood—just above his bill, often hanging down over it. The top of his head is pale, almost white. The rest of his head and neck are pinkish with some pale blue, especially about the face. When a tom struts before hens or threatens another male, the naked skin flushes red.

GAME BEHAVIOR & HUNTING HABITAT: In rich habitat, twenty or thirty hens of mixed ages may be flocked together with several yearling gobblers when the mating calls are first heard. Some of the old males prefer solitude, but most are in small bachelor groups. They gobble occasionally at all times of the year, but it is late February or March in the South, early April in the North, when gobbling begins in earnest. An experienced hunter can sometimes tell from a tom's sound whether it is a big one. Young birds have high, hoarse voices that deepen as they grow older. Most turkeys barely reach maturity, the average life span being less than two years, but some live twice that long.

As the days lengthen, males begin to squabble, establishing a pecking order. Not all bachelor groups disband completely. Sometimes two or three toms perform as a team to court hens. Though all may gobble, one dominant bird does the strutting and the mating. The birds remain inactive when noise can cover a predator's stalk, but on a calm day their gobbling is sometimes heard for more than half a mile. Since most gobbling erupts right after the birds leave their roosts, spring hunting is best during the first two or three morning hours, beginning half an hour before sunup.

The flocks soon break up. Yearling toms form separate groups. Hens form cliques of three or four, as do some of the toms. Gobblers shot at the beginning of this season are apt to be the heaviest a hunter ever bags, for in late winter and early spring they accumulate fat, particularly in the form of a frontal pad called the breast sponge. They feed very little during the mating time but take energy from the accumulated fat.

A gobbler attracts several hens to an area, where he struts and parades for them and guards them from interlopers. Each hen tamps a shallow nest in grass or brush or behind screening vegetation and incubates her ten or twelve eggs for about four weeks. Cold weather can cause hatching failure, and in a wet spring some nests are flooded. Hatching occurs as early as March in some regions, as late as June in others. During a cool, rainy spring many chicks die of exposure or exhaustion. Dust baths keep mites and lice to a minimum, and although at least sixty kinds of internal parasites attack turkeys the losses from infestations are seldom high. Sometimes, however, severe losses result from blackhead—enterohepatitis caused by a blood protozoan. Turkey numbers are also thinned by predation, but no more than is normal for upland birds.

By early fall new flocks form. Some of the hens and their half-grown poults are joined by other families and broodless hens, while the males begin to re-gather in small bachelor bands. Since the birds are still eating quantities of insects, the habitat must have grasses and brush to support insect life. There must be ponds, creeks, or swamps for water, trees for food and roosting. Most good hunting spots have sizable hardwood stands to supply mast—acorns, beechnuts, or hazelnuts by tradition, although turkeys also eat the seeds of conifers. Other foods that attract them are chufa grass, dogwood, sumac, wild grapes, ragweed, berries of many kinds, corn, sorghum, and oats. The birds feed intensively for a few hours after dawn and again for a few hours before dusk, when they fly up into roosting trees, but they feed intermittently all day and may be found in woods at any time.

The wild turkey is the wariest as well as the largest of American game birds. The average time spent by an experienced turkey hunter to take a bird is a full week. Whether a hunt is made in fall or spring, it should be preceded by scouting to find likely feeding areas, sign, and, if possible, roosts. The birds prefer to roost in tall trees, usually higher than 60 feet and located on a ridge or above a clearing, so that unobstructed flight is possible. In the South they often roost in cypresses over water—a natural moat to hamper predators. Elsewhere they use oaks, cottonwoods, pines, spruces, firs. They may use the same roost for several nights or try new ones each night, but roosting sign is promising because turkeys often remain in an area as small as 600 acres all year. Sign usually takes the form of droppings and molted feathers. Few hunters know that droppings reveal a turkey's sex: A hen's scat is looped, spiral, or bulbous, a tom's longer and straighter, with a knobby twist at one end. There may also be tracks. If a print is more than 4¼ inches long, it is probably a tom's, and if the stride is over 11½ inches, it is almost certainly a tom's.

In fall a man can still-hunt through bottom-land woods if there is screening brush, or he can stalk the brushy hills, topping out every few hundred yards to peer down the opposite slopes. But such hunting is not the most productive because turkeys have superb hearing and vision. Like most diurnal birds, they can distinguish colors, so hunters usually wear drab or camouflage clothing.

Those who scout the hills or go on stand overlooking open valleys often use rifles—a .22 rimfire Magnum or .222 with a 2½-power scope is a good choice. In eastern turkey habitat the birds are more often seen at shotgun range than at long distance, and they are running or flying before the gun comes up. A full-choked 12-gauge repeater loaded with No. 4's or 5's is a good choice, as is a 20-gauge Magnum with maximum loads. Many hunters use a combination firearm that provides a rifle barrel over a smoothbore; a few use drillings that feature a pair of shotgun barrels over a rifle.

Regardless of the firearm chosen, still-hunting is less productive than stand-hunting or "roosting." If sign is found or birds are seen feeding in the area, a man may decide to go on stand near the edge of a field or clearing, on the side of a small wooded

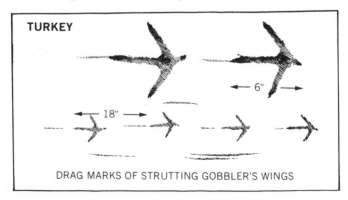

TURKEY

DRAG MARKS OF STRUTTING GOBBLER'S WINGS

valley, or beside an old road or trail where birds may travel, dust, or pick grit. Dusting spots are shallow ovals, not obvious but sometimes marked by tracks, feathers, or droppings. Often they are under sumacs or small trees, or beside logs or burned brush piles. A hunter on stand must be silent, motionless, hidden. Roost-hunting, or roosting, is merely taking a stand near a previously discovered roost, usually long before sunrise though another chance may come before dusk if a bird returns early.

In a few areas dogs are legal and used. No turkey lies to a point, nor is it likely to let a flushing dog put it up within range. What the dog does is locate and scatter flocked birds. They have the rallying instinct common to some of the other upland species, so if the hunter takes a stand where they were scattered, he has a fair chance of calling one back with clucking, gobbling, and trilling sounds.

In spring, however, what brings most gobblers into range is an imitation of a yelping hen. Calling is best done from a ridge or knoll; gobblers expect hens to invite them uphill to places that facilitate fast escape from predators. Many kinds of sounds will stimulate a response (though not an approach) and some hunters begin with an owl hoot.

There are old hunters who blow convincingly through a pipe stem or through a hen turkey's wingbone from which the ends are cut. A few use only their vocal chords, and many scrape a cedar peg across a thin, chalked slate. Among commercial calls, there are diaphragm types that are worked between the tongue and the roof of the mouth, leaving the hands free. After much practice they produce realistic yelps. Wooden or slate and wooden box calls are most common. With practice and close attention to the manufacturers' instructions they can be made to yelp, gobble, or yodel when a lid is rubbed over the box rim. When a turkey seems to lose interest in the yelps, sometimes a gobble prods him along, afire to chase any rival. In a few areas phonographic calls are legal; most of us use them only for self-instruction.

Turkeys become quiescent during hard rain, and box calls sound best in dry weather. But the birds are most active on overcast or drizzly days, though they avoid moving through wet foliage. Under such conditions a hunter might do well to take a stand near a road, trail, or clearing where birds can move about without wetting their feathers.

VOICE: A tom's high, throaty, yodeling sound is something like *grrddle, gl-obble-obble-obble.* The hen's call to him is a vaguely plaintive yelp: *keowk, keowk, keowk.* Softer yelping may accompany flight from a roost, and turkeys sometimes cluck or trill while feeding.

Woodcock *(Philohela minor)*
COMMON & REGIONAL NAMES: *timberdoodle, bogborer, bogsucker, whistler, mudsnipe, night partridge, night peck, becasse.*

DESCRIPTION & DISTRIBUTION: A certain small piece of farmland in southern New York always seems to have woodcock and woodcock hunters. On opening morning in the first week of October we give little thought to whether flight birds are in; barring a freakish cold snap, the native birds are still there, and the season is open on grouse, as well. The dog is a little too eager on the first morning. She plunges across the ancient orchard, splashes through the brook, and turns sharply to work the edges of an alder run. A woodcock goes up before she can check herself. We hear a light, whistling twitter and catch a glimpse as the bird corkscrews out of the alders, hangs above them for a motionless instant, and flicks away.

After that the dog usually works well and the birds go up almost at our feet. Even where the ground cover is no more than a leafy forest mat, their brown and black mottling renders them almost invisible until they move. Woodcock flush close, are not exceptionally fast, and fall when hit by very few pellets, but clean misses are common. A woodcock, after all, is hardly larger than a man's fist and is inclined to rise on a steep, erratic, sideward-veering course. Once up, it often flies at less than 20 miles an hour, though capable of reaching 30. Small though the bird is, it can be fairly easy to hit when flushed on an open pasture. More commonly, the hunter can barely swing his gun among clustered saplings.

A woodcock is a round, short-winged creature, 10 or 11 inches long if the needle of its bill is counted. The bill is the most reliable means of telling male from female. A female's is

almost always at least 2¾ inches long, whereas a male's rarely exceeds 2½ inches. A male is also smaller bodied—about three-quarters as large as a female. In early October an average cock weighs a shade more than 5½ ounces, while a hen weighs a shade over 7 ounces.

In regions between the northernmost breeding grounds and the wintering range, resident woodcock move south during the open season. Sometimes before they leave, sometimes afterward, successive waves of migrants arrive from the north. Hunters wonder why the transients, or flight birds, are usually larger than the native birds that departed earlier. It is because woodcock eat heavily in the fall, gaining weight in preparation for possibly lean winter months. When flight birds and natives mingle, no one can distinguish between them.

The American woodcock, a close relative of the snipe and the European woodcock, belongs to an order of shorebirds but has evolved strange adaptations for life in the uplands on a diet consisting chiefly of angleworms. Its legs have shortened, its oversized head is set close to the body, giving the bird an almost neckless appearance, and its eyes have shifted to an

Male woodcock lying close under point.

extraordinary position far back on the skull, enabling it to probe the earth deeply—injecting its bill to the hilt. The evolutionary shift of the eye sockets has forced the brain rearward and down, tipping the cerebellum ventrally. The woodcock is a unique bird with an upside-down brain. The bill is also unusual: It has extremely sensitive nerve endings that feel and perhaps taste for subterranean prey. A sprinkling of little round "bore holes," or "drill holes," in a limited area indicates a good covert where birds are feeding well. A woodcock's membranous upper mandible is prehensile. It hinges open and shut from about the midpoint.

Either sex has a mottled brown appearance. The head is buff with a black line from bill to eye, a small black ear-covert patch, and wide crossbars on the back of the skull and the nape. The breast is cinnamon; the underparts buff; the back, rump, and scapulars mottled and barred with black, gray, brown, and reddish yellow. The round tail has black and white tipping, and the primaries are slaty.

There is cause for astonishment at the 1,500-mile migrations of birds that appear so ill-suited to flight. Some woodcock nest in the South, but the principal breeding range extends through eastern Minnesota, Ontario, Wisconsin, Michigan, New Brunswick, Nova Scotia, and Maine. Smaller but important breeding populations summer in Ohio and from parts of New England to West Virginia. The birds winter chiefly in the Deep South, down to Tampa, Florida, and across the Gulf Coast into eastern Texas, with immense concentrations in Louisiana. They follow three main routes, one along the Atlantic, one west of the Appalachians, and one along the Mississippi Valley. Although the greatest numbers use the central corridor, there is hunting —usually good hunting—in thirty-seven states as well as in New Brunswick, Nova Scotia, Prince Edward Island, Quebec, and Ontario. New Brunswick is famous for woodcock, and the annual harvests are impressive in Michigan, Wisconsin, New York, and New Jersey. The seasons are set within Federal guidelines to coincide with the presence of flight birds as well as natives. In New Brunswick the season begins in mid-September, but does not open until about two weeks later in New England and the Lake states, and not until October 20 in New Jersey. In Louisiana it begins in early December, when the largest woodcock gatherings start to arrive, and ends in early February, when northward migration begins.

GAME BEHAVIOR & HUNTING HABITAT: Southward progress is slow and at low altitude, yet migratory flights are not often seen because woodcock do most of their traveling after twilight. Sometimes we have good shooting for a few days in our southern New York alder thickets and then one morning we move no birds. We put the dogs into other coverts and in desperation begin to look for sign. The bore holes are hard to find, but the "chalk" —white spatters of liquid droppings about an inch wide—show up very well. We find a few chalk marks, cannot judge their freshness, fail to find any woodcock in the immediate vicinity, and decide to concentrate on grouse. All or most of the natives are gone; so are any flight birds that may have come in.

The southward journey is a chain of short flights punctuated by marvels of flying stamina. Several hundred woodcock will congregate in a single small bushy spot behind a beach at Cape May, New Jersey. The habitat looks poor, but Cape May is renowned for such swarms of birds, resting there, gaining strength and perhaps nerve, maybe awaiting good flying weather, too, for the long crossing over Delaware Bay.

Most of the birds return in the early spring and are on their northern singing grounds in April, though some that stay in warm latitudes have already bred by then. Usually at twilight and sometimes at dawn a woodcock rises out of a glade or meadow or brush-bordered field, uttering a nasal, buzzing call as he ascends in wide circles. When the cock is about 50 feet up he usually accelerates and, for a moment, the wind can be heard twittering through his primaries. His circles are wide enough to cover several acres but tighten as he rises. He is a dim speck in the dusk, nearly 300 feet high. He hovers and then, with liquid chirps, dives to the ground in a zigzag glide. He struts for a few minutes, buzzing nasally again, then repeats the aerial performance. His efforts usually continue for half an hour or more and are rewarded by a visit from a hen.

After mating she leaves. Though she nests close to the cock's singing ground she has no more to do with him unless her eggs are destroyed. (European woodcock produce two broods a year, American woodcock only one.) On a rudimentary nest in grass or brush or under a shrub, the hen incubates her four eggs for about eighteen days. Hatching is most frequent in April, May, and June. House cats, crows, owls, hawks, and a few other predators destroy eggs or kill chicks, but predation is relatively light. So are the effects of the common poultry diseases and parasites. Pesticides have become a threat, however, and surprising numbers of woodcock are also killed during night flights, when they collide with power lines and other obstacles. The greatest cause of mortality is a long freeze on the wintering grounds. Frozen earth prevents boring for worms, and starvation ensues unless plenty of other food is available. But woodcock are hardy. Most live about two years, many live three, and some—chiefly females—live four.

The finest habitat provides food to supplement worms. Woodcock eat insects, as well as a few seeds and berries, particularly sedge seeds and blackberries. There is a nearly unshakable old belief that woodcock are flushed only from hiding and resting coverts, that they feed exclusively at night. But they also feed heavily at dawn, again at noon, and again at dusk. In most instances when hunters tell of seeing "flight birds settle into a field at dusk," they have seen birds come to a good feeding field. If the woodcock are gone in the morning, it is not necessarily because they have resumed migration. They have probably retreated to brushy edges or nearby woods after an early feeding, or they may be watering. Seeps, springs, marshy bottomlands, and brooks make good hunting.

There is a certain look about good woodcock areas: The earth is dark and soft, and there are shrubs and young trees and openings. The best habitat has trees 10 to 20 feet high—close and somewhat tangled for concealment and escape, but with light ground cover to facilitate boring. One season in Maine, a study showed that almost half of all flushes were from alder thickets. In New Brunswick, most birds are moved from alder, gray birch, or evergreens. In Louisiana birds may be on a variety of alluvial bottomlands or among pines. A Pennsylvania study showed that when they were absent from alder bottoms they could be put up in crab apple and hawthorn on slopes.

Any experienced woodcock hunter reading of those locations will probably bet that the slope flushes occurred in cool weather. On hot days woodcock rest in deep shade, particularly under evergreens. On mild days they are most often in alders but may also be in overgrown pastures, boggy fields, old orchards where the rotting apples have enriched the soil, sometimes in uncut cornfields next to alder cover. On cooler days they like sun-warmed slopes but, being reluctant to abandon thick cover, are most often in stands of birch or aspen on such slopes.

They are reclusive, but they migrate in loose groups, and it is very common to put up doubles. Many hunters assume that pairs are mated. Since woodcock are not monogamous and many of the migrating groups are sexually segregated, the hunter who puts up a double often sees two males or two females. Unless he is a good, fast wingshooter, he will probably bag one of them, at best, which is why few hunters discover that doubles may be birds of the same sex.

Dogless hunters—pitiable creatures—habitually plunge into the thickest alders. Birds may be there or almost anywhere else in the vicinity, of course, but most are flushed near the edges of coverts and not in the middle. It is the combination of feeding field and escape woods that attracts them. A dog is certainly not essential when native or flight birds abound. A man without a dog will pass many birds he never sees, but whereas they hold still and rely on camouflage at a dog's approach, they tend to flush within good range as a man towers near. The dogless technique is to move slowly and reasonably quietly on a zigzag course, pausing frequently. The author confesses to having put up many birds that way, and confesses with greater embarrassment that he did not find every bird he shot. Some dogs dislike retrieving a woodcock, but as a rule even they will show where it has fallen.

There are many people who hunt woodcock with springer spaniels, those finest of pheasant dogs, and Labs, those finest of waterfowling dogs. Probably there are people who would run a cutting horse in the Preakness. The rest of us employ setters, Brittany spaniels, or pointers.

We are inclined to carry light, short-barreled 20- or 28-gauge doubles, bored improved and modified, though a repeater with an improved cylinder will do. No. 8 or 9 shot in field loads provides the requisite dense patterns.

VOICE: Many hunters believed the whistling twitter of a flushed woodcock to be vocally produced until the game biologjst William G. Sheldon plucked the three narrow outer primaries from several birds, thus silencing the rises. The nasal, buzzing call of a woodcock on the singing ground is best transliterated as *skre-e-e-e-et* or *skre-e-e-e-nk*. On rare occasions the same sound is heard in the fall, and there are chirps and little quacking notes on the wintering ground.

Common Crow *(Corvus brachyrhynchos)*
COMMON & REGIONAL NAMES: *American crow, eastern crow.*

DESCRIPTION & DISTRIBUTION: A New Jersey cemetery is fringed by mixed hardwoods, tall and fairly dense, a fitting roost for black-clad birds. A little before sunrise the crows begin to scatter in all directions, in groups of three or four, a dozen, a score. Soon most will head along direct flyways, the shortest distance "as the crow flies" toward cornfields, truck farms, and orchards within a radius of several miles. We see them regularly on their favorite routes, and we rotate our blind locations from day to day so they will not abandon a flyway or feeding area.

We set up a couple of rolls of camouflaged wire mesh about 50 yards apart in shady tangles on the upwind edge of a flyway, facing downwind to ensure that our calling will carry far and the majority of birds will approach into the prevailing breeze. With two men to a blind, each takes birds only on his own side. We wear camouflage clothing, and our faces are netted or smudged. No birds are more cautious or more sensitive to reflections, colors, and movements than crows in hunted areas.

The belief that feeding crows post sentinels is nonsense —each bird is its own sentinel—but in the air advance scouts frequently precede a flock. They sail over, black silhouettes, bustling, always noisier than expected or disconcertingly silent, and large enough to make range deceptive. If we are unsure of bringing them down we let them go, but if the scouts bore in close we make a point of bagging them. Short, intermittent volleys of gunfire seldom seem to daunt advancing flocks, yet a scout that sees men shooting will turn back and usually warn the others away. At the first shots the flock peels to the sides, the birds often dipping rather than rising. We rush to hide most of the

Crow hunter setting up decoys (top), and timber edge used as natural crow blind.

kills, since curiosity can turn quickly into suspicion.

Crows make difficult targets for reasons other than their speed, which is seldom more than 30 miles an hour. All of us are so accustomed to seeing various smaller blackbirds that we underestimate a crow's size—typically 18 or 20 inches in length, with a wingspread of 3 feet or more at maturity. The sexes are indistinguishable, and each is apt to weigh a full pound. As a crow careens over a treetop it either looks surprisingly large or, more often, is much higher than it seems. A hunter fails to lead the target sufficiently and vows to correct that at his next opportunity. But his next opportunity may be a crow that drives in straight and low, a looming black flurry that is slower than it looks; this time he overleads the target and begins to comprehend the pride of crow-shooting virtuosos who carry repeating shotguns not for second and third tries but for double and triple kills.

There are half a dozen American subspecies of crows, all of them totally black with purplish glints in very strong sunlight. Several races are relatively small—notably the fish crow *(C. ossifragus)* and northwestern crow *(C. caurinus),* both of which ply coastal flats and rivers for shellfish. The largest, most gregarious, most migratory, and most hunted is the common crow *(C. brachyrhynchos).* (The protected raven is considerably larger

than the crow. It has a shaggily feathered throat and a heavier bill. In the air it has a more hawklike, measured flapping and soaring flight than the crow, and it soars with wings held horizontally whereas the soaring crow angles its wings upward.)

The breeding range of the common crow extends across all of the United States and most of the Canadian provinces; the primary wintering range is almost entirely within the United States. In many temperate regions the flocks are virtually sedentary or migrate only a hundred miles or so. In Canada and across the Great Plains they undertake much longer migrations. Families begin to flock together in August or September and soon move southward, following ripening crops. Sometimes the migration is prolonged into winter. Although northward flights may begin in February in the South, the birds remain plentiful all winter in most states. The finest crow hunting takes place in winter on the farmlands from lower Kansas and Missouri through Arkansas and Oklahoma into Texas. The Missouri Department of Conservation issues an annual guide to the state's heavily populated roosting areas, which usually lists more than a hundred.

Crows traditionally have been considered a varmint species. Game departments once advocated poisoning, trapping, and even resorted to dynamiting roosts; more than 26,000 birds

Fair-sized New Jersey crow roost.

were killed in an Oklahoma roost-bombing. Crows are omnivores, and there is no question that where overabundant they cause significant agricultural losses. They also take the eggs and sometimes the young of waterfowl and other game birds, but such prey constitutes less than one percent of their diet. The Federal government has at last recognized crows as migratory game birds, and has limited the shooting season to 124 days or less in the forty-eight contiguous states. (The Hawaiian and Alaskan subspecies are neither abundant nor really migratory.) Bag limits may be set regionally, and split seasons are permitted, but crows can no longer be killed in excessive numbers or during the peak nesting period. Exceptions are made only where large concentrations damage crops and trees or create a health hazard.

GAME BEHAVIOR & HUNTING HABITAT: In April, male crows squabble, chase females, and display for them. They seem to do most of the nest-building, usually rather high in trees, and they help with incubation, which requires about eighteen days. Clutches average four to six eggs and most hatching occurs from April to early June. Fledging takes about five weeks. Mature crows are so hardy that a life span of eight or ten years is not uncommon.

The owl-and-crow rig is a traditional crow lure. A mock or stuffed owl is propped in a tree or on a tall bush where it is clearly visible from the air, and a little higher, in front or more or less on the sides, two or three crow decoys are placed. The tableau represents crows holding an owl's attention and calling for reinforcements. Behind this type of stool, our calling mingles wailing caws with short, raucous, angry blasts.

After migrants begin to crowd the roosts, a larger rig of crow decoys, without the owl, is even more effective. Though some of the decoys can be stick-ups before a blind or natural hiding spot at the edge of a cornfield, a dozen decoys set on fence posts or tree limbs will be more visible from the air.

A good shooting site is between a roost and feeding area or between two feeding areas. In the North, roosting places often seem to be in dense, tall conifers surrounded by open terrain, but hardwoods are as promising in many areas, willow clumps are often used in the South, and even relatively low shrubs are used in parts of the West. A roost is noisy and birds are seen flying from it in the morning, returning in small clusters during the early afternoon and in large groups shortly before dusk. Corn is a favorite food wherever it grows. Also preferred are wheat, sorghum, oats, barley, rice, peanuts, acorns, cherries, and apples. If crows sometimes damage crops, they also help to control insects and they eat other small animals, such as mice, frogs, and snakes.

There are hunters who practice long-range riflery on perched crows, using calibers ranging from the .17 Remington to the .22-250, bullets ranging from 25 to 55 grains, and scopes ranging from 6- to 12-power or even greater magnification. But crow hunting is chiefly a shotgun sport, and a common hunting error is the use of needlessly large pellets. Big crows fall easily in a dense pattern of small shot—No. 7½, 8, even 9. There are masterful shooters who use full-choke guns, but for most of us the pattern must be wide as well as dense, and a modified boring is best. Birds should be allowed to swoop close enough for field or skeet loads to be effective.

VOICE: Commercial records, reproducing the calls of live birds, are effective, but tend to be too loud when crows approach. Some hunters use them in combination with a mouth call, others use a notched mouth call that can be held between the teeth to free both hands for shooting. Calls carry best and are most effective on still days. Strong wind, overcast, or rain reduces the activity of crows.

The safest call (least often detected as artificial but not always irresistible) is a spaced-out series of rallying notes—*caw . . . caw . . . caw*—blown from the diaphragm but with the vocal chords imparting a moaning quality. An underlying wail makes this a distress call that will bring birds to investigate but may not draw them into range. A hunter can then mimic the pounding repetition of excited birds, or with a partner switch to the quick babble and occasional long notes of food discovery, or the slightly more strident fighting and scolding notes (though not so choppy that they imitate the alarm call), or the lower-pitched, longer mourning caw of crows wheeling over an injured companion, or the rallying call of two short, then two slightly longer blasts, a signal to be used sparingly, with a rest after two repetitions. What sounds at first like monotonous crowing is a wide repertoire, differentiated by subtle changes in stridency, pitch, and tempo.

GENERAL DESCRIPTION & DISTRIBUTION: Caroming off the dusk like bats but in unison and with the speed of snipe jumped in a salt meadow, tight flocks of blue-winged teal begin to swarm southward as reflections of September's moon fleck the riffles of streams. On a higher, straighter course fly loose formations of sprig—sleek, long-necked pintails whistling and quacking their flight calls over blinds still vacant. Blacks and ruddy ducks are in the air as well, and a few scoters are traveling ahead of the other diving species. Shallow waters along the migratory routes are soon spangled with dabbling baldpates, gadwalls, mallards. The harvest moon is followed by the hunter's moon, when goldeneyes and greater scaup begin a protracted cavalcade of sea and bay ducks; but for most hunters on the upper stretches of the four great flyways—Atlantic, Mississippi, Central, and Pacific—October means dabbling ducks and upland birds. The choices are harder in November. Breezes harden into winter squalls and still the birds come: canvasbacks, lesser scaup, and other hardy divers.

Men dab at wind-tears as they watch for sloping lines, blotches, knotlike flurries, wavering chevrons. Ancient rites are honored on wide and lonely marshes. Cave-dwelling forebears of the Paiute Indians fashioned canvasback decoys two thousand years ago. For 50 million years or more, America's ducks have been evolving toward an awesome fusion of similarity and diversity, slowly altering with the environment. Scattered over the world are seven tribes, thirty-four genera, more than a hundred species. Twenty-nine species and subspecies are hunted in Canada and the United States. All are characterized by more or less spatulate bills and webbed feet; they are smaller than most geese, have shorter legs, tend to be more omnivorous, and are better adapted to aquatic feeding than to the field grazing of geese.

Mallards jumped from farm pond.

NOMENCLATURE USED IN DESCRIBING WATERFOWL

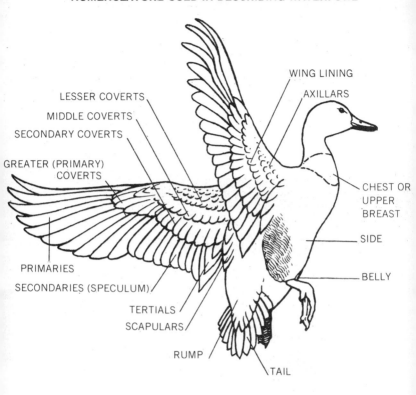

WING LINING

AXILLARS

LESSER COVERTS

MIDDLE COVERTS

SECONDARY COVERTS

GREATER (PRIMARY) COVERTS

CHEST OR UPPER BREAST

SIDE

BELLY

PRIMARIES

SECONDARIES (SPECULUM)

TERTIALS

SCAPULARS

RUMP

TAIL

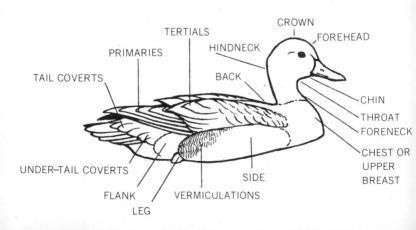

CROWN

FOREHEAD

TERTIALS

HINDNECK

PRIMARIES

BACK

TAIL COVERTS

CHIN

THROAT

FORENECK

CHEST OR UPPER BREAST

UNDER–TAIL COVERTS

SIDE

FLANK

VERMICULATIONS

LEG

With so many species on the wing, a primary concern of the hunter is preparedness: an ability to identify ducks in flight and a patient watchfulness. Since all ducks are gregarious, a marsh, pond, or bay that attracts a few wildfowl will soon draw more, not necessarily of the same species. To flying ducks, the sight of wildfowl below—either live birds or convincing decoys—signifies safety and the probability of food. If the breeding season has been poor for one of the species trading over a blind, it may be protected by Federal or state regulations. Perhaps there can be no shooting at the canvasbacks that have been stringing across the sky since daylight, but the hunter waits, still and quiet. A flock alights beyond his decoys. Feeding and loafing, they have drifted nearer when several scaup come down into the wind, eager to splash in at the fringe of the can flock. The hunter rises when the scaup are hardly more than head high. As they flare, his gun swings through the track of a plump and legal bluebill.

The pond and river species, the dabbling ducks, belong to the tribe *Anatini* of the subfamily *Anatinae.* Also called dippers or puddle ducks, they include the black duck, gadwall, mallard, pintail, shoveler, the continent's three kinds of teal, and the widgeon. Taxonomic purists now rank the wood duck as the sole North American member of the *Cairinini,* the perching tribe. In behavior, distribution, and habitat the woody is closely allied to the dabblers and is grouped with them in this book. There is likewise but one North American representative—the ruddy duck—of the tribe *Oxyurini,* the stiff-tailed ducks.

Older hunting references place the canvasback, redhead, ring-necked duck, and scaups in a general category of bay, sea, and diving ducks; although they do sometimes frequent brackish and salt waters during migrations and in wintering areas, they are freshwater diving ducks, properly classified as pochards, or *Aythyini.* Mergansers, on the other hand, are no longer listed as separate by some leading taxonomists but as true sea ducks, together with the bufflehead, all the eiders, the two varieties of goldeneye, the harlequin, oldsquaw, and all three scoters. In recognition of a close physiological relationship, these ducks have been shifted from the *Aythyini* to the *Mergini* tribe.

Most of us are less concerned with anatomical subtleties than with a knowledge of where a desired species is abundantly distributed, how to recognize it, what habitat is congenial to it, how it is likely to behave—knowledge that enables us to see and bag game. Since average sizes and weights can aid in identification of some species, these details are given in the descriptions. A hunter who wonders about the practical matter of dressed weight will discover that dabbling ducks usually lose at least a third of their weight upon removal of feathers, innards (including a few ounces of giblets), feet, and outer wing digits. The loss is slightly greater for diving species that feed primarily on animal matter, because they are often skinned, and it is important to trim away as much of the oily fat as possible. (And, of course, some epicures use only the breast meat.) But wide variations occur: A migrating duck is likely to be leaner than a wintering duck; a very full crop—which may be worth examining to see what is being eaten and thus where the game is feeding—adds to the total weight; and a gizzard may be heavy with grit.

Several species, too scarce or limited in distribution to be generally hunted, do not merit full individual descriptions but should be mentioned. Two are *Dendrocygnini,* whistling ducks or tree ducks. The black-bellied tree duck *(D. autumnalis)* is rarely seen north of Mexico. It has a small, ducklike body but long, gooselike neck and legs, and there is no difference in coloration between male and female. The head is gray; the crown, lower foreneck, breast, and back cinnamon-brown; the wings darker, with black secondaries and white coverts that are visible in flight; the underparts and rump black, with white speckling on the lower belly; the legs and feet pink; the bill pinkish red with a blue nail. The fulvous tree duck *(D. bicolor)* is rather similar but with a bluish-black or gray bill and feet, yellowish-brown head, a little white on the neck, and cinnamon or buff rump and underparts. It ranges slightly farther north but is largely nocturnal and not hunted much in the United States.

The Florida duck, the Mexican duck (sometimes called New Mexican), and the mottled duck of the Gulf Coast—all formerly ranked as separate species—are localized, sedentary races of the mallard in which the male resembles the female and does not acquire the nuptial plumage of typical mallard drakes. The reasons for such anomalies are not understood, nor is it clear why some wildfowl have lost or never acquired the migratory urge.

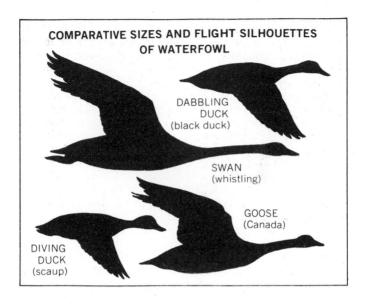

COMPARATIVE SIZES AND FLIGHT SILHOUETTES OF WATERFOWL

DABBLING
DUCK
(black duck)

SWAN
(whistling)

GOOSE
(Canada)

DIVING
DUCK
(scaup)

Among ducks of the genus *Somateria,* only the American, or common, eider and king eider will be accorded individual treatment. The northern eider and Pacific eider are regional strains of the American. Their physical distinctions and ranges will be mentioned in connection with the latter. The spectacled eider, named for distinctive black-rimmed white patches about the eyes of the drake, breeds on both sides of the Bering Strait and winters on the Aleutians; it is too rare and localized to warrant detailed description. This is also true of the little Steller's eider, which inhabits the same regions and is identified by the drake's white head, black eye ring and throat, chestnut underparts, and a small green tuft behind the head.

Whereas there is no difference in color between genders of swans and geese, most anatine birds exhibit a marked dimorphism. An outstanding American exception is the black duck, but among the majority of species the autumn and winter plumage of the male is far more colorful than the female's, and a wildfowler can distinguish the sexes even in flight. The downy young may be yellow, buffy brown, tan, gray, or white, depending

PACIFIC FLYWAY

CENTRAL FLYWAY

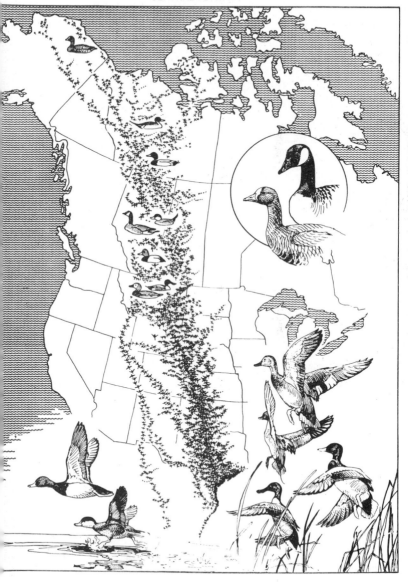

MISSISSIPPI FLYWAY

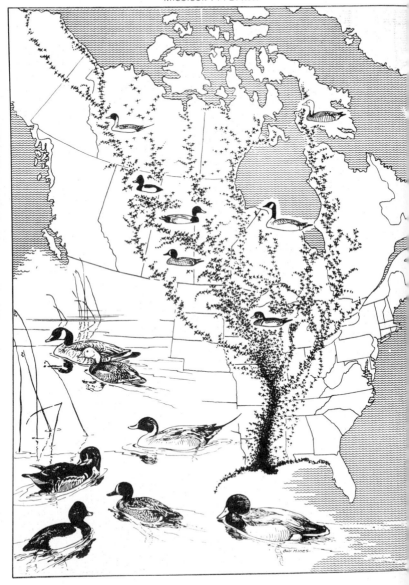

ATLANTIC FLYWAY

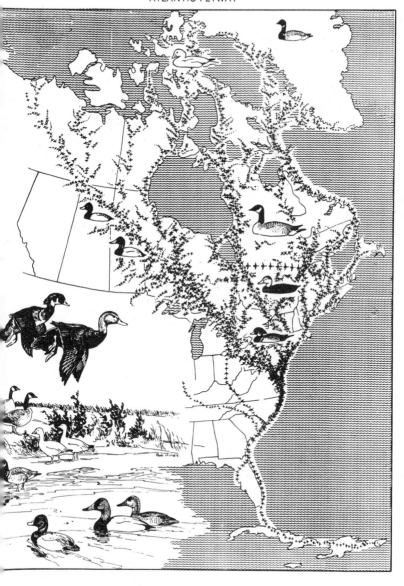

on species, and are usually spotted or barred on the body and head. A hunter who bags a bird of the year can often tell its age because some of the first-season feathers are notched at the ends, where the down tips of infancy have broken away.

But from a blind or duck boat, juveniles are usually indistinguishable from females, and the hen's description will suffice. Where bag limits are based on a point system to discourage the taking of females, a drake may count for only 10 points of the permitted total, a hen for 90, and hunters concentrate on adult males. However, juvenile scoters ("gray coots") will be described separately since they are often recognizable and are preferred by many hunters; scoters are either "bonus" ducks or are assigned low point values.

Ducks undergo two molts each year rather than the single postnuptial molt of swans and geese. During winter and early spring a hen gradually loses and replaces all of her plumage except the wing feathers. As nesting time approaches, she acquires longer, softer, stronger down—"nest down"—which she plucks from her breast to line the shallow cavity of vegetation where she lays her fragile eggs. Scaup and ringneck hens become browner during the breeding season, but females of most species show no color change. In late summer, when the ducklings are somewhat self-reliant, there is a second, postnuptial molt of a hen's entire plumage. For as long as three or four weeks she may be flightless, her only protection a watery retreat or concealment in vegetation near the shoreline. Yet a young and healthy hen usually survives to embark on the arduous fall migration with thick new plumage. The dense winter feathers of either sex can deflect shot pellets if loads are insufficient.

In the Northern Hemisphere, the drake's double molt does not coincide with the hen's. (In the Southern Hemisphere, drakes of many species retain their gaudy cloak of masculinity the year around, never developing the drab "eclipse plumage," and their molts are more gradual than those of northern drakes.) On this continent, a drake's postnuptial, or eclipse, molt begins in late spring or early summer, soon after he abandons the incubating hen and joins a bachelor flock on some relatively safe pocket of water. During this flightless period, when camouflage is important, the bright mate-attracting colors are replaced by muted plumage like the female's.

A few weeks later, when the power of flight has been regained, a second, slower molt begins. The newly gained flight feathers are retained, while the body takes on the nuptial, or winter, colors that reveal the species to the hunter. A bird in "autumn plumage" or "autumn molt" has not yet completed the transformation. Because most ducks begin their migration while in this phase, a gunner in Canada or the most northerly states may rarely see drakes in full winter array. However, their patterns will be recognizable, and most species attain full coloration during autumn. Under the heading *Game Identification in Flight*, males in winter plumage will be described first, then females. Drakes in eclipse plumage look like females; a bird that corresponds to the male description but is somewhat drab or mottled may be in the autumn molt or—if notched feather tips are discovered—be a drake of the year. (Juveniles tend to be small, but not so small that they can be recognized in the air.)

Prenuptial dimorphism is evidently important to many species which seek new mates annually and breed close to other species. Habitat is often shared by a profusion of races, particularly among dabblers, and it is noteworthy that no two dabbling species breeding in the same region have the same color patterns or repertoires of courtship displays. Yet hybridization is fairly common. Parentage is sometimes obvious because "mongrel" ducks tend to carry distinct markings of both species. Since hybrids are poor breeders, the array of species is not reduced by interbreeding.

Ducks are shorter-lived than geese or swans, usually surviving no more than about five years in the wild, and they are quicker to mature. Some breed successfully when only a year old, and many (particularly early nesting species) commonly renest if a clutch is destroyed, yet a hen generally produces only a couple of broods during her life. Swans and geese have a reproductive advantage because they are usually monogamous and form permanent pair bonds. A gander or cob helps to guard both nest and mate, helps to raise the brood, and sometimes does the brooding if the female is killed. Typical clutches of four to six eggs assure reproductive success. Ducks take new mates each year (sometimes more than one). Among most species, a drake deserts his hen soon after she begins laying. Incubation lasts three to four weeks, during which the female fends for herself, and then she must tend the ducklings alone. These disadvantages are offset by clutches averaging from eight to twelve eggs.

Mortality is high, but a mallard population can maintain itself by producing less than two young per adult each year. Enemies of the various species include tapeworms, roundworms, leeches, botulism, and fowl cholera, together with a large array of predators. Now and then ducks are also killed by collisions with farm fences on the southerly breeding grounds—chiefly in the Midwest and in Canada's Prairie Provinces—but drought is by far the greatest killer. Ducks that nest chiefly in the arctic or subarctic are less drastically affected by climatic cycles. However, about 80 percent of the game ducks are hatched in lower Canada and the upper United States.

Although Alberta, Saskatchewan, and, to a smaller extent, Manitoba form a tremendous cornucopia of American waterfowl, some species have a much wider summer distribution and others have relatively limited breeding grounds elsewhere. The prairie-pothole nesting habitat of south-central Canada extends down through the Dakotas and western Minnesota. Other major hatcheries occur as far south as Utah's Bear River Marshes, and minor ones are located farther south. The tidal flats and marshes of British Columbia and Ontario also are excellent incubators. The Maritimes produce large numbers of waterfowl, and the arctic islands are vital to some sea ducks.

Alaska, too, is a major producer. The remote, prairielike tundra attracts each year at least 13 million dabblers and divers. From the Yukon Flats and the Yukon Delta, canvasbacks and lesser scaup stream onto the Atlantic as well as the Pacific Flyway, and other species head for the Central or the Mississippi corridor. Every flyway is dotted with wetlands, and during the hunting season ducks of many species are seen almost everywhere in the United States, except for arid locales.

GENERAL HABITAT: The bleak shores of Greenland, Baffin, and other arctic islands are nesting havens for species that seem impervious to cold and can subsist on relatively sparse vegetation and invertebrates. The tundra regions become lush during a brief summer period and are far richer hatcheries. But the most productive habitat is in the prairie-pothole country. The best of it is not on the true prairies but slightly to the north, on terrain properly known as parklands—gently undulating glacial moraines between the dry, flat, shorter-grassed prairies and the fringes of the boreal forestlands and taiga. The knob-and-kettle topography of the Prairie Provinces is ideal for nesting and brooding, yet it is also a periodic reducer of duck populations. Many species prefer relatively small, shallow potholes, the first to vanish during prolonged droughts.

Knowing that most ducks are ground-nesters, misinformed hunters sometimes overestimate the damage of predation on the nesting range. Major predators include foxes, crows, gulls, magpies, skunks, raccoons, badgers, weasels, coyotes, ground squirrels (which destroy nests and eggs), owls, hawks, snapping turtles, northern pike, dogs, mink, bobcats—anything with an appetite for eggs or fowl. But some of these animals in turn become prey for larger carnivores, thereby serving as a buffer. Simplistic predator control is usually less effective than the maintenance of a balanced ecosystem—one with a diversity of fauna and flora. Given that, the birds are so hardy and prolific that the average fall flight of ducks is estimated to total a hundred million.

Along the migration routes and in wintering areas, ducks are attracted to a wide variety of habitat offering sufficient vegetable or animal food, together with water for rest and protection. The northern sea ducks subsist chiefly on crustaceans, mollusks, and other marine organisms. They can be hunted on salt marshes or sheltered bays and often on rough coastal waters where reefs provide forage. The mergansers are primarily fish-eaters, and the ruddy is truly omnivorous, but the dabblers and pochards are partial to marsh and aquatic vegetation. Nuts and berries are of little consequence, though acorns are sought by wood ducks, black ducks, and mallards. Corn, rice, wheat, and other domestic crops attract many ducks, especially the dabblers. Now and then a farmer may curse the appetite of wildfowl, but for the most part the birds take the leavings and are themselves part of the autumn harvest. Many farmers build ponds for them and cultivate or encourage Japanese and browntop millet, bulrush, smartweeds, widgeongrass, and other plants that attract ducks.

Additional details of food and hunting habitats will be

given for individual species, but a valid generalization is that ducks will tarry on any healthy wetlands where they can rest and feed in relative security. Though they flare from the sight of an ill-concealed hunter and sometimes from the sound of gunfire, they will return to an attractive marsh even if it is hunted regularly. Since their survival is more dependent on wariness than on seclusion, the hunting problem is not so much finding them as enticing them into range or approaching without alerting them.

BLIND & DECOY POSITIONS: There may be some truth in the old belief that diving ducks are less wary than dippers, but all wildfowl distinguish colors and see well enough to detect slight movements or the glint of sun on a gun barrel, eyeglasses, or skin at more than a hundred yards. Even when hunger or fatigue makes them eager to pitch in among decoys, they usually remain alert. Camouflage and stillness are essential in pass- or decoy shooting.

For pass-shooting (which is best on mornings after moonless or stormy nights, when the ducks have done little nocturnal foraging) a hunter can hide at a preselected site along a heavily

used route between resting and feeding spots. The length of such routes varies from a few hundred yards to several miles, and if the ducks must travel a considerable distance they are likely to fly high until close to their destination. The place of concealment should be close to where they rise or come down —where they will be low enough to be within range. A blind is superfluous if the hunter can hide in a thicket, hedgerow, high reeds, brush, a ditch, or standing sheaves and stalks in a stubble field. Otherwise, a pit blind can be dug or a standing blind can be built of slats or wire and camouflaged.

A roll of chicken wire, thin cane, or bamboo can be opened quickly and staked in high vegetation as a portable blind. It is extremely useful for either pass- or decoy shooting. The best blind is a natural one: high reeds and rushes, driftwood or rock piles along shorelines. Ducks are quick to detect any new or unnatural topographical features.

For shooting over decoys, a pit blind is sometimes installed on a point, island, or beach that edges resting or feeding waters. An alternative is a standing blind, masked with vegetation native to the area and erected at the same type of location or on an attractive cove. Ducks often come to rest on the lee side of a

Wildfowl resting at migratory way stop.

shore or sand bar. When they pitch in or make a low pass over decoys, they generally try to fly into the wind, and it is best to position the blind so that the prevailing breeze is at the hunter's back or from one side, encouraging birds to approach directly toward the gun or across. As with geese (see decoy recommendations for *Geese*), the nearest decoys should be about 20 yards from the blind, in a natural, unregimented arrangement. If each block is strung and anchored several feet from all others, and if there are a couple of large openings in the rig, birds can see the decoys from afar and will be attracted to the landing spaces. Where a shoreline interferes with the view of the stool, stringers of decoys can be angled out or placed farther away to draw in flights.

When two or more species mingle, they tend to orbit about in groups of their own kind. A rig may be enhanced by the combination of canvasback and scaup decoys, for instance, and will be most effective if the cans are grouped in a loose raft with the bluebills, not quite segregated but vaguely to one side. If goose decoys are used with the ducks they should be placed at a slight distance from the bulk of the smaller blocks, as if tolerating but not fraternizing with the ducks. Decoys mimicking one species will attract other species that favor the same type of habitat. Black-duck decoys on a shallow pond or close to a shore will lure mallards and sprig.

A dozen or even half a dozen decoys will turn pond and river ducks toward a food-rich pothole, stream, or cove, but the diving species congregate in large rafts on wider, deeper waters. For them it is advisable to use as many decoys as possible—several dozen or more if they can be left out overnight or placed before the first flights come over at daylight.

Decoys are used with many types of blinds. In addition to pits and standing reed enclosures, there are elevated reef blinds—wooden affairs on pilings high enough for a boat to be tied underneath, hardly disguised but not frightening to sea ducks if erected before migration begins. There are also floating blinds, covered with bushes or brush to look like islands, and overwater blinds staked to the bottom like hedgerows and spacious enough to hide a boat between their brushy walls. There are low reed enclosures that accommodate several Barnegat sneakboxes (or similar shallow-draft duck boats) in a line, and there are sunken blinds barely higher than the surface, walled with concrete and pumped out after each high tide. Regional preferences all reflect the universal principle of concealment.

JUMP-SHOOTING: Two types of jump-shooting are also popular. The more common method is to creep to the bank of a creek, pothole, or woodland pond in the hope of flushing puddle ducks as if they were upland birds. The other technique is to drift, pole, row, or paddle down a stream for the same purpose. The vessel may be of any kind, from a raft to a canoe or more conventional duck boat, but it should be low and camouflaged with reeds, grasses, brush, or branches. It is, in effect, a mobile blind.

GEAR & CALLS: See gear recommendations for *Geese* and calling descriptions under the heading of *Voice* for each duck species. Except where otherwise noted, duck sounds are best duplicated with a mouth-operated commercial wooden call employing a reed. Practice is needed to attract rather than flare the birds, and merely cupping the hand over the call's end in one way or another changes the sound drastically. Learning can be accelerated by the use of instructional phonograph records available at sporting-goods stores.

GUNS, LOADS, RANGES: As a general rule, the 12-gauge gun is best for all waterfowl, though a good wingshot can perform admirably with a 20 gauge when jump-shooting or luring dabblers in close over decoys. On a small pond or the edge of a feeding field, puddle ducks are often shot at only 15 to 30 yards. Quick shooting may be required, and an improved-cylinder or modified choke is needed to spread the pattern, as in upland hunting. Many gunners prefer No. 6 pellets for this sport, but unless the water is deep or the mud soft, No. 4 or 5 will sink faster and is therefore less frequently ingested by birds seeking grit. When lead shot is entirely replaced by an improved iron alloy, this will be a problem of the past. Though lead poisoning accounts for only a very small percentage of the fall flight, there is no need to blanket hard-bottomed wetlands with lethally light shot.

For the majority of shooting over decoys (at both dabblers and divers) the recommendations are No. 4 or 5 shot and a modified bore. Pass-shooting usually calls for No. 4 and a full

choke. High-velocity or Magnum loads are generally best. The barrel length for jump-shooting or short-range work with decoys may be 26 or 28 inches, but a 30-inch barrel is helpful in pass-shooting and with decoys, too, if long shots are common. Geese are frequently hunted at the same time, and a goose gun and load will bag the smaller birds efficiently. For species that provide exceptions to the rules, gun-and-load suggestions will be included in the sections dealing with *Game Behavior & Hunting Habitat*.

Range estimation is difficult with small, swift targets. But a duck brushed by the edge of a shot pattern at more than 50 yards too often dies slowly and miserably, miles away. Few shot-gunners can hit ducks consistently at more than 40 yards or so. Stakes, fishing bobbers, or decoys can be set out as range markers, but it is more useful to remember that by the time a duck flies into range its color pattern is probably discernible even on a dull day. If there is any question as to whether it is among the season's and flyway's legal species, there is no choice but to wait until the drake's colors or other characteristics can be confirmed, and range estimation then becomes integral with the greatest problem for most of us—species identification.

RETRIEVING DOGS: See recommendations for *Geese*.

Shooting ducks from lakeshore blind.

Dabbling Ducks
Black Duck *(Anas rubripes)*
COMMON & REGIONAL NAMES: *black, blackie, blackjack, black mallard, brown duck, brown mallard, beach duck, marsh duck, velvet duck, redleg, red-paddle.*

GAME IDENTIFICATION IN FLIGHT: Loose wedges, chevrons, or down-sloping lines of blacks come in over the waiting guns high and fast, evenly spaced, rarely more than a dozen in a flock after the first sweep of migration. Sometimes singles, pairs, and trios cross the sky. While in formation they fly a straight course, but a black flying alone or with only one or two companions may abruptly rise, dip, or break to the side and is more likely to fly low—within range. They can sustain a speed of 45 or 50 miles an hour.

Blacks are large, almost 2 feet long from bill to tail tip, with a wingspread of about 3 feet and an average weight of 2½ to 3 pounds. In the distance they do, indeed, look black, as do many kinds of waterfowl, but gunners learn to recognize their long, sooty, almost flat-bellied profiles, their large, slightly lighter heads, and the glow of silver flashing from underwing plumage. The wings are wide and their leading edges arc back smoothly, with less curve than those of many ducks, while the rear edges taper gracefully. The wingbeat is high but only moderately long, with never a dip very far below the body, the rhythm of strokes faster than that of geese but seldom approaching the whirr of smaller ducks except in a rough wind. They often approach at a height of 70 yards or more, then make several cautiously wide circles before dropping into range. On occasion they flurry down erratically, but the typical descent is smooth and steep, with wings rigidly cupped like curled autumn leaves.

When a black duck is close to the gun or in hand, it is no longer black but dark brown, stippled with thin buff or creamy feather edgings. The sexes are so much alike that it is usually impossible to distinguish male from female in flight. Once a black duck has been fetched by the retriever, the surest way to determine sex is to examine the small feathers on the sides of the chest. Most of them will bear a central U-shaped line of buff if the bird is an adult male in winter plumage, whereas the line forms a sharp V on an adult female. (A corresponding feather on a juvenile bird or a drake still carrying eclipse plumage has no central marking but only a light edging.)

Although the female tends to have a slightly smaller body, browner feet, and a shorter, greener bill than the male, there is great variation. The bill ranges from olive-yellow to orange-yellow, and sometimes—especially on females—has a dark ridge or small black spots on the upper mandible. The dark-crowned head and the neck are paler than the body but streaked with dark, thin lines. A thicker dusky streak curves from the bill through the eye. The outer wing feathers are as dusky as the body, but the speculum is purplish blue with a black bar at its front and rear. Usually the rear bar has a narrow white edging. The underlinings are silvery white. The feet may be buffy- or olive-brown with a salmon tinge, but on most males and some older females they are coral-red or orange.

DISTRIBUTION: The most abundant and popular game duck of the Atlantic Flyway, the black accounts for about half of the total yearly harvest of all ducks in much of the Northeast. Although the percentage declines rapidly below the mid-Atlantic, the species winters and is hunted as far south as the Gulf, from the tip of Florida west into Texas. The major breeding habitat extends across Ontario, Quebec, Labrador, Newfoundland, New Brunswick, Nova Scotia, Prince Edward Island, and the Gulf of St. Lawrence.

Western hunters may have read with premature delight that the black appears to be extending its winter range, but at present it remains a duck of the Atlantic and (to a much smaller degree) Mississippi flyways. There is a considerable overlap of breeding and wintering habitat, particularly along the eastern seaboard where occasional enclaves of black ducks nest from New England down into Virginia and on the famous shooting grounds of North Carolina: Hog Island, Pea Island, Bodie Island, Mattamuskeet Lake. Additional breeding areas exist in Manitoba, North Dakota, Minnesota, Wisconsin, Illinois, Indiana, and Ohio.

For years sportsmen and naturalists tentatively accepted the existence of two subspecies, the common black duck *(A. r. tristis)* and the red-legged black *(A. r. rubripes).* The common black, a smaller bird with olive-brown feet and an olive bill, seemed to be an earlier migrant with a more southerly range than the redleg, which was a big, more heavily feathered duck (thus harder to bring down) with a yellowish bill, coral-red feet, and subtle differences in plumage. The red-legged black was also rated as a more nocturnal feeder, harder to decoy, quieter, and more inclined to rest on big, open bays or even rough ocean waters than on ponds. The differences proved to be only indications of age and season. Among some ducks there are two surges of migration, the earlier sweep dominated by juveniles, which are small, lightly feathered, and dull in color. Similarly dull are those early migrating adults that are molting. The fall migration of blacks starts in early September and lasts into late October or November. The late arrivals from the upper reaches of the breeding range may look and act differently but they all represent the same subspecies.

GAME BEHAVIOR & HUNTING HABITAT: Black ducks seek pondweed, wild rice, cordgrass, bulrush, eelgrass, wild celery, smartweed, naiad, and a miscellany of grasses, algae, sedges, and aquatic seeds. Like mallards, they visit grainfields for wheat, corn, or other grains, and dip into the woods for acorns, beechnuts, and such fruits as huckleberries. Thus a set of decoys on a farm pond is sometimes enhanced by a scattering of blocks in an adjacent stubble field. As the season ages, black ducks resort more and more to coastal salt marshes, brackish bays, and even the open sea. Though they seldom fly far offshore, they begin to forage where mallards are rarely seen, eating a higher proportion of shellfish and insects. Fortunately, the intake of marine animal matter hardly ever increases enough to impair their fine flavor. They continue to make short flights inland and sometimes, when they seem to be avoiding the blinds, can be flushed by jump-shooting—stalking the brackish holes and tidal creeks of a salt marsh, or the ponds in the fields and woods beyond.

A wildfowler has to check the impulse to fire as black ducks circle, until his chosen bird drops quite low. It will often float down on the far side of the decoys, barely within range. Though it is a misconception that dabblers never duplicate the running takeoff of diving ducks, they do tend to leap up almost vertically, sometimes rising a dozen feet or more, before

leveling off. At the top of the rise the bird seems frozen in the air for an instant, an instant of advantage for the jump-shooter. An incoming dabbler, especially a cautious black, prefers to alight at the edge of a flock to avoid colliding with any abruptly rising birds. Many hunters therefore arrange their stool with the outermost decoys fairly close to the blind or with wide landing gaps in the rig.

VOICE: At high altitude, blacks are often silent but for an occasional sharp or reedy chuckle, yet they can be as noisy as mallards and the voices of the two breeds are virtually identical. Females are especially vociferous, emitting a loud, resonant quack, while male blacks utter a lower, shorter note: *queck . . . queck-queck-queck-queck.* Frequently these sounds seem to be hailing calls as the ducks start to circle over resting birds or decoys. A reply in kind may overcome their suspicions, but some wildfowlers find it easier to draw them with a softly glottal feeding chatter of clicks or coughs: *tick-a-tick-a-tick, a-tick-tick-tick-tick.* Feeding and hailing calls can be mixed.

Blacks crossing, as seen from salt-marsh blind.

Gadwall *(Anas strepera,*
formerly classified as *Chaulelasmus streperus)*
COMMON & REGIONAL NAMES: *gadwell, gaddy, gray duck, gray widgeon, prairie mallard, creek duck, redwing, specklebelly.*

GAME IDENTIFICATION IN FLIGHT: A dozen gadwalls, keeping no precise formation and traveling with pintails, can be mistaken for sprig hens or immature drakes. In some regions both species are called gray ducks, a reference to the dominant color of the drakes, but the long-necked, lance-tailed sprig does not resemble a gadwall. Though a hen or juvenile of either breed has mottled brown feathering, the pintail has a longer, more pointed rear and a longer profile.

Hunters also mistake gadwalls for baldpates. The colors look alike at a distance, and a baldpate is only a little smaller than an average 2-pound gadwall drake. Since the gaddy is the only surface-feeder with a substantially white speculum, it should be easy to identify on a freshwater hunting marsh, but the baldpate has white patches on the *foreparts* of its wings, which may flicker like the gadwall's secondaries.

A pair of well-fed gadwalls, high over the horizon on a line-straight course, can also be taken for mallards until they abruptly switch or swoop. But the wings are more slender and sharply pointed than a mallard's, and beat faster. Some hunters claim gadwalls are swifter, though less skittish, than either mallards or pintails. All of these birds probably can achieve 60-mile-an-hour bursts with a tail wind.

The drake has a short blue-black bill with a trace of orange at the base. The head and neck are pale grayish brown, duskily streaked and dotted, with a lighter throat. The breast, back, and sides are gray, the breast scaled with cream or buff and the other parts rippled or lined. The underparts are a faintly mottled white, the tail dusky gray with light edging. The black rump is seen clearly enough from a blind to help in identification. The wings are brownish gray and buff, with the middle coverts forming a rusty or chestnut patch. The white speculum has a black center patch. The hen's bill is dull orange, duskily ridged and spotted. Her plumage is mottled brown with light feather margins and an almost white belly. She, too, has a white speculum, but her black and chestnut wing patches are smaller and duller. Both

sexes have yellow feet with gray or black webbing.

DISTRIBUTION: This species probably has a wider global distribution than any duck except the mallard, yet it is not extremely abundant. Gunners on the Pacific Flyway usually see the most fall flights. Gadwalls appear with fair regularity on the Central Flyway and the lower reaches of the Mississippi, less so to the east.

The summer range spreads down into areas of heavy agricultural and urban encroachment. Some gadwalls nest as far north as Hudson Bay, but the primary breeding region ends in a curve from southwestern Ontario up across the central latitudes of the Prairie Provinces and down through lower British Columbia. Breeding grounds extend into western Minnesota and Iowa, and across the plains and mountain states almost to the Pacific. The winter range covers the lower part of the continent down into central Mexico and as high as the Chesapeake on the Atlantic Coast, Oregon's Rogue River on the Pacific, but with a sharp central dip into the lower Mississippi Valley—an outstanding hunting region where the largest numbers congregate by the end of autumn. The migration begins in September and subsides by the end of October.

Ducks making low pass despite exposed tidal-flat blind (top),
and gadwall hen and drake (r.).

GAME BEHAVIOR & HUNTING HABITAT: Despite an almost exclusively herbivorous diet, the gadwall is not universally acclaimed as table fare. It may be that the birds are inferior along some western and Gulf shores, where now and then they feed heavily on algae. Their chief foods are pondweeds, widgeon-grass, bulrush, algae, sedges, coontail, miscellaneous grasses, arrowhead, and cultivated grains. Essentially birds of the interior, they winter mostly on ponds, sloughs, swamps, and lakes, but along the lower coasts and in southern Louisiana and Texas gray-duck hunting is sometimes fine on estuaries and brackish marshes. In addition to tipping up in the shallows, gadwalls can submerge like the diving species to feed at depths unusual for most dabblers.

Both decoying and jump-shooting are possible, for the birds are less alert than most ducks. However, they are not abundant enough to be the principal object of many hunts, though welcome in a mixed bag. When jumped, they leap into flight with a celerity that can call for snap-shooting.

VOICE: A shrill whistle occasionally bursts from a gadwall drake. His chief sounds are a deep but reedy *whack* and a loud, frequently repeated croak rather like a raven's call. Females quack like hen mallards but with a higher pitch and less volume.

Mallard (Anas platyrhynchos)

COMMON & REGIONAL NAMES: greenhead, ice duck, frosty-beak, ice-breaker, twister, yellowlegs, redlegs.

GAME IDENTIFICATION IN FLIGHT: When a long echelon or wide chevron beads the sky over a freshwater blind, the birds are most frequently mallards. Often enough, a trio separates from the flight and comes over in a precise little spearhead, but mallards tend to fly in larger formations than any dabblers except sprig. Sometimes they bunch or swarm raggedly—as all ducks do on short flights between resting and feeding sites or when milling about in search of a place to alight. On migratory flights they more commonly draw themselves across the sky with a precision almost approaching that of Canada geese, yet a lone mallard is apt to skitter or flare unpredictably. The wingbeats are relatively shallow, reaching high but not deep, and slower than those of smaller dabbling species. The momentum may not appear swift, but mallards can accelerate suddenly from their 40- to 45-mile-an-hour cruising speed to 60 or more.

Easily tamed birds like mallards and blacks can be strangely timid in the wild. Mallards are not quite so cautious as blacks, but they will circle widely before cupping their wings over a decoy spread. When flushed either on water or land, they generally spring up almost vertically, although they can also make a running takeoff.

They are large—more than twice the size of teal, almost two-thirds as long as Canada geese, the drakes averaging between 2½ and 3 pounds, the hens not much smaller—and can often be recognized while still far from the blind. The head and neck seem to point slightly upward, positioned above the body during flight; the male's rump and foreparts appear dark, though sometimes the white neck ring is visible, and the underparts are white; the hen's belly is tawnier but pale. The ample, gently tapering wings have white undersides rimmed by dark primaries and a white-bordered blue speculum.

Before the moment comes to stand and shoot, details begin to emerge: white outer tail feathers, yellow or orange legs, the drake's chestnut-red breast sometimes glowing as dark as a splash of burgundy below the white collar, his glossy green-black head above it. A drake crossing low may clearly show his profile with its unique, jaunty upward curl of tail feathers. The female looks like a pintail hen but with an abbreviated neck, rounded tail, white wing lining, and white-barred speculum.

A few sportsmen, particularly in the West, still speak of an early migrating subspecies, small, red-legged, darkly billed and drably feathered. Such early arrivals are young or incompletely molted birds from the southerly breeding grounds. They soon grow larger and brighter, their reddish-orange legs fade to yellow, and the drake's bill, olive or greenish yellow in September, turns yellow as winter nears. His dark, iridescent green head has subtle purple glosses that catch the light. At the base of the neck is a narrow white collar, not quite complete at the rear, contrasting with green above and a chestnut-red breast below. The back is brown, the scapulars grayish white and chestnut, all duskily stippled. The glossy black rump shines with blue-green reflections. The sides, belly, and flanks are a vermiculated white that looks silver-gray. The wing coverts and primaries are ashy brown, the linings and axillars white. The speculum is blue with purple highlights, bordered fore and aft by black inner and white outer bars. The brownish-gray tail has white outer feathers and broad white edging with purple-black coverts. The tail's arc of white is familiar to jump-shooters as an identifying mark visible from the rear even in poor light. The upper central tail coverts form the cocky black drake's-curl worn as a trophy in many a hunting cap.

The hen's bill ranges from orange to olive-green, usually with dark mottling, especially on top. She is a speckled and streaked brown duck with lighter head and neck and dark wings that have the same striking speculum and white lining as the male's. Her breast, belly, and tail edgings are pale.

DISTRIBUTION: As the most abundant and adaptable duck in the Northern Hemisphere, the mallard has come to symbolize American duck hunting. It breeds throughout most of Canada, lower Alaska, and the upper western and midwestern states. Its winter quarters on this continent stretch from British Columbia down through nearly all of the United States and into Mexico. Its autumn passage touches every part of the country.

Favorite nesting sites are amid tall grasses where potholes quilt the prairies, but it also thrives on tundra, undeterred by

cold snaps or short brooding seasons. In September some of the restless birds begin a desultory wandering, though the full thrust of migration awaits October and some mallards dawdle on the Canadian sloughs until late in November. They can roost on ice, and a few winter as high as the coasts of Alaska, more of them in British Columbia. Most continue southward. They are prodigious fliers, cruising steadily at high altitudes. They have been known to fly from Alberta and Saskatchewan to southern Louisiana in less than two days—a nonstop flight of 2,000 miles. But they are also prodigious idlers. Some of the waystops on the southward route are food-rich marshes or wetlands close to grainfields, where they may remain for a month or more. Their major wintering area is the lower Mississippi Valley, but after a good breeding season they are populous on every flyway.

GAME BEHAVIOR & HUNTING HABITAT: During the summer, when ducks (especially the young) require a high protein intake, mallards are probably second only to a few species of fish in their consumption of mosquitoes and various aquatic insects. They also relish tadpoles, newts, frogs, worms, crawfish, and a host of small animals found in or around ponds. Yet they are principally herbivorous at all times of year. During lean fall or winter periods they can manage without food for a couple of weeks, but they often gorge themselves to build up reserves.

Where food is plentiful, hunting prospects are always fine. In the flooded oak flats of eastern Arkansas, mallards have been known to devour so many acorns they could not fly back to roosting water.

Though seen along all American coasts, they are fundamentally inland birds. Their renowned predilection for domestic grains notwithstanding, the most heavily used feeding sites in many regions are the shallows of lakes, ponds, sloughs, and streams. The foods of greatest importance in the Northeast are wild rice, pondweed, smartweed, wild celery, and wild millet; in the Southeast, wild millet, smartweed, bulrush, duckweed, spikerush, pondweed, and rice; in the West, pondweed, bulrush, sorghum, and horned pondweed; and on the Pacific Coast, pondweed, bulrush, and barley. They also feast on many other kinds of vegetation, from coontail to cypress cones, and they pick through the woods for acorns, beechnuts, and rock-hard hickory nuts. They have an immense appetite for the small seeds

Mallards circling in response to good calling.

of bulrush, duckweed, pondweed, wild celery, primrose willow, and other such plants.

Domestic crops do, however, attract great numbers of mallards. They sometimes rob significant amounts of wheat on the nesting prairies, and their wintering habits have been strongly influenced in the East by the use of the mechanical corn picker and the proliferation of cornfields near the Delaware and Chesapeake bays. The picking machines shatter ears and spew grain so generously that the stubble fields of the Delmarva Peninsula and the midwestern corn belt have become prime habitat for mallards and mallard hunters. Yet the undisputed mecca is the Grand Prairie of Stuttgart, Arkansas, where an estimated 1,200,000 mallards gather annually on the flooded rice fields, oak flats, and reservoirs. In still other areas crops of barley, sorghum, oats, or buckwheat may bring the ducks. Mallards that have been feeding for a while on any grain are above comparison with most culinary delights.

They decoy well but usually avoid rough or wide-open water. A good location for a stool is the lee shore of a marsh or the quiet water of a little cove or bay. Small ponds near farmlands or woods are fine, and a sandbar or creek bend may be productive either as a blind location or for jump-shooting. Mallards will come to small sets of decoys, and blocks should never be crowded for the sake of numbers, but if there is space for three or four dozen the rig will be all the more effective—for other species as well as mallards.

Early in the season, if the nights are clear, they may come to stubble fields only between sunset and sunup. As winter sets in they become less wary, at least on gloomy days when visibility is low. A day of snow flurries in early winter is ideal for "cornfielding," and white camouflage can be as effective as drab colors are at other times. Jump-shooting is usually best on ponds or sloughs that are wooded or surrounded by fairly high brush, and on streams with bends or high banks to conceal the approach. Since swamps furnish both shelter and food for puddle ducks, the hardwood bottomlands of the South hold numerous wintering mallards as well as woodies.

VOICE: Mallard hens, the most loquacious of American ducks, quack loudly in single, frequently repeated syllables, the first

often louder and longer than subsequent quacks. The drakes have a lower, more staccato call—*queck-queck-queck, queck-queck-queck-queck-queck*—which gives way occasionally to a reedy syllable that almost sounds like the word "reed." Harshly resonant, the voices of both sexes can be heard afar, and mallards respond to good calling. When they are nearly ready to pitch in, their cries often quicken into a soft, busy chuckle. All of

Jump-shooter flushing pair of mallards at close range.

these sounds may be heard when they eat, but the primary feeding call is a sharper, ticking chatter. The sounds can alert a jump-shooter scouting creeks and ponds, or can be imitated to draw birds to a blind. Both the chuckling and ticking are best mimicked by grunting quickly and softly into the call, and are most alluring if preceded or followed by one, two, or three loud, long quacks—a hailing signal.

Pintail (Anas acuta)

COMMON & REGIONAL NAMES: *pinnie, sprig, sprigtail, spring-tail, spiketail, split-tail, sprit-tail, picket-tail, spindletail, sharp-tail, kitetail, kitetail widgeon, gray duck, pheasant-duck, water pheasant, longneck, smoker, cracker, smee, smethe, pile-start, trilby duck.*

GAME IDENTIFICATION IN FLIGHT: A quadrant of morning sky is etched by a wide crescent, still miles out of gunshot but swelling forward, a gorget torn from the throat of the North. For a moment as the line advances, it becomes a perfect bow transected by dozens of miniature arrows, the long necks and tails of loosely spaced birds, but the form shifts constantly, rippling, billowing. The first ellipse is followed by another, a little to one side and more ragged, festooning a cloud bank with sprig.

Widgeon, too, sometimes group themselves in arcs, but seldom do they or other dabblers gather in such large flocks as pintails. There may be well over a hundred birds garlanded on a migratory flight. Later the formations will break up into little chaplets trading over the marshes. Some of the birds will fly singly, some will escort mallards, gadwalls, or other puddle ducks, but they are likely to be high and fast.

The beat of their raked and pointed wings, spanning almost a yard, is deeper and quicker than a mallard's. They are not at all heavy (even the drakes average hardly more than 2 pounds), but to a hunter below they can seem larger than mallards, and indeed they do have a slightly greater length of profile because of their long necks and tails. An average male in full plumage may measure over 2 feet from tail to bill tip; the shorter-tailed female perhaps 5 inches less. Sprig are among the fastest of ducks. They can move along steadily at more than 50 miles an

hour and have been clocked at an air speed of 65. Some gunners believe they can fly a great deal faster, at least on the diving descents to which they are addicted. Flocks sometimes approach decoys at great heights, then plummet with a loud rush.

They may swoop within gunshot or level off 300 yards away to glide on rigid wings, a few yards above water, slanting in—impossible targets at one moment and easy the next. When flushed from the water, they bound up like other dabblers and sometimes bunch closely on the rise. Leveling off almost without a pause, they can be nearly beyond range before a startled wild-fowler singles out a target and swings through to gain a lead that may be as great as six bird lengths.

The pintail's bill is gray-blue, and the feet range from that color to olive-gray. A drake's dark brown head, flickering faintly with purple, pink, and green, blackens at a distance and seems to slice the air independently of the body if the white, slender neck fades out against cloud or sky. The back of the neck, almost as long as that of a small goose, is black or dark brown, shading into the gray of the back. The white at the sides and front of the neck extends into a thin stripe up onto the head almost

Pintails milling high and fast over feeding waters.

as high as the eye and behind it. White also spreads down over the breast, becoming pale gray on the belly. Fine black and white vermiculations make the back and sides look gray, but the outer scapulars shade to glossy black edged with gray or white and forming a big dark patch when the wings are folded. The rump is ashy brown with pale flanking and a black rear border. The tail feathers are mostly brownish gray with light edgings and black coverts, the lower ones edged in white, but the two central tail feathers are black, pointed, strikingly elongated. (The only other long-tailed American duck is the oldsquaw, a seagoing northern diver easily distinguished by its small, chubby profile and piebald pattern.) The wings are brownish gray, with black stripes on the tertials, gray underneath, and a white rear edging that can be seen before the speculum is clearly visible. The speculum is a blend of bronze, violet, and green, with a cinnamon front border and rear black bar edged with white.

The female is buffy, speckled and streaked with darker brown except on the pale chin and belly. Her speculum is like the male's but speckled with black and so dull as to be almost unnoticeable. The pattern is somewhat like a gadwall hen's, but her figure is more graceful, her neck longer and thinner. Her tail lacks the drake's elongation but has an almost dovelike point visible from the blind.

DISTRIBUTION: Taken together, the several pintail subspecies—pile-starts, as they were known to the old Long Island gunners—have a circumpolar breeding range. The most heavily used nesting region in America is the vast subarctic and arctic tundra of Alaska, the Yukon, and the Mackenzie District of the Northwest Territories. However, the prairies of Canada's interior are also densely inhabited, and the major summer range stretches from Ontario, Minnesota, and Iowa to the Pacific, as far south as Utah, as far north as the Beaufort Sea.

Among the earliest fall migrants, a few sprig head southward or southwestward in August, closely following the blue-winged teal. They begin to trickle onto every flyway before the season opens, but fortunately their numbers swell late enough for wildfowlers on the interior flyways to include them in early-season mixed bags. Hunters on the Atlantic and Pacific flyways and across the South continue to watch the sleek and lordly

Pintails in fast flush (top) and drake on water.

rush of sprig throughout the season, as the wintering grounds lie chiefly along the Gulf Coast and the eastern and western seaboards. Large numbers also fly farther south, and a few of the Alaskan flocks turn out over the Pacific to the Hawaiian landfalls 2,000 miles away.

GAME BEHAVIOR & HUNTING HABITAT: Great numbers of sprig assault the rice fields of Texas and Louisiana, but since they cannot walk as well as mallards they spend less time foraging on land. The aquatic food preferences of the two species are much alike. From Maryland and Delaware northward, wildfowlers often put sprig and mallards into the same day's bag until December's cold weather pushes the sprig farther south. Although they winter chiefly on the lower coasts and are sometimes found in bays and brackish pools, they prefer fresh water.

They fly so high and fast that relatively few are taken by pass-shooting. The method lends itself only to dark and windy weather when decoying or jump-shooting can be even more profitable. A hunter who lies low in a Texas or Louisiana rice field may see clouds of pintails and blizzards of snow geese, and may count no other species in his limit. Elsewhere, pintails most often go into a mixed bag collected at small wooded waters in farm country. Now and then they slant in over a shallow slough, but long, fast shots are in the majority. Most misses result from underleading them.

VOICE: A pintail hen is demurely quiet except for an occasional low quack, hoarse and muffled. The drake's loud, throaty flight quack terminates less positively than a mallard's. The call is *qua, qua.* There is also a low, mellow, wheezing whistle, reminiscent of green-winged teal. Whether in the air or feeding, pintails are not very noisy; they are more readily attracted by decoys than by calling.

Shoveler *(Anas clypeata,* also classified as *Spatula clypeata)*

COMMON & REGIONAL NAMES: *spoonbill, spoony, broadbill, broad-faced mallard, broady, mesquin, mud duck, mud lark, mud shoveler, scooper, shovelbill, shovelmouth.*

GAME IDENTIFICATION IN FLIGHT: Shapeless little flocks of shovelers push slowly along, but when startled (and sometimes for no obvious reason) they whisk about erratically, behaving like teal in all respects except speed. To shoot a putative teal and collect a mud duck is depressing, but since shovelers have blue wing patches and are early migrants, they may be taken for teal when heading away so that their oversized bills are hidden. The hen is teal-brown, and sometimes a drake is no brighter because its molt begins late and is exceptionally protracted. Moreover, an average shoveler is barely larger than a teal, weighing only a pound or so.

Occasionally spoonbills are also mistaken for mallards, as there is a partial similarity of colors when the drakes are in winter plumage. However, the shoveler's wings are narrower than a mallard's, raked rearward more sharply, and set farther back on a leaner body. In flight the thick head and short neck are level or slope downward, and the broad, light-blue wing patches are often visible. If shovelers pass fairly high, they may look almost black, but when viewed from below, the bills usually show and the drakes have a distinctive black and white pattern: dark head, white breast, dark belly, white band, dark tail. They

Shoveler drake's eclipse plumage in early autumn.

alight slowly, almost vertically, with little splash but with loud wing rattling, and take off in a rattling bound.

The bill is the most outstanding mark. Longer than the head, it spreads toward the rounded tip, which is about twice as wide as the base. It looks disproportionately huge and spatulate, and the sides of the upper mandible swell downward near the front end. Its color is yellowish brown during the molt, but in winter the drake's bill turns black. His head is dark green, like a mallard drake's. The upper breast and foreback are white, the scapulars white with blue and black streaks toward the rear. The back is slaty brown, the rump black with a greenish gloss, the lower breast, sides, and belly chestnut or rusty, sometimes whitely mottled. The rear of the belly pales to white on the flanks at the base of the tail, which is sooty brown with whitish outer feathers. The wing coverts are chalky blue, cobalt, or blue-gray, the primaries dusky, the speculum a white-bordered green strip, the linings whitish. Both sexes have orange feet, and the hen's bill varies from yellowish or greenish brown to mottled olive-gray. Her plumage is buff, with streaks, spots, and stipples of darker brown.

DISTRIBUTION: The main breeding range on this continent is

Spoonbills in flight, easily identified by plumage contrasts.

similar to the pintail's but does not extend as far north in Alaska and the Canadian Territories, as far west in British Columbia, or as far east in Ontario. The shoveler is a warm-weather duck, southward-bound by mid-September and on the wintering grounds before October ends. The Pacific Flyway receives the traffic, with the Mississippi Flyway next. The Central and Atlantic corridors attract smaller numbers. The primary winter range is along the middle and lower Pacific Coast, through Mexico, across the Gulf states, and along the Atlantic from Florida up into the Carolinas. Some of the Alaskan flocks migrate to Hawaii.

GAME BEHAVIOR & HUNTING HABITAT: The shoveler paddles about, head partially submerged, so that algae, vegetative debris, or any other edible particles flow into its large open bill. The sensitive tongue and roof of the mouth sort out what is edible, while rejected matter is sifted away through lamellae at the sides of the bill. Sometimes several shovelers form a more or less circular flotilla, so that each can sift water stirred up by a paddling companion. They also slush mud through their bristle-edged bills, taking more bottom food than any other ducks. More than a fourth of the intake is animal matter. The birds are scrawny, mediocre table fare. They may be found winnowing through any fresh, brackish, or salty shallows and, while not eagerly sought, are occasionally taken to fill a mixed bag on a poor day.

VOICE: The shoveler is a weak-voiced bird, usually silent, though the female now and then quacks feebly and the male produces a low, guttural croaking and cooing.

Blue-winged Teal *(Anas discors)*
COMMON & REGIONAL NAMES: *bluewing, summer teal, fall teal, autumn teal, southern teal, white-faced teal, breakfast duck.*

GAME IDENTIFICATION IN FLIGHT: A swarm bobs and weaves, twists, swoops, darts, in a kind of synchronized chaos and to the occasional consternation of inexperienced gunners who become so entranced with the wonder of how the birds avoid collisions that they forget to shoot until too late. Bluewings often fly in moderately large flocks, and a group numbering more than a score can remain tightly massed. Occasionally a cloud of teal opens as some of the birds break away, straggle, or wheel; more often they keep together in a dense swath that brings to mind songbirds, and the illusion is heightened by their little wings, spanning hardly more than 2 feet and blurred with the speed of the beat.

Since teal sometimes fluster those of us who ought to have grown imperturbable, we like to perpetuate incredible estimates of their speed. It is true, though, that they are adept at spurting out of danger. Because of their small size and habitually erratic flight, they seem to rocket through the air even when flying only 30 or 40 miles an hour on short foraging trips. They can easily sustain greater speeds, are capable of astounding bursts and maneuvers when alarmed, and can spring into the air with awesome agility.

Some duck hunters say that teal seldom fly high enough to be out of gunshot. Actually, they may pass only a couple of yards overhead, or skim the treetops, or pass at 5,000 feet in clear weather, unobserved because of their small size. They measure only about 15 or 16 inches from bill to tip of tail, and even males seldom weigh quite a pound.

The drake's bill is bluish black. His head and neck are slate-gray, with motley reflections and a big white vertical crescent, its convex edge forward, in front of each eye from forehead to throat. The side crescents sometimes meet in front. A pale, rosy cinnamon begins high on the breast or base of the neck and flows down over the belly and sides, marked with round black spots that give way to bars on the sides and sometimes on the belly. The back is gray-brown with U-shaped buff markings. A white patch marks each flank ahead of the rump and tail, which are pale-edged olive-brown on top, black or blackish brown underneath. The wing coverts are cobalt or chalky-blue, whitely tipped at the rear and occasionally appearing entirely white if the sun is bright. The primaries are dark brown, the linings shadowy white. The iridescent emerald speculum, darkening to black on each side, is hard to tell from that of a green-winged teal, but the large blue patch ahead of it is visible in good light. The feet are dull yellow or yellow-orange, regardless of sex.

In dim light, bluewings cannot be distinguished from cinnamon teal or greenwings and, regardless of light, there is just

Bluewing drake, showing conspicuous facial crescent.

no way to tell a blue-winged hen from a cinnamon hen as the bird flits by a blind. Fortunately, where the two species occur the hunting regulations coincide.

The hen's bill is lighter than the drake's, edged with a little yellow or ocher, and darkly mottled near the base. Her head and neck are tawny or buff, streaked with brown except on the pale throat. Her lower breast and belly are white, with gray-brown mottling near the rump. Her body and primaries are brown or olive-brown, showing pale streaks and U-shaped edge markings, and her wings are like the drake's but duller.

DISTRIBUTION: Though related to teal species on other continents, the bluewing is found only in America. The summer range, centered in the Prairie Provinces and prairie states, reaches west to British Columbia, Idaho, and Oregon; east across the Great Lakes; south to Colorado; north to the Canadian Territories.

Blue-winged teal migrate earlier and farther than any other American ducks. Some of them winter along the Atlantic, from Connecticut down to North Carolina, particularly in the Chesapeake area, but they are more plentiful in the lower parts of the Gulf states, from Texas through Florida, and still more numerous in Latin America and the the West Indies. A considerable population flies to Chile and Argentina—some 7,000 miles. In most years, hunting is best on the Central and Mississippi flyways. The thickest wintering concentrations above Mexico are in the marshes and flooded rice fields of Louisiana and Mississippi, but wildfowlers in Atlantic states also bag good numbers.

When migration swells with the harvest moon, early morning and evening are the peak periods of flight. It is not uncommon

for a teal hunter to quit his blind only an hour or so after legal shooting begins, not to return until an hour or so before it ends. The birds tend to segregate themselves by age and sex; many of the mature males gather in northern staging areas and launch their migration in August. Unless breeding has been poor, a special September season is opened for teal in a number of states; by then the females and birds of the year are on the wing and they account for a high proportion of the bag. The migration ebbs in October, except on the lower reaches of the flyways.

GAME BEHAVIOR & HUNTING HABITAT: Bunches of teal sometimes paddle through flooded rice fields to pick fallen grain. Their appetite for it seems insatiable, yet rice is far less important

Shooting dabblers from canoe amid outline-breaking cattails.

to them than the wild harvest along the reed-bound shores of lakes and freshwater marshes, shallow sloughs, muddy little ponds, creeks, and ditches. Major foods, particularly in the East, are duckweed, naiad, pondweed, smartweed, bulrush, and widgeongrass. In the West there are times when bristlegrass is almost equally important. The birds also eat considerable quantities of insects, tiny mollusks, and other animal matter, yet the little "breakfast ducks" are as delectable as they are small.

Sometimes bluewings are jumped from brushy shoreline waters but decoying is more common, for they fly about frequently, searching for food, and are easily lured. A few puddle-duck decoys on shallow waters will bring repeated inspection. Early in the season they sometimes make pass after pass or try to splash in even after shots have been fired. They are near enough to be reasonably easy targets for accomplished duck gunners, some of whom prefer a modified choke and No. 6 shot instead of the tighter choke and larger pellets favored for bigger ducks. A 20-gauge Magnum is adequate for a shooter who can judge range.

VOICE: Bluewings are quiet birds. In flight the female may utter a feeble quack, while the male chirps softly and repeats a peeping whistle. Having approached decoys eagerly, they flee just as eagerly if alien sounds warn them off. Unless a gunner has heard them often and mastered their soft calls, wisdom lies in silence or the imitation of other dabbling species in the same locale.

Cinnamon Teal *(Anas cyanoptera)*
COMMON & REGIONAL NAMES: *red teal, red-breasted teal, bluewing, silver teal, river teal.*

GAME IDENTIFICATION IN FLIGHT: Cavorting like skittish doves, cinnamon and blue-winged teal are identical in their manner of flight, except that cinnamon teal seldom travel in big flocks. Most often they pass by singly, in pairs, or, shortly after the breeding season, in small family groups numbering from half a dozen to a dozen. They are as swift as bluewings, as easily decoyed, and as agile in bounding up from land or water to twist and dart away. But they are more innocent; when jumped, they frequently alight again only a short distance away.

Like bluewings, they are very small, not often weighing a pound, and they have the same blue wing patches that can glow with cobalt brilliance or blanch in the sun. The name "silver teal" may have derived from this illusion.

The drake's long, narrow bill is black, sometimes tinged with pink on the lower mandible. His head, neck, sides, and upper breast are cinnamon-red, darkening to blackish brown on the crest and lower breast or belly, where black bars may show. The back and rump are dusky brown with lighter cinnamon scallops and streaks. The tail and its coverts are almost black, the scapulars cinnamon with smoky accents. The wings are like those of blue-winged teal: brown with blue covert patches and a green speculum bordered in front with white. Both sexes have dull yellow or yellow-orange feet, and a cinnamon hen darting over the stool looks just like a bluewing hen. Either female would be nearly indistinguishable from the white-breasted, buffy-brown hen shoveler were it not for the mud duck's ungainly bill.

DISTRIBUTION: The only North American puddle duck whose

(text continued on page 177)

Male cinnamon teal foraging on marsh in Utah.

▲ Black duck on takeoff flashing silvery underwings.

▲ Black duck in shallows.　▼ Gadwall drake (l.) and hen.　▲ Black duck in flight.

▲ Blue-winged teal jumped from slough.   ▼ Bluewing drake.

▼ Green-winged teal in flight.　▼ Young retriever at work.

▼ Shovelers.

▲ Mallards in flight.   ▼ Mallard drake (l.) and hen.

▲ Gull mounted on boat as confidence decoy.   ▲ Wood duck taking off.

▲ Woody drake (l.) and hen.   ▼ Baldpates passing over.

▲ Greater scaup hen (l.) and drake.   ▼ Lesser scaup drake (l.) and hen.

▼ Raft of canvasbacks.

▼ Ringneck drake. ▲ Pintail-shooting on coastal river. ▼ Redhead drake.

▲ Shooter and Lab on eastern marsh. ▼ Bufflehead taking off.

distribution is restricted to the western third of the continent, the cinnamon teal has a migratory pattern that is hardly more than a shift to the warmer part of the range, with summer and winter quarters substantially overlapping. The breeding grounds stretch from southern British Columbia and Alberta into Mexico and from the Rockies to the Pacific. A few migrating birds stray over the prairie states, but very rarely east of the Mississippi. In September and October, those in the north meander down the Pacific and Central flyways to join other red teal inhabiting Mexico and southern California and Arizona. North of Mexico, hunters find the largest gatherings in central and lower California and in Texas.

GAME BEHAVIOR & HUNTING HABITAT: At the tule-rimmed margins of western ponds, lakes, streams, and marshes, cinnamon teal paddle quietly through thick vegetation. They feed on the surface and sometimes come ashore but seldom wander far from water. The principal foods are bulrush, pondweed, horned pondweed, grasses, sedges, and miscellaneous seeds, stalks, and leaves.

Where rushes and reeds grow high, jump-shooting may be reasonably productive. Cinnamon teal often permit a close approach, and when they take flight they are unlikely to go far. But since they neither travel nor feed in sizable groups, they are sometimes regarded merely as a bonus by hunters decoying other species. More of them are bagged in Mexico, where hunting guides know the best wintering marshes for pass-shooting or decoying.

All ducks will, on occasion, dive to escape danger, and the cinnamon teal is among the most adept at swimming great distances underwater. Teal are easily killed, but they are so small that it is not uncommon to miss a bird with most of the shot pattern. If a second shot is needed, it should be made quickly, before the teal can dive. (For recommendations regarding guns and loads, see *Blue-winged Teal.*)

VOICE: Cinnamon teal are even quieter than bluewings. The hen's occasional quack is weak and timid. The male's infrequent call is a low rattling chatter. Imitation is hardly worthwhile since teal can be lured by the calls of other dabblers.

Green-winged Teal *(Anas crecca carolinensis)*

COMMON & REGIONAL NAMES: *greenwing, common teal, butterball, lake teal, mud teal, congo, redhead teal, winter teal, partridge duck, water-partridge, breakfast duck.*

GAME IDENTIFICATION IN FLIGHT: "Flurry" is the most common word for the sudden approach or departure of greenwings. They swarm like bees or wheel about like a rush of pigeons but with gyrations even more abrupt than the antics of other teal species. Whether a group numbers fewer than a dozen or more than a score, the birds twist, dip, rise, turn, circle in bunched unison or occasionally in succession. They may spread out, bunch, then flare again.

Smallest of American ducks, they generally weigh only three-quarters of a pound, with an average length of 16 inches or a little less and a wingspan of 2 feet or so. They are also the fastest of the small dabblers, faster even than the bluewing. The big canvasback (probably the speediest American duck) can outdistance them, but undoubtedly greenwings can sometimes ride a tail wind at better than 60 miles an hour. When flushed, a greenwing explodes into the air—hence the name partridge duck or water-partridge. The lightning rise is not, however, a sure defense. Startled greenwings tend to bunch together even more tightly than usual as they lift away, and a shot occasionally brings down more than one despite the gunner's efforts to single out his target.

The drake has a slender black bill and a green and chestnut mask. The chestnut of the head and neck darkens to purplish black at the rear, where a crest of longer feathers slopes out and down the neck like a little mane. The green marking is a large, glossy, curving but almost horizontal teardrop on each side of the head, its wide front end enclosing the dark eye. Below and behind the eye it darkens to black, and is entirely bordered by a faint buffy line which often extends forward to the bill. The European teal *(A. c. crecca),* which visits the Atlantic Flyway, is probably counted in the bag as an American greenwing with fair frequency, although it has a more pronounced—often white—line bordering the green patch. A clearer differentiation is a horizontal black and white side stripe above the European's wing, formed by long upper scapular feathers. The American

has a black patch on the upper sides but no white stripe there; instead, it has a vertical white stripe extending down the side from the front of the wing.

The back and sides are gray, a fine etching of dusky and white lines. Round and crescented black spots cascade down the rosy-buff breast and fade at the bottom of the white side stripe and into dusky or buffy white on lower breast and belly. Beneath the slaty-brown rump a black stripe runs around the underparts, separating the light belly from the tail's lower coverts, which are black centrally and pale ocher or yellow-gray at the sides. The tail is slaty brown narrowly edged with white. The wings are grayish brown, the speculum green with a narrow inner and wide outer stripe of black, bordered in front with buffy brown and at the rear with narrow white or buff tipping on the outer black feathers. The linings are dusky white. But the wings beat so fast that they blur, sometimes rendering the markings invisible until a bird is brought to hand.

Both drake and hen have gray feet. The hen's bill is also dark gray, spotted with black and often tinged with violet. Her wings are like the male's but more subdued. Like the cinnamon and blue-winged hen, she is a mottled brown bird with white breast and belly, though she is even smaller than those two.

Greenwing hen.

DISTRIBUTION: The greenwing is hunted on all the major fly-ways. It nests from the Mississippi to the Pacific. The most pro-ductive breeding grounds blanket the Prairie Provinces, the upper portions of the plains states, British Columbia, and the northern tier of states from Montana through most of Washington, but some of the birds nest farther south and great numbers summer far to the north.

Whereas bluewings are the earliest fall migrants, green-wings vie with northern-bred mallards as the last of surface-feed-ers to leave for the South. Many green-winged teal begin the journey with the first frost, but the main surge comes later and most of the birds linger at waystops until driven on by heavy snows or closing ice. The most heavily populated winter range covers the upper half of Mexico and the southern United States, particularly the Gulf Coast. However, greenwings are abundant all winter from the Rockies to the West Coast as high as southern British Columbia, throughout the Southwest, and along the East Coast from Virginia downward. In addition, small enclaves some-times endure a New England winter if they find open water in springs and coastal streams.

GAME BEHAVIOR & HUNTING HABITAT: Greenwings prefer inland sloughs, marshes, ponds, lakes, creeks, rivers, and rice fields, but they do visit coastal estuaries, bays, and stream mouths. Early in the season, teal dawdle on Maine's famous Merrymeeting Bay, and later they congregate on delta wetlands

Greenwing drake picking grit.

and lagoons in the Gulf states as well as on smaller waters. Many of them winter on the big tule marshes in lower California, and they show up throughout the season on open but smooth waters —a sheltered bend of the Platte in Nebraska, perhaps, or a backwater of Oregon's Willamette.

They feed chiefly by plucking seeds and vegetation in the shallows and by tipping up to reach bottom growth. Sometimes they wander about on land to glean berries, acorns, chestnuts, and other wild foods, as well as domestic grains, but their staples in the West are pondweed, bulrush, wild millet, smartweed, and spikerush; in the Northeast, muskgrass and wild rice are also important, and in the Southeast so are panicgrass and duckweed. Unfortunately, during the salmon run on the Pacific Coast they feast on decaying fish that renders them almost unpalatable. But as a rule the species is a gastronomic prize, even though about a quarter of its diet consists of mollusks, insects, and other animal matter.

Jump-shooting is not invariably a short-range effort analogous to upland hunting. Depending on local habitat and prevalent species, and particularly in the case of green-winged teal, it may consist of sculling wide waters such as Merrymeeting, or poling rice flats or tule-fringed sloughs where birds tend to flush at long range. This calls for a tightly choked gun, preferably in 12 gauge, and some wildfowlers prefer shot as large as No. 4 or 5. Where birds are more likely to get up close, however, less choke is needed, 20 gauge may be adequate, and smaller shot can be used.

Greenwings decoy readily. A flock may circle and dart by a set repeatedly even after one of the birds drops. They may also splash in just beyond the decoys. Some hunters gamble, waiting in the hope that birds will set down so that they can be flushed and one or perhaps two can be taken on the rise.

VOICE: Some of the male greenwing's calls have been likened to the song of spring peepers, but the bird has a much wider repertoire—trills, twitters, a short, mellow whistle, and a higher, staccato whistle. The hen utters a fast and frequent series of quacks, high-pitched but not loud. A stuttering quack—*eck-eck-eck*—seems to signify curiosity. It can be imitated by gently grunting into a mechanical call if care is taken not to make the sound too loud or resonant, for the hen signals alarm with a similar but deeper belching note.

American Widgeon *(Anas americana,* also classified as *Mareca americana)*

COMMON & REGIONAL NAMES: *baldpate, baldy, bald widgeon, bald-faced widgeon, bluebill widgeon, green-headed widgeon, gray duck, specklehead, whiteface, wheat-duck, whistling duck, whistler, poacher.*

GAME IDENTIFICATION IN FLIGHT: During high, long migratory flights, widgeon sometimes form a ragged arc or blunted chevron, after the manner of pintails but in smaller numbers. On lower, shorter foraging flights they are more apt to pass a blind in a compact, shapeless little flock. After approaching steadily, they may erupt into disconcerting swoops, climbs and turns—like teal but with less dazzling velocity. Their speed is generally between 40 and 50 miles an hour, the beat of their sharply curved wings midway between the teal's blur and the pintail's quick but measured rhythm.

A widgeon's profile is stocky, short-necked, stubby-billed, with a pointed but broad tail. It is a duck of medium size, generally weighing less than 2 pounds, about 20 inches long and with a wingspan of about 30 to 33 inches. In the air, the drake's big white forewing, or shoulder, patches and black tail are easy to spot, and both sexes are white-bellied. They approach decoys with dull-witted confidence, yet there is a nervous quality to their flight and they are exceptionally quick to take alarm, flushing from water in perpendicular haste with rattling wings and loud, terrified quacks, then careening away in panic.

Both sexes have gray or bluish-gray feet and a short, almost gooselike bill of the same color, with a black lower mandible, nail, and base. The drake's forehead and crown are whitish—hence the name baldpate—and the marking is often visible as birds approach the rig or when the tops of their heads show as they rise. A glossy green patch extends rearward from each eye, thinning and curving downward around the back of the head. The lower head and neck are cream, beige, or grayish, speckled with black. The upper breast is lavender-pink, turning somewhat grayish or rosy brown on the sides and white or rusty white on the lower breast and belly. The dark gray tail has black coverts, and the back and scapulars are rosy, duskily stippled brown, graying at the rear. The wing coverts are white, with a brownish-gray front edge—white patches that glimmer in the air before the time comes to stand and shoot. The primaries are brownish gray, the linings and axillars white and ashy, the speculum green, blackening toward the rear, with a black bar in front and a white bar at the inner side separating the secondaries from white-edged black tertials.

The hen's head and neck are gray or ivory, thickly speckled and streaked with grayish brown. The upper breast and sides are rusty or yellowish brown, the lower breast and belly white, the rest of the body grayish or yellowish brown with pale feather edgings. Her speculum is black or dark brownish gray with only a spot of green or sometimes none at all. Her covert patches are grayish but can look almost as white as the male's because of their contrast with the brown primaries.

A baldpate hen can be taken for a gadwall, but the latter has a substantially white speculum. There is an even closer resemblance to the female European widgeon *(A. penelope),* which is distinguished only by a more reddish body tone and duskily mottled underwings. The European widgeon sometimes visits this continent during hunting season, and is bagged now and then on the Atlantic and Pacific coasts. The European drake

Widgeon drake.

is easier to recognize as he makes a close pass over the rig. He has a cinnamon or chestnut head with a tawny or buffy cream forehead and crown; there is no eye patch, and his upper body is silver-gray rather than rosy brown.

DISTRIBUTION: The American breed, or baldpate, nests chiefly on the central and western Canadian prairies but also north into the Canadian Territories and Alaska, as well as south into the plains and mountain states. The migration is a leisurely fanning out over all of the flyways to the lower segment of the North American coasts, Mexico, the West Indies, and Central America. Birds bred in Alaska and Canada take wing early in September but do not reach the United States in force until October.

A few of the hardy ducks from the far Northwest winter in lower Alaska and British Columbia, and a few others fly to Hawaii, while most head for the coasts and south-central states. Only the pintail and mallard are more plentiful in the West during hunting season. On the Pacific Coast they winter from Washington to Mexico, and on the Atlantic from Long Island or lower New England to the Florida Keys. Concentrations grow progressively heavier in the South and along the Gulf Coast.

GAME BEHAVIOR & HUNTING HABITAT: Baldpates can graze like little geese, and they occasionally become a minor nuisance in western locales, where they raid alfalfa and garden crops. They also enjoy wheat, barley, and other coarse grains; farmlands along flyways are always worth reconnoitering for waterfowl. But they are primarily aquatic feeders. Wild celery would constitute an important part of their diet if they could obtain it at will, but they are poor divers. To compensate, they often lurk near diving species, scavenging remnants scattered on the surface by canvasbacks, redheads, and such. They dabble in the mud as well as in the shallows, but consume very little animal food. Pondweed, widgeongrass, naiad, bulrush, and muskgrass attract them throughout much of their range. In the West, alfalfa, eelgrass, and various algae also mark good hunting sites. Widgeon and gadwall have similar feeding habits, and it is strange that neither is as great a delicacy as some less fastidious dabblers.

Frequenting fresh ponds and marshes, brackish and salt marshes and bays, widgeon consort with other puddle ducks as well as with pochards. Like black ducks, they depend on much nocturnal feeding where hunting pressure is severe, hiding in dense reeds during the day, resting in open water far from shore, or sunning on remote banks. Even on lightly hunted waters, the best hours to be in a blind are early in the morning and again toward dusk, though the offer of this advice is qualified by the memory of several busy forenoons on a California marsh.

Because baldpates are so alert and high-strung, jump-shooting is less productive than decoying or pass-shooting. By imparting their nervousness to other species, they can become a hindrance even to the gunner in a blind. Once, in that California marsh, we made the mistake of letting them splash down. Their terrified racket when we flushed them reached all the wildfowl in the vicinity, and their departure was followed by a complete lull. But, paradoxically, they later flew at and over our decoys with no trace of caution when we remained hidden and still.

VOICE: Widgeon are sometimes called whistlers. The drake has a mellow triple note—*heew, heew, heew*—at times repeated interminably either in flight or on water. The female intersperses a weak, guttural, drawn-out *qua-awk* with occasional loud caws. If the caw turns into louder, panicky quacking, all widgeon within earshot flee. So may all the ducks on a marsh. Ducks have excel-

Hunting for widgeon and other ducks from camouflaged canoe.

lent hearing and react quickly, even to the danger signals of a different species. It is hard to identify most ducks positively by voice alone, but the whistling of baldpates, recognizable when they are a couple of hundred yards away, warns hunters to keep still and low in the blind.

Wood Duck *(Aix sponsa)*
COMMON & REGIONAL NAMES: *woody, wood widgeon, acorn duck, swamp duck, tree duck, summer duck, plumer, squealer.*

GAME IDENTIFICATION IN FLIGHT: As dusk thickens, a hen and drake scud swiftly over the trees. They are stubby-billed and plump as widgeon but the male's regalia is a shattered rainbow. They approach straight from some wild-rice marsh or acorn-strewn riverbank to a wood-encircled roosting pool. The small, darting forms catch the attention of an upland hunter trudging homeward with a brace of partridge. He notes the direction of flight and the pool's location. He even notes the time.

The birds splash in carelessly, spattering water before composing themselves and gliding about, as buoyant as dry leaves. A single hen soon arrives on a lower course, flying less like a duck than a grouse as she threads the canopy of forest, dodging and flitting. Before the light fails, half a dozen little wood ducks float quietly, another swoops in to perch and preen on a mossy limb, and one mutters and clucks while scurrying along the bank to peck at mast.

Migrating woodies usually travel in small flocks, seldom more than a dozen or so together, often fewer. In their winter quarters, they are frequently seen singly or in pairs or little clusters, but sometimes the clusters accumulate, filings on the magnet of a safe communal tree limb, food-rich swamp bottom, or secluded creek.

Their wingbeat is fast, and when they dart low among the trees they look somewhat like oversized teal. The average length of a wood duck is about 1½ feet, the wingspan 28 or 29 inches, the weight between 1¼ and 1½ pounds. They streak by at 45 or 50 miles an hour. When at a height of 50 yards and the light is too poor for colors to stand out, they can be mistaken for widgeon or sometimes gadwalls. The pronounced crest on the

head of either sex flattens somewhat in flight and is not a good identifying mark for the hunter. However, a woody flies with its head at a distinctive tilt—above the body and with the short bill angled downward.

Readily seen by a hunter huddled flat against a drowned but upright tree are the long, dark tail (narrower than a widgeon's and almost square-ended), white belly and lower breast, dark upper breast and wings, and the drake's vertical black and white bar on each side of the breast at the front of the wings.

But when a drake plummets almost vertically, with wind whistling through his primaries, the hunter's impression is of bright shards poured from a broken kaleidoscope. Startled, he may be slow to get his gun up. If he keeps still the bird may alight within range. As he wades forward to flush it, he congratulates himself. But with a shrill squeal of panic the drake rips itself off the water, rising at an unexpected angle midway between the skitter of a diving duck and the leap of a dabbler. The gun follows but the woody abruptly fans its tail, tipping it downward, braking, almost stopping in midair, makes a tiny swoop, sideslips, and is hidden by a maze of timber on which the pellets rain in harmless sibilance. The next attempt may smack of snap-shooting at grouse.

The wood duck's short, high, narrow bill has a sharply hooked black nail, regardless of sex. Black, too, are the drake's

Woody hen (l.) and drake.

lower mandible and the ridge. The central portion of his bill is rose or pinkish white, and the remainder is purplish red—bright during breeding season but somewhat faded in autumn—with a narrow yellowish border about the base. A thin white streak curves up from that point over the large crest, which terminates behind the velvety black nape. The sides of the head gleam with bronzes, greens, purples, brownish blacks, vermilions—shifting vapors. Above the white streak, the feathers are mostly metallic green and bronze, darkening on the luxuriant crest into a white-streaked cascade mixed with purples and blues behind the head. Reaching up from the white chin, throat, and foreneck are two white crescents, one ending on the cheek, the other almost circling the neck.

The body is a blend of dark greens, bronzes, smoky browns, and bluish blacks; the tail is black but with glints of other colors and with glossy brown undercoverts. The upper breast is dark chestnut, often with brown or violet overtones, marked with rows of white spots some of which are triangular, like little arrowheads. The chestnut fades to white on the lower breast and belly; on the sides it ends abruptly against a vertical bar of white backed by a second bar of black. Behind these, the sides are vermiculated buff; a border of long, broad, black and white feathers runs rearward between the scapulars and sides, curving down the flanks to separate the buff from a chestnut patch near the base of the tail. The primaries are grayish brown, tipped with smoky blue, and the grayish-brown wing coverts shimmer with vague greens and purples. The speculum is a metallic greenish blue, darkening at the rear to a narrow black band tipped by white; its inner edges shade to chestnut and dark purple where it merges with black tertials. The axillars and linings blend white with dusky brown—quite dark looking as the ducks pass over.

The darkly webbed feet of both sexes are dull yellow, sometimes tinged with olive or orange. The hen's bill is bluish gray. Her head is ashy brown, glossed with green on crown and crest. A white ring around each eye tapers to a little streak at the rear. The chin and throat are white, the upper body brown, with subdued glints of bronze, green, and purple. The belly is white, the breast and sides a mottled and streaked olive-brown, the tail is a green-glossed olive brown. Except for a little patch of red-violet on the inner great coverts, broader white tipping on

the speculum and brown tertials, her wings are a muted reflection of the drake's.

DISTRIBUTION: Though usually classified as a dabbler, the wood duck is technically the sole American member of the perching tribe *Cairinini*. It breeds in small numbers across the United States and the southernmost Canadian forests but has only two major nesting areas: the temperate woodlands from the Atlantic to the states just west of the Mississippi, north to the Canadian border and south to the Gulf; and a smaller stretch from lower British Columbia down into central California.

Woodies on the Pacific Flyway migrate into southern California, Nevada, Arizona, and Mexico, and some sprinkle onto the Central Flyway. Those breeding from the plains states eastward winter chiefly in Mexico, the Gulf states, and the Southeast

Wood ducks coming down on pond.

up to the Carolinas, though a few stray as far north as Virginia, Kentucky, and Illinois. Most plentiful on the Mississippi Flyway, they are also hunted on the inland waters of every other migratory corridor. The short migration from nesting range into overlapping winter quarters is accomplished in September and early October.

GAME BEHAVIOR & HUNTING HABITAT: Nesting areas in the Southeast and the lower Mississippi Valley continue to shelter birds during hunting season. Most ducks, though they occasionally nest on elevations, prefer ground level. But, like the hooded merganser, goldeneye, and bufflehead—and unlike any of the dabbling species—the woody habitually nests in a rotted tree cavity or woodpecker hole. This tree-nesting tendency almost eradicated the species when the swampy eastern timberlands were cleared, but in recent decades the same characteristic has renewed its value, for wood ducks take readily to predator-proof nesting boxes attached to trees or atop posts. The specialized nesting and feeding requirements also help a hunter to judge whether an area might hold birds.

Where they nest they forage, seeking wild grapes, berries, the seeds of many trees and shrubs, beechnuts, hickory nuts, pecans, acorns (especially those of burr and pin oak). They scuttle

Hunter and Lab watching for incoming flights.

about on a forest floor almost as nimbly as they swim. Although oak and hickory provide their chief staples in the South, they rely more heavily in other areas on wild rice, pondweed, arrow arum, dogwood, and various other marsh and swamp vegetation. The same river cove, slough, or beaver pond that furnishes a hidden resting place may also provide sufficient food to hold the woodies throughout the day, and ducks flushed over water are easier targets than the "incomers" darting among trees. They thrive in the timbered borders of open marshes, as well as among bottomland hardwoods, tree-rimmed ponds, lakes, wild-rice marshes, and swamps.

They are very fond of spiders, but animal matter comprises no more than a tenth of their diet. Their flesh is a delicacy.

Between an orchard and a slatternly hardwood sprawl close to the Neversink River in New York is a high-banked, easily stalked creek where woodies stay for a while every fall. The day's grouse hunting ends with a walk among the apples. If no partridge whirrs from ground or tree, the creek sometimes holds a duck or two that will flush like a grouse and fall to an upland gun. In early autumn, the birds are also trusting inspectors of decoys, but gunfire soon teaches them to avoid blinds and blocks. The best hunting method after that is the simplest: jump-shooting or hiding at a previously observed feeding or loafing spot, or at a roosting site toward dusk. Brush or timber facilitates stalking and hiding, usually rendering long shots both unnecessary and impractical. A 20-gauge gun can serve well, and there is no need for large shot or a tight choke.

VOICE: Wood ducks peep and whistle in flight. Drakes, especially, emit a cheep with a rising inflection that has been likened to the call of a finch, and they intone a mellow, hooting flight call— *hoowett, hoowett.* When startled, they let loose a high, hooting squeal, while females are likely to intersperse squeals with chirping quacks. Woodies are sometimes located by their chattering, squeaking, and clucking as they feed or poke about the woods. Having thus pinpointed them, a hunter can steal through a forested swamp and flush them; he may even achieve success by a rapid approach, relying on quick surprise rather than silence, since woodies in cover are not terribly wary. Sometimes they scatter like chaff when nervous, and one or two may dart over or past the jump-shooter.

However, it is probably more often productive merely to locate them by sound or sight, then quietly wait and watch. Flocks follow habitual patterns—flying to a feeding area at dawn, for example, resting through much of the day on nearby waters, feeding again toward dusk, then flying to roost. After several days, a hunter knows where they will come; from a strategic hiding spot he might bag his limit in a few minutes before legal quitting time.

Stiff-tailed Ducks

Ruddy Duck: *(Oxyura jamaicensis,* also classified as *Erismatura jamaicensis rubida)*

COMMON & REGIONAL NAMES: *booby, bumblebee coot, deaf duck, leatherback, butterball, biddy, blackjack, bluebill, bobbler, bristletail, spiketail, stifftail, wiretail, brown teal, bullneck, chunk duck, creek coot, dapper, dipper duck, dip-tail, dumpling duck, dummy duck, fool duck, sinker. (Note: The ruddy has more colloquial names than any other species; some of the most common and colorful are listed here.)*

GAME IDENTIFICATION IN FLIGHT: Ruddies migrate in big bunches—irregular sprays of fat little ducks following the courses of streams, long lakes, or other waterways whenever possible. They fly low, and lower still when they reach the coastal feeding and roosting waters. In an island blind on some brackish Virginia or North Carolina estuary or on a California bay, a gunner watches them trade about in their bumbling way, making fair speed but pitching jerkily and looking tail-heavy, as if rearing up slightly to breast the wind. Their stubby wings, raked and rounded, beat very rapidly, producing a buzz the gunner can hear by the time he rises to fire; the nickname bumblebee coot alludes both to sound and appearance.

Not many hunters bother with ruddy decoys any longer, but there are eastern baymen who still talk of their "booby blinds," and ruddy ducks seem no less dull-witted (nor less delicious) now than they were in the era of market shooting. Sometimes they shy away from big rafts of canvasback decoys but will bustle right in over a sprinkling of scaup or coot blocks—true coot, not scoter. Strangely, the coots themselves ignore the decoys but shallow-feeding ducks investigate them, and ruddies like the company of coots and broadbills. They may even alight, coming down with a moderate splash to look for wild celery swaying up through the current. If flushed, some will submerge and swim out of range before surfacing. Like grebes, they can sink from sight without diving. But some choose the labor of getting airborne, lumbering along the surface with their big feet pedaling to gain momentum, wings pumping to lift their blocky bodies.

A winter-garbed ruddy might almost be a miniature scoter hen, but it is smaller than any of the continent's divers except the bufflehead. Neither a true sea duck nor a pochard, it is the only North American stiff-tailed species, a bird easy to identify as it bobs past a blind or skitters off before a boat.

In changes of plumage, the male ruddy is the antithesis of other drakes—drab in winter, bright in summer. Instead of a normal eclipse molt, he acquires prenuptial plumage in spring and duller feathering in early fall. At the opening of the fowling season, hunters see many ruddies in full or partial courting raiment—gleaming black cap, white cheeks, bright sky-blue bill, scaled silver and gray belly, and a neck and upper body of the rich chestnut red that gives the ruddy its name. But soon the drakes can hardly be told from hens. (On the water, a drake

Ruddy drake in winter plumage.

sometimes can be distinguished by the jauntier angling of his tail quills, upright or even tilted forward like the fan of a strutting tom turkey.)

The ruddy's upcurved bill is wide and short, and the neck is short and thick. Both sexes have absurdly large blue-gray feet, set so far back that they have difficulty walking. The stiff, narrow, gray-brown tail feathers fan out and up. The wings are a blend of dull browns, with no contrasting patches. The body plumage is so dense that a diminutive ruddy can be difficult to bring down; "shot pouch" is one of the breed's old names, and some hunters still call the ruddy a leatherback.

In late fall the drake's bill turns gray. He retains whiter cheeks than the hen but assumes her general coloring: brown or blackish-brown crown with lighter flecks; ashy neck; brown back and scapulars specked with ash; mottled gray, silver, and rusty upper breast, paling on the belly, darkening on the sides.

DISTRIBUTION: The species is purely North American. It nests on prairies from Manitoba, Saskatchewan, and Alberta down through the plains states and in scatterings across the West. Never very plentiful, ruddies were severely reduced by market shooting, and by the Dust Bowl years, but they still spray over all the continent's flyways each September and winter in fair abundance on the Atlantic and Pacific coasts—from Massachusetts to Florida and from Washington to Baja California. They also pour over lower Arizona, New Mexico, Texas, and Louisiana. A few reach Guatemala, and some of those on the Atlantic Flyway winter in the West Indies.

GAME BEHAVIOR & HUNTING HABITAT: Ruddies often gather on muddy ponds and creeks but they prefer the quiet shallows of bays and estuaries. Nearly helpless on land, they will not often come ashore, yet they are commonly jumped close to the banks. In a few bays they have to partake heavily of animal matter (chiefly insects, with a smattering of mollusks and crustaceans) but on most of the open waters they seek plant life. Their favorites are probably pondweed and bulrush, followed or equaled by wild celery in the East, widgeongrass in the West.

Though restless, and capable of fast, long dives, the birds are so stupid or lacking in protective timidity that they can be approached closely. "Deaf duck" is another old nickname. Easily decoyed, they frequently go into a mixed bag at estuarine blinds. But some of us, being incorrigible jump-shooters, like to scull or wade toward a consortium of the little butterballs. Since they can elude the gun by submerging or paddling away tantalizingly, just out of range, the technique is to come at them from open water and herd them toward the shore until they rise. Because of their tough feathering, a small pellet size such as No. 6 is best employed in Magnum loadings; an alternative is the use of No. 4. A fairly open bore is recommended.

VOICE: Ruddies can chuckle and cluck, but when migrating or wintering tend to be so silent that listening for or calling them is pointless.

Pochards

Canvasback *(Aythya valisineria)*
COMMON & REGIONAL NAMES: *can, canny, gray duck, white-back, bullneck, horse-duck.*

GAME IDENTIFICATION IN FLIGHT: To a hunter scanning the veil of morning, the first indications of canvasbacks are the large formations and distinctive flight characteristics. High over a bay or estuary come surging V formations in late autumn, small flocks at first, then larger ones, sometimes as large as flights of Canadas and as precisely regimented. Their necks stretch to a taper of long, sloping heads and bills. The long, pointed wings, set well back, beat rapidly, with a whirring, rattling force that occasionally is audible in a blind while birds are still beyond the stool. The strokes appear labored, perhaps because they are deep and lifting obviously heavy bodies. Yet cans are probably the fastest of all ducks. They have been clocked at more than 70 miles an hour. Curiously, the wingbeats seem to be noisiest and most rapid during short flights, when the birds seldom strive for top speed.

Although a mature canvasback has slightly less wingspan and length than a mallard drake, its wide body is larger. An average male whose wings spread less than 3 feet is likely to

weigh 3 pounds. The species is heavier than any of the dabblers or the other pochards, heavier than all but a few sea ducks. While the birds are still beyond range, identification is often confirmed by the pointed wings—long in relation to the broad, flat bodies—and by the long, slender heads and necks as well as the contrast of white bodies with dark tails and foreparts. Hens are darker and slightly smaller than drakes.

Over feeding grounds, wedges give way to lines or compact but irregular groupings. They are addicted to long morning and evening flights, sometimes trading back and forth for miles on seemingly aimless forays that have been called "constitutionals." They take off ponderously, running over the water as many diving species must, and then suddenly are away and powerfully cleaving the air.

They closely resemble redheads, but differences may show as they drop low over the rig. The redhead has a darker, slimmer body, brighter head, shorter neck. Most noticeably, it has a round, puffy head with a shorter bill rather than the can's sloping forehead and long, sloping bill.

The canvasback drake's bill is black, and he has a reddish-chestnut head and neck. The breast and the back just behind the neck are brownish black. The remainder of the back and the scapulars are white with black linear stippling which, at a distance, looks like coarsely woven canvas. (The ornithologist Alexander Wilson described a flock's "broad flat bodies wrapt in pencilled snow.") The sides have fainter stippling, and the lower breast or upper belly is almost pure white, darkening under the brownish-black rump and tail coverts. The tail is slaty. The wings are dark: brownish-gray primaries; brownish-gray coverts stippled with white; whitish tertials and linings; white-tipped,

frosted, oyster-gray speculum barely lighter than the primaries.

Both sexes have large, dark-webbed blue-gray feet, sometimes with a hint of olive. The hen's bill is charcoal-gray. Her
head, neck, upper breast, and foreback are fawn-brown, varying
from reddish to yellowish. Her rump, tail, and tail coverts are
dusky brown, whitening underneath. The rest of her body is like
the male's but darker. Her wings, too, are like the drake's.

DISTRIBUTION: The canvasback is a close American relative
of the European pochard *(Aythya ferina).* It breeds in sizable
numbers from central Alaska east into the Yukon. Far more nest
on the north-central parkland and prairie sloughs, from Great
Slave Lake down through the Prairie Provinces and eastern British
Columbia into the United States, west to Washington and Oregon,
east to Minnesota and Nebraska.

Hunters begin to watch the northern skies for cans in mid-
October, though sometimes the birds hold back until ice forces
them out. In many areas the hunting is best late in the season.
Eventually, canvasbacks traverse all major flyways, appearing
over blinds across the continent on their way to coastal wintering
grounds: the Pacific seaboard from Washington almost to Acapul-
co; the Atlantic seaboard from Connecticut to upper Florida; the
Gulf Coast to Veracruz. Some of the birds winter on or near
large inland waters such as New York's Finger Lakes.

Their once vast numbers have never fully recovered from
market shooting, drainage, and drought. After a good breeding
season they show fair abundance on the Pacific wetlands, but
the mecca for canvasback hunters has always been on the shores
of Delaware, Maryland, Virginia, and upper North Carolina, the
labyrinth of bays and river mouths between the Susquehanna

Raft of canvasbacks on Chesapeake Bay.

Flats and the lower end of Currituck Sound.

GAME BEHAVIOR & HUNTING HABITAT: The canvasback's specific designation, *valisineria,* reveals the best kind of hunting areas in the Northeast, for it alludes to *Vallisneria spiralis,* wild celery, the bird's favorite food. A long, tape-leafed aquatic plant, slightly broader than eelgrass, it may be deeply submerged but never in very salty water. It attracts ducks to lakes, ponds, streams, and mildly brackish coastal marshes.

Some hunters stubbornly attribute the delicate flavor of cans to their love of wild-celery roots. Yet on stretches of the Pacific Coast where wild celery is absent, the ducks rely on the arrowhead known as wapato and are equally delicious unless they have been fishing for spawning salmon. Pondweed is almost as important in the West and Southeast as wild celery in the Northeast, and the ducks feed on many other aquatic plants. Since canvasbacks easily dive 30 feet or more to reach food, they need not rely heavily on animal matter.

During the day they commonly frustrate gunners by rafting up in large flocks, far out on large bodies of water. But in the early morning and again near dusk they fly in near shore to feed, engaging in their long "constitutional" flights and searching for aquatic pastures. Those are good times to be in a blind behind a big decoy spread.

Since rafted cans are sometimes hard to approach even when cover is present, jump-shooting has always been problematical in the various areas familiar to the author. Early in the season the birds are easily decoyed, but after a few encounters with gunfire they flare upon sighting movement, an unnatural-looking blind, a flash of metal or color, or an unconvincing decoy spread. Sheer numbers of decoys help to overcome their hesitation: the larger the group, the safer it looks to birds that habitually congregate in huge flocks on the water. The blocks should be glareless, close imitations of cans, redheads, or scaup, set not too close to shore.

It seems as if the birds love to bore in toward the stool, sweeping low into the wind and then veering up and away. Long passing shots are frequent, requiring large pellets such as No. 4's in a tightly choked 12-gauge gun; a wing-tipped canvasback may swim so far underwater that the hunter will never see it again. But the breed's timidity is tempered by curiosity. These and other pochards sometimes alight out of range, beyond the stool, then rise and come closer to investigate a handkerchief or cap waved above the blind. The stratagem has succeeded with acceptable frequency for generations of gunners on Long Island Sound and the Eastern Shore of the famous Delmarva Peninsula.

VOICE: Cans are often lured by a low, insistent grunting or growling into a call, punctuated by a few hoarse croaks—typical flight notes of the drakes, which also have a repertoire of bass peeps and coos. The hen quacks like a mallard. When alarmed, she erupts into a screaming croak, higher-pitched than the male's alarm croak.

Redhead (Aythya americana)
COMMON & REGIONAL NAMES: *American pochard, red-headed broadbill, raft duck, fiddler, fool duck, grayback, mule duck.*

GAME IDENTIFICATION IN FLIGHT: Men who have lived their lives on Puget Sound or the Chesapeake may still mistake distant redheads stitched over a gray morning for canvasbacks, but redheads are darker and a trifle shorter, their flight less steady, their wingbeats faster, and at 2½ pounds a good-sized drake is a half pound lighter than a can. Nonetheless, as a big wedge of redheads approaches, the birds are barely distinguishable from cans despite these and other differences—round, high foreheads and shorter, slightly concave bills.

When they come in over the rig, the air can be heard whirring through their primaries. They fly great distances at more than 40 miles an hour and easily make faster dashes, but they would probably be hard put to keep up with cans on a long flight.

The females look pretty much like scaup and ringnecks as well as cans. However, the scaup hen is smaller and has a wide white face patch around her bill and a white speculum; the ringneck hen's white eye ring may be invisible but she is smaller still. The wings of redheads are quite ashy, those of ringnecks and scaup browner.

Shortly after a hunter arrives on a bay in the morning or again in the late afternoon he may see huge rafts, low in the water though not so low as cans. Several dozens of the birds shake their wings open, patter over the surface, and rise, soon to be followed by another few dozen and another. Each detachment is likely to form a high, long, oblique line on these morning and evening promenades. At other times over the feeding grounds, lines and chevroned phalanxes give way to formless bunches.

A redhead of either sex has a blue-gray bill with a whitish ring behind the black nail, but the drake's is lighter and brighter. His head and neck are chestnut red, blending at the base into a black or very dark gray bib, paling into duskily marked white on the belly. The black-lined white and gray of back, scapulars, and sides look dark gray. The tail is blackish or charcoal-gray with darker coverts. The wings are almost entirely gray but with faint white flecks on the coverts, brownish clouding on the primary tips, and a lighter, pearl-gray speculum with thin whitish edging. The underwings are also gray.

Both sexes have large bluish-gray feet. The female's head is yellowish brown with gray overtones, paling almost to white near the bill. The body is mostly dark gray-brown (grayer above, browner below) but the lower breast and upper belly are grayish white. The wings are like the drake's but smokier.

DISTRIBUTION: The redhead ranges from coast to coast during migration and from north-central Canada in summer to central Mexico in winter. After a good breeding season, hunters on every flyway await the redhead flocks. They nest in clumps of vegetation

Redhead drake (l.) and hen.

over the waters of sloughs, chiefly in the Prairie Provinces and the midwestern United States but also in states farther west. In October, shortly after canvasbacks have started south, the redheads begin their journey, at first unsuspicious of blinds that resemble little islands or shoreline hummocks and thickets, but becoming progressively warier. The greatest densities occur on the Pacific Flyway, yet many flocks pour down the Central Flyway and considerable numbers use the Mississippi route or cross it to the Atlantic. The primary winter range extends from the lakes and marshes above San Francisco south into Mexico and east over the Gulf states to Florida's panhandle. Smaller but heavily populated wintering grounds run from Delaware and Maryland through Virginia into the fine hunting sites on Pamlico Sound in North Carolina. Some western flocks migrate no farther south than Washington, and there are eastern flocks that stop around the Great Lakes, settling on nearby waters from Wisconsin to New York.

GAME BEHAVIOR & HUNTING HABITAT: Redheads like big waters but seldom wander out where our dories waylay the true sea ducks. They frequent bays, lagoons, and estuaries, but even in winter when redhead shooting is best on and near the coasts they choose lakes or large ponds if such waters provide sufficient forage. Now and then they dabble in the shallows with surface-feeding ducks, at which times they are usually feeding on mollusks or insects. But they consume even less animal matter than canvasbacks and provide equally fine table fare. Pondweed is a staple. In the Northeast, wild rice, wild celery, and bulrush are probably next in importance. In the Southeast, widgeongrass and waterlily are major foods, as are muskgrass and bulrush in the West.

The name "fool duck" was bestowed on the redhead by market gunners, evidently because of the way flocks raft up in huge gatherings at night and during the midday hours, and because of their strange habit of "boiling up"—suddenly rising a few feet off the water and then settling back. The boiling is noisily chaotic and would seem to attract predators, including duck hunters, but it occurs out on open water where the birds feel secure. Many of us have seen the same commotion among dabblers on a crowded pond; it seems to be a reaction to overcrowding, an irritability rippling through the flock when too many birds mass in a small area.

If hunting pressure is not excessive, redheads eagerly approach a large decoy set, and sometimes can be approached when feeding close to shore—unless they are being hounded by thieving baldpates, skittish sentinels as notorious for panic as for pirating the wild celery dredged up by the diving ducks.

A redhead shooter has to learn patience. Sometimes the stool draws birds but at first they refuse to drop down into range. They may fly back and forth over a long body of water, descending a little on each cautious pass, then, finally, setting their wings to drop splashily among rafted companions—or possibly rafted decoys. While there may be no need to wait for the final sailing descent, restraint is essential until the ducks cross low enough.

On calm, bright "bluebird" days the characteristic approach can change unnervingly. Once in a while, when visibility is good, the birds dispense with reconnoitering and drop from great heights, plummeting in a "broken-wing" zigzag. But there is no counting on this. It is well to be armed as for canvasbacks: large gauge, large shot, tight choke.

VOICE: The hen raps out raucous, sometimes squeaky quacks in flight. On the water or in the air she is also capable of a growling croak: *r-r-r-rrraw!* A convincing imitation can be produced by vibrating the tongue while growling into a call. The drake, too, growls on occasion or mutters a desultory *qua-qua,* but his usual sounds are loud, deep meows and a rolling guttural purring. Redheads can be coaxed in by a restrained imitation of a house cat, without the aid of a call.

Ring-necked Duck *(Aythya collaris)*
COMMON & REGIONAL NAMES: *ringneck, ringbill, bastard broadbill, bastard redhead, creek redhead, pond bluebill, ring-necked scaup, blackhead, blackjack, bullneck, buckeye, bunty, butterball, dogy, fall duck, tufted duck.*

GAME IDENTIFICATION IN FLIGHT: Ringnecks tend to fly in small, loose groups, perhaps half a dozen or a dozen. Pairs and trios are also common and are more likely to decoy or pass low. When migrating, their flight is steady and moderately swift, but a hunter is more apt to see them fly past the blind erratically, with great speed, their small wings beating very fast.

They come in reasonably low and they seldom circle hesitantly but pitch right in, regardless of whether other birds are on the water. They may splash in among the decoys unless a hunter flares them by shooting, and even then they are likely to return shortly. Light and agile on the water, they rise quickly, at a steeper angle than other diving ducks and with a pronounced whistle of wind through the primaries.

A mature ringneck usually weighs about 1½ pounds, and a drake weighs a few ounces more. They are fat little ducks, almost rotund, perhaps 16 or 17 inches long, their wings spanning about 26 or 28 inches, but in the air they resemble scaup or small redheads. In good light, a scaup's white speculum may flash with each downstroke and a redhead's rich chestnut neck and head may show well, but until the birds are almost close enough for shooting, a more obvious distinction is the ringneck's

Ringneck drake, showing characteristically high crown.

black back, confirming the clue of the small, open formation.

A faint, narrow, chestnut collar around the base of the drake's neck is barely discernible until the retriever brings in the bird, and then only if the duck is in full winter plumage. The popular name ringbill is more appropriate than ringneck. Both sexes have a short, slightly upturned bill, dark bluish gray, often white along the edges, with a narrow, light ring around the base and a wider one near the tip, just behind the black nail. If the light is good, the forward ring can sometimes be spotted once the birds are well within range.

Loose, slightly raised feathers on the drake's crown give the effect of a tuft or short, puffy crest. His head and neck are black, with purple reflections and minor green glints. The collar may be absent but usually there is a small white triangle on the chin. The breast, back, rump, tail coverts, and greenly glossed scapulars are black. The belly and sides are white, with vermiculated gray toward the rear, and the tail is slaty brown. The wings are grayish brown—darkest on the primary tips and the green-vapored coverts—with greenish-black tertials, white axillars, gray-white linings. The speculum is soft gray, tipped with white.

The hen's feet, like the drake's, are buff or bluish gray with dark webs. Her head, neck, and body are mostly grayish brown, paling near the bill and whitish on chin, lower breast, and upper belly. A narrow whitish ring surrounds the eye and a pale, sometimes indistinct line behind it fades away toward the back of the head. The longest scapulars are greenly glossed. The wings are like the drake's but slightly lighter and grayer, with brown tertials and little or no green.

DISTRIBUTION: Closely related to the scaup, the ringneck breeds chiefly in swamps and potholes from north-central Alberta and Saskatchewan down through Manitoba and lower Ontario into the eastern Dakotas, Minnesota, and Wisconsin. A smaller breeding range blankets New Brunswick and northern Maine, and a few ringnecks remain always in the South, having lost their instinctive yearning to migrate.

The exodus begins in mid-October, and ringnecks continue to arrive from Canada until almost the end of November. Even where they run a gauntlet of blinds or jump-shooters, they stubbornly follow chains of ponds, lakes, swamps, and rivers, the majority tracing the Mississippi Flyway into the southern states. Fair numbers take a southwestern course to the Pacific Flyway, wintering in lower Washington, Oregon, and upper California, while the northeastern breeders move almost due south on the Atlantic Flyway. A few travel as far as South America, but the principal winter range covers the southeastern United States, from the Carolinas, Tennessee, and Arkansas down through eastern Texas, Louisiana, Mississippi, Alabama, Georgia, and Florida.

GAME BEHAVIOR & HUNTING HABITAT: Ringnecks can haul food up from 40 feet of water, yet their favorite haunts are forested ponds, swamps, sloughs, and creeks. They prefer brush-rimmed pockets, trusting to cover rather than the broad protective waters sought by other divers. A favorite feeding or resting pond is visited again and again, hunting pressure notwithstanding, while similar ponds nearby are ignored.

The mainstays of diet are pondweed, wild rice, waterlilies, wild celery, sedges, rushes, widgeongrass (especially in the South), muskgrass, and similar plants. The ringneck grows very fat on this fare, supplementing it with only small quantities of animal food, and is a better table bird than the scaup.

Wooded edges of ponds afford cover for jump-shooting, and ringnecks will charge at decoys as if attacking. A modified choke, therefore, is sufficiently tight under typical conditions. Some hunters use a 20-gauge gun rather than a 12, with shot as small as No. 6.

VOICE: Ringnecks remain silent much of the time. The alarm cry is a strident croak like the call of the greater scaup, but the normal flight call is the same contented cat's purr that rumbles from lesser scaup. It can be mimicked by trilling into a wooden call, using the tongue in a kind of Scottish burr, but no mechanical aid is really needed to produce a coaxing imitation: *b-b-r-r-r-r, b-b-r-r-r-r.*

Greater Scaup *(Aythya marila)*
COMMON & REGIONAL NAMES: *broadbill, broadie, bluebill, blackhead, bay blackhead, blackjack, blue-billed widgeon, bullhead, bullneck, butterball, flock duck, raft duck, greenhead,*

grayback, laker, lake bluebill, mussel duck, saltwater broadbill, troop duck, winter duck.

GAME IDENTIFICATION IN FLIGHT: Migrating scaup often fly too high for positive identification until they sweep down for a pass over decoys. On occasion a flock seems to ignore the rig, staying high until, without warning, birds drop so suddenly and steeply that hunters talk of broadbills falling out of the sky. Later in the season, as they traipse about over feeding grounds, they often fly only 30 or 40 feet above the water. Their primaries rustle loudly with the extremely rapid wingbeats.

High or low, they commonly move in large, compact formations that shift from a wavering, bulging, ragged wedge or arc, perhaps, to a ball and then a string, stretching and contracting as if beaded on invisible elastic. An old guide on the Eastern Shore, watching a ball disintegrate, is apt to speak of broadbills "smoking the sky." Soon they bunch again, flying swiftly, erratically, twisting, turning.

The hens at first are gray or white-bellied brown blobs, their wings blurred—though if they pass overhead the grayish-white wing linings show. By then a wide white patch is visible about the bills of the females. Drakes at a distance are simply black-and-white bodies whose dark front and rear ends look

almost disconnected.

At rest in huge rafts on wide waters, they sometimes string into a line or lines parallel to shore, facing into the wind, yet a single file of decoys is never so effective as a large, grouped set. When the birds leave, the first in line skips along splashily and lifts off, followed by the second, and then the next, until the whole line has snake-danced into the air.

They are ducks of medium size, averaging about 2 pounds, with a length of perhaps 1½ feet, a wingspan of 30 inches or so. The greater scaup's bill is broad and heavy-looking. The drake's is grayish blue and black-nailed, the female's dark gray, turning somewhat blue near the black or nearly black nail. The feet of both sexes are gray with a bluish or greenish cast. It is difficult to be certain at first whether scaup or ringnecks are coming toward the blind, but a hunter can soon make out the gray backs of scaup drakes, whereas ringnecks have sable topcoats. Even before that, white speculums may flash, much brighter than the secondaries of ringnecks.

The drake's head and neck are black with a strong green lacquer and sometimes a few violet reflections. His upper breast and foreback are black, his back and scapulars blackly vermiculated white (producing a gray effect). The lower breast, upper belly, and sides are white, shading to sooty brown on the lower flanks and belly. The tail and its coverts are blackish brown. The dull, slaty, grayish-brown wings have white secondaries with brown rear edging and a greenish glow on the tertials. The greater scaup's white speculum extends into a few of the inner primaries—a longer stripe than that of the lesser scaup. But the distinction is hardly apt to be clear when a partner whispers something about broadies coming in high at nine o'clock.

The female's head, neck, and most of her body are a relatively uniform dark brown. Her face bears a conspicuous white patch around her bill. Her lower breast and belly are also bleached, though commonly mottled or stained rusty. Her wings are a trifle duller and browner than the male's.

DISTRIBUTION: The greater scaup is the only pochard hunted both in North America and Eurasia. It breeds and winters farther north and is more maritime in habit than the lesser scaup, but the ranges overlap. Broadbills marked from blinds or boats on

Greater scaup drake.

the East Coast are predominantly greater scaup. Lessers out-number them on midwestern lakes and marshes. It is difficult to say which variety is more numerous in the West. Both races use segments of all four major migratory funnels, though the route along the Mississippi Valley is almost monopolized by lesser scaup.

Alaska's tundra ponds and potholes are the greater scaup's most famous breeding grounds but the species also summers in the Yukon, the western half of the Northwest Territories, upper British Columbia, Alberta, and Saskatchewan. In the southern-most nesting quarters some of the birds, chiefly juveniles, begin sporadic migratory travel before the hunting season opens. The main flight begins later, and greater scaup are still arriving in the United States in late November.

Some wait out winter on the Aleutian Peninsula, in northern British Columbia, and in Maine, while a few range as far as Mex-ico. Others winter on the Great Lakes—especially about Lake Ontario, Lake Erie, and the southeastern end of Lake Huron—where the fine shallow-draft duck boats are vaguely reminiscent of Barnegat sneakboxes. However, more are bagged on the coasts, from lower New Hampshire or Massachusetts to North Carolina and from central British Columbia to California's San Luis Obispo Bay.

GAME BEHAVIOR & HUNTING HABITAT: The name of the species occasionally provides a clue to good hunting habitat. The scaup, like the scallop, derives its name from an old Scottish word for an oyster or mussel bed. About half of the greater scaup's diet during migration and at winter shooting sites is animal mat-ter, chiefly mollusks. Broadbills furnish exhilarating sport, and both greaters and lessers are hunted as "bonus" ducks when bag limits are lowered for prairie-nesters that have been hit by drought, but they are less tasty than some of those species. The greater scaup, though quite palatable, becomes less savory through the winter.

The flocks haunt salt marshes, bays, and estuaries, as well as brackish and fresh waters. In the West and Northeast, pondweed is their favorite plant food, while in the Southeast widgeongrass takes precedence.

Even during migration, broadbills rest and feed on the

largest ponds, lakes, and rivers they can find, gathering in enormous rafts and diving for animal or vegetable matter. The flocks are not excessively wary, and sometimes a duck boat can approach while the birds are foraging. Jump-shooting is occasionally productive on waters rimmed by high reeds or rushes, especially early in the morning or late in the day when scaup may feed close to shore. But since they gad about over their feeding waters at moderate altitudes, there is more to be gained by waiting in a blind (particularly near oyster or mussel beds) to which they can be attracted by big sets of decoys.

In view of their moderate cruising altitude and readiness to decoy, a relatively open-bored gun may be adequate except on windy days when ducks tend to flare. But since scaup are tough and, like most "winter ducks" densely feathered, a 12 gauge is best, usually with shot as large as No. 4. An injured scaup can dive before a second barrel can be fired; once underwater, it is unlikely to be retrieved.

VOICE: The notion that the scaup was named for its voice, though mythical, indicates the sort of bleating caw that a wooden call can accurately mimic. *Scaup, scaup*—loud, discordant, frequently repeated—is a characteristic flight call. But since it sounds like the alarm cry of the lesser subspecies, it is not recommended where both races visit the same waters. An easily imitated, frequently repeated call of both greaters and lessers is a mellow cat's purr—*b-b-b-r-r-r-r-r*. It is not uncommon for broadbills to settle in on the far side of a wide decoy spread, and sometimes we have brought them closer by purring at them—with or without whetting their curiosity by fluttering a handkerchief above the blind.

Lesser Scaup *(Aythya affinis)*
COMMON & REGIONAL NAMES: *bluebill, little bluebill, broadbill, broadie, blackhead, blackjack, booby, bullhead, bullneck, butterball, river bluebill, creek broadbill, freshwater broadbill, lake duck, grayback, raft duck.*

GAME IDENTIFICATION IN FLIGHT: Lesser scaup are as swift as the larger variety and perhaps even more erratic in flight, yet migrating birds often form broad arcs or long lines and fly a steady course for some time before bunching again. On the water they seem more nervous—harder to jump—than greater scaup, glancing about warily before diving. Ponderous running takeoffs and low flights over feeding areas are typical. Lesser scaup average a quarter pound lighter than greater scaup but there is an intergrading of size. The lesser, fundamentally an inland bird, visits coastal marshes but prefers smaller lakes, ponds, streams, and freshwater marshes. Locale, therefore, is often a clue to identification.

The black head of the lesser scaup drake has a purple sheen and only a trace of the green reflections that gloss the greater scaup's head. It also has a more pronounced crown—loose, fluffy feathers almost like the ringneck's cap. But these features rarely stand out as birds make a pass over decoys. The white of the lesser scaup's speculum does not extend into the primary feathers as on the greater scaup but this means of recognition, too, is blurred until after the shot. In other respects, the races are alike. (See *Greater Scaup.*)

DISTRIBUTION: The lesser scaup inhabits no other continent but has a wider American distribution than the greater scaup and is hunted over more inland waters. It breeds in eastern Alaska, the Canadian territories, British Columbia, the Prairie Provinces, eastern Montana, the Dakotas, western Minnesota, and Nebraska. Nesting density is greatest on the potholes of the central prairies.

Late breeders, lesser scaup are necessarily late migrants, and because they travel in leisurely fashion the journey may continue from October until December in the southern states. Using all of the flyways, they winter along the coasts, across the lower third of the United States, and as far south as the Panama Canal. On the East Coast, where greater scaup are more common, lessers are also bagged occasionally from New England to Florida, and along the West Coast they winter from Vancouver Island to Mexico. They provide the best hunting in the Gulf states and as far up the Mississippi Valley—a heavily used flyway—as Tennessee, Missouri, and lower Illinois.

GAME BEHAVIOR & HUNTING HABITAT: Lesser scaup, somewhat more desirable table birds than greater scaup, are slightly more herbivorous. They are tastiest when they have been living on wild rice, a favorite plant. They feed on it especially in the Northeast, where they also eat a high proportion of wild celery and pondweed. Widgeongrass is of greater importance in the South, and in the West bulrush, widgeongrass, and pondweed are all of major importance.

Except in their preference for smaller waters, often inland, lesser scaup exhibit the same behavior patterns as greater scaup and they decoy about as readily though they tend to be more alert. Gunning suggestions are the same as for greater scaup.

VOICE: Both types of scaup purr, but lessers tend to be silent for long periods during the day and, unlike greater scaup, seldom croak unless startled. (See calling recommendations for *Greater Scaup* under *Voice.*)

Sea Ducks

Bufflehead *(Bucephala albeola)*
COMMON & REGIONAL NAMES: *butterball, bumblebee dipper, buffalo-head, butter duck, butterbox, dapper, dipper duck, marionette, robin dipper, Scotch dipper, Scotch teal, woolhead.*

GAME IDENTIFICATION IN FLIGHT: As many as fifty buffleheads may sometimes rest and feed together on open waters, but flocks

Lesser scaup at rest.

on the wing usually number no more than eight or ten, and it is common to see a lone bufflehead make repeated passes over decoys or flit about over a bay or lake. Singly or in shapeless little bunches, the birds fly low on a straight, swift course, their small wings beating rapidly.

The species is only slightly larger than a teal but with an oversized round head that looks all the more enormous because of its puffy crown. (The name bufflehead is a corruption of "buffalo-head.") The drake resembles a miniature goldeneye but with a much larger white face patch. There is also a resemblance to the hooded merganser, which has a darker body, more extreme crest, black neck, and pointed bill.

In flight a bufflehead drake appears purely black and white (mostly white) though his short bill is blue-gray and his head gleams with traces of lavender and green. The white face patch is almost an inverted triangle, whose wide top caps the rear part of the crown and whose blunted narrow end is below the eye. The neck, chest, belly, and sides are white, with dusky shading near the dark gray tail. The back and rump are black. The primaries are black or very dark gray, while most of the secondaries and coverts are white—a wide white wing patch. The underwings are mottled gray-white.

The drake's black-clawed feet are flesh-colored, the hen's gray. Her bill is darker than the male's, her face patch a small white horizontal oval behind the eye. Her head and neck are grayish brown, almost black. Her upper body is slightly lighter,

Diving species winging over New England duck boat (above), and buffleheads, marked in flight by black-and-white feather pattern (above, r.).

her sides gray, breast and belly lighter gray or dull white, wings dark grayish or blackish brown with only a small white patch on the inner secondaries.

DISTRIBUTION: The bufflehead is taken on every flyway, but because it often has a rank taste and is not among the most challenging targets (despite small size and fairly swift flight), it is generally hunted only as part of a mixed bag. Its breeding population is sparsely distributed from lower Alaska down through parts of the Canadian territories and provinces as far east as Ontario. The birds also summer in the Pacific states, in Montana, and around the Great Lakes. The upper limit of the primary wintering grounds is a continent-sweeping V extending from British Columbia down to Texas and up to New England. The southwestern states and Gulf Coast form the lower limit of major winter habitat. Flocks move south in October and November.

Though allied to the seagoing *Mergini* tribe, the bufflehead is a freshwater diver that inhabits the interior as well as the coastlines. (Some ornithologists group the bufflehead and goldeneye in a separate tribe, *Bucephala,* since they are broadheaded tree-nesters more closely related to each other than to ordinary sea ducks.)

GAME BEHAVIOR & HUNTING HABITAT: Buffleheads winter on lakes, ponds, and rivers, salt bays, estuaries, and tidal marshes.

Hunters on the West Coast consider them inedible when they have been devouring dead fish on fall spawning runs. Insects are their chief food, and these, together with crustaceans, mollusks, and a few fish, make up about four-fifths of their diet. The birds are most likely to be adequate table fare in areas where they can easily supplement animal matter with aquatic plants.

A bufflehead will come readily to decoys representing common game species, sometimes dropping right in among them with a splash. But only a gambler lets it alight in the hope of taking it on the rise. It may dive, or may rocket upward almost as steeply as a dabbling duck. A flying bufflehead sometimes ignores movement in a blind, or it may circle, or flare, or plummet like a stone and swim away underwater. Occasionally it comes up again within range, flying as it breaks the surface.

VOICE: Both sexes tend to be quiet. The hen can quack hoarsely and sometimes produces a series of liquid gulps; the drake has a weak, squeaky whistle and a harsh, rolling, guttural note.

American Eider *(Somateria mollissima)*
COMMON & REGIONAL NAMES: *common eider, Eskimo duck, sea-coot, black-and-white coot, sea duck, shoal duck, squam duck, pied wamp.*

GAME IDENTIFICATION IN FLIGHT: Eiders migrate in small flocks, flying low over shoal and reef waters along the coasts but seldom over land. They often travel in file or abreast until they reach their destination, where they skim about over the waves in formless bunches. The flight is straight and so low that birds can be hidden by wave crests, and when the wind is up they may follow the troughs of a rolling sea. Several of us, spray drenched and shivering in a rock blind, once listened to the hooting of five successive flocks that remained invisible until we tolled them in over our blocks.

With their heads held low, and their wings beating sluggishly, they look awkward but are moderately swift. Big, chunky birds, the eider drakes of the East Coast average more than 4 pounds and have a wingspread of about 40 inches, though they are only about 2 feet long. Hens are much smaller, averaging

a little over 3 pounds. (Both sexes of the Pacific eider, largest of American ducks, are likely to weigh over 5 pounds, while the rare little Steller's eider of the same region usually weighs less than 2.)

The male American eider has a glossy black crown with a whitish streak from the center to the rear. There is a light sea-green patch on the hindhead and rear part of the cheeks, sometimes extending forward almost to the bill, which varies from gray to green (turning orange-yellow in the spring) with a light nail and a round-tipped leathery extension running up onto the forehead. (The northern eider has less green on the head, a narrower bill extension, and sometimes a black V on the chin and throat, like the marking under the bill of the Pacific and king eiders.) The neck and forward part of the face are white, as are the upper breast, back, and scapulars. The underparts, tail, and rump are black, the flanks patched with white. The wings are mostly black but with a large white patch formed by the coverts, inner secondaries, and tertials. The underwings are gray and white.

The duskily webbed feet of both sexes are yellowish or greenish gray. The hen's bill is gray or greenish gray. Her head, neck, and body are brown, streaked on the upper parts with black, rust, and buff. Her wings are dark brown with white tips on the greater coverts and secondaries.

American eider drake of northern type.

DISTRIBUTION: Tame and stupid by the gunner's standards and undistinguished by those of the epicure, eiders nonetheless are hunted when other birds are in short supply on the upper Atlantic Flyway. The common eider has a circumpolar distribution. On this continent it breeds chiefly along the shores of Hudson Bay and Hudson Strait and on the coasts and islands of Newfoundland, Labrador, and Quebec. The overlapping winter range, to which it comes in November and December, lies from Newfoundland through New England to Long Island, and small flocks sometimes wander farther south.

The closely related northern eider (*S. m. borealis*) seldom winters below Newfoundland, and its breeding territory extends farther north. The Pacific subspecies (*S. m. v-nigra*) winters along the arctic coasts of the Bering and Beaufort seas and is rarely seen below the Aleutians. These related races, described in the introduction to this section, are similar in habits and habitat.

GAME BEHAVIOR & HUNTING HABITAT: The favorite food of eiders is the small blue mussel common to the shoals of northern coasts. Scallops, other mollusks, and miscellaneous shellfish are also eaten. Eiders often sleep on coasts and islands, but during the day they feed offshore, frequently within gunshot of rocky islets and ledges that provide natural blinds. In northern New England they are sometimes hunted from dories and skiffs. The safest procedure is to have a small craft of this sort towed by a powerboat within rowing distance of a ledge; at half tide it is then easy to reach the ledge, while the large boat—piloted by a local lobsterman or other guide who knows the waters— stands by to take the gunners aboard if the weather turns dangerous.

Pass-shooting is often good offshore, and eiders also decoy eagerly, but they are big, hardy, densely feathered, thickly skinned. Large shot and Magnum loads in full-choked 12-gauge guns are recommended.

VOICE: Eider drakes coo softly, moan harshly, or chuckle and hoot like loons. Hens often utter a series of quacks. The sounds sometimes alert a hunter to the approach of unseen flocks. Few of us bother to entice eiders vocally, but a call will arouse their curiosity if it imitates any common diving duck.

King eider drake on water, hen on nest.

King Eider (*Somateria spectabilis*)

COMMON & REGIONAL NAMES: *king-bird, passing duck, sea duck, mongrel.*

GAME IDENTIFICATION IN FLIGHT: Kings are slightly smaller than common eiders but fly in the same labored manner that fools hunters into shooting behind them. Though less plentiful, they migrate in larger flocks; groups of fifty are common, and occasionally several hundred travel together. They sometimes fly overland but prefer to stay a mile out to sea during coastal journeys, flying abreast in long, loose, wavering lines 30 or 40 feet above the water. Some of the birds in a large formation bunch together, particularly near the center of the line.

The drake's bill has a wide, fleshy, almost knoblike extension on each side, reaching high onto the forehead and bordered by a narrow inverted U of black feathers. The extension itself is usually bright yellow or yellow-orange, reddening on the forward portion where it blends into a bill of same brilliant color except for a gray-brown nail. The crown and hindhead are light gray or blue-gray, the cheek sea-green with a narrow whitish streak running down and back from the rear of the eye. A thin black V spreads rearward on the throat below the bill. The neck, breast, and foreback are creamy or rusty white and, but for a

large white flank patch, the rest of the body is black. The wings, too, are black, with a white covert patch and gray and white undersurfaces. Feet are yellowish or dull orange with dark webs.

The hen's feet tend to be yellower. She has a greenish or yellowish-gray bill with only a small upward extension. Her head, neck, upper breast, sides, and rump are buffy cinnamon with fine black streaks and U-shaped markings, while her back and scapulars are almost black with tawny edgings and her belly is dark brown. At a distance she appears smoky brown, a shadow of the spectacular drake.

DISTRIBUTION: The king eider breeds on most of the arctic and subarctic islands and coasts of North America, Europe, and Asia. On this continent a slow southerly migration begins in August, and kings generally arrive in the United States in November. Some of the western flocks winter on the Aleutian Peninsula while others fly on into Washington or Oregon. Some of the kings from Greenland and upper Canada winter on the Great Lakes but larger numbers fly to the Atlantic Coast, from Newfoundland to Long Island, and occasionally as far as South Carolina.

GAME BEHAVIOR & HUNTING HABITAT: King eiders prefer the outer islands and ledges. They can dredge mollusks from deeper waters than other eiders but are similar in diet and general behavior. Birds of the year decoy readily, yet mature kings are so suspicious that they usually provide only pass-shooting for hunters who endure the cold and chop of outer reefs for the sake of a mixed bag of sea ducks.

VOICE: Both sexes can coo softly, but seldom do so after sunrise. They utter an occasional series of three rolling, increasingly loud *burrs*. Though they tend to be silent on winter days, the juveniles sometimes come to calls imitating other sea ducks.

American Goldeneye *(Bucephala clangula)*
COMMON & REGIONAL NAMES: *common goldeneye, whistler, whistle-wing, whistle diver, whistle duck, wiffler, brass-eye, bullhead, cobhead, ironhead, jingler, oyster duck, pie duck, pied whistler, winter duck.*

GAME IDENTIFICATION IN FLIGHT: Sometimes before golden-eyes are within sight of a blind, much less within gunshot, a shrill of whistling wings identifies them: *wee-wee-wee-wee-wee-wee*. The wind whistles sharply through the primaries of their short, raked wings with each rapid beat, cutting through mist or snow that would stifle most sounds, and is multiplied by half a dozen or a dozen birds in a formless bunch. Even a single or a pair can be heard far off. Larger groups tend to segregate themselves by sex during migration so that 80 or 90 percent of a flight may either be drakes or hens.

They are fast fliers, and when visibility is good may pass too high, stubbornly resisting the allure of decoys. But they are very active in the meanest weather, when squall, fog, or overcast presses them down into range, perhaps only 10 or 15 yards above the water. The hunter who wants goldeneyes wears foul-weather gear and is on the water before the sunup flights have dwindled.

They are recognized by their big, round, dark heads; short, thick necks; white wing patches; and light bodies. In flight, the drake's body and wings exhibit more white than any duck except the American merganser. He is of medium size, unlikely to weigh much over 2 pounds. His puffy, high-crowned black head is

Shooting American goldeneyes from rock blind.

glossed with green, sometimes with traces of violet. Between his short black bill and bright yellow eye is a round white patch. White, too, are the neck, breast, belly, and sides, though the long flank feathers are narrowly edged with black. The back, rump, and inner scapulars are black, the outer scapulars white edged with black. The tail is slaty gray, the wings gray-black with a large white patch over the coverts and secondaries. The linings and axillars are gray. At a distance the bird appears starkly black and white.

Both sexes have orange or yellow feet with dark webs. The hen's bill is like the male's (though its tip turns yellow at breeding time) and her head is brown, patchless, and not so puffy. Her neck, lower breast, and belly are white or gray-white, but her upper breast is scaled with white-edged ash or brownish-gray feathers. The scaled gray covers her sides, scapulars, and foreback, darkening toward the rear into a sooty rump and tail. Her wings are usually somewhat lighter than the male's and have a smaller white patch.

DISTRIBUTION: When frosts give way to November's coastal snow squalls, fog, and blustering winds on the northern part of the Atlantic Flyway, an enormous build-up of goldeneyes and other divers descends on New England. The swelling flocks of whistlers are the vanguard of 80,000 goldeneyes that winter on the flyway, the thickest concentration of a species scattered widely but never densely across the continent.

American goldeneyes breed from northern Alaska down through most of Canada. They nest in tree cavities or occasionally rock clefts over or near water and are partial to coniferous forests. Their nesting range dips into the Dakotas and overlaps wintering grounds eastward to the Atlantic. Considerable numbers winter on the Pacific Coast, from the Aleutians into southern California; some follow the Central Flyway as far south as New Mexico; more are bagged on the Mississippi Flyway from the upper Midwest to the Gulf; and still more veer onto the eastern seaboard from Maine to the Carolinas, and in smaller numbers continue into Georgia and Florida.

GAME BEHAVIOR & HUNTING HABITAT: About three-quarters of the goldeneye's diet consists of animal matter—mostly small crabs and other crustaceans, followed by insects, mollusks, and occasional fish. Vegetation is not important enough to determine prime hunting sites. Wintering flocks prefer coastal salt marshes and ponds, but also gather on bays, estuaries, the mouths of tidal rivers, and inland lakes or wide fresh rivers.

Goldeneyes are hard to bag unless a hunter knows their ways. In placing a blind and decoys it is well to consider their feeding and flying habits. They like to fly upstream, sometimes for several hundred yards, then ride the current down as they dive and feed. They often fly along the windward side of a river or other body of water, and they often feed on smooth water between rapids, lifting off when they reach rough water. A rig on a smooth section but near a fast or windy stretch is therefore attractive, as is a rig on the windward side or downstream tip of an island. Since whistlers follow shorelines but almost invariably remain over water, a blind should be on an island or point or out on the water.

Sculling and other jump-shooting methods are more often than not futile, for goldeneyes are wary even though they swing about in low circles as they skitter off the water. They will come to a spread of several dozen oversized whistler or scaup decoys. (Scaup, on the other hand, are not often enticed by whistler decoys, and broadbill rigs are therefore a better choice where there is the possibility of a mixed bag.) If the spread is large and at least 30 yards from shore, passing whistlers frequently brake themselves and drop like hailstones toward the blocks. The range calls for tightly choked 12-gauge guns and Magnum No. 4 or 5 loads.

VOICE: Though the drake sometimes makes a piercing, squeaky cry and the female is capable of a low-pitched, harsh quack or, when startled, a sharp croak, goldeneyes are not voluble. Mimicry is not necessary, and it is the whistle of their wings that the hunter listens for.

Barrow's Goldeneye *(Bucephala islandica)*
COMMON & REGIONAL NAMES: *Rocky Mountain goldeneye, whistler, whistle-wing, pie duck, pied whistler.*

GAME IDENTIFICATION IN FLIGHT: The Barrow's goldeneye flies

as high, straight, and fast as the American, often maintaining a speed of perhaps 50 miles an hour, and in the same unregimented little flocks that seldom number more than a dozen. The whistle of its wings, though not quite so loud and sharp, is distinctly audible. A few large drakes may weigh close to 3 pounds, but most specimens are of medium size.

Few hunters can tell the two breeds apart in flight, though the crown of a Barrow's drake puffs rearward more than upward, the sheen on his black head is purplish rather than green, and the white marking between bill and eye is a rearward-pointing crescent rather than a round patch. He also has a larger expanse of black on his back, smaller white markings on scapulars, sides, and wings, and a heavy black border along the sides and down the flanks, but these differences are impossible to make out at a distance. As a rule, females of the two races are virtually indistinguishable. (See *American Goldeneye.*)

DISTRIBUTION: The Barrow's goldeneye, like the harlequin duck, has widely separated eastern and western populations with little or no interchange between them. In the East, the species nests chiefly in Iceland, Greenland, and upper Labrador, wintering from eastern Quebec and the Gulf of St. Lawrence down through New England. The western population is larger, with nesting grounds extending from Alaska and the Yukon through British Columbia and Alberta and then dividing into two prongs,

Barrow's goldeneyes.

one through the Rockies into Colorado and the other near the Pacific Coast into central California. The primary winter range fills these two prongs and the coastlands to the upper border of British Columbia. Migration takes place in October and November. Straddling the Pacific and Central flyways, the species is probably most populous along the Continental Divide, where hunters call it the Rocky Mountain goldeneye.

GAME BEHAVIOR & HUNTING HABITAT: Inland as well as along the coasts, Barrow's and American goldeneyes seek the same bays, inlets, lakes, and rivers. Although the Barrow's consumes a higher percentage of insects, dietary differences may arise from distribution rather than preference, for western hunters know that the Rocky Mountain goldeneye is attracted to the strongly alkaline lakes that support plenty of crawfish and similar crustaceans.

In two important respects the races differ: The Barrow's is more easily decoyed, and on small mountain lakes where hunting is light, jump-shooting the Barrow's can be effective, using a relatively open choke and shot as small as No. 6.

VOICE: The Barrow's can squeak and quack like an American goldeneye, but a low croak is more characteristic.

Harlequin Duck *(Histrionicus histrionicus)*
COMMON & REGIONAL NAMES: *painted duck, blue-streak, circus duck, mountain duck, rock duck, sea-mouse, squealer.*

GAME IDENTIFICATION IN FLIGHT: In compact flocks, low over the water, harlequins twist and turn. At first they seem to bob along laboriously, but the swift strokes of their short, pointed wings propel their chunky little bodies with an agility approaching the abrupt maneuvers of teal. Inland hunters watch for the species to fly a precise course along any river, turning with each bend, looping over hairpin meanders instead of cutting across. On the coasts, harlequins sometimes trace the convolutions of rocky shorelines, ledges, spits, and reefs, but they may fly out over deep water if the shallows hold too little prey.

Harlequins usually weigh less than 1½ pounds, not much

bigger than buffleheads or much smaller than oldsquaws. At more than 60 yards or so they might be mistaken for either of those ducks. The bizarre pattern of the drake's plumage does not show clearly until he is close, but whereas bufflehead and oldsquaw drakes look black and white in the distance, the male harlequin looks dark gray. As he nears the blind, his reddish sides show and then his white collar, vertical white stripe in front of the wing, and white face patches. Positive identification is accompanied by a fast decision: Is the bird worth taking for a dish comparable to coot stew and an unusual array of fly-tying feathers, or should it be passed up in the hope that something tastier will come along?

The harlequin's Columbine looks like a hen bufflehead —dark with a whitish breast— but lacks the white speculum and has three dim whitish facial smudges instead of a white cheek patch. The oldsquaw hen is similar but with more white on underparts and head.

The drake has a short blue-gray bill with a yellowish nail. His head and neck are dark, slaty blue-gray. Between eye and bill is a roughly triangular white patch tapering above the eye to a backswept chestnut streak. Behind the eye is a roundish white spot and behind that a vertical white streak. At the base of the neck is a white collar. A long white crescent, almost vertical in flight, runs from the shoulder onto the lower breast. The white

Harlequin drake (above), and
sea-duck shooting on Atlantic Coast (r.).

markings stand out, bordered with black. Most of the body is slaty blue-gray but with a white bar running rearward over the scapulars, a white spot on the flank at the base of the long, pointed black tail, a black rump, reddish-brown sides, and a brownish lower belly. The wings are dusky brown and slaty but with small white spots on the coverts and a dark blue speculum bordered inwardly by white tertials. The western harlequin, often classified as a separate subspecies (*H. h. pacificus*), has similar but slightly duller plumage.

Eastern or western, the female has dark gray feet like the male's and an almost black bill. She has several indistinct splotches on her face, and her lower breast and belly are grayish white. The remainder of her plumage is brown, olive-brown, or gray-brown.

DISTRIBUTION: The harlequin usually falls to hunters seeking other ducks. Essentially a marine carnivore, it is less palatable than the herbivorous ducks and is relatively scarce. The eastern harlequin nests chiefly on the coasts of Iceland, Greenland, Baffin Island, and northern Quebec and Labrador; beginning in November, it shifts to the lower coasts of the Maritimes, and small flocks trickle along the rocky New England shores but seldom below Massachusetts. The western harlequin breeds in southern Alaska, the Yukon, British Columbia, and the northwest-

ern states, with some of the birds drifting through the interior as far as Wyoming. Their fall migration is predominantly westward to the Pacific Coast, as high as the Gulf of Alaska and as low as central California.

GAME BEHAVIOR & HUNTING HABITAT: Aquatic animals, insects, and a few fish make up the harlequin's diet. In the interior the birds love to hunt in rough mountain streams, coasting down tumultuous riffles and playing in the rapids. On the coasts they splash among breakers, ride the surf, and dart about the jagged rocks and reefs. Not especially wary, they sometimes inspect decoys representing ducks common to the area.

VOICE: The colloquial name "sea-mouse" refers to the squeaks of harlequins. They also produce hoarse, whistling squeals, harsh grunts, oinks, and quacks.

American Merganser *(Mergus merganser)*
COMMON & REGIONAL NAMES: *common merganser, goosander, fish duck, sheldrake, freshwater sheldrake, pond sheldrake, gony, sawbill, spike, tweezer.*

GAME IDENTIFICATION IN FLIGHT: Hunters on every flyway now and again see a handsome merganser skim over the water, slice in and under as the wings fold back, and fly out moments later clutching a fish in its tweezer bill. To many wildfowlers, pursuing their sport under a point system of limits that places a high value (thus a low bag limit) on scarce or heavily hunted game species, the American merganser is a bonus target that counts only 10 points against a permissible 100. To hunters who are also trout and salmon anglers, the merganser is a fish-killing villain that must be recognized and shot on sight. But merganser decoys are no longer carved, and most hunters regard the bird as worthless, nearly unpalatable, to be recognized before a shotshell and 10 points are wasted.

Small, irregular flocks of southward-bound mergansers fly high and very fast, but at waystops and on the wintering grounds they almost always stay close to the water, alone or in a straight file of two or three. A female is apt to weigh nearly 2½ pounds,

sometimes more, and a male is often a full pound heavier. Long-bodied, narrow billed, with wings spreading 3 feet and beating deeply, a big merganser might be mistaken at a distance for a loon, equally unsavory table fare and generally protected. But the loon's wings are even longer, its back is checkered, its feet trail behind a skimpy tail, and both neck and feet sag slightly in the air, whereas the merganser is a streamlined, horizontal projectile. And no other duck shows as great an expanse of white on body and wings.

The bill and feet of both sexes are red. The mandibles are "sawtoothed" and the bill is long, narrow, almost cylindrical, hook-nailed. The drake's upper neck and head are greenly gleaming black. The lower neck, a small foreback area, and the breast, sides, and underparts are white suffused with a faint salmon tint, graying near the rump. The undercoverts of the tail are also white, as are the underwings and outer scapulars. The back is black, ashy on rump, tail, and upper tail coverts. The dull, brownish-black wings bear a large white patch—white coverts behind a black front edge, black and white inner coverts, black-edged white secondaries and tertials forming a wide speculum.

A drake in eclipse has a crest, but in December, when full winter plumage has developed, the species is unique among American ducks in that only the hen is crested. Her chin and throat are white or pinkish-white, her tufted head and upper neck chestnut, sharply defined against an ash-white lower neck. Her back, tail, sides, and flanks are gray, with white or whitish bars, her lower breast and belly white mottled with gray or faintly salmon-tinted. Her wings are darker than the drake's, with gray

American merganser drake.

coverts and nearly black tertials and outer secondaries, so that she shows only a small white speculum.

DISTRIBUTION: The American merganser breeds from lower Alaska across Canada and the northernmost states to the Atlantic, down the Pacific Coast to central California, and down the Continental Divide to Colorado. In October and November, its population flows southward onto an overlapping winter range that also spans the continent, dwindling only in the prairies and the southernmost states.

GAME BEHAVIOR & HUNTING HABITAT: Of the three merganser species on this continent, the common, or American, is the most insatiable fish-eater, but it also hunts crawfish, shrimp, frogs, mollusks, and insects. It frequents both fresh and salt water. Substantial numbers winter on inland lakes and rivers. Trout and other game fish may constitute nearly a third of the prey for American mergansers residing on good trout streams, but a larger proportion of their food normally consists of "rough" fish and in some areas they devour no game fish at all. Their destructive reputation probably is overblown except in the vicinity of hatcheries or where game fish are the only abundant prey.

VOICE: Apart from a harsh croak of alarm, the American merganser is usually silent.

Hooded Merganser *(Mergus cucullatus,* also classified as *Lophodytes cucullatus)*
COMMON & REGIONAL NAMES: *fish duck, California fish duck, sawbill, lake sawbill, spikebill, bastard teal, cock-robin duck, cottonhead, fuzzhead, hairyhead, hooder, frog duck, goosander, sheldrake, pond sheldrake, pied sheldrake, summer sheldrake, swamp sheldrake, pickaxe, sharpy, smew, wirecrown.*

GAME IDENTIFICATION IN FLIGHT: A hooded merganser in a stream or a swamp is no threat to fish, and the sight of one heartens those of us who recognize its presence as a sign of wood-duck waters. The two species favor the same forested ponds and streams, though the merganser has a much wider distribu-

Hooded merganser, vaguely resembling woody as crest is lowered.

tion than the woody.

A plump hooded merganser drake infrequently weighs more than 1½ pounds. It is almost as small and fast as a teal, and its wings blur with the same rapidity of beat. Flocks are small even during migration. It is common to see a single, a pair, or at most a loose string of five or six, flashing low overhead.

Having risen from water with the agility of dabblers, they hold their bodies straight as they cleave the air but dip their heads a trifle. Both sexes flatten their crests while on the wing, so that head and neck form a dark oblong block. The drake's white crest patch narrows like a folded Japanese fan until it becomes a thin horizontal streak flashing from the eye rearward against black plumage. His body appears black on top, white beneath, that of the female brown and white, and both sexes show white patches on dark wings.

Their feet are olive, ocher, or light brown. Their bills are shorter than those of other mergansers but equally narrow and cylindrical. The drake's is black, the hen's blackish with yellow and orange tinges. Over the male's black head the feathers fan up and rearward in a hairy, black-bordered white crest. The neck is black, the upper body and tail dark brown. Two dark brown bars curve diagonally from the foreback onto a white breast. The sides are rufous brown, darkly vermiculated. White patches and streamers of folded coverts, tertials, and secondaries separate the sides from black scapulars. The open wing shows dusky-brown primaries, gray-white coverts, long tertials striped black and white, and black and white secondaries forming a white speculum.

The hen has a gray-brown head—reddish on the fanned crest, which is smaller than the male's and has no contrasting patch. Her chin and throat are pale, her lower breast and belly white, her upper breast and sides gray, her back, scapulars,

and rump dark brownish gray. Her wings are like the male's but with darker coverts and speculum.

DISTRIBUTION: This smallest of the continent's fish ducks is a tree-nester that breeds in watery timberlands from the Atlantic to the Pacific, up through central Canada and down to the northern states west of the Mississippi Valley and the southernmost states east to the Atlantic. Major wintering areas are on the Pacific Flyway from Washington to the Mexican border, on the Atlantic from lower New England southward, and along the Gulf from Florida through southeastern Texas. Many of the birds migrate in October and November but hooded mergansers remain in some areas throughout the year or merely drift slightly southward to find open water.

GAME BEHAVIOR & HUNTING HABITAT: The hooded merganser is a shy bird but often enough skims over a blind near the timbered edges of a marsh, flits across watery swamp openings where a hunter is shadowed by trees, or passes a camouflaged duck boat sculling a pond or drifting a river for woodies or other ducks.

Though the species prefers fresh water even in coastal areas, it is not a significant predator of game fish. It prowls quiet pools for frogs, tadpoles, crawfish, snails, insects, and a few fry. It also eats more vegetation than other mergansers do and is more palatable though certainly not comparable to the woodies sharing its habitat.

VOICE: When on the water a hooded merganser may now and then grunt harshly but it is a quiet duck, especially in the air.

Red-breasted Merganser *(Mergus serrator)*
COMMON & REGIONAL NAMES: *fish duck, red-breasted fish duck, red-breasted goosander, sawbill, garbill, sheldrake, Indian sheldrake, Long Island sheldrake, pied sheldrake, saltwater sheldrake, fuzzyhead, hairycrown, jack, scale duck, sea robin.*

GAME IDENTIFICATION IN FLIGHT: Red-breasted mergansers habitually fly low over the water in the same manner as American mergansers but they show less white of wing and body. The

drake's black-speckled, reddish-brown breastband under a white collar is an aid to identification. Smaller than the American, a redbreast seldom has a yard-wide wingspan, and drakes average less than 3 pounds, hens less than 2.

Most landlocked wildfowlers consider the redbreast worthless, but a different opinion is held by some of the sea-duckers of New England and the Maritimes. Saltwater mergansers, trading over the crests with scoters, may well go into a mixed bag with those birds and the higher-flying oldsquaws. A New England "coot stew" occasionally contains more than scoter and is nonetheless delicious to those who have acquired the taste.

A redbreast drake differs from an American merganser in having a ragged, hairy, rearward-flaring, double-pointed crest; a white neck with a vertical black line down the nape; a reddish brown bib spotted with black; a patch of black and white checkering or short stripes on the forward bend of the folded wing; grayer sides and darker wing linings than the American's. In the air the races look much alike.

The hen bears an even closer resemblance to the American but has a double crest smaller and less hairy than the male's, though shaggier than the American hen's, and the contrast between the whitish foreneck and the reddish brown of her nape and head is blurred rather than sharp.

DISTRIBUTION: On this continent, red-breasted mergansers breed from Alaska across almost all of Canada, some as far north as the Greenland coasts or as far south as upper New England and the Great Lakes. Unlike other mergansers, they nest on the ground and in general behave more like true sea

Red-breasted merganser hen on nest.

ducks. The fall migration, cresting in October and November, takes them chiefly to coastal areas: the Pacific Flyway from lower British Columbia to Mexico, the Gulf Coast, and the Atlantic Flyway from Maine to Florida. Substantial numbers also follow the Mississippi, and some of them winter on large inland bodies of water, but they prefer a salt or brackish habitat.

GAME BEHAVIOR & HUNTING HABITAT: Owing to their maritime habits, wintering redbreasts rarely destroy game fish. They prey on other kinds of fish, mollusks, crustaceans, and insects. Just as wheeling gulls may lead an angler to a school of bluefish slashing through a herd of menhaden, gulls over a shoal may lead a sea-duck hunter to spawning herring that will soon attract a few mergansers or a frenzied flock. If the same shoal or reef is bedded with mussels, clams, or oysters, it is likely that scoters and perhaps eiders will also come within gunshot. A full-choked 12-gauge gun firing No. 4 Magnums is recommended.

VOICE: Except for an occasional hoarse croak, the seagoing merganser is habitually silent.

Oldsquaw (Clangula hyemalis)
COMMON & REGIONAL NAMES: *longtail, granny, hound, jackowly, old-wife, organ duck, scolder, singing duck, siwash, squaw, winter duck.*

GAME IDENTIFICATION IN FLIGHT: Sometimes in file, more often in spatters, oldsquaws are black-winged flakes of snow swirling in from the north on the high winds. But they rarely flutter down like the snow. More typical is a sudden drop, accompanied by noisy gabbling, punctuated by a noisy splash. Having arrived, little foraging bunches flit a few yards above the water, but they can be hard to hit; beating the air in short, swift strokes, they veer off unexpectedly or circle a rig widely, twisting like shorebirds so that a breast and then a back winks alternately at the hunter. They are small ducks, with wings usually spanning less than 30 inches. A hen is likely to weigh 1½ pounds, and a heavy drake weighs only a few ounces more.

It seems odd that wildfowlers should mistake oldsquaws

Oldsquaw hen (top) and drake.

Labs with mixed bag of surf scoters and oldsquaw.

for buffleheads or goldeneyes. In winter plumage the oldsquaw drake has a long, dark needle of a tail like that of a sprig but has a much shorter neck and appears to be almost all white with black wings and chest. The hen is the only duck that presents a flight picture combining mainly white underparts with solidly dark wings.

The drake has a short black bill with a pinkish smudge near the nail. The head and neck are white if the molt is finished, with a tawny gray stain surrounding the eye and darkening to a brown patch high on the sides of the neck. The foreback, belly, sides, lower tail coverts, and scapulars are white or very pale gray. The breast, back, rump, upper tail coverts, and two long, central tail feathers are blackish brown, sometimes virtually black. The outer tail feathers are margined with white. The wings are brownish black, too, except for a slightly lighter speculum and grayish-brown linings and axillars. The duskily webbed feet are gray, as are the hen's.

Her bill is dark gray, blackish, or smoky green. Her head and upper neck are mostly white, splashed with dark brown on cheek, chin, forehead, and crown. Her lower neck, upper breast, back, rump, and scapulars are dark brown or gray-brown; her tail is darker still and lacks the drake's long, trailing points. The brown feathers of the back are broadly rimmed with cinnamon. The sides and underparts are white, the wings like the male's but duller and sometimes lighter.

DISTRIBUTION: Western duck hunters pay little attention to oldsquaws because few of the birds stray below Washington. On the Atlantic Flyway, the "grannies" have traditionally supplemented scoters as winter targets for seagoing New Englanders but were formerly considered "trash ducks" by most wildfowlers below New York. During recent years gunners on the Chesapeake have taken increased notice of oldsquaws and scoters—species that account for about 250,000 of the ducks wintering on the bay—and Maryland's special sea-duck season has substantially lengthened the regular waterfowling period and our scaup-only season. Opening day for sea ducks is typically in September's last week, when scoters have begun to arrive; oldsquaws begin migrating the following month and we see them over the upper bay early in November. Still more arrive later, though many flocks spend all winter on the New England Coast or the Great Lakes. Oldsquaws and scoters are famous for decoying with alacrity, but hunters are only now discovering that oldsquaws make good eating if breasts are marinated, then stewed or flour-fried.

The oldsquaw has a circumpolar distribution. American flocks breed on Alaska's coasts, Canada's arctic coasts and islands, Greenland, and Iceland. The primary wintering ranges are the Pacific Coast, from upper British Columbia to northwestern Oregon; the Great Lakes area, from central Ontario and Wisconsin to New York; and the Atlantic Coast, from New Brunswick to the Carolinas.

GAME BEHAVIOR & HUNTING HABITAT: Though oldsquaws nibble at miscellaneous plants, almost nine-tenths of their diet consists of crustaceans, mollusks, insects, and a few small fish. They are most often hunted on big, open waters—bays, the ocean, large lakes. Together with scoters, they feed at any time of day. Offshore blinds are used but it is more common to shoot sea ducks from a fairly large, seaworthy boat. In some areas, when the season on other wildfowl is closed, the duck boat must be anchored at least 1,200 yards from the nearest shore or emergent vegetation; this, however, is no hindrance to the hunter with game of such maritime inclinations.

"Poor man's decoys"—gallon plastic bleach jugs painted flat black—have become perhaps the most popular stools for sea ducks. They toll both oldsquaws and scoters (and scaup if a wide white band is left around the center of each bottle). Four strings of about fifteen jugs apiece will make a good set. The decoys are spaced about a yard apart and trailed from a heavy anchor line. A string is floated on each side of the boat as well as fore and aft, with the most distant jug only about 30 yards off. No camouflage is needed, and a hunter can sit upright if he remains reasonably still. Oldsquaws are not so foolish as scoters; they often veer off at 40 or 50 yards, but they come in low and close enough to be taken with No. 4 or 5 Magnums in a full-choked 12 bore.

VOICE: The name oldsquaw is a comment on loquacity. Flying or on the water, oldsquaws are the noisiest of wildfowl. Some of their calls resemble the words *south, ow, owl,* and *owly.* Whis-

American scoter drake.

tles, hoots, yodels, and honks may signal a flight, but they decoy so easily that the mastery of a call is superfluous.

American Scoter (*Melanitta nigra*, also classified as *Oidemia americana* and *O. nigra*)

COMMON & REGIONAL NAMES: *common scoter, black scoter, coot, sea coot, broad-billed coot, yellow-billed coot, butter-bill, butter-nose, copper bill, bay muscovie, beachcomber, booby, deaf duck, Indian duck, iron pot, rock coot, scooter, whistling coot, tar bucket.*

GAME IDENTIFICATION IN FLIGHT: Flocks of American scoters are extremely variable. A flight may number only a few birds, or it may be a great mass of black dots in shapeless disarray, long straight lines, ragged chevrons, or crescents. However, the larger the flock, the less likely it is to descend into shooting range.

Unlike other scoters, the American seldom ventures inland once it reaches the coasts. It prefers to fly over water, following the shoreline. In gentle weather migratory flight is apt to be high, but wind or storm will press the flocks down low, where they often remain when trading about over feeding areas. A scoter of any species will occasionally fly right through a wave crest. American scoters are more active than the other breeds, flying about frequently through the day in small bunches. These little flights usually approach at low level and sometimes circle the decoys, dangling their legs as the first shot is fired.

They are heavy-bodied, the drakes averaging about 2½ pounds and the hens not much less, with a wingspread of perhaps 30 to 32 inches. Their flight appears slightly nimbler than that of other sea coots, but all scoters look ponderous and the usual reason for missed shots is that the ducks are flying much faster than they seem to be. Some shooters are convinced that an American scoter can make 60 miles an hour, an estimate not greatly exaggerated.

The wings of all three scoters whistle, each with a recognizable tone. Birds can often be turned by whistling back at them, without any precise imitation. The sound of an American scoter's wings is relatively sharp; that of a surf scoter is deeper, almost a hum when the bird is well under way; that of a whitewing is low and bell-like, heard only at intervals, usually repeated six to eight times, and believed by some gunners (and naturalists) to be produced vocally.

The male American is the only duck on this continent whose plumage is entirely black, yet a fast-flying American can be difficult to tell from the other breeds since a hunter may get no glimpse of a surf scoter's white head patches or a whitewing's speculum. Where the species mingle, all are legal game.

On the black, lump-nailed bill, a yellow-orange mound rises from the nostrils to the face. The feet of both sexes are brownish black, sometimes olive on the female. Her blackish bill is tinged yellow about the nostrils, behind which it rises somewhat abruptly but lacks the drake's bright mound. Her feathering is all dark, dusky brown—black-looking at a distance—relieved only by pale gray, brownly streaked and speckled, on cheeks, chin, throat, and foreneck. Juveniles of either sex are like the adult hen but paler, their breasts whitish and marked with gray-brown. They are called "gray coots."

DISTRIBUTION: The American, or common, scoter is actually least common of the continent's three varieties and merely an American strain of a circumpolar species. Flocks breed on the western and northern coasts of Alaska, the Yukon, and an adjacent stretch of the Northwest Territories. They winter chiefly on the Pacific and Atlantic coasts, from the Aleutian Peninsula to Puget Sound and from Maine to the Carolinas or sometimes farther south.

The traditional winter lodestones for American scoters and scoter hunters have been Martha's Vineyard and Nantucket, where big flocks patrol the bays, reefs, and small islands to feed on mussels, clams, and scallops. However, the birds drift up or down the seaboard to the best shellfish beds; sometimes they are very plentiful north of Massachusetts, and in recent years have increased on more southerly bays, though they are far less common than other scoters on the Chesapeake.

They sweep over New England in mid- or late September, ahead of the other scoters, but the first arrivals are almost invariably mature. Though the sea-duck season may be open and the limit as high as seven a day, some hunters wait for the October surge of juveniles, which decoy with the greatest eagerness and are less oily and rank than their elders. (Coot stew is a New England specialty; if a scoter is quickly skinned, it can also be broiled or roasted in a hot oven, but all the oil should be drained off before it is served.)

GAME BEHAVIOR & HUNTING HABITAT: Since mussels and barnacles are favorite foods of the American scoter, sea-ducking expeditions are best where these mollusks and crustaceans abound. The birds also seek other prey and small quantities of aquatic plants. Scoters are undismayed by rough seas but prefer to feed on the tidal flats of bays and sounds. American scoters are also partial to reefs, islands, and the rocky points and ledges of the coasts. They are daytime feeders and dull-witted, easily attracted to an uncamouflaged boat surrounded by relatively crude decoys (see *Oldsquaw* for details applicable to both species). If the wind is up, they may not hear the hunter's whistle to draw their attention, but are so inquisitive that, having passed without noticing the decoys, they frequently can be brought back by shouting.

Yet they are not easy to bring down. They pass with great speed, often flaring almost to the edge of effective range, and they are tough, densely feathered birds. Particularly on waters where brant are as likely to pass as scoters, eiders, or oldsquaws, 12-gauge No. 4 Magnums are recommended in a tightly bored gun. Some wildfowlers using double guns load the more openly choked right barrel with high-brass No. 5's or 6's, the tighter barrel with 4's for the long shots.

VOICE: American scoters rarely call, though a female now and then growls and a male can utter a long, cooing whistle, lower-pitched than the wing whistle.

Surf Scoter *(Melanitta perspicillata)*

COMMON & REGIONAL NAMES: *coot, bay coot, surf coot, river coot, rock coot, sea coot, specklebill, bald-headed coot, whitehead coot, horsehead, patch-head, skunkhead, skunkbill, blossom-bill, bottlenosed diver, mussel-bill, patch-bill, beachcomber, bay muscovie, booby, deaf duck, Indian duck, iron pot, scooter, surf scoter, surfer, tar bucket.*

GAME IDENTIFICATION IN FLIGHT: On bluebird days, it is frustrating to watch shapeless clouds of black specks pass high overhead. But when the winds rise and visibility lowers, the same big flocks—even if they are still migrating—ripple along above the waves. They follow the shores, sometimes rising to cut over a cape but as often turning indecisively or coming down to rest and feed before changing course. Their wings whistle as they

(text continued on page 249)

Surf scoters rafted on Alaskan coastal waters.

▲ King eider drake.   ▼ Common eider drake.   ▼ Common eider drake and hen.

▼ Common eider hen.

▲ Wildfowler modulating call with his hand.   ▼ Cattails rimming wildfowl refuge.

▲ Offshore blind for diving species.

▲ Mallards.

▲ Barrow's goldeneye flock.　▼ American goldeneye.

▼Ruddy drake in winter plumage.　▼ Widgeon drake.

Geese
(see pages 254-299)

▼ Ross's goose with lesser snows.　▲ Emperor goose defending nest.

▼ Black brant in Alaska.　▲ Whitefront flying over tundra.

▼ Canada geese.   ▼ Blue goose.

▲ Lesser snows during migration. ▼ Canadas alighting.

▲ Greater snows. ▼ Field-hunting for snow geese.

drop their legs to settle and as they rise into the wind. Once scoters are airborne, the whistle deepens to a hum and they attain surprising speed. Smaller and nimbler than whitewings, they may be indistinguishable from American scoters until they swing in close over the decoy strings. They usually weigh 2 pounds or so, and their wings span about 30 to 33 inches.

The nickname "skunkhead" derives from two oblong white patches on the drake's long, sloping, lumpy black head. The front patch is an almost round cap above the eyes, from behind the bulbous bill back over the low forehead. The rear one is a rough inverted triangle on the back of the head, with its point on the nape. Apart from these marks, the plumage is totally black. The base of the great, thick, heavily nailed bill is a distinct swelling from the chin up to the forehead, built for digging and grasping prey. It has a roughly round (or almost square) black patch on each side, margined below and in front by white, behind and above by an orange streak that extends forward and spreads, reddening on the ridge and about the nostril, yellowing on the nail. The feet are dark red-orange, turning quite red on the outer surfaces, with black webs and blackish bands on the joints.

The hen's feet are duller, usually with a yellow or brown cast. Her bill is less bulbous and is gray, almost black, with a black side patch surrounded by a paler area. Her plumage is mostly a dark grayish or blackish brown. She has two vague whitish cheek patches, one behind the bill and one behind the eye, sometimes almost invisible or blended into a single pale area. Her hindhead, where the male displays a white triangle, has a dim whitish or pale patch. Her underparts are mottled or silvered gray. The cheek patches of a gray coot, or juvenile, are clearer, sometimes white, but the hindhead patch is absent. The breast is whitish or pale gray.

DISTRIBUTION: The surf scoter's primary nesting range lies in northeastern Alaska, the upper Yukon, and the Mackenzie District of the Northwest Territories. In September and October, flocks sweep down onto the Pacific and Atlantic flyways. Most of the gray coots arrive over the hunting waters a couple of weeks after the main flights of mature birds, and these younger ones, easily decoyed and tastier than adults, are eagerly awaited by New England connoisseurs.

The Pacific wintering range stretches from lower Alaska

into northern Mexico, yet cooting has never attracted western gunners to the degree that it preoccupies the boatmen of the northeastern coast. While fair numbers of surf scoters end their migration on the Great Lakes, the majority pushes on in search of salt water. On the Atlantic, the area of density extends only from the Bay of Fundy, just above Maine, to the Carolinas. Few wildfowlers below Block Island or Long Island Sound took much note of scoters until recent years, but some of us are reviving the sea-ducking arts on the upper Chesapeake, where lengthened sea-duck seasons were established in the 1960s.

GAME BEHAVIOR & HUNTING HABITAT: Surf coots share the diet of American scoters but prefer to fish for their mussels and bits of vegetation in shallower water. Whole flocks ride the swells near beaches, diving as the breakers rise over them. Where hunting from a boat is not permitted near land, a gunner can string out his decoys on a bay, as for other scoters, and await the frequent flights between the feeding flats. Four lines—about five dozen simple black blocks or jugs—will toll these and other species (see *Oldsquaw* and *American scoter*). Surf coots also frequent shoals and reefs farther offshore, and some boatmen manage to jump-shoot them. When they sight a skunkhead flock on the water, they approach from upwind. Although the birds often lift off before a dory or even a sneakbox can be brought within range, they rise into the wind and may fly just close enough. (For additional gunning details, see *Oldsquaw* and the other *Scoter* entries.)

VOICE: Surf scoters may flare from gunfire or the sound of an outboard motor, yet sometimes they investigate other noises, including a moderate shout. Aside from this hailing them into range, it is advisable to attract them vocally only by whistling—echoing the wing whistle. Their infrequent calls are low clucks and croaks.

White-winged Scoter *(Melanitta fusca)*
COMMON & REGIONAL NAMES: *coot, whitewing, whitewing coot, bay coot, bell-tongue coot, brant coot, rock coot, sea coot, bay muscovie, beachcomber, booby, channel duck, deaf duck, ice*

duck, *Indian duck, velvet duck, halfmoon-eye, white eye, iron pot, scooter, sea horse, tar bucket.*

GAME IDENTIFICATION IN FLIGHT: Whitewings migrate in large flocks, occasionally strung out in a long line, an arc, or a blunt V, but more often in no real formation. Like other scoters, they follow coastlines, but are more inclined to cut across small bays and over long capes. Flock after flock chooses the same crossing, where a neck of land dips or narrows or curves sharply seaward, or near its outer end. Hunters watch for them on the capes, and whitewings are shot from land more often than other scoters, especially when migrating against a south wind. In calm, clear weather they cross too high, but drop lower when visibility is poor, still lower when pushing against a headwind. In rough weather they sometimes fly along through the troughs between waves.

To take off they splash over the surface, on occasion running for many yards if there is no strong wind to lift into. They are powerful fliers, much swifter than they look as they waver and buffet the sky, but they are the largest and least agile of the scoter species. The drake—aptly called a "bull whitewing" by New Englanders—usually weighs over 3 pounds, sometimes closer to 4, and the hen usually weighs between 2 and 3. The average wingspread is more than a yard, almost 40 inches on many large bulls.

Although the species is named for a bright white speculum—fairly wide and flashing from the wings of both sexes—these scoters can look completely black at long range. The remainder of the male's plumage is black except for dusky or silvery-brown wing linings, a brownish tinge on the underparts, and a small white marking about the eye. The eye itself is peculiar—pale bluish gray or almost white. A narrow white border encircles it, and a short white streak curves back and up from the bottom of the border to form a stubby half-moon. The low black forehead slopes to the base of the upper mandible, which is a black knob. The bill edges are black, the ridge white but sometimes with a narrow black line, the nail and sides orange. The lower mandible is orange at the tip, white centrally, black at the base. The feet are orange on the inner sides, redder or purplish on the outer surfaces, with dark webs and black bands

or spots. The female's feet are similarly marked but brown or red-brown.

The black knob on the female's bill is much less prominent than the male's, and both mandibles are dark gray or black, paling on top and sometimes tinged pink on the sides. Except for her white speculum and sometimes one or two pale cheek areas, she is dark brown or blackish brown.

Juveniles are dark grayish brown, with pale underparts that may be almost whitish, and with two white cheek patches, one behind the bill, one behind the eye. Known as gray whitewings or (like other juvenile scoters) gray coots, they are the best table fare and are disposed to circle decoys closely and repeatedly.

DISTRIBUTION: Whitewings (also called velvet scoters in Europe) breed from eastern Alaska through the Yukon and the Northwest Territories, northeastern British Columbia, the Prairie Provinces, and the north-central states. They nest late but begin to show

Retriever fetching white-winged scoter.

up on the eastern and western seaboards before the end of August. Juveniles and additional flights of adults swell the migration in September and October.

A few whitewings join the surf scoters on the Great Lakes, but most of them winter on the coasts, from the Aleutians to Baja and from New Brunswick to South Carolina. Famous whitewing-hunting spots include Cape Cod, Plymouth Bay above it and Monomoy Island below, the sound between Martha's Vineyard and the Elizabeth Islands, Long Island Sound, Barnegat, Brigantine, the Delaware and Chesapeake.

GAME BEHAVIOR & HUNTING HABITAT: Whitewings consume negligible quantities of aquatic plants. The place to hunt them is a mollusk-rich bay or stretch of shoals, particularly where water of moderate depth—perhaps 15 feet—is known to hold beds of rock clams, oysters, or mussels. They are often on the wing during shooting hours, flying low as they search for food. In calm, clear weather a flock may become restless and make long, high flights. However, scoters passing at 200 feet or more can sometimes be whistled or hollered down if the boat is surrounded by big black decoys.

On a good bay at the peak of migration or shortly after the wintering population has arrived, scoters seem to be in the air almost all the time. A careful boatman may scull into range of feeding birds before putting them up, but more commonly the flocks are decoyed. A hunter may work alone, or his anchored boat may be one link in a chain extending out from shore if scoters are still following the coastlines south. The chain of boats turns some of the birds seaward—but often not until they fly within gunshot—while other flocks cross the chain just as they cross low capes where hunters wait. When a flock does flare, it is not unusual for a couple of tender juveniles to come back and circle the decoys. Like other scoters, whitewings require tightly choked guns and high-brass loads of fairly large shot (see *American* and *Surf Scoter*).

VOICE: Whitewings are silent on the water, but during low flights a series of six or eight low, bell-like whistles is heard often enough to have inspired the nickname "bell-tongued coot." Whistling, and sometimes shouting, can draw a passing flock.

Geese/3

GENERAL DESCRIPTION & DISTRIBUTION: Each autumn, along the four great migration corridors of North America, hunters await the vague, edgeless advance of yelps and bayings from wild geese. A clearer bugling chorus follows, and the first sight of fluctuating columns and chevrons under scudding clouds; then come the teetering, leg-dangling swarms descending on fields or in waters. Geese are the wildfowler's big game. Their sovereignty is not a simple matter of size, either individually or in vast formations. Stately, swift, graceful, aloof, they have a beauty and a wild intelligence that draw goose hunters to the blinds while saner men sleep warmly. Wildfowlers regard such creatures as worthier adversaries than ordinary prey.

Memory still preserves the first spearhead of Canadas ever seen by the author, velvet-black ripples in an iron-gray sky. Another memory concerns the first goose killed, thudding into the stubble after four were missed because they loomed so large above the blind. They are always higher, always faster than they seem, and each one brought to hand is a trophy.

There is a paradox in the contrast between the shrewdness of some species and the gullibility of others, which long ago attained proverbial status in the expression "silly goose." Many ducks have an instinctive yearning for the company of Canadas; since these eerily intelligent geese are too alert and perceptive to be easily surprised by predators, they attract satellite ducks into their sphere of safety. The most efficient predator has made a practice of employing Canada decoys as "confidence stools" to enhance a rig of duck blocks. Such a spread is usually more effective in luring ducks than Canadas.

Yet snow geese are easily fooled, even when they swing in close enough to see details sharply. At the other extreme is Alaska's emperor goose, regarded by northern hunters as craftier than the Canada, since the latter will decoy to well-placed stick-

Snow geese, whitefronts, and cacklers on Pacific Flyway.

ups or floating blocks. It is true that somewhat similar contrasts exist among ducks: Ruddies and scoters are called "boobies" for good reason, and there are times when normally wary mallards seem to court death or domestication, while black ducks are invariably alert. However, the contrasts are more extreme among geese.

Geese exhibit great diversity of appearance, distribution, and habitat, as well as demeanor. About forty species are scattered over the planet. Of these, only seven are North American, but there are numerous subspecies. Though some authorities provide no listing for the tule goose, it is generally accepted as a subspecies of the white-fronted goose. In addition to the Ross's goose—a mallard-sized duplicate of the snow goose —there are two subspecies of snows, the greater and lesser. Recent studies have concluded that the blue goose is not a separate breed in the usual sense, but a color phase of the lesser snow; still, it differs in ways affecting the hunter and is commonly accorded a separate listing. And many game biologists divide the ubiquitous Canada into as many as eleven subspecies, ranging from a giant race to the tiny cackling goose of the West Coast.

All are birds of the family *Anatidae,* subfamily *Anserinae,* closely related to swans. A goose, however, has a neck shorter than its body, while a swan's neck is slightly longer than its body. Another distinctive difference is in the lore, the area between the eye and bill, which is naked on the swan, feathered on a goose. The relationship to ducks is not quite so close. Apart from the obvious difference in size (notwithstanding such exceptions as the little brant, the cackler, and the Ross's goose), the most striking distinction is that of color. The males of most duck species are easily separated from females by their gaudier plumage, whereas the male and female of any goose or swan species are alike in hue, and their colors are not so spectacular as those of most male ducks. All three subfamilies go through similar immature stages of plumage, but geese and swans mature more slowly and molt only once a year, postnuptially, rather than twice. During summer the entire plumage is renewed and, as with ducks, there is a short flightless period.

Further differences concern bill and body stucture. A goose or swan lacks the duck's cere, a soft swelling about the nostrils.

A goose's bill is also more bluntly triangular than a duck's. (A swan's is longer but it, too, has a triangular profile.) Geese and swans have rounder bodies than ducks and slightly longer legs. The legs of most geese are farther forward under the belly than those of typical swans and ducks. Geese are built to get about on land better than most waterfowl, thus widening the hunter's realm.

GENERAL HABITAT: Geese nest, migrate, and are hunted on every flyway. They blanket the continent in the course of a year. Three Prairie Provinces—Manitoba, Saskatchewan, and Alberta —form North America's greatest waterfowl hatchery; but geese have an immense breeding habitat that sprawls from Greenland and the arctic islands westward to Alaska and southward through Canada and large portions of the United States, particularly the Great Plains and the belt of the Rockies. Innumerable sloughs and potholes, lake shores and tidal flats provide the food, water, grit, and security essential to the hatching and rearing of young. In autumn most of the birds course down the flyways to winter in the middle and southern states, and considerable numbers fly on into Mexico.

On the coastal breeding grounds of the North, geese must fend off glaucous gulls voracious for eggs and goslings. In more temperate regions the crow, the bulldozer, and the plow are similarly constant threats. And everywhere there are other enemies, as almost all carnivores hunt fowl or eggs or both. Yet the geese flourish where man has not replaced wetlands with pavements or dust bowls.

Like most ducks, geese usually build simple ground nests, lined with down. But unlike most ducks they mate for life, and the gander guards the incubating female and her nest, and then helps to rear the young. Geese that achieve maturity in the wild, escaping disease, accidents, and predators (man included), have an average life span of six or eight years. Even discounting far more impressive but atypical longevity records, there is no doubt that they live longer than ducks. All of these factors enable them to maintain a successful reproductive cycle with relatively small broods. Though the number of eggs to a clutch depends not only on species, but on age, habitat, and other factors, the average is from four to six.

Most species mate during the second or third year. There is evidence that until a goose mates it remains close to its siblings and parents. The family migrates as a unit, joining other families but retaining a kind of integrity within the flock. With each migration a young bird becomes more certain of the way and more suspicious of sights or sounds connected with hunters. Its marvelous migrational powers and wariness are reinforced by experience.

Strangely, in spite of the fact that geese are extremely adaptable, and that the different species encounter a wide variety of ecosystems along the migratory corridors and on the wintering grounds, they are so remarkably alike in their feeding requirements that gunners seldom have difficulty finding good hunting habitat. Most geese obtain at least some of their sustenance by grazing on dry land, and all of them are predominantly vegetarian. Canadas and snows get so much of their food by grazing that they can often be hunted more successfully over grainfields than over water. Brant are America's only true maritime geese, and they, too, have such definite feeding preferences that the best blind locations will easily be enumerated in the entries for the two species.

BLIND & DECOY POSITIONS: A blind should be camouflaged with vegetation natural to the area, but surrounding earth should not be denuded for the purpose or scarred in any way, as waterfowl have excellent vision. They detect suspicious markings while far out of range, perhaps a hundred yards or more. And since they perceive colors clearly, a hunter's clothing must be as drab as his blind. The glint of spectacles or the planes of a man's face will also flare geese, so an experienced hunter keeps his head low until he is ready to shoot.

All wildfowl prefer to head into the wind when they are about to alight or make a close pass over decoys. A head wind acts as a brake and helps the birds control their maneuvers. If the breeze is in the gunner's face, therefore, geese and ducks seldom fly close over the decoys spread before him. They veer off, seeking a place to alight into the wind, or may approach from the rear of the blind, pass too high over the decoys, and come down (if at all) far beyond the rig. An ideal position is on a lee shore, with the wind coming from behind the hunter.

The birds are then likely to fly in over the water, directly approaching the blind as they breast the wind. They will make a low pass over a good decoy spread and may even attempt to splash in among the blocks. The nearest decoys should be about 20 yards from the blind.

If the breeze is coming from the right, the bulk of the decoys can be set to the right of the blind—or to the left if the breeze is from the left—so that the birds will cross directly in front as they approach, heading upwind toward the spread.

No formal arrangement is needed, but for aerial visibility each block should be several feet from all others, and one or two fairly wide openings should be left in the pattern to persuade incoming birds that there is room to pitch in. Natural, unregimented appearance and good visibility are the requisites.

Waterfowl nesting habitat in eastern Canada.

Oversized decoys are not essential, but may be helpful in open areas where an attempt is made to attract birds from great distances. If a spit or sand bar or the crescent shore of a cove hides part of the rig from the birds approaching on either side, stringers of decoys can be lined out at angles from the main rig to draw in flights appearing to the left or right.

Specialized rigs, such as Canada-goose stick-ups on grazing fields and sheet decoys for snows, will be described in connection with individual species, as will the blinds that are particularly appropriate for certain species or areas. Additional information on pit and hedgerow blinds—of great importance in grazing areas—will be found under the heading of *Blind & Decoy Positions* in the section on ducks. Regarding the number of decoys, the general rule is to use as many as possible. Geese, like the diving species of ducks, are most strongly attracted to large spreads.

GEAR & CALLS: Since waterfowling is often best when the weather is worst, and since the season extends into winter, warm clothing is essential. Chest-high insulated waders are recommended for shooting over water, even when a retriever is used, as it may be necessary to wade about to set out decoys and pick them up. Waterproof boots are recommended for shooting over land, as fields are often quite boggy. The most common calling device is the mouth-operated commercial type, the wooden cylinder enclosing a reed. Other types (as well as unaided vocal calling) will be mentioned where applicable, and calling suggestions will be offered for individual species under the heading of *Voice*. In general, calling should be restrained and must be closely imitative or it will flare the birds instead of attracting them. Skill can be attained only with practice, and there is no substitute for time spent in a blind, listening to waterfowl, but instructional phonograph records, available in sporting-goods stores, can be extremely helpful.

GUNS, LOADS, RANGES: Although some expert marksmen bag their game consistently with 16- or 20-bore guns, the 12-gauge is best for all geese, large or small. It should have a 30-inch full-choke barrel (or modified and full if it is a double and will be used over decoys). Jump-shooting is rare because cover is sparse where geese congregate, and some species—particularly Canadas—are too alert to be approached within flushing distance. In many areas, moreover, the geese habitually rest in sanctuary areas where stalking obviously is not permitted. High-velocity or Magnum No. 4 loads are recommended for shooting over decoys. For pass-shooting many hunters prefer a gun chambered for 3-inch Magnums, and pellet size should be No. 4 or (if long shots are frequent and the species large) No. 2. Federal regulations stipulate that a gun for wildfowling must hold no more than three shells, including a chambered load. A repeater capable of holding more than three must have its magazine plugged to reduce its capacity.

Estimating the size and distance can be difficult over water or fields where reference points are lacking. A rule of thumb among goose shooters is that if the front bead of a shotgun obliterates a bird's head, the range is more than 50 yards. However, the head of a small species (or a duck) is slightly smaller than that of the average goose. A decoy placed at a precise distance from the blind—or a stake driven into the mud—can serve as a range marker. A simpler method is to compare the size of an incoming bird with that of decoys below it. The bird itself furnishes another means of range estimation. Even though it is possible to identify the colors (and shapes and sizes) of some wildfowl at considerable distances, a duck or goose is usually no more than 45 or 50 yards away when its plumage pattern becomes sharply detailed. Most geese and ducks are bagged at ranges between 25 and 50 yards. It is best to refrain from shooting at geese more than 60 yards away.

RETRIEVING DOGS: Most geese are stronger fliers than ducks, more heavily shielded by plumage, and more tenacious of life. When brought down by a shot that fails to kill, geese and ducks will try to escape, heading for cover if there is any, and often diving to evade detection. A well-trained retriever may be even more important for hunting geese over water than for hunting ducks. A swift current increases this importance. Labrador, golden, and Chesapeake Bay retrievers are the most popular for hunting geese, for they have the stamina, strong swimming ability, intelligence, and resistance to cold that are requisites for a good water dog.

American Brant *(Branta bernicla hrota)*
COMMON & REGIONAL NAMES: *brant, common brant, eastern brant, white-bellied brant, brant goose, burnt goose, clatter goose, crocker.*

GAME IDENTIFICATION IN FLIGHT: While crossing long overland stretches, migrating brant fly as high as most waterfowl, but along the coast they stay low, a little above treetops or cliffs, a few feet above open water. On short foraging flights they often travel in ragged bunches, but the typical grouping is a long, wavering line, a wind-rippled streamer, sometimes relatively straight, sometimes curving, sometimes headed by a cluster. On reaching feeding areas a migrating string, perhaps fifty or more, disintegrates into small groups that may surge right over decoys.

Males average about 3¼ pounds, females half a pound less, hardly bigger than a plump mallard. Because their short wingbeats are somewhat more rapid than those of larger geese,

American brant and Canadas on wintering grounds.

and because they dip and bob in the air like cork floats on a rolling swell, their flights lack the aura of power associated with other geese. If they seem to push slowly through resisting currents of air, it is an illusion. Over eelgrass flats their average speed of 40 or 45 miles an hour equals that of many ducks. Though brant are not the fastest fliers, it is a common shooting error to underestimate their speed. Moreover, a brant flying directly in or away tends to look larger and closer than it really is because its pointed wings are long in relation to its body. The gunner who misses a brant most likely has shot behind it.

Each bird is at first a teetering black silhouette. Soon the long wings become distinct, and the round black head on a thick neck as short as a mallard's, and the sharply contrasting pale underparts. Europe's easily duped barnacle goose (*Branta leucopsis*) occasionally visits the Atlantic Flyway and mystifies hunters who afterward tell of having shot a "white-faced brant." Its short-billed, pure white face, surrounded by a black cowl that extends down to the breast, inspires French hunters to speak

of it as the "little nun."

A brant flying away reveals long white tail coverts, and the upper ones form a broad V similar to the white crescent visible above the tail of a Canada goose, rimming the dusky rump. The brant's bill, head, neck, and breast are charcoal-black, relieved only by a broken stripe, patch, or crescent of thin white slashings on each side of the neck. (The absence of white slashings distinguishes juveniles even when they appear fully grown.) The American brant is the continent's only goose with a black breast clearly terminating against pale underparts. The back, too, is dull black, fading into dusky brown toward the rump. The scapulars are brown, the wing coverts grayish brown, the flight feathers black, the linings grayish brown. A brant coming directly toward the blind is a somewhat startling spectacle. The long black forward edges of the wings curve down to join the black pedestal of breast supporting the upright black head, and this bowsprit of ebony looms almost disembodied from the white hull. The sides and forepart of the belly are pale ash, fading toward the tail coverts, where the feet are black wedges against pure white.

DISTRIBUTION: The American brant, a variety of the European species known to English wildfowlers as brent or brent goose, is a true maritime goose, in fall and winter seldom seen anywhere but along the Atlantic seaboard. The breeding range lies on the coasts of Greenland, on several arctic islands, and the Boothia Peninsula above Hudson Bay.

By the end of September the largest flights have reached the Gulf of St. Lawrence, and in mid-October and early November they arrive in full force on the wintering grounds, from New Hampshire's little bays down to North Carolina's Outer Banks. Along the wrinkled coasts are spots renowned for brant hunting: On the New Brunswick shore there is Tabusintac; below Massachusetts Bay there is the gigantic windbreaking hook of Cape Cod, where Pleasant Bay and Monomoy Island provide feeding shoals and isolation; to the south Rhode Island Sound and Long Island's Great South Bay, New Jersey's Barnegat Bay and the Brigantine shoals below Egg Harbor, Delaware Bay and Chincoteague, Currituck Sound and Hatteras and Ocracoke on Pamlico Sound. And there are scores of others.

GAME BEHAVIOR & HUNTING HABITAT: Brant rest far out on a bay or upon the open sea unless bad weather forces them shoreward. On calm days a hunter waits for the water to ebb on the eelgrass flats. At the approach of low tide the birds head for shallow coastal waters where strands of eelgrass rise to the surface. Whereas most wildfowl feed on a variety of plants, brant depend as much as they can on eelgrass (*Zostera marina*). Before a fungus blight struck the eelgrass of the eastern seaboard in 1931, the plant accounted for almost 90 percent of the American brant's diet, the remainder being widgeongrass and algae. By 1935, only about 2 percent of the former brant population clung to life. The estimated 20,000 birds that remained must have been the most adaptable of their race. Until the early 1940s, they subsisted chiefly on sea lettuce and other algae, supplemented by widgeongrass, cordgrass, and rare windfalls of eelgrass. As the blight finally passed, the brant slowly increased again.

Now they are fairly abundant, though in some years, after a poor breeding season, low bag limits are imposed or the birds are stricken from the game list. Once again they feed on eelgrass, but they are slightly less selective than before the long famine. When a gunner brings down his first brant of the day he may examine the down about its cloaca. If he finds a green algal taint he may decide to concentrate on other game for a week or so. But if the down is white or tan, eelgrass has probably been the food and he will want to bag his limit. Brant that have been feeding almost solely on eelgrass are among the most succulent of wildfowl.

They do not graze on land, and the eelgrass shallows are often far offshore, but during feeding periods flocks are likely to explore a cove, estuary, or the lee of a point or island where decoys can be floated. The tide usually rises before their hunger is appeased, and they fly about in search of new beds. They are generally most active when the tide is at half flood, or half ebb. At these times the birds also search for resting spots on sand bars and sandy points.

The morning tides are considered best for shooting, because brant are hungriest then. A lantern bobbing across the black shore of night on a coastal marsh probably means a hunter is racing an early tide; when the sun rises he will be hidden at the water's edge, his decoys spread. His anticipation will be whetted if the barometer has been falling and the bay's leaden cast foretells a storm. Yet during every season there are barren mornings at Assateague or on Cape Cod's Chatham Bay. One cold, pallid morning three of us huddled on a tump and watched a birdless Chincoteague horizon. Noon passed. It was after two when we rose in the blind, ready to pick up the decoys, and abruptly crouched as a dozen brant appeared unaccountably. Disorganized little clusters continued to come in, and for the next hour no one raised his head above the blind except to shoot.

At sea, brant are wary, but some hunters have had good shooting from sneakboxes. In autumn the boats are painted the color of sedge and sometimes camouflaged with reeds and grasses; in winter they are painted white to look like floating ice or shoreline mounds of snow. Along the Outer Banks some of the guides rent out curtain blinds—concrete boxes sunk in the shallows, with canvas and wood extensions that are raised and lowered with the tides. More common elsewhere is the elevated reef blind, a reed-camouflaged box on pilings high enough for a boat to be tied under the floor. It stands out as prominently as a lighthouse, yet spooks no birds if the structure is up by the time of migration. There are also floating blinds that look like clumps of vegetation on little islands, and on some waters stake blinds are permitted. A boat can be eased in between the rows of stakes, which are driven into the bottom and covered with vegetation. Permanent blinds are not essential. A roll of cane or bamboo can be opened and propped in shoreline brush. A hunter in a thick stand of bulrush or an island fringe of beach myrtle may need no blind but the habitat itself.

The birds become curiously reckless during feeding periods. Though a stool that simulates the species is most effective, brant will come to rafts of scaup or canvasback decoys—all the more eagerly if a few Canada blocks fringe one side. They come in low and sometimes hover even while a hunter wades among the decoys to pick up a fallen bird.

Many birds will dive if injured. Brant more often try to escape detection by flattening themselves with neck outstretched on the water, looking quite dead but capable of suddenly swimming off. If the head comes up at all, a *coup de grâce* should be prompt.

Black brant with young.

VOICE: A babbling rondelay of short honks and grunts includes deep, loud notes—*ronk-ronk-ronk*—that can be imitated with short blasts on a goose call. Brant may come to the feeding chatter of a duck call, as well, and can also be imitated vocally, without a mechanical call. Sometimes the babble diminishes to a clucking interspersed with metallic honks and a double-noted exclamation whose closest representation is *torok*. The alarm cry, to be scrupulously avoided when calling brant, is a single ducklike squawk. Only an occasional honk is needed, and hungry brant will come to well-placed decoys without the added attraction of calling.

Black Brant *(Branta nigricans)*
COMMON & REGIONAL NAMES: *brant, China goose, Eskimo goose, sea brant.*

GAME IDENTIFICATION IN FLIGHT: The black brant of the West Coast is, on the average, a few ounces heavier than the eastern brant. There is an extreme similarity in general appearance, particularly at long range, but the western strain is darker. The bill, head, neck, chest, and upper body are black, the wings black with grayish-brown linings. The white slashings below the head are more distinct than on the American brant, and they meet in front. (They are absent or barely discernible on birds of the year.)

A black brant flying away shows the same white crescent between tail and rump that hunters recognize on the eastern birds, but the Pacific subspecies has far less white elsewhere. The black upper breast blends into slaty-brown or brownish-gray underparts. The sides are the same color but with vague white or pale bars running up to the scapulars. The lower belly and flanks are white or whitish, the feet black. Until a flock passes close to a blind, the pale tones are lost in smoky velvet.

Black brant tend to fly in slightly smaller flocks than American brant. They fly in a wavering line, sometimes head to tail, sometimes side by side. Occasionally they make an abrupt detour for hundreds of yards before returning to a straight course, and they may rise or dip in a follow-the-leader progression, though they seldom lift out of gunshot.

DISTRIBUTION: The breeding range is the northern coast of Alaska, the Yukon, and the Northwest Territories, and still farther north on Victoria Island and Banks Island. Occasional flocks nest farther east, just as some American brant nest farther west than the main colonies. Interbreeding is uncommon, yet hunters occasionally report bagging intermediate specimens. Black brant pass along the shores of the Bering Sea and the Gulf of Alaska during the last half of September, appearing on the coastal waters of Washington, Oregon, and California from mid-October until late in November. Some winter in British Columbia, others continue as far south as Baja.

The Pacific Coast has as many rich brant-hunting harbors as the Atlantic. The sea geese raft up in Kotzebue and Norton sounds, pass through Shelikof Strait and Yakutat Bay, then down through the island chain shielding British Columbia's coast. Hunters reminisce about the rainswept headlands of Vancouver Island's western side—Brooks Bay, Nootka, Tofino, Barkley Sound. On the eastern side the brant file through Queen Charlotte Strait and on across the Juan de Fuca Strait. Conclaves soon appear at Puget Sound, Grays Harbor, Willapa Bay, the mouth of the Columbia, Tillamook, Newport, Reedsport, Coos Bay, Humboldt Bay, Tomales Bay above Point Reyes, Monterey, the Santa Barbara Channel, Santa Monica, and San Diego.

GAME BEHAVIOR & HUNTING HABITAT: Although the Pacific

brant are less dependent than the eastern flocks on eelgrass, the plant probably makes up at least half their diet. The rest consists of widgeongrass, surf grasses, algae, and assorted other aquatic plants. Like the eastern birds, they forage on offshore beds, trade over sand bars and islands, explore bays, and seek the shelter of coves and estuaries when a storm blows.

Just as scaup (and for that matter, pronghorns and caribou) are tempted to investigate a fluttering object, so are brant. Sometimes they can be waved in by raising a handkerchief just above the blind. They decoy as readily as American brant, responding to the same techniques, rigs, and blind locations. A natural simplicity is always best—blocks spread in the lee of a bar, for instance, within range of a pit dug in the sand.

VOICE: The most frequent flight and feeding call is a low, guttural trill that sounds like a growl; it sometimes becomes rapping-sharp, and is interspersed with mellow honking and double-noted cries that sound like *wah-oook.* Black brant respond to calling more eagerly than most geese. As with eastern brant, vocal mimicry can be effective without a call. Volume and tone should be realistically modulated by cupping the hands before the mouth. A wooden goose call also works well for a hunter who can honk and trill convincingly.

Canada Goose *(Branta canadensis)*
COMMON & REGIONAL NAMES:*Canadian goose, honker, Canada brant, French goose, Mexican goose, Eskimo goose, prairie goose, bay goose, big gray goose, black-headed goose, black-necked goose, blackie, cravat goose, wild goose, long-necked goose, wavey, white-cheek, white-chin.*

GAME IDENTIFICATION IN FLIGHT: In the gray half-hour before the statutory minute of sunrise, the tension of the sky watch is the same whether a hunter is in a stubble-field pit behind stick-ups, or pass-shooting from a hedgerow blind, or in a marsh blind thatched with cordgrass and bulrush behind a floating raft of oversized decoys. Sometimes, as the first wide chevrons and oblique lines take shape in black silhouette against the distant sky, their sound identifies them: yelping, baying, houndlike cries

COMPARATIVE SIZE, BODY TONE, AND NECK LENGTH AMONG REPRESENTATIVE SUBSPECIES OF CANADA GOOSE

CACKLING GOOSE

LESSER CANADA

VANCOUVER CANADA

ATLANTIC CANADA

deepening and echoing as the Canadas approach, becoming a wildly assertive honking, bugling chorus. Even at fairly close range the geese appear darker than they really are, the gray of storm clouds framed by black wings, black tail, black neck. Though the darkness of body and blackness of wings are illusory, identification is sure, not only because the most common subspecies are so large but because of distinctive markings, shape, and flight characteristics.

All races can be recognized by a wide white chin strap, or bar, which is almost always visible and marks no other birds. (On a moderately foggy morning in corn and soybean fields near Chestertown, Maryland, the author used a range-finding device to verify that he and four other hunters could plainly make out the chin straps before honkers came within 65 yards, flying high. To rely on the white marking as a range indicator is therefore a mistake. Many goose shooters sensibly wait to fire until they can see the pale stippling or barring on the gray-brown breast.)

When Canadas are taking off or heading away, and often when crossing, a white bar between rump and tail is conspicuous. As seen from the rear, it takes the form of a broad V or crescent, sharply contrasting with the dark plumage bordering it. The big, dark wings are wider from front to rear than those of most geese. The long neck, with its distinctive black stocking that ends abruptly over the breast, is sometimes held straight forward in flight and sometimes curved gently; though relatively short on the smaller subspecies, it is a reliable element in identification.

Regardless of many subtle differences among the subspecies—geographical races—the short bill, round head, and long neck are a glistening black. The wide white chin strap is a patch that begins up behind the eye and spreads down the cheek and around under the chin. The back and scapulars are brownish gray (or often grayish brown) with a light tipping that produces a softly barred effect. The breast is a pale, ashy gray, usually with a brownish tinge and dim whitish barring. The belly and flanks are white, sometimes stained rusty, the sides brownish gray barred with white. The rump and tail are black, the feet black or grayish black, the tail coverts white, the wings dusky grayish brown with paler linings.

From the blind, first-flight birds are hard to tell from their elders, but their colors are darker and more blended, their edgings vague, and their light parts usually speckled or tinged with darker shades. Among the larger subspecies, birds of the year are almost a third longer than mallards by late fall, and look still larger as they swing over the rig. They may weigh a pound or so less than average mature birds, but size is an unreliable indication of age. An adult Atlantic, or common, Canada *(B. c. canadensis)* usually weighs between 8 and 10 pounds. Field research for this book, conducted at Remington Farms in Maryland, verified an average weight of somewhat over 8 pounds, 3 ounces for birds wintering there. A Canada's dense, tough feathering, known for its ability to deflect light shot charges at pass-shooting distances, actually weighs more than the bones. Plucking and dressing reduces the weight by about a third, more after draining; the Canadas bagged in the Maryland experiment averaged just under 5 pounds, 3 ounces after dressing and draining.

The number of Canada subspecies has long been disputed, and their common and scientific names have undergone more than one reshuffling, but at present eleven distinct strains are widely accepted. They range in size from the tiny cackling goose *(B. c. minima),* rarely larger than a plump brant, to the giant Canada *(B. c. maxima)* which sometimes weighs 20 pounds. The cackler is primarily a bird of the upper West Coast, and it probably interbreeds occasionally with the rare, protected, almost equally small Aleutian Canada *(B. c. leucopareia).* The latter can usually be identified by a unique white ring encircling

Canada geese, showing white rump chevron in flight.

the base of the neck, but cacklers frequently show a whitish, incomplete ring. The giant Canada, thought to be extinct until a flock was discovered wintering near Rochester, Minnesota, in 1962, looks like an oversized common Canada. Its average weight is over 16 pounds. It looms most often over blinds on the Mississippi Flyway but is rapidly expanding its numbers and distribution.

The traditional image of the honker—a stately bird weighing from 7 to 12 pounds and having a wingspread of 5 to 6½ feet and a length of about 3 feet—applies not only to the Atlantic Canada, but to the Todd's *(B. c. interior),* the western *(B. c. moffitti),* and the Vancouver *(B. c. fulva)* subspecies. The ranges of some subspecies overlap, interbreeding occurs, and it can be impossible to tell one of the large races from another unless a hunter knows which is most prevalent in his region and can detect very subtle differences in coloration. All the races, large and small, are much alike in habits and choice of habitat. The large ones employ at least nine major flight lanes interwoven over the general flyways—the Atlantic, Mississippi, Central, and Pacific. Generally speaking, and with exceptions, the westernmost Canadas are darker and smaller than those of the Midwest and the East.

The large and medium races are the ones that concern the greatest number of hunters. Even when these honkers are flying at top speed—a little over 60 miles an hour—the wingbeats are deep and slow. Between resting and feeding areas they may

be going no more than 40 or 45 miles an hour unless they have a tail wind. They can slow down abruptly, setting their wings to glide or dip and teeter down. Still, their speed is often greater than it seems owing to the combination of their large size, direct flight path, and deep, rhythmic wingbeats. When other waterfowl are in the sky, the steady, leisurely surge of Canadas quickly overtakes the ducks whose wings are a frenzied blur, yet a gunner's natural inclination is to give ducks the greater lead. In goose shooting the most common error is too slow a swing, too little lead.

During long flights, particularly in migratory travel, the characteristic formations are a great sweeping V or a long, staggered line that hunters can recognize from afar. Some gunners refrain from shooting a lead bird, believing that it always is a tough old gander or that the flock will be lost without a leader. The myth may be a blessing since a large V formation is probably flying much too high for a clean hit, but the lead position is taken by any strong, adult member of the flock and is relinquished when fatigue sets in. In clear weather, long flights are made at great altitudes, normally at speeds close to 50 miles an hour, sometimes faster. But storms, dense cloud cover, overcast, or strong cross winds hold them back a little and force them down —occasionally just over the treetops—where they can watch for landmarks and sheltered resting spots. A head wind sometimes keeps them low, but it may also have the opposite effect.

On short flights over or between resting and feeding areas, Canadas fly in irregular bunches, and sometimes singly or in groups of two or three. Of course, the birds are immediately identifiable regardless of number, but the ease or difficulty of bringing them down is another matter. Sometimes they form a skein that seems to cover the sky. Unless some of them are quite low, it can be harder—for some of us, at least—to choose a target and pluck it from the skein than to bring down a high single or one of a lone pair or trio.

Like all wildfowl, geese prefer to land into the wind, and it is also from downwind that they most frequently reconnoiter a feeding or resting spot, a set of decoys, or another flock of birds. To rise from the water again they usually run a few steps, but if jumped they can get airborne with a bound, either from land or water.

DISTRIBUTION: No large section of America is without at least one race of Canadas at some season. The breeding areas of one subspecies or another extend from Labrador and Newfoundland in the East to Baffin Island in the North, and westward to Alaska and the Aleutians. The largest populations nest in Canada's Maritime and Prairie provinces but breeding colonies also thrive as far south as Nevada, Utah, Colorado, and Nebraska. There are flocks that make only short migrations, wintering in southern Canada and the upper states, but most Canadas fly on into the middle and southern states or into Mexico.

On the uppermost breeding grounds or when cold weather comes early, southward flights begin, fitfully, during the first part of September. The great migration really gets under way at the end of that month or in the first days of October. It begins to taper off in late November but shooting remains good—especially in the southern regions, where most of the birds winter—through January.

GAME BEHAVIOR & HUNTING HABITAT: Those of us who are addicted to goose hunting give thanks that the anserine preference for grazing on dry land is most pronounced among Canadas.

Western Canadas on breeding grounds.

In wild areas they feed on a tremendous variety of terrestrial and aquatic plants, as diverse as wild rice and sedges, clover and buds and berries, supplemented by occasional small shellfish, insects, worms, and fish. But they like domestic crops best of all. The fact that corn heads the list probably has as much to do with availability as with inclination. Canadas also love rice, wheat, soybeans, barley, oats, and alfalfa; it is not taste, but safety and the proximity of roosting waters that will determine which fields are in greatest need of a blind.

Although a shooting site on or near a cultivated field is likely to be visited by large numbers of geese, it is also true that hunting pressure can eventually keep birds away from a field during daylight. There is usually plenty of food on nearby marshes where hunting pressure may be less severe. The best locale for a blind may be determined in part by the region's most prevalent wild plants—cordgrass along much of the Atlantic Coast, saltgrass on Utah's Bear River marshes, sago pondweed and rushes near the Pacific. Geese will also come to decoys where there is an abundance of such plants as widgeongrass, spikerush, bulrush, bromegrass, wild barley, wild oats, and so on.

Atlantic Canada taking off (above), and
good pass-shooting site for Canada geese.

Fields may be best in agricultural regions, especially in fall, but in winter, when fields have been picked bare or are blanketed with snow, good shooting is to be had along the shores where wild vegetation is adjacent to water. The birds prefer to rest on the water and on bars and shores near feeding grounds. They are likely to pick the lee of some slight windbreak, especially on blustery days, but the protective barrier is sometimes no more substantial than tall grasses. The extreme intelligence of Canadas shows in their preference for those refuge waters where shooting is illegal. Inevitably, the best hunting is as near as legally possible to such resting areas.

During a full moon the birds do most of their foraging—and therefore most of their flying to and from feeding areas—at night. The tendency is accentuated during clear, starlit weather. Con-

versely, a great deal of daylight feeding and flying must occur in cloudy or stormy weather, on the day of the new moon, and during the week just before and after the new moon. Those are the days when Canadas veil the air, beginning to head for their feeding grounds after dawn or shortly before sunrise. Usually the aerial activity continues almost unabated for an hour or so after legal shooting begins. Before noon some of the birds are in the air once more, returning to water; additional flights occur in midafternoon, when the geese revisit the fields, and at dusk, when they retire to the waters.

Just as whitetail deer follow habitual runs between bed and browse, Canada geese use established routes—generally a direct line unless heavy shooting has provoked a detour. The best blind locations are between resting and feeding areas, as near as possible to one or the other. Most elevated blinds are on water or shorelines, though cornstalk blinds and hedgerows are also used at or near the edges of grazing fields. The best concealment on land is a pit blind near the edge of such a field. Where geese spend much of the day on water, camouflaged sneakboxes and sunken curtain blinds are also effective.

If the decoys are on water, a few mallard, black duck, or baldpate blocks can be set a little to the side of the Canadas to add realism. Since Canada geese are not easily duped, lifelike positioning is essential; whether on land or water, a few decoys may have their heads turned back between the wings in preening or dozing attitude, but it is more important to have a few with their necks bent as if feeding. Because Canadas post sentinels, at least one or two decoys near the fringe of the spread should have their heads up in alert attitude. Bagged geese can be set on land as additional decoys, but they must be naturally positioned or they serve as an alarm rather than an inducement. Stick-up decoys should be employed in large (hence, reassuring) numbers dotting the stubble rows. Many can be in feeding positions, but geese do not keep their heads constantly lowered while grazing, so a number of heads should be up.

An Atlantic or Todd's Canada looks bigger at 60 yards than a mallard at 30 yards. Because of the Canada's speed, vigor, and dense, hard plumage, 60 yards is the maximum at which shots should be attempted. Most successful hits are made at ranges between 25 and 50. (For additional recommendations,

Giant Canadas (top) and
upper West Coast's dusky Canadas (*B. c. occidentalis*).

applicable to other geese as well, see *Guns, Loads, Ranges,* page 260.)

VOICE: Stentorian, clarion, magisterial—these adjectives describe the flight calls of honkers. In flight or on the water they habitually engage in loud, resonant honking interspersed with a sound close to *ong, ong,* and a frequently drawn-out *h-r-r-ronngk.* This last cry appears sometimes to be a greeting between flocks or a summons from feeding birds to new arrivals, and it can be imitated effectively with a mouth-operated wooden call. The cry is composed of two notes: a guttural, imperative tone held for a long moment before sliding into the second, higher, punctuating note. Such cries are mixed with quieter, shorter, conversational honking. Occasionally, while a flock feeds in relative quiet, a bird utters a long honking cry or a *woof.*

Though the descriptive term honker is appropriate to the several large, widely distributed subspecies that most of us hunt, the smaller races have higher voices and indulge in much cackling, yelping, or ducklike chuckling. The little Aleutian Canadas and cackling geese, especially, are prone to squeak, yelp, cluck, and chatter.

Canadas rarely mingle intimately with alien species, but various subspecies sometimes mingle, and they will feed and rest next to ducks and other geese. Often, therefore, a call that convinces one race will attract another. Though poor calling will flare these extremely perceptive birds, it is not essential to render an exact imitation of a particular subspecies.

The wood-and-reed goose call has never been superseded, though there is also a good rubber bellows type that is shaken or manipulated like a miniature concertina. Most lifelike of all is the unaided vocal mimicry of hunters who have spent their lives near the haunts of Canada geese.

Emperor Goose *(Philacte canagica)*
COMMON & REGIONAL NAMES: *beach goose, painted goose, white-headed goose.*

GAME IDENTIFICATION IN FLIGHT: Out beyond a wide, northwestern beach, almost skimming the breakers, an emperor goose looks ash-gray, barred with black and white. Even when, as usual, it swerves just beyond range, its contrasting head and neck help identify it, for the chin, throat, and front of the neck are brownish black, sharply outlined against the back of the neck and the face, which are white, usually suffused with rust or amber. It looks rather like a blue goose except for its darker, shorter neck —as short as a brant's. The short, rapid wingbeats also make a hunter think of brant, though the emperor is heavier-bodied, less speedy and agile.

The birds generally travel in pairs or in flocks or four or five, sometimes grouped haphazardly. They often fly so low that their wing tips barely miss the water on the downstroke.

A typical emperor is a medium-sized goose, a little over 2 feet long, with a wingspread of slightly more than 4 feet and a weight of 5½ to 6½ pounds. The bill is pale purple or flesh-colored, white on the nail and around the nostrils. The underparts of the silvery-gray body are finely patterned, scaled rather than barred as on top, and often yellow-stained. The rump is a pale tipped ashy brown, ending in a white tail. The wings are gray, duskily tipped, with darker white-edged coverts and secondaries. The feet are yellow-orange. Juveniles have paler feet, a duller bill, dusky spotting on head and neck, and brown rather than black barring on the back.

DISTRIBUTION: The emperor breeds only along Alaska's western coast from the Kuskokwim River up to Kotzebue Sound, on St. Lawrence Island in the Bering Sea, and on Siberia's eastern coast. The bulk of the population winters on the Aleutians but small numbers fly farther south. By October they are seen on the coasts of British Columbia, Washington, Oregon, and California, but emperors rarely penetrate a dozen miles inland.

GAME BEHAVIOR & HUNTING HABITAT: Emperors, America's only primarily carnivorous geese, pluck mussels and other shellfish at low tide along beaches and mud flats, and sometimes browse various heath berries on the tundra near the water or wander farther ashore for cranberries or mossberries in the foothills. Most hunters who have tasted emperor goose declare it to be almost inedible, yet it has also been described as quite palatable. The flavor probably depends on whether birds have

been diluting their mussel diet with berries.

Not many hunters occupy blinds within the narrow limits of the primary wintering grounds, and those who do seldom bring emperors into range. Neither calling nor decoying is very effective since emperor geese—almost as maritime in habit as brant and much warier—hesitate to approach landing spots that attract other birds. Were it not for their very low flight even fewer would be bagged, for passing shots are usually the best that can be expected, even from pit blinds or camouflaged boats.

VOICE: No other goose utters the emperor's shrill, strident flight call—*kla-ha, kla-ha, kla-ha*—repeated in two-syllable raps. The staccato cries identify the birds and alert a hunter to their approach, but flocks will not respond very eagerly to calling.

Ross's Goose *(Chen rossi,* also *Anser rossi)*
COMMON & REGIONAL NAMES: *China goose, galoot, horned wavey, little wavey, scabby-nosed wavey, wart-nosed wavey.*

GAME IDENTIFICATION IN FLIGHT: The miniature white geese shimmer in the air, their wings almost translucent except for tapering black primaries. The flock is a bow or ragged chevron or perhaps a diagonal line. Or, if the fifteen or twenty birds have flown only a little way from some valley stream, they may be loosely bunched as they sidle out of the sky at the edge of an oat field.

At a distance they look like exceptionally small snow geese, and sometimes they match the 50-mile-an-hour speed of snow geese. Lesser snows are hunted along segments of the Ross's migratory route and on its California wintering grounds. It is essential to tell the species apart, because, despite rising numbers. Ross's geese are sometimes protected. Fortunately, long before the most optimistic hunter would think of raising his gun, size ensures recognition: The Ross's goose, hardly more than 2 feet long, with a wingspan of about 4 feet and an average weight of 2½ to 3 pounds, presents only half the apparent bulk of a lesser snow. It is the smallest American goose. And also, before a flight moves into shooting range, sound may be revelatory. Lesser snows are vociferous in flight, Ross's geese nearly silent.

Emperor geese in Alaska (opposite above), and Ross's goose in California.

Other differences are perceptible only at close hand: A snow goose has broad black edging, known as a "grinning patch," on the sides of its bill, while the black edging on a Ross's mandibles is a mere line. The Ross's bill is oddly furrowed and, by maturity, acquires lumpy, warty-looking protuberances near the base. But in coloration the Ross's and the snow are virtually identical (see *Lesser Snow Goose*).

DISTRIBUTION: The Ross's flocks nest close to the upper rim of the Northwest Territories, in a small area at the base of the Boothia Peninsula, east of Victoria Island and west of Baffin. Early in September they arrive over Great Slave Lake and Lake Athabasca; in October they reach Montana, then fly southwestward over the Rockies to winter in California's central and southern valleys, arriving in October and November.

GAME BEHAVIOR & HUNTING HABITAT: During migration, Ross's geese graze heavily on grasses and rushes. Upon reaching the California valleys they descend on the oat fields with lesser snows, cacklers, Canadas, and white-fronted geese. Barley crops also attract them. They are somewhat "tamer" than the other geese on the stubble fields, and long ago earned a reputation as fine table fare. Before the prohibition of commercial shooting, large numbers were sold in the California markets. Federal law may have saved them from extirpation, but only recently have they begun to regain their numbers. If they continue to increase they will eventually become an agricultural nuisance and will be hunted more frequently. For wildfowlers it is not an unpleasant prospect.

VOICE: The most common feeding call is a repetitive but rather subdued clucking. Ross's geese are very quiet in the air.

Greater Snow Goose *(Chen hyperborea atlantica)*
COMMON & REGIONAL NAMES: wavey, white wavey, common wavey, white brant, white goose, arctic goose.

GAME IDENTIFICATION IN FLIGHT: Snow geese converge over the mid-Atlantic beaches in November or early December.

Grouped against the sky like Canadas, not quite so swift but with a look of indolent power in the strokes of their black-tipped wings, broad wedges of seventy or eighty white birds surge overhead. Some of the formations soon disintegrate into graceful clusters of half a dozen or so on short flights of reconnaissance for feeding and sanding places. No hunter can tell greater from lesser snows in flight, and at present snow geese may not be shot on the Atlantic Flyway because the larger subspecies, strongly predominant there, has never been populous. However, flocks are increasing and a snow season will probably be opened in the East before many more years have passed.

In the air, snows appear pure white except for their broad black wing tips. On the ground they often appear mud-stained their heads and breasts almost always rustily streaked and mottled. Preferring a few inches of water to dry land, they waddle about clumsily on big, dull red, black-clawed feet. The homely

Greater snow geese on Atlantic Flyway.

bill of the species is high, narrow, and short, varying from pale pink to deep carmine, tipped with a whitish nail. The saw-toothed edging is distinctly exposed, and a broad black convex band along the sides of the mandibles forms a grotesque ellipse called a grinning patch.

The average weight of a greater snow is from 5 to 7½ pounds, the length slightly over 2½ feet, the wingspread 5 feet. Females and birds of the year tend to be slightly smaller, but color is the clue to maturity. In its first autumn a snow goose is ashy gray, darker above and lighter below, with slaty primaries, dusky bill, tawny feet, and brownish-gray mottling on head and neck.

DISTRIBUTION: *Chen hyperborea atlantica*—"Atlantic goose from beyond the north wind." The Greco-Latin nomenclature is not merely poetic but accurate. The greater snow goose nests in the upper reaches of Canada's Arctic Archipelago and in northern Greenland. The wintering range is similarly small, reaching only from southern New Jersey to North Carolina. Early in the fall, great concentrations linger at two legendary waystops, St. Joachim in Quebec and then Fortescue in New Jersey. In late November, when migration is virtually over, sizable flocks are most often seen on the marshes of Chesapeake Bay and Currituck and Pamlico sounds.

GAME BEHAVIOR & HUNTING HABITAT: Whereas the lesser snow is an inland grazing bird, the greater comes down near coastal blinds to feed on grasses that thrive in a few inches of salt or brackish water. Among its foods are saltgrass, horsetail, and cordgrass. Flocks like to rest on wide bays or the ocean, or stand in a long line on a sandy shore, too wary to be approached. With the coming of ice and snow, they frequently retreat to hollows among the dunes of the outer beaches. Sometimes they fly over a blind to look closely at a rig of Canada decoys. At favorite feeding times—early morning, late afternoon, and moonlit nights—flocks plow meadows or grainfields near such havens as the Blackwater Refuge in Virginia.

VOICE: Greater snows are less loquacious than the western race but sometimes engage in a fairly noisy conversational gabble—

ga-ga-ga—and in short honks, higher and less sonorous than the cries of Canadas, although snows respond to a Canada goose call.

Lesser Snow Goose *(Chen hyperborea hyperborea)*
COMMON & REGIONAL NAMES: *wavey, white wavey, common wavey, little wavey, white brant, white goose, Alaska goose, arctic goose, Mexican goose.*

GAME IDENTIFICATION IN FLIGHT: Lesser snow geese are far more abundant than greater snows and far more likely to pass over the gun in massive formations or waves—one group closely following another as hundreds or thousands of birds descend from the northern sky in long, oblique lines and bluntly curving V's. Migratory flight is high, steady, at times exceeding 50 miles an hour. The shallow wingbeats make flight seem effortless. Suddenly, attracted by feeding birds or decoys in a field, they dip or dart or tip, more acrobatically than other geese. With wings cupped downward they glide toward earth from great heights, zigzagging, and an instant before alighting they brake their descent with quick, short wingbeats.

The fondness for altitude is usually forgotten when the geese approach a remembered feeding area. Hunger overcomes caution as they search for waste grain in stubble fields, flying only 30 yards or so above the heads of white-garbed hunters, decoying to scattered rags, frequently ignoring visible danger that would deter Canadas. Anxious to land, they probably pass overhead no faster than 40 miles an hour, but an abrupt twist or turn can be difficult to follow with a gun.

White birds accompanied by dark ones are lesser snows and blues, but the mixed flocks are familiar only on the Gulf Coast and in Texas. Farther west the snows arrive alone, though they mix with other species in the fields. To the east, where most of the flocks are greater snows, no snow-goose season will be opened until the larger race becomes more plentiful. A lesser snow is apt to weigh between 4 and 6 pounds, only a shade lighter and smaller than a greater snow goose, and for practical purposes the races are indistinguishable. Both have white plumage, rusty stains on head and breast, black primaries, saw-

toothed reddish bill with a black grinning patch, and reddish feet. The juveniles are grayish, with dusky bills and tawny-olive feet.

DISTRIBUTION: After Canadas, lesser snows are the most abundant of American geese. They nest from northern Alaska eastward along the upper Yukon and Northwest Territories, on Victoria Island, across the base of the Melville Peninsula, throughout the lower reaches of Baffin Island, and on Southampton Island at the top of Hudson Bay.

At the beginning of September they trend southward in a leisurely progression, some of them stopping for a whole month on the shores of James Bay. In October big flocks are spotted over the Rockies and fanning out above the California grainfields. There are early arrivals over Arkansas and on the Texas and Louisiana rice fields, but it is November before the geese swarm over the Gulf Coast and through central California. New flocks may still be arriving in December, as easily duped by white rags or stick-up decoys as were the first flocks. The finest hunting regions encompass California's grain lands and the Gulf Coast

Lesser snows near rice-field hunting sites in November.

from Florida's western tip and Alabama's Mobile delta across lower Mississippi, Louisiana, and Texas into northeastern Mexico. Large populations also winter in Nevada and Utah, and in the Mississippi Valley as far up as southern Illinois. For reasons not fully understood but thought to involve climatic changes, lesser snows are extending their range northward and eastward, a good portent for Atlantic Flyway hunters who would like to augment their take of Canadas.

GAME BEHAVIOR & HUNTING HABITAT: Snow geese eat rushes, berries, and insects in early autumn, but they prefer grains and grasses. Southern rice fields have become famous hunting grounds. Other important food sources on the Gulf Coast are cordgrass, panicgrass, and roots of cattails and bulrush pulled up in typical wildfowling marshes. At Utah's Bear River marshes the hunting is good near wheat or bulrush, and the birds also consume wild barley, buffalograss, glasswort, horsetail, and saltgrass. Like Canadas, they come to fields of rye, corn, soybeans, and sorghums. On the Pacific Flyway, fields of oats and barley are spread with decoys. Snows are addicted to the easy foraging in stubble.

They are often shot from a blind and over decoys intended for Canadas, but on the bogs, bars, and flats of the Mississippi delta many hunters draw in snows and blues with the simplest of mud decoys—mounds adorned with bits of white paper or rag. In California's San Joaquin Valley, pit blinds are favored in open fields, rice flats, and the fringes of marshland. "Shadow," or profile, decoys are sometimes used, but the classic Texas method is simpler, and so effective that it has become popular in fields from Mexico and Louisiana to Utah. The standard decoys are white rags—old bed sheets, napkins, shirts, and the like.

The best stool is a generous scattering of rags on a feeding field. Dispensing with a blind, the hunter himself becomes a giant decoy by camouflaging himself with a sheet or white coveralls. He lies on his back, and as flocks of snow geese pass over he sits up and fires fast. Those who have done it are entitled to an admission here that the position can put a strain on anyone whose muscles have lost the tone of adolescence, hampering a smooth gun swing and follow-through, but under a constant surge of geese most of us conquer hardship with obstinacy and

Hunter bagging lesser snow, and bringing in the birds.

liniment. The height of activity comes just after sunrise, and again shortly before sundown when the geese head back toward resting sites. During these peaks, even snows that have been flared by gunfire or sudden movement will often return shortly to the limp decoys.

VOICE: Lesser snows fly silently for a while, then one calls out, another answers, and soon the flock is singing. The cries are falsetto, sometimes nasal, honks, repeated over and over and punctuated by double-noted exclamations: *we-hongk, we-hongk.* A babble of murmurs, chattering, and honking often emanates from a feeding flock. The shrill honking can be mimicked vocally or with a mouth-operated goose call. A conventional imitation of Canadas will also toll in snows.

Blue Goose *(Chen caerulescens)*

COMMON & REGIONAL NAMES: *blue wavey, gray wavey, bald brant, blue brant, gray brant, silver brant, eagle-headed brant, Alaska goose, blue snow goose, blue-winged goose, white-headed goose, skillet-head.*

GAME IDENTIFICATION IN FLIGHT: The blue goose is a color phase of the lesser snow and is about the same size—4 to 6 pounds. It flies as fast as its white counterpart but with fewer gyrations. Flocks travel in broken combinations of chevrons, curves, and crooked lines or mix with flights of other geese. During the hunting season they are most often seen with their own kind or with lesser snows. In a flight of white geese, the dark bird—darker than the juveniles—is a blue goose. The common name for the breed derives primarily from the blue wing tone, while names like skillet-head and eagle-headed brant are reminders that it is the only dark-bodied goose with an entirely white head and neck. The cheeks and upper neck are almost always amber-stained, and the bill is like the lesser snow's, pink or reddish, with a white nail and black grinning patch. The orange, pinkish, or lilac feet are also like the snow's.

The white feathering ends irregularly and the lower neck is a dusky slate, blending into a grayish brown that is fairly even on the breast but with wavy cinnamon or ashy markings on the

upper body. The rump varies from blue-gray to white. The under-parts are slightly lighter than the breast on most blue geese of recently pure lineage but may be ashy or white on blue-snow crosses. The flanks are white, the tail slaty or grayish brown with broad whitish edging. The primaries are black, paling at the bases, the secondaries and tertials black with grayish or white edges, the wing coverts light grayish-blue patches with black and white streaks. The underwings are gray and whitish, finely speckled.

By the time of migration, first flight birds look rather like their parents, but their heads and necks are slaty tan, with a white patch only on the chin. The bill and feet are dusky and the plumage is darker than that of adults. Blue geese can bewilder a hunter with their color variations, a result of crossbreeding between the blue color phase and the more populous snow geese. In a flock composed mostly or entirely of blue geese, the color is usually dark. On the western fringe of their range, where a few blues are often included in a large flight of snows, some or all of the blues may be white-bellied or piebald.

DISTRIBUTION: Though interbreeding with the lesser snows is

Blue goose in shallows.

common, the blue's breeding range overlaps that of the white variety only on the western side. Large colonies of blues nest on Baffin Island, on Southampton Island in upper Hudson Bay, and in the Perry River section of the Northwest Territories.

By far the greatest concentrations winter on the Gulf Coast of a single state, Louisiana, where the goose shooting is excellent, but blues have vastly extended their range in recent decades. They now come to Texas rice fields in flocks of their own as well as with snow geese, and they also winter across the coast of Mississippi. In smaller numbers, they are bagged still farther to the east and north, together with lesser snows. In the future they may become common game birds on the prairies and perhaps on the Atlantic Flyway.

They begin to leave Baffin Island during the first half of September but dally along the way, particularly on the salt marshes of James Bay, where goose shooting is superlative during the earliest part of the season. At about the same time, other blues join migrating snows or depart by themselves, heading down the Mississippi Flyway in late October.

GAME BEHAVIOR & HUNTING HABITAT: The blues feed heavily at James Bay, and a good many come down again around Saginaw Bay in Michigan, an excellent hunting area, but they make hardly any other stops on the way to·the Gulf and are ravenous when they arrive. Up on the prairies they feed gluttonously on cattail rhizomes, grasses, and horsetail. On the Gulf marshes where blues are traditional game, close to half of their diet consists of bulrush rootstocks and seeds; the other important foods are cattail, cordgrass, saltgrass, and spikerush. Blue geese like to rest by day on the Mississippi delta mud flats, which have attained legendary status among goose shooters. Some of the flats, covered with dense stands of rice cutgrass, sorghums, and flags, are denuded each fall. Like snow geese, blues are fond of rice, but where snows do not outnumber them in the flocks, more blues are taken in marshes than in fields.

Blue geese usually show at least a passing interest in any goose or brant decoys but are most attracted by snows, and therefore any white object will lure them. The rag decoys used for lesser snow geese are standard on fields visited by mixed flocks. Even on the marshes, big scatterings of white decoys have worked well.

Standard goose guns and No. 4 loads are suggested, but the method of getting to a blind is slightly out of the ordinary on some of the flooded Gulf Coast swamplands. Around Louisiana's famous Vermilion Marshes, there are wetlands too soggy to be crossed with a conventional vehicle or on foot, yet with insufficient water for a boat. On navigable bayous some hunters use shallow-draft sneakboxes or air-propelled boats of the kind used in the Everglades; on quaking bogs, a wide-wheeled "marsh buggy," built on an old automobile chassis, is giving way to commercially produced amphibious "all-terrain" vehicles.

VOICE: Blues have a wide vocal repertoire. Hoarse, raucous honking and quacking are typical, and there is a high-pitched plopping sound that sometimes rises out of a gabble like that of greater snows. When the birds are feeding the gabble can swell into a canine yapping. The honks, quacks, and plopping sounds can be imitated with a goose call, which will attract both blues and snows. But loud honking should be avoided, since that is the blue's alarm signal.

White-fronted Goose *(Anser albifrons albifrons)*
COMMON & REGIONAL NAMES: *whitefront, specklebelly, speck-lebelly brant, speckled brant, pied brant, speckled goose, speck-lebreast, checkerbreast, checkerbelly, yellow-legged goose, yel-lowlegs, laughing goose, California goose, China goose, Texas goose.*

GAME IDENTIFICATION IN FLIGHT: As high and fast as Canada geese, a thin line or spearhead pierces the sky. The birds might easily pass for Canadas until they come close enough to reveal the splashed black-and-white breast plumage. Only when they are quite near can a hunter make out the yellow legs and little white face patch. Deliberation marks their approach. They cautiously circle, lower and lower, steady, almost silent, suspicious of decoys or possible blind locations unless the presence of other wildfowl allays their fears. When only 25 or 30 feet up, they suddenly begin an excited gabbling, flapping, tumbling, and straighten out just before alighting.

At close range, no hunter is apt to mistake a whitefront for either a Canada or a snow, but in general color and in the type of bill there is a close resemblance to blue geese. Were it not for the white head and neck of the blue, errors of identification would be common. The whitefront has a pinkish bill that blends into a light blue at the base, with pale orange about the nostrils and a slight black grinning patch. The head and neck are grayish brown except for a white forehead patch extending around the bill. It is only this small patch that justifies the name whitefront.

The body is mostly grayish brown, with pale barring and a lighter breast that fades to grayish white on the upper belly, which is marked with splashings and specklings of dark brown and black. Toward the rear, the belly whitens. White, too, are the flanks and tail coverts. The tail is dark, dull brown or gray, tipped with white. The primaries are black or ashy gray, the secondaries brownish black, the tertials and coverts mouse-brown edged with ashy white, the linings slate-gray. Birds of the year are more uniformly gray, and paler on their underparts. They lack the white face patch and black breast and belly markings. The bill is dull yellow or lilac-gray and without a grinning patch.

DISTRIBUTION: The specklebelly, as it is commonly called by American and English gunners, probably has a wider global range than that of any other goose. In the Western Hemisphere, nesting grounds span the upper parts of Alaska, the Yukon, and the Northwest Territories east to the Queen Maud Gulf, and the southwestern coast of Greenland.

Whereas lesser snows and blues have expanded their domain eastward, white-fronted geese have retreated westward. They wing toward winter quarters in September and October, following the Pacific and Central flyways to Washington, Oregon, California, and a large west-central portion of Mexico, and coursing down the Mississippi Flyway to the Gulf Coast of Texas and Louisiana. A few winter as far north as British Columbia. Substantial numbers sometimes arrive in California early in September but "soft" weather can delay migration until October. They are plentiful throughout the West during the hunting season, drifting down all the flyways and fanning out to permeate wetland

bivouacs from the Pacific to the Mississippi. One of the great hunting areas is at the Big Bend of the Platte River in central Nebraska, where specklebellies, sandhill cranes, and assorted other migratory game birds gather in force each autumn and spring.

GAME BEHAVIOR & HUNTING HABITAT: Whitefronts like to roost on the shallows of ponds, lakes, rivers, and bays. They can tip up to reach aquatic plants but prefer to graze on land. Observations as they passed through Oklahoma during a fall migration indicated that they feed heavily on wheat during the hunting season there. On the Gulf in winter they seem to rely to a considerable degree on panicgrass and sawgrass, but they probably were influenced by heavy hunting pressure on the stubble fields. In California, rice accounts for up to a quarter of the fall and winter diet; various grasses and sedges are equally important, and barley and wild millet also attract specklebellies.

They are elusive when traveling alone, but mingle freely with other species and are influenced by them. In the Sacramento Valley, where they often feed with cacklers and snow geese, they can be hunted simultaneously by the methods used to hunt snows. They are also quite likely to come to a Texas rice field with flocks of snows, and seem to be attracted to the rag decoys that entice the white geese. On the Gulf Coast marshes—and marshes on the flyways to the north—hunting specklebellies is

"Specklebelly" view of white-fronted goose.

often a matter of pass-shooting from a reed blind or the concealment of growing vegetation, with or without goose and duck
decoys.

VOICE: Hunters on some of the western marshes call the whitefront the "laughing goose." Its cries are like hysterical laughter
or the eerie hooting of loons. Rapid and clanging, the flight notes
come in long, quavering sequences—*wah-wah-wah-wah-wah-
wah*. No mechanical call reproduces the laughter, and few hunters learn to mimic it. While circling to come down, the birds
grow quiet, and if whitefronts are the only birds passing over,
silence is probably the best hunting tactic.

Tule Goose *(Anser albifrons gambelli)*
COMMON & REGIONAL NAMES: *tule whitefront, timber goose;
all names (except Texas goose) applied to the white-fronted goose
(see page 295).*

GAME IDENTIFICATION IN FLIGHT: The tule goose is a large,
localized subspecies of the whitefront. By the time a tule comes
within gun range, it looks considerably bulkier than an ordinary
specklebelly and, indeed, it is between 20 and 30 percent larger.
It has a noticeably longer neck, a total length of about 30 inches,
a wingspan of twice that figure, and a weight of 5½ to 7½ pounds.
Tule geese fly lower and in smaller groups than other
whitefronts, and often come over as singles or pairs. They are
less vociferous and much less cautious, frequently swooping low
over decoys in a silent, headlong approach, without any prelimi-
nary circling. Their coloration is darker than that of whitefronts,
particularly on head and neck. But there is an intergrading in
size and hue—probably due to occasional hybridizing—and the
whitefront description (see page 295) fits the tule goose.

DISTRIBUTION: The word "tule" refers to several large species
of bulrush that flourish in sprawling tracts called the tule
marshes, or tule lands, around the junction of the Sacramento
and San Joaquin rivers in California. The name is also loosely
applied to cattails and other marsh plants. Until recent times
the rushes, supplemented by cattails, furnished the primary food

and cover for the tule goose, but their importance has been diminished by grain farming, and the name is now more indicative of the tule goose's wintering region in the Sacramento Valley than of its dietary selectivity.

The breeding range is unusually small, covering only the Perry River area of the Northwest Territories. Even more restricted is the wintering range. Arriving in the Sacramento Valley during September and October, the geese settle on tule marshes near fields of barley or wheat. The best hunting areas are on the Sacramento and its tributaries, above the confluence with the San Joaquin.

GAME BEHAVIOR & HUNTING HABITAT: In the early morning, when most other geese are already on the stubble fields, tules often fly low over ponds, wooded sloughs, and marshes shielded by high rushes, cattails, and willows. As the morning wanes, they sometimes settle on watery resting spots and remain inactive until late afternoon, when all of the wildfowl again take off in search of food. They are more likely to feed then with other species on the fields as well as in the marshes.

A conventional marsh blind or a simple platform in a high, dense tule thicket offers ample concealment for hunting, but it is not really necessary to have a blind at all in areas where a boat can be pushed in and hidden among the tules. During the active periods of the day, pass-shooting can be productive. The site can be enhanced by the use of goose decoys—either dark or white—with or without a spread of duck blocks to imitate locally plentiful species. In the fields, a pit blind is recommended, whether for pass-shooting or to use with stick-ups. Tule geese sometimes make low passes over decoy spreads, and the various species of geese seem to urge one another on as they succumb to the blandishment of a stubble field.

VOICE: The tule's laughing flight call is noticeably louder but less frequently uttered than that of the whitefront. The tone is also coarser—abrasive. Landings are accompanied by very little cackling, and the birds sometimes approach in silence. Even the feeding gabble is relatively subdued. For most of us, the best hunting tactic is either silence or the sparing use of a wooden call in imitation of Canadas or snows.

GENERAL DESCRIPTION & DISTRIBUTION: ". . .snow white birds, glistening in the sunlight . . . their long necks pointing northward toward their polar home, their big black feet trailing—their broad translucent wings slowly beating. . ." Thus the naturalist Arthur Cleveland Bent described swans, largest of American waterfowl.

The cygnets of this continent's wild swans—whistlers, feral mute swans, and the great trumpeters—all are grayish brown, and yearlings are termed gray birds. The shadow vanishes early in the second year of life. Tannin or other waterborne substances sometimes tinge underparts and slender necks with russet but the unstained plumage of both sexes is as white as the winged constellation Cygnus. Even if there is no chance to see the black-pointed lance of outstretched neck or the black feet against the tail, recognition is certain, for the absence of black wing tips separates swans from snow geese or other large white water birds trading over a blind.

The wingbeat is deep and slow, yet swans fly faster than any of the ducks or geese. Whistlers—at this writing the only swans legally hunted in America—are probably the fastest of the three breeds. In Montana, Nevada, and Utah, special permits authorize a limited number of wildfowlers to take one whistler each during the duck season, and these men almost always find that their targets are higher, faster, trickier than they seem. Whistlers can cruise at nearly 60 miles an hour and are capable of 80-mile-an-hour spurts.

Migrating swans often reach an altitude of 8,000 feet and rise considerably higher if wind or weather prompts them. On feeding waters they are restless and gregarious, making short, low, swift flights to group and regroup. They are slow only when pattering over the water to gain takeoff momentum or during a sailing descent. They often set their wings while hundreds of

Whistling swan in flight.

yards from a destination, circling, tipping, gradually settling.

All American swans were fully protected for many years after the signing of the Migratory Bird Treaty in 1918. Mute swans, originally imported from Europe, have never spread far from the East Coast, and trumpeters remain relatively scarce. However, in some areas where the effects of land drainage and market shooting were least severe, or where the refuge system has been outstandingly successful, a resurgence of whistling swans has had to be balanced with habitat and competing species. This is why several thousand a year are now taken in three states.

Some whistlers breed as well as winter in these states, but the species nests chiefly along the western and northern coasts of Alaska, the upper Yukon and Northwest Territories, and the shores of Hudson Bay and the arctic islands. Male swans —cobs—battle ferociously for a chosen female, or pen. Mated for life, they zealously guard their bulky ground nests on lowlands near water. Most clutches number from two to seven eggs.

Migration begins in September and early October. Considerable numbers follow the Pacific Flyway down through California to Baja, while still more fly southeastward across the continent. Vanguard flocks reach the eastern seaboard in October, followed by innumerable waves until rafts of thousands appear on Chesapeake Bay or some Virginia impoundment or North Carolina sound. In most years the majority of all American swans can be found wintering on this part of the Atlantic Flyway. The long ban on shooting has transformed them into brazen idlers, preening within shot of duck blinds and poking about decoy rigs, yet once they rivaled black ducks in wariness—and they may do so again.

The mute swan was brought to America as a "park bird," and here, as in Europe, it sometimes reverted to the wild. Swans are irascible, and when mature their flesh is tough, but ill temper and epicurean mediocrity are counterbalanced by the elegance of serpentine neck and frequently arched wings, doubled in stately reflection on smooth water. Feral flocks now breed on Long Island, along the New Jersey coast, and in the Hudson Valley. Some wild mutes undertake short migrations, extending their range up into Massachusetts and down through the Chesapeake region.

The trumpeter faced extinction in 1933, when the last thirty-

Whistlers taking off, trumpeters on nest.

three specimens were counted at Red Rock Lake in Montana. A few years later Red Rock became a national wildlife refuge. With habitat improvement and game management, the population mounted. Several hundred trumpeter swans nest there now, and small but viable populations exist in Oregon, Wyoming, Idaho, South Dakota, Alaska, and the Canadian Rockies. Unlike whistling swans, trumpeters never were abundant, but their slow increase continues and they are no longer endangered.

GAME BEHAVIOR & HUNTING HABITAT: Though whistlers and other swans often hoot vociferously in the air, they feed in comparative silence. They are indifferent to whether water is fresh, brackish, or salty, but prefer shallows where they can dip their long necks to the bottom or tip up like dabbling ducks to extend their reach. In western marshes where whistlers can now be hunted, important foods are pondweed, horsetail, bur reed, and

Whistlers crossing within range.

various grasses. Wild-celery roots, widgeongrass, and foxtail are favorites in the East. Whistlers are voracious and they root up their food plants, sometimes severely damaging a duck-hunting area. They also eat small shellfish and insects. Mute swans are partial to the same types of vegetation but are not sufficiently widespread to threaten duck habitat significantly. The huge trumpeters, too scarce to be competitive, rely most heavily on sage pondweed, water buttercup, arrowheads, rushes, and mosses. All swans feed more or less destructively along the margins of bays, ponds, and lakes.

Mute Swan *(Cygnus olor)*
With the neck stretched in flight, a mute swan averages between 50 and 60 inches in length. Its wings stretch more than 7 feet. It weighs between 20 and 30 pounds—more than the whistler, less than the trumpeter.

Cygnets of all three species have dusky bills, but that of a yearling mute swan becomes suffused with a flesh color and then turns orange or pinkish red, tipped and edged in black and with a black fleshy knob at the forehead, easy to distinguish from the knobless bills of other American swans.

The mute has a peculiar posture, habitually riding higher in the water than the others and often arching its neck in a flowing S-curve with the bill inclined downward. Whistlers and trumpeters usually hold their necks and heads more erect unless preening or feeding. All swans can raise their wings in a sweeping arch while on the water but the position is most pronounced and frequent among mute swans.

The species is misnamed. All swans tend to be quiet when feeding or at rest, but they will hiss in anger or warning. A female mute swan can also bark like a small dog to call her young and may trumpet exuberantly in the spring. The myth of an eerily modulated dying call, the "swan song," has persisted since before the time of Plato, but swans lack the vocal apparatus for musical modulation.

Trumpeter Swan *(C. buccinator)*
Averaging more than 65 inches in length and 28 pounds in weight, with a wingspan often exceeding 8 feet, the trumpeter dwarfs

Mute swans on East Coast.

all other North American waterfowl. Audubon recorded one that weighed over 38 pounds and spread its wings nearly 12 feet. A mature trumpeter's bill is almost entirely black, but with salmon-red edging.

The call is a loud, low-pitched, resonant note, followed by several higher, softer notes. It has been compared to the lowest tones of Canada geese.

Whistling Swan *(C. columbianus)*

Mature whistlers are usually over 50 inches long, have a wingspan of about 7 feet, and weigh 16 or 17 pounds. A bird that looks like a whistler but weighs more than 20 pounds is likely to be a small trumpeter, probably a female. An adult whistler's bill is black, and sometimes there is a yellow spot on the featherless skin fronting the eye.

"Whistling" hardly describes the call, which has the mellow tone of an archaic wooden flute and is sometimes interspersed with whoops, clucks, murmurs, honks, and clucking chatter.

Each autumn, attenuated lines of whistlers rise from the northern muskeg and tundra, sometimes 500 birds in a wavering file. As migration gains momentum the birds separate into small flocks, probably family groups. Countless tight wedges descend over coastal marshes, often to the consternation of duck hunters and the rage of clam dealers. Predation of soft-shelled clams by swans has been exaggerated, but whistlers do injure duck habitat and interfere with hunting. When they tear up a mud flat or sit among decoys, ducks and geese may flare off. Feeding swans may also attract ducks but can scare them off, as well.

If an occasional whistler fell to a Magnum No. 2 load from a full-choked 12-gauge fowling piece, swans would soon have to be coaxed into range by huge white decoys such as once floated on Currituck and Pamlico. Those swan blocks sometimes rode to one side of a duck or goose rig as confidence decoys, a stratagem that might be revived if swans were legal game there. Perhaps within a few years seasons will be opened on the coasts as they have in Montana, Nevada, and Utah, with a turkey-style single-bird limit for permit holders. When hunted, swans soon regain their slyness, flaring at the slightest movement in a blind and retreating like shreds of white cloud across a bay.

Shore & Marsh Birds

Lesser Sandhill Crane *(Grus canadensis canadensis)*
COMMON & REGIONAL NAMES: *little brown crane.*

DESCRIPTION & DISTRIBUTION: Arriving over eastern New Mexico and western Texas in October, loose lines and chevrons of sandhill cranes are often so high that the birds look no bigger than high-flying geese. Still, the cranes are easy to recognize by their fluting, rattling flight calls, their very long, outstretched necks, and their long black trailing legs. Their manner of flight is equally distinctive—a hawklike glide alternating with vigorous flapping. They flick their wings up, above body level, rather than lowering them in the deep, bowed downstroke of herons and some of the other large marsh birds. Hunters watch with eagerness tinged by the recollected dismay of frequent misses. At the end of the month, when the season opens in much of this area, there will be great shapeless clouds of cranes, as well as columns and V formations. On windy days many will fly low, but among crane hunters the word "low" sometimes means just within range of a 10- or 12-gauge Magnum, choked full or modified and full, and firing heavy loads of No. 2's.

Pecking about in stubble or wading the shallows on its stiltlike legs with knees bent backward, its long inner secondaries tufting over its short tail in a bustle that distinguishes it from herons and egrets, a crane does not look capable of powerful flight. It stands over 3 feet tall and moves with stiff deliberation. Yet hunters hope for a head wind and some shoot only while a crane is gliding, for then the bird is probably traveling at less than 45 miles an hour; with a tail wind or when flapping hard, it can hit 60. Some hunters also listen for the whistle of wind through primaries, a fair indication that the target is close. A typical mature lesser sandhill is a 7- or 8-pound bird with

Sandhill cranes in New Mexico, rising with great clatter of wings.

a wingspread of 5 feet or more. While still out of range, it can look as if it means to land on the blind. There is no use in relying on the old goose shooter's trick of waiting to make out the eye; even with geese it is no guarantee, and a crane's eye is larger. Several misses are the rule before most hunters begin to judge the range and lead their targets adequately—by several bird lengths.

Although game regulations and hunters often refer to the subspecies by the name "little brown crane," only juveniles are predominantly brownish. An adult has black-tipped brownish-gray flight feathers, soft gray underwings, a dark gray back with rusty feather tipping, and mouse-gray underparts, paling on belly, neck, and head. A bald, bright red cap extends from the long, pointed, blackish bill back over the eye. Birds of the year lack the red patch, but both males and females acquire it at maturity, and the sexes are indistinguishable.

There are two scarce and protected subspecies, the non-migratory Florida sandhill crane *(G. c. pratensis)* and the greater sandhill *(G. c. tabida)*. A greater sandhill can be told from a lesser only by size: It stands over 4 feet tall, is apt to weigh 15 pounds, and may have a 6- or 7-foot wingspread—but fortunately the races inhabit different ranges. The lesser sandhill breeds in Siberia, Alaska, and northwestern Canada, migrates chiefly along the eastern slopes of the Rockies, then fans out to widely scattered wintering grounds from the Gulf Coast across the Southwest to central California. The greater sandhill nests from Oregon to Michigan and migrates chiefly to the west and north of the lesser's winter domain. An intermediate strain (intermediate in size as well as range) is called the Canada sandhill; interbreeding must be common, but the Canada sandhill has recently been described as a separate subspecies *(G. c. rowani)* by the ornithologist Lawrence Walkinshaw.

Federal regulations restrict crane hunting to states where only the abundant lesser sandhills are usually found during the hunting months. Alaska's season (with a daily bag limit of two) generally runs through September and early October, when the migrating birds are still plentiful in the North. Lesser sandhills are legal game in federally stipulated parts of eight other states—North and South Dakota, Montana, Wyoming, Colorado, New Mexico, Oklahoma, and Texas. The bag limit is three. Open-

ing day in each district depends on average migratory and arrival dates, and seasons in some places last almost to the end of January. Probably the best shooting is to be had in eastern New Mexico and western Texas, where the scattered crane populations begin to concentrate as winter progresses. The greatest density may be around the Muleshoe Wildlife Refuge, southeast of Muleshoe, Texas, near the New Mexico line. Cranes begin to appear there in October and keep arriving until more than 10,000 have gathered.

Hunter crouching in hiding spot near stick-up crane decoy.

As with many birds, fall and spring migrations follow slightly different routes. By March, more than 200,000 sandhill cranes—the majority of the total population—funnel northward onto a 60-mile stretch of the Platte River between Lexington and Grand Island, Nebraska, where warm ground water causes an early thaw and shallow sand bars provide ideal roosts. From these "staging grounds" they head north in March and April. If sportsmen and other conservationists continue to thwart recurrent "reclamation" plans, including proposals to divert the river, sandhill cranes should remain in good supply.

GAME BEHAVIOR & HUNTING HABITAT: By May, cranes are breeding on northern tidal flats and around prairie potholes. The nests are grass-lined scrapes on lowland knolls. Cranes are seasonally monogamous and the male helps to incubate the eggs —usually two—which hatch in late May or June. The precocial young can soon roost with the adult birds in shallow water far enough from shore to minimize predation. They are strong fliers by August. Beset by the same enemies as geese and swans, they are equally hardy and seem to have comparable longevity.

Heatherberries and lemmings are among their foods in the North, and in temperate regions they obtain protein from grasshoppers, snails, frogs, aquatic insects, and so on, but they are remarkably vegetarian for marsh birds. The hunting is good where bur reeds, grasses, and various aquatic plants thrive near farmlands. During migration and in winter quarters they rely heavily on corn, sorghum, wheat, rice, or other grains, making daily flights to stubble fields.

Hunters in some regions have revived the old practice of using stick-up crane decoys. Since the birds are exceedingly gregarious and inquisitive, decoys can work well if they are set naturally about fields and if the hunters remain well hidden. However, cranes are also exceedingly shy. They can spot movement, a man's face, or a glinting gun barrel 3 miles away over fairly flat terrain. In many areas they learn to flare from automobiles more than a mile away. Many of the gunners in New Mexico and Texas leave their cars far from the blinds. Pit blinds are popular, but constant shooting in a small area can detour foraging flights, so a degree of hunting mobility is required. A shooter may crouch in a brushed gully or a drainage or irriga-

tion ditch, or he may use a natural blind or pile sagebrush or tumbleweed against a fence or embankment.

Sandhills prefer surprisingly shallow roosting waters. On the Platte and some other rivers they roost on barely submerged sand bars moated by deeper channels that deter terrestrial predators. They spend their fall and winter nights on farm ponds, sloughs, wide streams, potholes, and the shallow, temporary playa lakes of the Southwest. A blind is well situated near such a roost and between the water and grainfields or wet meadows. Though the big flights occur in early morning, and again in late afternoon when the birds return from feeding, some activity continues through the day on the wintering grounds. Singles and

Texas hunter running for downed, but lively, crane.

doubles come over, as well as small groups of a few or a dozen and occasional flocks of forty or fifty. Windy, overcast days make for good pass-shooting. On bright, still mornings the cranes may circle over their open roosting waters until they gain tremendous altitude, and shooting will be good only where they descend to feed.

VOICE: Sandhill cranes do not respond well to calling, but they do announce their approach with loud, low-pitched flight calls. The sound is a monotonous, liquid fluting—*k-r-r-rrroooo, ku-r-r-r-roooo*—irregularly punctuated by a soft, throaty clacking or rattling.

American Coot *(Fulica americana)*

COMMON & REGIONAL NAMES: *common coot, freshwater coot, marsh hen, mud hen, rice hen, crow duck.*

DESCRIPTION & DISTRIBUTION: When a duck hunter arrives late on a midwestern wild-rice lake—with sunrise coming and legal shooting hours already begun—he can compensate for lost time as he poles through the plumed stands toward decoys left in place the previous evening. With gun loaded and close at hand he watches black, ducklike marsh birds paddle away, heads bobbing like the heads of gallinules; the coots retreat from his advancing skiff into the tall, swaying grass. At the edge of open water three of them panic and run across the surface, their big feet splattering, their wings flapping in an effort to get airborne. Finally they are flying, 40 or 50 yards out, low but accelerating. The gunner fires twice and brings one down.

Later, if he is lucky, some Indian harvesters may come beating through the rice, pushing out ten or fifteen times as many coots. The flock will line across the water in the same running takeoff and some of the birds will rise into range. At Back Bay, Virginia, and in California's tule marshes—almost anywhere in the country—other hunters will see coots. Some will reject them as hardly worthy to be called game; others, lacking the chance convenience of wild-rice harvesters to flush their coots, will do a bit of jump-shooting amid the rushes. The initiated know that the coot is a tasty bird when skinned and trimmed

of fat, that it flies as fast as a pheasant once aloft, and occasionally, unexpectedly, can ride a low, buffeting wind almost with a canvasback's 60-mile-an-hour speed.

The American coot is 13 to 16 inches long, with rounded wings and a superficial resemblance to a duck. It belongs to the family of rails and gallinules—*Rallidae*—and is the sole American member of its subfamily. Its olive legs are longer than a duck's, and its toes are not webbed but individually fringed with spatulate lobes for paddling, diving, plodding through reeds, walking over floating vegetation. In the air its legs trail behind its stubby tail, dangling slightly and providing one of several identifying marks for a hunter who must decide quickly whether to shoot. It is the only ducklike marsh bird that appears black or blackish with a white bill. The undercoverts of its tail show as a white patch and the tips of its secondaries form a thin, white line along the rear edges of its flapping wings. The thick, short, white or whitish bill has a couple of brownish spots near the nail and a brown extension, or frontal shield, running up

Flock of ducklike American coots.

the bird's forehead, as on gallinules, probably for protection from cutting blades of marsh grasses.

The sexes are alike: black heads and necks, blackish or dark gray bodies fading slightly on the underparts. Juveniles are a paler gray and have duller bills.

The flight seems labored and is almost invariably low—no more than 5 yards off the water. Coots migrate in small clusters, sometimes even alone, attaining much greater altitude, but the migratory flights are mostly nocturnal and seldom seen. Upon reaching their wintering places, coots congregate in flocks, sometimes very large flocks, and are found more often on the water or on a shoreline than in the air.

More numerous than any of the duck species except mallards and pintails, they breed in lower Alaska, the Canadian provinces, and the northern states, mostly from Indiana westward, but with a few colonies in the East. Some also nest in the South, and there are resident populations in Latin America and Hawaii. The northern, migratory coots, though they winter chiefly in the Gulf states and on the Pacific Coast, use all the flyways and are plentiful enough for good hunting almost everywhere. Flocks continue to swell from October into winter. Seasons in most states are long and conform roughly to duck seasons. A bag limit of twenty-five is normal on the Pacific Flyway, fifteen in Alaska and on the Central, Mississippi, and Atlantic flyways. Limits are generous because coots are underharvested and in many areas they are overabundant.

GAME BEHAVIOR & HUNTING HABITAT: Nesting occurs as early as April in warm regions, as late as June in parts of the North. Breeding behavior is somewhat like that of ducks, marked by displaying, squabbling, and chasing until pairs are formed. The female builds a floating nest basket, attached to reeds or rushes or on a raft of vegetation. She incubates her clutch for about three weeks, while the male guards the territory. The eight to twelve eggs do not hatch together, and the male seems to tend some of the first young to emerge while awaiting completion of the brood. The young—queer little black creatures with fiery-orange heads—quickly become self-reliant. Being late migrants, however, some coots die in unseasonable freezes. In matters of predation, disease, and longevity, they are comparable to most large marsh birds and to ducks.

They eat a few insects and small shellfish but subsist during the hunting season almost entirely on aquatic vegetation and shoreline seeds and grasses. Like dabbling ducks, they prefer surface feeding in the shallows; however, they also walk the banks or swim out a little way and dive, particularly where emergent plants screen them. The jump-shooting is good wherever coots are attracted by preferred foods: naiad, pondweed, bulrush, wild rice, widgeongrass, muskgrass, or wild celery. Though they nest on fresh water, they winter on brackish or salt bays and estuaries, as well as freshwater rivers, marshes, bogs, shallow ponds, reedy creek pools.

They are far less wary than ducks, yet seldom come to decoys since they do not locate their own kind from the air. The true purpose of the coot blocks used on some waters is to attract ducks, which often feed or loaf with coots. The ducks flush if the coots show alarm, and in most cases probably escape while a predator pursues the slower coots. Sometimes coot blocks are used together with duck decoys, and sometimes jump-shooters put up a teal, mallard, or scaup together with coots.

The surest hunting method is to walk, pole, drift, or scull a reed-choked shoreline. A flock strung out in the shallows will flush a few at a time, but the birds tend to swim before rising and are sometimes out of range midway through the lumbering takeoff. One way to overcome the difficulty is to approach from open water, herding birds toward shore, where they lift more readily. Another is to work with several hunters and boats, driving coots to open water, ringing them, and trying passing shots as they rise, higher than usual, to break out.

VOICE: Coots are no more attracted to calls than to decoys, but they are sometimes located in dense reeds by their rough, noisy, guttural clucking, grunting, and croaking.

Common Gallinule (Gallinula chloropus)

& Purple Gallinule (Porphyrula martinica)
COMMON & REGIONAL NAMES: *water chicken, mud hen.* For common gallinule—*Florida gallinule, American gallinule.*

DESCRIPTION & DISTRIBUTION: The common gallinule and the less abundant purple gallinule are quite alike except in coloration and distribution, and neither is a great game bird. Nonetheless, a "water chicken" can discomfit an overconfident hunter. It usually happens on a coot or rail hunt, for these species occupy the same habitat. A man walks the rush-fringed shore, sculls along the cattail edges, or takes his ease on a rail-boat seat, while his pusher silently slides the skiff through wild rice with a long, splay-ended pole. Gallinules are as reluctant to flush as rails, and birds of one kind or the other may skulk invisibly through the thick vegetation. The hunter looks toward a sound of clucking and rustling. Instead of a rail or coot, a red-billed bird with the body and cackling voice of a small chicken skitters across an opening, struggling to rise, and takes off through a sawgrass veil.

Its flight is slower and lower than a coot's. As the hunter mounts his gun, the bird skims along the sedge tops and suddenly drops straight down out of sight before he can fire. His next effort will be quicker, cutting a swath across the grasses to collect a gallinule.

A long-legged, long-toed wader that can walk on lily pads,

snake through rush tangles, swim strongly, or dive from sight, a gallinule is a marsh bird with a length of 12 to 14 inches or so. The undercoverts of its abbreviated tail form a white patch. Its chickenlike but colorful bill merges into a wide, hard frontal shield—protection from sharp grass—that runs up to the crown. It swims with its head nodding, walks daintily with its bill down and tail up, lifting its legs high, runs with its body stretched forward and wings raised for balance like a startled barnyard hen, and flies laboriously with its legs trailing and dangling. It can, however, fly higher, straighter, and moderately fast when migrating or when crossing land from one pond to another.

The common gallinule has a bright red frontal shield and bill, tipped by a yellow nail. The upper parts of its legs are also red, but grade into dull greenish yellow above the first joint. Its plumage is slate-gray, washed on back and scapulars with olive-brown, paling on the belly. It is dark-headed and dusky-

Common gallinule (l.) and
purple gallinule, showing immense feet.

winged, but the wing edges and outer webs of the first primaries are white, and a long white streak runs along its sides. The sexes are alike, but juveniles are duller, paler, with brownish bill and frontal shield.

Still browner and paler is a juvenile purple gallinule, which has no white stripe. An adult has a yellow-tipped red bill and a pale blue or bluish-white frontal shield. The legs are yellow, the head, neck, and underparts deep purplish blue. The wings and tail are dusky, with bluish-green outer webs. The back is olive- or bronze-green, browning toward the rear.

The common gallinule breeds from upper New England and the Great Lakes southwestward to central California and down through most of the United States, the West Indies, and parts of South America. Birds in the northern portion of the range migrate in September and October; some of those in warmer locales fly farther south in October and November. The North American populations winter chiefly in the lower states, from southern California to Georgia, South Carolina, and points south. Especially plentiful in the marshes of Alabama, Mississippi, and Louisiana, they are also found in most other states during some part of the wildfowling season, since they move down all the flyways. As with coots and rails, bag limits are generous.

The purple variety has a much smaller range in this country. It breeds from the Southeast and the Gulf states down to Ecuador, and winters from the Gulf Coast southward. It is strangely scarce in Florida, where, at this writing, only common gallinules may be taken.

GAME BEHAVIOR & HUNTING HABITAT: The breeding behavior of gallinules is rather similar to that of coots, except that the male shares in the 3-week incubation of six to twelve eggs. The nests are constructed of dry reeds, flags, or rushes, usually hung amid reeds a foot or two over the water but sometimes on a floating mat or mired log. There is, of course, predation by snakes, crows, and other enemies. Land drainage is a more serious threat but, in spite of severe habitat reduction, common gallinules remain plentiful.

They are primarily seed-eaters, though they also feed on insects, worms, and shellfish. Plants that attract them include rice, wild rice, windmillgrass, knotgrass, and duckweed. Like rails, they often thread favorite paths through thick stands of marsh grasses—good places to put up either species. The edges of open water, where emergent grasses end, are also promising, and there coots may flush as well.

Gallinules do not gather in true flocks, but sometimes ten or twelve are found fairly close together in a small feeding area. They can be harvested with the open-bored guns and small shot used for rails or with the heavier loads used for coots.

VOICE: Gallinules are more active than rails in the daytime and often announce their presence noisily. They have a wide repertoire of harsh, chickenlike clucks, cackles, and grunts.

Rails *(Rallinae)*
COMMON & REGIONAL NAMES: *marsh hen, mud hen, meadow hen.*

DESCRIPTION & DISTRIBUTION: A shallow-draft skiff slithers along at high tide, nudging rails out of the tall aquatic grasses. Standing on an oversized stern seat, a guide or experienced hunter, called a pusher, poles the boat forward swiftly. On the platform with him may be a retriever. The shooter stands near the bow or uses a high gunner's seat affixed nearer the center thwart. The pusher's view is higher than the gunner's, and he watches intently for a flush. Whatever species of rail is prevalent on the marsh, he may speak of it as a marsh hen or mud hen, but there is nothing derisive in his tone. "Mark left," he calls, and a dangle-legged bird comes up out of the stalks as if trying to run through the air.

The gunner tracks his target over open water, waiting it out and then almost spot-shooting when the rail nears thick rice or cordgrass. The bird lifts its wings straight up and drops straight down out of sight, as rails often do after a short flight and before a shooter can catch them. But this rail hits the water on its side and the pusher grins and tells the dog to fetch. Or, if a double has flushed, he may toss out a painted float to mark the first fall, while he watches the second. Downed rails can be lost in thick growth.

There are several protected species, all so tiny that there

is no danger of mistaking them for a huntable rail. The four that are classified as game range in size from the sora, which is comparable to a quail or meadowlark, to the king rail, which is twice as large. All are wading birds that prefer running to flying, and all fly so low and feebly before the gun that some hunters scorn them. Others discover that rail shooting is seldom quite so easy as it looks. Amid tall, dense wild rice there is sometimes little room to swing a gun, and the view of the bird may be fleeting. On a flooded salt marsh, rails pitch into cordgrass after just a short flight. They wobble and sometimes wheel, and a rail shooter learns to "read" his birds, timing his shots to their expected actions but not leading them; he must stay right on each target, holding a trifle low, because a rail seems to begin descending almost from the instant of rising. And if the pusher is not strong and skillful enough to stop the skiff and keep it still when birds take off, success is uncertain.

Rails in profile are plump, deep-bodied birds, but they can thread their way through dense reeds and rushes because they are so compressed laterally as to have inspired the expression "thin as a rail." They are mostly brown or gray, with short, rounded, brownish wings and stubby, cocked tails that show a white undercovert patch. They have long legs for wading and—except for the sora, a relatively herbivorous species—long, slightly downcurved bills for capturing insects and plucking up shellfish. The four game varieties are the sora *(Porzana carolina),* clapper *(Rallus longirostris),* Virginia rail *(R. limicola),* and

king rail *(R. elegans)*. The clapper and sora are by far the most abundant and most hunted.

Rails on the Pacific Coast are not widespread or plentiful enough to be harvested. Federal migratory-bird regulations permit rail hunting on all three of the other flyways, but the sport is traditional only on the Atlantic Coast from Connecticut southward and on the Gulf Coast. Because rails are underharvested, the daily limit on soras or Virginia rails—or a combination of both—is generally twenty-five. (Limits on Virginia and king rails are academic, since both species are so shy and solitary that no one sees more than a few in a full day.) In Connecticut, Rhode Island, New York, New Jersey, Delaware, and Maryland, the limit of twenty-five is complemented by a 7-bird limit on clappers or kings, or both; in a larger number of southern Atlantic and Gulf states the sora-and-Virginia limit of twenty-five is complemented by a clapper-and-king limit of fifteen.

The open season in most northern states lasts from early September into early November, by which time most of the birds have flown south. Many rail populations are sedentary, or nearly so, as far north as the mid-Atlantic states, but they are fundamentally migratory birds. Although the season in some southern states corresponds to that in the North, it is more commonly set from early November (when migration is virtually complete) through early January. But rail hunting—particularly clapper and sora hunting—is good only during a few hours of a couple of days each month when tides are so high that the birds have little or no solid ground on which to run.

When the water is low, they hide in the thick marsh grasses, and skulk or run at the hunter's approach. When the water is very high, it submerges the thickest cover, and rails are often plainly visible; even in stands where they can hide, running is impossible. Since they feel safer flying than swimming, they flush. On the salt marshes of the Carolinas and Virginia, it is possible to bag fifteen clappers in an hour, but only during the highest flood tides that come at the full moon and new moon. Veteran hunters at Barnegat Bay, New Jersey, seem to do equally well when a nor'easter blows the tide abnormally high, but the efficacy of such factors depends on locality.

Rail shooting is a traditional sport in a number of East Coast areas. Sora hunting has always been excellent on the Con-

King rail, reluctant to flush.

necticut River, near Essex, Connecticut, and on the Patuxent in Maryland. Nearer the sea, in the Connecticut marshes sprinkled around Nell's Island, close to the mouth of the Housatonic, a hunter may move a few Virginia rails as well as soras. The marshes near Cape May, New Jersey, hold soras and clappers. Virginia's freshwater marshes hold lots of soras, and her salt marshes are rich with clappers. Perhaps the best of all clapper marshes stretch from Beaufort, North Carolina, down to the South Carolina line and from Charleston down to Port Royal Sound in South Carolina. Clappers are also plentiful around St. Simon's Sound in Georgia, around St. Augustine and Tampa in Florida.

The sora—sometimes called the Carolina rail, Carolina crake, or chicken-billed rail—is the smallest of the group and the most widespread. It breeds across most of Canada and the upper United States; it winters from the lower fringe of the nesting regions—Kansas, Illinois, Long Island, New Jersey—down through the West Indies and Central America to Peru. It prefers to nest on fresh marshes, but it winters on fresh, brackish, or occasionally salt marshes.

It is a plump rail, 8 to 10 inches long, with a 13- to 15-inch wingspread. The bill is short, thick, and yellow, with a bit of black at the tip. There is a narrow black patch in front of the eyes and down the throat. The crown, hindneck, and back are olive-brown, with thin white streaks and wider dark ones along the back. The breast and the sides of the head and neck are pure gray. The belly and flanks are crossbarred with white and dark gray or olive, and the legs are light yellowish green. The sexes are alike, but juveniles are buffy and without the black frontal patch.

Clappers occur chiefly on the Atlantic Coast (though there is a Pacific subspecies), breeding from Connecticut to the Carolinas and wintering from New Jersey to Florida and on the Gulf Coast west into Texas. They are the most plentiful species on the grassy southern salt marshes. A typical mature clapper is 14 to 16 inches long—about the size of a coot. It has a very long, slender, slightly downcurved, dusky-yellow bill. The head, neck, back, and breast are pale, olive-tinged ash, with brown streaking on the back. The throat and a streak over the eye are whitish. Like most rails, the clapper has thin white and broader dark crossbarring on the flanks and belly from legs to tail. Its

Sora rail (top) and rail hunter with guide.

legs are pale gray-green. Juvenile clapper, Virginia, and king rails are darker than adults.

The Virginia rail breeds across lower Canada and the upper United States and winters from the southern states to Guatemala. A little larger than the sora, it has the crossbarred belly, brown-streaked back, and white eye streak and throat of most rails but is rustier-looking than the clapper, with a rich chestnut breast. The legs and long bill are reddish.

The king rail is the largest, measuring about 15 to 19 inches long, with a wingspread of more than 2 feet. Its long bill is yellowish and dusky on ridge and tip, and its legs are dusky greenish or brownish. Its breast is somewhat lighter than a Virginia rail's, its back more olive-tinged, but its appearance is very similar except for size. It breeds from the Great Plains eastward and winters chiefly in the southern states. The king, like the Virginia rail, is sometimes flushed from sora meadows or waters, but it prefers habitat of a more inland character. Along the coast it is bagged almost exclusively on freshwater marshes like those around Currituck Sound.

GAME BEHAVIOR & HUNTING HABITAT: Rails build ground nests in wet meadows or reed nests over marsh waters, lay eight to twelve eggs, and have precocial young that hatch mostly in May and June after a 2- to 3-week incubation. Their mating habits, life span, diseases, and predation are much like those of the other marsh and shorebirds described in this book.

Kings, clappers, and Virginia rails subsist chiefly on insects and shellfish, supplemented by seeds and—in the case of the king—tubers such as arrowhead. Soras eat less animal matter and more seeds. They are flushed most often on fresh or brackish tidal rivers, where they can feed on wild rice, bulrush, and sedges. Virginia rails seek the same plants but often on more brackish waters. Clappers, salt-marsh birds, are fond of cordgrass.

When an old Connecticut pusher mentions oats, he means wild rice. The best way to hunt soras is to push through rice at high tide. Tall, long-leafed, tasseled, pale green—the wild rice stands out like bamboo groves among the common brown and ocher aquatic plants. Early in the season a pusher may look for the darkest husks, because rails like ripe seeds. Later he may also look for openings where the rice has been flattened

by boats or wind; the birds are drawn to the easy feeding on downed stalks and floating seeds.

Regardless of which rail species is prevalent, a good pusher knows productive spots where birds return each year, and he has scouted the marshes in late summer, noting where the most calls were heard. Rails will be there long past opening day.

A rail boat should be pushed along swiftly, forcing the birds to fly. Even then some refuse, lowering themselves into the water until only their heads show. They may flush close or after the skiff passes. When the water is down, a briskly moving man can walk up soras or clappers on flats, along tidal creeks, and on grassy islands. Birds can also be flushed by a retriever or a springer spaniel. Some hunters leave their skiffs to walk exposed islands. They wear waders or sneakers, and are resigned to getting wet, if not to the possibility of stepping from knee-deep water into a head-deep, tide-hidden creek.

In Connecticut's thick wild rice, shooters prefer the dense patterns of very small shot—No. 10 or 11 when they can get it—but on the more open Carolina cordgrass marshes they use No. 8 or 9. Skeet loads are fine and a 20- or 28-gauge gun is sufficient. It should be cylinder- or skeet-bored.

VOICE: Soras whistle and cheep; clappers tick, cluck, clack, and squawk; Virginia rails grunt, tick, and make a sound almost like

Virginia rail.

a duck quacking; and kings grunt and cluck, rather like Virginia rails, but with a deeper pitch.

Wilson's Snipe (Capella gallinago, formerly classified as C. delicata and Gallinago delicata)

COMMON & REGIONAL NAMES: snipe, jacksnipe, common snipe.

DESCRIPTION & DISTRIBUTION: Even when the rubber boots drag like anchors, there is quiet pleasure in slogging over water-skinned snipe meadows while the earth is still green though the trees are copper and gold. The dog goes along. She is not flawed by the aversion of some retrievers to fetching snipe, woodcock, or soras, and sometimes she points a jacksnipe lying as close as a woodcock. More often a bird flushes before it can be scented, catapulting from behind some little hummock that makes an island in the inch or two of water filming the boggy ground.

Snipe rarely flock, but on a good day they may be sprinkled through the swales. Nocturnal migrants, they materialize one morning, swelling the numbers of resident snipe, then disappear again a week or two later as mysteriously as woodcock or soras. But they are faster than woodcock. If they are not quite so swift as teal, their small size and superlatively erratic flight produce an optical illusion of exaggerated speed. Their size also makes them seem beyond range while they are still well within gunshot. A common embarrassment is to shoot behind a snipe and then forgo a second attempt because the bird already looks too far away. The initial phase of escape flight after the hurtling flush is low, twisting, zigzagging. The jacksnipe is among the most bewildering of wingshooting targets. Since it is subjected to little hunting pressure, Federal regulations permit a daily limit of eight, but we seldom fill the limit. We congratulate ourselves at scoring three birds for five or six shells.

The Wilson's snipe is the American subspecies of a bird more often hunted in Europe. It is a migratory shorebird closely related to the woodcock and sometimes mistaken for that uplander. However, its body is trimmer than a woodcock's. It has longer, narrower, more pointed wings, prominent dark striping on the head, and a tail that looks orange in flight.

The sexes are alike, and juveniles are recognizable only on close examination of their drab feathering and pointed primaries. A typical snipe is about 9 to 12 inches in length, with a very long, slender bill of a dusky flesh color. The tip of the upper mandible turns down over the lower one. The head, neck, and upper breast are pale tan, longitudinally streaked with brown. Two broad, brownish-black stripes run from the bill up over the crown and down to the nape. The back and sides are a mixture of brownish black, chestnut, and buff, with white edging that forms lateral streaks. The wings, too, are a blend of rufous brown, black, and white. The belly is mostly white, with brown transverse streaking on the flanks. The legs are greenish gray. The wide, stubby tail is orange-brown with a black subterminal band and white tipping.

The North American race breeds from upper Alaska across most of Canada and as far down as California and Colorado in the West, Pennsylvania and New Jersey in the East. A few snipe winter in the middle tier of states, but most seek milder latitudes—from the southern states to Brazil. Since they probe spongy ground for insects, as woodcock do for worms, frost spurs autumn flights. Snipe are migrating through the upper states by mid-September, stopping so frequently that some arrive in the South in December and stay only a couple of months.

Early fall snipe hunting is productive in much of Canada as well as in the upper states, where a typical season lasts from the first days of September to early November. On the Pacific Flyway the season is more commonly from October to the beginning of January, and in parts of the Deep South the snipe is purely winter game. The meat is tasty but meager—an average bird's live weight is less than half a pound—and the heavy work of bog walking has never gained the popularity among sportsmen that it had among market shooters. There are no truly renowned snipe resorts, but the birds travel along all the migratory flyways used by waterfowl, and are plentiful enough to be hunted in a majority of states.

GAME BEHAVIOR & HUNTING HABITAT: Breeding peaks in May and June in the North, earlier in warm regions. A hunter who rambles on marshy meadows in the spring may see the courtship

flights of snipe, which resemble the circles and dives of wood-cock, or he may flush a hen from a grass-lined nest in a tussock, where for eighteen or twenty days she incubates her four darkly streaked and speckled olive-gray eggs. A strong similarity of breeding patterns, enemies, and mortality is exhibited by the snipe and woodcock (see page 115).

As with woodcock, a hunter may find sign in autumn—the same chalky dropping spatters and the holes drilled by long, flexible beaks probing the ground for food. Snipe feed in boggier habitat, however, and their prey is less often earthworms than insects, insect larvae, and freshwater snails. They also eat some vegetation and may be flushed from smartweed, bulrush, panic-grass, sedges, or other marsh plants.

Before land drainage and market shooting devastated the game, decoys were effective where snipe and other shorebirds occurred in very large numbers. Decoys are no longer used, nor are dogs employed as commonly as in former times. But a dog is of some help in finding birds and can be essential for retrieving where snipe fall amid willows, brush, or tall grass.

Wilson's snipe.

Wintering snipe sometimes find shelter and food in woodcock alders, birches, or maples near water. But productive habitat usually consists of quiet, open, short-grass bogs, flooded meadows, swamps, and grass patches about marshes or on stream, lake, and pond shores. To a snipe hunter the finest terrain is a meadow with a thin film of water over most of it and with scattered hummocks, tufts, or brush to provide cover. The birds linger on brackish and salt marshes as well as fresh water.

The best way to hunt snipe is to move with the wind. They almost always jump into the breeze, then fly against or across it. A missed snipe will occasionally climb high and dive right back, almost at the hunter, so there is reason to stay and await developments after a poor shot. Snipe also tend to return to a resting or feeding spot soon after fleeing from intrusion. A hunter develops the habit of coming back in a little while to the place where he flushed birds.

Some hunting books advise shooters to fire as fast as they can at wild-flushing snipe, the theory being that the targets are too difficult for long shots and pass beyond range in a moment. Yet a seasoned expert waits out his birds, having observed that snipe usually twist and zigzag for only 10 yards or so, then straighten. He pulls the trigger as flight becomes direct, and gets a preponderance of crossing targets, broadsides that are easier than incoming or outgoing twisters. When he flushes his bird from windward, he knows it will most likely fly toward him and past him before flitting out of range. If it gets away, he marks it down and quickly flushes it again.

A man who knows snipe likes to carry a 20- or 28-gauge double gun with improved and modified borings, and his shells are loaded with No. 9's or even smaller pellets; the range is shorter than it seems, and dense, wide patterning is needed.

Two hunters can put up birds by moving together along opposite edges of a swale, but the windward man will have most of the shooting. Several hunters can take turns driving and standing, with the stander in front of the nearest water or at a gap in a tree line. Once a snipe has smoothed its flight, it seeks gaps and heads for water.

VOICE: Snipe sometimes broadcast their presence with chirps and low, nasal rasps. When flushed, they utter a harsh squeak.

Small Game/6

Bobcat *(Lynx rufus)*

COMMON & REGIONAL NAMES: *wildcat, bay lynx, red lynx, pallid lynx, desert lynx.*

DESCRIPTION & DISTRIBUTION: A stalking bobcat is the essence of silent stealth. A treed bobcat is a back-crawling sight —20 pounds of disdain or hissing ferocity with the pointed ear tufts of some mythical woods demon and wildness itself lighting the vertical black pupils of the golden eyes. Some men devote decades to the breeding and training of cat hounds, while others take justifiable pride in tolling bobcats into range with a predator call. But apart from these coteries of specialists, few hunters ever glimpse the mottled brown blur of a bobcat dissolving into shadowed cover, though plenty of bobcats gaze at passing hunters in most parts of the country. More often than not, *Lynx rufus* is an invisible presence. Amid arid western canyons where cats are numerous but snow is rare on the dry rimrock and lava rubble, a lifelong outdoorsman may never have seen a cat track.

With predator poisoning and bounties at last being discredited, bobcats can maintain a stable population or multiply as their prey multiplies. In some places where rabbits and deer have increased after mature forests gave way to small second-growth timber and brush patches interspersed with openings, bobcats are more abundant than they were a century ago. They are also infiltrating farmlands from which they were long absent, because grain attracts small rodents and rodents attract cats to the brushy edges of fields. After one or two raids on poultry and small livestock, a rancher or farmer is eager to kill a cat or hire a trapper. However, vendettas are no longer frequent because most bobcats avoid human habitation, resorting to domestic prey only if wild prey is scarce.

Except for enclaves along the Mississippi and Ohio rivers

Bobcat refusing to stay treed.

and in the Appalachians, the cats have not returned—perhaps never will—to the central and lower Midwest or to the Southeast above lower Georgia and the Gulf Coast. These two barren regions aside, the animals range from coast to coast and from southern Canada into Mexico. The best bobcat hunting is in the Far West, from Washington down to Baja and as far into the interior as Idaho, Nevada, and Utah.

There are eleven subspecies of bobcat—geographic races that differ in size and coloration. Generally speaking, the largest cats are northern; the darkest, most strongly marked are those of northern woods and southern swamps. As with horses, the word "bay" designates a reddish-brown shade, and the cats of the Northeast are often called bay lynx or red lynx (the latter being a literal rendering of *Lynx rufus*), while western and southwestern cats are often called pallid lynx or desert lynx.

A bobcat looks larger than it is, especially in winter when the coat is long and thick. A typical mature male stands a little less than 2 feet high at the shoulder and a female is slightly smaller. Length averages 3 feet or so and weight usually ranges from 15 to 30 pounds, but 50-inch cats are not uncommon; a trophy Colorado cat weighing 69 pounds was taken in 1951.

Light or dark, the basic reddish, grayish, or yellowish brown color becomes grayer in winter. The fur around the eyes is usually white or whitish, as are the muzzle, chin, underparts, and the underside and tip of the stubby tail—a thick 4- to 7-inch "bobtail" that gives the species its most common name. The nose is tawny pink, the lips black. Thin, often broken, black lines radiate back along the muzzle, up from the eyes, and out along the cheeks onto a broad ruff on each side. Dark or black horizontal bars generally mark the upper legs and vertical slashes sometimes mark the body, but flecks and spots predominate, giving the more strongly marked subspecies a somewhat checkered appearance. Two or three wide black bars cross the top of the tail; the rearmost bar is widest, bordering the white tip. The large, triangular ears, jutting out and up, are light in the center but rimmed with black and tipped with thin, upstanding black tufts.

GAME BEHAVIOR & HUNTING HABITAT: A bobcat would not survive in the cold upper realm of the Canada lynx but can adapt to a much wider array of habitat—mountains, woods, deserts, swamps, farm country. Almost any region may offer good hunting if it is not too densely settled, has plenty of rocky or brushy cover, and supports enough prey.

One reason cats are seldom seen without the aid of dogs or a mechanical dying-rabbit call is that they are nocturnal. From dusk until a little after dawn (unless they are sated) they stalk what prey they can find by sight or sound. Scent is less important, yet bobcats are too cautious to be fooled by a wooden call if they wind the hunter. Calling is most productive very early in the morning and at dusk from a brush clump, amid rocks, or on an elevation, a hiding place commanding a wide view. A strong breeze is a detriment because no one can be sure what approach route a bobcat will choose. A hungry fox or coyote sometimes rushes headlong through an opening, whereas a bobcat—even though it likes to hunt abandoned roads and old trails—will probably make at least one wide, slow circle.

Total frustration is to blink away sweat, straining to see the vaguely checkered pattern of a slinking bobcat, nearly invisible against brush, earth, or mottled rock, only to have the animal sense danger and fade away or spin out of its low-bellied crouch before the sights are up. In some situations little can be done about scent, but an experienced caller gives nothing else away. The key is to stay motionless and silent except for the calling, repeated frequently in an operatically prolonged rendition of a rabbit's demise. Camouflage clothing is a good idea, and many hunters wear headnets or daub their faces with dirt. If, despite all precautions, a half hour or so goes by without response, move on. Any cat within a mile would have heard the squealing.

Rabbits and hares are staples, but bobcats will comb appropriate locales for mice and rats of all kinds, pocket gophers, ground and tree squirrels, chipmunks, marmots, turtles, frogs, lizards, mountain beavers, muskrats, prairie dogs, opossums, skunks, raccoons, and assorted birds but especially ground-nesters. The cats are hunted with intensified zeal when they have been marauding quail, ruffed grouse, sage grouse, or turkeys, but such depredations seldom threaten game-bird populations. The same statement can be made with respect to deer. Though a big wildcat has the strength and weapons to pull down a full-grown whitetail, there is a marked preference for easy kills. It is most unusual for a bobcat to attack any deer weighing more than a hundred pounds, and predation nearly always occurs in winter when the smallest, weakest yearlings can be culled from yarded herds made vulnerable by snow and hunger.

Bobcats are more reluctant than most predators to eat carrion, but they will try to cache a deer carcass or other large kill by sprinkling twigs, leaves, and grass over it, and they will usually return at least once. A hunter who discovers a fresh cache has discovered a stand that may produce a bobcat if he hides and waits for dusk.

Porcupines are also numbered among the prey, and the cats evidently suffer only minor damage from the quills, but nothing more dangerous is stalked. Under ordinary circumstances, a bobcat will not pounce on a badger, much less a man. Attacks on humans are very rare and invariably are made by animals surprised at a fresh kill, or females defending their young, or hopelessly cornered or rabid cats. Most females will abandon their young in an effort to lead an enemy away instead of fighting.

Rabies is no more prevalent among bobcats than among many other species. A few die of distemper, and a virulent type of mange can kill the kittens. Other afflictions include the usual internal and external parasites. Predators such as owls and cougars may catch a kitten or half-grown cat now and then, but not often. Few enemies will attack a wildcat.

Good hounds are a courageous exception. A bobcat would rather run from a dog than fight but can kill a hound three times its size and will take on several or a dozen when necessary. A dog that becomes overconfident and careless for an instant can be disemboweled by a rake of the extended rapier claws. The cat's snapping teeth, long, sharp, set in powerful jaws, are almost equally dangerous.

Some fine packs consist of nondescript dogs, but in the East foxhounds are favorites, and in the West—where the same dogs may trail a bobcat or a cougar—foxhound-bloodhound crosses are popular. They need great stamina, fine scenting ability, strong voices, pugnacity, and an instinct for wolflike teamwork that will keep a furious cat at bay.

The finest hound work is done on snow: a fresh snow that displays only last night's tracks, a light snow that will not hinder progress. Under those conditions a hunter can scout old roads,

trails, brushy draws, rocky slopes, the known resorts. His dogs can help if the search becomes wearying, but ordinarily he will release them only on a fresh track. Without snow, many hunters prefer to put down only one hound—an especially sharp-nosed "strike dog." The others are turned loose when the strike dog calls "hot trail."

During the day a bobcat "lies up" in a rock cleft, in a thicket, under a blowdown, in any convenient hideaway. Desert cats survive the heat by using caves, crevices, and recesses shaded by overhangs. A cat may have traveled only a short distance the previous night or may have prowled several miles through a vague territory. It will seldom hunt the same spots for two nights running, but revisits favorite vantage points where it can watch for prey—a boulder, ledge, or low tree crotch ideal for pouncing on small game. The dogs may find strong scent at such spots though the cat has been long gone. There is no way to be sure whether the pack will jump a cat from its lie almost immediately and tree or corner it within 200 yards, or take most of the day to close with the quarry. Sometimes they

North Carolina bobcat at bay.

lose one trail and pick up another while the exhausted hunters try to estimate distance and direction by the pack's voice, hoping to catch up soon after the hounds bellow "treed."

Some hunters follow the hounds as best they can, on horseback or afoot, hoping not to lose the pack as well as the game. In the northeastern woods and some of the thickly brushed southern areas, where a cat tends to run like a fox in a rough, wide circle, hunters often take stands at openings, ready to make a quick shot at a crossing. Large packs seem to be favored in the South, partly for the purpose of hemming in an evasive cat and partly to handle one that will not stay treed. In the North and the open terrain of the West, many hunters have consistent success with only two or three dogs.

Opinions differ sharply regarding guns. The predator-calling purist may install a 2½-power scope on a carbine or light "varmint rifle"—one of the .22 centerfires—for long shots, and will take pride in being able to sight the same rifle fast in the event of an unexpectedly close, sudden approach. The man who goes on stand where his hounds may push a cat out of the brush at high speed will choose a full-choked 12-gauge shotgun, prob-

ably loaded with an ounce and a half of BB's or No. 2 or 4 Buckshot. The man who walks up to a tree or rock ledge can bring a bobcat crashing down with an open-sighted .22 rimfire rifle or pistol, preferably with hollow-point bullets.

Some hunters carry no gun unless a cat has been sampling poultry or small livestock. Not everyone agrees that bobcat tastes a little like veal—there are those who call it inedible—and not everyone wants a cat pelt for the den. An old caller in Texas counts coup when his shutter clicks to film his trophy, and there is a Florida hound fancier who says that a fox run to ground or a cat treed should be left to run again. Much can be said for restraint, though the bobcat population is not endangered by hunting for sport.

Bobcats are solitary creatures, but the males are sexually active all year and will travel 20 miles to find a mate. Most females are in oestrus in February or March, and the litters, averaging three kittens, are born a couple of months later in rock dens, in hollow logs, beneath windfalls, in root holes, occasionally in mine shafts and abandoned houses. They are weaned in a couple of months, learn to hunt with their mother in late summer, and

Eager hound in tree with bobcat.

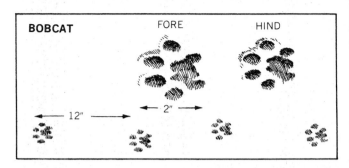

BOBCAT   FORE   HIND   12″   2″

strike out on their own by winter. Acknowledging that they kill more rats than chickens or grouse, some states have at last accorded them the status of game animals to insure the maintenance of a huntable population.

TRACKS & SIGN: The tracks of a 20-pound bobcat are comparable to those of a middleweight hound or a bird dog, about 1¾ to 2¼ inches across and often slightly longer than wide. Since the claws retract, no claw marks are left—but a dog print sometimes shows no claw marks, either. If the print is clearly outlined, look at the front of the heel pad. That of a dog, coyote, or wolf is convex in front, while the rear edge is scalloped into two or three lobes. A bobcat's heel pad likewise prints three lobes at the rear edge but is also concave—lobed—at the front edge.

It is a generality, true enough but far from invariable, that a bobcat sets its hind feet on the prints of its forefeet, thereby leaving a very narrow trail that looks as if it were made by a two-legged animal. The cat evidently does this because it can only see where to place its forefeet noiselessly; a similar placement of the hind feet ensures silence, and evolution has endowed the animal with an ideal stalking gait since a cat hunts as it travels. Often, however, the rear feet merely come down close to the front prints and are not superimposed.

A cat establishes scent posts (a means of communication with other cats) by urinating; the spots are visible in snow but can be identified only by the tracks. Scat looks like a dog's droppings when it is visible at all. The bobcat usually buries its scat but sometimes only scrapes a little dirt about, leaving identifiable scratch marks in the earth. Tree trunks are used for claw sharpening, and such scratching posts reveal that a cat has been in the vicinity. A freshly cached kill will be scantily covered by ground litter; the cat will probably return to it at least once if the hunter disturbs nothing and hides downwind.

VOICE: A bobcat's vocal repertoire is the same as a house cat's but considerably louder. It is generally silent when being trailed, however, and stories of its "hunting cry" are myths. Yet in late winter hunters may decide to scout an area where they have heard savagely wild, piercing yowls. It is the breeding season. Fights are few since the males tend to avoid one another, but mating is accompanied by tremendous caterwauling.

Canada Lynx *(Lynx canadensis)*
COMMON & REGIONAL NAMES: *loup-cervier*—European and French Canadian.

DESCRIPTION & DISTRIBUTION: Hunters seldom get a close look at the Canada lynx, a gray wraith slipping through timber where deep snows hamper pursuit. A lynx can crouch invisibly in the light-filtering sieve of a conifer swamp or flat on a thick tree limb, and it climbs trees habitually—much more often than its relative, the bobcat—using them to watch for prey and as ambush points from which to leap down on hares and other small animals along the game trails. A mature male commonly stands about 2 feet high at the shoulder and measures 3 feet or so in length. Females are slightly smaller. A 40-pound trophy has been recorded, but weight averages from 15 to 25 pounds. A lynx appears bigger than a bobcat only because of its longer, thickly furred legs and exceptionally large, furry paws, adaptations for climbing trees and padding through soft, deep snow.

Its body is smoky or silvery gray, usually with a weak intermixture of brown or tan and a few very faint black markings, but color and degree of darkness vary slightly among several subspecies, depending on primary regional habitat. The tail is black-tipped, bushier than a bobcat's, seldom more than about 4 inches long, and sometimes a mere stub. The upright black ear tufts, more pronounced than a bobcat's, are usually a couple of inches high, and the cheek ruffs are very large and sharply tipped, forming a double-pointed beard at the throat. The ruffs are light or whitish with black barring. The inner fur of the legs is also whitish, and there is a sprinkling of white on the muzzle, rimming the eyes, and in the ears. Typical heads show indistinct black lines.

The lynx was never abundant, but when winters were colder and forests were uncut it inhabited the northern United States. Its major range still covers Alaska and all of Canada, except the arctic barrens. Hunters still come across its tracks in Maine, upper Michigan, Wisconsin, Minnesota, Washington, Oregon, western Montana, and northwestern Idaho. A separate small group remains in the Rockies of Wyoming, Utah, and northwestern Colorado.

GAME BEHAVIOR & HUNTING HABITAT: The lynx is somewhat less nocturnal than the bobcat; in the Far North, where summer has little darkness and winter almost no light, it may hunt at any hour. Yet few of the cats are taken except by trap or snare. Much of the habitat is remote, some of it nearly inaccessible, and most of it lies amid dense evergreens and heavy snow. Hounds that trail cougar or bobcat will hunt lynx, and they are

used. But thick cover and deep drifts favor the game. Ironically, the lynx is a poor runner, incapable of reaching 15 miles an hour, even when it resorts to a rocking gallop punctuated by 12-foot leaps. More than once, coming across a lynx by sheer good fortune, hunters have outrun it, and a lynx jumped by dogs will tree very quickly.

The problem is to jump one. Trailing hounds soon tire in the drifts, and dry snow holds scent poorly. The hunters may have difficulty bulling their way through conifer swamps, and horses are often useless in such country. Snowmobiles have come into use where forests are not too dense, but many hunters will agree that mechanization impairs the sport, and the noise overwhelms the hound music and shatters the peace of the wilderness.

Sport is the only reason to hunt the lynx, despite its inflated deer-slaying reputation. A lynx will kill a small, winter-weakened deer (or caribou or sheep, for that matter), but its staple food is the varying hare. The lynx population grows and declines following the varying hare's cyclic rises and falls. The cats also feed on arctic hares, grouse, ptarmigan, lemmings, squirrels, voles, and other small inhabitants of the North.

Mating peaks in March, producing litters of three or four kittens a couple of months later in makeshift dens beneath tree roots, blowdowns, tangles, or in hollow logs. The young sometimes remain with the mother through their first winter, and tracks of family groups can create an illusion of many cats in a limited area. They hunt chiefly by sight and sound over small territories when prey is abundant; however, they do roam far in times of scarcity. Lynx will investigate the dying-rabbit squeals of a predator call but are not sufficiently numerous to tempt many hunters into taking a stand in the northern cold. Lynx meat is palatable but no great inducement.

Regardless of hunting method, long shots are so unlikely that any iron-sighted rifle of medium power will suffice. A treed cat can be dispatched with a hollow-point bullet from a rimfire, standard or Magnum, but most lynx trophies fall to deer rifles.

TRACKS & SIGN: Scent posts, scat, scratching posts, cached kills—all resemble the bobcat's (see page 340). But the tracks are much larger and quite round. There is nothing unusual about

Canada lynx searching for prey.

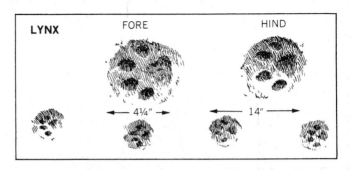

a print 4 inches wide, or more than 4 inches when the woolly toes spread and blur in powdery snow. The "straddle," or trail width, is almost as narrow as a bobcat's, seldom more than 7 inches across, but a lynx sometimes varies its normal short strides with a leap, as if practicing kills.

VOICE: Same as the bobcat's (see page 341).

Coyote *(Canis latrans)*
COMMON & REGIONAL NAMES: *prairie wolf, brush wolf, barking wolf, cased wolf, medicine wolf.*

DESCRIPTION & DISTRIBUTION: The Aztecs attributed supernatural powers to the *coyotl,* as did many northern Indians who knew the smallest American wolf by other names. Not many sportsmen relish coyote meat, as some Indians did, but those who hunt the species will agree that the coyote is among the cleverest of American game animals. No other carnivore has doubled or tripled its range despite man's intrusion (or because of it).

Though the coyote is not a migratory animal, it will follow concentrations of prey from place to place. Sometimes, too, when hunting and trapping pressure mounts or when food dwindles, it slowly probes new areas, traveling mostly by night. Even in daylight it can skulk across brushy flats or along river valleys and rocky draws without being detected until its hunting urge leads it up a ridge to be silhouetted on the skyline. A wiry, nimble

wild dog, built and colored for escaping large enemies as well as stalking nervous prey, it fades into a background of rock, desert sand, prairie grass, brushy timber. "Desert-running" hunters, relying on the patient technique of cruising and scanning, often have to make "bragging shots" at distant targets about a third the size of a timber wolf. There are also "bragging trophies" (almost invariably males) which are hard to tell from a wolf, and a few of these may be coyote-wolf hybrids or the coyote-dog crosses commonly known as coy-dogs. A coyote weighing more than 50 pounds is a rarity, the norm being between 20 and 25.

A mature male coyote is likely to be barely 2 feet high at the shoulder and 3 feet long—or a foot or so longer when his brushy tail floats out behind as he breaks from a dog-trot to lope out of gunshot. He would look like an undersized German shepherd dog if it were not for his narrow, pointed, almost foxlike snout. The rough coat tends to be browner in summer, grayer and much thicker in winter, darker in the wooded North, paler in the arid South; in many regions the basic tannish- or buff-gray color varies considerably, from the ocher of wild hay to dusty brown to the gray of tree bark. The black tips of long guard hairs sprinkle the body, and there are usually rusty shadings about the muzzle, ears, and legs. The underparts and muzzle rim near the black lips and nose are pale, or even whitish.

Coyote mousing in snow.

Unable to compete with timber wolves, coyotes were formerly confined to the plateaus, prairies, and deserts west of the Mississippi, from southern Canada to central Mexico. But they followed the settlers' livestock down to the grasslands of lower Central America and up onto the high Canadian meadows and mountain parklands. They now populate Alaska, where they were unknown before the Klondike Gold Rush, and have spread through western and southeastern Canada. They have also come to most of the states east of the Mississippi, though hardly in huntable profusion except for limited northern pockets, where they seem to be multiplying, filling the ecological gap created by the extermination of wolves.

GAME BEHAVIOR & HUNTING HABITAT: A blend of slyness and audacity has helped the coyote to outlive an era of poisoned baits, traps, and bounties, and to flourish in proximity to man.

Virtually anywhere, February is a supreme month for coyote hunting, not only because pelts are prime and snow discloses tracks and sign, but because the rut is at its height. During the breeding season coyotes are most active and least wary.

Hunter using predator call for coyotes and bobcats.

Moreover, pairs and small groups are seen more often than at other times, even though coyotes occasionally hunt in pairs or family groups throughout the year.

Strangely, whelping tends to be somewhat later in the South than in the North. Most litters are born in April, after a gestation of about 60 to 65 days. The female usually digs more than one den, and then may decide on a natural cave, a log or culvert, or may enlarge an abandoned badger or fox burrow. Usually, however, her den is a conspicuously wide-mouthed tunnel, a foot or two in diameter, anywhere from 5 to 30 feet long and terminating in an enlarged nesting chamber. Favorite sites are riverbanks, well-drained slopes, and the sides of gulches or canyons. If the area is disturbed she will move the pups (about half a dozen in an average litter) to a new den. But a hunter who locates a den and refrains from going near it has reserved a good hunting site for fall or winter; though the den will be empty, the locale will be frequented. In sandy or soft-dirt areas, a den is sometimes found by the tracks radiating from the mound of earth marking the wide entrance.

Mated coyotes frequently remain together for several years, and some probably mate for life although a few are polygamous. The potential life span is perhaps ten years, but not many coyotes survive half that long in the wild. The behavior of a family pack is much like that of wolves. The male has little to do with the young at first, but he does bring food. Pups usually are weaned when they are between five and eight weeks old. Soon the den is abandoned and the pups tag along as the parents wander and hunt. Most families gradually disperse in early fall, but sometimes the young stay together, with or without parents, through the first winter.

No longer is the wolf the coyote's major enemy in the northern part of the range, but pups and half-grown coyotes may be attacked by cougars, bears, great horned owls, and golden eagles. More insidious population controls include summer drought and severe winter weather (which can devastate the food supply), mange, tularemia, distemper, rabies, and all the internal and external parasites that attack canines.

When rabbits are in good supply, they are the dietary mainstay. Carrion, mice, rats, ground squirrels, marmots, prairie dogs, and other rodents, together with a few unwary birds, make up the remainder of the basic diet.

Heavy stock depredations are almost always the work of a few rogues, usually coyotes that have escaped from traps and are unable to catch wild prey because of leg injuries. In the West, many ranchers are at last treating coyotes as valuable game animals, having discovered that they help to control jack rabbits and undesirable rodents, whereas their extermination has little effect on losses of lambs, kids, calves, and poultry.

Coyotes need water, and sometimes dig for it in a dry wash, but a cruising or predator-calling hunter will probably have better luck on high ground overlooking a water hole, particularly at dusk. Predators come there both to drink and to lie in wait for prey. Few hunters seem to realize that coyotes eat more vegetation—particularly fruits—than most predators. It pays to scout areas that offer both fruit and flesh: orchard edges, prickly-pear patches, mesquite, hawthorn, juniper, chokecherry, and so on.

A coyote cannot outrun a jack rabbit or a pronghorn fawn that is more than a couple of weeks old, but two coyotes will often pair to kill difficult prey. They run in relays to tire an animal, or one of them waits in ambush while the other herds the victim. Being intelligent opportunists, coyotes also use badgers as involuntary hunting partners. Mutual caution prevents fighting as a badger digs for rodents while a coyote waits to pounce on any prey that eludes the badger by emerging from an escape hole at the far end of a burrow. Digging areas are good places to hunt for coyotes, as are prairies and meadows used by gophers, prairie dogs, or marmots.

If prey is plentiful and hunting pressure reasonably light, a coyote may spend its life within a few miles of the den where it was born. Like the wolf, it hunts habitual runways, meandering routes that may snake out for 10 miles over the home territory. Such runways and their environs can sometimes be recognized by tracks, scat, scent posts, den sites, or bones and other debris that have been buried and then dug up for later use. However, a hunter must bear in mind that a coyote frequently leaves its runway, and the entire area merits scouting. Equipped with binoculars and a light but accurate "varmint-caliber" rifle (one of the centerfire .22 bolt-actions or something in the 6mm to 6.5mm class, mounted with a 2½- or 4-power scope and sighted in at 150 or 200 yards), a hunter can cruise coyote country on

foot, on horseback, or in a sturdy vehicle with four-wheel drive. Some hunters use their prairie-dog or chuck rifles, while others prefer the rifles they use for pronghorn or deer or larger game; either type will serve well. Accuracy—high velocity to produce a low long-range trajectory—is more important than power. For winter cruising or coursing (chasing game on open, relatively flat terrain), snowmobiles are quite sporting since the coyote has a better than even chance of eluding pursuers. The same cannot be said of aerial hunting, even where the law condones it. The only excuse for shooting any animal from a plane or helicopter is to eliminate predators in isolated instances when they are preying heavily on local domestic stock.

A hunter cruising the prairies or running the desert must be alert for sign (unless he has prior knowledge that coyotes are in the vicinity) and for distant targets. Probably the most common shot is at a silhouette on a ridge or hilltop. Coyotes favor elevated lines from which to spot enemies or prey.

Hungry coyote racing toward dying-rabbit call.

Those who have never hunted coyotes with dogs may wonder why scent hounds are seldom used. The reason is that few scent hounds can overtake a coyote, though once in a while they are employed to find fresh tracks and put a pack of sight hounds within coursing distance of the game. Even the speedy sight hounds—whippets, greyhounds, wolfhounds, Scottish deerhounds, and various crossbreeds—often fail to outdistance a coyote before it vanishes into scrub or rocky mazes. A light snow helps, since it enables the hunters and dogs to pick up a trail again after losing it. The average successful chase lasts a mile or two and ends when the coyote begins to tire, abandons more or less straight flight, and takes to running in tight circles. Whether the hunter is mounted or in a vehicle, he strains to catch up before the hounds close in and finish the coyote in a bloody fight. It is a matter of fast shooting at short range, using a rifle, a pistol, or even a 12-gauge shotgun loaded with No. 2 or 4 Buck.

Predator calling furnishes another kind of suspense, and is often more productive. Windless days are best, as coyotes are likely to come upwind toward the call and they are not only exceptionally keen of eye and ear, but so sharp-nosed that they can sniff out mice. Some of the best coyote areas are treeless, but where trees grow near trails, water holes, or any good rabbit or rodent habitat, it is hard to understand why more predator callers do not use a wide limb or crotch as a stand. Little or no scent drifts down, nor do coyotes look for danger from above, and a treed hunter has a good view of all approaches. Bluffs or brushy slopes above water holes are also excellent calling stands.

It must be admitted that a coyote will be tempted by a rabbit squeal almost regardless of the spot from which it emanates. Wearing camouflage clothing, a hunter need only find a place with a good view where he can conceal himself. The best calling times are early morning and late afternoon or evening. After half an hour or a little more, a hunter might as well try elsewhere, watching for unexpected targets as he moves. A hungry coyote often dispenses with caution and dashes toward the call. Since range and speed are unpredictable, the most practical arm is a light, fast-handling rifle in a varmint caliber, equipped with a low-power scope.

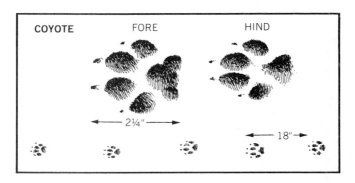

TRACKS & SIGN: A coyote leaves smaller, narrower tracks than a dog of comparable size, but they are not so dainty as fox prints. Still, in country frequented by dogs or foxes, coyote tracks can be hard to recognize. Typical foreprints are about 2¼ inches long and perhaps 1¾ inches wide—slightly larger in snow or soft mud. Hind prints average about ¼ inch smaller. A walking stride is apt to measure about 13 inches; a trotting stride may be almost twice as long, and stretches to 30 or even 40 inches at a fast lope or run. A running coyote also makes occasional leaps, spanning 3 feet or as much as 3 yards.

On dry, rocky terrain, tracks may be scarce until the first snow, and a hunter may not be certain about the identification of any tracks he does find. But scat and scent posts can be found along the narrow, somewhat meandering trail of a coyote. The scat is like that of any dog, except that it is often quite full of hair and is usually deposited right on a runway—most likely where the trail comes over a hillock or crosses a small flat or opening, the places where a coyote lingers to look for prey. Scat commonly accumulates where a couple of trails meet or cross. A dip in a ridge would be a likely place, or a saddle between ridges. Like other canines, coyotes urinate on trees, bushes, stumps, rocks, grass tufts. These scent posts are not always easy to spot unless freshly used, but since they are visited repeatedly they mark good locales for stands.

VOICE: The coyote's song is a higher-pitched version of a wolf's typical howl, most often lasting only ten seconds or so but sometimes considerably longer. Coyotes answer one another, and no one who has heard them doubts that howling sometimes is a means of signaling or locating hunting partners or members of a family pack. Whether it starts right off as a smooth wail or is preceded by a few short yaps, hoots, and yowls, it most often ends with sharp yaps sometimes described as notes bitten off the tail of the refrain. Barking alone, without any howling, seems to be commonly used as a threat display. A hunter who hears it can figure that he is probably not far from a den or prized bit of territory. It is pure bluff and an indication that hunting ought to be good in the locale.

Gray Fox *(Urocyon cinereoargenteus)*
COMMON & REGIONAL NAMES: *tree fox, Virginia fox, grayback, swamp fox, mane-tailed fox.*

DESCRIPTION & DISTRIBUTION: No animal seems better attuned to the woods than a gray fox, a rust-washed patch of dusk oozing through the brush. Yet red-fox purists belittle or curse the species. One reason is that where gray foxes are numerous, red foxes tend to be scarce, for grays are more aggressive and tolerate no close competition for prey. But since grays prefer forest habitat and reds are adapted to the fringes and partially open terrain, they can thrive in the same general region. In such cases it is not for lack of effort that fewer grays are taken. Most hunters fail to tell one kind of fox track from the other, and some remain in doubt when they glimpse the animal. Only in a race with hounds is the gray inferior. The excitement seldom lasts more than an hour, and sometimes only a few minutes, because the gray fox is relatively short-legged and soon tires. The only American canine with real tree-climbing ability, it scrambles up a leaning or thickly branched tree or it holes up when pressed. Often enough, however, it eludes hounds and hunter by plunging into dense cover, weaving through every thicket and tangle at 20 or 25 miles an hour.

Most gray foxes weigh between 7 and 12 pounds, no more than a house cat, and stand about 14 or 15 inches at the shoulder, but long, bushy fur adds substantially to their size. Length varies from less than a yard to about 45 inches, including 12 to 15

inches of brush, which is bulky despite its paucity of underfur beneath the stiff guard hairs. A manelike black tail stripe runs along its top from rump to black tip. The salt-and-pepper gray of the bristly fur is washed with rust on ears, face, neck, and flanks. The underparts are white. There is often enough red on the body to confuse any hunter who is unaware that a red fox (even in the dark silver phase) always has a white brush tip while a gray fox always has a black brush tip.

The gray fox is absent or uncommon in much of the West, but it is abundant from the eastern seaboard to the Dakotas, from coast to coast in the South and in Mexico, and along the Pacific from southern Washington to Baja. Though it prefers temperate habitat, on the eastern half of the continent it has extended its range into bits of southern Canada, and western hunters find it as far north as upper Colorado. The country supports a score of subspecies, including dwarf strains on the Santa Barbara Islands off southern California. Races differ in shading and size but are much alike in a preference for dense cover that is hard to hunt.

The southwestern part of the range is shared with the kit fox, or desert fox *(Vulpes macrotis),* smallest and fastest of American foxes but no more capable than the gray of sustaining its speed over long distances. A lean animal weighing from

Gray fox on foraging run.

3 to 6 pounds, it is buff-yellow and gray, with a black-tipped tail. It is probably a subspecies of the swift fox *(Vulpes velox)*, an almost equally small buff-yellow breed with a black-tipped tail and blackish snout patches. The swift fox ranges from the Southwest up through the Dakotas and across the Rockies. Less wary than most foxes, both breeds have been decimated by predator poisoning and ranching operations. They have been added to the protected list in some areas and—regardless of area—should not be shot. Any hunter can tell these miniatures from gray and red foxes.

One other American species, the arctic fox *(Alopex lagopus)*, inhabits northern Canada, Alaska, the arctic islands, and Greenland. It is not a true fox but is closely related. It has a blunt, puppyish face and rounded ears, may weigh 5 or 6 pounds or as much as 12, sometimes stands a foot high, and is brownish gray during the brief northern summer. There is a "blue phase" which in winter turns smoky blue-gray or gray-black. The much more common white phase turns winter-white, except for black nose, eyes, claws, and a few tail hairs. The arctic fox preys on lemmings, voles, hares, and occasionally the young of seals and sea lions, commonly scavenges the kills of polar bears, and eats the eggs and young of ground-nesting birds.

Forefoot of gray fox (l.) and of red fox.

There are nesting grounds where arctic foxes perhaps ought to be thinned somewhat for the sake of game birds, but the species is of more interest to trappers than to hunters. Its range is so remote that it commonly shows little fear of man, is very easily trapped, and will approach a hunter. A sportsman on a far-northern big-game trip may shoot an arctic fox for its handsome pelt, but the animal presents so little challenge that it is more often shot by a hungry man making his way through an area where other game is scant. The meat should be thoroughly cooked to avoid trichinosis, and the liver should not be eaten, as its high vitamin A content can be toxic.

GAME BEHAVIOR & HUNTING HABITAT: Gray-fox hunting is most enjoyable from midfall, when a few of the males, or dog foxes, grow restless with sexual stirrings, through the peak of mating activity in February. Unlike red foxes, grays use dens all winter long for warmth, shelter, or safety, but after mating the male helps the vixen select and, if necessary, clean out a special maternity den. As a rule several auxiliary or escape dens are situated within a few hundred acres, but there is little use in searching the open areas where red foxes often den, or looking for conspicuous mounds of dug-up earth. Grays do no digging if they can find suitable cavities in woodlands or among boulders and rocky ridges. They use hollow trees—especially oaks—as well as logs, rock piles, slash piles, clefts, and small caves.

Annual litters, averaging from three to five pups (also called kits), usually are whelped in late March, April, or early May after a gestation of about fifty-three days. The pups venture out at about five weeks, are weaned after about two months, and follow their parents on hunts a month later. Until then, both parents feed the pups on small prey and regurgitated meat. Although foxes are the least gregarious of canine game, a hunter who takes a gray should be on the lookout for a possible second. Grays are more clannish than reds; occasionally a gray remains with its mate all year or seeks the same mate at the return of the rut. Foxes are supposed to have a life span of eight or ten years, but it is doubtful that many survive beyond three or four. Their enemies—apart from irate farmers and overzealous protectors of upland birds—include all the larger predators and the usual canine diseases and parasites, as well as a form of encephalitis which is not transmitted to man but is lethal to foxes.

Gray foxes slay grouse, quail, and pheasants, but not in the numbers generally supposed. Even in the absence of tracks, a kill can be illuminating. If a pheasant carcass is pretty much intact, with only the head, neck, crop, and perhaps a bit of the back gone, an owl swooped there; the fox is exonerated since it would have eaten much more, cached the remains, or carried the prey to its den. Devoted fox hunters hardly want their favorite game extirpated, but other sportsmen sometimes do. The result is the removal of a species that helps control unwanted rodents, provides a buffer form of prey for larger predators, and serves as a strengthening pruner of the weak or sickly in the game populations. Even the great horned owl is more beneficial than harmful.

Unlike red foxes, grays so consistently avoid the exposure of open farmland that they would present no very serious menace to domestic birds even if most of today's poultry were not raised indoors. They sustain themselves chiefly on mice, rats, rabbits, hares, insects, fish, wild birds, eggs, and all types of carrion, supplemented by fruits and other vegetation. Northeastern hunters know that it pays to inspect apple orchards in the early morning, at dusk, and on overcast days. The edges of southern peanut fields are likely spots to track or start the hounds, and in the Southeast and Southwest persimmons attract foxes. Oak and beech stands are good, and cherries and grapes are perhaps their favorite wild fruits.

In prime habitat a gray fox roams over a vague territory of some 10 square miles but moves more during breeding season or when food is meager. Good hunting areas are laced with overgrown trails marked by tracks, scat, scent posts, and cache holes, but foxes detour at very short intervals to weave about on mousing excursions. A shooter on stand must be still and quiet, even when a fox is being pushed toward him by hounds, and a still-hunter must pause frequently, for a fox sees and avoids anything that moves, yet often fails to notice anything that does not. On dull, dark days a gray fox may be active at any hour but is not easily caught unaware as it hunts upwind. Though it seldom bothers to track prey, it can locate a mouse by scent under grass and can hear one squeak several hundred feet away.

Without snow, still-hunting is a mediocre gamble unless there is a heavy infestation of gray foxes. The places to check are bottomlands, rocky ridges or draws, woods in general, heavy second growth in particular, and, in the West, mesquite thickets and chaparral. Man-made trails and woods or brush along roadsides may also be productive. Where traffic is light, foxes are bold enough to patrol roads, looking for car-killed animals and birds; and simple curiosity seems to draw them to trails. Sometimes sign is in evidence. Foxes habitually defecate along roadsides and establish scent posts along customary routes. A spot that looks as if something has recently been buried there is just that—a cache. When a fox digs up the meat, no attempt is made to conceal the hole.

There is reason to watch and listen for crows and birds of prey, which sometimes worry a fox or try to rob it of a kill. There is also reason to watch for natural cavities of all types in the woods and along wooded edges. Some of them are likely to be den sites, and the more of them that are available, the more appealing the vicinity will be to a gray fox. An area holds special promise if caches or discarded bits of bone, fur, and feathers are in evidence near the dens.

Upon finding so choice a locale, anyone who has had foxing experience can turn still-hunting into predator calling. A mouse squeak, easily produced after a bit of practice by sucking the back of a hand, is often just as effective as a rabbit squeal in thick cover, where a hunter wearing drab or camouflage clothing can find instant concealment. Battery-operated phonographic predator calls, utilizing a loudspeaker, have also become very popular. There is no denying their effectiveness, but for some of us they diminish the atavistic pride of achievement in luring foxes. Moreover, some of the very best fox, coyote, and bobcat callers insist that they bring in more animals in thick eastern cover with a mouth-operated wooden or plastic call or by using the back of the hand.

The haughtier gentry may protest, but one of the finest fox guns is the unprepossessing little Savage combination rifle-shotgun in the version with a .222 rifle barrel over a 20-gauge Magnum smoothbore. The more elegant European over/under combinations and drillings are also excellent, if substantially more expensive. For hunting with hounds, and for hunting without them in thick cover, especially before snow, the ideal firearm is a 20-gauge Magnum or 12-gauge repeating or double shotgun, full-choked or modified and full, and the ammunition is the express or Magnum No. 2 or 4 load. But hunting without dogs on snow or in relatively open country usually calls for a rifle, preferably mounted with a 2½- or 4-power scope and sighted in at 100 yards. Good chamberings range from the 5mm and .22 rimfire Magnums up through the outstanding .22 centerfires and slightly larger calibers. In many areas the range is totally unpredictable for the tracker or caller (for that matter, he may not know what species he will find or whether the target will be moving or still). In those situations a rifle-shotgun has self-evident advantages.

There is a feeling of mild absurdity about donning white coveralls and cap and wrapping white tape around a gun, but camouflage is too important to be sacrificed to mere dignity, and early-morning tracking on a light, fresh snow is the most rewarding way to hunt foxes without dogs. This, too, can be effectively combined with calling, of course. Fox tracks that weave aimlessly about are mousing tracks. The trail to seek and follow is the purposeful one, made when the fox has filled its belly and heads for a safe bedding area to lie up. In the case of a gray, success on a very cold day depends on finding the fox before it reaches a den, or else using a small, pugnacious terrier to run the fox out. But on milder days a gray may behave like a red: seeking some secluded little elevation, out of the wind and perhaps in the sun, approaching upwind, circling, then curling up to face its back trail.

With its brush over paws and nose, a fox looks deceptively torpid. It naps like a cat but is ever alert, raising its head at intervals as short as half a minute to sniff and look about. The way to get a shot is to spot the game at a distance, stop dead-still, then advance only when the fox's head is down. Crouch low and use every bit of cover.

Hounds and hound-running techniques are the same as for the red fox, and they will be discussed in connection with the red (see pages 362-368).

TRACKS & SIGN: A fox track might have been left by a very large house cat except for the four sharp marks of the nonretract-

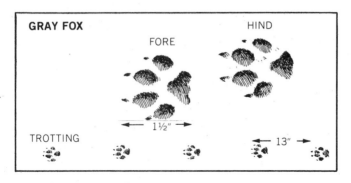

GRAY FOX
FORE
HIND
1½"
TROTTING
13"

able claws. Foxes dig in when running, often making claw marks even in hard-packed dirt that takes no pad impressions. The foreprint usually measures from 1¼ to almost 2 inches long, the hind print is a trifle smaller, and both front and rear are slightly longer than wide. The toes are widely spaced and far forward of the heel pad, which is wide from side to side, thin from rear to front. But on hard ground the heel pad leaves only a round dot if the lateral portions fail to print. The trail is almost line narrow, and a fox with a very thick brush leaves a drag line in the snow. With practice, it is possible to tell a gray-fox track from a red's; grays have smaller feet with larger toes.

Sometimes the droppings of the two can also be distinguished. Since the gray fox eats more berries than the red, its scat is darker—very dark where cherries abound. The droppings are small, narrow cylinders, usually sharply tapered at one end. Scent posts are visited on small prominences along a run but may go unnoticed except when snow is stained and melted. Caches are easier to see: mounded or loosened dirt, turf, or moss, often lighter than the surrounding color. A dug-up cache hole is typically shallow but wide since foxes rarely bury very small prey, except in whelping season near a den. Tufts of hair are sometimes snagged at den mouths.

VOICE: Foxes bark, growl, yap, and make other typical canine sounds. The gray's yapping is lower and harsher than the red's and is not heard much except at the peak of mating activity and when the young are first led on hunts.

Red Fox *(Vulpes fulva;* also classified as *Vulpes vulpes* or *Vulpes vulpes fulva)*
COMMON & REGIONAL NAMES: *reynard, renard, colored fox, upland fox.*

DESCRIPTION & DISTRIBUTION: Like blind men describing an elephant after touching one part, hunters tend to define the red fox by the differing images of their favorite hunting methods. To those who don the pinks and ride to hounds, the game is an orange or grayish-yellow flicker, skimming over a stone fence as if consciously imposing a difficult jump, or it is a seldom visible magnet drawing twenty or a hundred frenzied hounds across rolling fields, or the blurred vortex of a whirling pack that must be lashed off if the fox is to be spared, as it often is. To the still-hunting tracker, it can be a darkling ripple, studied through a binocular and then through a rifle scope against a distant slope as it hunts mice, chucks, rabbits, but more frequently it is an oblong mound on some little bedding knob from which it scans a snow-blanketed field quite bereft of stalking cover for hundreds of yards. To drivers and predator callers it may be either shotgun or rifle game, depending on terrain and cover, but is always an adversary that can freeze and vanish into its surroundings, slink into the sparsest cover, or, perhaps most disconcerting, slink and run simultaneously. To a "hill-topper," the red fox is usually not a target at all but a presence conjured by the chorus of hounds, an unseen fiddler calling the midnight tune of "jug-hunting" revelry. And to those who guess at daylight crossings while their hounds run, the coppery fox is a burnished ground-level comet streaking through an opening somewhere below the shotgun.

Though there are a dozen subspecies of red fox in North America alone, and others in Europe, Asia, and Africa, the European and American races are the same species. Distribution maps must be misleading to hunters in many states; they show no red foxes on the lower southeastern coast, in much of the Southwest, or in the Rockies and high plains from central Alberta and Saskatchewan southward. While these regions are, indeed, the poorest hunting sections, the red fox is now established in Florida. North of Mexico, it is everywhere.

Though Minnesota has very big foxes and the northwestern

Red fox stalking ground squirrel.

states very small ones, the eastern strain can be taken as fairly representative of the various geographic races. It is longer-legged than a gray fox but likely to stand no more than 15 or 16 inches at the shoulder. The tail is about 14 to 16 inches long, and the body length, including this brush, averages only a little more than a yard. By the time a hunter has plodded home with a big male slung down his back he will swear to having shot a 15-pounder, but those are uncommon, the norm being between 7 and 12.

Summer sun can bleach the bushy coat to pale gold, but a prime winter pelt is usually copper, deep rust, or reddish yellow. The nose, lips, whiskers, feet, lower legs, and rear ear surfaces are black, as are the elliptical pupils—more feline than canine in appearance—of the coppery gold eyes. Some of the guard hairs are black, particularly on the tail, but the invariably white brush tip enables a hunter to tell the red fox from the gray or any other American species. Also white are the underparts, throat, and rim of the snout.

A sportsman unfamiliar with northern red foxes may sooner or later run across a rather bewildering color phase called the silver fox, a melanistic red fox with a white-tipped black coat. The pelt is prized, a rarity except in high country or in the northern part of the range. Color gradings are innumerable, and some melanistic trophies are magnificently frosted, while others look like gray foxes, and still others are quite black except for the

white brush tip. (This compounds possible confusion, as grays were called "black foxes" in early American accounts.) In the same regions is a slightly more common intermediate color phase, the cross fox, which at shooting distance looks like an ordinary red but has a dark brown, sometimes almost black, cross on its back—a stripe from nape to rump, transected behind the withers.

When a hunter or trapper speaks derisively of a Sampson, scorched, or burnt fox, he means an animal with a skin affliction which halts the development of guard hairs, rendering the pelt worthless. A "bastard" fox can be either a Sampson or a healthy red fox with a dark gray coat.

The long, steady decline of the fur trade has benefited the red-fox population enormously. In some of the states where fox hunting is an esteemed tradition, foxes have long been protected from trapping, yet in others the harvest remains virtually unregulated. Predators are still bountied in a few states, and foxes account for about nine-tenths of all bounty moneys, but change is gaining momentum. Rhode Island, for example, abolished the fox bounty in 1968 and four years later declared the fox a game animal with a closed season from March through September. Game managers have proved that red foxes do no appreciable damage to poultry or wildlife. There are probably between 3 and 4 million in America. They continue to extend their range, and the change in control policies brightens the hunting outlook.

GAME BEHAVIOR & HUNTING HABITAT: The red fox exudes a sharper musk than the gray (and trapping lures concocted for sprinkling over hole sets or blind sets are potent), but the legendary "reek of a fox" is not so aromatic as to alert a hunter to nearby game, regardless of tall stories passed with the jug around an old-fashioned hilltoppers' fire. Storytelling and good natured heckling are traditional to the southern jug hunt, an informal nighttime gathering of hound owners and their friends, commonly around a hilltop fire unless a fox leads the dogs so far that a back-road motor cavalcade becomes necessary. The hounds run as a communal pack, too intent upon the quarry for many fights to erupt, while the men follow the chase by sound alone. Much faster than the gray fox and able to run much longer,

Red fox bringing ground squirrel to den.

a red can sprint at more than 40 miles an hour and gallop considerable distances at 30 or more, leading the dogs on for miles.

A red fox will not hole up or tree in the manner of the gray, nor is it invariably run to ground. It may lope in a stream to break the scent, or leap onto a stone fence, gallop along it, double back, and head off in a new direction while the milling dogs try to unravel the trail. It will climb bluffs and go through hollow logs and culverts. It has been known to enlist the aid of another fox, making a hatch of trails and then separating. It has also been known to jump onto a sheep's back and ride the terrified beast across a meadow. Enjoying the race, it may wait on the far side to see if the pack can find the vanished trail. When hounds do catch a fox they usually kill it, but few hilltoppers are unhappy if a fox escapes after a good chase.

In some states the season is open only in fall and winter, a good time to hunt because pelts are prime and tracks show well on snow. In the northern part of the range some of the prey hibernates, forcing the foxes to search more actively for other food, and the rut accelerates this activity. A majority of matings occur in January and February. Since gestation lasts a little over fifty days, most litters are whelped in March. The pups, or kits, usually number from four to eight.

Shortly after mating, the female selects several den sites and the male helps her to enlarge them before making a final choice. The most common dens are renovated marmot or badger holes on slight hummocks or knolls in fields, providing a view of all approaches. Alternative sites include stream banks, slopes, rock piles, and hollow trees or logs. The typical den is a long tunnel with a nest chamber somewhere along it and several shafts leading to escape ports. If the den is in the open, its main entrance is often easy to spot: a hole commonly less than a foot wide but higher than that, marked by a fan or mound of packed earth excavated from the tunnel and sometimes by a scatter of bones, feathers, bits of fur.

Pups begin to come out at about six weeks and are weaned a couple of weeks later. Both parents bring food, dropping it farther and farther from the den mouth to coax them into exploration. The adults soon lead the young on hunts, and family groups begin to disperse by late August, red foxes being less gregarious than grays. A few may seek the same mates in succeeding years, but they are almost always found alone in the fall, foraging over areas as wide as 10 square miles. Nonetheless, any locale that yields a fox is a good place to try for more—first because another

Red fox with kit at den.

will probably take over the vacated foraging grounds, and second because foxes, like many canines, maintain vaguely defined territories, overlapping and shared to some extent by the peaceable means of mutual avoidance.

Their numbers are held in check by larger predators, including domestic and feral dogs, and by inclement spring or fall weather, flooding, internal and external parasites, and such diseases as distemper, encephalitis, and rabies. Since modern poultry-raising methods have reduced depredations by red foxes to an insignificant level, a local paucity of prey will also limit the fox population. However, meadow mice and rabbits are rarely in short supply. In times of plenty, foxes cache surplus prey for leaner times.

Red foxes also eat upland birds and their eggs (though not in sufficient numbers to warrant severe control), ground squirrels, marmots, muskrats, insects, frogs, lizards, and worms. Marshes as well as uplands are worth scouting, as are stands of nuts and fruits. Like coyotes, red foxes are sometimes shot while raiding melon patches; like raccoons, they are shot while raiding corn; like gray foxes, they are shot while browsing on fallen apples, plums, peaches, and persimmons—especially apples in the North, persimmons in the South. Calling is sometimes effective in stands of nut trees—beechnuts, acorns, pecans are sought—and hounds can also be cast in such woods. In the East, it seems as if tracks show up most consistently on mousing fields and around patches of wild fruits, findings confirmed by those who have done much western fox hunting. The animals are fond of wild strawberries, blueberries, gooseberries, crowberries, blackberries, shadbush (serviceberries), and the like. Wild cherries ripen during hunting season in many regions, and grapes may attract as many foxes as grouse.

Whether seeking prey or vegetation, foxes prowl upwind, frequently departing from habitual runways on meandering circuits to listen, watch, sniff, even feel for grass- or snow-hidden mice to pounce on. Their senses are exceptionally keen to everything except stationary downwind or overhead objects—factors to be taken into account when calling or when taking a stand while hounds work. Calling techniques are the same as for grays, requiring a high or downwind point of concealment with a wide view, and the use of a rabbit-squealing mechanical call, a mouse squeak produced by sucking the back of the hand, or a phonographic call with a hidden amplifier. Hunters who have used phonographs (or learned calling from them) will probably agree that the most effective records employ a diminuendo series of squeals, beginning with the screech of a suddenly hurt or terrified rabbit but gradually changing to last-gasp whimpers. The same dirge can be played on a mechanical call. The terminal whimpers should be followed by a silence before repeating the series, and one should wait a half hour before moving on.

Since reds are more partial than grays to mixed or open terrain, good hiding places for calling include lightly wooded ridges or the fringes of brush and woods—the sort of place from which either a chuck or a fox might be spotted. In most regions, rifles or combination rifle-shotguns are probably used more than smoothbores. A combination of .222 in the upper barrel and 20-gauge Magnum in the lower is excellent. For patchy cover, a rimfire Magnum bolt-action can be mounted with a 2½-power scope and sighted in at 100 yards, but if the locale promises long shots, a better choice is one of the .22 centerfires or a slightly larger caliber, perhaps with a 150-yard zero and a 2½- or 4-power scope. That sort of arm is also best for tracking, particularly on snow in open country. As with the gray fox, a latticework of tracks indicates mousing, while a more or less straight trail often leads to a slightly elevated morning bedding site from which the fox can watch its back trail as it catnaps. Most shots are made over wide, snowy fields; long though the range may be, white camouflage (of rifle as well as hunter) has great value—foxes are color-blind but alert to contrasts—and a slow, crouching approach from downwind is *de rigueur.* Use every bit of available cover and stop, perfectly still, each time the fox raises its head. Tracking is more effective with reds than grays, especially if the fields are glassed frequently with a binocular featuring wide view and good magnification—something in the 7x35mm class. Despite the utmost caution, a fox may spook and move on before a shot can be made. The best tactic is to wait a while before following. It will soon bed down again if it does not suspect it is being trailed. If no shot can be made by midafternoon, most of us head for home. A fox jumped after that will probably keep moving and hunting into the night.

When solitary tracking fails, some hunters stage drives across woodlots. Several standers take positions at the downwind end of the woods, where their scent is least likely to make a fox backtrack or slip out to one side. A couple of drivers start from the other end along opposite sides of the patch, soon followed by drivers going through the woods. Spacing depends on the density of cover, the object being to maintain safe distances without letting a fox slip through too easily. A mistake common to both fox and deer drives is an excess of noise that frightens the game into slipping back between drivers—a common enough occurrence even when sound is kept to a sensible conversational level meant to push the animal toward the standers. In a variation known as belling, one hunter intermittently rings a cow bell as he follows a fox track, and he is flanked by two men who move slightly ahead of him and 100 to 200 yards to each side. A red fox is inquisitive enough to backtrack toward the sound, but cau-

Successful fox hunters with hound.

tion soon prompts a retreat or a cut to one side—past a flanker. The gun for driving or belling is governed in some degree by safety (that is, by the distance between men). A rifle can be used in some instances. A 20-gauge Magnum or a 12 gauge loaded with high-velocity or Magnum No. 2's or 4's is recommended, but with the admission that this is a matter of regional opinion. Choke should be full or modified and full. The same shotgunning suggestions hold, without any regional concessions, for hunting on foot with hounds.

Most of the dogs used for equestrian hunting are foxhounds of English bloodlines, which are more single-minded and tractable than the modified American breeds, and are also excellent for hunting grays. But at ranging wide, then bringing a red fox around or keeping with it on a long chase, they cannot match the famous American strains—black-and-tan, bluetick, Arkansas traveler, redbone, Trigg, Trumbo, Walker, July, and others, all having the requisite nose, stamina, voice, and fox sense. Racing ahead of hounds and horses, a red fox often flees into unfamiliar country. But if not pressed too hard, a red fox will stay inside a couple of square miles, circling almost like a rabbit though on a much wider scale. An unmounted hunter wants the fox moved, not chased too closely. If he has worked the area before, he knows the favorite routes of escape and stations himself to intercept the fox. Otherwise, he must gauge the direction and distance of his dog or dogs (northerners commonly have fine hunting with just one or two hounds). Then he picks a stand on high ground overlooking a likely crossing, and the odds are improved if he has at least one or two companions who can race for other likely crossings. Having arrived on some bald bluff or saddle, each man stands as quietly as if he were still-hunting, because dogs do not distract a fox from watching and listening for new dangers. A red fox rarely panics; it is accustomed to slipping past human beings who would be astonished to discover they had ever been within shooting distance.

TRACKS & SIGN: Red-fox dens are more easily spotted than those of grays because they are normally situated in more open country, often in the middle of a meadow or field, well marked by excavated earth, cache mounds, holes, and indigestible scraps. The catlike tracks resemble the gray's (see page 358).

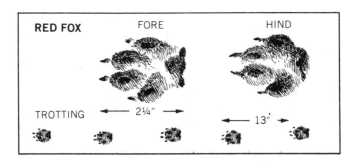

RED FOX   FORE   HIND

TROTTING   ← 2¼″ →   ← 13″ →

but are larger and have smaller toe prints. Red-fox scats are generally somewhat lighter in color than those of grays, but sign is otherwise similar.

VOICE: A harsh, high, coughing bark is the alarm signal of the fox. Upon hearing it, an experienced hunter drops low and stays still, knowing that a fox is nearby but alert. Terrierlike yapping is normal, but useful only as proof that a fox is in the vicinity. As the red fox is not gregarious, imitation is futile.

Cottontail Rabbit *(Sylvilagus)*
COMMON & REGIONAL NAMES: *cooney, coney, bunny, brush rabbit, gray rabbit, wood rabbit, hotfoot.*

DESCRIPTION & DISTRIBUTION: Most of us who hunt can remember when we first trudged the scraggly edges of fields lying fallow or planted to corn or clover, alfalfa or soybeans or wheat; whatever the crop, in retrospect it is the color of indolence hiding rabbits the color of action, whether in Minnesota or Nebraska, Connecticut or Virginia or Oregon. Somewhere, in one way or another, each of us is the Missouri farm boy who ambles along a weedy fence row, pausing to kick at a heap of prunings where previous success is marked by a couple of spent shotshells in the fading bluegrass. The details differ, of course. But in every instance the quarry is the cottontail: most abundant, most widely distributed, most hunted of all American game.

More than a dozen species and nearly seventy subspecies

hide in their forms—resting spots like miniature deer beds in shrubbery, high grass, or brambles—from the Atlantic to the Pacific and from lower Canada to South America. Cottontails are the continent's only native rabbits (jacks and snowshoe rabbits being hares). There are five major groups: The eastern, or common, cottontail *(Sylvilagus floridanus)* ranges from the Atlantic Coast to the Rockies; the somewhat grayer Rocky Mountain cottontail *(S. nuttalli)* ranges from the plains states and the Southwest to the Sierra Nevada; the bigger, browner Audubon cottontail *(S. auduboni)* ranges from Oklahoma into the Rockies and down through the entire Southwest; the small, dark marsh rabbit *(S. palustris)* and closely related but lighter and very large swamp rabbit, or cane-cutter *(S. aquaticus),* both range from Virginia to Florida and across the Gulf states into Texas; and the smallest and darkest of all, the brush rabbit *(S. bachmani),* ranges throughout the West. Perhaps a sixth should be added—the New England cottontail *(S. transitionalis)*—which is bagged by hunters from upper New England to Georgia and is usually taken to be the common cottontail, though it can be distinguished by a black spot between its ears.

The closely related European rabbit *(Oryctolagus*

cuniculus) has been introduced in various parts of the United States, partly because it is so large—occasionally as heavy as 5 pounds and measuring a foot and a half from nose to tail—and partly because its reproductive capacity may surpass even that of the native cottontail. Hunters in this country sometimes call it the San Juan rabbit, a reference to the San Juan Islands off the coast of Washington, where it was first introduced and is still found in the wild. Some hunters continue to clamor for European rabbits but local infusions have been disheartening. They dig extensive tunnels, forming dense colonies known as warrens, and are so nocturnal that they seldom venture out before dark. Since ferreting is illegal in most states, the best way to hunt them is by using small dogs such as toy terriers to drive them out—a method tried occasionally and with better results on cottontails, which hole up in abandoned woodchuck, badger, and skunk burrows during very cold weather. The only cottontail that digs its own burrow is the Idaho pigmy rabbit (classified as S. idahoensis or Brachylagus idahoensis), a 10- to 12-inch midget that vies with the brush rabbit for title of smallest breed.

Habitat with a good carrying capacity can support as many cottontails as European rabbits, and the cottontails provide better hunting while causing less agricultural damage. Still, European rabbits are encountered in scattered localities, bewildering the hunter who bags what appears to be a substantially oversized cottontail with normal grayish-brown coloring above, white below and on the underside of the tail, but an unusually buffy hindneck and black ear tips.

Most cottontails have a sprinkling or vaguely defined blaze of white on the forehead, and all of them have grayish-brown bodies, sometimes with a darker salt-and-pepper area on the back. Relatively dark species such as the brush rabbit spend their lives in thick cover, while lighter varieties such as the Texas cottontail blend with a background of more open, arid terrain. Even the larger races of the East can easily conceal themselves. They usually weigh between 2½ and 3½ pounds at maturity, measure from a foot to a foot and a half in length, and stand half a foot high at the shoulder. Hugging the ground and flattening their 2- or 3-inch ears, they are almost perfectly camouflaged when they remain motionless in their customary hiding, feeding, and basking areas.

Eastern cottontails.

The first defense upon the approach of a hunter or predator is to "freeze." A rabbit can keep perfectly still—not twitching a muscle or blinking—for at least ten minutes. But if the hunter comes close, the second defense is to bolt. With the first leap, the tail flicks up like the flag of a deer, and its underside is white (except on the tiny brush rabbit and the peculiar swamp rabbit, a bog-loving creature with webbed hind feet). The underparts are also white. When a cottontail bounds, camouflage is shattered by a conspicuous white flashing which is not only a target for the hunter but a marker for any pursuing predator.

The bouncing beacon cannot be an alarm signal to other rabbits since the cottontail is a somewhat territorial animal that spends most of the day in thick cover, not far from others of its kind but far enough so that a visual signal would have doubtful value. The "theory of flash pattern" accounts for its function and can be a definite aid to the rabbit hunter. To appreciate the function, bear in mind the rabbit's ability to stop short and to twist and turn, sometimes making acute switches in midair as well as with each bound. When a cottontail stops the white blob vanishes. Often it is also invisible from the side as a rabbit runs. The predator chases after or pounces at the white flash pattern, sometimes overshooting the mark or losing it altogether when it suddenly disappears. Although cottontail rabbits suffer a mortality rate almost as astounding as their birth rate, the vanishing flash saves enough of them to help ensure survival of the species.

The hunter's eye, like that of a pursuing animal, follows the bouncing white ball. As he swings the bead just ahead of the scurrying rabbit, misses are frequently caused by overshooting when the target abruptly vanishes. The cottontail has a maximum escape speed of no more than 18 or 20 miles an hour, but its bounding and zigzagging produce an illusion of greater velocity. Shotgunners who bag grouse or woodcock by snapshooting usually are adept at taking rabbits in the same manner, rather than by maintaining a steady lead beyond the winking white and brown target. Another method that is effective for shotgunners with fast reflexes is to put the bead on the rabbit at the top of the bound, judge the landing spot, and pull ahead to that spot. Those who hunt rabbits with a rifle generally prefer their targets distant and stationary or nearly so, but there are

Well-used rabbit run (top l.), twigs chewed by cottontails (top r.), and beagling on Tennessee farmland.

riflemen who take pride in bagging cottontails by hitting them as they touch down.

When feeding or moving undisturbed between foraging spots and a form, a rabbit makes short hops and sometimes walks on all fours like most animals. But its short front legs serve primarily as a landing platform and pivot. The hind legs, about 12 inches long and powered by very strong back, haunch, and thigh muscles, fold under the animal like a pair of leaf springs. A fleeing cottontail is likely to cover about 3 to 5 feet at a bound and can occasionally leap 15 feet, fooling the hunter who has misjudged the animal's trajectory or failed to shift with a midair turn.

GAME BEHAVIOR & HUNTING HABITAT: Obsolete guide books notwithstanding, leporids—rabbits and hares—are not rodents. They belong to the *Lagomorpha* (hare-shaped) order, characterized by an apparently useless second pair of upper incisors hidden behind the larger functional ones, and by the location of the scrotum in front of the penis rather than behind it. (No other mammals except marsupials have this genital structure.) However, rabbits and some rodents are alike in having an almost

Cottontail in brushy cover (above),
and cottontail bounding in snow.

infinite reproductive capacity. Cottontails are the most delicate, easily killed game animals and probably have more enemies than any other American species. A high death rate is offset by the birth rate. If no young were killed, a single pair of cottontails, together with their offspring, could produce 350,000 rabbits in five years. Over most of the country the long breeding season lasts from late February until September. An average female has four or five litters during that period, and three to six young per litter.

In the third week of a 28-day gestation period the "doe" scoops several shallow, oblong depressions in the earth, and after some indecision lines one with grasses and leaves mixed with fur plucked from her breast and belly. She makes a nest coverlet of the same materials, and although the site is seldom hidden in the thickest cover available, it is so well camouflaged as to be invisible. On the day of birth she usually mates again with one of the nearby males that are squabbling over her. She suckles the young once in the evening, once at dawn, and sometimes during the night, but in the daytime she sits in a form perhaps 25 or 30 feet away or wanders farther off to feed.

She probably spends her short life on a 2-acre plot from which she drives other adult females. A male's territory may cover 6 or 8 or even 30 acres, encompassing the ranges of several females and overlapping those of other males. The males now and then battle each other, and they perform hopping, leaping

courtship ceremonies, but a hunter who strolls rabbit fields on a midwinter night to see the spectacle of groups romping on crusted snow is witnessing nothing more than play.

Because a female is inclined to hole up sooner than a male when cold or alarmed, more males are probably shot. But hunters account for a very small percentage of fatalities of either sex. The annual national harvest, probably more than 25 million, is a paltry fraction of the breeding population. In a year when more than 6 million are bagged in Missouri—long known as the best cottontail state—more than 10 million are left to breed, and at the population peak in May there might be more than 50 million. Where habitat is not spoiled by "clean" farming or pavement, population slumps usually are evidence of a 9- or 10-year cycle like that of grouse: Numbers increase until the habitat cannot support them and a decline sets in.

Unlike hares, rabbits are blind and almost furless at birth.

More than half die in the nest or shortly after leaving it in the third week. Some of the females born in early spring will breed before autumn, but about 85 percent of the population will fail to survive a year, and very few live two years. Winter spares 15 or 20 percent to renew the population.

Apart from automobiles, house cats are the greatest enemies in many regions. Other major predators include dogs, foxes, coyotes, weasels, bobcats, owls and hawks, nest-raiding crows, badgers, and skunks. Every carnivorous or omnivorous animal kills cottontails, and they are also beset by cold snaps, nest-flooding rains, agricultural burn-offs, plowing, mowing, trampling cattle, and many parasites.

"Rabbit horn"—warty bumps produced by the insect-borne virus of Shope's fibroma—is fairly common but not serious, and man is immune. The warts, only skin deep, have no effect on rabbit meat. Lumps known as "bots" or "warbles" are caused

Beagle running cottontail across open snow patch.

by burrowing botfly larvae. They, too, are harmless to man, but a heavy infestation may kill a cottontail. Watery, bladderlike cysts—"bladder worms"—may sometimes be found in a cottontail's body cavity. They are larval tapeworms of a species that cannot mature in a rabbit or use man as a host, but can be very dangerous to canines. They are easily removed if noticed, but raw rabbit meat or entrails should never be fed to a dog. Some hunters will not dress a rabbit in the field, much less reward a beagle with a bit of raw meat.

A cottontail can die of tick-induced anemia or a number of other diseases and parasitic attacks. All are harmless to man except "rabbit fever"—tularemia, which is carried by biting insects and occurs in at least forty-seven species of birds and mammals but is most prevalent in leporids and rodents. While American hares are relatively resistant to the bacterium, it is fatal to a cottontail within a week. The danger to man has been exaggerated, and tularemia is no longer considered an important or common disease in this country. Deaths are very rare. There is no vaccine, but the illness responds quickly to the mycin drugs. Mild cases are usually untreated, dismissed as a touch of influenza. Symptoms of more severe cases are fever, tender and swollen lymph glands (especially in the neck or under the arms), and sometimes ulcerated sores.

Since tularemia can be contracted through the skin or,

Southwestern cottontail.

more easily, through cuts or abrasions, it is wise to wear rubber gloves when dressing or skinning a rabbit. Tularemia and other diseases are also avoided by thoroughly cooking the meat—and by opening the hunting season as late as November in some states. The insect carriers hibernate after the first heavy frosts, and infected rabbits soon die off.

For cottontails that remain, cover is more important than food because rabbits eat such a wide assortment of vegetation that hunger is seldom severe. Desert cottontails thrive on prickly pear, mesquite, and sage, but in most regions the preferred foods include grasses and sedges, clover and other herbs, sorrels, plantain, brambles, lespedeza, goldenrod, wild rye, domestic grains, soybeans, truck crops—and more. In winter the rabbits subsist well on bark, twigs, and buds. When orchardmen defend their fruit trees by wrapping the lower trunks with hardware cloth or aluminum foil, it is a good time to walk up cottontails in willow thickets and clumps of sumac—particularly sumac, the bark of which has a high fat content, required by rabbits in cold weather.

Many of us who were, in a manner of speaking, weaned on rabbits make it a rule to hole up when the cottontails do. When the temperature falls below 10 or 12 degrees rabbits seek the warmth of woodchuck burrows or badger holes and the hunter might as well seek the warmth of his own den. The best hunting times are early in the morning and from late afternoon until dusk, particularly during a warm spell following a cold snap, snow, or rain. Rabbits are most active when the temperature is between 10 degrees and freezing.

With or without dogs, the spots to jump rabbits are where food is combined with concealment and protection from the wind: woodpiles, brush piles, brushy fields, weedy fence and hedge rows, overgrown ditches, patches of honeysuckle, bramble hells, windbreaks, brushy edges between fields and woods, the lee sides of abandoned farm buildings, brushy stream banks, pastures dotted with shrubs.

Rabbits do not rely much on scent to warn them, but on hearing, sight, and the sense of touch. A cottontail's ears swivel about and catch the sound of a distant hunter or dog. Nervously the rabbit thumps a hind foot and other cottontails, a little farther off, are alerted by the ground vibrations even before they feel the heavy-footed thudding of the hunter. Seeing movement

through the brush, they freeze. As the hunter nears a thicket he should be alert because rabbits are getting set to erupt from the bushes. A cottontail may ripple away, unseen, through high cover or may pause in the open. Or there may be nothing more to shoot at than a hurtling white blur, a glimpse as the cottontail bounds erratically from bush to brush.

A silent walk through the fields blends repose and suspense, but there are those who prefer the accompaniment of a yapping, yodeling hound—the urgency of its belling voice when the trail warms. And if one hound is good, three or four are better. No breed is more proficient than the beagle, but other keen-nosed hounds will do if they are small enough to squirm

Day's bag of large cottontails.

under briers and slow enough to stay out of the line of fire and keep the rabbits above ground. If pressed too hard, a rabbit will dive for a hole. Otherwise it moves in a rough circle, usually no wider than a few hundred yards, clinging to a familiar area where it knows every concealing clump and burrow and where previous enemies have been eluded. Most of us, in our eagerness, have made the mistake of trying to follow, though we know the wisdom of waiting patiently in a relatively open spot or on a stump, hummock, any slight elevation, preferably close to where the hounds started the rabbit. It will probably come back, bounding before the muzzle.

A rabbiting shotgun may be of any gauge from 12 to 28 if it has an improved-cylinder or modified boring. Tight chokes do not mix well with scurrying rabbits at a range of 30 yards or less. No. 6 low-brass loads are ideal.

An exceptionally fine time for rifle hunting is when the ground is thinly covered with snow, or a couple of days after a heavier snow when a crust has formed and cottontails have emerged from sheltering chuck holes. Tracks will reveal areas of concentration—south-facing slopes, for example, where rabbits contrast with a white background as they bask in the sun or browse amid protruding grass or thin sumac stands. Any accurate .22 rimfire rifle will serve well, especially with Long Rifle match cartridges. The medium velocity is adequate and hollow-points are not needed. A 2½-power scope is best for such shooting, but the rifleman who walks up his targets will want open sights since he must shoot almost as fast as the shotgunner.

TRACKS & SIGN: The neat leaf-clipping of rabbits is easily distinguished from the ragged tearing of deer, and in winter a sign of cottontails is the low girdling of fruit trees, saplings, and shrubs, particularly sumac, white and black oak, dogwood, and sassafras. Since cottontails never roam far, browse marks reveal good hunting spots. Every hunter acquires personal convictions about sign, and the author admits to a scatological predilection because droppings are often more noticeable than browse marks or tracks if the ground is snowless and thinly grassed. The enormous potential of a cornfield edge in North Dakota was displayed to him, for example, by droppings scattered everywhere as thick as spilled beans. The pea-sized pellets are dark and usually round

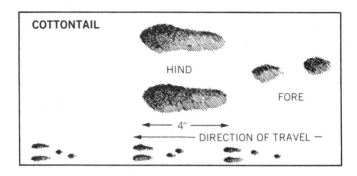

COTTONTAIL

HIND

FORE

◄—— 4" ——►

◄———————— DIRECTION OF TRAVEL —

but sometimes slightly flattened.

The tracks are most conspicuous in snow. The hind feet leave oblong prints up to about 4 inches long (much shorter when movement is fast and less of the leg touches down) and widening toward the front, while the forefeet leave much smaller, almost round prints. Sometimes four toe or claw indentations terminate each print, fore or hind, but they are blurred or obliterated in soft snow by the cottontail's long winter hair. A sitting rabbit leaves foreprints close together, side by side, and more widely spaced hind prints to the rear, but when a rabbit hops the hind prints are in front of the foreprints. The forefeet touch down first—one ahead of the other if the animal is moving fast —and on their fulcrum the body clenches, pulling the hind legs down and ahead for the next spring. This reversal of foot position occasionally fools a novice hunter into following a trail in the wrong direction. Sometimes a trail leads to a rabbit's form but walking a single track is often unrewarding. What should be sought is a profusion of runs, converging and diverging, where a dog can be started or a hunter can poke about brush piles or thickets.

VOICE: Infant rabbits squeal almost inaudibly and a doe may grunt or purr softly while nursing, but rabbits during hunting season are silent unless captured or injured by a predator. Then they can scream like a newborn human infant. The sound—duplicated with a mouth-operated predator call—is commonly used to lure foxes, bobcats, and coyotes into range of a hidden gun.

Jack Rabbit *(Lepus)*

COMMON & REGIONAL NAMES: *jack, jackass rabbit, donkey rabbit.*

DESCRIPTION & DISTRIBUTION: About 90 miles above the Big Bend in Texas, the butte-strewn painted desert crawls with life—blue quail, javelina, mule deer, cottontails, wiry blacktail jack rabbits. Local hunters hoot at the notion of going out just to hunt jacks. "All ears and legs, as tough as leather and just as dumb." But when a man walks alone in that country with a rifle or pistol, he is not unlikely to sharpen his javelina marksmanship on a much smaller target snugged against some hilltop knot of prickly pear or cluster of Spanish bayonet. If he hits a jack running, he may dance a jigstep.

Some of the hunters on the plains of Kansas and Nebraska are less furtive about the jack-rabbiting addiction. At the height of the breeding season in February or early March, a 4-acre hillside may be dotted with forty whitetail jacks. They catapult for a strolling shotgunner, but the winter sport is best with a long-range rifle. If a hunter keeps his distance, the jacks sit like woodchucks. They can be hard to spot against snow, but if the hill is bare a rifleman may move back, as an eastern chuck shooter sometimes does, to test his long-distance marksmanship.

Originally named "jackass rabbits" by settlers who were understandably impressed by their long ears, jacks are not rabbits but hares: larger than rabbits, longer-legged, longer-eared, born furred and with their eyes open, so precocious that they are weaned and abandoned in a week. There are three accepted species and a debatable fourth. Most widespread and abundant is the blacktail jack *(Lepus californicus),* which thrives from western Arkansas and Missouri to California and Oregon and south into Mexico. If jacks are frequently derided as tough and stringy table fare and easy targets, blacktails are sufficiently esteemed to have been released in New Jersey and Kentucky. It is a strange experience for a Jersey hunter to jump what ought to be a cottontail and suddenly see it in the clear—2 feet long, with 6- or 7-inch ears, and with kangaroo haunches and legs that account for a good portion of its 3½ to 7½ pounds. The average escape speed is less than 25 miles an hour for blacktails and all other

Antelope jack rabbit (top),
and northern whitetail jack.

jacks, but they can go nearly twice that fast when pressed. A panicky leap can span 15 feet, sometimes 20.

The blacktail is a grayish-tan or sandy hare with whitish underparts, black ear tips, and black on the upper surface of the tail and the base of the rump. (The underside of the tail is white on all jacks and is flashed during escape in the manner of deer and cottontails; jacks are gregarious, and the flash is a warning signal to all nearby hares, as well as a confusing distraction to pursuing predators.) Like other jack rabbits, the blacktail prefers open terrain but may be the most adaptable of its clan, flourishing on farmland, grassy prairies, or sparsely vegetated desert.

The whitetail jack *(L. townsendi)* provides better table fare than other jack rabbits, and better sport in the opinion of many. It ranges from south-central Canada into New Mexico and from Wisconsin to the Sierras. Its ears are 5 or 6 inches long, as are its hind feet from the toes to the first joint, and it weighs from 5 to 10 pounds. It is tannish gray in the summer and early fall, with black ear tips, white tail, and white on the underparts that sometimes reaches up the lower sides. In the northern part of its range it turns winter-white or very pale gray except for the ear tips, and is sometimes mistaken for an arctic hare or the shorter-eared, shorter-legged varying hare. In the South it merely pales or turns buffy white in winter. The whitetail is a lover of grass and sage on plains and open mountain slopes, in some regions foraging higher than the timber line.

The antelope jack rabbit *(L. alleni)* is usually a lean 4 to 6 pounds but sometimes heavier. It has huge ears—occasionally more than 8 inches long—with no black on the tips. Now and then a hunter bags a dusky-backed specimen but as a rule the coloration is pale, fading to whitish sides and haunches. A southwestern desert animal, it gets along on a diet of coarse grasses, prickly pear and similar cacti, mesquite, cat's-claw, and the like. There is some question as to whether the Gaillard jack *(L. gaillardi)* is a separate species or an antelope subspecies. It is somewhat shorter-eared, seldom weighs more than 5 pounds, and has a rather buffy back and slightly darker sides than the antelope. It inhabits grassy plains from New Mexico south.

GAME BEHAVIOR & HUNTING HABITAT: Jacks begin feeding

actively before twilight and keep at it until long after dawn. A hunter's best chance to catch them moving about is in the late afternoon and again in the morning until about eight o'clock. Sometimes they feed together—a couple or a couple of dozen—for they are not territorial except perhaps with regard to their forms. And they can be jumped from those resting spots at any time of day. A jack usually has several forms, shallow depressions scraped in the earth under clumps of such vegetation as rabbitbrush, sagebrush, and snakeweed, or against tussocks of gramagrass, filaree, bristlegrass, and similar plants—shrubs and grasses providing edible cover. On cultivated land they infil-

Blacktail jack rabbit.

trate crops, especially alfalfa, and if no legumes or grains stand high, they will hide in plowed furrows.

The breeding period lasts as long as ten months in some southwestern areas. Mating usually peaks in late winter or early spring, and gestation lasts about six weeks. A southern female may have four litters per year, a northern one only two, but larger, litters. Four is the average number of young. Jacks scatter their infants, hiding them but making only rudimentary nests or none at all. Owls and coyotes are their major predators, and they are also killed by bobcats, hawks, snakes, foxes, and so on—but they must be taken by stealth because they can soon outrun all four-footed enemies. Like cottontails, they are resistant to myxomatosis, which is lethal to some leporids, and more resistant than cottontails to tularemia. They are afflicted with parasites and ailments but are so hardy that in good habitat the life span may be five or six years.

Jack-rabbiters seldom use hounds, partly because hares can be spotted so often without a dog's help, and partly because jacks—which can easily outrun any breed but the greyhound—are not inclined to circle in the manner of cottontails. A jack rabbit may habitually wander in an area of 3 or 4 square miles, feeling no compulsion to circle back to familiar territory at the first sign of danger. Except for juveniles, jacks seldom enter burrows, but they do attempt to hide when alarmed by remaining dead-still. Their long ears, twitching about to catch all sounds, provide an early warning, and sometimes if there is no intervening cover—on a snow-blanketed hillside or prairie, for example—a hunter cannot get within shotgun range. In many areas, jacks are the favorite small game of pistol hunters and riflemen. High-velocity .22 rimfires, standard or Magnum, will do nicely up to 100 yards (half that with a pistol, of course), and some hunters use hollow-points, since jacks are much tougher than cottontails. There are also hunters who prefer .22 centerfires and even larger calibers because they specialize in long-range shooting—excellent practice before a hunt for larger game. A 2½-power scope will suffice.

Where cover is adequate, a shotgunner can jump or even stalk jacks. Having heard the enemy at a considerable distance, they sit still, counting on concealment at first. Though their eyesight is excellent, they seem to ignore a hunter while he remains stationary, losing interest and looking the other way. Like cottontails, they sense ground vibrations and will signal danger by thumping their feet, but a shotgunner is often within easy range before they panic. Then they spurt away, rising especially high with every fourth or fifth leap to look for the source of danger. If a first shot misses, there is usually a second chance because a jack rabbit commonly stops and looks back again after fleeing only 30 or 40 yards. At that moment it matters little whether a hunter is using a smoothbore or a rifled arm. The shotgun may be 20 gauge or larger, choked modified or full, and loaded with high-velocity No. 4, 5, or 6 charges.

TRACKS & SIGN: Good jack-rabbit areas may be marked by scarred or bitten cactus, small, light tufts of fur on barbed wire, or concentrations of dark, round droppings, slightly larger than those of cottontails. Jacks often defecate repeatedly in one place, evidently for some communicative purpose. The long hind tracks and smaller foreprints—with the hind feet printing in front of the forefeet when the animal hops—are similar to the cottontail's but larger and more widely spaced. Tracks and sign are not very important in finding jacks, however. If they are in the area they will be seen frequently, for places of concealment are scarce on grasslands and deserts.

VOICE: A jack rabbit is silent unless injured or caught by a predator, in which event it shrieks piercingly. The sound resembles the cottontail's scream of terror but is louder and slightly lower-

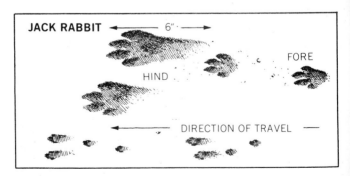

pitched. It can be heard for a mile. A predator call that imitates the scream will toll in bobcats, coyotes, and foxes.

Varying Hare *(Lepus americanus)*
COMMON & REGIONAL NAMES: *snowshoe rabbit, snowshoe hare.*

DESCRIPTION & DISTRIBUTION: It can be startling if not down-right unnerving for a New York hunter to kick out a big, white, slab-footed hare while hunting for deer in a Catskill hemlock swamp. The snowshoe rabbit, as most of us call the animal, is supposedly gone from there—forced northward long ago by clear-cutting lumbermen and the leveling of forests for pastures and fields, changes favoring the cottontail rabbit and whitetail deer but ruinous to the hare. Few hunters are yet aware that a trap-and-transfer program has been slowly returning snowshoes to the Adirondacks and to parts of the Catskills where the habitat has been improved by reforestation and, to a smaller degree, by the abandonment of some tilled acreage. The resurgence is especially marked in the Franklin County area of the upper Adirondacks, where we can again work our dogs on hard-packed snowshoe runs without heading east and buying a Vermont or Massachusetts license.

Release experiments have been less successful in the Kit-tatinny Mountains of New Jersey, where hares cannot compete with the overabundant whitetails. Some snowshoe rabbits remain in the Appalachians as far south as West Virginia, but good hunt-ing for this species usually means northern hunting. Varying hares abound throughout Alaska and Canada, as far north as the taiga regions, across the northeastern and north-central United States, down through the Rockies to Colorado, and in the Cascades and California's upper Sierras. Easterners are sur-prised to discover how good the hunting is in the Cascades and Sierras, and more surprised to find that varying hares do not necessarily vary. In those westernmost mountains they remain brown all year long. Still more disconcerting is the occasional sight of a black hare in the Adirondacks, where a melanistic strain—heretofore considered very rare—has been showing up with increasing frequency. Black hares remain black right

through winter. Perhaps they are becoming more plentiful because we are too puzzled to shoot when we see one.

Typically, varying hares in summer are brown, sometimes rusty, sometimes grayish, darkest on the ridge of the back and rump, white on the underparts and the underside of the tail. Near Joe's Pond, in north-central Vermont, some of them seem —in memory, at least—the pure brown of chocolate Easter confections edged on the bottom with frosting. As the daylight hours diminish in autumn, they begin to acquire a white-tipped winter coat, at first as patchy as the first light snow on a forest floor. Before long they look almost pure white except for their eyes and the tips of their 3½- or 4-inch ears, black specks that occasionally betray them to archers, handgunners, and other hunters who sift conifer, aspen, and willow swales without a dog.

Unseasonable weather can also betray them. A partly brown hare on a blanket of snow may blend with the forest or

Varying hare at summer's end (above),
and in winter.

stand out like a bull's-eye. Strangely, however, a hare that has turned white before the first snows can be difficult to spot unless it has been started by a dog. The snowshoe rabbit seems to sense danger when the days are short but snowless, and therefore seeks screening cover. When daylight begins to lengthen again, the winter coat is slowly shed and replaced by summer brown.

In Canada and Alaska, hunters occasionally confuse the snowshoe with the closely related arctic hare *(L. arcticus),* which is, indeed, very similar. But the arctic hare is usually much larger than a snowshoe—up to 28 inches long, nearly a foot high at the shoulder, and weighing 6 to 12 pounds, as against the snowshoe's average length of 19 or 20 inches, 8- or 9-inch height, and weight of 3 to 4½ pounds. Arctic hares live so far north that they are not hunted much, but if identification is dubious even after the game is in hand, a close look at the fur settles the matter. It is white all the way through on the arctic hare, dark at the base on a varying hare. In relatively temperate parts of its range, the arctic hare turns brown or gray-brown in summer but its tail remains white.

The name "snowshoe" is accurately vivid. The hind feet are almost 6 inches long at maturity and they broaden considerably from rear to splay-toed front. Long, thick hair, especially about the toes, enhances the snowshoe effect, supporting the hare well even when running on deep, soft snow, preventing wet snow from sticking to the feet, and providing traction on ice and insulation from cold, while also cutting the scent left in tracks. If powdery snow impedes progress, the effect has gone unnoticed by those of us who have watched hounds and hares conduct a 30-mile-an-hour chase. The first move may be a short hop or a 10-foot leap, after which the snowshoe has enough momentum to cover 15 feet at a bound if the dogs close in. It is a tireless runner, even more adept than the cottontail at making right-angle turns in midair, and never holing up as a cottontail does.

GAME BEHAVIOR & HUNTING HABITAT: "A good winter for running cat hounds is a good winter for running rabbit hounds." There are numerous versions of the old hunting proverb, but the snowshoe hare is a staple of the lynx; where man has not annihilated the predators, populations of the two species tend to fluctuate in rough harmony though the hares exhibit much sharper cyclic increases and decreases. In one part or another of snowshoe range, other major predators include bobcats, weasels, wolverines, foxes, minks, owls, and hawks.

Whitetails compete for winter forage; in summer, ticks and other parasites plague the hares and they are sometimes weakened by a mild form of tularemia or by other leporid diseases such as coccidiosis. None of these factors accounts for the violent population cycles which mystify hunters and are not yet fully understood by scientists. In normal habitat and without benefit of game stocking, snowshoes become exceptionally plentiful every nine to eleven years, then swiftly and drastically decline. The fluctuations are most pronounced in the Northeast, but the best hunting years can be predicted almost everywhere: Peaks occur with fair regularity during the first, second, and third year of each decade. This is being written as a peak period dwindles.

No devoted snowshoe man plans to give up the sport during the expected meager years, but we do look forward to 1981 or 1982.

The greatest mating activity, marked by fighting among the males, occurs in March. After a gestation of about thirty-five to forty days, a female bears her young in a concealed form. No real nest is made for the precocious infants, which begin nibbling at vegetation within a week, though they may continue to suckle for almost a month.

From personal observation and reports of other hunters and naturalists, it seems unlikely that varying hares hole up even in very cold weather. Their forms are often on slight elevations, probably for drainage rather than vantage, and, except for the natal hideaway, they are seldom in such concealing cover as that of cottontails. On snow, a form packs and melts until it becomes a slight depression reflecting the sitting hare's contour, a miniature of the bed made on snow by elk and other big game. More conspicuous than the forms are the networks of trails, or runs, emblazoning areas of good forage. Packed by repeated use, the trails often sink well below the surrounding snow.

When winter has ravaged the last grasses, clover, and similar succulent greens, a hunter can look for trails and other sign where snowshoes browse on the bark, twigs, and tender tips of many plants but especially pine, spruce, fir, white cedar, aspen, willow, and paper birch. Dense fir and cedar swamps are good places to release the hounds, for the hares love conifers.

In light powder snow, the dogs sniff about uncertainly, taking a long and frustrating while to pick up a fresh trail. A wet snow—a thawing snow—holds scent better. If the day is dark and overcast, so much the better, for then snowshoes feed pretty actively without waiting for dusk. A leveret—a hare in its first year—sometimes circles before the dogs almost as tightly as a cottontail. An older snowshoe is generally bolder and wiser. Though it dislikes traveling more than a few hundred yards from its favorite cover, except when avoiding intruders, its first circle may well cover a mile. The game does not always come within view that first time around, but subsequent circles shrink.

When the hounds return, you will want to be alert and very still. The hunter's stand must have a good view; ideally, it will keep him inconspicuous if not hidden, but a view of possible

crossings is the paramount consideration. A chase can be short or the waiting can go on for several hours. If the hounds pass out of hearing very quickly and seem to have taken a more or less straight course, it is wise to follow for some distance before taking a stand. An old hare occasionally runs straight out—more like a red fox than a rabbit—before circling. A hound for this work needs a strong nose, a strong voice, and great stamina. Most hunters prefer something leggier than the 13-inch beagle of the brier patches. Favorites are foxhounds, 15-inch beagles, and beagle-foxhound crosses, the sort of dogs that plow through drifts and run without tiring.

The hare will not tire, either. A bounding, skittering, side-slipping snowshoe is game for a 12- or 20-gauge shotgun with a modified choke and No. 4, 5, or 6 loads. For still-hunting, on the other hand, a .22 rimfire rifle or pistol is proper. Long shots are so unlikely that a scope is superfluous, and bullets may be solid or hollow-pointed. The man without dogs must walk slowly through areas thick with tracks and sign, searching for

Hunting in snowshoe-rabbit country.

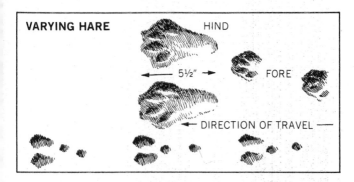

a twitch before a hare disappears by freezing in position, and for the black specks of eyes and ear tips, for something like a patch of thawing snow—a subtle shadowing where dark hair shows through the white outer layer—under a tree, against a log or bush or blowdown.

TRACKS & SIGN: The round droppings of a snowshoe are about as large as a jack rabbit's—almost a third larger than a cottontail's. The girdling of trees for winter food is also noticeable, just above the snow, even in a dim forest. As with jacks and cottontails, the hind feet print in advance of the forefeet when a snowshoe hops, but the hind prints are larger than a cottontail's and broader at the toes, forming wide triangles. The long furred toes may leave no individual indentations in powdery snow. Tracking looks easy but is too often futile on the deeply trodden runs and complex networks of trails. A hare will leave its run at any point to forage or to avoid a strange sound or sight, turning the networks into an endless maze. Without a dog, the hunter's best chance is to look for thickly marked foraging areas and hunt them carefully without attempting to unravel the trails.

VOICE: Like other hares and rabbits, a snowshoe squeals when injured or caught by a predator but is otherwise quiet. The piercing squeal tends to be slightly louder than a cottontail's and has great carrying power. A lynx, bobcat, fox, or coyote will come to investigate when a hidden hunter imitates the sound on a wooden predator call.

Squirrel *(Sciurus)*
COMMON & REGIONAL NAMES: *bannertail, bushytail.*

DESCRIPTION & DISTRIBUTION: For minutes at a time, the silence in the woods is perfect as night evaporates. Pierced by a shrill bird call, it mends itself and remains absolute—at least to the human ear—for another few minutes before a sibilant rustle lifts the hunter's gaze to the branches of a white oak. There is almost enough light to shoot; he cannot make out the source of the rustling, but he is betting on a squirrel, perhaps more than one, and he makes no sound to spoil the beginning of the day's finest squirreling hour. On windless mornings, when squirrels are most active, they are often heard before they are seen. The hunter's back rests against a tree, and he faces west so that the rising sun will light the game and not blind him when it punctures the timber openings. He hears another rustle, then sees a plume of tail whisk from the top of a limb and drape itself downward, 10 inches long, sapling-thick and diaphanous. Very slowly he raises his iron-sighted rimfire rifle. A dark knurl materializes atop the swaying plume, and he knows it is not a knurl but a haunch. The squirrel is flat against the limb, watching and listening. Detecting no danger, it reveals a sinuous gray cylinder of body as long as its flicking tail, and now there is light enough to shoot the day's first bannertail.

It may be either a gray squirrel *(Sciurus carolinensis)* or a fox squirrel *(S. niger),* depending on region and, to some degree, on subtle factors of habitat, and the woods are probably but not necessarily in the eastern half of the United States. After rabbits, these tree squirrels and their closest relatives are the most hunted of American game. Gophers and all the other ground squirrels are important as prey for carnivorous animals, but not as game except to small boys. Among the arboreal species, the flying squirrel is much too minuscule and nocturnal for hunting. The several red squirrels, or chickarees *(Tamiasciurus),* also known as pine squirrels, seldom weigh much more than half a pound and are likelier to scold a hunter than to hide or flee. In many northern and western coniferous forests, where they thrive on nuts and cone seeds, they are abundant enough to require no special protection, but are not classified as game animals and are only occasionally shot. They look like reddish,

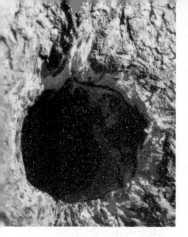

skimpy-tailed miniatures of the gray and fox squirrels that contributed more than any other game to America's early reputation for marksmanship.

Closely related to the eastern, or common, gray is the California, or western, gray *(S. griseus),* whose range is restricted to the West Coast of the United States. Very much like its eastern kin—though a little larger and narrower-tailed—it provides good hunting in the pine and oak groves of California and Oregon. Similar habitat is favored by the Arizona gray squirrel *(S. arizonensis),* which also looks like the eastern type, except for its yellowish belly. Additional western relatives are the tassel-eared squirrels *(S. aberti)* of Arizona, New Mexico, and Colorado. (They also occur in Utah but are scarce there, and protected.) Since they subsist chiefly by chiseling the seeds out of yellow-pine cones, the best hunting habitat for tassel-ears is self-evident. There are two color phases, both with dark, conspicuous ear tufts. One is the Abert's: chestnut on top, gray on the sides and upper tail surface, white on the underparts and usually on the lower tail surface. The other is the Kaibab squirrel, which generally has a white tail and mainly black underparts.

But when hunters speak of squirreling, they generally are talking about eastern gray or fox squirrels. A half-dozen races of the gray range from southernmost Canada to the Gulf and across the eastern half of the country. It is said that at one time they could have journeyed through the trees from Maine to Florida or from Virginia to Kansas without touching the ground. At long intervals they have, indeed, made lemminglike emigrations to relieve overcrowding in some of the richest forests, but not across

Gray squirrel's den (l.) and nest.

such long distances. They remain abundant where tracts of nut-bearing hardwoods have been spared, but lumbering, farming, and mining have diminished their range, and they will never again number in the billions as they once did.

Agriculture has actually extended the range of the fox squirrel, which originally inhabited the sparse woods fringing the midwestern prairies. Heavier than the gray, it spends far more time on the ground and (although the two species coexist in many regions) it prefers woods that are interspersed with clearings or croplands. There are ten subspecies, distributed from the Dakotas, Nebraska, Kansas, Oklahoma, and central Texas across all of the East, except upper Wisconsin, upper Michigan, and the northeastern states down to lower Pennsylvania.

Adult northern grays are commonly almost a foot long from nose to rump, with a bushy tail of equal length and a weight of a little more than a pound. They tend to be a trifle smaller in the South, where many hunters still call them by the traditional name "cat squirrels." They can be almost as playful as kittens, occasionally mewing and purring as they tumble about or chase one another. A squirrel will scratch at fleas and use its claws as tail combs, but—like a cat—it grooms its body by licking, and, if it falls out of a tree, it can right itself in midair.

Silvery or peppery gray is the dominant color of a typical gray squirrel. The effect is produced by guard hairs banded with

Gray squirrel feeding on acorn.

black or gray, brownish or buff, black near the ends with white tips. The bands are more conspicuous in the long tail hair, edged with white. The underparts are white, very pale gray, or (in the Midwest) yellowish or buffy. The eye rings and muzzle are pale, often light rust or yellowish tan, causing large grays to be confused now and then with fox squirrels.

However, a fox squirrel's tail is rust-edged, its underparts generally yellowish or yellow-orange. It tends to be both stockier and longer than the gray. The average length is a little over 2 feet, including a foot-long orange or rusty banner of tail. The weight is usually between 1½ and 2 pounds, or occasionally up to 3. But tree squirrels are genetically unstable, color variations are wide and common, and identification is sometimes dubious where both species are hunted.

On the ground, a fox squirrel lopes in a manner reminiscent of the fox, and it has a luxuriant foxy plume, but it was probably named for the suffusion of red in its fur. (In some areas it is also known as the red squirrel, a name more properly applied to the little pine squirrels.) A northeastern fox squirrel is most often salt-and-peppery with a foxy orange wash. In the western part of the range a bright rusty tinge predominates—which may surprise southerners who are accustomed to black fox squirrels, often with white face blazes and tail tips. A typical South Carolina fox squirrel is unmistakable—black with white ears and nose. If memory can be trusted, no handsomer animal has ever gone into the game pocket.

Melanism is rather common, but not among both species in a single region. Oddly, black fox squirrels are pretty much restricted to the South, whereas grays become darker in the North (most Canadian grays being black or very dark). Albinism is more common to grays than to most species. Around Olney, Illinois, there is a sizable colony of white squirrels, protected by state law. Elsewhere, albino grays are generally legal. If neither size nor fur positively reveals the species, recognition is simple when the game is dressed; a gray squirrel's bones are white, those of a fox squirrel pinkish.

GAME BEHAVIOR & HUNTING HABITAT: City parks, purged of predators and closed to hunting, spawn squirrels that will eat out of one's hand. Squirrels in hunted woodlands and groves are so different that any consistently successful squirrel hunter has a basis for vanity. They learn so quickly that most of the yearly bag is taken during the first couple of weeks of hunting, even in some states with long seasons.

Seasonal protection is a continuing controversy. Most states permit hunting from September or October to January or February, but some have slightly earlier or later seasons—and a great many Ozark hunters would rather go squirreling in mulberry time than in acorn time. Spring hunting produces great quantities of Brunswick stew where hungry squirrels—having subsisted mostly on winter buds, bark, and twigs after the buried nut supply dwindled—congregate about mulberries and other fruit trees. In Missouri, Kansas, and Oklahoma the season generally lasts from May or June through December, and squirrel hunting is better there than in many states with short seasons. Squirreling no longer amounts to much in South Dakota, which permits year-long shooting, but the reason is too little habitat rather than too much hunting. Studies by game biologists indicate that hunters account for an extremely small fraction of "surplus" squirrels, those doomed in any event by winter hunger and competition because man has so drastically reduced the habitat.

On the other hand, squirrels are so hardy that in most hunting regions they now maintain stable, relatively large populations. West Virginians bag more squirrels than cottontails, North Carolinians almost as many. Gray and fox squirrels together account for a larger harvest than rabbits in Tennessee. Counting both species, a couple of million are taken in an average year in Wisconsin, Ohio, Missouri, and Louisiana.

Yet, as rodents go, squirrels are not prolific. A typical female of either species brings forth two litters per year, averaging three young to a litter. The gestation period lasts six weeks or a trifle longer. A winter breeding season, in late December and January, produces young mostly in February and March (or a little later in the North), and a May breeding season produces chiefly in July. Hunters who worry about seeing "fall litters" in September have encountered weaned young, only just beginning to explore outside the den entrances, but which nonetheless are self-sufficient. Spring and summer hunting, despite the kill of some pregnant or nursing females, does not limit the population—the habitat's carrying capacity does that—but some

of us refrain from squirreling when orphaned young may be unweaned. Hunting during the mating periods is less cruel and more exhilarating. The squirrels are not so wary then. Several males are often seen in frenzied pursuit of a female, nipping and squabbling among themselves until a dominant male chases away the last rival.

A male gray dallies with his mate for a couple of days, then wanders off, rests, and seeks another. A male fox squirrel takes a single mate and remains with her almost until she bears her young (but not for life, as some hunters believe). The preferred den for either species is a tree cavity—sometimes a woodpecker hole, more often a decayed spot in a hardwood where a shaded limb died and fell away. The den may be a couple of feet deep and half a foot across, but its entrance must be no larger than 3 or 4 inches to prevent access by possums and owls. Such cavities usually form in large trees, anywhere from just overhead to about 30 feet up. Since squirrels use dens all year long, groves that include some stout, mature trees or standing dead ones hold promise of a good hunt. Holes are most common in white oaks, beeches, elms, and red maples—as well as the corpses of the blighted chestnuts.

However, leaf nests are easier to spot. Most squirrels build at least a couple of big nests each year even where tree cavities are numerous. Some females build sturdy nests as nurseries or move their litters back and forth between den and nest. Both

Young gray squirrel at den.

males and females weave summer and winter nests, the summer abodes having a looser construction, but all look pretty much alike. They appear to be great, ragged, leafy balls anchored in high crotches. Solid as they look, they are hollow. The few ramshackle ones are commonly practice nests made by juveniles or temporary bivouacs close to crop fields.

Less thick and elaborate than nests are the loafing platforms, known to many of us as "cooling beds" because they are most frequently used in warm weather. A leafy couch probably means a squirrel in the immediate vicinity, even if no true nest is in evidence. However, the man is not a sportsman who shoots into a nest or cooling bed instead of relying on hunting skill and marksmanship. The squirrel almost never tumbles out, is usually impossible to retrieve, and will probably be wounded—not killed outright. Any nest-shooter who manages the climb and

Fox squirrel.

reaches into the leaves deserves all the lacerations the anima can inflict.

Squirrels are apt to be abundant and active in the fall, for neither the young nor the old have many enemies. Some are killed by bobcats, tree-climbing snakes, weasels, red-tailed hawks, and red-shouldered hawks, but few predators can squeeze through a den or nest opening, much less catch a squirrel in the trees. Fleas often infest a den, but a squirrel escapes most of them by taking to a leaf nest. Ticks occasionally attach themselves but rarely cause serious damage, and a few diseases and internal parasites are no more dangerous. Some squirrels contract the viral wart growth known as rabbit horn, or Shope's fibroma; it is not lethal to them and it comes off with the hide, leaving perfectly good meat. Warbles—botfly larvae burrowing under the skin—are a summer problem in the South and one reason why some states open the season late. A severely afflicted animal is weakened, and the sores are so unsightly that hunters tend to discard warbly squirrels even if they know that the meat is never affected. Where squirrels are undernourished or winter-weakened, they sometimes also suffer from mange. Most of them recover, and where the habitat keeps them strong they tend to resist mange mites. Life expectancy varies from about a year and a half in typical regions to six in prime woods.

The reason for heightened fall activity is the need to store nuts, and the caching becomes most frenzied while the nuts are green and on the trees. Fallen ones are often eaten but seldom buried. The little cache holes, covered with sod or leaves, are difficult or impossible to spot, though in winter the holes become visible where nuts have been dug up. Regardless of popular beliefs, squirrels recover most of what they cache, and they do so not by memory but by scent. They can smell a buried nut under a foot of snow, and when that becomes difficult they tunnel under the snow to get closer. (Fortunately for hunters, squirrels do not rely on their sharp noses to detect danger. Their exquisite hearing and sight make the sport sufficiently difficult.)

Nut-rich woods are almost inevitably good hunting sites in the fall, as are fruit trees that ripen then. Squirrels have a special fondness for the nuts of shagbark and other hickories, white and black oaks, pecans, beeches, and black walnuts; they can be sought among whichever of these is prevalent in a given region, or among wild cherries, hackberries, and black gum. As winter progresses, they are similarly attracted to the twigs and immature buds of maples, oaks, and elms. And in farming country they will be near cornfields. Raccoons are often blamed for corn thefts that are obviously the work of squirrels. A gray squirrel nibbles the kernels off a cob and then eats only the germ portion, dropping the remainder of each kernel. A fox squirrel prefers to haul a cob away to a nearby feeding perch—a stump, log, low branch—where the ground is strewn with husks and bits of cob.

Similar food preferences do not mean that both species will be abundant in a single kind of habitat. Gray squirrels prefer forests so thick that they can travel through the tree crowns. They like heavily wooded bottomlands or big, mature forests with an understory of smaller trees, and they chiefly inhabit the eastern hardwoods—especially oak and hickory. Where both breeds reside, intermingling is uncommon, the grays occupying the depths, while the fox squirrels seek uplands, creek drainages, and edges. Except during mating seasons and when the young spread to less crowded parcels of habitat, neither species likes to roam more than a few hundred yards from nest or den tree. Fox squirrels prefer small groves, clearing edges, or open woods. In the northern and western parts of their range, the hunting is best on dry ridges and in well-drained valleys among oaks, hickories, or walnuts. In the Deep South they also populate longleaf pines, the edges of cypress swamps, and stands of red and black mangroves. Though many are shot in dense southern swamps and midwestern flood-plain forests, a limit is usually collected faster where plenty of sun penetrates. Hunting is good in the small woodlots of farms, in windbreak strips or clumps, and among field-border trees.

The game is sporadically active through the day, but hunting is best in the early morning—very early for grays—and late afternoon. It is poor in extremely cold or stormy weather, when squirrels doze for several days in nests or dens. They also tend to be inactive on blustery days, probably because the noise of wind might hide an enemy.

In parts of the South and Midwest, many hunters sustain the tradition of using a squirrel dog. A dog scents squirrels a hunter would never see. The method is unexcelled early in the

season when squirrels are on the ground burying nuts. For reasons that defy analysis, mongrels are among the best squirrelers. Any fairly small, quiet, close-working dog can be trained to the task, but mixed breeds with terrier blood often combine the right size and working style with drab colors. Anything bright is a long-distance danger signal to squirrels, but (perhaps because they escape most foxes and coyotes) they are not panicked by a small, quiet dog sniffing along a carpet of mast. A treed squirrel may escape or present a fast, difficult shotgun target, but almost as often it will scamper part-way up, then hug a branch or—more inquisitive than alarmed—flatten itself against the trunk to look down at the dog. A smart hunter comes up quietly from the opposite side, while the dog holds the squirrel's attention. Fox squirrels are easiest. They inhabit fairly open woods, spend much more time on the ground than grays do, and cannot scurry along branches as fast or leap as effortlessly through the crowns. When caught on the ground, they head for a den tree, rather than the nearest tree, and often go no farther. Grays therefore provide better sport with dogs (an opinion, admit-

Fox squirrel on feeding stump.

tedly, that will invite some disagreement). Moreover, squirrels are not very fast on the ground, and only the grays are adept at dodging, so fox squirrels are overtaken by dogs now and then.

Without a dog, the surest way to bag squirrels is to search out well-populated spots before the season opens and then combine several hunting methods. Begin by arriving before dawn and sitting silently to watch the forest waken (an especially valuable approach late in the season, when squirrels have become so wary that inexperienced hunters wonder if they have all moved out or been killed). If nothing happens in twenty or twenty-five minutes after first light, move on, but slowly. This kind of stalking is true still-hunting, the technique that brings success with whitetails as well as bannertails.

Move quietly, without a steady walking rhythm, pausing often. There is no need to cover more than 10 yards in a minute. Watch for bulges that look too smooth, too soft for tree knurls, for flickers of movement, for breeze-ruffled tail hair. Hiding squirrels seem to forget about their tails—which are used chiefly for balance, as parachutes, and to fool diving hawks into missing their strikes. Listen for rustling, scratching, chirping chatter, and the little quacking barks that are a squirrel's signal of alert. When hunting with a partner, stay 30 or 40 yards apart so that each man's movement pushes squirrels to the other man, and watch for dim forms flattened against trunks or limbs. A sandy, waterless creek bed makes a path for near silent walking, and some hunters canoe along shorelines. There are streams and ponds where squirreling can be combined with jump-shooting for wood ducks. In other areas, where the cover is very thick, squirrels can sometimes be flushed by shaking vine tangles and brush. But to follow a squirrel round and round as it circles a shielding trunk is an exercise in futility. A stone or small branch tossed into the brush on the far side is more likely to bring the game back into view.

If all else fails, walk without any attempt at stealth into a grove of foraging and den trees, and then sit quietly for a quarter hour. Believing the danger is gone, the squirrels will probably come out again to sun, feed, and play. They may need reassurance, however, in the form of calling. Among the best commercial calls is the bellows type, which has a little rubber sounder—an accordion in principal—on one end. Tapping this end rapidly against the palm of a hand, the knee, or the chest produces a squeaky barking chatter. Squirrels also click and cluck, and some hunters manage a reasonable facsimile by clucking their tongues. It is easier and more realistic to rap a couple of apple-sized stones together, tap a coin against a gun stock, or tap the edge of one coin on the flat surface of another. If a rapid clicking is answered by squirrel chatter, repeat it only briefly and then watch in silence for a curious squirrel to approach through the branches or start down a tree.

An everlasting argument pertains to the choice between rifles and shotguns. With dogs, or whenever there is much foliage on the trees, the shotgun has a definite advantage. Sometimes it is the only possible choice, even if a landowner makes no objection to rifles. And if the shooting is restricted to moving targets, it is just as sporting as a rifle. As shots may be long and squirrels are tough, modified- or full-choked 12 gauges are common, but Magnum 20's will also serve well. Moderately heavy No. 6 loads are widely used, and 5's may be still better for large fox squirrels.

A few hunters use scoped pistols, though handgunning squirrels is difficult at best, especially for any woodsman who agrees that head-shooting enhances the sport and is the only sure way to avoid excessive meat damage. Depending on the density of local cover and the distances at which a hunter shoots most of his squirrels, a good rifle may be iron-sighted or equipped with a 2½-power scope zeroed at 50 yards. In some areas, for that matter, a 4-power scope might be better. Nothing more powerful than a .22 Long Rifle cartridge with a solid bullet is needed for conventional squirrel shooting. However, a few traditionalists shoot muzzle-loading squirrel rifles of larger caliber. The relatively heavy ball used in such a rifle is ideal for "barking" squirrels. This difficult method, almost forgotten since the era of black powder, is feasible only when a squirrel is seen in profile, tightly flattened against a limb or trunk. The object is to hit the bark just beneath the animal, knocking it down and killing it by concussion though it is untouched by the ball.

TRACKS & SIGN: Tracks are seen occasionally in mud, commonly on snow. A squirrel bounds somewhat in the manner of a rabbit, bringing the hind feet down ahead of the forefeet to leave tracks resembling small rabbit tracks but with distinct differences. The claws usually leave sharp indentations. The print is smaller than a rabbit's and more sharply triangular—splay-toed. And the foot placement is straighter, so that the long hind prints, followed closely by the short foreprints, look rather like a pair of exclamation marks. A profusion of tracks indicates squirrels in the trees nearby.

The dark little oval droppings are rarely found, but three types of sign are obvious. The first is the round, leafy nest or flatter cooling bed high in a tree. The second is a ragged hole in earth or through snow where a nut has been dug up. The third is a litter of gnawed nutshells or acorn husks amid the mast where squirrels have fed. Debris left by fox squirrels is especially evident when they carry nuts to a favorite feeding perch, using it repeatedly until the ground is covered.

VOICE: Fox squirrels are less noisy than grays, but both species bark sharp alarms. A hunter who calls too stridently can defeat himself by sounding the squirrel's own hysterical alarm. An imitation of feeding and playing chatter should sound busy but unruffled: chirps, clicks, clucks, squeaky little barks. This is most effective with a hand-operated bellows call. There is no point in mimicking the gray squirrel's playful mews and purrs or the squeal of injury and fright common to rabbits and squirrels —unless, of course, the object is to call in a predator.

Marmot *(Marmota)*
COMMON & REGIONAL NAMES: *chuck, whistler, whistle-pig,* siffleur *(French Canadian).* For eastern or flatland species— *woodchuck, groundhog, monax, pasture pup.* For western species—*yellow-bellied marmot, yellow-footed marmot, rock-chuck, mountain marmot.* For northwestern species—*hoary mar-mot, rockchuck, mountain marmot.*

DESCRIPTION & DISTRIBUTION: Down on all fours grazing, waddling through meadow grass, or scrambling over rocks, a 10-pound marmot is a squat, blunt-nosed, slothful-looking, lub-berly mound of grizzly brown or gray. It bulks that way in the

(text continued on page 417)

▲ Common gallinule.   ▼ Purple gallinule.

▲ King rail. ▼ Sora rail.

▼ Sandhill crane.   ▲ Virginia rail.   ▼ Clapper rail.

▲ Wilson's snipe.   ▼ American coot.

▲ Bobcat approaching caller. ▼ Hunters, hounds, and bobcat.

▼ Blacktail prairie dog.   ▲ Bobcat running from pack.   ▼ Author aiming for javelin

▼ Tracking Texas peccary.

▲ Hoary marmot.   ▼ Peccaries rooting.

▼ Varying hare in summer coat.　▲ Cottontail sign.　▼ Hunter with brace of varying

▼ Blacktail jack.

memory of anyone who spent boyhood days on elbows and knees in itchy alfalfa trying to stalk close enough to use an open-sighted .22 before the chuck plopped with sudden agility into a burrow. But now that the hopelessly loose-jointed .22 has been stored by a son in an attic corner, the chuck is studied most often while it sits straight up on its haunches, perfectly pear-shaped even across 300 yards of clover, a trencherman with a look of mild surprise magnified as the scope's fine crosshairs meet above its neckless, apple-sized head.

Despite adaptations to widely separated environments —accidents of distribution—the woodchuck and the western and northwestern marmots are so alike that they can be logically treated as one animal; they are three distinct but very closely related species of the genus *Marmota,* totaling thirty-one subspecies. The woodchuck *(Marmota monax),* representing nine subspecies, is best known because it is a flatlander that resides chiefly in farm country and offers targets both plentiful and problematical to long-range marksmen. It alone was responsible for the development of specialized "varmint" rifles and cartridges. Before the forests were swept away it was indeed a chuck of the woods, though it required wide grassy spaces during the summer to fatten itself for hibernation.

The rolling pastures and fields from New England to the

Eastern woodchuck emerging from den.

central southeastern states encompass the traditional purlieu of long-distance chuck shooters, but the bookish designation "eastern woodchuck" is misleading—and annoying to a writer who, at the age of ten, shot his first groundhog while hunting gophers near the hedgerow of a sprawling Minnesota pasture. That particular woodchuck was of a reddish subspecies ranging from North Dakota to Ontario, New York, and parts of New England. Other races are hunted as far west as Alberta and north

Chuck as seen by rifleman (above) and close up.

to Great Slave Lake in the territories, from the Atlantic to Kansas and Arkansas, from British Columbia to Idaho, from the lower Midwest to Nebraska, from British Columbia north into Alaska and the Yukon. Woodchucks are most plentiful in the eastern half of the United States but are found across all of Canada. It is hardly unusual for a western hunter to shoot a "rockchuck" that is really a woodchuck.

The true rockchucks are the yellow-bellied, or yellow-footed, marmot *(Marmota flaviventris)* and the hoary marmot *(Marmota caligata).* The dozen yellow-bellied subspecies reside chiefly in the mountainous terrain of South Dakota's Black Hills, the Rockies from Colorado northward, and the far western ranges from lower California into central British Columbia. They share the northwestern part of the range with the hoary marmot, whose ten subspecies inhabit alpine meadows and stony slopes from Alaska and the Yukon down into Washington, Idaho, and western Montana.

The woodchuck, smallest of the three, usually weighs between 6 and 10 pounds at maturity, but loses weight during hibernation and for a month afterward, until spring·vegetation comes up. It gains a couple of pounds by late summer or early fall, when fat reserves must be accumulated for winter. Stretched

flat, a big woodchuck may be over 2 feet long, but it stretches only when sunning, and its chunky build makes it appear shorter. Its fur is basically brown—blackish brown on the thick feet and short, bushy tail—but varies from quite dark (occasionally melanistic) to light reddish brown, and silver-tipped guard hairs give its body a grizzled tone. It has small, round ears, long digging claws, a blunt head, and long incisors, whiter and more conspicuous than those of other gnawing animals.

The yellow-bellied, or yellow-footed, marmot averages between 6 and 12 pounds and may weigh as much as 17. Its underparts and feet are usually light yellowish brown or tawny yellow, its body a somewhat paler, grizzled brown than the woodchuck's. Its shoulders are buff-washed and the muzzle has a white or whitish band around the mouth, usually with additional bits of white between the eyes.

The hoary marmot, 9 inches high when standing on all fours, over 30 inches long, sometimes as heavy as 20 pounds,

Hoary marmot.

outweighs all American rodents except the beaver and porcupine. Its feet and tail are black or blackish, its body gray or almost white with small black specks. There are black patches about the eyes, ears, and on the forehead, and frequently a black band around the snout. (Some authorities recognize the big brown chucks of Washington's Olympic Mountains and a similar group on Vancouver Island as two separate species, and a much lighter breed in northern Alaska as a third, but they are generally accepted as races of hoary marmot.)

GAME BEHAVIOR & HUNTING HABITAT: Chucks are the only true hibernators among the continent's game animals. Bears, raccoons, skunks, and chipmunks spend much of the winter in a torpid state, but the only North American mammals to undergo full, prolonged hibernation are ground squirrels, jumping mice, bats, and marmots. Immature woodchucks commonly remain in their summer dens for hibernation, probably because they have had a shorter fattening season than the adults and must keep to the pastures as long as possible. Occasionally two juveniles will share a meadow burrow, and if they are a male and female they mate the following spring. Most mature woodchucks, however, leave their field burrows in September or October (depending on regional climate) and excavate winter dens in the shelter of woods, where cold penetrates less deeply. Some rockchucks hibernate in meadow burrows, while others use natural rock dens or dig burrows under timbers. Those remaining in the alpine meadows are now and then killed in their sleep, when bears—particularly grizzlies—sniff them out and dig them up in early spring.

Woodchucks and rockchucks are fairly similar in most other aspects of behavior. On a mat of grasses in the winter burrow, a marmot curls into a ball and gradually goes into a deep sleep. Body temperature falls from almost 97 degrees to less than 40, the heartbeat drops from a rate of more than one hundred beats per minute to four, circulation slows, a breath is taken only once in about six minutes, all growth stops, and fat is absorbed to keep the animal alive. A chuck is lean when it groggily emerges from its den in late February or March—later in northern regions. This is the time of mating. Females dig burrows in the pastures, while males wander from burrow to burrow seeking mates. Often repulsed but steadfast, a typical male eventually settles into a female's den, though an old one may dig his own burrow and spend only part of his time with his mate. Four is the average number of a woodchuck litter, but northern rockchucks are slightly more prolific. Since gestation requires about a month, most births occur in April. Shortly before the young are born, the male usually leaves or is evicted and wanders off to dig his own den, but a female with an unmanageable mate will leave and dig herself a new burrow.

For six weeks or more, the young are totally dependent on their dam, and since there is no way to tell a male chuck from a female before he squeezes the trigger, no genuine sportsman hunts chucks before mid-June. Where they threaten vegetable gardens, clover, or alfalfa crops, killing them in early spring is a control measure, not sport. Until recently, control has been overemphasized in some intensively farmed eastern states, where landowners, justifying massacre with traps, poisoned grains, cyanide cartridges, and hoses leading from tractor exhausts down into plugged burrows, chose to believe the myth that cattle and horses break their legs in chuck holes.

Acceding to the prejudices of the agricultural establishment, game departments have failed to classify the marmot as a game animal. Officially it remains a "varmint," though the species is beneficial. A peculiarly hygienic creature, it defecates in an excrement chamber separate from the burrow's nesting chamber, and the droppings add fertilizer to the soil. By digging, it loosens and aerates the earth, brings up subsoil for transformation into topsoil, and lets in moisture and organic matter. Farmers who weary of turning the soil might ponder the fact that chucks in New York State alone are estimated to turn 1,600,000 tons of it annually. Hunters notice that abandoned chuck holes are used by cottontails in winter and enlarged by red foxes in spring, but few realize that the burrows also provide occasional dens for other furbearers (raccoons, skunks), rodent killers (weasels), prey species (chipmunks), and upland birds escaping predators or mean weather. A woodchuck can eat more than a third of its weight in clover or alfalfa per day, but reasonable hunting pressure will control chuck infestations.

For several years, avid hunters in several states have advocated an open marmot season only from the last week or

two of June until the animals hibernate, thus halting the kill of nursing females and consequent destruction of entire litters. Bag limits have also been proposed. At this writing neither suggestion has been heeded, but informed hunters (and particularly those who write about hunting) will continue to press for reform while setting an example of restraint.

Rockchucks subsist chiefly on wild grasses and forbs—including locoweed, which evidently has no effect on them—supplemented by roots, berries, flowers, and shrubs. Hunters look for mountain meadows in proximity to rocky retreats. No matter how quietly a meadow is approached, it may at first appear deserted if it has been hunted recently, but where there are

Yellow-bellied marmot.

mounded chuck holes there are usually chucks, and there is time while they remain below to get into a solid shooting position; after a quiet wait, generally lasting only a few minutes, heads will begin to pop out. However, the wait may be futile on very hot days in the southern part of the range because chucks escape extreme summer heat by denning for brief periods of estivation. Yellow-bellied marmots in this part of the range often inhabit agricultural lands and feed on alfalfa, pasture grasses, beans, and truck crops. Though the preferred eastern foods are clover and alfalfa, woodchucks are also fond of garden crops, soybeans, and a large assortment of wild fruits and greenery. Hunters always seem to regard a chuck in a tree as an unusual phenomenon, but marmots are good climbers with an appetite for an occasional change of diet. In view of the fodder, it is no surprise that chuck meat rivals cottontail in a beer hasenpfeffer; the mystery is how such a delicacy can go untried by hunters who should campaign for wider recognition of the chuck's game qualities.

In the East, men and farm dogs are the chief slayers of chucks, and throughout their range marmots are prey for all carnivores. Yet malocclusion may be almost as important in controlling their population. A chuck's incisors grow throughout its life (up to ten years in captivity, half that in the wild if enemies are eluded). When the upper and lower teeth fail to meet and grind down—a strangely frequent condition among chucks—they grow in long curves until they interfere with eating and sometimes pierce the skull.

Hunters occasionally puzzle over spring-shot chucks that have patchy or balding coats. They are quite safe to eat. A patchy coat generally results from normal spring shedding (though mites transmit mange to a few chucks) and baldness may result from the hibernating position or from pushing earth and stones while burrowing. Fleas, ticks, and internal parasites afflict some chucks, and yellow-bellied marmots attract ticks that carry Rocky Mountain spotted fever. This is no longer a common disease, however. Chucks resist most ailments and carry no other diseases communicable to man.

Hunters, as well as farmers, ought to be apprised that holes dotting a field seldom indicate the local chuck population. By mid-June chucklings are weaned and, since many weigh a pound or more, dens become overcrowded. The female then leads each timid juvenile away to its own burrow, which she has prepared in advance. She visits them daily for a while, gradually breaking off contact. In mid-July each juvenile again leaves its den and migrates to a new field, where it digs another burrow. The population spreads, inbreeding is reduced, and young chucks settle into burrows surrounded by the pasturage they need to fatten quickly for hibernation. By fall they will weigh 4 or 5 pounds.

Most holes are on open slopes providing drainage and a wide view. The main entrance, marked by a big mound of excavated dirt which serves as an observation platform, may be a foot wide but it narrows to a tunnel so constricted that foxes normally must waylay chucks rather than invade burrows. Often there are two or three entrances (making holes all the more unreliable as an index of local chuck numbers), and always there is at least one smaller observation and escape hole, unmarked by any telltale mound. Some tunnels are short, others long and branched, the average length is about 14 feet. The shaft dips down, then rises, for maximum drainage of a large grass-matted nesting chamber. A hunter has his best chance of spotting a chuck at or near a burrow entrance; chucks seldom venture far from the safety of their tunnels.

A chuck per acre or two signifies a healthy local population. Still, eight times as many may be spotted on big, gently rolling clover or alfalfa fields in the East, and a great many more populate some of the high, benched mountain meadows of the West where rockchucks are hunted. It is not that rockchucks gather in colonies like prairie dogs, but that a need for grass, closely edged by rocky hideaways, forces them to converge in ridge-backed pastures and cirques above the timber line. Hunters know that if they cull too many from such a group no seed stock will be left.

Sometimes, especially where hunting has been infrequent, a chuck ignores the report of a rifle, grazing contentedly after a bullet spatters rock chips or dust a foot away or kills another chuck a few yards off. Such behavior gives rise to a belief among hunters of small experience that chucks are dull of sense or wit. But on a calm day or with a breeze blowing toward them they can be spooked by the crunch of a boot on leaves 200 yards away and they can spot movement at 700. They generally show no fear of livestock or of men mounted on horses or tractors; yet they plunge into their holes at the approach of dogs, foxes, or men on foot. In some eastern locales where hunters drive along back roads, stopping to glass fields and getting out when they spot game, chucks often drop from sight at the approach of an automobile, and some are intelligent enough to wait and see whether the car stops.

Even on eastern flatlands, a few hunters enjoy stalking close enough to use a rimfire rifle or a scope-sighted pistol chambered for .22 Magnums or high-velocity centerfires. As a rule, such stalking must be done with exquisite slowness—fine practice for hunting larger game—because a chuck rises on its haunches at frequent intervals to check for danger. Most easterners prefer long-range shooting; chucks often ignore a distant hunter until the first shot cracks the air, then dive for their burrows but reappear after a few minutes. Western marmots usually behave similarly.

The aged .22 Hornet still shoots 150-yard chucks, but it is eclipsed by modern cartridges, preeminently the .222 Magnum and .22-250. Caliber choice depends on common shooting distances in a hunter's home region. Between 150 and 250 yards, the .222 Magnum and .223 are outstanding, and they make less noise than those designed for longer range (an important consideration in thickly settled farm country). Out to 350 yards, ideal calibers are the .22-250, .224 Weatherby Magnum, and .225 Winchester. Medium-game calibers such as the .243 Winchester and 6mm Remington are sufficiently accurate at 450 yards if properly scoped and fired by an expert marksman. Those who hunt on foot mostly use relatively light "sporter" rifles with scopes from 6- to 10-power or featuring variable magnification and sometimes a range-estimating scale on the reticle. Those who scout in automobiles and then settle down for hours with rifle stand and spotting scope favor heavy-barreled target or varmint rifles with very high-powered scopes that demand much practice because they magnify a shooter's heartbeat as an apparent wobble in the field of view.

The head alone is the target of the experts, for humane reasons as well as vanity. Chucks are so resistant to shock that a very high-powered, fast-expanding bullet will not always stop a body-hit marmot from retreating into its burrow to die slowly.

Long-range woodchuck shooting is unsurpassed practice for hunting pronghorns, mule deer in open country, and other such game. Rockchuck shooting is unsurpassed practice for hunting sheep and goats. The yellow-bellied and hoary marmots inhabit the mountainous terrain of bigger game. Hunting them hardens muscles to the rigors of climbing, improves stalking skill, hones marksmanship. It is the rockchuck that often teaches a sheep hunter to hold low when shooting at a steep angle. The trajectory is pulled earthward by gravity only along the horizontal distance from shooter to target, which is shorter than the distance along the up- or downhill angle—a hard concept for most of us to visualize. How much pleasanter to master it by missing a few chucks than by missing perhaps the only good trophy on a big-game trip.

Mountain-meadow grasses rarely grow high enough to hide rockchucks, but woodchuck hunting is more seasonal. It is best at the end of June, before the crops grow high, again after the midsummer haying, and again between the second haying and hibernation. With the cover gone, chucks are spotted at great distances, nothing blocks the target, and no vegetation deflects or shatters the light, high-velocity bullets. During these periods chucks are most alert, another sign of intelligence in underrated game.

TRACKS & SIGN: A marmot's long-toed, flat-footed hind prints and handlike foreprints somewhat resemble raccoon tracks, but few chucks are out when it snows, and their tracks are invisible in grass. When the hay is high, on the other hand, grassland chucks tramp down distinct trails from burrow to burrow, radiating from holes that might otherwise be hidden in high cover. All the same, a conspicuously mounded chuck hole is the most easily spotted sign in the East. This is sometimes true even in rockchuck country, where there may be no sign at all if the animals are denning only in the rocks. Watching for scat is useless; the dark, more or less cylindrical droppings usually are deposited underground by woodchucks, buried or left in stony recesses by rockchucks.

VOICE: Disregarding the squeaks and grunts typical of large rodents, hunters need concern themselves with just one of the marmot's calls, the only one generally heard: a short, shrill whistle common to all species though loudest among rockchucks. The sound is very close to that of a man whistling with two fingers between his teeth. The call's primary function is a warning, but chucks hearing it are less apt to scurry than to rise up on their haunches and see for themselves whether retreat is indicated. They almost always sit up before whistling, and at times seem intent not on alerting others but on startling an approaching animal heard or smelled though concealed by vegetation. The whistle sometimes prompts the intruder to halt, or to move again if it has halted, thus revealing itself as a possible foe, since another chuck would react by sitting up. Though whistling alerts a hunter to the presence of chucks, they are more often seen than heard. When the grass is high, a hunter scouting a promising pasture may whistle and then watch for any chucks to rise out of concealment. More important, if he has spotted one but cannot get a clear shot, he can whistle to raise it, in effect calling for his target. Results may be nil, but the trick works just often enough to try.

Opossum (Didelphis marsupialis)
COMMON & REGIONAL NAMES: *possum.*

DESCRIPTION & DISTRIBUTION: If nothing about the opossum strikes anyone as particularly imposing, hardly anything is merrier than an old-fashioned southern possum hunt—with half a dozen lights twitching beams across a coal-black night, men yelling, the stinging whip of sapling sprigs, and at least one rasping crash in brambles accompanied by a liturgy of cursing before the hunters, hardly able to laugh for panting, reach the yelping hounds. One dog is dancing, rump high, chest almost in the leaves. The other stands on his hind legs, straining upward against a spindly, bushy-topped tree. With a low howl he jerks his hindquarters up and struggles into the dogwood's lowest fork, determined to climb the tree if need be. A dark, shaggy clump sways far out on a thin branch, its eyes shining dull orange, face white, hair silver-fringed in the lights. One of the men raises a stubby old single-shot .22 rifle, and his holler can be heard above the subdued crack: "Roast possum and 'taters!"

Other marsupials inhabit Latin America, Australia, and New Guinea, but the opossum is unique on this continent, above Mexico. A fat little animal, at maturity it usually has a length of about 2½ feet, including a foot of tail. Weight averages 5 or 6 pounds, though some of the largest males weigh 10. The scaly-looking, almost hairless prehensile tail is nearly white, darkening to black at the base. A possum of moderate size can hang from a branch by its very flexible tail, but a larger animal normally uses it only for an auxiliary hold. Sometimes a female brings her tail forward over her back when carrying her young there to give them something more than fur to cling to. The ears are naked and black, pinkly tipped as a rule and sometimes rimmed with white. The eyes are black, the nose pink, the long, narrow-snouted face mostly very pale or white. The body is gray, usually dark on the back, growing lighter down the sides to the belly; the underfur is cottony, the long black guard hairs white-tipped. A female's furred, muscular pouch closes too firmly to show. The legs and feet are black but the toes are white. Those of the forefeet fan out widely; the fifth toe of each handlike hind foot is clawless, an opposable thumb for grasping thin branches when a possum climbs.

Female opossum with young riding her back.

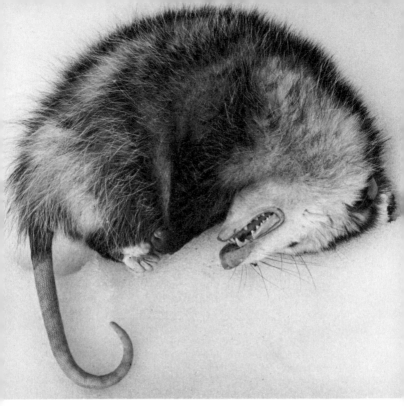

Playing possum, a rarely used last defense (top),
and the strange foot structure
responsible for unique possum tracks.

Possums in the Deep South are darker and slightly smaller than the more northerly strain and have relatively longer, thinner tails. A century ago they were purely southern animals, but they have expanded their range steadily northward since the 1890s. Having been introduced some years ago in California, Oregon, and Washington, possums have spread north and south along the Pacific Coast to British Columbia and Baja. Meanwhile, the originally southeastern population has reached lower Ontario.

The species is ill-adapted to cold. During frigid weather it dens up briefly, but cannot hibernate and often loses parts of its naked tail and ears to frostbite. Evidently it has a high pain threshold and a toughness that defies adversity.

GAME BEHAVIOR & HUNTING HABITAT: Possum-hunting novitiates are commonly disappointed when the animal refuses to play possum. Some other animals (including such diverse species as grass snakes and hog-nosed snakes) feign death as a last defense, but the possum is supposed to be the exemplar of the phenomenon. When hopelessly cornered, an occasional possum does indeed fall on its side, mouth agape, totally limp. It is an involuntary defense mechanism believed to be roughly analogous to shock or the release of adrenalin. Once the animal appears dead, most dogs and other predators usually lose interest, having no appetite for the meat. The supposed victim retains at least partial consciousness; it quickly recovers and flees after the enemy turns away. Yet it is much more common for a chased possum to scurry for a tree or hole, and if cornered at close quarters to face its attacker with mouth open wide, hissing loudly, showing all fifty teeth, and salivating.

The possum's mating period usually begins in January and lasts until April or May in the North, September in the South. A male breeds with any and all available females, and while a northern female generally has only one litter a year, a southern possum produces two, separated by about three and a half months. After a gestation period of only thirteen days, she may bear eight or nine young or twice as many. They are so small that even the largest litter would fit in a tablespoon. Blind, hairless, embryonic in appearance, they have sufficiently developed forelegs to crawl through the mother's fur into her pouch, where they attach themselves to elongate nipples—most often, but not invariably, thirteen in number—and remain that way for at least a month. Slow infants and the last born fail to secure a nipple; they soon die and are expelled from the pouch. After a couple of months seven or eight survivors emerge, mouse-sized and furred, to ride the mother's back. They continue to go into the pouch to feed but are weaned and gone a month later.

They are primitive creatures, equipped with an unusually small brain case, stupid and slow. Yet most of them probably survive about three years in the wild, for they have few enemies other than dogs, men, and automobiles. An owl will eat a possum, and a fox probably will if hungry enough, but for unknown reasons most carnivores seem to find the meat distasteful. Possums also seem to be unattractive to most external parasites, though they host various internal ones. They have been known to contract a form of tularemia, but in general they are relatively resistant to diseases.

Possums den wherever shelter can be arranged—in leaf-lined hollow trees, logs, abandoned chuck burrows, rock clefts, woodpiles, culverts, drain pipes, holes under old buildings. They like open woods, swamps, and marshes, but have such flexible feeding requirements that hunting them is often a matter of luck, except in the South. Possums are inordinately fond of the persimmon fruits that ripen there in the fall, and hounds are often started at a 'simmon tree. Until winter, insects may constitute the possum's chief food, but mulberries and corn are also eaten, and quantities of grapes and acorns when the time comes. The animal is truly omnivorous. Now that hen houses are generally impenetrable, the possum has gone back to natural mainstays: mice, shrews, moles, infant rabbits, eggs and the young of ground-nesting birds, carrion, worms, frogs, newts, lizards, a bit of grain, and assorted greens. Strangely, it does most of its foraging on the ground even though it is more agile in trees.

Hunting is good in the fall because the possum population is very active, partly on a pre-winter feeding spree and partly because the young ones are dispersing to unoccupied land. The home territory is small, no more than 10 or 15 acres for a typical mature possum, though a few individuals preside over 40-acre spreads. There is little point in hunting them without a dog except after snow, when they can be trailed. It is easy enough in farm country because a hunter can count on finding the trail's end a couple of fields from where he first saw tracks. But if the sun is up, the possum will probably be denned for the day, and few northerners ever bother to hunt specifically for possum. The animal has mediocre eyesight, uses its keen sense of smell only to locate food, and shows little or no reaction to enemies until they come quite close. Still, it has acute hearing and feels sufficiently insecure in full light to stay hidden much of the time or hide when an intruder approaches.

Real possum hunting is the night hunting in the South, and the darkest nights are best. Coonhounds will tree possums, to the disgust of coon-hunting purists but to the delight of those who savor mixed adventures and a mixed bag. Any hound with a good nose and a treeing voice can be used, and any open-sighted .22 rifle or pistol. Lanterns and flashlights have been largely replaced by powerful, hand-freeing headlamps of the kind used by spelunkers and miners. The hounds are cast where dens, tracks, or possums have been seen, or near crop fields or persimmon trees, or in any appropriate area. They may pick up a scent immediately, or not for hours, but once they strike a trail the chase is brief. In thick brush it may be chaotic, but the possum is too slow to go far before treeing.

TRACKS & SIGN: Gray hairs are sometimes seen around a den mouth. Scat usually goes unseen or unrecognized, as it has no

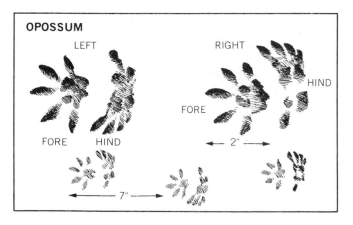

OPOSSUM

very constant form and is often not solid, but the tracks are easily recognized on snow or in mud. The trail pattern commonly resembles a raccoon's, with hind prints close to foreprints, almost side by side. The stride is about 7 inches, but the prints themselves are like no other animal's. The five long, narrow toes of the front foot spread so widely that a print covers a couple of inches and is nearly star-shaped. The hind foot leaves a slightly larger and distinctly longer, outward-pointing track, with three inner toes closely spaced, the small outer toe separated, and the thumblike fifth far to the side pointing inward or rearward.

VOICE: The possum can emit low grunts and growls, and sometimes hisses when cornered.

Peccary *(Pecari angulatus; also classified as Tayassu tajacu and Pecari tajacu)*
COMMON & REGIONAL NAMES: *javelina, collared peccary, musk hog.*

DESCRIPTION & DISTRIBUTION: An account of personal experience sometimes delineates a game animal more sharply than pages of anatomical detail. On a December morning in 1965 a scouting truck jolted across a desert flat in southwestern Texas and stopped before a ranch gate. Beyond lay slightly higher ground, seamed with arroyos, backed by pastel buttes, splotched with prickly pear, Spanish bayonet, spiny mesquite. The place was far below the Pecos River in Brewster County, east of Alpine

and almost in the shadows of the Glass Mountains and the San-tiagos. The rancher was guiding two northern sportsmen to a 640-acre section called Hell's Half Acre, known for thorn bushes, cacti, and javelinas. They planned to walk the rim of a shallow gully where tracks were numerous, prickly pear and agave heavily browsed. As one of the hunters unlatched the gate he spotted a bristly black pig, only 40 yards off on a brushy hillock. Even with its massive head down, rooting among the desert shrubs, it stood almost 2 feet high and a yard long, big for a Texas peccary, and a good trophy. It was feeding alone, as old boars occasionally do, perhaps no longer tolerant of company, perhaps outcast because an old animal may become irascible or attract predators to the herd.

The hunter's rifle was still in the truck. He crouched, thumbed off his holster flap, and drew a .22 Magnum revolver as he quietly advanced, unaware that somehow the rear sight had loosened slightly. His partner eased up behind him with a camera. At the first shot the pig flinched, but the bullet had gone high, scratching its back and spewing up sand on the hillock. The animal's head came up and turned from side to side, its weak little black eyes searching for the source of the noise. The hair on its withers lifted into a black mane above its ears, and then the hair along its backbone rose as it trotted toward the shooter. Scent or sound had given the hunter away. A trace of pungent odor drifted to him, like a skunk's reek though not nearly so strong. The javelina's musk gland had discharged. Tusks clicked as the old boar came stiffly forward on stubby legs that appeared dainty under the thick shoulders and haunches. The

Typical band of peccaries in Southwest.

tusks were short and straight, yet the animal had the look of a miniature wild boar. Close and with its back up, it was no longer black but dark grizzly gray, most of the face and side hair tan beneath coarse black tips. Its head swung low and a second bullet seared the top of its blunt snout. It turned, then came again, snapping and very close, when a better-placed shot at last spun it around. It stumbled but got to its feet and started over the hillock at a fast run, while the second hunter unholstered a .44 Magnum. Both men fired and the animal crashed into a thorn bush, lifeless even before its shoulder flattened a clump of mesquite grass.

A tight rear sight or a head shot would have ended the incident sooner, but the hunter feared he might ruin a trophy mount by damaging the head, and a large peccary is so tough-hided and tough-bodied that a rimfire Magnum is not fully reliable even when its bullet strikes the chest cavity. If the animal had not spun around, momentum and stamina would have driven it the last three yards. Yet neither the hunters nor the watching rancher could be quite certain the animal had meant to charge.

Exaggerated tales of ferocity have been spawned by the javelina's poor eyesight and resemblance to a small feral pig or severely dwarfed wild boar. Natural selection has not sharp-

Large Texas javelina running from hunter.

ened the vision of this short-legged animal whose ancestors fed in thick brush. When alarmed and confused, a javelina sometimes runs toward an enemy rather than away. Ferocity is not characteristic, although peccaries have been observed to charge deliberately on occasions other than that December morning in 1965, and they will fight furiously if cornered—especially after being wounded—by men or dogs.

The jaws are powerful. The upper tusks, thick, sharply pointed, averaging 1½ to 2½ inches long, snap down close behind a pair of equally wicked lower tusks. On the author's Texas trophy, both sets are just over 1½ inches long and may have been worn down with age. The animal weighed a bit over 45 pounds, large for that desert region, but peccaries tend to grow heavier in New Mexico and Arizona, particularly where scrub oak provides good food and cover. Mature animals vary from about 30 to 65 pounds, stand about 18 to 22 inches high, and measure about 30 to 38 inches in length. The name javelina, more current than peccary in the Southwest, is said to be a Spanish metaphor referring to "javelin tusks," but is actually a corrupted diminutive of the much more impressively tusked *jabali*—wild boar.

Descended from giant pigs that lived 25 million years ago, peccaries are related to swine and wild boars, but belong to a separate family distinguished by fewer teeth, a more complex stomach, small size, straight tusks, a single dewclaw rather than two on each hind foot, and a strong, functional musk gland located on the back just forward of the rump. When a javelina raises its back hair in agitation, the musk evidently discharges involuntarily. The gland, which resembles a navel, should be cut out promptly after the game is killed. If this is done when the animal is field-dressed, the meat of a young javelina is delicious—light, dry, much like pork—contrary to a statement in at least one widely respected hunting book that "it holds its odor" in spite of every precaution.

The North American species is often called a collared peccary. In much of its range it is typified by a white or whitish band extending from the throat up the shoulders or neck (there is hardly any neck to speak of) and across the foreback. The collar tends to be irregular and is often incomplete or absent, particularly on the dark animals found in Texas, where the hunting is best. All javelinas look black or blackish at rifle range, but at shorter distances those of New Mexico and Arizona are a bit lighter—peppery gray. Black, black-tipped, and lighter hairs are mixed, the light color being whitish or tan depending on region. The coat, hiding a vestigial tail, is more copious than the wild boar's and so coarse that it feels bristly to the touch. As with true pigs, the hoofs are small, the body short and thick, the back rounded, the pinkish-tan nose pad a tough, flattened circular disk for rooting.

The collared peccaries familiar to American hunters are also found in Mexico, and other geographic races are found all the way to Argentina. A slightly larger species, the white-lipped peccary, inhabits dense rain forests from Mexico to Paraguay. The collared variety once ranged northward into Arkansas. Settlers killed the animals indiscriminately for meat and to protect crops, although agricultural damage probably was never severe; later, peccaries became a cheap source of "pigskin" and were exterminated except in the southern portions of Arizona, New Mexico, and Texas, which have at last set limits and seasons. Despite very short February seasons and special permit drawings in Arizona and New Mexico, the present hunting can be called good only in Arizona's southeastern and New Mexico's southwestern corner, but it is quite good in much of southwestern Texas, where the season during the last few years has been from the beginning of September through January, with local variations.

GAME BEHAVIOR & HUNTING HABITAT: The future looks better. Fortunately, peccaries have few natural enemies; their life expectancy may well exceed ten years under normal conditions. They are a favorite prey of jaguars, but jaguars (unfortunately) are now extremely rare north of Mexico. Southwestern cougars are not plentiful in the lowlands, and only a few young shoats can be taken by coyotes or foxes. Dust baths keep ticks, lice, and flies to a minimum. Internal parasites are comparatively minor nuisances, except for the nematode that causes trichinosis. The disease is carried to humans by way of infected meat, so javelina, like pork, should be well cooked.

Having evolved where cold and seasonal food shortages rarely impede reproduction, javelinas breed intermittently throughout the year, and being herd animals they are polygamous. Females breed at two years, whereas males of that age are probably deterred by older, more dominant males. Gestation requires about four months. Before giving birth, the female searches out a cave, an interstice amid rocks, a hollow log, or, if no better den is found, a bed in thick, overarching brush. She bears a single piglet or, more often, twins. They are well-haired, brown with a black stripe down the back. Within hours they can walk well, and after three or four days the mother leads them to the band, which may number half a dozen, sometimes many more.

They inhabit arid brush country and scrub-covered foot-hills, and hunters occasionally find them foraging as high as 6,000 feet on the gentler mountain slopes of New Mexico and Arizona. There they eat quantities of scrub-oak acorns, whereas prickly pear is their primary food on the desert flats. They consume the cactus fruit and pads, thorns and all, with no ill effects. They eat little grass, but like pigs root up many tubers and rhizomes. Other plant foods include agave, mesquite beans and pods, berries, and nuts. With the tubers they sometimes root up a welcome mouse nest, for they are omnivorous. They eat insects, worms, frogs, toads, lizards, eggs and young of ground-nesting birds, and all the snakes they can find. Armed with sharp hoofs, a peccary kills a rattler as a pronghorn or deer does, by jumping and stomping.

Javelinas can probably survive with little moisture other than that which is contained in cacti, yet they do seek water, often moving along washes and browsing near them. Even a dry wash may be a good place to hunt, as are springs, creeks, water holes of any kind. The age of tracks can be impossible to judge on sand or parched soil, but wet prints dry so quickly in desert country that a hunter can easily tell if tracks crossing a wash or coming from a water hole are fresh. If they are, javelinas are probably within a quarter of a mile. They generally browse over an area no more than 5 or 6 miles wide, traveling neither fast nor far. Even when panicked they run only a short way, then slow to a trot, then to a meandering walk. However they do run much faster than the 11 miles an hour stipulated in some field guides; they can disappear over a fairly steep Texas foothill at 25 miles an hour. When spooked, a band invariably scatters, some of the animals dodging with great agility. After the danger has gone they regroup by scent and sound. They have a keen olfactory sense and fine hearing. It is sensible to hunt upwind when possible, not only for these reasons but because a man with a sharp nose can sometimes smell javelinas before he sees them. It is also important to watch for tracks, droppings, wallows, freshly turned earth, and tooth marks or bitten pads on cactus from about 1 to 2 feet above the ground. The search should include periodic backward glances. A peccary feeding alone may stand still while a hunter passes, and until it moves again its dark coat can fade into the shadows.

Javelinas are most active in the early morning, late afternoon, and at night. It is not that they have a nocturnal instinct to hide when the light is strong, but that they try to stay cool during midday. Hunters who are not similarly inclined can investigate caves, old mine tunnels, cool hollows, and protected draws where the animals find shelter from heat and also from cold, hard rains, and sometimes from merely cloudy days. Musk, combined with the odor of accumulated droppings, is often detectable at javelina caves. Not many men evince a desire to crawl into one even when it is large enough, and the game is not often visible in the dark recesses, but a couple of stones tossed in may bring a javelina dashing out.

At other times the best places to hunt are washes, gullies, and the patches of prickly pear, mesquite, oak, brush, and even Spanish bayonet. Brush pants are recommended, and many hunters scout on horseback or in four-wheel-drive vehicles, stopping frequently to look for sign if no animals are spotted.

The use of hounds, while not unknown, has disadvantages. Since javelinas have more speed than endurance, they are not the finest game for hounds. The dogs can be badly lacerated by thorns (and by an enraged javelina, if they are inexperienced), and rattlers can endanger them. They sometimes single out one animal in a band, but not invariably. And they usually select the nearest or easiest one, not necessarily the hunter's choice. Hunting without them is better sport.

Most hunters use rifles. (The javelina taken at a couple of yards with the .22 Magnum pistol was a fine trophy but too old for fine eating; it was followed by a smaller, younger animal, a clean one-shot kill at about 230 yards with a .264 Magnum bolt-action under a 4-power scope.) Because there is no way

to foretell range, some hunters use iron sights, but most of them prefer 2½-power scopes or even greater magnification since open terrain offers more shots at 300 yards than at 6 feet. The .30-06 remains popular, as the same rifle is often used for larger game. More popular are both the venerable and modern chamberings in the .25 group, the 6mm group, and slightly larger classes. The .22 centerfires are not heavy enough except perhaps at moderate ranges. Some handgunners use varmint calibers—the .256 Magnum and still smaller chamberings—but the .38 Special, .357, and .41 are more widely accepted. Such pistols are fine if the hunter forswears long-distance shooting.

TRACKS & SIGN: The lobes of a javelina's cloven hoof are rounded oblongs, not sharp-pointed, and the cleft is narrow. A foreprint is generally about 1½ inches long if the animal is mature, and as wide or nearly so. A hind print is similar but a trifle smaller. The tracks are much smaller and rounder than those of desert bighorns, and the stride is only about 6 to 10 inches long, so recognition is not difficult. The tracks do resemble those of pigs but are smaller; in any event, there are no wild boars in peccary country, and the feral pigs of Texas reside farther north and east. Since javelinas do not form single files to cross gullies or washes, the size of a band is often known by the tracks; and since they do not travel far, fresh tracks are worth following.

Fresh peccary tracks showing darkly in sandy desert wash.

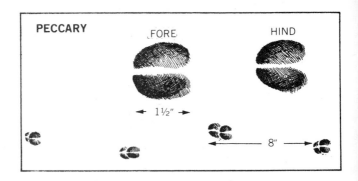

Scat is usually composed of large, irregular segments—not the small pellets dropped by sheep—and sometimes is deposited in flattened disks when the animals have been feeding on succulent vegetation. Other promising sign includes freshly rooted-up ground and chewed cactus or other low vegetation. At times, a light skunky odor is also valuable sign.

VOICE: Soft grunts help to keep a herd together. Hearing them faintly coming from the far side of a rise or down in a draw, a hunter knows he is close. A barking cough tells him to slow up; it is an alarm call. Javelinas can squeal loudly, but do so only when injured or terrified.

Prairie Dog *(Cynomys)*
COMMON & REGIONAL NAMES: *prairie pup, little dog,* petit chien *(French),* pi-spi-sa *(Sioux), barking squirrel, Louisiana marmot, picket pin.*

DESCRIPTION & DISTRIBUTION: Some 100-acre dog towns still sprinkle the plains, now that a century of poisoning by stockmen and government exterminators is conceded to have done more agricultural harm than good. Spreads of twice that size, once considered small, will probably be uncommon for several more decades, while sportsmen, conservation leaders, and a new alliance of enlightened ranchers and wildlife agencies work to bring back the rotund, squeaky-voiced, grayish-tan burrowers that used to populate the western prairies in astonishing numbers. A published estimate of 400 to 600 million prairie dogs must have amused any hunter or rancher who saw the single extended Texas dog town that covered 25,000 square miles in 1901. That concentration alone probably numbered 400 million blacktail prairie dogs, the miniature volcanoes of their den mounds scattered to the fading horizon.

The mounds furnished ideal dust wallows for bison, and large herds milled over the dog towns. The tramping of buffalo, as well as the digging and eating habits of the prairie dogs, fostered the growth of forbs that also fattened herds of pronghorns. It is true that an overabundance of prairie dogs can be ruinous to domestic livestock, since 250 of the rodents can rival a 1,000-pound cow in the daily consumption of grass. However, a reasonable population of them—controlled by natural predators, the rifles of sportsmen, and modern habitat modification—can actually improve range land.

Today's hunter may find a colony numbering hundreds or, much less frequently, thousands. In either case he has found a practice and testing ground for long-range shooting. If he has hunted prairie dogs much, he knows they soon become very cautious. On his first couple of visits he may see twenty or thirty animals at assorted distances, all within range, popping out of burrows like animated targets at a shooting gallery, or sitting bolt upright on their close-cropped pasture. But if they have been subjected to shooting gluttony, most or all will disappear into their holes after a few yaps of alarm. Quiet though the hunter may be and low though he may crouch as he approaches, they are gone before he comes within range. Even if this were not so likely, he would be sensible to set a limit on his take in order to leave game for tomorrow and next year. In the deplorable absence of legal bag limits, his take may also be regulated by a landowner. Many ranchers who formerly tried to eradicate prairie dogs now maintain a profitable supply, controlled by fee-paying hunters.

Most riflemen reject the example of Indians and settlers who feasted on prairie dog. The meat, if not as good as chuck, is quite palatable, but the marksman's image of the prairie dog has nothing to do with food. We are all conditioned to see the animal as a picket-pin target, shimmering in a heat mirage that ripples from the prairie dust a couple of hundred yards away. We see it through eye-stinging sweat that blurs the reticle and across the sway of grass in a breeze that never seems to stop shifting. To hit the pin is to count coup.

Biologically the animal is a ground squirrel, but far larger than animals that usually go by that name. Regardless of subspecies, a mature prairie dog is about 5 inches high when down on all fours, a foot high or more when it sits up. Its length averages about 14 inches, excluding a 3-inch tail. Many an adult prairie dog weighs only 1½ pounds when the grasses begin to sprout, but it is twice as heavy by fall. There are two subgenera: the whitetail prairie dogs of mountain meadows and high pastures, and the blacktail dogs of the flatter plains and semi-desert country. A hunter who speaks of the whitetail variety usually has in mind a prototype subspecies, *Cynomys leucurus,* and he thinks of the blacktail prairie dogs in terms of another prototype, *C. ludovicianus ludovicianus.* There are three other whitetail subspecies, but they are endangered, and they may be protected where they occur—in parts of Utah, Colorado, New Mexico, and Arizona. However, they resemble the more abundant varieties, and hunters ought to check with game departments if there is any doubt about a local breed. There are also two additional blacktail subspecies, a Mexican strain that seems to be maintaining its numbers and an endangered strain, which is probably now extinct in Arizona, yet survives in Texas and New Mexico.

The various subspecies are commonly grayish tan, paler on the underparts, but range to reddish brown, buff, or pale cinnamon. Some of them in western North Dakota are so saturated with coal dust that they look black, and some in Oklahoma are stained red with clay. The blacktail and whitetail subspecies are distinguished not only by the tipping of their tails but by region, habitat, and type of mound. A loose ring of earth or sometimes none at all marks a whitetail burrow, whereas a blacktail's is surrounded by a big, hard-tamped crater or dome. Whitetail prairie dogs now inhabit the Rocky Mountain region from the high country of southern Montana to Arizona and New Mexico. Blacktails range from above the Canadian border into Mexico and from the eastern fringe of the Rockies across the plains into the Dakotas, Nebraska, Kansas, Oklahoma, and Texas. Hunting prospects fluctuate, but there have always been sizable dog towns in South Dakota, and at last inspection in Oklahoma and Wyoming.

GAME BEHAVIOR & HUNTING HABITAT: When all residents of a dog town are underground, escaping midday heat or hiding from a predator, the colony remains easy to spot by a wide scattering of holes, and a town of the blacktail mound builders especially can be seen at a considerable distance. Great activity is noticeable in a blacktail town after rain has made the excavated dirt workable. The animals spend hours tamping the adobe with their noses, foreheads, and feet to shape lookout platforms that also serve as dikes to prevent dens from flooding. Some domes are only a foot high while others rise 3 feet, and they may be 10 feet across or less than a yard. The roomy entrance narrows to a tunnel perhaps 5 inches wide and dropping or angling at least a few feet before leveling off. Whether a tunnel is short or very long, it has at least one turning and listening chamber, where a prairie dog can pause on the way in or out and reverse directions if danger is detected. Usually there is a defecation chamber, where the dog deposits and covers its scat, steadily renewing the space by digging. As a rule, there is a spare room above a widened, grass-matted nest chamber; in the event of flash flooding, air trapped there can save an occupant from drowning. Finally (but not invariably) there is an escape hatch unmarked by any mound.

Except when seeking new territory, a prairie dog dislikes traveling more than about 50 yards from its burrow. Therein lies refuge for an animal that feeds during daylight and is fed upon by golden eagles, rough-legged hawks, prairie falcons, coyotes, badgers, bobcats, and other predators. The prairie dog probably has a well-developed sense of smell and definitely has keen hearing, but relies chiefly on its extraordinary vision. Only half an inch of head shows above the mound when a prairie dog first peers out at sunrise. After a few minutes it bounces out and sits upright on the lookout platform. A few companions appear on nearby mounds. Soon an exuberant, squeaky, double-noted braying yap is heard—an all-clear call—and several animals join in the barking for which the species was named. It may last for seconds or hours, and may erupt intermittently until the animals retire when the sun becomes too hot; the perfor-

mance is repeated as the day begins to cool.

The alarm bark is also a double-noted yelping, but progressively more rapid and strident as an intruder approaches. When a bird of prey circles, only a few terrified yaps are heard before every dog dives into a hole. Badgers are almost as much feared as birds, for their lack of speed is counterbalanced by their digging ability. But when a coyote comes within sight, only the nearest prairie dogs flee. The others sit up and yap until the enemy is within a few yards. Unless there has been much recent shooting, their reaction to a hunter is much the same, except that the man's size evidently makes him seem much closer than a coyote spied at an equal distance. As he walks around a dog town's fringe the animals within 100 yards or so may rush to their burrows, and if a town has been hunted they may become alarmed at twice that distance. Most of those at greater range will bark and keep watching. Some hunters scoff at the notion of crawling, since there can be no true stalk where there is no cover. All the same, the man who walks upright may have to sit and wait before dogs within range come out again. The man who crawls into position looks much larger than any coyote but

small enough not to be frightening.

Prairie dogs are gregarious in the extreme, yet they must have foraging room between burrows. About 50 feet of pasture from den to den may be nearly ideal, so a tight cluster of dens does not always mean a rifleman will see several targets all at about the same range. Some dens are probably vacant and some occupied by the burrowing owls or rattlers that live with prairie dogs. The leggy little owls are more interested in grasshoppers than in anything as formidable as a prairie dog, and if rattlesnakes killed as many prairie dogs as they are supposed to, the rodents would be gone. No doubt a few pups are killed in the spring, but rattlers hardly seem worth a bark. The black-footed ferret, a mink-sized weasel that invades the burrows at night, was once a greater scourge than golden eagle or badger. But it was never a plentiful species, and the mass poisoning of dog towns, starving some predators and indirectly poisoning others, has brought the ferret near to extinction. The other carnivores still exert some control on population. Floods and prairie fires also kill a few prairie dogs but not many, and such parasites as fleas, ticks, and mites are minor nuisances. The animals are susceptible

Prairie-dog town.

to sylvatic plague—bubonic plague carried by wildlife—and although the disease has become increasingly rare, there is no sense in handling any rodent that appears sick. Today, however, the remaining prairie dogs are remarkably free of serious diseases. The life span is four or five years (twice as long in captivity), giving a female time to bear four or five spring litters averaging five pups.

In a blacktail enclave, breeding peaks for two or three weeks during March in cold regions, as early as January in warm southerly areas. The high-country whitetails breed chiefly in late March. Gestation requires only a month, but the young do not appear at burrow entrances until May or June, when they are fully furred, can see and hear well, and are about to be weaned. After that, the shooting of females will not doom the young. As summer blooms, the pups become independent, but the adults and yearlings are the ones that most often move out, crossing territorial boundaries to dig new burrows or renovate deserted ones on more open pasture. Thus towns expand, change shape, and shift, eventually disappearing and popping up again nearby.

.Prairie dogs are incapable of the deep hibernation that typifies smaller ground squirrels, but they do remain underground and become torpid during the coldest weather. Whitetails on mountain meadows may den up as early as September or October and stay in their snow-covered burrows for months. They probably awaken occasionally and nibble at roots and seeds. Where wind sweeps the snow from a prairie, blacktails come out on bright winter days to graze the dried grasses. The full renewal of activity depends on climate; in the Wyoming mountains it does not come until late March or April, while on the Kansas plains and in Oklahoma's Wichita Mountains mating begins by the end of January, and hunters spend evenings making up a future supply of long-range loads or tinkering with winter-stored rifles.

Devoted marksmen know where the local towns are situated, but they are always eager to discover new ones. Vegetation is the key. It has to be low so that the prairie dogs can watch for enemies. They eat what necessity dictates, but they have favorite types of nutritious pasturage: wheatgrasses, blue grama, buffalograss, fescue, young Russian thistle, dandelion, foxtail, sand dropseed, bromes. Before the grasses sprout, they

eat seeds and ground-runners and often dig little holes a couple of inches deep and a couple of inches across to get at the roots of perennials. The whitetails in some areas have to rely heavily on saltbush even in summer, but all prairie dogs become increasingly selective with opportunity. A dog town is likely to be discovered on patches of prairie that look cropped. For the sake of visibility they cut even the plants they dislike—spiderwort, wild indigo, and ironweed, for instance—and this promotes the growth of the low green grasses they prefer.

There is no reason for an old-time varmint hunter to relinquish his .220 Swift, since he can load 55-grain bullets to keep the wind from fishhooking his shots at ranges beyond 150 yards. After decades of prairie-dog shooting, a man gauges his Kentucky windage without thinking about it, just by seeing how the grass sways near the target. Still, the younger shooters can outdistance the .220 with their more modern .22 centerfires, .25's, and 6mm chamberings that are used for chuck hunting (see page 426). Some sight their rifles at 200 yards with scopes of 6- or 8-power, while others prefer variable magnification.

Prairie dogs barking.

TRACKS & SIGN: The swollen rims of burrows are, of course, the chief sign of prairie dogs when the animals are out of sight. Whitetail burrows are less conspicuous than those of blacktails, but the cropped look of a pasture draws the hunter's eye. A scattering of mounds in good repair (or fresh, loose earth piles and fans in the case of whitetail dogs) marks a town in use. A hunter scanning the low-grass expanses of a prairie with a 7x35mm or 8x35mm binocular can discern bald domes at distances that render the little mound builders invisible. Other sign is of minor importance. The scat, small pellets or segments sometimes strung like beads, is mostly deposited underground. Both fore and hind tracks are narrow and about 1¼ inches long. A front print shows four long, strongly clawed toes, while the hind print is more handlike, with a fifth toe in thumb position. The tracks tend to sidle, or veer laterally, though not as sharply as a skunk's, and the stride is naturally very short.

Blacktail prairie dog at burrow entrance.

VOICE: Barking can be so varied as to baffle interpretation. Some of the feeding and territorial barks are single, smooth notes reminiscent of a lap dog's shrill pitch. Chirps and squirrelish chatter can also be heard at a bustling dog town, and the animals snarl when fighting and squeal when very frightened. A braying, double-noted all-clear bark seems to serve as a territorial proc-lamation; it usually is accompanied by an upward toss of the body and sometimes by an upward fling of the forelegs. Virtually the same call, but rapped out stridently to a fast rhythm of tail flicking, is an alarm signal; its first syllable quickens to a chirp, followed by a longer, wheezing sound. When such barks become truly urgent the prairie dogs rush for their holes, but a hunter need only wait for them to reappear. Intense curiosity, probably a defense mechanism for animals that must be visually alert to danger, is also their undoing when heads again lift cautiously above the earthworks.

Raccoon (Procyon lotor)
COMMON & REGIONAL NAMES: *coon, ringtail,* shoui *(Louisiana Creole, from Choctaw).*

DESCRIPTION & DISTRIBUTION: Few game species have the amusing appeal of a fat, bushy-coated raccoon, low to the ground, with a thick, ringed tail, upright round ears, and a broad, innocent face wearing an improbable burglar's mask. But apart from hunt-ers (and farmers besieged for corn or poultry), few Americans have any idea that raccoons probably pad invisibly through the night in the nearest woods.

They are scarce in the Rockies and absent from southwest-ern deserts to which the closely related little ringtail cat and coati are adapted, but they exist in every continental state. Rac-coons have lived in Alaska since 1945, when they were introduced near Ketchikan, and they are found along the Alberta-Sas-katchewan border. Elsewhere the upper limit of distribution is southernmost Canada. The same species inhabits Mexico and Central America, with close relatives residing to the south. In the United States there are probably about 5 million raccoons, as many as when the country was settled. During the coonskin-coat fad of the 1920s, they were nearly exterminated but afterward multiplied astonishingly. A few coons can take a large toll of corn, and only the newer hen houses—veritable poultry fortresses—are impregnable to them, yet they have never suffered widespread, intensive bountying. In fact, they have been restocked in states where they had declined. On the other hand, they are not seasonally protected as game animals, and fur-trapping regulations in some states have been lax. The absence of limits or seasons, plus trapping and shooting by farmers, have sufficiently controlled their numbers to forestall eradication campaigns.

Hunters are grateful, as there is no finer way to spend an autumn night than by following coonhounds, and sportsmen reap a large ringtail harvest. At the time of year when hunting is best, a mature coon is accumulating winter fat in the abdominal cavity and an inch of it between skin and body. It can ruin the flavor of the meat, just as it can ruin an ill-scraped pelt. Removing all of it is a painstaking but necessary chore. A proper roast is a hunting reward, almost akin to hearing the hounds bellow "treed," or seeing a coon's disks of eyeshine, orange or green, flicker into the circle of light in answer to a predator call.

Even in spring a raccoon looks portly. There are nineteen subspecies and some of the pale southern varieties are small—as small as 3 to 6 pounds on the Florida Keys—but most average between 12 and 16 pounds at maturity, with a shoulder height of 9 to 12 inches, and a body ranging from about 2 feet long to nearly 3. A predator caller in Washington has good reason to claim that the largest, darkest raccoons are those of the Pacific Northwest, while a Down East hound fancier can dispute the claim in favor of Maine. Plenty of 30-pounders have been taken in both regions, and either man may be right on the basis of averages. But in late fall, when fat can account for close to half the total weight, some midwestern specimens are monstrous. To the author's knowledge, the largest raccoon recorded was shot in Wisconsin by Albert Larson in November, 1950. It weighed 62 pounds, 6 ounces, and measured 55 inches from nose to tip of tail.

A northern raccoon's back may appear almost black, but the general body tone varies from yellowish gray to grayish tan with black peppering, white frosting, paler grayish or yellowish underparts. Out of thick, reddish-tan underfur on most coons

grow long, copious, white-tipped guard hairs that mix gray, yellow, tan, and black. The nose and eyes are black, and a black band about 2 inches wide crosses the whitish face from the cheek just in front of the neck ruff, fading out between the eyes. The bushy 10- or 12-inch tail has a black tip and four to six black rings.

GAME BEHAVIOR & HUNTING HABITAT: Raccoons are supremely adaptable. They require just a bit of woods, some water, and a sufficiently long fattening season to prepare for winter. Although they have favorite foods, they can thrive on such diverse prey and forage that they need only a small home range. Some of the young disperse in autumn; others are driven away in spring when the females that bore them are again pregnant and can no longer share den space. A few adults wander to new territories, and males travel for miles seeking mates. Still, a typical coon

Treed raccoon.

spends most of the year on perhaps a square mile of land. Except for those killed by automobiles, they are rarely seen in daylight.

During early spring a raccoon subsists chiefly on grasses, worms, and newly emerged insects and frogs. As the season warms, crawfish become a staple, supplemented by shiners, minnows, small rodents, birds' eggs and nestlings, and miscellaneous vegetation. The raccoon and the bear evolved some 30 million years ago from primal dogs, and the raccoon has become even more omnivorous than the bear. On coastal marshes it modifies its nocturnal woodland habits to pick edible debris as the tides recede. A great raider of muskrat houses, it tears in to devour the young and to prey on little rice rats nesting in the walls, after which it often uses the lodge as a den instead of searching or a tree hollow. It preys on rabbit litters, and on squirrel litters when it can get at them. Occasionally it will open up a squirrel nest for use as a den, though more often it merely sprawls atop an empty squirrel or hawk nest to sun itself without being seen. Where wildfowl breed, it destroys duck nests, and tracks are not needed to disclose the culprit. A coon eats an egg by biting it in half, leaving half shells about the nest or at the base of a nearby rock or log where it can look about for enemies while eating. The nest itself is usually shredded, because a raccoon habitually kneads and tears at food.

Hunters puzzle at the spectacle of a coon at a stream or pond, "washing" morsels in the early morning or late evening. Its teeth and salivary glands easily manage dry food of every kind, and if water is more than a very short distance away a coon will not bother to wet its catch. Evidently the moistening serves but to heighten the animal's exquisite tactile sense, and kneading is a way of inspecting food. To a species with so all-inclusive an appetite, perhaps it is important to feel for matter that should be rejected. The forepaws are more sensitive than any other American animal's. None of the five long toes is an opposable thumb, yet they can hold food, lift the lid of a garbage can, open a door latch, and clasp the thinnest branch or grape vine.

The summer diet, principally vegetable, includes every sort of wild or domestic berry, other fruits, garden peas, potatoes, and quantities of sweet corn "in the milk"—almost ripe for harvesting. Hounds often pick up a trail at the edge

of a cornfield. A coon sneaks to the outer rows from the cover of brush and woods. It climbs a stalk, which usually breaks under the weight, shreds the husk, and gnaws away the kernels and sometimes a cob end. In its hurry the animal often wastes as much as it eats and then scrambles to the next stalk. The farmer's reaction is predictable, as it is when a raccoon manages to squeeze through a 4-inch hole in chicken wire or stretch a leg through untorn wire mesh to reach a bird.

A coon also eats tadpoles, clams, small fish, turtles, and turtle eggs. During hunting season it takes dead or crippled game and, like the fox, will patrol back roads for carrion left by automobiles. Many hunters drive slowly along, while a hound runs ahead to check ditches and brush patches until a scent trail is struck. On the Pacific salmon rivers and Atlantic shad rivers the dead fish during spawning runs attract raccoons, and some hunters start their dogs near streamside.

Young raccoon venturing from old maple den tree.

With the coming of fall, raccoons feel a desperate urge to fatten. In addition to animals, insects, grubs, and honey, they can now feed on grapes—wild or cultivated—and pecans, hickory nuts, beechnuts, hazelnuts, acorns. And in the South a persimmon tree is a likely starting point for hounds trailing either coon or possum. Chestnuts used to be important, too, and the blight may have caused the increase of corn raiding in recent years. Coons now feed voraciously on field corn, not only in the milk stage, but when they can find only dried leavings.

In the South they shuffle their way through winter and even in the North can be hunted effectively until the temperature remains rather steadily below about 28 degrees. Then they become lethargic, slumbering in their dens for weeks if no warm spell brings them out. Unable to hibernate, they are easily aroused by any disturbance, but they lose their appetites when cold reduces the food supply and, being short-legged, they are reluctant to move in deep snow. Typical hollows are in large basswoods, elms, beeches, maples, oaks, and sycamores, but a coon will den beneath a limestone overhang, in a cave or rock cleft, an unused drain tile, an empty mine, a chuck burrow, a high-grass tussock on a marsh, even a duck-nesting box that has not been predator-proofed and has a large-enough entry hole.

For a few weeks of February (a month earlier in the warmest areas, a month later in the coldest), males wander from den site to den site looking for mates. A female accepts only one male, and he remains in her den for at least a week, then seeks another mate while she subsides into lethargy for most of her two-month pregnancy. The annual litters average four or five young. Their eyes open in about three weeks, and they clamber about the den entrance at seven or eight weeks, although full weaning may require another month and a half. By then the mother is cautiously leading them about on foraging expeditions, and they are fat miniature replicas of her.

Some are killed by great horned owls, bobcats, and other predators. Young and old may be attacked by internal parasites and bothered by fleas, lice, or ticks, and there are many devastating diseases: distemper, meningitis, septicemia, toxoplasmosis, pneumonia, tetanus, rabies, and a semi-paralyzing, convulsive form of encephalitis sometimes mistaken for rabies. The encephalitis, though not communicable to man, can be transmit-

ted to dogs. Any game that looks or acts ill must be treated with the utmost caution. Despite natural dangers, coons have a life expectancy of eight or ten years in areas where local hunters abide by a gentlemen's agreement to spare the younger, smaller ones that begin their nightly forays early and are most often treed.

Hound work is finest on warm, moist nights in late fall when the coons are very active and the scent is heavy. There will never be agreement between advocates of silent coon dogs and the majority who favor open trailers. No breed dominates

Bluetick hound announcing that raccoon is treed.

the silent ones, which are very effective workers when meat or pest-control is the main objective. A raccoon has excellent night vision, but in heavy cover it cannot see the dogs until they are close. Its hearing, too, is excellent, but a coon on a feeding orgy often ignores quiet dogs until they are so near that the chase will be as brief as with a possum.

Vociferous hounds alert a coon so far in advance that the chase can be more like the running of a fox, even though the game can do no better than about 15 miles an hour when it switches from its waddling shuffle to a bounding run. But open trailers permit hunters to follow part or all of the pursuit. Then they bark "treed"—and, since a coon does not invariably stay treed, the men race for the sound with due haste. Silent dogs probably tree more coons, but they also lose more. An old coon is tricky. It may break up its trail by climbing a tree and leaping down again from a long limb; it may walk a fence rail, or circle and double back, cross water, or ride a drifting log. In the water it is easily overtaken by a dog but can whip and sometimes drown a single hound. And it is no easy adversary on the ground. There are advantages to releasing at least two or three dogs rather than one. Favorite full-voiced breeds are such as the treeing Walker, black-and-tan, redbone, and bluetick.

Hunters usually wear the spelunker's headlamps that have largely replaced lanterns. They carry open-sighted .22 rifles or pistols, since treeing means short range. Where coons are not so numerous as to be a problem, they sometimes haul their dogs away without shooting if everyone in the party has meat in his freezer; the sport is in the dog work.

Most hunters like traditional coonhound music, but a few use mouth-operated or phonographic predator calls, taking a stand in a clearing or field where approaching animals can be seen. A couple of hunting partners in Texas have demonstrated that good calling draws coons close enough for archery to vie with the .22. The dying-rabbit squeal works as it does with a fox (see page 365), except that night hunting is recommended. A call that shrieks like a wounded bird is even more effective. If a headlamp is adjusted to point just a trifle high, enough light spills to reveal the game or its eyeshine without scaring it off by throwing the beam at it too soon. An alternative is to use a red lens in the lamp, as red light does not spook animals.

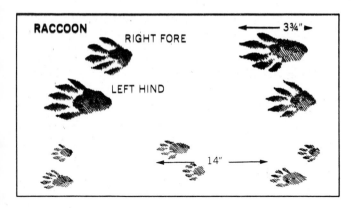

TRACKS & SIGN: Raccoon droppings are inconsistent but tend to be cylindrical, uniform in diameter, with some segments a couple of inches long. Unless bleached, they range from black to reddish. Deposits on tree limbs or on log or stone stream crossings are scent posts of a sort, marking a coon's prowling area. When scat is accumulated about the base of a tree, the trunk merits inspection for scratches, torn bark, and perhaps a den hole. A rough-barked entrance may also have snagged hair.

The tracks are almost bear-shaped but a walking coon pairs them—left hind foot beside right forefoot—and a running coon bounds heavily, bringing the hind feet down ahead of the forefeet in a pattern like oversized squirrel tracks. The stride varies from 6 inches to 20 or more. Being plantigrade, the animal makes large tracks. A typical foreprint measures 3 inches, with long, sharp-clawed toes spread like an open hand. A rear print, typically 3½ to 4 inches long, looks as if it were made by a flat-footed human baby with abnormally long toes.

VOICE: Coons can purr and whimper at each other, and they snarl, growl, and hiss at dogs or other foes. Once in a great while they utter catlike screams at night, or deep, rasping, tremulous whinnies suggestive of a screech owl. The reason for the calls is speculative, but they indicate activity and promise a good night's hunting.

Whitetail Deer *(Odocoileus virginianus)*
COMMON & REGIONAL NAMES: *whitetail, flagtail.*

DESCRIPTION & DISTRIBUTION: Whitetail deer have an uncanny ability to suit appearance to circumstance. A whitetail in a game park or gazing at automobiles from a roadside crop field looks nothing like the deer of the hunter's quest. In summer's chest-high hay and later in an orchard when the apples have begun to drop, the animal looks much bigger than it really is—perhaps the unexpected always appears larger than life—and even if the autumn molt has begun, its coat may seem tawny or even russet. Back in the woods it appears gray as a beech trunk, small as a weathered log, unobtrusive as brush.

A little stretch of Maine woods near Merrymeeting has a carpet of oak and beech mast latticed with deer trails. Yet the deer are seldom seen in that open part of the forest. They feed there at night, and they come through early in the morning and before dusk, moving between lower browsing areas and higher bedding grounds. Once in a great while, when a soft snow or recent rain dampens the crunching sound of booted steps, a hunter jumps one there. In most instances he sees no blob of flank or chest—nothing but a flashing white flag of tail, bounding so high that the deer assumes record-book dimensions in memory though no antlers were glimpsed. More often still, he sees not so much as the flag, but only hears a whistling snort.

On a wet fall morning three of us worked our way above those woods to where we had a better chance of detecting game before it detected us. A deer run crossed a saddle between ridges and dipped in among thickets of willows and alders. Soon, alerted by a light pattering, we watched a typical doe amble slowly up the trail, nipping twigs along the way, and enter a dense jungle of saplings. Had she brushed against us, her back would have

Wide-racked whitetail buck in Ohio woods.

reached only belt-high. Her head would have come barely to our chests until she reached up for dangling twigs. Several storm-smashed trees overhung the trail, so low she could have stepped across them, and whitetails often leap such obstacles, but she slithered under with an effortless ripple that brought her belly almost to the ground as her long legs folded beneath her. We watched her out of sight and waited an interminable twenty minutes in the hope that a buck was following her. And at last the buck (if buck it was) drifted up through the woods, at least 20 yards to the side of the conspicuous trail taken by the doe. We caught only a flicker of gray ghosting by.

Much later, drawn on by frustration, one of us followed while the other two waited at the edges of the copse, where an alerted deer might sneak out. Without crashing about noisily, the only way to penetrate was on hands and knees, stopping frequently to rest and peer about. At first nothing looked out of place. There were merely thin gray saplings, some as close together as fence pickets. Only in a vague, slow way did the realization come that several of the pickets thickened as they rose. Sometimes a hunter sees no more than deer legs that mimic saplings, and he may not know he has seen that much until the chance is gone. There was no twitch, no betraying shift of weight before the deer rustled away, turning and ducking so that a whitish throat patch glimmered for an instant. Solitary

Browse line clearly visible above deer run.

stalking, the epitome of deer hunting, would have been foolish in that tangle. But one of the standers at the edge had his shot.

The deer was a buck, a nice eight-pointer that probably weighed about 140 pounds since it went a little over 110 hog-dressed. Those weights are fairly typical for a northeastern whitetail, although Maine still produces bucks weighing 300 pounds or more, as do Missouri, Nebraska, the Dakotas, Minnesota, Wisconsin, Michigan. But the national average for mature bucks is probably between 135 and 165 pounds, while does usually weigh between 125 and 150 pounds. (As a rule, live weight is 25 percent more than field dressed—eviscerated but with carcass intact.)

After dragging a 110-pound field-dressed carcass out of the woods, a hunter may well overestimate its weight. A whitetail's dimensions are peculiarly deceptive. There are some thirty subspecies, distributed from the southern half of the Canadian provinces down through Central America. On Coiba Island, off Panama, mature bucks seldom weigh more than 50 pounds. Not much bigger is the Florida Keys deer *(O. v. clavium),* smallest of whitetail races in the United States and comparable to a lean collie dog. Until recently the Keys deer was endangered; it has protected status and seems to be recovering, especially on refuge lands. Far more abundant, but elusive and difficult to hunt in its arid realm, is the Coues deer, or Arizona whitetail, *(O. v. couesi),* which was once thought to be a distinct species. It is a thin-coated, dove-gray, mule-eared animal that seldom weighs a hundred pounds, is crowned with a lightly graceful rack, gets most of its water from cactus, and has adapted to the Sonora Desert and mountains of Arizona and northern Mexico. Most whitetails are incapable of surviving in such dry country. They are scarce or absent in much of California, Nevada, Colorado, northern Arizona, southwestern Idaho, and parts of Washington and Oregon (though mule deer or blacktails are plentiful in some of those areas). But whitetails are abundant throughout most of the United States. There are more than a dozen subspecies in this country.

The most familiar are the northern whitetail *(O. v. borealis)* of Canada and the upper United States; the Virginia whitetail *(O. v. virginianus)* of the Southeast; the Kansas whitetail *(O. v. macrourus)* of the Midwest and much of the Southwest; and the

Dakota whitetail *(O. v. dacotensis)* of the Midwest and upper West. Since subspecies overlap and interbreed, physical characteristics often blend. But generally speaking, the southerly strains are smallest and palest; they tend to be sandy-gray, while northern deer turn reddish-brown in summer, rich tannish gray or smoky in winter. A winter-clad northern woodland deer is said to be "in the blue," and is "in the red" after spring shedding.

The northern whitetail is the largest, the only one that frequently weighs more than 200 pounds, and it is found in the finest whitetail-hunting regions—southern Canada, New England, New York, Pennsylvania, Wisconsin, Michigan, and Minnesota. A 400-pound Adirondack buck shot in 1890 measured 51 inches high at the withers and 9 feet, 7 inches from nose to tail tip, but an average northern buck stands about 38 inches at the shoulder and is 5 or 6 feet long.

Regardless of race, the belly and inner leg surfaces are white, and a white patch covers the chin and upper throat. The nose is black, the forward part of the snout light or whitish with a black spot on each side extending down onto the chin. The

Whitetail scat (top l.), swamp-country
whitetail's long dewclaw and hoof (top r.), soil gouged at salt
lick (bottom l.), and browsed red-maple sprouts.

eyes are brown, with big black pupils. The tail, sometimes more than a foot long and widely furred at the base, tapers like a pennant. Its outer surface is the color of the back, sometimes streaked with black. (A mule deer's tail is narrower, more rounded, white all about and tipped with black, while a blacktail deer has a rounded tail with a dark brownish or blackish outer surface and white inner surface.) The whitetail is named for the inner tail surface—the most conspicuous feature when the deer is spooked. Its tail goes up, showing the bright white inner surface, and it wags and bobs as the deer bounds away, occasionally tossing its hindquarters high in leaps that may cover 20 feet.

Mule deer are generally bigger than whitetails and bounce more when they run, but at a distance identification is sometimes difficult. The tail may not be visible, and some whitetails have mulish ears. A buck's antlers are often a clearer indication of species. A whitetail's main beams curve back, out, up, and forward, hooking in near the tips if they are beyond the spike stage, and the tines grow directly from these beams. A muley's rack forks more evenly and forks again in a series of Y shapes like hardwood crotches. The mule deer's antlers also tend to be higher in proportion to their spread, and the brow tines less pronounced. But there are exceptions. A mule deer can have wide, low antlers, and on a good rack the brow tines can be massive. Moreover, the Carmen Mountains whitetail *(O. v. carminis)* of the Rio Grande has such even forks that it looks like an undersized mule deer.

During the 15 or 20 million years since the forebears of the American whitetail crossed the land bridge from Asia, they have developed into a unique species found nowhere else in the world. We can only guess at the number of whitetails when the country was first settled but, since they fare poorly in climax forests, there must have been substantially fewer than 5 million. Today there are more than 16 million. Even so, whitetails had been brought to the verge of extinction by the turn of this century. At first their population had soared with the clearing of agricultural lands and the cutting of timber. Then a decline set in, partly because of flooding, uncontrolled slash fires and forest fires, and the abandonment of ravaged lands as lumbermen moved westward. The second-growth trees and shrubs, sprouting on heavily lumbered tracts, eventually grew too tall for browse, again turning into climax forests that could not support large herds. Simultaneously, settlers were massacring deer for food, hides, and the protection of crops. As a market developed for meat and skins, the slaughter accelerated.

The crisis hastened an unprecedented conservation movement. Whitetails were restocked in states that have since become famous for them. In some areas the animals were fully protected for many years and in others hunting was restricted to adult —noticeably antlered—bucks. Many states have retained the bucks-only law, a restorative that has worked all too well. Since deer are polygamous and one buck will breed with all the does he can find or win from rivals, potential herd size is governed by the number of does. The problem is that, with predators eliminated from most of the range, the severely reduced habitat has a limited carrying capacity. Deep snow forces whitetails to yard up, and inadequate browse turns a yard into a cemetery.

Game commissions have experimented with party-permit doe harvests, which can be put into effect throughout a state or within overpopulated "management units." Typically, a party of four hunters obtains a permit to take one doe among them in addition to the normal buck per man. But the issuance of too many party permits can be disastrous, as many of us discovered not long ago when herds were severely thinned in some parts of New York. Results have been better in states that set short doe seasons or allow a hunter to take one deer of either sex per season. Most hunters yearn to take an antlered trophy, so they do not become overzealous doe killers unless the doe is a party bonus.

GAME BEHAVIOR & HUNTING HABITAT: About nine out of ten hunters go home without venison. They fail so often because whitetail deer are the most adaptable of all the larger species. They were once primarily diurnal in their feeding habits, and during the summer they still revert to daytime feeding in some sparsely settled areas, but they become chiefly nocturnal when hunted. Although they prefer certain browse plants, they are known to eat more than 600 kinds of vegetation. Bold when unmolested, they also skulk invisibly through woods and farm lots within sight of the Empire State Building.

But three factors favor the hunter. The first is that whitetails do not migrate seasonally as muleys do. Throughout most of the year a whitetail buck's home range covers only about a square mile, and even when seeking does he rarely expands that territory to more than 2 or 3 miles. If driven out, he travels only as far as he must and returns as soon as possible.

The second factor is that within the small home range most deer repeatedly use the same routes between bedding and feeding areas. They follow terrain contours that make for easy, unobtrusive travel—benches, saddles, shallow draws, creek banks, dry brook beds, all the natural paths a man might take between high and low ground. A heavily used deer run is well marked with tracks and droppings, and sometimes becomes grooved with tramping. It can, however, be misleading. Within a few weeks it can be abandoned or can shift hundreds of yards if it becomes too watery or muddy or is blocked by a tangled deadfall, or if the deer are attracted by vegetation sprouting in a new location or happen to come on an easier route as they amble off while browsing. The better a hunter knows his woods, the more consistently he takes game.

The hunter's third advantage is that, in most areas, the hunting season coincides with at least part of the breeding season. A rutting buck, preoccupied with finding does and challenging rivals, loses some of his caution. And by moving about in daylight more than at other seasons, he increases the chance of being spotted or ambushed.

It is astounding that a buck can live for years without being seen on a mile-square parcel of land, land which includes low growth or relatively open spaces for feeding. Almost always he detects the hunter before the hunter detects him. Like the majority of mammals, the whitetail is color-blind, but has an extraordinary ability to perceive motion. As a rule, a deer either fails to notice or ignores stationary objects and animals unless sound or scent gives warning. But the slightest movement will cause a buck to freeze and focus on a hunter. Anyone who has spent much time on stand knows that an alerted deer can detect the blink of an eye at 50 or 60 yards. In a situation of that kind, the hunter's best chance is to remain perfectly still until the buck looks away, then raise his rifle smoothly. Any fast or sudden movement is like the release of a spring.

The buck will not go far, but he will be very difficult to find. After running a short way he will probably slow to a nervous,

"single-footing" walk, holding one forefoot high, as if to stamp, trotting two steps with the leg up, then bringing it down and lifting the other forefoot for a couple of steps. He is a runner on his mark, ready to spring away at the expected signal. As he becomes calmer he circles or fishhooks to scan the back trail, test the wind, and listen. Scenting ability is the first line of defense, for a whitetail prefers to feed or retreat into the wind and can probably smell a man at a third of a mile if the breeze is right. Some hunters lightly sprinkle their clothes with one of the commercial scents, or "lures." Probably the most popular is the kind that smells like frostbitten apples, an almost irresistible autumn food. The most appetizing scents do not really seem to lure bucks, but they mask the human odor.

Having slowed to a walk and begun to circle, the buck pauses often, rock-still, almost invisible in screening brush. If he continues to sense danger, he then proceeds by skulking rather than walking or trotting. A 150-pound buck can squirm under knee-high tangles and fence wires almost noiselessly, and can then leap from a standing position to clear an 8-foot fence.

His hearing is almost as acute as his sense of smell. His big ears twitch and turn incessantly. A scolding squirrel or the alarmed squawks of jays, crows, and other birds can sometimes lead a hunter toward a buck but will more likely provide an early warning for the game. The whitetail's hearing seems to be most

Eastern whitetail doe jumped from bed.

finely attuned to high-pitched sounds—a snapping twig, a cough, a loosely clinking sling swivel.

Still-hunting holds promise only for the careful hunter. (In this book the term "still-hunting" is used in the old-fashioned sense of stalking silently rather than going on stand and remaining still; the two methods can be effectively combined.) A deft still-hunter may get no farther than a couple of hundred yards in half an hour. He pauses, looks, and listens more than he walks. And he seldom walks at the steady, rhythmical pace that deer recognize as human sound; he takes a few unevenly timed steps, waits, takes a few more steps, like a browsing animal.

Certain sounds can fool a buck instead of warning him. A few hunters use calls to mimic the calflike bawl of a doe or the whistling snort of a buck on the prod, but such calling seldom works. More effective is the southwestern technique of rattling for bucks. The hunter takes a concealed stand where he has found plenty of sign. It may be at ground level, but a tree crotch provides a good view and raises the scent and sight of a hunter above detection. Man-made towers, sometimes called "high-sits," are also used. Rattling is done with a pair of fairly heavy antlers collected during some past season. Though there is no definite time limit, it seems best to rest every few minutes just as bucks usually do when they fight.

By September in most areas a buck's antlers are fully grown and hardened, and the velvet begins to dry and peel away soon thereafter. By October, with diminished daylight stimulating hormone production, his neck begins to swell, the blood supply having increased to bulge and harden muscles needed for battle. The rutting fever usually peaks in November and begins to subside in December. Bucks may meet while trailing the same doe, and if they are fairly evenly matched a fight is apt to ensue. With heads lowered, they come together in a contest of strength, balance, and shoving ability, each trying to push the other over while watching for a sudden chance to dip under the adversary's guard with a goring or slashing lunge. Occasionally a spike buck defies an older animal and wins by stabbing his straight, slender horns through the opponent's branching rack. More often, after a seemingly even fight that has lasted minutes or an hour with brief rests between desperate rounds, one animal breaks away and quits the area. The victor returns to his pursuit of the doe.

Deaths are infrequent, but now and then a buck is fatally gored or trampled, and occasionally the rivals lock antlers inextricably.

A buck, having shed his antlers soon after the rut, begins to grow new ones in the spring, usually in May. Their velvet covering is a membrane of modified skin, laced with veins to nourish them and covered with short, bristly hairs.

Whitetails collect no harems, though a buck may sometimes squire two does at a time. Usually he stays with a receptive doe for several days, then seeks another, trailing by scent. Deer of both sexes have musk glands between the lobes of their hoofs, on the outside of the hind legs below the hocks, and on the inside of the hind legs at the hocks. The musk does not endanger them since predators would be able to locate deer by body scent alone. It forms a tracking bond between mother and young and among herd members, and it is a sexual attractant during the rut. Many hunters take care to cut away the knoblike, swollen musk glands from the inner surface of the hock joints for fear it will taint the meat. This is unnecessary if the glands are not rubbed or cut while the deer is being dressed out. It is more important to avoid getting hair on the meat (or to wipe it all off), since hair can sour the venison.

It is essential to approach a downed whitetail cautiously, even if the eyes are glazed. Be ready to fire a *coup de grâce* if there is any sign of life. Then position the carcass on its back, preferably with the hindquarters slightly lower than the head. A small, sharp knife is ample for dressing; a blade longer than 5 inches can be awkward, and a shorter one is fine. It should be fairly straight and sharpened only on one edge, though a sharp top hook behind the point can help in opening the animal without slicing the paunch. Some hunters begin by bleeding big game—slashing the jugular vein or plunging the blade in at the juncture of neck and chest to sever the carotid arteries where they come together between the shoulders. It is not really necessary. The bullet has usually bled the animal fairly well, and draining continues during the dressing process.

Begin by slitting all the way around the anus. If local law requires that the scrotum be left in place, a small detour will have to be made in opening the carcass. Otherwise, simply sever the genital root from between the rump bulges and cut off the genitals. With a forefinger held along the back of the blade to guide it and prevent pricking the viscera, the knife is then inserted with the cutting edge up, and the belly is slit to the chest.

Next, cut around the ribs to free the diaphragm. Reach in and up as far as possible to grasp and sever the windpipe and esophagus. A few additional freeing cuts will be obvious, after which the organs and viscera can be rolled out of the carcass. Most hunters carry a plastic bag or other receptacle for the liver and heart, which are delicious.

Unless the viscera have been cut, it is best not to flush the body cavity with water but to wipe it dry with a clean piece of burlap, moss, leaves, or grass. The thin blood glaze that forms is desirable at the onset of cooling and aging, and it helps seal the flesh from blowflies. A liberal sprinkling of black pepper also repels flies and other pests, but if the deer is to hang in camp for long a wrapping of muslin provides better protection.

If a buck is so large it must be left behind while dragging help is obtained, the body cavity should be propped open with one or two sticks to facilitate draining and cooling. If it must be left for very long, it should be raised off the ground as much as possible. Some hunters carry hauling ropes or harnesses, which can also serve as hanging rigs. At camp, the deer can be hung head up, by lashing the antlers.

A small deer can be shouldered and carried out of the woods with its head and forelegs draped on one side of the hunter's chest, its hind legs on the other side, its body behind the man's head. A bright handkerchief or rag should be tied to the antlers and another to the tail, and the carrier is well advised to whistle or sing all the way out of the woods because in dim light a bobbing rack may entice one of those fortunately rare cretins who shoot at shadows and sounds. A better way is to stretch the deer's forelegs straight out to the front, lash the head to them, and drag the animal out with a rope tied to the forefeet. Another good way is to lash a short pole crosswise through the antlers, grasp the pole ends, and haul; it is easiest with a partner but can be done alone. For that matter, two men can drag a deer out by its antlers.

Antlers are not only a hauling aid but the principal object of the hunt to men who want venison strictly in conjunction with a fine trophy. There are nontypical racks—congenital oddities or the result of an injury during growth—that sometimes become

very large, assume strange asymmetrical shapes, and may sprout tines like thorns on a cactus. The world's record nontypical whitetail was shot in 1892 at Brady, Texas, by Jeff Benson, and it rated an unbelievable 286 points on the Boone and Crockett trophy-scoring system. The record typical rack, shot by an unknown hunter and discovered on a wall in Sandstone, Minnesota, scored 206⅝. Discounting the anonymous trophy, the record typical head scored 202 on the Boone and Crockett chart. It was shot by John A. Breen in 1918 at Funkley, Minnesota, and it has 16 points (tines more than an inch long) symmetrically positioned 8 to a side. The left main beam is 31 inches long, the right a quarter inch longer, and the inside spread is 23⅝ inches. A recently shot Missouri deer nearly matched it, proving that the age of great trophies is not past, but most whitetail hunters are happy to collect an 8-point trophy.

A whitetail's basket-shaped antlers are very difficult to judge in shadowy woods, through screening foliage, or when the buck is moving. But if the deer is seen from behind and the rack is wider than the body, it will be excellent. Other favorable indications are thick-looking bases, a sweep that seems disproportionately large for the head, or an antler height comparable to the length of the tail or the distance from chin to bottom of brisket.

Antler development is no sign of age once a buck matures. In his first autumn he usually grows knobs which may be invisible

Florida buck, poised to flee at slightest movement.

except for the twin hair swirls between the ears, or as much as an inch long. A "button buck" is a yearling with substantial knobs. In his second autumn he will probably be a "spike buck," with smooth, fairly straight horns averaging 4 or 5 inches but sometimes longer. In habitat with ample and nutritious browse, containing calcium and phosphorus, the spikes may begin to branch during the second summer to produce a forkhorn. That usually occurs with the third set of antlers, but two-year-old bucks occasionally have 6 or 8 points. Commonly, antlers are largest and heaviest in the fourth or fifth autumn, but after three years the number of points indicates only the quality of habitat. A very old buck may revert to spikes, or fail to sprout any antlers.

At about the time when antler growth begins, most of the does are bearing fawns, gestation having lasted some 200 days. A 2½-year-old doe almost invariably bears a single fawn; in succeeding years twins are the rule, and triplets are not uncommon where good browse is plentiful.

A doe usually seeks solitude but not concealment when she gives birth. The young can stand about ten minutes after they are born, and an hour or so later the mother leads them to a hiding spot in the woods, where they snuggle down as low to the ground as possible. Incredibly, they are almost odorless for about the first month of life. Even a keen-nosed dog cannot find them by scent, and they remain motionless if an intruder approaches. At birth their weight is comparable to that of human infants, but they weigh about 30 pounds by August. The typical coat is russet, with some 300 immaculate white spots on sides and back. The spots vanish when a deer acquires its first gray winter coat.

Predation is light. Some are killed by cougars in the West, wolves in the North, but most victims are old animals, defective fawns, or winter-weakened individuals, but none of these adversities severely limits the population.

A greater menace is the domestic dog. Nearly every rural or suburban dog owner thinks his pet harmless, but even hounds carefully trained to ignore deer in favor of other game sometimes yield to the deer-running passion. New York dogs have been known to kill over a thousand snowbound whitetails by the end of January. Even deadlier is the automobile. Every day, motorists run down a million American animals of various kinds. In a state with a high whitetail population and considerable road traffic, a yearly toll of 10,000 deer is not unusual.

The survivors thrive until deep snow claims an even heavier toll. Deer can move quite well on a firm crust but flounder in a soft 2-foot snow. Before it gets much more than half that deep they band together and yard up on south slopes, in valleys, or other relatively sheltered spots. Often the snow prevents them from moving on when the area is overbrowsed, and they are reluctant to leave when able to. Instinct hinders them from defying snow, wind, and cold in a dubious search for better forage.

In some regions men go out to the yards with bales of fodder, but winter feeding can be disastrous without the guidance of a game biologist. Weakened deer quickly become addicted to the dole and refuse to leave the area when the weather breaks.

Plantings are more effective than winter feeding. A deer will dig through 2 feet of snow to browse herbs such as rape down to ground level. Cutting and bending certain trees can also help ensure the survival of next season's game. Aspen and yellow birch, which have little commercial value, can be cut part way through and bent over so that deer can reach the upper branches, and the trees will continue to grow. Another fine winter food is the red maple, the stump of which sprouts new shoots every time it is cut back.

When deer are not yarded, they are certain to be near one or more of their preferred foods. Tender maple buds appear as the days lengthen, and in spring and summer whitetails seek oak, sassafras, willow, sumac, blackberry, blueberry, sweetfern, clover, buckwheat, corn, alfalfa, soybeans, truck crops, and an assortment of less important wild foods, including waterlily. They leave their cool, high, secluded beds when the afternoon is waning and go to water before they do much feeding. Until snow ends the need to find water, late afternoon is a good hunting time near springs, ponds, and streams.

But a hunter will find the most heavily worn game trails and the largest tracks leading to concentrations of preferred fall and early-winter foods. Acorns, especially those of white oak, are a mainstay wherever they occur. The edge of an apple orchard, abandoned or cultivated, attracts deer from all the neighboring woods. They nibble leaves and twigs, but what they love most are fallen apples softened by frost. Some of the favorite foods differ from one part of the country to another. In the Northeast they include waste corn and truck crops, the mast of black oak, beech, and hickory, berry bushes, and the twigs and foliage of white cedar, hemlock, yew, maples, witch hazel, sumac, aspen, sassafras, wintergreen, dogwood, basswood, and birch. The list is much the same in the Midwest, with the addition of white pine, jack pine, ferns, arborvitae, viburnum, bearberry, rose, and fir. In the South and some of the Midwest the list also includes blueberry and strawberry bushes, Christmas fern, grape vines, greenbrier, mountain laurel, antennaria, fringe tree, sweetbay, mulberry, swamp ironwood, holly, jessamine, dewberry, honeysuckle, sweet pepperbush, rhododendron, raspberry, lespedeza, snowberry, persimmon, and buffalo nut. In the Southwest live oak is very important, as are mountain mahogany, snakeweed, buckthorn, cliff rose, silk tassel, and red-oak mast. In various parts of the West there are buckbrush, chokecherry, red osier, juniper, bur oak, yucca, Oregon grape, serviceberry, spruce, and willow.

Deer feed most actively at night in the lowlands. The cooling air produces descending thermals, and on low ground, where many favored browse plants proliferate, the whitetails can most clearly scent and hear approaching danger. By first light some of them are climbing and a few may already be on the high benches and ridges. When the air warms, producing rising thermals, they want to be where scent and sound will drift up to them, and where they can watch for dogs and men. Both usually approach from below. It is a good time to be on a stand overlooking a gap, brushy spot, timber edge, gentle slope, bench, or perhaps a funneling valley—the traveling routes between feeding and bedding grounds. The best location of all is close to, but not on, a game trail or an intersection of game trails. It should be upwind and far enough off the run so that the hunter will not be readily detected and will have a fairly clear view for at least 25 or 30 yards even in timber. Full concealment may be impossible, and is not essential if a man hides in a hillside tangle or blowdown that breaks his outline, or up on a large boulder, a ledge, or a big tree crotch. A deer pays little attention to anything much above the height of a man. Some hunters wear red plaid or black-spotted red camouflage clothing that is easily seen by other hunters but not by deer; bright red or orange, worn for safety and in some locales required by law, cannot be discerned by a deer, yet shiny material or a big solid patch of any tone may lift a flag. The tone and outline should be broken.

In cold weather deer are drawn to south slopes for warmth, sun, and protection from wind, and they like hillsides where seeps, swamps, or running springs maintain good browse after feeding becomes meager on the ridges. An excellent location for a stand is high on the hill, at its top, or on a promontory overlooking it, but en route to the chosen spot a hunter can drive the unseen game ahead of him and right over the summit. The way to reach the stand ahead of the deer is to circle and come over the top from the far side, starting as early as possible in the morning and utilizing the climb as a still-hunt, in case a whitetail is poking about on the poorer side of a mountain.

An oak ridge or high beech flat is an ideal place to be until midmorning, unless the season has been so dry that the nut and acorn crops are scanty and the deer are browsing in the valleys. Though whitetails head for their bedding areas early in the morning and are generally inactive during the warmest hours (except when an influx of hunters churns them up), they feed intermittently throughout the day. They are drawn back to favorite bedding areas but not to previously used beds. A buck will find a suitable spot to bed wherever he happens to be when he wants to rest or ruminate. He may lie down in a concealing thicket or just a small clump on a slope or promontory where he can watch the approaches. Usually he circles around somewhat to bed facing his back trail and facing downhill if possible.

When a hunter finally leaves his stand, therefore, he wants to work downhill, slowly and quietly. He wants to advance from above the deer, except perhaps at the end of day, when he can take a last, lower stand near a trail to ambush game descending from the ridges. He may also work lower on drizzly days when the rain masks his sounds and the game is sheltering in thick swamps, wooded draws, and hollows.

There is little point in following a deer's trail directly, but a hunter can often take his game by moving in the direction of the trail, crossing and recrossing it in wide, long, serpentine swings to intercept a suspicious buck that fishhooks or circles to look back. When two men find a fresh trail—usually on new snow—a frequently productive technique is for one hunter to move along perhaps 15 or 20 yards to one side of the tracks while his partner parallels him much farther out on the other side, anywhere from 25 or 30 yards to a hundred or more, depending on cover density. If the wind is crossing, the wide man should be on the upwind side. Should the deer fail to become suspicious, the close man may get a shot, but a buck is more apt to swing upwind, coming into view of the other man.

When three men work a trail, one walks the tracks and the other two parallel him, far out on each side. The same technique is effective in hunting long ridges; one man walks slowly along the top while a flanker on each side stays a couple of hundred yards below.

Such hunting is really a small version of the traditional northeastern deer drive, which is best confined to an area of less than a square mile and limited to half a dozen or a dozen men. It is well suited to brushy gullies, notches, swamps, woodlots, old road cuts—fairly small natural hideaways that can be thoroughly combed and offer good shooting visibility at their borders. Half the men spread out wide on the downwind or higher edge and part way along the sides. They are the standers. The drivers, or pushers, spread out on the opposite edge, clear across to the sides, with the wind at their backs since they want the deer to catch their scent as they move through. They walk quietly and steadily toward the standers. For safety and efficiency, one man should be in charge, and he gives a prearranged signal to begin and end the drive.

A quiet drive usually produces shots at walking or trotting deer. A noisy one can push them out at a top speed of about 35 miles an hour. The hunter catches only a glimpse of his quarry. If does are illegal and he is not certain he has spotted antlers, he has to forgo the shot. In any event, he usually carries a shotgun rather than a rifle because he must swing quickly through a fast-moving target.

The same kind of shooting is the rule in deer-hounding, a more sporting pursuit than is commonly supposed. It is illegal in most states but a social event in parts of Canada and the South. Hounds are generally used in swamps or woods containing extensively thick cover that is difficult to hunt by ordinary means. No particular breed is best. The dogs are of the same types used for other game, from coon to cat, boar to bear. The hunters go on stand overlooking natural crossings or openings, and ideally trained dogs will not push too hard. The deer come through ahead of them, fast but almost never in full flight and neither exhausted nor terrified.

For hunting with hounds, for big noisy drives, and in heavily populated areas where the law permits nothing but buckshot, the arm of choice is a full-choked 12-gauge shotgun firing high-velocity loads of No. 00 Buck. Some shotgun-only areas permit the use of rifled slugs. In slug-choked or cylinder-bored guns they are unquestionably more accurate and lethal than buckshot, but even when the gun is equipped, as it should be, with rifle-type sights or a scope, slugs are unreliable at more than about 65 yards. Of course, shots at whitetails in timber are often at such short range that speed and good general slug placement are more important than pinpoint accuracy. The permissible targets are the brisket, neck, upper spinal column, shoulder, and the lung-and-heart area in the forward half of the rib cage. Scopes with virtually no magnification or up to 2-power gather sufficient light and furnish an improved sight picture for slug shooting. Similar scopes are used by handgunners who hunt deer with .357 Magnums.

The .308 is probably the best rifle chambering ever employed for whitetail hunting, but many other calibers are also excellent. In relatively open terrain, a hunter may have more faith in a .243 bolt-action, whereas in thick northern woods the .30-30 and .32 Special lever-actions are as popular as they are venerable, and some deer-stalking traditionalists use muzzle-loaders ranging in caliber from about .30 to .50. Included among cartridges almost as popular as the .308 are the 6mm, 6.5mm, .44 Magnum, .45-70, .35 Remington, .300 Savage, and, of course, the ubiquitous .30-06. In very dense woods, some riflemen prefer open or aperture sights. Where shots are apt to be a bit longer, the 2½-power scope is a favorite.

After shooting, any conscientious hunter searches for a blood trail unless the kill was instantaneous or he is absolutely certain he missed. A whitetail is slow to succumb to shock. Occasionally, no flinch or jump is visible upon impact, and a deer sometimes runs more than a hundred yards after being struck in a vital organ. Going immediately to where the deer was when he fired, the hunter searches for blood and possibly hair. Then, if he doubts that the animal was well hit, he may wait a few minutes before following the blood trail. A wounded deer tries to keep moving if it senses pursuit. Otherwise it soon lies down and begins to stiffen. The hunter then has a better chance of finding it quickly. A short wait is humane as well as efficient.

TRACKS & SIGN: The print of a deer's cloven hoof is a split heart, with the pointed end forward. Size varies greatly from region to region and from one subspecies to another, but most tracks are between 2 and 3 inches long on relatively hard ground. If they are much smaller, a fawn probably made them.

Many experienced whitetail hunters are convinced that they can tell a buck's track from a doe's. They say a buck's hoof lobes splay, sometimes so much that the front of the track is wider than the rear. But a heavy old doe often has splayed hoofs. Both sexes run with a rocking-horse motion, causing the hind prints sometimes to register ahead of the foreprints but forming a slightly zigzag line and not bunching in the manner of a bounding mule deer—except in deep snow, which forces high, leg-bunching leaps. The trail is apt to be perhaps 5 or 6 inches wide, the walking stride a foot or so long but the running stride 6 feet or more.

Buck rubs—long polished scars low on saplings and

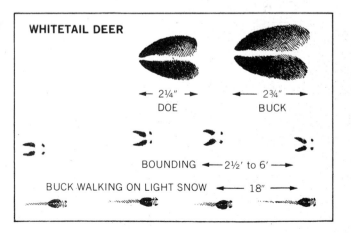

WHITETAIL DEER

← 2¼″ → DOE   ← 2¾″ → BUCK

BOUNDING ← 2½′ to 6′ →

BUCK WALKING ON LIGHT SNOW ← 18″ →

bushes where the deer's antlers have scraped away bark—signify that a buck inhabits the area.

Before first snow, bedding spots are merely slight depressions or ovals where the leaves have been pressed by body weight. Unless a deer has been scuffling up the leaves and brush, a bed may be almost indiscernible. A bedding depression on snow is more noticeable.

Browsed vegetation is also recognizable, even when low enough to have been nibbled by rabbits, as a deer has no upper incisors for snipping. Bites are ragged rather than trim. Droppings, too, are readily identified. Very early in the season, scat is sometimes tubular and segmented or even amorphous if the animals have been feeding on succulent vegetation. But throughout most of the fall and winter it takes the form of hard, dark pellets, sometimes round but more often slightly oblong or acorn-shaped and averaging about three-quarters of an inch long.

VOICE: Whitetails, especially does and fawns, sometimes communicate by bleating like a lamb or bawling like a calf. Bucks and mature does also snort, and a buck's snort is often characterized by a kind of whinnying or whistling.

Apart from horn rattling, no calling technique has ever proved very effective.

Mule Deer *(Odocoileus hemionus)*
COMMON & REGIONAL NAMES: *Muley, burro deer.*
For Columbian blacktail subspecies—coast deer, redwood deer.
For Sitka blacktail subspecies—Sitka deer, coast deer, Alaskan deer.

DESCRIPTION & DISTRIBUTION: A hunter from the East may be unprepared for his first glimpse of a mature muley buck across some high meadow in Montana's Rockies or on a sweeping Colorado plateau. The antlers are as high as they are wide, and the animal appears monstrous at more than 200 yards. Magnified through binoculars and then through a rifle scope, it dwarfs the memory of a heavy New England buck that was shot at 60 yards.

But if an awesome buck poised on the horizon is the most widely recognized image of the mule deer, it is hardly all-

(text continued on page 489)

▲ Whitetail buck makes flagging bound.   ▼ Southern whitetail buck.

▲ Whitetail jumped near Pine Barrens, N.J.   ▼ Muley buck and doe.

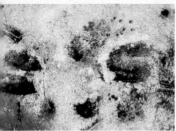

▼ Muley tracks.

▼ Tower-type deer stand popular in Texas.

▼ Whitetail rubbing off velvet.

▲ Desert mule deer. ▼ Glassing for mule deer.

▲ Cougar in Utah mountains. ▼ Stalking fine pronghorn buck.

▼ Bighorn ewe.　▲ Band of Alaskan Dall rams.　▼ Excellent desert ram and juveni[

nting bighorns in Alberta. ▼ Rocky Mountain bighorns—one with full, but small, curl.

▲ Gray wolf. ▼ Male mountain goat high in Rockies.

encompassing. Equally valid is the recollection of a guide feathering his paddle, then letting the canoe drift closer to one of the
thickly timbered little islands below the Alaskan panhandle to
search the borders of green-black conifers for the little Sitka
bucks that often venture out. The hunter nods toward the woods.
Silently the guide beaches the canoe upwind of a browsing deer
no larger than an eastern whitetail. Many miles down the coast,
in British Columbia, a man conceals himself in a thicket and
uses a call to mimic the bawling of a nervous fawn. A doe and
a high-antlered buck, much like the Alaskan deer, raise their
heads from succulent tufts of streamside grasses and turn
inquisitively toward the sound. Not far from Oregon's bays, a
hunter jumps a deer out of woolly fog below a canyon rim. It
may look a trifle leggier than the Sitka deer stalked on the northern
island, but it is virtually indistinguishable from the buck that
followed a doe toward the fawn call. It, too, is a coast deer,
a Columbian blacktail, as is a doe bedded in ferns under a California redwood. All are subspecies of mule deer.

An especially vivid recollection concerns a pale desert
muley, larger than the blacktails and with more imposing antlers
but not quite a match for the Rocky Mountain race. At about
four o'clock, with the Texas sun still vicious on December's first
Friday, the guide had turned the truck west to check a remote
string of broken mesas where few hunters had wandered that
season. The only road was a flat, wide coulee bottom. With the
truck jouncing like a lame horse, the hunter tried to steady his
binoculars on a slope that should have been called Pyramid
Mountain. His partner glassed the other side, a considerate ges-
ture since he had a fair five-pointer (by western, one-sided count)
riding the truck bed.

The guide swung around a curve, coasting slowly on a
smooth northward stretch that looked like a salt flat. And there
lay a much bigger buck, bedded halfway up on the right bank.

The guide, Biddy, knew better than to horse the brake.
The stop was almost noiseless, but the buck rose to its front
knees, lifted its rump, and stood up stiffly. The door opened
without much sound, but time was lost fumbling for rifle and
cartridges as the buck turned, walked up toward the rim, and
disappeared behind an uptilted prow of sandstone. What had
looked almost too easy at 90 yards now looked almost unattain-

able. There was nothing to be done but crouch and follow quietly, around chimney rocks and brush, over lava slabs, avoiding brittle sandstone flakes and loose gravel, trying to hurry. The first trace of the buck to reappear above the rock palisade was a thin, perpendicular white needle—sun glinting on an antler tine, jogging up and down. He was trotting. There was just time to sink down and wonder whether to hold low for an uphill shot or dead on at a range that could hardly be much more than a hundred yards. Almost at the crest the buck stopped for a fraction of a second and looked back. At the report of the .264 Magnum he sprang forward smoothly, without any humping pitch to signify a hit. Yet he was falling, perhaps already dead, when a second bullet passed over his shoulder and spattered the rimrock.

Since he weighed a little over 170 pounds field-dressed, his live weight must have been about 215 pounds, quite heavy for the desert muley *(O. h. eremenicus)* though it would not be for the Rocky Mountains mule deer *(O. h. hemionus)* that ranges the plains and mountains from Canada to Arizona and New Mexico. The latter is the most abundant and widely distributed of eleven subspecies, and in lush habitat it grows very large. While an average buck may weigh 200 pounds or so (a bit more than a doe), a big buck may be a hundred pounds heavier. Most of the very large ones—bucks that look almost like elk—are said to be British Columbian.

The 215-pounder on the coulee rim was probably one of the finest taken in 1965 in lower Texas but the mount would score only about 154 on a Boone and Crockett chart, essentially because the rack was not outstandingly wide nor were the beams extremely thick. Unfortunately, the right antler had a sixth tine, precisely an inch long and therefore scored, but as a penalty. Symmetry counts heavily in record-book scoring for the category of typical trophies, and nontypical ones have so many tines that a barely asymmetrical rack is out of the running. The first-place typical mule deer, shot in Wyoming by an unknown hunter, has six tines on each side and a Boone and Crockett score of 217.

Whereas a whitetail hunter revels in counting abundant matched tines (up to 7 per side on a normal rack), a typical mature mule deer has only 5 to a side—or only 4 if brow tines are lacking, as they often are. Each main beam forks twice, forming long, relatively straight points and providing a fast way to

tell a small muley from a large whitetail. Because blacktails rarely weigh more than 150 pounds and were once considered a separate species, they are accorded separate records. The current high score of 170⅛ is for a coast deer shot in 1963 in Oregon by W. W. Gibbs.

Mule deer are thought to number between 7 and 8 million. Of these, the mule deer of the Pacific Coast—the Sitka blacktail *(O. h. sitkensis),* ranging from southeastern Alaska into upper British Columbia, and the Columbian blacktail *(O. h. columbianus),* ranging from that province down into central California—probably account for a million and a half. Except for the antlers and the ears (which are large though not as long as those of other muleys), a blacktail looks like a whitetail. Its tail, somewhat wider, shorter, and brushier than a mule deer's, is brown or blackish with a skimpily haired white underside. A spooked muley tucks its tail in so tightly it is sometimes said to be "lowtailing out of danger," while a whitetail "hightails" it. A blacktail usually lets the appendage droop limply.

Coloring differs among geographic races, but a typical mule deer is bay or tannish gray in summer, a somewhat purer gray in winter. Discounting its size, antlers, ears, and tail, it too looks much like a whitetail. The ears may be nearly a foot long in some regions. The tail is roughly cylindrical, white with a 2-inch black tip.

Oregon hunter aiming at skylined mule deer.

Mule deer range through the three westernmost Canadian provinces, southward into Mexico, and from the Pacific states eastward to a vague line running along the eastern borders of the Dakotas down through west-central Texas.

GAME BEHAVIOR & HUNTING HABITAT: Blacktail mule deer are best hunted near clusters of preferred foods such as oak, filaree, bromegrass, fescue, wild oats, manzanita, buckthorn, mountain mahogany, ferns, berries, and acorns or other nuts. In the lower part of their range they are also attracted to cactus, and in the North they often browse conifers and other evergreens. Because the snow never becomes deep in the rain forest of the upper Pacific Coast or in some of the drier terrain to the south, blacktails do not make such long fall migrations as most mule deer. (Similarly, many desert muleys remain in a single general area throughout the year.) They do tend to move toward lower ground in winter, however. Some hunters spot Sitka deer by cruising about the coastal islands in boats or working upriver from tidal flats. Columbian blacktails respond fairly well to calls mimicking a fawn's querulous bleating (and it may be that some Sitka deer are equally responsive, although other mule deer are no more enticed than whitetails by such calling).

Because of thick rain-forest habitat and precipitous terrain, blacktails in some regions use game trails almost as habitually as whitetails. In remote areas where the hunting pressure is light, they are less nocturnal, but their biology and behavioral habits are so similar that they can be hunted in the same ways.

Other mule deer are quite different. In most areas, there are loners among the mature bucks but some band together before and after the breeding season in small groups or occasionally with twenty or thirty comrades. A hunter fortunate enough to find such a bachelor band as he scans the slopes may have a bewildering choice of trophies. A whitetail rack with an inside spread of 20 inches is a great trophy, but a truly outstanding muley rack must be closer to 30. It may look larger at close range, smaller at a distance or when seen from above. An exceptional rack usually appears boxy—about as wide as it is high, and with heavy beams and long tines. If the hunter gets a front view, he tries to see whether the first main fork on each side is out beyond the buck's big ears. It helps to know the average

size of deer in the locale so that the antlers can be compared with body features. Most muley bucks stand a little over 40 inches at the withers and are about 6 to 6½ feet long. In some locales the shoulder of a really fine buck may be 4 feet high. A good rack looks at least half as long vertically as the shoulder height. When seen from behind, a muley's pale rump usually stands out clearly. On a big buck it measures about a foot and a half across. If the antlers appear to stand out half again as wide on each side of the body, they must have a spread of about 30 inches, maybe more, and the deer is worth a long stalk.

The buck's relatively peaceful nature does not deter him from occasionally gathering three or four does, an entourage that would be very unusual among whitetails, but he is not a harem guardian like the bull elk. The does wander off at will. If the rut has begun, a hunter may see solitary bucks, does alone or with fawns, and both sexes mingling in small groups.

Gestation consumes about 210 days, a trifle longer than the average whitetail pregnancy. Aside from that difference

Muley bucks with nontypical (l.) and typical antlers.

and the somewhat duller spots on a muley fawn's coat, the facts of birth and infancy are much the same.

Predation is more severe (and undoubtedly more helpful in strengthening herds by pruning away weak breeding stock) among western than eastern deer. In Utah it has been found to account for more than half of all mule-deer losses. The chief predator is the cougar, a reaper whose kill rate is almost a deer per week in prime, undisturbed habitat. In the North, wolves also take some mule deer, and black bears occasionally slay a fawn. Arthritic old deer and malnourished young with defective teeth are easy kills. Bobcats and even coyotes probably account for a few of the aged, the fawns, the sick or malformed, and the winter-starved. Yet careful studies have proved that the deer population is limited by winter forage, not by carnivores. Mule deer are subject to brucellosis, pyobacillosis, hoof rot, and the same diseases and parasites that attack eastern deer, none of which will obliterate a large, normal, well-fed population.

Instead of yarding like eastern deer, muleys migrate seasonally to habitat where the snow depth does not excessively hamper movement or browsing except for short periods or during the most severe winters. The extent of travel varies from an almost imperceptible and chiefly vertical shift in some regions to long journeys in others. The differences may be governed primarily by terrain and climate, but there are probably local genetic influences, too. The Tehama herds at the south end of California's Trinity Mountains have been reported to move as far as a hundred miles, and another group to the north migrates that far to summer

in Oregon. Few other muleys wander such long distances, but even where the autumn descent covers only a few miles the migration trails usually become well marked and well known. Snowfall dictates the time of descent. Mule deer on the high summer range graze more than they browse.

When grasses are flattened under a foot of snow, the deer begin to drop toward winter browse—snowberry, bearberry, serviceberry, cedar, oak, mountain mahogany, cliff rose, jack pine, sagebrush, fir, poplar, sunflower, snowbush, buckthorn, bitterbrush, and juniper.

"Nest hunters"—riflemen on stands, or "perches," overlooking the migration trails—glass the slopes with 7- or 8-power binoculars, usually 30 or 35mm, searching for good racks or summer-heavy does. Those who want an impressive trophy climb high and seldom take the first good buck they see. As a rule, the biggest bucks stay above, lingering behind the does and younger males, reluctant to set foot in a valley until forced down by deepening snow. However the rule is flexible. It generally holds true in the Rockies, or in any rough mountain country where hunters have to work up toward the animals from below the timber line. On Colorado's wide mesas, however, buck-hunting parties sometimes reach the top from a road or high connecting ridge. They comb the pastures there and then hunt downward. Since the big bucks are the ones that have survived several earlier seasons, they react quickly to hunting pressure. When many hunters are up on the mesas for the season's opening week, the grandest bucks may be the first to descend.

Muleys have a slightly longer life span than whitetails, and adults that react evasively to human intrusion or are located in remote fastnesses may often reach an age of eight years. It is among the unhunted young that mortality is high; about a third of all Utah fawns die before the state's hunting season opens in October.

Assuming no abnormal flurry of hunting pressure, a good general policy is to look for mule deer high in the mountains and on cool north slopes during Indian summer weather, then drop down to scan the warmer south slopes when a foot of snow accumulates on the summer range, and hunt the lowland flats, draws, and canyons—paying particular attention to those with lush stands of oak, cedar, or piñon. Cover, not food, is the

Blacktail doe in British Columbia.

searcher's object. A knowledge of the area's preferred browse is helpful but less important than in whitetail hunting because desirable food is scattered all over the flats and hills.

Where disturbances are few or thickets are sparse, mule deer may bed down to rest and ruminate wherever they happen to be feeding. The big buck in the Texas coulee had merely curled up on the relatively cool, shady north slope of the depression. But muleys are not so trusting as some hunters believe. In open country they simply cannot skulk in the style of the whitetail, so they rely on keeping distance between themselves and intruders. Where cover is conveniently located, many will penetrate deep into conifer stands to rest and hide. Others bed in thickets just inside the forest edges but near overgrown escape cover. Still others bed on slopes or shady ridges that provide

Blacktail buck with rack almost ready to shed velvet.

a good view and rising thermals to carry sound and scent.

Dense, dark conifers sometimes provide good still-hunting even during the warm midday hours when deer bed down and there is little or no activity in the open. Woods are especially productive during rain or snow, but muleys move out to browse as soon as a storm begins to abate.

Still-hunting is best at daybreak, toward sunset, and in rain, snow, or fog. Working downhill is not very important since there is no need to contend with the whitetail habit of nocturnal lowland feeding and a dawn ascent to ridgetop retreats. It is, of course, important to hunt into the wind when possible and to be slow and quiet. A stalker may come upon a column of moving deer (in which case any buck is most likely walking to the rear of the does and fawns) or a browsing group. Bunched muleys tend to face in several directions while feeding. No particular herd member is serving as sentinel but most of them will be alert. A mule deer does not flick its tail before raising its head, as a whitetail often does, but very frequently licks its nose and looks all about before moving off. The hunter has to remain still at such times or when a deer is looking his way.

If a buck takes fright he comes bouncing out like a jack rabbit. The high, jack-in-the-box leaps probably function to give him a clear view of danger. Lacking the whitetail's grace, he can nonetheless attain the same 35-mile-an-hour speed. But he commonly makes a fatal mistake: Just before going over a rim or into the woods he pauses to see if he is being pursued.

In the mountainous states, quiet drives of moderate size are sometimes conducted in cedar and piñon woods that are cut here and there by ridges or draws. Such drives also work well in forested basins or thickets surrounding streams, and in groves of lodgepole, fir, aspen, oak, or other trees that provide shelter and browse. The principles are the same as in driving whitetails. Drivers sometimes work without standers, though, merely moving the deer about for one another on wooded flats.

On open prairies and desert flats, the most popular technique is to scout from a horse or vehicle, in the manner of pronghorn hunters. Binoculars are put to use every few minutes but, even so, more game is overlooked than seen. Woodsmen realize that they must watch not for deer but for parts of deer. Open-country hunters tend to forget that a deer may be hidden by low, sparse cover. Often on the flattest plain a deer is camou-flaged by brush or background color, but a muley's big black nose or pale rump patch is often detectable.

Unless mule deer are sought in conjunction with elk, sheep, pronghorns, or other game, the choice of rifle is governed by the prevalent type of terrain. Much of the hunting is in open country where long shots are common, and a traditional caliber is the .30-06, which is equally effective for other game or in somewhat thicker cover. Other good choices are the 7mm, .264, .270, .280, 6.5mm, .250-3000, .308, and .348. Some riflemen abide by a 4-power scope, others use variable-power models.

Field-dressing procedures are the same as for other deer. But for sportsmen hunting their home areas without a guide, the handling of a trophy is crucial when the game is large. If a head is to be entrusted to a taxidermist, only he should be permitted to do the skinning. A hunter or guide only has to cape and sever the head, taking care to leave enough hide for a full shoulder mount. A sharp, reasonably short knife is held with its cutting edge up, and the point is used to slit the skin straight from the top of the withers up the back of the neck to the center point between the ears. At the rear end of this cut, make another to encircle the body—down behind the shoulders and across the front legs at the very bottom of the brisket. Then peel the hide forward to the bases of ears and jaws. Then, with the carcass on its back, sever the neck directly behind the jaws. No ax or saw is needed. Cut into the axial joint between the skull and spinal column, grasp the head at the antler bases, and twist the head off. Rub fine salt liberally into the flesh and the flesh side of the cape and freeze it as soon as possible.

TRACKS & SIGN: Blacktail tracks resemble large whitetail prints. A big muley buck leaves a substantially larger track that can be mistaken for an elk's. However, it usually has a more definite heart shape than an elk's. In wooded areas where soft soil pre-dominates, the lobe tips are rather pointed, but they become blunted by rocky terrain. Tracks of mature muleys vary from about 2½ inches long to more than 3, and a big buck's forefoot may leave a print closer to 4 inches. In sand or thin snow, bucks often leave drag marks as they walk. Does and young males seem to point their feet along a straighter line than do heavy

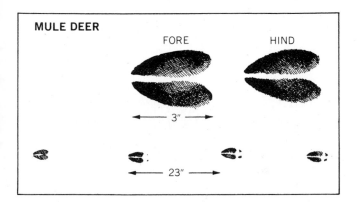

MULE DEER

FORE   HIND

← 3" →

← 23" →

old bucks; prints turned outward somewhat from the direction of travel may be the spoor of a good trophy.

At a walk, the stride may be less than 2 feet long, but a fast trot can lengthen it to 9 feet or more. A sure sign of muleys is a tight clump of four deer tracks or several clumps widely spaced. The bunching results from the muley's high, stiff-legged bounces when fleeing or when running nervously.

As with whitetails, direct trailing more often leads to exasperation than to game, but tracks and sign denote a general direction or area to be hunted carefully. The ragged browse marks often reach to ground level but sometimes rise considerably higher than those of whitetails. Autumn and winter droppings are apt to be hard and oblong, frequently with a boat-shaped taper, and they average about ¾ inch long. If the dark brown pellets have a greenish cast they are probably quite fresh.

Back rubs and beds are like those of whitetails. Few hunters claim perfection in reading sign, and the author was unaware, until it was pointed out by Rollo Robinson, that a freshly used bed sometimes reveals a mule deer's sex. Both does and bucks urinate when they rise, but a doe urinates to one side and a buck wets the middle of the bed.

VOICE: Fawns and occasionally does bawl or blat, but not vociferously. Adult muleys of either sex snort when curious or alarmed, and the sound often has a whinnying or whistling quality.

Wild Sheep *(Ovinae)*

GENERAL DESCRIPTION & DISTRIBUTION: In the Rockies of Alberta a heavy-headed ram picks its way across a knoll to an alluvial fan debouching from a cleft granite bluff. The ram peers out over a muskeg valley at a strange animal squatting on a crest. The hunter squints through a spotting scope, finds the ram in the cramped field of view, centers on the corrugated curl of horns, and feels a twinge of surprise as his attention shifts to the animal's eye. More than 2 miles away, the trophy he studies is studying him. There is no sign of alarm in the ram's dark obsidian and amber eyes, perhaps eight times more powerful than the man's.

The sheep hunches slightly and bounds upward, hoofs caroming from side to side of a rock chimney in 6-foot ricochets. Half a dozen brown shadows, unseen until now, erupt from the periphery of the knoll. They are all big males, a bachelor band, none quite so impressively crowned as the sentinel but equally agile. Several follow the first ram up the cleft while the others ascend by a different route, bounding from one invisible rock projection to another. They stream along the bluff and step off into space. It is a 30-foot leap into a draw where each animal's legs fold at the instant of impact, absorbing the shock of a 200-pound body landing on unyielding rock. The rams melt into the shadows of the gulf. Something has made them nervous, but they should be bedding down soon, and the hunter sees a way up the sheep mountain to an outcrop above the likeliest bedding spots, just a little higher than the grazing meadow where he spotted the band. The climb will be rough, but sheep hunters are almost as indomitable as sheep.

Some of America's wild sheep endure almost perpetual snow and ice, others endure heat and thirst where the annual

Trophy bighorn, with broomed, but full, curl.

rainfall averages little more than 3 inches. Biologically there are but two North American species, for *Ovis canadensis* includes the desert bighorn as well as the Rocky Mountain bighorn, while *O. dalli* encompasses the white Dall sheep and the nearly black Stone sheep. The Boone and Crockett record book, arbiter of American trophy hunting, recognizes all four varieties as they differ in horn formation, appearance, and range. Within these groups there are numerous, more or less localized subspecies. (Following the general coverage of sheep, each of the four major types will be listed separately, with additional details.)

The Dall sheep is principally Alaskan, but it ranges into northern British Columbia and across the Yukon into the Mackenzie Mountains of the Northwest Territories. The white strain blends with the darker Stone in the southeastern part of the range and is then eclipsed by it. Where their realms overlap, interbreeding produces color variations from almost white to gray. Blackish brown or almost blue-black are the pure Stones that

Hunter in Yukon glassing for Stone sheep.

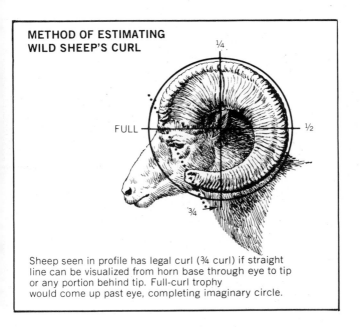

**METHOD OF ESTIMATING
WILD SHEEP'S CURL**

¼

FULL ½

¾

Sheep seen in profile has legal curl (¾ curl) if straight
line can be visualized from horn base through eye to tip
or any portion behind tip. Full-curl trophy
would come up past eye, completing imaginary circle.

range from the mid-Yukon eastward to the Mackenzie District
and southward to British Columbia's Stikine River.

Bighorns vary from rich brown in the northern mountains
to pale buff in the deserts. The tail is usually darker, with a
whitish edging that runs part way down the back of the hind
legs. A light or whitish rump patch is conspicuous on the dark
animals, less so on the light southern sheep. The muzzle is pale
or white, and there is usually a pale ring around the eye. These
sheep have more massive but much less flaring horns than Dalls
and Stones. Bighorns range from the western slopes of the
Rockies in British Columbia all the way to Mexico, and as far
east as the Dakotas, as far west as Washington and Oregon.
The familiar bands of Alberta, Montana, Idaho, Wyoming, and
Colorado are Rocky Mountain bighorns, while the sparser bands
in arid regions—principally in Arizona, Nevada, and Mexico, but
also in Utah, lower California, New Mexico, and Texas—are desert
bighorns. The desert tribe furnishes half a dozen examples of

subtle differences among localized races, from the small, pale, slim-horned sheep of southern Nevada to the darker, heavier-horned Arizona bighorn and the pale little Mexican *cimarrón* with its thin, flaring curl.

The progenitors of these closely related animals crossed the Bering land bridge during the Pleistocene Epoch. Several very similar species are scattered through Asia and Europe. In general, wild sheep have thick undercoats and long, coarse, cellular, air-filled hair that provides excellent insulation. The horns differ from one breed to another in girth, length, and flare, but American rams develop massive horns, curling up and back over the ears, then down and around and up past the cheeks in a C shape, generally terminating below the eyes but sometimes higher on old sheep. Horns that have grown long enough to terminate as far forward as the bases are known as a full curl. An occasional big ram has a curl that exceeds a complete circle, but "brooming" is more common. Broomed horns are broken off near the tips, sometimes by accident or during rutting battles, but an old ram files his horns down deliberately by rubbing them on rocks when the curl begins to block his peripheral vision. Ewes of all breeds have short, slender horns that form no more than a half curl.

Brooming is more common and pronounced among the close-curled bighorns than among the Dalls and Stones whose flaring, more slender horns are less of an impediment to vision. Record scoring depends on symmetry as well as length, girth, and spread, yet many hunters seek broomed bighorns. A curl blunted for the sake of constant watchfulness and chipped in countless battles symbolizes a regal patriarch.

Glassing a sheep mountain, a hunter finds a head that looks good. His guide has already seen the ram and, training his spotting scope on it, confirms that the curl is full or nearly full and equals almost a third of the animal's height. Therefore it is probably of trophy size. The guide is already planning the stalk. A clearer view may be impossible before the long climb is made, but he studies the curl a little longer, hoping the head will turn. In profile, a ram may display a breathtaking curl, but final judgment is withheld until the far horn is revealed. Even then, assessment is not always easy unless, by rare good fortune, the sheep is encountered at moderate range.

If not cut down by predation, accident, starvation, or disease, wild sheep have a potential life span of about fifteen years. Many of the most impressive trophies are thirteen or fourteen years old, though they usually attain fine curls by the age of seven or eight. Age can be calculated from the winter growth rings of the horns, which form dark, narrow bands.

GAME BEHAVIOR & GENERAL HUNTING HABITAT: A sheep's lobed hoofs are much like a mountain goat's, but the spongy sole tissue, the gripping portion, is more concave at the front, and the outer shell is slightly more pointed and forms a deeper, sharper rim. Both sheep and goats use their hoofs in a clawlike, gripping manner, but whereas a goat excels at walking razorbacks and hairline ledges, the sheep excels at bounding from point to point. On fairly level ground, it can leap about 17 feet; when ascending, it can cover 6 or 8 feet at a bound, and 25 or 30 feet is not uncommon for a downward jump.

A sheep's useless-looking dewclaws help in braking headlong runs down steep slopes, but the animals prefer to travel at a leisurely walk. Mild alarm sends them into a jogging trot, sometimes for a short distance, sometimes for miles. While a band grazes, at least one ram often remains watchful. Sudden alarm spurs a sheep into a heavy gallop, and the sight or sound of a sheep galloping causes its companions to flee. Spooked rams can cover short distances at more than 35 miles an hour.

During the daytime they feed and rest in the open, but they are alert and seldom stray far from steep escape routes. Of all American game, only the pronghorn equals or surpasses sheep in keenness of vision. A ram may fail to notice a hunter who remains quite still, even at relatively short range, yet sheep can probably spot the movement of a man in the open at a distance of 5 miles.

In hot, arid, desert-bighorn country, rising thermal currents often lift away the scent of a hunter concealed near a water hole or mineral lick, but in northern regions of capricious wind shifts, thermal drafts can more easily betray him. While he is circling out of sight, rams may catch his odor and drift off. Mountain animals also have acute hearing but are only mildly alerted by the common sound of sliding or falling rocks. An unfamiliar noise—the human voice or metal scraping stone—will

instantly alarm them. The exhilaration of sheep hunting is in the long, rigorous stalk, not in the shot. Most trophies fall at less than 200 yards. Since sheep are not as tough as goats and are more often taken at moderate range, rifle power and low trajectory might seem unimportant. But caliber selection is dictated by the possibility that the terrain will demand a long shot. A Magnum in the 6.5mm class is a good choice. If larger game is to be sought on the hunt, a heavier caliber may be desired, but the rifle should be light because of the interminable climbing for mountain game. The preferred telescopic sight is 4 power, and a powerful spotting scope and binocular are needed.

The various breeds of sheep exhibit roughly similar rutting, foraging, and resting patterns. From mid-December until October, northern rams almost invariably disdain the company

Rocky Mountain curl, showing animal to have been 12 years old (above), and Larry Koller and guide taping excellent bighorn.

of females and young. A few of the eldest rams lead a solitary existence, but most of them gather into bachelor bands. The more animals in a group the greater is the chance that one will detect danger; there may be only three or four, more likely five to a dozen. As many as 200 Stone rams, a loose confederation of smaller groups, have been seen dotting a single sheep mountain in British Columbia.

Sometimes one ram moves off a short distance to keep watch. He may remain on guard until the animals bed down or he may abandon sentinel duty after a while. There is no predicting whether another sentinel will take his place.

Because rams tend to segregate themselves into age groups, it can be difficult to tell which member of a band is the best trophy. Even prolonged scrutiny may leave a tense doubt until the climax of the stalk. Occasionally the selection is influenced by chance. Perhaps the best curl is hidden from view and there is no way to improve the vantage point or move the sheep (by whistling or otherwise arousing their suspicion) without panicking them into headlong flight. Or the stalk may be aborted by a sentinel, more curious than suspicious. A ram leaves his bed or feeding site to investigate a strange sound. Coming around a point, he stops and gazes at the hunter. In a moment he will bound away, alarming the others. He has a massive curl, and since there is no longer any way to reach the original quarry, the choice is to take this trophy or—for the present—none.

In October the males begin to search for their abandoned ewes. Scuffles erupt as their necks swell for the rut. Two rams interlock their curls in a wrestling bout, pushing and pulling until one disengages and retreats. Large, evenly matched rivals clarify the origin of the term "battering ram." They walk away from each other with a show of casual contempt. When separated by 30 feet or sometimes twice that, they turn, suddenly and simultaneously rear up on their hind legs, then charge. If they are heavy northern bighorns they may weigh 300 pounds each, and they crash head on at more than 20 miles an hour. A ram's horns, together with his heavy skull and the musculature of neck and shoulders, are his shield as well as his weapon. The combined speed and weight of adversaries can produce over a ton of impact. Sometimes a shoving contest follows, but more often the combatants shake their heads, separate, and repeat the head-on collisions until one groggily withdraws. In most cases no lasting damage is inflicted and the victor turns his attention to the ewes until another rival intrudes. A ram usually dominates no more than three or four ewes, because frantic competition prevents the maintenance of a true harem.

Breeding in the North generally reaches a peak in November or early December and ends soon thereafter. The rams separate from the ewes, again forming tranquil bachelor bands. They are miles away when lambs are dropped in May or June. Single births are the rule, but twins are not unknown.

Desert rams seem to be a trifle less savagely combative than northern sheep, perhaps because the populations are more thinly spread, perhaps also because they cannot build up comparable vigor during the parched months preceding the rut, and perhaps because their breeding season is longer than that of any other American medium or big game. It begins in late July and lasts until September or sometimes October. Thus a large percentage of lambs will be born a couple of months earlier than their northern relatives—in winter or early spring.

Regardless of breed or locale, a ewe prefers to bear her lamb in a hidden or inaccessible spot such as a ledge, the base of a steep cliff, or a shallow cave. A lamb gallops within a few days, nibbles vegetation within a week, and is usually weaned in two months, though some ewes permit nursing until winter. Horns begin to sprout by the time of weaning. Yearlings and even two-year-olds are reluctant to leave the flock, but maturing rams wander away with other males of about the same age. Their horns, which now arc in a half circle, will reach a three-quarter curl by the age of four or five and a full curl between the ages of seven and eleven.

Weather and food are the chief factors in lamb mortality. The young are occasionally killed by wolves, coyotes, cougars, bobcats, eagles, and bears. Old, sick, or injured sheep are also gleaned by the large predators, but a healthy adult is rarely caught, much less felled. The most hazardous season is winter, when deep snow can hamper flight while also weakening the flocks by preventing access to food. Where enemies are abundant, northern sheep may be driven to high escarpments during periods when they should be grazing at lower elevations, but predation is generally light. Tick or mite infestations can weaken sheep, and several internal parasites—especially lungworm—can kill them. Serious diseases include necrotic stomatitis and coccidiosis. In most regions sheep populations withstand disease if they have enough food to keep them strong, but in the Southwest a problem not yet fully solved is the bluetongue virus, introduced by domestic sheep and carried by the blood-sucking gnat *Culicoides veripennis*. Efforts to re-establish desert bighorns in Texas have continued since 1957, when a ram and ewe were brought to the Black Gap Wildlife Management Area from Arizona, but the herd has remained small owing to the viral infestations.

Desert bighorns have a paucity of forage, shade, and channels of escape. Therefore they may be attracted to almost any mountainous area, canyon, maze of hills, or rocky bluffs. The more remote and inaccessible, the better they like it. Elsewhere sheep are more selective. They wander much more than goats, seeking new slopes from day to day and in some instances traveling 20 or 25 miles from summer to winter range, but they frequently return to a hospitable mountain.

A good sheep mountain usually has a definite character. Even where sheep share the same general habitat with goats, they prefer more open, less precipitous slopes. If they detect danger at sufficiently long distance to remain calm, they are more apt to trot away than to make a spectacular, bounding escape. The relatively gentle slopes and wide basins where they congregate are usually high and invariably close to more rugged terrain, so that a bounding, ascending escape can be made if necessary. Rams may dot a grassy alpine hill or basin, a col at the foot of a shale slide, a saddle on a ridge or between bluffs, or a wide point projecting from a ridge. They are rarely content to remain where they do not have a wide, clear view in at least a couple of directions or where there is no option for an upward retreat.

In summer and early fall the rams keep to higher, rougher terrain than the ewes and lambs, often at altitudes of 10,000 feet, but wintering elevations may be only 2,000 feet. During hunting season the rams are still on the upper slopes as a rule, or making a very leisurely descent. They are primarily grazers, feeding in the open and resting during the day at random bedding spots, shaded in hot weather, exposed if the day is cool enough for sunning. Nighttime beds are used repeatedly, sometimes for years. A well-worn sheep bed may be a foot deep; it usually has an odor of urine and is edged with droppings, yet high altitude and dry air prevent it from becoming damp and unhealthy. Sheep begin feeding and rambling at first light, then lie down to rest and ruminate at nine or ten in the morning, rise again in the early afternoon to graze briefly, then rest again until late afternoon. By about five they begin feeding once more and keep at it until dark.

While a hunter steals through timber or over ridges, he cannot keep the grazing area in view, and the rams may have disappeared when he arrives above their meadow. If possible, it is better to wait while they graze and watch where they go to rest, then stalk the bedded band. The rams will remain there for five hours or more, rising only for a brief midday feeding near their bedding spots.

TRACKS & SIGN: Where sheep have disappeared, tracks and sign sometimes lead to their destination or indicate a slope that merits watching. A sheep trail may be no wider than a man's boot. This is not unusual among ungulates, and bighorn tracks can be confused with those of goats or mule deer, Dall or Stone tracks with those of goats or blacktail deer.

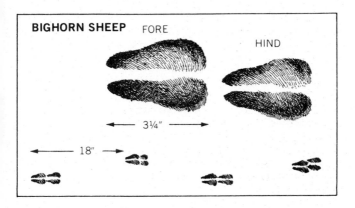

BIGHORN SHEEP FORE HIND

←――― 3¼″ ―――→

←――― 18″ ―→

A sheep's track is not quite so square as a goat's because the lobes of the hoof are not so widely splayed. Each lobe tapers toward a slightly more pointed front, and forms a more definite crescent. In soft ground, particularly when headed downhill, the dewclaws may leave small twin impressions behind the hoof tracks, which are larger but more closely spaced than those of deer. The print of a mature ram in soft ground is 3 or 3½ inches long.

Tufts of white hair are sometimes left by Dalls as well as by goats. Since sheep generally keep to easier inclines than goats but higher country than deer, location helps to identify trails. Bighorns shed more than deer and have longer, darker hair.

A nighttime sheep bed is a depression about 4 feet wide, almost always marked by droppings. The pellets are usually bell-shaped, sometimes massed as a result of succulent feed, sometimes elongated and clayish if dropped by a salt lick. Curiously, Dalls and Stones that have been licking minerals drop scat as round as marbles, perhaps because of differences in the content of the licks, which they visit a couple of times each week. Desert vegetation results in less uniform droppings than those of northern bighorns, but the pellets tend to be somewhat bell-shaped.

VOICE: Sheep bleat, and rutting rams emit a deep, rasping blat to challenge rivals. The danger signal is similar. In some regions the hunting season opens at summer's end or the beginning of fall and may close in September or early October, before the rut is well under way. However the southwestern breeding period is very long, and as far north as Utah, where a typical season might be set in late September and early October, it is possible that a ram's challenge or crashing horns will disclose the location of a flock. Elsewhere, hunting sometimes extends into November. Occasionally in Montana and Wyoming, and usually in the Yukon and Northwest Territories, the open season stretches well into the time of the rut.

As a rule, however, sheep are first spotted on slopes too far away for rams to be heard, and the rut is the toughest time to acquire a trophy. A late hunt may end in a sudden, dangerous snowstorm. Moreover, the rams will be bunched with the ewes. Although the reproductive drive dulls the wariness of males, the females remain very watchful. Even if a hunter manages to stay downwind and out of sight until he can climb above some open basin where a flock feeds, the ewes can block his view.

Desert Bighorn (*Ovis canadensis nelsoni* and related subspecies)

TROPHY DESCRIPTION: A ram in the arid Southwest rarely attains a height of more than 3 feet at the shoulder or a weight of more than 180 pounds. Mature ewes of all American races average a fourth smaller than rams. Remarkably large desert trophies have been shot, but a ram with an outside curl of 33 inches is considered good. The current record is close to 44 inches. Most of the finest trophies come from Arizona, Baja California, and Sonora, Mexico.

Some of the desert dwellers are almost as brown as their northern counterparts, but most strains are tawny or buff. They blend so well with sand, sandstone, and brush that they are more difficult to sight than other American sheep. They are also the least populous of sheep. Where a subspecies is rare or endangered, hunting is prohibited. Where seasons are opened, permits are stringently limited and it is legal to take only rams with substantial curls.

DIFFERENCES IN GAME BEHAVIOR & HUNTING HABITAT: Possibly because of the open vistas and light predation, southwestern bighorns are more inquisitive than other sheep. If a hunter tells of luring a bedded ram into the open by rolling a pebble, he is most likely speaking of a desert bighorn. However, there are as many stories of long searches for elusive rams or for bands that were impossible to stalk as they drifted beyond gun range day after day.

The habitat is as savage for the hunter as for the game: jagged, crumbling rock; searing sand; labyrinths of thorns; rattlers and scorpions; blinding sun; swift changes from terrible heat to cold. Desert bighorns have remarkable stamina. Water holes are heavily used, but the sheep can go for a week without any liquid except that taken from saguaro or barrel cactus. The plants are chewed open or a barrel cactus is butted over. Thorns become imbedded in a ram's horns, and the thickly calloused muzzle seems impervious to sharp needles.

As desert sheep wander from one salt lick to another, they can rely on all sorts of cacti for food. Like all sheep, they prefer grasses and forbs when they can find them—cottontop, hilaria,

Desert ewe (l.) and exceptionally good ram.

galleta, gramagrass, needlegrass, desert trumpet, and so on. They browse on shrubs and small trees, such as yucca, century plant, ocotillo, paloverde, silktassel, Sonora ironwood, piñon, juniper, mesquite, catclaw, saltbush, buckthorn. They feed heavily on almost any plant that exists in arid country—from club moss to evening primrose, from sagebrush to sunflowers.

Rocky Mountain Bighorn *(O. c. canadensis)*

TROPHY DESCRIPTION: These are the largest of American sheep. A prime ram may well stand over 40 inches high at the shoulder and weigh 300 pounds. The coat is thicker, longer, and darker than the desert sheep's, but there is the same light muzzle, belly, and rump patch. The horns are dark, the curl tight but massive. The world's record measures 45 inches long on the left side, an eighth inch shorter on the right, but any sheep with a 40-inch curl is a sporting trophy. Alberta, British Columbia, and Montana produce the majority of them.

The dark brown of Rocky Mountain sheep is almost as effective a camouflage as the lighter hue of desert sheep. Shadows and brush can break up the outlines of the animals, hiding them until they move or unless the hunter notices a glint of horn, or a flicker of light rump or belly. The knack of watching for small movements and parts of animals is most important in early fall, when mountain bighorns sometimes drift down into patches of timber.

DIFFERENCES IN GAME BEHAVIOR & HUNTING HABITAT: Mountain sheep seek bluegrass, wheatgrass, fescuegrass, needlegrass, sedges and rushes, sage, mountain mahogany, twinflower and mountainlover, berry bushes, rabbitbrush, and greasebush. If winter snows cover the low growth, they nibble at willows and alders, and even reach up for pine, fir, or maple.

Bighorns sometimes wander downward in search of mineral licks, water, or better forage. A hunter comes through the timber and surprises a band on a low knoll, scant yards above a muskeg glade where a cow moose dips her muzzle in a valley stream. There is no jumble of crags or steep bluff for escape. Confidently the hunter advances toward the fringe of

the clearing, but he had better not wait too long, pressing his luck for an easy shot. In a moment the sheep can disappear into a timbered draw.

Dall Sheep *(O. dalli dalli* and *O. d. kenaiensis)*

TROPHY DESCRIPTION: Only slightly larger than desert bighorns, Dall sheep seldom weigh more than 200 pounds. The dazzling white Dalls of the Kenai Peninsula are smaller and have relatively close-curled horns but are otherwise difficult to tell from the white flocks of central Alaska. Some of the Dalls in the upper Yukon also look pure white, but usually have a few black tail hairs. Farther south the tails sometimes become black, and finally, where there is a large infusion of Stone sheep, flocks of Fannins occur. Also called saddlebacks, Fannin sheep are quite gray, particularly on the back. Sometimes the saddle is almost black. Sometimes, too, they are slightly heavier in body and horn than the white sheep, but they are only a color phase.

The Dall's horns are yellowish, and they flare gracefully outward, often with a spread of more than 2 feet. The horns are comparatively slender, usually a bit longer than those of Rocky Mountain sheep and with less brooming or none. The record outside length is over 48 inches. Because of the flaring,

Rocky Mountain bighorns in moment before head-on collision.

full curls are harder to come by than among bighorns, but it is nevertheless illegal to take less than a three-quarter curl. The Yukon and Alaska's Chugach and Wrangell mountains yield many of the record listings.

Against green vegetation or the gray of cliffs and rock slides, white sheep are the easiest of all to spot. The light flanks, rumps, and heads of Fannin rams also are spotted with comparative ease. Scanning is simplified by the tendency of Dalls to stay far above timber line, speckling a panorama where there are few obstructions.

DIFFERENCES IN GAME BEHAVIOR & HUNTING HABITAT: Dalls prefer rather dry as well as very high country. They have little difficulty finding food and water since the melt and subterranean seeps below snowcapped peaks irrigate the open alpine meadows, slopes, and cirques.

Primary foods are alpine grasses and forbs, leafy ground plants, mosses, and lichens. Most Dalls hesitate to venture below

Bachelor band of Dall sheep (above), and hunting author Charles F. Waterman with fine Stone ram.

timber line except when crossing from peak to peak, but they do occasionally come down for brush and shrubs if they have not been harassed much by wolves. They wander less than bighorns and seem more inclined to follow an old leader. A hunter who spies a far-off band can feel moderately confident that they will be there when he arrives, and if he has trouble determining which curl to try for, his guide may advise him to concentrate on the lead ram.

Stone Sheep *(O. d. stonei)*

TROPHY DESCRIPTION: Hardly larger than Dalls, the Stone sheep of the Yukon and northwestern British Columbia seldom weigh more than 225 pounds. Yet their horns tend to be slightly heavier, sometimes longer, closer to the face, and more severely broomed. The world's record has an outside curve of more than

50 inches on both sides. All of the top hundred Boone and Crockett entries are from British Columbia.

Color varies from gray-brown to gray, to a charcoal- or blue-gray verging on black. Still, these sheep are easier to spot than bighorns. They have the same light patches, and the pale color of the belly extends quite far up onto the brisket. Most important, the contrasting whitish rump flickers against a mountainside's somber tones.

DIFFERENCES IN GAME BEHAVIOR & HUNTING HABITAT: In range, food, and habitat the Stone is intermediate between the Dall and the bighorn. It tends to explore lowlands to a slightly greater extent than the Dall, and perhaps browses a bit more on willows and other small trees and shrubs, but has the characteristic preference for grasses, forbs, sedges, and alpine ground plants. Though less abundant than Dalls, Stone sheep maintain satisfactory numbers throughout their limited range. During most years they are both plentiful and sizable in the area of the Muskwa and Prophet rivers in northern British Columbia, where L. S. Chadwick brought down the world's record Stone ram in 1936. Sheep trails still lattice the ridges there, beyond the timber line, where a mountain caribou tugs at a bearberry twig.

Mountain Goat *(Oreamnos americanus,* also classified as *O. montanus)*
COMMON & REGIONAL NAMES: *Rocky Mountain goat, white goat.*

DESCRIPTION & DISTRIBUTION: As the September sun shot pale lancets among the dark needles of alpine firs and hemlocks at the timber line, five mountain goats slowly grazed their way across a meadow's edge. If they survived a dozen winters it might be that none of them would wander more than 5 or 10 miles from that grass-carpeted cirque in the Bitterroots, near the Idaho-Montana line. Creamy splotches against a blue-green background, their coats were soft robes of pile, not yet thickened and lengthened for winter. Two were mature nannies, the smaller of them 3 feet high at the humped shoulder, 5 feet from square nose to stubby tail. She probably weighed a bit over 150 pounds with her summer accumulation of fat that would help her through the lean months. The other was slightly larger, an older animal with a stronger yellow wash tincturing her coat.

Both had thin black horns rising and curving 8 or 9 inches from bases to sharp points. At a distance they might be mistaken for billies of average size (they would look even bigger in their winter shag), though neither would ever pass for one of those rare 300-pound trophy males that stand aloof on the highest crags. Closely following each nanny was a fluffy, belly-high kid. The fifth goat, a yearling male, eyed the others but dared not come close. He was somewhat smaller than the nannies and had rather straight horns, hardly 5 inches long.

One kid nuzzled its mother for remembered milk, though weaning must have been completed a month or more before. The nanny pushed the kid away, then stepped closer again as she lifted her head, testing the air. She ambled to a pocked glacial bounder and hopped up with ponderous agility. Poised like a dancer on point, she gazed down into the timber—toward us.

The guide had already confirmed the absence of a trophy, and we hoped to retreat without sending this band over the ridge where they might spook a fine billy before we could circle and glass the high terrain beyond. All the goats now peered toward the timber. The nanny hopped down from the boulder and nosed her kid. Then she turned away, and the band crossed the meadow at a pace between a gallop and an awkward trot toward a ledge that streaked diagonally up a steep rock wall. In single file and with solemn deliberation, they picked their way upward, nature's wire-walkers shuffling onto pinnacles where no enemy could pursue them. We found no billy beyond the ridge, and two days passed before we had a trophy to pack out.

Far to the northwest, some other hunter and guide may be exploring talus-strewn slopes above the Kenai Peninsula. A 5-hour climb brings them to a crest overlooking a brushy, open flat where a trophy billy feeds. The distance is 400 yards—close enough for a shot—but the wind is in their favor and the range can be cut by half if they take care. On the previous day, after caping a Dall ram with a flaring full curl, they spotted this goat more than a mile away, a barely visible white blur against gray talus. Until the spotting scope was focused, they were uncertain whether it was a goat or another white sheep. Was it worth that kind of stalk? The billy's size persuaded them.

Now, prone on the ridge, they regain their breath before the final crawl. They watch the goat scrape at dirt in a little hollow a foot deep and 5 feet wide. As they descend, the goat rolls in the dust, ridding himself of ticks or other nuisances. After a few minutes the animal rises and resumes feeding. Suddenly a loud, rusty whistle pierces the air: the alarm call of the *siffleur*, the hoary marmot, loudest of its clan. The goat looks up. The time to shoot is now, but a hummock—undetected from earlier vantage points—blocks too much of the target. From the far side of the hummock a covey of rock ptarmigan bursts into the air. The billy pulls himself onto a ledge and is not found again until the next day. No more than a thousand yards from where he had first been spotted, he stands beneath an overhang, taking shelter from a downpour. The fiercest wind would not have driven him from pasturage, but goats dislike heavy rain. Shooting visibility is adequate, and his evenly curving horns prove to be nearly 10 inches long.

Such goat hunts might take place in the high country of Montana, Idaho, Washington, western Alberta, British Columbia, southeastern Alaska, or the central and lower portions of the Yukon. Some goats have drifted south of the primary concentrations, down the ridgelines of the Coast Ranges and Cascades into Oregon, down the Rockies into Wyoming. A few have been successfully transplanted to new habitat, particularly to South Dakota's Black Hills. But they are far from nomadic, evidently having required 600,000 years to spread over their present range after crossing the Bering land bridge from Asia. Appearance and name notwithstanding, the species is no goat but an antelope. Its closest relatives are the Himalayan serow and goral and the European chamois. A case has been made for the classification of mountain-goat populations by subspecies—*americanus, kennedyi, columbiae, missoulae*—but the differences have more to do with location than with evolution. Though very large specimens are hardiest and are more likely to be spotted in Alaska or British Columbia than in the lower parts of the range, the animals are all much alike.

The heaviest goat ever recorded was an Alaskan billy weighing just over 500 pounds. An average mature male weighs only about 225 pounds, perhaps 250 after a good summer, and a female rarely weighs 200. These figures pertain to the hunting season, generally September and early October in the lower part of the range, a month sooner in Canada and Alaska. By then the animals have acquired fat reserves for the long winter.

Male or female, a goat almost always appears larger than it is. In part this is because of its narrow, deep-chested, slab-sided build, which permits cliff-hugging travel over nearly impercepti- ble protrusions. In part it is because of the shaggy coat and the high, fatty shoulder hump which led western explorers to call the animal a "white buffalo." The deception is accentuated late in the season, when the undercoat of fleece is thick and the outer guard hairs may reach a length of 6 or 7 inches everywhere but on the lower legs.

A mountain goat on a summit is an aristocratic patriarch. At close quarters it suggests an improvisation from spare parts: the bisonlike hump, the mustang's rectangular head, the beard hanging from the sides and bottom of the jaw, the bovine aspect when the animal is stolidly grazing, the look of a great shaggy dog when it sprawls with its forefeet drooping over a ledge. It can also be quite invisible to a hunter glassing the snow patches of high peaks. Even at moderately close range, the black traces of horns, eyes, nose, lips, and hoofs, if they show at all, can look like wet stones, shadows, debris. Only against vegetation or snowless slopes does a goat stand out in contrast, and still its white or yellowish-white coat might be mistaken for a tatter of unmelted snow. But inaccessibility is more important to surviv- al than camouflage, and the hardest part of a goat hunt is the climbing—harder and harder as the air thins with altitude.

Trophy judgment is another difficult problem. Though the stiletto-pointed horns furnish no sure indication of sex, male horns tend to be slightly thicker at the base than those of females, and curve more evenly. Female horns generally rise almost straight for about two-thirds of their length and then curve back more acutely. An experienced guide can frequently determine sex as he trains the spotting scope on a potential trophy, but not from horn length. For many years the top record was a Cana- dian nanny with horns more than a foot long. She was eventually deposed by trophies whose horns were slightly shorter but heavier, more symmetrical, wider at their maximum spread as well as from tip to tip, where there is a slight inward curl. A length of more than 8 inches is acceptable, more than 9 excellent,

and anything over 10 may appear in a record book. The difference between good and mediocre horns is trifling, and a hunter must rely on his guide's judgment. As a rule, a 9-inch horn matches the distance from a goat's eye to the tip of its nose.

Recognition of sex is so unreliable that the shooting of nannies is permitted, but it should be avoided; an orphaned kid seldom survives until spring. Bands are usually composed of nannies, with or without kids, and young males up to three years old. A lone goat may be a dry female or a stray from a band but is probably a prime billy.

Mountain goat picking its way over rimrock.

GAME BEHAVIOR & HUNTING HABITAT: It seems miraculous that animals can live well at elevations beyond the line where tamarack and fir become wind-smashed dwarfs. But mosses and lichens grow far above the timber, and in summer there are succulent grasses as well as such shrubs as creeping willow. The mountain goat is primarily a browser, but it is a grazer also. A favorite grazing place is a slide near timber line, where trees and brush have been flattened and new grass sprouts. From spring through fall, grasses make up perhaps two-thirds of a mountain goat's food, with the remainder supplied by forbs and browsed twigs and buds. In late fall and winter, when low-growing forage becomes scarce or snow-covered, the diet includes a high percentage of woody and brushy plants: balsam, Douglas, and alpine firs, hemlock, aspen, red osier, bearberry, dwarf birch, and willow.

A goat begins feeding early, beds down by eleven o'clock or so to chew its cud, rises to feed again in midafternoon, and retires by sunset. On a warm day a shady bed may be sought against the northern face of a cliff, beneath a bush, or perhaps on an unmelted snow or ice patch in a gully. In cool weather, a resting spot may be on some high, breezy bench or slope or even atop a peak. Sometimes a shallow bedding hollow is dug in the shale and dirt along the side of a favorite cliff. Females and young animals sometimes descend during winter and early spring to glean the withered grasses below their normal habitat. But deep snow can make lowland foraging harder rather than easier, and safety increases with altitude. The old billies love windswept crags where large expanses are perpetually free of deep snow. They seem to be nibbling bare rock as they graze on moss and lichens.

Mountain goats have never been very numerous (even though a hundred may be spotted in a day along the Alberta-British Columbia line north of Jasper), yet neither have they suffered the decimations of some more plentiful species. A local population may increase sharply but only briefly, remaining nearly constant once the habitat's carrying capacity is reached. As many goats are believed to dwell in the mountains now as there were 400 years ago.

Able to withstand great cold and subsist on seemingly meager rations, goats are also favored by light hunting pressure.

The flesh of a worthwhile trophy—an old billy—is tough and strongly flavored, and to the uninitiated the trophy is far less impressive than an antlered mount or a massively horned sheep. There is the handsome white robe, but it becomes most luxuriant after the hunting season closes, when blizzards make the high crags inaccessible or immeasurably dangerous.

Predation is almost inconsequential. The white hair found in the wolf's scat is, more often than not, hair of a goat dragged from under an avalanche or rockslide, or perhaps a kid or weak old animal that plunged to its death from a high ledge. Mountain goats are the most sure-footed American game—better mountaineers than sheep though not enamored of spectacular dashes and leaps—but they occasionally falter or misjudge a foothold or step on a loose stone or lose their balance in a sudden slam of wind. Rockslides are the greatest killers of mountain goats, and during rain an eager guide is inclined to check the spots where they seek protection from slides.

The animals linger at salt licks, and during dry, warm spells visit water basins, but do not gather in large groups even when November's shortening daylight stirs the rutting instinct. A mature billy then relinquishes seclusion to join a small band of females and adolescents—as few as two or three, seldom more than eight or nine. (The difficulty of differentiating between the sexes when a billy has joined the nannies is an additional reason for early, pre-rut hunting seasons.)

Though the male gathers no true harem, he regards one or two females as his. If most rutting fights amounted to much more than bluffing and sparring, the wickedly sharp horns could reduce the herd to a critical level, but there are exceptions. Just as a female viciously rakes any predator that succeeds in approaching her kid, so will rival males sometimes gore each other.

The hollow horns, growing continually over bony cores, may be slightly less brittle during breeding season than at other times. Around each base is a black, crescent-shaped gland that exudes a musky oil, and the glands become enlarged during the rut. Evidently the oil is a sexual attractant; billies rub their horns against rocks and plants, and against the females themselves. The secretion also seems to accentuate the annual, well-defined growth ridges on the horns. A goat's age can be determined by these rings; a hunter who counts more than twelve or thirteen has shot an unusually old goat.

Between late April and mid-June, after six months' gestation, an average nanny bears a single kid weighing about 7 pounds. Occasionally twins occur. Within a few days the infant can follow its mother and after a week it nibbles plants. It is weaned in six or eight weeks. It spends the first year with its mother and may remain with the band for another year or two. First-year mortality is high, chiefly because of lack of adequate winter fodder, which is more critical than disease, accident, or predation.

Goats are most often hunted in combination with other mountain game, and a good rifle is the sort of bolt-action used for sheep—chambered for a cartridge ranging from one of the 6.5mm Magnums up through the .30-caliber Magnums. If elk or other big game will be hunted during the same trip, 7mm is the minimum. A telescopic sight is essential, preferably with 2½- to 4-power magnification. Distant terrain can be scanned with a 20-power spotting scope and a 7- or 8-power binocular.

The initial stage of a high-country hunt is most often a horseback exploration with frequent stops to glass wide vistas in search of a trophy. Then, while shortening the range, the technique is to get above the target because goats escape danger by climbing and expect enemies to approach from below. If a billy is alarmed by a hunter above him, he may actually trot closer in an attempt to climb toward refuge. But sometimes the stalk ends with a choice of forgoing a shot at a goat poised on a high pinnacle or attempting to make the animal move before shooting. A long fall can smash the brittle horns. This possibility and more important humane considerations require a kill to be instantaneous or as nearly so as possible. A lightly hit goat, too tough to succumb easily to shock, can move to the brink of a cliff before toppling.

There is no basis for the myth that goats see poorly. They can see for miles and may spot a man against a distant crest or crossing a far valley. Sometimes a billy watches calmly, certain that any predator can be avoided by a casual walk up the nearest cliff. A goat's hearing is sharp, but any mountain dweller is accustomed to howling winds, thunder, rolling rocks, sliding shale, cracking wood. The quarry will often ignore minor noises, though

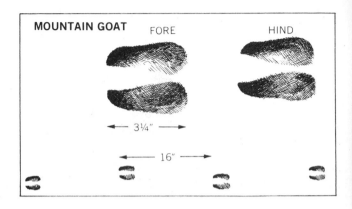

MOUNTAIN GOAT FORE HIND

← 3¼" →

← 16" →

a hunter does not chance it. If the goat's keen sense of smell has detected no danger, it may shuffle off without taking alarm, merely continuing its normal activity. A goat that was bedded down when first spotted may be on the move to nearby pastures; if it was feeding, it may head for a convenient bedding area during the hours consumed by a long, climbing stalk. Often, then, a hunter succeeds by calculating where the game will probably be located later on.

TRACKS & SIGN: Tracking is less important than with many kinds of game, but an abundance of sign indicates goats in the vicinity, whether or not an ivory speck is seen on a distant mountain. Even on rocky ground where a game trail is subtle or nearly absent, droppings and perhaps hair can lead to a vantage point from which game is visible.

The hoofprints are hard to tell from a sheep's. A goat's hoofs are double-lobed, blunt, squarish, with high dewclaws that rarely leave a mark. Prints average from 2½ to 3½ inches long for mature animals; anything over 3 inches indicates the probability of a large male. The lobes spread a bit more than a bighorn's, and the separation widens at a point closer to the rear end. The print is therefore a little squarer, blunter, with less crescented lobes. Unique hoof structure dictates the goat's climbing technique. A slightly convex, rubbery sole projects below the hard outer rim. The rim of the goat's hoof hooks projections while the sole gains traction. A sheep's concave sole can grip small projections but may slip on smooth surfaces, so a sheep bounds from perch to perch where a goat walks.

Half the summer or more is required for a goat to shed its winter coat. Shag blows away in patches until, from a distance, the animal looks like a giant milkweed pod that has split to release its batting. Tufts clinging to the ground or brush indicate a likely goat mountain. Scat, easily confused with that of sheep or deer, often reveals where goats are feeding. If they are subsisting chiefly on succulent grasses and the like, droppings tend to be massed. Separate, compacted pellets result from browsing on drier, brushier foods, perhaps just inside the timber line, hidden by trees. The pellets may be oblong or nearly round but are more commonly bell-shaped.

VOICE: Although young goats bleat like sheep, adults rarely utter any sound louder than a soft grunt or snort.

Pronghorn *(Antilocapra americana)*
COMMON & REGIONAL NAMES: *antelope, American antelope, pronghorn antelope.*

DESCRIPTION & DISTRIBUTION: Hardly more conspicuous than the small gold sage blossoms spattered on the gray and ocher prairie is a looser cluster of white and russel dots—a score of pronghorn antelope against a distant hillock. They move slowly as they browse, then halt abruptly. The fore end of each piebald speck is cocked upward, and a hunter is not surprised, upon raising his binoculars, to find that the animals have turned their heads toward him in distrustful curiosity. Then one of them kindles a burst of white, like a mirror flashed at the sun; the animal is flaring the rosette of its rump patch. The alarm signal crackles through the herd, rosettes igniting, and the pronghorns dash over the rise. Each one raises its four legs and brings them down almost together, yet its back remains nearly level. Unlike the bobbing escape of deer, the pronghorn's run is a smooth stream.

At a steady speed of more than 30 miles an hour the pronghorns can keep going for perhaps 15 miles without resting, and they can sprint for a mile or two at twice that speed. No animal in the world can stay with them for long. The hunter has no hope of overtaking them, but he knows they will not run far unless pursued, and if he fails to locate them again today he can try tomorrow, staying even lower to the ground, making an even slower, more cautious approach, using the concealment of gullies and low stream beds, brush and hillocks, hoping for a close look at a chosen buck and time for a careful shot at a stationary or walking target.

Though mature bucks have been known to weigh 140 pounds, the average is between 100 and possibly 115. The length from nose to tail is 4 to 5 feet at most, the height at the shoulder never much more than 3 feet. The species has a long-legged, deerlike build, yet a prime buck is hardly taller than a desert sheep, and does are slightly smaller. At several hundred yards they are difficult targets.

Pronghorns on the pale southwestern deserts are considerably lighter in hue than those in northern regions. Generally, a reddish-tan or fawn color covers the upper body and legs as well as the top of the head and the top and sides of the neck. The creamy white of the belly extends halfway up the sides and up the brisket to the front of the neck, where a white shield is formed by an interrupted band of the tan body color. Above this is a complete band of tan and then a wide slash of white up near the throat. The cheeks and lower jaw are also white. Facial color varies, but there are reliable sexual markings. A buck has a broad black or very dark brown band from its eyes down the snout to its black nose, and a black patch from the rear of the jaw onto the throat.

Both sexes have a conspicuous white rump patch, bisected by a narrow strip of tan running down off the back onto the top side of the short tail. A number of other species have light rump patches, and a few (including elk and mule deer) sometimes raise their rump hair slightly when excited, but the pronghorn is unique in the possession of a complex musculature that sharply erects its long rump hair, flaring it out for several inches in all directions. The white flash is a danger signal comparable to the lifted flag of a whitetail deer; it is instantly repeated by all pronghorns within sight on wide grasslands or desert flats. The rosettes may reveal distant groups of antelope to a hunter scanning the prairie, but later, after a difficult stalk, the shimmering heliographs can mean that a shot has to be made immediately or the chance may be gone.

Most does have horns, usually prongless, very seldom more than a few inches long, and sometimes hardly more than bumps. They are almost never visible from more than a few yards away. The buck's black lyre, jutting up above his eyes with a slight forward tilt, exhibits an unusual degree of variation in contour. Conical near the tip, each of the two beams is laterally compressed from the base to the prong or slightly higher. Normally the tips curve rearward and slightly inward, but on some of the finest trophies they turn forward. Each beam has a single prong at the front, jutting forward and most commonly curving slightly upward from a point about half to two-thirds of the way from the base, but on some bucks the prongs are quite close to the skull and on others almost at the tips. The characteristic prong shape is a broad, blunt triangle, slightly concave along the upper surface, yet prongs may also take the form of sharp points. They are not weapons but shields—a marvelous adaptation found on no other animal—for they serve to catch the lowered horns of opposing bucks during rutting duels and thereby prevent fatalities. The horns are useful at no other time because the sharp hoofs alone are employed to kill or drive off predators, and the headgear is shed soon after the rut.

The shedding, too, is unique among horned animals, though typical of antlered species. The horns are not velvet-sheathed antler bones but a hardened keratoid substance allied to that of hoofs, claws, hair, and feathers, and nourished from inside by a circulatory system in a pointed bony core. Between mid-October and mid-November, as a general rule, the horn sheaths fall away. New sheaths then grow and harden until they reach their ultimate size in spring or early summer. Strange, atypical horns—spiraled, stunted, or bent—are believed to result from damage to the core.

Bucks develop more impressive horns each year until they reach their prime, at four or five years in most cases, although the average trophy is probably three years old. Fawns (sometimes called kids) are born in spring, and a "long yearling" buck, approaching its second autumn, may have 8-inch horns. A fully mature buck that has dropped its horns in October may have longer ones than that by mid-December. The hunter wants horns measuring at least 13 inches. A length of 14 or 15 inches is very good and anything exceeding that is excellent. The current record is 19½ inches, with one prong measuring 7 inches, the other 7⅛; slightly longer horns have been collected but with smaller prongs, and both factors are considered in record scoring, as is circumference. Because of the curvature near the tips, trophy judgment can be difficult even with powerful binoculars. However, the horns of an immature buck do not look as deeply black or massive as those of a good trophy. The horns of a worthy buck are usually thicker from front to rear than the ears and project considerably higher. The height from base to tip should nearly equal the length of the head—anything longer will be a very fine trophy—and the prongs should be conspicuous.

Because the pronghorn requires a prairie or desert-prairie habitat, pioneers found no herds east of the Mississippi, but immense concentrations of the animals shared the Great Plains with the bison, prairie dog, sage grouse, and prairie chicken. Over 90 percent of today's populations are the common "American" pronghorn *(A. a. americana)* of the plains. There are four other subspecies: the Oregon pronghorn *(A. a. oregona),* inhabiting a vaguely limited range in eastern Oregon's sagebrush country; Mexican pronghorn *(A. a. mexicana),* in the western tip of the Texas panhandle, lower New Mexico and Arizona, and northern Mexico; Sonora pronghorn *(A. a. sonoriensis),* in southern Arizona and the Mexican state of Sonora; and Peninsula pronghorn *(A. a. peninsularis),* in Baja California. Most fine trophies are of the American or Oregon subspecies, which are so similar as to be virtually indistinguishable. The others are paler, and the Sonora strain tends to be smaller.

The fencing of range land killed many millions of pronghorns. For animals like the whitetail deer, accustomed to jumping deadfalls, low fences are easily surmountable. But the pronghorn is a creature of gently rolling prairies and open flats. Though there are records of panicked antelope clearing fences 8 feet high, the animals seldom attempt to jump an obstruction. They slip under or between barbed-wire strands—occasionally becoming fatally entangled—or run parallel to the obstruction until they find a gap, or may veer off in a new direction. Sometimes they make long horizontal leaps to cross a shallow gully, a cattle guard, or the shadow of a telephone pole, but they prefer to

walk across a gully if the incline is gentle, swim it if it is water-filled, or circumvent it entirely. A fence can mean death if a herd is barred from relatively sheltered areas or from forage during blizzards. If the pronghorns do not die of malnutrition or exposure, in their weakened condition they become abnormally easy prey. A pair of coyotes can pull down a full-grown buck caught at a fenceline, floundering in crusted drifts that support a coyote.

Pronghorns do not overgraze a range, but early ranchers, resenting even a semblance of competition for their livestock, slaughtered great numbers. Pronghorns were also shot and used as poisoned bait to eradicate predators that never seriously

Mildly spooked pronghorn, beginning to flare rump patch.

threatened livestock production. Finally, there was uncontrolled killing for meat and hides, in spite of the fact that pronghorn meat is only moderately good and the hide lacks durability.

After the turn of the century, when the western states began to prohibit the shooting of pronghorns, the herds were already gone from much of the best habitat. There are still only a couple of thousand in Mexico, and hardly more than another 20,000 in Canada, but the United States now has more than half a million. The numbers remain quite stable. Hunting, usually on a permit basis, has become a necessity because the remaining habitat cannot accommodate any great increase.

Today Wyoming has the biggest herds, Montana the next biggest. Pronghorns are found on grasslands and semiarid plains throughout the West, north into lower Alberta and Saskatchewan, south into upper Mexico, east into the high plains of the Dakotas, west into the central portions of the Pacific states. Experiments continue, with herds established in Kansas and even on Florida's Kissimmee prairies. Though pronghorns are hunted in only fourteen western states, their popularity as "big game" is surpassed only by deer.

GAME BEHAVIOR & HUNTING HABITAT: There is a widely held misconception that it is useless to hunt antelope where there is no sage. Pronghorns in most regions are partial to sage only because it is the most plentiful and palatable food on the range that has been left to them. They also thrive where sage is scarce but various grasses, forbs, and browse plants are abundant. Though they like woody species, they probably graze as much as they browse. They eat rabbitbrush, snowberry, snakeweed, cedar, saltbush, wheatgrass, buffalograss, alfalfa, bitterbrush, juniper, even prickly pear. Whether antelope country is hunted on horseback, on foot, or in a vehicle, game is likely to be spotted on distant grasslands, sage-dotted plains, or where splashes of vegetation relieve a monochrome of desert.

Sometimes, caught between the magnets of distrust and curiosity, pronghorns are seen at close range. More often they are miles away, watching suspiciously. It does not take much to spook them into a run. Their mouths quickly come open, but they are neither winded nor tired. They are gulping great draughts of oxygen to power their astounding long-distance

sprints. Some hunters believe that does are faster than bucks, because a herd buck tends to lag behind. The band is usually led by a mature female. She is quick of reflex, knows her domain, and is not apt to lead her companions into the lair of a predator, against a fence, onto a mud flat where miring is a danger, over the brink of a deep gully or high bluff. There are accidents, but not frequently. The buck, serving as rear guard, is fleet enough to herd any hesitant or straying members of the band.

Sometimes one man remains in view of the pronghorns, a diversion while his partner stalks. Sometimes the hunter reaches a point from which he is confident of his target. Sometimes the stalk ends unexpectedly, not quite within range but with no more cover. Gambling on the notorious curiosity

Pronghorn does and buck in full flight.

of pronghorns, he raises his hand above the brush and wiggles his fingers or flutters a handkerchief. Perhaps the herd buck looks toward the hunter, snorts softly, and comes closer. Or perhaps a dozen rosettes flare and the chance is lost.

There is also the possibility that nothing at all will happen, and in desperation the hunter gambles again. Slowly he rises, in full view of the band. If curiosity overcomes fear and the animals still choose not to flee, he approaches—obliquely, quietly, steadily. Finally he eases himself to the ground, hoping for a moment more, hoping he will be steadier than he feels.

The other method is the ambush at a hiding place that commands a view of a frequently used water hole, a salt lick, or a pasture. Nibbling as they amble along, pronghorns seldom range farther than a mile in a day, and they often return to a favored area. Typically they feed from daybreak until perhaps eight in the morning, rest and ruminate for an hour or so, move on and feed for a couple of hours, rest through the heat of the day, and feed again from mid- or late afternoon until dark. But they may be active at any time. They usually go to water once a day but at no predictable time, and in arid country or during a drought they can do without drinking for several days.

Their eyes, larger than a horse's and set in protruding sockets, give them almost a 360-degree arc of vision. Though rain does not bother them, they may lie with their backs to the wind or in the lee of a hill; more often, however, they will face different directions, dozing lightly, jerking their heads up every few minutes to look about, turning to gaze at objects or animals more than half a mile away.

Their hearing is excellent (though not comparable to their eyesight) and strange sounds will alert them. Scent is evidently more important in foraging than for defense, as they see enemies at distances much too great for scenting. Still, a hunter prefers to wait where no strong breeze will carry his scent to the animals. Whereas mountain game expects danger from below and is therefore best approached from above, the pronghorn tends to look out toward the skyline, expecting to see danger at a great distance. Low places therefore favor either an ambush site or a stalking route.

In the northern part of the range, particularly in Saskatchewan and upper Montana, a hundred miles or more may separate winter and summer habitat, yet in other regions there is little or no seasonal migration, and any wandering in spring or fall is nothing more than a search for food, water, and safety. Where storms are severe and snow is deep, the onset of bad weather generally prods them away from the highest plains to slightly lower, more protected areas. Groups remain together, often traveling in single file. The route is likely to be along a drainage, a relatively sheltered valley that has good forage. But if snow accumulates in the lowlands a winter migration may lead to higher plains. Pronghorns will nose away a thin layer of snow or eat what protrudes from it, but they do not paw through it, and a cover of 10 inches can force them to move on.

Their long, brittle outer hair grows over such a fine, sparse undercoat that it is difficult to understand how they survive a hard winter. In spring they shed the long hair, and they have the muscular control to ruffle the outer coat so that air plays through it; in cold weather, they compress it for warmth, an ability that gives them a sleek look in winter. The insulation of the outer coat is enhanced by large air cells inside each coarse hair.

Pronghorns gather into winter herds that vary from a score to more than a hundred. There is a degree of safety in numbers when crusted and deeply drifted snow hampers weakened antelope from outrunning or fighting off coyotes and bobcats. In spring there is less need for mutual protection and the bucks form small bachelor bands. The does also form smaller groups, thus thinning the competition for food. In May or June, or as early as April to the south, after a gestation period of about eight months (longer than that of many larger animals), females wander off to bear their young in solitude. A first pregnancy frequently brings a single fawn; subsequently twins are most common. The birth site is apt to be a shallow depression with prairie grass or brush 9 or 10 inches high furnishing all the concealment needed. The two fawns are dropped a little distance from each other. If one is discovered by a predator, the other has a good chance to survive.

The drab, dun-colored fawns are almost invisible in grass and brush even at a short distance. They are also nearly odorless for the first few days, before they can run well. A doe nurses her young for very short periods, then moves away to feed so that she will not attract enemies to them. If a predator does approach, she drives it off. She can catch and trample a coyote. Rattlers, too, are stomped with the sharp and nimble hoofs. Sometimes a golden eagle may outmaneuver a doe, a bobcat may outwit her, or perhaps two or three coyotes will be more than she can manage, but a greater toll is taken by congenital defects, spring and fall storms, summer droughts, poor forage, and a wide variety of diseases and parasites common to ungulates. Half of spring's fawns are the scattered bones of autumn. Those that survive have an average life span of about seven years, long enough to maintain a stable population on good range.

In September, or earlier in southern regions, bucks begin leaving their bachelor bands to gather harems, and the rut generally lasts into October. Hunting seasons vary considerably from state to state, and in districts within some states. Men who have lived in antelope country will probably agree that hunting is best just before the breeding period and during its first few weeks. The bucks are in their finest physical condition, with horns fully developed and not to be shed for some time, and the animals are at their boldest and most active. Any harem master that is felled will quickly be replaced by another, so the coincidence of hunting with the rut does not endanger breeding, nor does the rut turn wary bucks into dullards that might be vulnerable to 40-yard shots.

One of the finest trophies on record is an Oregon buck shot by Eugene C. Starr from 510 yards. The rifle was a .270 Magnum with a 2½-power scope. Very few pronghorns are shot at quite such long range. The usual distance is between 200 and 400 yards. A hunter needs a binocular (at least 7x35mm) to search distant hills, and if he is mounted or scouting in a vehicle, he usually packs a high-powered spotting scope. The .270 has long been a popular caliber for pronghorns; other good choices range from the old .25-06 and various 6mm rifles to the .30-caliber Magnums. The bullet should be the fast-expanding soft-point type. Most hunters prefer a 4- or 6-power rifle scope or a variable model with settings from 2- or 3-power to 7 or 9.

For brief periods of glory, a buck may be lord of a dozen or more does, but a harem of three or four, being easier to control, is much more common. The smaller the group, the easier it is for a hunter to avoid hitting a doe—and the easier for a buck to keep track of them while on the watch for rivals. An interloper approaches, circles, eyes a doe hopefully. The harem master trots forward and the rival most commonly retreats or is chased off. If intimidation fails, the bucks advance with cautious dignity until their horns touch. A brief but vigorous shoving and slashing contest ensues. Serious injury is infrequent because of the shielding prongs which catch an antagonist's horns. As a rule, one of the bucks abruptly accepts defeat by breaking and running. He is not chased far, since the harem cannot be left unattended.

The buck's concern for his does can serve the hunter when a band is spooked. There is no way to ensure a clean hit with a rifle at a distant, deceptively small target going 60 miles an hour, but the buck, herding his does from the rear, very often stops to look back while still within range. If the hunter is ready, that pause may last just long enough to give him his trophy.

TRACKS & SIGN: A pronghorn's front hoofs often measure 3 inches or more in length, the rear ones about half an inch shorter. A trail that wavers slightly to the left and right, with front tracks larger than rear ones, is sometimes obvious as pronghorn spoor, but where mule deer share the prairie habitat identification may be difficult or impossible. Both species leave the heart-shaped double imprint of cloven hoofs.

The scat, too, is similar: segmented masses when the ani-

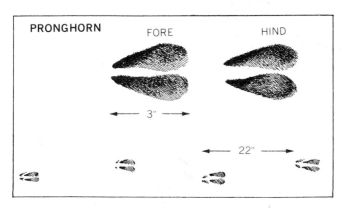

PRONGHORN   FORE   HIND

mals have been grazing preponderantly on succulent grasses, or distinct small pellets produced by browse. The pellets may be bluntly oval or elongate, or they may be bell- or acorn-shaped. However, pronghorns frequently scrape the ground, then urinate or deposit droppings on the cleared spot. This vestigial territorial habit may reveal the presence of antelope in the vicinity, though tracking is not of great importance where a hunter scans enormous open vistas for game to be stalked.

VOICE: Most ungulates whinny, snort, and grunt; the pronghorn also emits a forceful, whistling snort when annoyed at a disturbance but not yet fully alarmed. It sometimes signals a slow, stately retreat. A frequent variation is a reedy blowing, almost like a sneeze, which led the Klamath Indians to call the pronghorn *cha-oo*. Among does and fawns there is also some bleating and mewing. Rarely does a hunter get close enough to hear pronghorn voices before the shot is made, but in a few instances the sounds may warn him to stalk no closer for a while; if he remains still, the herd may resume feeding or move closer.

Cougar *(Felis concolor)*
COMMON & REGIONAL NAMES: *mountain lion, American lion, puma, panther, painter, catamount.*

DESCRIPTION & DISTRIBUTION: Trailing a cougar without hounds is fool's work. A cougar may trail a woodsman for miles, too cautious to get close enough to confirm that the two-legged creature is not a prey species; the woodsman never sees the lion, but later, returning over the same route, he finds the tracks following his own. A lion that outweighs a human can slip through the forest so smoothly, slink through canyons and over bluffs with such fluid, low-bellied stealth, that a hunter may run lions all his life without seeing one that has not first been treed or bayed by his dogs.

A mature male cougar is usually almost 9 feet long from its nose to the flicking tip of its 2½-foot tail. The average weight is about 140 pounds, but the largest mountain lion ever killed weighed more than twice that. Though females are often a third lighter, either sex stands over 2 feet high at the shoulder. The usual color is tawny, with pale or creamy-white muzzle, chin, and underparts. Like deer—their favorite prey—the cats turn grayer in winter, tanner in summer, and shadings differ slightly from region to region. Most of the localized races are much alike, but the subspecies *F. c. coryi* of southern Florida is sometimes rich brown and occasionally black. Usually the tip of the thick tail is dark or black, as are the backs of the ears and a patch on each side of the muzzle. The nose is light, the lips dark, the eyes yellow around dark pupils that narrow to vertical slits in strong sun. The fur is short, thick, and soft. The slack skin of the belly ripples and sways when a cougar runs and stretches smooth when it leaps.

It is a purely American species that once ranged from lower Canada to the Strait of Magellan. Having been obliterated from much of its former habitat, it remains the most widely distributed of cats. It is found as far north as the Peace River in British Columbia, eastward through Alberta, and southward into Latin America all the way to Patagonia. Sizable numbers no longer exist east of the Rockies, but there are a few in lower Texas, Louisiana, Mississippi, and Florida's Everglades, Big Cypress Swamp, and the mangrove thickets of the Ten Thousand Islands. Northeastern cougars, until recently considered extinct, have sifted back like ghosts through the woods of Canada's Maritimes.

Most cougars avoid human contact, but there have been attacks, generally and inexplicably by young males. It is also generally a young lion that unwittingly terrorizes settled areas as it searches for an unoccupied territory after leaving its mother. Rabies is uncommon among lions because of their solitary habits, but it cannot be ruled out as a possible cause for unprovoked attacks. A more probable cause is starvation or the recognition of man as a competitor in hunting territory.

The American lion is sufficiently adaptable to thrive in hilly northern forests, semiarid mountains, or subtropical and tropical jungles and swamps, but it is a solitary, strongly territorial hunter that needs a game-rich wilderness. As settlements or roads carve up the habitat, the cougar declines. The single good omen is that game departments have become champions of the predator's ecological role; the age of bounties has ended. The species is now protected in the eastern regions where it is rare, and has been granted status as a game animal in its western strongholds: British Columbia, Washington, Oregon, California, Idaho, Nevada, Utah, and Colorado. Harvesting limits are set, and where the cats are scarce the hunting season is shortened or suspended. Pure trophy hunting may also be declining, as the reduced habitat has led many sportsmen to forswear killing a trophy animal unless it will be eaten.

GAME BEHAVIOR & HUNTING HABITAT: Hunters have always assumed the cougar to be nocturnal, but cats studied in the Big Creek Basin of the Idaho Primitive Area proved to be as active in daylight as at night. They are unseen because they are so furtive, well camouflaged, alert to sight and sound and smell. Working silently into the wind, a lion tests for scent along a customary patrol route through its territory. After a while it pauses to rise on its hind legs and rake a tree trunk with its claws, sharpening them. Later it scrapes together a loose little mound of dirt, snow, or twigs and leaves, then urinates on the heap. If the scent post is fresh when another cat passes this way, the newcomer will add to the heap and then leave the area. Scat as well as urine may be deposited. Hunters watch for the sign heaps—starting spots from which good hounds can often unravel a cold trail.

After marking its post, a lion usually continues walking in the same direction. Eventually it scents prey and pauses. Its eyesight and hearing are perhaps as important as its sense of smell. The game may be a ground squirrel or other small rodent, rabbit or hare, beaver, marmot, raccoon, coyote, bird, porcupine, elk calf, or aged moose; a hungry cougar can even sustain itself for a while on grasshoppers. But its preferred meat is deer, particularly mule deer, and a cat hunter knows where deer browse.

The cougar catches the faint sound of browsing and there is no need yet to see the grizzled buck. The cat slinks forward, slowly, belly almost on the ground, using every patch of cover. It can outrun a deer, but only for a short distance. Before pouncing it tries to stalk within 30 feet, perhaps less.

The kill is dragged to the nearest brush patch, deadfall, or other cover. After devouring 7 or 8 pounds, the lion heaps branches and debris loosely over the carcass and wanders off a little way to a brushy ravine or high, rocky shelf where it can sleep undisturbed. It will keep returning, perhaps for several

days, until the kill is consumed or begins to putrify. A cougar will not touch tainted meat; it is left for the ravens or magpies or the golden eagle that has been visiting while the lion slept.

By then perhaps a hunter has noted the circling birds or found the scent heap, and the lion hears the distant barking of dogs. He can kill a hound with one rake of a paw and yet he fears them more than he fears men. They can overtake him on open, level terrain, but he heads upward, crosses a shallow stream, weaves through a rocky canyon that ends in a cul-de-sac, where he climbs the boulders and benches to a jagged rim. He crosses a flat-rock plateau, too dry to hold scent well, edges along another canyon rim for half a mile, backtracks, and crosses, leaping and rippling, into a sandstone maze that resembles a stand of gigantic tree stumps in the twilight.

Snow-sprinkled cougar climbing over blowdown in muley country.

At the end of the first canyon, where the climb is impossible for horses, two hunters unsaddle. The dogs circle in confusion, lathered, panting, willing to give up until dew releases stronger scent. At dawn the men climb the blind canyon. The dogs, clambering ahead, bellow that the trail is found. At noon the distant calling of the pack changes in tone, the cat is treed. The dogs—a mongrel and four foxhound-bloodhound crosses—can keep a cat treed for hours. But this one snarls and spits, reaches down from the swaying limb to jab at a leaping hound. A sudden gust unbalances the lion. Raking wildly, he plummets into a bedlam of fangs and is gone up a rubble chute. He comes to bay again in late afternoon, on a ledge jutting from a bluff. He tenses and glares in calm defiance as a hunter at last approaches, thumbing back the hammer of a lever-action carbine.

Since a cougar does not expose itself to long shots, lion hunters have little concern about long-range accuracy and power. They use fast-operating rifles, often but not necessarily of the .30-caliber family, or sometimes rely on handguns. They move in as close as possible to try for a head shot that will kill instantly. If a wounded lion falls among the dogs there is a risk of hitting one of them with a second shot, or a hound may be injured or killed by the cat.

There are not many packs of really fine lion hounds—tireless, adept at trailing, and trained so thoroughly that they will not run deer, coyotes, or foxes. An ideal hound is undistracted even by hot bobcat scent. It takes years to develop a good pack, and such dogs are generally owned only by professional hunters and guides.

Chance can bring quick hunting success, but a long search for a hot trail is common, since a cougar's home range may cover 15 square miles or 30. The primary territory sometimes overlaps that of other lions, particularly females. However, there is mutual avoidance of contact except when a female is in heat. A lioness will lead a large cub on short forays, but otherwise the search for prey is a solitary, careful circuit of the territory, scouting and stalking, covering ground. Only in legend does the cougar leap down on prey from a tree limb, though on rare occasions it will crouch in brush or on a ledge by a game trail.

It seldom wastes energy by killing what it does not want for food, yet there are rare and mystifying killing orgies when a lion slaughters several deer or a score of domestic sheep in a night. Though such incidents bring on attempts to exterminate a region's lions, raids on livestock are infrequent and the cougar is beneficial to its wild prey. A 6-year study in the Big Creek Basin has proved that cougars, abundant there, weed out defective young and old and weak among deer and elk, deter the spread of disease by removing the ill, and alleviate overbrowsing in restricted winter habitat. Where game abounds, a lion kills about a deer per week, mildly reducing a doomed surplus.

Locality determines when lions can be hunted with the least chance of orphaning cubs, because there is no set breeding season. Vancouver Island has an abundance of cougars (*F. c. vancouverensis*) and, probably because of the mild climate, they most often give birth in winter. In Idaho most births occur in spring or early summer.

A roaming male, attracted to a female in oestrus, stays with her for about nine days. The appearance of a rival may draw blood, but battle fatalities seem to be uncommon. The female accepts the victor. Later, while he is sleeping or distracted, she may wander off to mate with the vanquished, as well. The gestation period is about ninety to ninety-six days, and the den is a temporary, makeshift shelter—a small cave, rocky fissure, or a recess shielded by overhanging rock. Most females mate every two or three years and produce a litter of two or three cubs, sometimes four. A male takes no part in their rearing, and in fact, if the region's population is dense, he may kill and eat any cubs he encounters though the lioness tries to defend them. Cannibalism seems to function as a check on population, which tends to remain stable for long periods.

The cubs, spotted somewhat like bobcats and with tigerlike black tail rings, weigh only about a pound. After two weeks their eyes are open, and after four the mother may bring them bits of meat, though nursing sometimes continues for several months. At six months, the cubs weigh 30 or 40 pounds, and the lioness, abandoning the den, begins leading them to her kills. Occasionally she takes one on a hunt—but only one at a time, as more than one would interfere with stalking. In the Big Creek Basin, tracks revealed how one lioness stood by to let her cub pounce on an elk calf, then completed the kill herself. A yearling male is almost full-grown and may leave to establish its own territory.

More often, the young remain with the lioness until they are nearly two years old.

Apart from man, they have no natural enemies. Neither do they suffer from serious diseases, other than very rare instances of rabies. Parasitic infestations, internal or external, are usually minor, and the average life span is eight years.

TRACKS & SIGN: The print of a cougar's forefoot may be 3 or 4 inches across, slightly larger in soft snow, and quite round. The slightly smaller hind print may overlap but seldom registers precisely in the front track. Each foot leaves indentations of four toes—sometimes blurred by winter fur—as the fifth front toe is too high for contact. The retracted claws leave no marks. The tracks, somewhat spread if a lion is moving fast, are spaced about 2 feet apart and follow a rather direct line. In snow, the tail sometimes leaves drag traces between the prints.

The general direction of travel may also be revealed by a sign heap or scratchings where a cat has defecated, because cougars usually face their line of travel while scratching. They sometimes cover their droppings with earth but often leave them exposed on a sign heap. The scat, usually copious, varies from masses to pellets, and commonly shows a suffusion of hair and scraps of bone. Claw-sharpening tree scrapes and cached kills may also be found along the territorial circuit. A loosely covered kill is typical, though a cat occasionally buries meat as bears

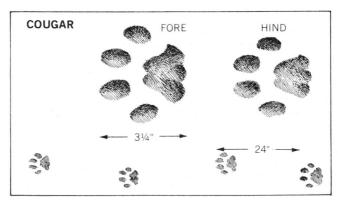

COUGAR   FORE   HIND

← 3¼" →   ← 24" →

and wolves do. A fairly fresh kill, with plenty of meat and little disturbance by scavengers, probably means the cat is near.

VOICE: Cougars are comparatively silent but can make the same variety of sounds as most cats. The legendary scream of the panther is really only a loud, deep caterwauling, seldom heard and probably connected with mating activity. The species can growl, hiss, and spit, but does not roar. Its strangest utterance is a shrill whistle, more piercing than a bird's, usually a female's alarm call to her cubs. It also signals the hunter to watch for a lion—running, treed, or cornered.

Gray Wolf *(Canis lupus)*
COMMON & REGIONAL NAMES: *timber wolf, tundra wolf, lobo, lobo wolf.*

DESCRIPTION & DISTRIBUTION: "They go in droves by night, with dismal yelling cries," wrote the naturalist Mark Catesby in 1743. Wolves do go in droves, or packs, by night, but also by day, and some wolves wander alone. A few of us have had the good fortune to hear them while hunting moose or sheep or bear in the north woods; the remembered sound of a howl—a wild, piercing resonance, more vibrant than dismal—is trophy enough at a time when wolves are in critical need of protection.

Eskimos, who share the caribou with wolves, comprehend the role of predators in culling weak, diseased, or otherwise inferior prey from vigorous herds. "The caribou feed the wolves," they say, "and the wolves keep the caribou strong." The white man's fear of wolves is heightened by their invisibility in regions where their survival has depended on eluding the human enemy. Though tracks and other sign abound, a man can live in wolf country for years without encountering one. It is a strange state of affairs, for wolves are often located by howling at them. If they are within hearing, they usually answer and sometimes approach to investigate. There are some of us who no longer shoot wolves, even where packs are abundant, but hunt them nonetheless and count the sight of one as a bloodless coup.

It is a sight worth hunting. Discounting wide variations in size and color, the wilderness traveler hopes some day to see a typical mature timber wolf—a male weighing between 70 and 90 pounds, a bit over 2 feet high at the shoulder, or a female almost equally imposing. A wolf is an extremely intelligent wild dog that looks much like an extremely large German shepherd, but with a bushier tail, longer jaws, longer, shaggier coat, grizzled and gray, with lighter underparts, and slanted yellow or brown eyes often lit by a greenish flicker. The tip of the tail is usually black or very dark, and there is a small oblong black spot over a scent gland on the upper tail, about 6 inches from the base.

There are several subspecies in Europe and Asia, and scientists disagree as to how many subspecies inhabit North America. The races interbreed (for that matter, they will hybridize with large dogs) and they exhibit an extreme variability of characteristics. Two dozen subspecies of American gray wolf have been catalogued, as well as three subspecies of American red wolf *(C. rufus,* also classified as *C. niger),* but many of the geographical races are now extinct.

The several types inhabiting the arctic islands and Greenland are almost entirely white or cream-colored, sometimes subtly shaded with black or gray. These subspecies, of about the same size as the common gray timber wolf *(C. l. lycaon),* are substantially smaller than the eight or nine varieties of tundra wolves inhabiting Alaska and northern Canada. Tundra wolves are chiefly gray, but a single litter can include creamy pups and black ones. The races of Alaska and the Mackenzie District of the Northwest Territories are the largest in the world. Adult males exceeding 100 pounds are not unusual. The largest ever taken was a 175-pound male trapped in east-central Alaska in 1939 by the U.S. Fish and Wildlife Service.

Smaller and probably more closely related to eastern timber wolves are those of British Columbia and Vancouver Island, where they are still relatively common. A few wolves have been seen in Washington and Oregon in recent years, and a few in isolated pockets of habitat in Wyoming, Colorado, Utah, and Arizona. Very small numbers may survive in the arid Mexican mountains, the southern boundary of a range that once covered most of North America. But gray wolves have been virtually extirpated from all of the United States except Alaska, Minnesota, Michigan, and Wisconsin. Fortunately, they are still relatively common across the tundra and forests of Canada. In Ontario's

Algonquin Provincial Park, where they were shot and trapped for many years but have recently gained protection, they are believed to be more numerous than when fur traders began to map the region. There are probably close to 25,000 wolves in Alaska and an equal number scattered throughout Canada.

Below the Canadian border, the last major concentration lives in delicate balance with the whitetail deer of Minnesota's Superior National Forest. Until 1965 a live wolf was officially considered vermin in Minnesota, a dead one was worth $35. They are no longer bountied, and Forest Service researchers believe that the influence of trapping and hunting has become negligible. Healthy packs have been bounding through the snows of Michigan's Isle Royale National Park since 1948 or 1949, when they crossed the ice of Lake Superior to the island. The

Gray wolf patrolling its home range.

park's moose herd—chief source of winter food for the wolves —will probably dwindle as park utilization is intensified. In Michigan and Wisconsin, wolves have been granted full protection, but no more than a thousand are thought to remain in these two states and Minnesota.

They are the common gray subspecies *C. l. lycaon,* sometimes called the "eastern" timber wolf, which is also prevalent in Quebec, Ontario, and other forested regions across central Canada. Among these timber wolves there is a very high percentage of gray (or "normal phase"), though many animals have a reddish or brownish cast, some are melanistic, and a few are nearly white. Black and white color phases were far more common in the neighboring subspecies *C. l. nubilus,* the Great Plains wolf, which fed on the immense herds of bison (it was also called buffalo wolf). It was believed extinct, but game biologists have noted an abnormally high incidence of black wolves, as well as some white ones, in northeastern Minnesota, within 150 miles of the buffalo wolf's former range. The buffalo wolf may have survived the rancher's traps and poisons, and bred with the timber wolf to produce an intergrade between the subspecies. A deer hunter who sees a black specter glide into the shadows of Superior National Forest is perhaps witnessing a phase of evolution.

The red wolf of the Southeast is classified by some taxonomists as a subspecies of the larger gray timber wolf and by others as a separate species, perhaps closely related to the coyote with which it readily interbreeds. Of the red wolves that once occupied a large portion of the eastern United States, remnant populations survive chiefly along the Gulf Coast of Texas and in Louisiana. A few packs of reds or hybrids may also exist in Mississippi, the Ozark National Forest of Arkansas, and possibly southeastern Oklahoma.

The names "red wolf" and "black wolf" are interchangeable. Color variations include red, black, brown, yellowish, and gray. A typical male weighs between 50 and 75 pounds, a female between 40 and 60. A red wolf looks like a lean, leggy cross between its bigger relatives and a coyote, admirably built for long runs on coastal prairies or for plodding through river-bottom swamps and bayous. Den sites include hollow trees, stream banks, sand knolls in coastal areas, and enlarged burrows of

other animals. Red wolves occasionally run deer but, like coyotes, subsist mainly on hares and rabbits, mice, squirrels, and other small rodents.

In southern Europe there have been authenticated attacks by rabid wolves, but rabies has always been rare among American wolves. It is possible that the American breeds have some slight degree of resistance, but more important factors are the wide, thin spread of the packs—a deterrent to epidemics—and the tendency of a pack to keep to itself. In all of America's history, the only verified attack by a wolf occurred in Ontario in 1942.

A stronger basis for man's hatred has involved livestock. When settlers turned the wilds into ranch- and farmland, the wolf's normal prey animals were replaced by easily caught sheep, cattle, and poultry. Consequently wolves were slaughtered, and still more were killed in the mistaken belief that they were reducing the remaining game. Enmity was compounded by misinterpretation. Because travel through deep snow can be wearying, a lone wolf or a pack sometimes follows the trail of men or dog teams. Occasionally the shadowing wolves veer off in search of game or become curious about the strange animal that is

Gray wolf following shoreline on territorial circuit.

breaking trail, and they circle ahead. A hunter finds they have trod his back trail, and then he finds they have crossed ahead of him. They refuse to show themselves, and a pack seldom howls when traveling or hunting. It is an eerie silence of wolves, an unheard and invisible presence until evening, when howls reverberate through the woods where the man makes camp. In the morning, tracks encircle his campsite, and he wonders if he is being stalked.

GAME BEHAVIOR & HUNTING HABITAT: While glassing sheep mountains in Alaska or the Yukon a hunter may have the good luck to come upon wolves prowling gravel bars or ranging above the timber line in quest of Dalls, and a caribou hunter may sight a pack on the tundra. But wolves are rarely seen in heavily timbered deer country or in the vast taiga where moose plod through spruce swamps. Very few men have the skill or experience to hunt specifically for wolves, which may be just as well in this time of diminished numbers. Many of us hunt only for sign while looking for other game. A lone wolf or a pack will frequently follow game trails, since a trail makes for easy traveling, and scent posts even appear on logging roads. Wolves also walk along the natural paths formed by lake shores and stream banks. A knowledge of such habits increases the chance of finding sign —reward enough—or of some day seeing a gray form or a file of half a dozen drift through the forest.

They mate only in February and March. A gestation period averaging sixty-three days usually brings forth young in early May. The degree of successful breeding is somewhat influenced by the size of a wolf pack. A group of more than eight or ten is uncommon, the average number being six in most habitat.

Several weeks before whelping, a bitch establishes a den—sometimes a new one, sometimes one that has been used by her pack for years. It may be a rock cave or hollow log, or it may be dug among pine roots or in the side of a sandy hill. On treeless tundra, slopes of eskers are favorite sites. An earthen burrow, the most common type, is sometimes dug from solid ground, but fox or badger holes are often enlarged for the purpose. Wolf dens are difficult to find, though a site is occasionally discovered by following tracks, listening for howls, or searching where sign is thick.

The brown, woolly pups weigh about a pound at birth, and are likely to weigh 15 after two months, when they are being weaned. During the first weeks only the mother enters the den, but soon her mate (or a dominant male assuming the mate's role) visits the pups. Once they emerge from the den, all members of the pack help rear them.

A wolf's long guard hairs and thick undercoat furnish protection in severe cold, and a healthy animal may curl up for a nap—tail over nose in the manner of a fox—during a blizzard at 40 degrees below zero. Yet a bad winter can occasionally cause hardship through a scarcity of prey, and there are other agents of infant and adult mortality: congenital defects, various worms, lice, and other parasites, mange, distemper, a mysterious lupine ailment called listeriosis, accidental injury, flash flooding of a den, or malnutrition during a pup's first winter, when it has not yet gained the experience, size, strength, and very efficient teeth of adults. Like dogs, some wolves live to be very old, but the usual longevity is between seven and ten years.

It is usually late afternoon or early evening when one of the adults rises, stretches, noses a companion, wags his tail, and perhaps utters a few sharp barks. Then, raising his snout and closing his eyes, he emits a low, querulous howl. The companion replies with a full-throated, steadier wail. The others join in a raucous chorus, a ritual of howling and tail-wagging that precedes the hunt. After a few minutes it melts away, ending frequently with a short series of barks, and the pack trots into the dusk. At least one wolf, not always the mother, stays at the den with the pups. The others return, sometimes but not always together, usually but not always the next morning. During their absence the guardian and pups may have caught a few mice, but they are famished. Returning, an old male carries a tattered deer hock in his mouth, and when two pups run up to him he drops it for them. The other pups bite at the throats and snouts of the returning hunters; it is a stimulus that causes the adults to regurgitate undigested meat, and the pups rush for it.

In midsummer the pack abandons its den for a new headquarters known as a rendezvous, rest area, or loafing spot. Here the pups rest, play, feed, and practice hunting until fall, when they begin traveling with the adults. The site is usually a large, grassy area that offers good mousing and a view of the surround-

ings. It might be a dry marsh, an old burn, or a former beaver pond that has turned to meadow. A curious hunter can locate it more easily than a den, not only because of the terrain but because there is much activity at a rendezvous. Many tracks, scat, and even beaten trails are produced by wolves leaving to hunt and returning.

For practice or the pure enjoyment of the hunt, wolves try to catch and kill many small animals they come across, but

Red wolves hunting for small prey.

if other prey is abundant, they usually leave the carnivores uneaten. They will eat hares, rabbits, grouse, ptarmigan, waterfowl, beavers, marmots, mice, and the like. A diet of small game is insufficient, however, and reports that mice constitute their chief fare are true only of occasional summer days when the mice are plentifully available. To survive on a diet of mice, a grown wolf would have to capture more than five dozen daily. Small game provides sustenance when larger prey is scarce, especially where caribou are the primary game but are present in great numbers only during migrations. Wolves prey chiefly on deer, moose, sheep, and caribou. They take a considerable number of fawns, calves, and lambs in spring and summer, killing some healthy ones but chiefly weeding out the flawed—the easiest to capture. In winter the old, arthritic, ill, or injured become the chief prey. In Mount McKinley National Park, most of the Dall sheep killed by Alaskan wolves are ten years old or more. The deer killed in northern Minnesota are frequently beginning to suffer the ailments of age. The toll per wolf averages one deer every two or two and a half weeks, enough to ensure a little extra winter forage for the breeding deer.

A wolf trots along at 5 miles an hour for half a day without tiring, then lopes after a deer at five times that speed, finally galloping and bounding at more than 30 miles an hour to attempt the capture. But a healthy deer is slightly faster unless deep, semicrusted snow hinders the pursued more seriously than the pursuer.

Though wolves will investigate a game trail, their chief hunting method is simply to wander over patrol routes until they encounter potential food. Then they test the prey by bounding after it, but long pursuits are common only in legend. The typical deer, sheep, or caribou kill involves a lunging run of less than a thousand yards, and a moose is likely to interrupt short runs by turning on the pack. The kill depends less on endurance than a sudden, short dash, with success hinging on luck, surprise, primitive teamwork and strategy, and the habits and condition of the prey.

An October snow filters through the conifers as an Ontario pack leaves its Smoke Lake rendezvous to begin a nomadic winter existence on a vaguely defined range, perhaps 10 miles across, perhaps as wide as 40. The territory slightly overlaps that of another pack, but there is plenty of room and the groups avoid each other. On light snow four or five wolves often travel almost abreast, with 50 or 60 yards between animals, increasing the chance that one or another will come across game. When snow deepens the pack moves in a single file so that only the leader has to break trail. Occasionally a wolf sniffs the ground—most often at a junction or turn of a wolf trail, game trail, or human trail—scrapes the earth, and urinates. Such scent posts are not territorial markers so much as calling cards, a means of communicating to later arrivals that one of their kind has recently passed this way. Some woodsmen speculate that members of a pack can recognize a comrade's scent post as easily as they recognize the howl of a mate.

TRACKS & SIGN: Wolf tracks are exactly like a dog's but larger —those of a big tundra wolf sometimes measuring nearly 5 inches long and almost as wide in soft snow, mud, or wet sand. There are times when the slightly smaller hind feet come down almost precisely on the prints of the forefeet, or the wolves step in one another's tracks so that a trail reader has difficulty determining the number of wolves in a pack.

The scent posts—scrapes, rocks, or stumps marked with urine—are typically canine. The droppings, too, are like a large dog's but frequently showing traces of hair from prey animals.

If game is plentiful in a limited pocket of range, packs

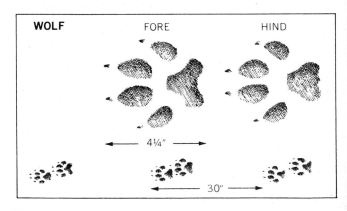

WOLF FORE HIND

4¼"

30"

and lone wolves sometimes establish heavily used trails that are easy to follow if not to interpret. The searcher for wolves must take note of other wildlife. Concentrations of ravens or magpies may reveal the site of a kill, as may the converging tracks of other carnivores, such as fox, bear, and lynx. Wolves may remain in the vicinity of an old den where a porcupine, using the vacant den in winter, has girdled the willows or spruces. A grassy rendezvous flat may be revealed by scat, tracks, and sometimes diggings where caches were uncovered.

There is a strong likelihood that a wolf or a pack will return to a partly consumed and reasonably fresh kill, or perhaps another pack will be attracted to it. A woodsman hiding near such a spot may be granted the sight of wolves.

VOICE: Not all wolves seem capable of barking, but many will answer a bark (or a crude human imitation) by howling. The bark is brief, harsh, usually uttered in a short series. It is sometimes a challenge or alarm call, but is also heard occasionally at the beginning and end of a communal howl. Less frequently heard but unmistakable is a deep growl when a feeding wolf feels crowded by a subordinate member of the pack.

Wolves seldom call during a chase, but may stop and howl to each other if they become separated or to signal arrival at an ambush point. Evidently because the actual hunt and final chase are silent, prey animals show no fear of howling.

Group howls are heard most often in the evening and to a lesser extent in the early morning. The howl of an individual wolf seldom lasts more than about five seconds, but may be repeated until the pack tires. Some howls rise and fall, some retain a constant pitch, some rise and break off abruptly. Wolves separated from a pack may utter what is known as a lonesome howl, a protracted sound that rises in pitch and falls away plaintively. If answered, it usually changes to a location, or assembly, howl—deep, even, and perhaps punctuated by a few barks.

Anyone who has heard dogs or coyotes howl can imitate a wolf passably by deepening the tone. Wolves are likely to reply, particularly in the evening. Since they can recognize the voices of pack members, certainly they are not fooled. They seem to answer out of curiosity, sometimes even replying to a hooting loon or screeching owl.

Black Bear *(Ursus americanus,* also classified as *Euarctos americanus)*
COMMON & REGIONAL NAMES: *bruin, blackie.*

DESCRIPTION & DISTRIBUTION: Once, leaning into the wind as we came over a timbered rise during an elk hunt in northwestern Wyoming, we surprised a big chocolate-coated bear as it stood on its hind legs and clawed at a Douglas fir, ripping diagonal scars in the bark 7 feet from the ground. Our own surprise matched the bear's, though we had seen a couple of other bear trees near our trail, aspens with long, festering slashes in their white skin. For an instant we were uncertain whether the animal was a black bear or a grizzly, since other species may be brown. It sank to all fours, turning, and came toward us in a slow, rolling shuffle, its head swinging, and then we saw that its facial profile was flatter, less concave than a grizzly's and it lacked the grizzly's shoulder hump. It made no sound—no cough or grunt or clicking of teeth. It was not attacking, merely reacting in confusion. The wind having held back our sound and scent, the bear's weak eyes may have perceived only three moving blurs before it caught the repellent man-odor. No one could predict its next move. It reared slightly and seemed to be swinging away as a hunting partner toppled it with a bullet from his .300 Magnum. The bear would set no record, but it was a large male, close to 400 pounds, with a thick and glossy pelt in prime condition.

That probably is more or less how black bears are most often seen and killed. The majority are shot during chance encounters by hunters seeking other game, though a planned bear hunt has dramatic appeal for a woodsman who uses hounds or, lacking dogs, has a higher regard for patience and solitude than for frequent success. A guide in northern New Hampshire, a man who takes inordinate pride in his six big brindle Plott

Black bear with chest blaze common among eastern races.

hounds, has proved on a number of occasions that he can tell from the way they bawl when they are onto a bear that has been run before. He tries to follow them as closely as possible and hopes the hunter can keep up. A bear learns by experience—other than the wolf and the raccoon perhaps no game animal is more intelligent—and one that has escaped previous chases almost invariably heads for the steepest terrain and thickest cover. Instead of treeing after a brief run it can maintain a steady 15-mile-an-hour lope through the morning and afternoon, circling, doubling, crossing water as cleverly as a fox. It may never tree. It may finally back against some great fallen log or an escarpment to face the pack. Being an eastern bear, it is most likely a glossy black, medium-sized animal—a 200- or 250-pound snarling black swirl that can break a dog's back with a quick cuff. The guide, after wearying hours of trying to keep within earshot of his dogs, hears their urgent cries and races through the timber.

A North Carolina friend prefers the traditional southern hunts involving thirty or forty men and as many dogs. His guests take stands along trails, on ridges, and at crossings. Sometimes a bear trees after a brief run. More often one of the standers hears a swell of wild yelping and bugling, then a crashing of brush, and he sweeps a buckshot pattern through a foliage-screened patch of bolting black. One of the guests some years ago brought several Airedales and a pair of redbones that had built a reputation for baying wild Tennessee boar as well as black bears. Leading the combined pack, they struck a hot trail almost immediately and in half an hour put a bear up a slippery elm directly in front of the host's stand. It leaped straight up the furrowed trunk in 6-foot stretches, its front claws digging in to hold while its hind legs pistoned.

Some states prohibit the use of dogs. Some, on the other hand, permit spring hunting, and some also permit the use of bait. Alaska has about 75,000 black bears, more than any other state, and year-around hunting is permitted in many sections. Washington is next, with a population fluctuating between 30,000 and 40,000. Sometimes the bears there kill significant numbers of pines and firs by girdling them to get at the cambium, a pre-ferred food, and timber firms welcome hunters on their lands in fall or spring. In autumn a hunter may stand watch near the entrails of a deer he has killed, and when spring weather draws the bears from their dens he may return and hang up a calf's head or a chunk of pork from some local slaughterhouse. If he can stand the insects and the waiting, he may eventually see a dark shape lumbering out of a devil's-club tangle or amid tall evergreens, pausing as if to decide between the scent of ripening carrion and the lure of sweet grasses and pungent skunk cabbage on a stream bank below. More likely, the hunter will return one morning to find the bait consumed, but now he can still-hunt along the stream, or he may have dogs with him to cast on the fresh trail. Some of the guides prefer to truck slowly along the logging roads, with strike dogs riding up behind the cab. A sudden babble of hounds lets the driver know where a black bear has recently come out to the road.

There are eighteen subspecies, distributed throughout Alaska and Canada (except in the northernmost latitudes), down both coasts of the United States to Florida and lower California, across the Great Lakes states and the well-forested portions of the Gulf Coast, and down through the Rockies into Arizona, New Mexico, westernmost Texas, and northern Mexico. Some of their original range has been floated away by the loggers. Good habitat may be anywhere from sea level into the upper coniferous zones, but black bears seldom dally for long above an altitude of about 7,000 feet. They fare best in relatively open forests combining dense hideaway thickets with spaces that provide fruits and grasses. Ideal locales have mixed stands of conifers and hardwoods, sprinkled with streams, ponds, or lakes for drinking.

Omnivorous though the species is, over three-quarters of its diet consists of vegetation and fruit; it may damage lumber and can inflict havoc on an orchard. When a black bear climbs an apple tree, it often eats leaves and twigs, but causes the most damage by breaking branches as it tries to reach every apple.

Conflict is inevitable where black bears live in proximity to man. Some of them lose their fear and all of them are unpredictable. Most horror stories about black bears are akin to the fables about wolves, but bears become irritable with age or injury, sows with cubs are always dangerous, and any bear may attack if startled at close range or disturbed while feeding.

Despite their intelligence, they have such insatiable appetites that they are easily caught in meat-baited, drag-set traps arranged in V-shaped log or rock pens that draw them directly over the steel jaws. At one time great numbers were trapped for their fur, meat, and fat. Bear oil was used for all manner of products, from liniment to hair restorative. Useless for most purposes, it was and is a superlative shortening and frying oil. Some of the hunters and guides on British Columbia's lower coast tell visiting sportsmen that only a barbarian would eat bear meat. Their prejudice must have originated from the taste of bears that had been eating lumber-camp garbage or feeding on dead fish along the spawning rivers. A few woodsmen in the Pacific Northwest still trap bears primarily for their flesh. Thoroughly cooked to avoid trichinosis, and with fat trimmed away to avoid oiliness or a rank flavor, it can be delectable.

Conflicts with bears and the demand for bear products led to uncontrolled shooting and trapping. Correction came so late that black bears are still scarce in many states where once they abounded, but there are probably about 250,000 of them in the United States, and some authorities postulate twice as many in Canada. After Alaska and Washington, the states with the greatest abundance at this writing are California, Oregon, Minnesota, North Carolina, Colorado, Idaho, and Maine.

Most of those in the East are black with a tan or grizzled snout and often with a white chest blaze. But color variations, often occurring in a single litter, become progressively more common to the west. The species may be brown, tan, blond, or cinnamon. In California, brown is much more typical than black. In Alaska, light brown is rare but dark brown common. Albinism is rare, yet the Kermode subspecies *(U. a. kermodei)* of west-central British Columbia—a scarce and fully protected variety—is creamy white but for its beige-gray nose, brown eyes, and reddish-brown pads. Another strange color phase is the glacier bear, or blue bear *(U. a. emmonsii),* of Yakutat Bay on Alaska's gulf coast. Most specimens are medium-sized and generally described as having luxuriant bluish-gray coats. Bud Branham, a well known Yakutat guide, says he has "seen them from a silver-black to almost midnight-blue." He estimates their total number at perhaps 300, for they occur only along a mountainous coastal strip less than a hundred miles long.

The state permits each licensed hunter to take one glacier bear per season and the Alaska Professional Hunters' Association now advocates "one in a lifetime." Even that may seem excessive to someone unfamiliar with the region, but very few of the bears are killed. For one thing, an Alaskan hunting trip is expensive and time-consuming; for another, blue bears are extremely wary and are shielded by high, steep, coastal slopes and glacial snow above bordering spruce and hemlock forests, dense alders, and high thickets of moose willow and the like. Branham guides sportsmen in May and June, cruising in a hunting boat past Disenchantment Bay and Hubbard Glacier into Russel Fiord. Game spotted from the boat is much too distant to be shot without an arduous climbing stalk that often takes several hours. Probably the first sportsman ever to shoot a blue bear was the famous hunting writer Warren Page, who returned to the area two decades later, in 1970, but had no chance to take a second blue-bear trophy. He and Branham spotted a beautiful silvery-blue specimen feeding in a high, grassy opening, but after a 25-minute climb to get within range they saw the bear disappear into the brush at the crucial moment.

A single subspecies within a single season may exhibit great variations in size. Before denning in late fall or early winter, a yearling cub (ten months old) may weigh between 30 and 95 pounds; the following autumn it is likely to weigh between 80 and 130 pounds; in the third year it will probably weigh between 215 and 295, and may reach its maximum weight the following season. Some authorities state that an average, fully mature black bear weighs a little over 300 pounds. Others, unwilling to accept specific figures, say that an average well-fed adult may weigh from 200 to 400 pounds. The shoulder height is not often more than about 3 feet, but the middle of its rounded back may be a little higher. Length averages between 4 and 5½ feet.

Males are much larger than females, and a number of boar bears have weighed more than 600 pounds and measured 9 feet from the nose to the tip of a tail so stubby as to be almost unnoticeable in the thick fur. Blacks of this size are comparable to mature sow grizzlies. The heaviest on record was an 802½-pound Wisconsin black bear killed in 1885. Fourth place in the trophy records is held by another Wisconsin bear, shot by Ed Strobel in 1953; after the removal of 150 pounds of viscera and fat, it weighed 585 pounds. In recent years very large black bears have been recorded in the Rockies. At one time trophies were

scored by measuring hides, but since pelts can be stretched, the scoring basis was changed to skull measurement. First place in the Boone and Crockett listings is held by a Utah bear that Rex Peterson and Richard Hardy shot in 1970. Its skull is $13^{11}/_{16}$ inches long, $8^{11}/_{16}$ inches wide. Second and third place are held, respectively, by Arizona and Colorado bears killed in the 1960s. Their skulls are only a trifle smaller.

GAME BEHAVIOR & HUNTING HABITAT: Like raccoons, wolves, dogs, and foxes, the various bears are descended from tree-climbing carnivores that lived 50 million years ago. There are closely related European and Asian species, but the black bear is distinctly American. It is the smallest and the most widely distributed American bear and probably the world's most abundant. It is also the only American bear that retains its tree-climbing ability beyond the cub stage. It has shorter, more acutely curved foreclaws than the grizzly, and uses them to dig into bark and cling, while the hind legs push upward. The animal can spiral a trunk like a squirrel or, under pressure from a hunter or dogs, go straight up in long bounds. Sometimes a moderately

Black bear searching decayed log for grubs.

large black bear appears to enjoy swaying in the top of a spindly sapling. But the descent is peculiarly awkward, a process of backing down, raking bark to slow a laboriously controlled drop, then letting go for the last few feet to land on its haunches. Before it reaches the ground there is time enough to shoot a bear that refuses to stay treed, and it should not be allowed to come down alive into a ring of frenzied dogs.

A sow is fiercely protective of her cubs during their first year. An adult male will usually try to kill any cubs he catches, for he regards them as food or, when they grow larger, as competitors. But an angry sow can often beat a larger boar. The animals bellow, snarl, roar, and click their teeth as they battle, sometimes on all fours, sometimes rising up to wrestle and slap. Since their short legs are ill-suited to squeezing, the bear hug is more fanciful than descriptive, but a bear sometimes tries to hold an adversary close so that it can claw and bite at the head and neck. Fights are so loud and furious that other adult bears in the vicinity leave or climb trees. Combat goes on until one animal breaks and runs or—in only a few instances—is killed.

More feared than males of the same species are grizzlies. Black bears make way for any grizzly that invades a choice feeding spot, and if many of the bigger bears move into an area the black bears forsake it. The same fear is, of course, exhibited toward the Alaskan brown bear, which is not really a species but the largest subspecies of grizzly. Cougars and wolves may kill a few cubs, but bears are subjected to no significant predation except by other bears and men. They have a remarkable ability to withstand infection, recover from wounds, mend fractured bones, and survive amputations. Black bears may be afflicted with any of two dozen or more external and internal parasites, but severe infestations are rare, and of the internal types only roundworms, filariae, and trichinae are at all common. Ailments include tuberculosis, anthrax, tumors, and pneumonia, yet black bears are so vigorous that they have a life expectancy of twelve to fifteen years in the wild.

Males and females travel and feed together, demonstrating great affection, for about a month during the mating season, sometime from June through July. Then they go their separate ways. Black bears are not strongly territorial. They may remain in one very small area as long as it provides plenty of food, but the average home range can be 5 square miles in some regions and many times as wide in others.

Bear gestation is unlike that of most mammals. The fertilized ovum develops little if at all during the summer and in the black species does not attach itself to the uterine wall until November, when the sow is almost ready to den. Thereafter the fetus develops so rapidly that birth usually occurs in January or early February. Most black bears begin to breed at about three and a half years, and usually a sow first produces a single cub. After that she usually bears twins but triplets are not uncommon. Though bears are not true hibernators, a sow is denned at the time of birth and is either sleeping or so drowsy that she is only minimally conscious of the event.

Like raccoons, bears feed voraciously in the autumn, preparing to den up by accumulating a 4-inch layer of fat beneath a thick hide and 3 inches of fur. In the southern extreme of their range, some bears remain active through the winter. Others den only intermittently, and even in the North a bear may awaken during a warm spell and groggily stagger about for a while before returning to its den. Its temperature and pulse remain almost normal and it takes four or five breaths per minute even during a period of deep dormancy. Denning may last from two to four months, through the season when food is most scarce, yet a bear loses only a little weight.

At denning time (late October for Alaskan black bears, late November or early December over most of the range) the stomach and intestines shrink and appetite disappears. No typical den is sought; it may be a cave, a recess under a ledge, a sheltered space among boulders, a large hollow in a tree or log, a space under a blowdown or a drooping conifer, or the angled root mass of a toppled tree. Some bears dig holes beneath logs or stumps or in hillsides. Some simply bed down in brushy tangles with only the trees overhead for protection. Some scoop out earth to enlarge a den, some rake in a matting or screen of twigs and leaves, some use a sheltered spot just as they find it. In a cold region with little snow, a southern exposure is favored, but north slopes may be preferred where they accumulate deep drifts, as snow furnishes excellent insulation and concealment. A woodsman may walk by a dormant bear, unaware of anything but a snowy hummock.

At birth a cub is about 8 inches long and weighs from 6 to 10 ounces—a five-hundredth or six-hundredth of what it will weigh at maturity. The disparity between newborn and mature sizes is greater only among marsupials. If cubs were larger, the mother probably could not manufacture sufficient milk during the long denning fast. Blind, almost naked and helpless, they nestle into the sow's warm fur and probably nurse at her two inguinal nipples. Later, when they are out of the den, they suckle at any of her four pectoral nipples, sometimes perching on her hind legs while she sits on her haunches in a disconcertingly anthropomorphic position.

Most bears emerge from their dens in March, later in regions of deep snow. After several days a sow brings out her tottering 5-pound cubs. Almost as soon as they leave the den, they begin to nibble at tender green plants and any insects they find. Before the August weaning they will probably weigh more than 30 pounds and may weigh twice that before the sow takes them back into a den with her for another winter. She breeds only in alternate years. The following spring she will be receptive to a male. The yearlings, ignored by the sow and intimidated by the boar, will leave.

The spring awakening is gradual. A bear is often so groggy that it returns to the den once or twice. Then it nibbles a few sprouts and goes immediately to water, drinking great quantities probably to start digestion and metabolism functioning normally. Favored spring foods include grasses, willows, snowlilies, starchy bulbs, skunk cabbage, the cambium of pines and firs, carcasses of winter-killed animals exposed as the snow melts. Buds, roots, and herbs are found on the slopes; ants, beetles, and grubs at lower elevations. Occasionally a bear can dig out a small rodent or a hibernating chuck. Later there will be honey, honeycombs, and bees, and berries—not only bearberries but any variety that can be found. A black bear may come across an unprotected deer fawn or an elk or moose calf, but the species is not an adept predator. Its meat consists mostly of rodents, frogs, lizards, insects, and carrion. A bear will try to eat almost anything. It will attack a porcupine, though if it takes many quills about the mouth it may be doomed to starvation. The black bear is no angler like the grizzly but can supplement its diet with dead fish and near-dead spawners. In the fall it consumes grapes, cherries, great quantities of acorns, pine and fir seeds, and what-ever nuts are available. A beech grove is often a good place to start hounds or look for sign.

Black bears are nocturnal only where hunting pressure makes them so, but they do bed down to escape heat, usually in a secluded timber thicket and preferably with a slope to the immediate rear. Dozing with its back to a talus slide, a bear is difficult to approach undetected, and can be equally difficult to find behind a screen of brush and trees. The bed is usually just a leafy nest or a shallow depression, a foot or so deep and a yard across, scooped out for the sake of coolness. If food is plentiful a bear may return repeatedly to the same thicket, though not always to the same bed. In such areas, black bears establish trails that follow the line of easiest travel. If there is plenty of sign, a hunter may want to take a stand overlooking a trail, a bedding area, or a stream or pond where tracks show that bears have been coming daily to drink, wallow, and swim.

But still-hunting is largely a matter of luck, even in a promis-ing stretch of forest. The difficulty lies in the acuteness of a black bear's sense of hearing and smell. In spite of its poor eyesight, it will seldom let a hunter come near. While camping near Wakeman Sound in lower British Columbia, the author stalked a tremendous black bear four times without success. The bear was sunning itself, sprawled belly down on a high, grassy bluff that formed a lawn before a deserted trapper's cabin. Below were mud flats, pebble beaches, and tidal waters. To the rear were dry, brushy woods that could not be stalked quietly. But on one side was a downwind corridor of sand and boulders between the water and tall, overhanging balsams, a perfect avenue for a silent, crouching approach. Each stalk was slow and careful and ended about 500 yards from the bear, when the wind abruptly shifted or an imperceptible flutter of breeze carried scent to the game. The bear rose, stood on its hind legs to look about and sniff, then retreated into the woods for an hour. Finally, there seemed to be no choice but to find a hiding place within range and wait for the bear. It did not return.

The same bear, or one equally black and huge, grazed on a neighboring ribbon of beach the next morning, swinging its head like a scythe and then resting with long strands of whis-kery beach grass drooping from both sides of its snout. The wind was right for an approach by canoe, and the bear, looking in our direction, gave no sign of seeing us. But as the rifle came up, the stock lightly bumped the gunnel. The bear spun away—pirouetted on its right hind foot—and leaped atop a 6-foot heap of driftwood and slash that abutted a low bluff. It was hard to comprehend how such a great hulk of beast, a shaggy black wine cask on short, thick legs, could jump so high and gracefully from a standing position. It jumped again, onto the wooded bluff, and took with it all hope of a shot. A better hunting tactic might have been to take a stand on a downwind promontory with a view of the narrow beach. A walk to the nearest promontory would have spooked any bears within hearing, but they probably would have returned before evening, and a 500-pound black bear is worth a very long wait.

Many of the southern hunters who watch for hounds to run a bear past their swamp-forest stands show a logical partiality to No. 0 or 00 buckshot in a 12-gauge shotgun with a full choke. A treed bear can be quickly dispatched with a .357, .41, or .44 Magnum handgun. Most black bears are probably killed by deer rifles, and any of the more powerful ones will suffice. For reasons of safety, a humane kill, and confidence that a bullet through the shoulder or in the chest cavity will result in a trophy, rather than a lost cripple, the caliber and bullet weight should provide at least a couple of thousand foot-pounds of energy at 100 yards. On that basis a .270 is about minimum on a planned bear hunt, and most of the .30 calibers will serve nicely. Something can be said for an open or aperture sight in very dense timber, but a 2½-power scope is normally better.

In selecting a stand it is well to try for elevation not only to keep scent high but because a large bear is going to roll—or run—downhill. Being in its way is inadvisable. Dressing and skinning should always be left to the guide. If a bear is taken on a local guideless hunt, the basic dressing procedure is the same as for a large deer. Skinning is more difficult. Slit from the chest toward one corner of the mouth, then from the rectal area of the belly out along the inner surface of each hind leg to the pads and from the chest out along the inner surface of each foreleg. Skin around the pads and turn the pelt inside out to unjoint the claws, which should remain on the robe. Proper skinning of a head is so delicate that—in spite of advice found in many hunting books—it is best left to a taxidermist if no guide is present. Simply sever the head at the axial joint, as with a deer, and let it remain in the skin. Fist and pare the hide away from the fat of the carcass. A sharp caping knife is excellent for the purpose. After removing all fat, salt the flesh side of the robe liberally and roll it up. A small or medium bear can sometimes be dragged out on a travois, but even if a vehicle or pack horses wait close by, a heavy bear will have to be quartered and packed out.

TRACKS & SIGN: Bears are plantigrade animals that walk with their toes pointed in somewhat and produce large prints with their sole pads. They have five toes on each foot. A black bear of medium size leaves a foreprint about 4 inches long and 5 inches wide. Its hind feet have much longer sole pads; prints are the same width as the foreprints but about twice as long, narrowing toward the rear. They look as if they were made by a moccasined man with very broad, flat feet. The walking stride measures about 12 inches and makes a double row of tracks with the left hind print a few inches ahead of the left foreprint, then the right hind print ahead of the right foreprint. A round dot is sometimes visible behind the main portion of the foreprint, rather like the mark of a dewclaw. This is because the forepad is analogous to the ball of a human foot, and there is a small pad behind it, higher up—a vestigial heel. A grizzly's tracks are

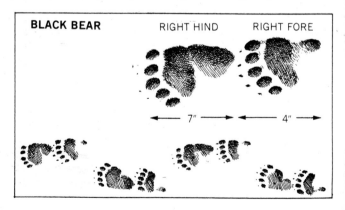

BLACK BEAR   RIGHT HIND   RIGHT FORE

← 7" →   ← 4" →

usually much larger, and its long claws stab the ground far ahead of the toes. A black bear's relatively short claws print closer to the toes or sometimes not at all.

Bear scat is roughly cylindrical (unless a heavy berry diet results in an almost liquid mass), and a black bear's droppings are likely to be an inch or an inch and a half in diameter. Often they show animal hair, insect husks, nutshells, fruit seeds, or root and grass fibers.

Hide is one of the few foods a black bear can leave alone. When it feeds on a kill or on carrion, it tries to peel the hide back, leaving pieces of skin with head and feet attached. Such leavings are a probable sign of bear.

Beds are so secluded and well-screened that the shallow depressions or brushy nests are not often found, but signs of feeding are common: broken fruit-tree branches, torn-up berry bushes or patches, logs or stones flipped over in the search for insects, decaying stumps or logs torn apart for grubs, excavated ant hills or rodent burrows, ground ripped up for roots, trees girdled or with large slabs of bark vertically pulled away (usually near ground level) for the cambium underneath.

There are two other types of "bear trees." One is the familiar clawed and bitten trunk. Tooth marks are usually vertical and may be as high as a bear can reach when standing upright on the ground. Claw marks may reach still higher. They are often diagonal but may be vertical or sometimes horizontal—long slashes that probably help a bear sharpen and clean its claws, assert itself, and perhaps leave a scent message to attract the opposite sex or warn away smaller bears of the same sex. New marks are obvious, whether neat or oozing sap. Old ones dry up and scab over; on smooth aspen bark they form dark welted scars. Another kind of bear tree is one used by shedding animals in spring to rub away annoying loose hair and relieve itching. When a bear finds a good tree, with deeply furrowed or shaggy bark, any other bears that pass are likely to use the same tree. They are probably attracted by scent. A heavily used bear trail may show depressions in a zigzagging line, where generations of bears have trod in one another's prints, and to one side may be a well-tufted rubbing tree. Bear pelts are no longer prime when tree rubbing becomes frequent, but bears are hunted that late in the spring in some regions.

Swamp, meadow, and beach grasses are often scythed off rather evenly by feeding bears, but patches of skunk cabbage in swamps or at streamside may be chopped up as if the plant intoxicated the bear (as frostbitten and fermenting berries actually may on occasion). Skunk cabbage is a favorite food.

VOICE: A hunter confronted by a coughing, grunting, or jaw-chopping, teeth-clicking bear is a hunter in imminent danger of attack. Bears make many other sounds—cubs whimper and bawl, fighting adults roar and snarl—but a lone bear is habitually silent, and a bear is usually alone when found by a hunter.

Grizzly Bear (Ursus arctos horribilis)

&AlaskanBrownBear(Ursus arctos middendorffi)

COMMON & REGIONAL NAMES: For grizzly—*silvertip, roachback, interior grizzly, bruin.* For Alaskan brown bear—*brown bear, big brown bear, Kodiak bear, brown grizzly, coastal grizzly.*

DESCRIPTION & DISTRIBUTION: In Montana, in southwestern British Columbia, or up in the Talkeetnas below Mount McKinley, a 450-pound grizzly is considered to be in the trophy class. Russell Annabel, an outfitter-guide of long experience and success, has written that 600 pounds is about the usual limit near the headwaters of the Healy River, a little farther to the north in the Alaska Range. These are not the largest of the interior grizzlies, though they are formidable, and they would be driven from the choice fishing pools by the dominant 750-pound coastal bears that gather along the McNeil River in July and August. When the salmon come in from Cook Inlet to spawn in the McNeil and other streams at the head of the Alaska Peninsula, more grizzlies collect there than anywhere in Alaska—more, therefore, than anywhere on the continent—though they are nearly rivaled in size and numbers by the bears of Admiralty Island, off Juneau, in the Alexander Archipelago. Largest of all but no longer so numerous are the great brown bears of Kodiak Island, just below Cook Inlet. One of those huge Alaskan browns was said to weigh 1,656 pounds—perhaps an exaggeration, but not by much.

An old boar grizzly, lifting his head out of the meadow barley and rising upright on his hind legs, may stand 9 or possibly 10 feet tall as he tests the breeze sifting up from the Kodiak beaches. When he resumes grazing, the hump of muscle atop his shoulders may be 4 feet from the ground, and his length from nose to almost tailless rump may be twice that measurement. If he has lived eight or nine summers, he probably weighs between 800 and 1,200 pounds. Some whales grow larger, as do several herbivorous land mammals, but there can be no definitive answer as to whether the brown grizzly or the polar bear is the world's most immense land-dwelling carnivore. Each is the most fearsome creature of its realm.

The four greatest trophies in the most recent Boone and Crockett listings are all male brown bears from Kodiak. The skull measurement of the largest, killed by Roy Lindsley in 1952, is $17^{15}/_{16}$ by $12^{13}/_{16}$ inches. The four largest interior grizzlies in the listings are all from British Columbia, and their measurements are nearly as imposing. Near Alexis Creek in 1970, Doug Edmon shot one whose skull measured $17^{1}/_{16}$ by 10 inches.

Because of size and characteristic color—some shade of brown or tan rather than a silver-tipped grizzly hue—the bears of the Alaskan islands and coasts were for some time described as a separate species and are still best-known as Alaskan brown bears. They are the largest of grizzlies, but a few miles inland they breed with others, intergrading in size, varying in color, causing difficulty in separating the two subspecies. Both types are of the same species as European and Asian grizzlies, having come over the isthmus that once joined Alaska to Siberia.

A century and a half ago, grizzlies ranged from the upper rim of North America down into Mexico and from the Pacific shores eastward to Ohio. Naturalists attempted to classify as many as eighty-six subspecies, most of which were evidently no more than local variations hardly meriting separate status. The smallest was the Sonora grizzly of Mexico and the Southwest, a variety comparable to the black bear. The largest, aside from the Alaskan brown, was the Tejon, or California, grizzly, which ultimately proved to be the same animal as the plains grizzly—the prototype that first came to be known as the silvertip. Both are now extinct and the remaining races are classified only as the interior grizzly *(U. a. horribilis)* and the Alaskan brown bear, or coastal grizzly *(U. a. middendorffi)*.

Grizzlies are wanderers. They require more open space and a slightly larger home range than black bears, and cannot adapt as well to man's proximity. Ironically, they can be more or less tamed if born in captivity or acquired as young cubs, and performing bears are invariably Asian or European grizzlies, yet in the wild they tend to be more ferocious and even less predictable than black bears. Where they have attacked human beings (with or without obvious provocation), revenge has some-

Silvertip grizzly bear.

times amounted to extermination.

However, it was the introduction of cattle and sheep that brought extinction to grizzlies over much of their former range. Like black bears, grizzlies are omnivorous, but they have a greater fondness for meat and are better able to kill relatively large prey, particularly such easy prey as domestic stock. Often they have been blamed for the slaying of stock when in reality they were only scavenging carcasses found on the range, but there have also been true outlaws that habitually raided livestock either because an injury hindered normal foraging or because a chance encounter with a domestic animal had revealed a plentiful food source. Cattlemen and sheepmen put a price on the head of any outlaw bear, and there were states that bountied all grizzlies. By the time the animals were accorded protection as game, they were gone from most of the United States.

Probably a few remain in Colorado's San Juan Mountains, but the species may be extinct there. In Idaho, fewer than a hundred are believed to wander the Bitterroot Mountains and the banks of the Snake River. A very small remnant group may still survive in Washington. Of the lower forty-eight states, only Montana and Wyoming now allow grizzly hunting, and in both it is tightly controlled by permit. A few hundred remain in the region, their population evidently stabilized by animals that wander out of the sanctuary of Yellowstone and Glacier parks. The morality of hunting grizzlies in either state is debatable, but they are sufficiently plentiful in areas to the northwest. Even in some parts of Alaska the bears—particularly the big coastal browns —have been severely persecuted by nervous ranchers. Yet in many sections they remain plentiful. At least 10,000 probably inhabit the state and a like number is estimated in British Columbia, where some game officials have privately wondered if a few relatively settled locales have too many bears for the remaining habitat. The Yukon and the Northwest Territories are the other regions where grizzly hunting is reasonably good and a sportsman can seek a trophy without fear of dooming the species.

Across this still-large range, grizzlies vary even more in color than in size. Some are true silvertips, while others are the color of taffy or chocolate, copper or bronze. Many of the Toklat grizzlies around Mount McKinley are pale blond. A few in Canada and the lower states are almost as dark as the blackest black

bear though never as glossy. The face of a typical grizzly is more concave in profile than that of a black bear, but the surest way to tell a small grizzly from a big black bear is by the grizzly's shoulder hump, which inspired the colloquial name "roachback."

GAME BEHAVIOR & HUNTING HABITAT: The Aleuts have a saying to the effect that a bear with his head down is unhappy, and a smart man stays away from an unhappy bear. When its head hangs lower than its shoulder, a grizzly is usually prepared to rush. Other threats of immediate hostility include coughing, woofing like a large dog, or salivating and jaw-popping.

It is not only the approach of a hunter that can rankle a bear. A big grizzly needs more food, more foraging space than a black bear—though the home range in lush habitat may be no more than a dozen square miles—and is even more solitary in habit, less tolerant of competition. Spawning salmon draw bears from many miles around, and crowding can occur at shallow riffles or little falls where the tiring fish become vulnerable. A bear makes its catch with a snap of the jaws or by pinning the fish with both forepaws and then dipping its head to grasp

Alaskan brown bear preying on spawning salmon.

the prize. Large, dominant boar grizzlies appropriate the spots where salmon have trouble climbing upstream. Less aggressive bears are driven back to less productive riffles, sometimes in savage battles involving tooth and claw but usually by bluff. Though sows are, on the average, much smaller than boars, a sizable sow with cubs can sometimes evict a boar.

Still, the salmon streams and the high berry patches near them offer outstanding chances for a careful hunter. Chum salmon spawn in the little McNeil and neighboring streams during summer. Though part of the area is a sanctuary where no shooting is permitted, hunting is excellent beyond the refuge, and Alaska's grizzly hunting season generally lasts from the beginning of September through about the first week in July. A grizzly has lost its prime winter pelt by July, of course, but in September, when the fur is thickening again, the coho are running on Kodiak and in many of the Alaskan and Canadian coastal streams. Runs are in progress in some portion of grizzly country from June to October. In recent years, British Columbia has generally opened the season at the beginning of September and again in the spring. The season in the Northwest Territories lasts from mid-July to mid-November, and it begins and ends about two weeks later in the Yukon.

Generally, when a bear emerges from its den on some high mountain slope it seeks the new grass shoots wherever snow has receded from a meadow, and supplements these with ants, grubs, trout, or char if it can find any, the carcasses of winter-killed animals, and an occasional ground squirrel or marmot. Like a black bear, it works its way to the lowlands for skunk cabbage, beach rye, fiddleheads and other ferns, bulbs, tubers, and assorted grasses, which it devours in tremendous quantities.

As all sorts of berries ripen in the summer, bears eat enormous helpings, and occasionally grizzlies will congregate uneasily at a high, open berry patch, as they do along fishing streams. A guide knows his country well, and he has good reason if he prefers to leave the rivers and glass the open mountain slopes and bushy swales. Among the grizzly's other favorite foods are wild oats, horsetail, grapes, pine seeds, nuts and acorns, spruce cambium, alder bark, aspen leaves and twigs.

In the fall, when a grizzly may acquire a 6-inch layer of fat before denning up, not even a copious seed and mast crop can totally meet its need for food. Ground squirrels and yellow-bellied or hoary marmots are then sought avidly, and a bear becomes more than usually reluctant to abandon any larger kill or piece of carrion before it is consumed. A hungry grizzly will attack an adult animal, but success is no more than sporadic, though it can make a rush at 30 miles an hour. It therefore caches what meat it cannot consume at one time. Often it digs a shallow depression, then rolls the kill in and covers it with a high mound of branches, earth, or any available debris. The hunter who finds a grizzly's cache ought to assume that the bear is not far off.

November or December is denning time in the lower part of the range if the weather is mild, but in the harsh North bears may be gone by late October. Unlike blacks, grizzlies seek high country for denning, often near or above the timber line on a well-drained slope. A natural cave will suffice, but more often the bear digs its own capacious den or enlarges a cave, scattering earth at the entrance to form a mound like an alluvial fan, perhaps 2 feet high and 6 feet wide. A tunnel 4 feet high and almost as wide is conspicuous before snow falls, but it is apt to be in remote mountains, and, when situated on a north slope to catch insulating snow, it may soon be buried under a 6-foot drift. A safe, warm den is used in some instances for winter after winter. During a rare, unseasonably warm spell grizzlies have been known to emerge for a short while since they are no more true hibernators than the black bears, but they are apt to remain denned until April or May—late in May if the climate is severe.

By then the breeding season has begun in some regions, though the mating peak may extend into mid-July in the North. In matters of breeding, prolonged gestation involving delayed implantation, and birth there are no substantial differences between the grizzly and the black (see *Black Bear*). For either species the average number of cubs is two. However, grizzly cubs develop at a slower rate, are less adept at climbing, lose the climbing ability before they are yearlings, and have greater need of the sow's protection. Sometimes she permits them to den with her for an extra winter and does not breed again until the third year rather than the second. Though the animals are sexually mature by their fourth spring, they grow until they are eight or nine years old, or even older, and have begot several litters of their own.

Despite the sow's fierce defense, an occasional cub may be killed by an irascible boar grizzly or by a wolf or cougar. But existence is no longer very hazardous when a lone yearling weighs 150 pounds or more. Mortality is relatively low and life expectancy in the wild is at least fifteen years, perhaps closer to twenty. Disease is infrequent, recuperative ability phenomenal, external parasites uncommon. Internal parasites include roundworms, hookworms, tapeworms, flukes, and the like. Since there is also a chance that a bear may harbor trichina nematodes, its flesh must be well-cooked. The vicious steel bear traps have been abolished, and a healthy, uninjured grizzly that reaches full size has nothing to fear except the rifleman.

To kill such a brute cleanly, as humanely as possible, and to prevent the likelihood of escape or attack requires a large, heavy bullet that transmits great energy upon impact and penetration. Nothing less than a .30-06 is recommended. Good choices include the several .300 Magnums, the .308 Norma Magnum (but not the standard .308), the .338, .358 Norma, the heavy Weatherby Magnums, and even the .375 H&H. A 2½-power or variable-power scope is needed, even on a spawning stream in late afternoon when fishing activity seems to be most intense. Like a great deal of northwestern hunting, the search for grizzlies often entails riding all the open terrain a horse can negotiate and then walking where no mount can proceed, glassing the slopes and swales. A bear is as likely to be shot at 250 yards as at 50, and it may appear at close quarters in an unexpected encounter or may first be sighted at a tremendous distance.

There is nothing unusual about finding a wide, clear trail stretching across a huge meadow or open valley, for all the world like a human path except that it may be deeply pitted or rutted. In familiar territory a guide may head directly for such a trail between feeding and resting or watering spots, but finding one—even if it is marked with fresh tracks and droppings—does not do away with the probable necessity of spotting, sizing up, and perhaps shooting at distant game. In addition to the telescopic sight, equipment includes a 7- or 8-power binocular with a wide field of view and a high-powered spotting scope.

TRACKS & SIGN: Finding trails and sign can be very helpful

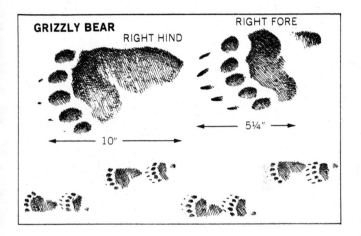

in determining approximately where a bear is feeding or hiding, but following tracks can be disheartening. A grizzly periodically swings off to check its back trail from windward. Its eyesight is as poor as the black's, but its hearing and scenting ability are probably even keener. If it hears or scents a hunter, it may circle back out of curiosity and actually toy with the enemy. Many hunters have been trailed by the grizzly they were trailing or have passed within 20 feet of a hidden bear they thought to be up ahead. Tracking is either cautious or dangerous.

The hind track of a large Alaskan brown bear can be 10 inches wide at the front and nearly 17 inches long; its forepaw leaves a print perhaps half as long but equally wide. The hind print of a good-sized grizzly of the interior may be about 10 or 12 inches long and 7 or 8 inches wide at the front, where it broadens. (The late Larry Koller, an eminent hunting writer, once found the track of an Alaskan brown bear that measured 16 inches long, 10 inches wide, and was sunk 2 inches into hard sand; this author has placed both of his booted feet in the hind track of a British Columbia grizzly on a soft mud slick.) The hind claws register only occasionally, and the long, relatively straight foreclaws print far in front of the toe pads. In other respects the tracks look like those of a black bear (see page 568) but much enlarged. The stride averages about 2 feet in

Bear scat in grassy feeding area (top l.), aspen scarred by bear claws (top r.), and tracks of male (l.) and female brown bear (bottom).

length but stretches to 8 or 9 at a bounding run.

Where snow piles up during hunting season, a wide, deep slide is occasionally gouged by a grizzly tobogganing down a slope on its haunches. Savage as grizzlies are, they also tend to be playful. A more frequent sign is a torn-up berry patch, a raggedly rooted patch of ground, or a gaping hole where a bear has dug for rodents. Yet more common is the wide, deep trail through high grass, visible at long distance and, upon close inspection, revealing round pits 8 or 9 inches across and as much as 6 inches deep, pounded by years of treading.

Grizzly scat is usually cylindrical (though it can mass in areas of succulent feed) and is often more than 2 inches in diameter. Like black-bear scat, it frequently shows husks, fibers of vegetation, animal hair, and similar rough matter. Overturned rocks, torn logs, and bark-stripped or girdled trees also resemble black-bear sign.

Beds, or "nests," are most often in thickets. They tend to be oval depressions perhaps a foot deep, more than a yard across, and about 50 inches long, matted with leaves, needles, and sometimes boughs of lodgepole or some other evergreen. Tufts of hair cling to rubbing trees, and some trees show spots polished smooth after use during several seasons or by many bears. On clawed and bitten bear trees, the deepest, widest tooth marks are seldom much higher than a man's head, but the claw slashes may be twice as high. Just below a fish ladder somewhere near Thompson Inlet in lower British Columbia there is a massive leaning balsam trunk, its top smashed away in some squall, with claw slashes 12 feet from the ground.

VOICE: Cubs whimper and bawl. Adults roar and snarl when fighting. But hunters seldom locate a grizzly by sound, for it is a quiet animal. Coughs, low woofs, grunts, and jaw-popping sounds are a final threat before an attack.

Polar Bear *(Ursus maritimus;* also classified as *Thalarctos maritimus)*
COMMON & REGIONAL NAMES: *ice bear, snow bear, white bear.*

DESCRIPTION & DISTRIBUTION: Napping among the tilted pressure ridges of an ice field, a polar bear looks like a wind-rounded, shadowed drift of snow. Thirty or 40 yards off, the ice is tattered with red and black, the remains of a hair seal. The blubber has been stripped away, the snow littered with shards of hide and bone, but part of the carcass has been left intact. Two small arctic foxes, whiter than the bear, gnaw ravenously at the mound of dark flesh. They, too, have black eyes and noses, and fresh blood reddens their muzzles. The bear, having taken what it wants, ignores them. It rises, yawns, snaps its thick jaws shut, stretches a neck that seems somewhat long for a bear, momentarily turns its tapered head toward its abandoned kill, sniffs the air, and ambles away at a fast, shuffling walk.

At noon an Eskimo guide in a bulky parka halts his dogs not far from the ragged outer edge of the ice field, miles offshore, and points to a dim trail that crosses a dune of wind- and current-packed ice. The hunter accompanying him is gazing seaward at an irregular line of shadow that splits into two dark cracks near the horizon, treacherous open leads. The Eskimo taps the hunter's parka with a heavily mitted hand and, grinning, tells him not to worry. He points again at a blurred print. The hunter can make out vague pad and toe marks in the thin mantle of powder. An ice bear's hairy paws leave indistinct outlines that may soon be erased by the wind, but the hunter can see that the tracks are larger and rounder than those of his mukluks. A little later the guide grunts and nods almost in the direction of his sled's trail, back toward a village at Eskimo Point, on the shore of Hudson Bay in the Northwest Territories. The hunter, straining to see some telltale spot or shadow in the white distance, wonders if his goggles have failed to prevent the onset of snow blindness. Then he sees the bear, ivory-white, trotting between upheaved chunks of slab ice. But it has already seen or smelled the men. It stops short and veers northward into a maze of pressure ridges. The guide only grins again, sure that the bear will head toward open water to hunt seals, almost as sure that he and the hunter can head the animal off without venturing too near the rot of ice at the edge of the lead. They will hide the dogs and sled behind a ridge. The hunter, peering upwind over the top, will perhaps first see the black traces of eyes, nose, lip line. But he will wait until the white body, jogging against a whiter background, is clear in the scope and slow enough and close enough to reveal the rippling, shaggy texture of thick fur.

If the bear is a mature male, it is probably 8 feet long and stands 4 feet high at the shoulder. It weighs between 800 and 1,100 pounds. The heaviest Canadian polar bear yet recorded was a 1,450-pound male, immobilized by narcotic darts from a tranquilizer gun for examination and tagging in the fall of 1970. It was encountered a hundred miles below Cape Churchill, Manitoba, on the western side of Hudson Bay. Several larger ones, killed in the arctic seas, have been reported to weigh about 1,600 pounds. It is possible that most of the giants inhabit the ice packs of the Chukchi Sea and the Bering Strait. Alaskan guide-outfitters ply the area, operating out of Kotzebue, Point Hope, Cape Lisburne, and as far north as Point Barrow. The three best trophies in recent Boone and Crockett listings were all taken off Kotzebue. The skull of the largest, shot by Shelby Longoria in 1963, measures $18^8/_{16}$ by $11^7/_{16}$ inches. Some of the largest polar bears outweigh the broader-skulled Alaskan brown bears. Fortunately, a mature female seldom weighs 800 pounds. Females and cubs are protected by regulations which would be impossible to enforce but for the fact that a hunter can take only one bear and he wants the largest animal his guide and he can find.

A polar bear's paws are comparable to those of an Alaskan brown bear, but the pads are smaller, almost haired over. Stiff hairs on the soles provide insulation and traction. The claws, short but sharp, also grip the ice or slick snow when the bear runs. A slightly pear-shaped taper of body and head is admirably suited to a large swimming animal; polar bears normally swim no faster than about 5 miles an hour but can probably achieve much greater speed, particularly underwater, can remain submerged for a couple of minutes before coming up for air, and can swim farther than any other large four-footed mammal. They have been known to go more than 40 miles without resting and have been seen hundreds of miles out in the open sea. Many of the males spend most or all of their adult lives on the sea ice, often beyond all international boundaries, and they seldom, if ever, den up. Insulated by thick fat and by an extremely dense undercoat of fur combined with thick, long guard hairs, the species seems completely impervious to cold. The fur, though it frequently has a faint yellowish cast, appears pure white at a distance. White is essential camouflage for a ponderous stalker of northern seals.

The circumpolar range is for the most part restricted to the arctic seas, islands, and coasts, though polar bears live as far south as Labrador and on the coastlands of James Bay, at the lower end of Hudson Bay. A global warming trend is slowly but unremittingly shrinking the polar bear's range, for the animal is adapted to a very cold environment. Pollution of northern waters by mercury and pesticides also menaces the species, as it subsists on prey and carrion that can accumulate dangerously concentrated poisons. An even greater danger until recently has been uncontrolled killing for meat, for the valuable hides, and for trophies. In 1965, after a severe decline in numbers became evident, a conference was held at Fairbanks, Alaska, by the nations possessing polar-bear habitat: the United States, Canada, Denmark, Norway, and Russia. International cooperation in research and protection is slowly taking effect.

Russia currently permits no polar-bear hunting at all, though poaching is believed to persist. Trapping, poisoning, and set-gunning are illegal but will continue as long as bear rugs bring high prices in Oslo shops. At this writing Norway still allows the use of seagoing boats not merely for the justifiable purpose of scouting but as shooting platforms from which to kill swimming bears. In the water, a bear's size is sometimes impossible to judge; females and juveniles are inevitably killed.

However, the situation has improved vastly in Alaska and Canada. For several years guides commonly scouted from ski-equipped aircraft, then landed nearby for a quick stalk or an ambush. In some instances one plane came down and a second plane flew low to drive a bear toward the waiting hunter. Such hunts hardly qualified as sport, regardless of an element of danger in flying over ice fields and landing on them. The Boone and Crockett Club discouraged the practice by disqualifying any trophy taken with the aid of aircraft, and in 1972 Alaska banned aerial hunting. A stringent permit system has been established, and the hunters travel out on the ice floes by dog sled or snowmobile. Under certain conditions, snowmobiles also may detract from the sport. Unfortunately, a few Eskimo guides use the machines for travel and pursuit while their dogs—no longer needed for sledding—chase and bay the bears.

Eventually snowmobiles may have to be banned for hunting polar bear in Alaska as they have been in the Northwest Territories. Elsewhere in Canada only Eskimos and Indians may shoot polar bears, but there each native village is allowed a yearly quota, and the Eskimos themselves can fill the limit or, under a special permit system, can guide nonresident sportsmen whose kills count in the quota. A hunting fee of $2,500 goes in part to the guide and hunting assistants, in part to a council for community use. Travel must be by dog sled, and the guest is offered no guarantee of a shot, but hē may hunt for as long as three weeks. A high success ratio is maintained without depleting the bear population.

Some authorities have estimated that North American polar bears number no more than about 10,000. The figure is probably conservative in the extreme, despite danger of extinction for the subspecies of Labrador's coast (the only place where polar bears fish for spawning salmon in the manner of grizzlies) and the subspecies of eastern Greenland. In contrast, ice bears on the western edge of Hudson Bay seem to be increasing. With the precise number of subspecies still uncertain, game biologists are studying geographic races that can be differentiated by blood characteristics and skull dimensions. In Canada, which now has the highest population of polar bears, old theories are being revised as a result of research using aerial surveys, tagging, and radio tracking by the Canadian Wildlife Service. Most of the global population was thought to be fluid in range, for polar bears appear aimlessly nomadic and many are carried vast distances on ice fields that shift across the arctic with dominant ocean currents. Tagging has now proved that Alaskan polar bears do not wander into Canada, nor is there a mixing of the Hudson Bay and James Bay groups.

But it is true that Hudson Bay polar bears come ashore as the ice melts in late summer, then move northward in early autumn, gathering on headlands and islands near shore until freeze-up, when they move out onto the ice to hunt seals. Thus the hunting season in the Northwest Territories (from the beginning of October through May) coincides with the heaviest influx of bears. In Alaska (where the season lasts from mid-October through May) hunting is best from February through March. The theory is that in spring the shifting ice fields carry many Alaskan

(text continued on page 593)

▲ Cinnamon black-bear sow with cub.   ▼ Yearling Alaskan brown bear.

▲ Male Alaskan grizzly. ▼ Massive head of mature grizzly. ▶ Polar bears.

▲ Cow bison, juvenile, and calves. ▼ Herd of plains bison.

Barren-ground caribou migrating. ▼ Perfect chance to take barren-ground trophy.

▼ Elk bed and tracks.　▼ Whistling for elk.

▲ Royal bull elk with cows.   ▼ Culmination of stalk for bull elk.

▲ Eastern bull moose in Canada.   ▼ Shiras, or Wyoming, moose in Montana.

bears to Siberia's northern coasts and that the currents return them to Alaska in the winter.

GAME BEHAVIOR & HUNTING HABITAT: Little is yet known about the polar bear's life cycle in its remote natural habitat. There is no certainty, for instance, about the normal age of weaning in an environment without plants or small prey for cubs and yearlings. Sows breed every two or three years. Mating usually takes place far out on the ice floes in spring or early summer, and gestation requires about eight months. A sow first breeds when she is less than four years old, long before she has stopped growing. Apparently only pregnant sows normally den up, coming inland in November or December and digging into hard-packed drifts or nestling into spaces beneath tilted pressure ridges. The cubs—most often twins—are born in late December or January, and most of them probably weigh less than a pound at birth.

Polar bear in characteristic swimming attitude.

One of the world's largest denning areas, on the lowlands of Hudson Bay and James Bay, remained undiscovered until 1969. It is the only known region where polar bears den in earth rather than snow. They dig to the permafrost, excavating large caves in peat hummocks and in lake and stream banks. The area is very far south for polar bears, and it is believed that the same permafrost dens are used for cooling off in warm weather. No large denning areas have been found in Alaska, so the origin of the state's white bears remains a mystery; perhaps they drift from Siberia on the ice.

Since a bear of any species may possibly carry trichinosis, the meat should be thoroughly cooked (and polar-bear liver must not be eaten by man or dog since its concentrated vitamin A content is toxic). Parasites and diseases are uncommon among bears living in isolation in a frigid environment. A few are slain by killer whales, still fewer in reckless attempts to prey on large bull walruses or musk oxen. With no significant enemy but man, life expectancy in the wild is probably fifteen to twenty years.

A female with young breaks open her snowed-over den some time between late March and early May. When her rich milk has nourished the cubs for about four months, they each weigh 20 or 25 pounds and are thickly furred and able to follow her onto the sea ice.

In the second year, when the young look nearly as large as the mother, she may abandon them and breed again. Adults remain alone most of the time but will gather about a beached whale or other feast of carrion. During their northward meanderings in October and November, several dozen sometimes gather at dumps outside of two small towns at Cape Churchill, and they are dangerous. They probably regard any relatively dark animal, man included, as possible food. They are unpredictable, they may have less fear than bears in areas of denser human habitation, and, like grizzlies, they are easily angered by interference with their feeding. Among themselves they seem somewhat more tolerant than grizzlies but do exhibit a vague order of dominance while gathered at a feeding site.

Once believed to be strictly carnivorous, polar bears eat some vegetation when it is available. They also eat fish, crustaceans, assorted carrion, and perhaps any land or water animal they can catch and kill. Hair seals are their staple.

It is because of seals that the hunting for polar bears is best near the rims of ice packs. A bear cannot catch a seal in the water so it searches for one resting on the ice. If a polar bear's small, low-set ears are not especially efficient, it has far better eyesight than other bears and will investigate any dark object it sees. Relying on extremely acute scenting ability, it may also locate prey hidden by drifts and ridges. When a seal is found dozing near the brink, the bear slips into the water, swims toward it silently, and suddenly heaves up onto the flow to kill the prey with a smashing blow. If the seal is using a plunge hole far from the floe's edge, the bear attempts a low-bellied stalk. Some authorities deny that a polar bear will use a paw to hide its black nose, but the species has been observed to pause during a stalk with one paw in front of the face so that its white camouflage is almost total. If no seal is found, the bear may settle beside a plunge hole and wait patiently in ambush.

The bear, in turn, is hunted by men who scout the floes or wait in ambush. Drifts and pressure ridges notwithstanding, long shots sometimes must be taken over wide, flat ice fields; a polar bear is too intelligent to proceed incautiously if it detects possible danger. A scope of 2½-power or slightly greater magnification is needed—2½–4-power variable scopes are favored by some trophy hunters—and many guides recommend sighting in at 200 yards. Also recommended are the same powerful calibers used for the largest grizzlies (see page 577). The rifle can be lubricated with graphite or some other preparation designed for arctic shooting since ordinary oil thickens in very cold weather and causes an action to stick.

White-camouflaged polar-bear hunter.

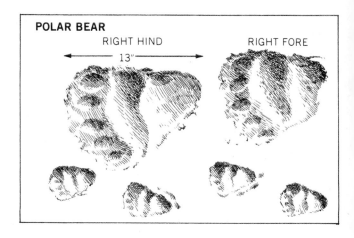

POLAR BEAR

RIGHT HIND   RIGHT FORE

← 13" →

TRACKS & SIGN: A polar bear's droppings are like a big grizzly's: large, dark, cylindrical. More often than not, scat and tracks are snowed over, and no prints are formed on hard ice, but a bear track on a floe is certain to be a polar bear's. The prints are like those of large grizzlies but blurred by hair and rounder; a hind track measuring a foot long, for instance, might well have a width of 9 inches or so.

Other sign may reveal that polar bears are about. Since they devour a seal's blubber but sometimes leave a substantial portion of the flesh, a seal carcass is occasionally found. Fox tracks or the arctic foxes themselves may lead to a freshly abandoned kill, or at least indicate that a bear has recently been in the vicinity. Wheeling, screaming gulls may similarly disclose the location of a seal carcass or some type of carrion that would attract bears. In a manner of speaking, the outer edge of an ice field or any large break in it is a kind of sign when a bear has been glimpsed but lost, because a spooked polar bear usually heads for open water.

VOICE: Cubs whimper, whine, and sometimes utter a humming sound. Adults can roar or snarl when aroused. But sound is of little importance where it is frequently overwhelmed by grinding, creaking, crashing ice, groaning wind, raucous gulls. Both the bears and the men who hunt them must rely less on hearing than on sight.

Bison *(Bison bison)*
COMMON & REGIONAL NAMES: *buffalo, buff, American ox.*

DESCRIPTION & DISTRIBUTION: A lean young stockman and his hunting guest scan a hill half a mile to the east, beyond a flat sea of buffalograss, needlegrass, and gray sage. At first the hunter can make out only a pall of dust drifting slowly away over the crest and then, drifting with the dust, the brown-black splotches that are bison, forty or fifty in two loose groups. Several of the largest animals, the bulls, plod along in satellite fashion a few yards from the herd's fringe. It would be difficult to overtake them from the downwind side by crossing the open plain. The hunter and his host walk back to the ranch car and drive up onto a ridge that commands a view of the entire 11,000-acre Little Buffalo Ranch. Cloud Peak is visible 80 miles to the northwest in Wyoming's Big Horns. Spotting the herd again is easy on this vast, almost flat plateau. Making a close approach would be equally easy with the car, because on working ranches vehicles no longer alarm bison.

However, the hunter has no interest in driving up to kill a dim-witted mountain of beast as if it were a penned Hereford. Much later, above a water hole, he makes the approach on foot and then on hands and knees and finally slithering on his belly like the rattlers that may be active on as warm a day as this. In his arms he cradles a forked shooting stick cut from a dead tree limb and a .45-90 Model 1885 rifle. Eighty yards from the stolidly feeding herd, he plants the stick, rests the antique buffalo gun in the fork, with his fingers cushioning the forestock, centers the bead in the laddered aperture, and holds on the neck of a huge buffalo. The rancher-guide touches his shoulder to call off the shot, but the hunter has already stopped himself. A woolly calf, cocoa and russet, has trotted up beside the hump-shouldered beast. So much for the rule that cows are invariably small. The hunter shifts to another big animal, unmistakably masculine and in the clear, away from the herd. A wounded bison assumes it has been hurt by the nearest living thing. It may gore another bison or charge into the herd and cause a stampede. The hunter knows better than to try for the invisible heart and lung area in the immense arched slab of forequarters. He holds on the neck, a few inches below and behind the ear flicking under a black horn. The bull subsides, hindquarters first, and dust billows when the chest crashes into the ground.

On the plains, most of today's bison hunts roughly follow that pattern, though few sportsmen go to the length of using an antique or replica buffalo gun. There is a general public impression that because the bison never have recovered from the butchery of the late nineteenth century hunting them is criminal. But the plains are fenced and roaded, and the grasses that fed the immense dark herds are reserved for cattle. Of the bison hunted today, most are privately owned herds on ranches that must also support livestock (and in some cases other game, such as pronghorns). The ranchers, some of whom have contributed significantly to the preservation of the bison, must consider their herds in terms of harvest. Surplus animals are rounded up for sale to stockmen and meat packers. Bison meat is similar to beef but slightly richer and certainly superior in the form of rare steaks or roasts. Yet to anyone who has seen a wild buffalo bull raise his tufted tail and lower his head in final warning of hostility there is something demeaning about treating the herds as livestock. A kinder fate is selective trimming by trophy hunters whose fees help maintain some of the big, well-known ranches in Wyoming, Oregon, South Dakota, and Arizona.

State-owned herds must also be reduced periodically to the grazing capacity of the available range. Limited numbers of bison-hunting permits have been issued in some recent years by Arizona, Colorado, South Dakota, and Utah, but the opening of seasons has been irregular except in Alaska and the Northwest Territories.

In the 1930s, twenty-two animals were shipped from the National Bison Range in Montana and released in Alaska's Big Delta region, near the Copper River. Penetrating that wilderness with a pack train is more difficult, more sporting than the taking of the largest bull on the western prairies. The herd today numbers 250 or 300 and is protected by stringently limiting the permits for a short September season.

Straddling the border of Alberta and the Northwest Territories is a 17,300-square-mile wilderness where a few surviving bison were discovered shortly before the turn of the century. In 1922 the area was established as Wood Buffalo National Park. It remains almost roadless, and it supports 12,000 to 15,000 bison, more than any other single area. For a number of years hunters reduced the multiplying population by a hundred trophies annually, until a siege of anthrax ended the practice in the 1960s. Though park hunting has not been resumed at this writing, the herds are again overflowing park boundaries, and limited permits are issued by the Northwest Territories for a season that generally runs from mid-September through December. (Hunting on private ranches goes on throughout the year, but the bulls down on the plains are not very richly robed until October, when they have regained some of the weight lost during the rut.) Hunting in the region of the park has been excellent in recent years. The game reaches trophy size because experienced guide-outfitters, old buffalo hands like Stan Burrell, long ago established a policy of encouraging their hunters to be very selective.

At one time the herds of Wood Buffalo National Park and the Territories were exclusively wood bison *(B. b. athabascae),* the larger and darker of the two surviving subspecies. In the 1920s several thousand plains bison *(B. b. bison)* were released on the range in the hope that they, too, would prosper there. Unfortunately, only a few pure wood bison remain, the rest being an intermediate strain—hybrids.

Those in Alaska and the lower states are plains bison. The humped withers of a mature plains bull may be 5½ or 6 feet high. From nose to the tassel of a foot-and-a-half tail, he may measure 9½ to 11½ feet. He probably weighs between 1,400 and 1,800 pounds. Bison tend to be smaller in some herds, but an old bull on lush grassland may weigh over a ton. Though bison are sexually mature at the age of three, bulls usually grow until they are more than seven years old. Weight also varies with season; during the rut (August in the Far North, July and August on the plains) a herd bull sometimes loses 300 pounds. Most five-year-old cows weigh between 800 and 1,100 pounds and are unlikely to grow any heavier.

The wood bison is even more formidable. Bulls often weigh 2,500 pounds and occasionally 3,000. Cows average 1,500 or 1,600 pounds. The subspecies is the world's largest hoofed ani-

mal. Its head is bigger and broader than that of the plains bison, but a plains bison has an almost equal chance of appearing in the records because its horns are big and widely curved. First place in the Boone and Crockett listings has been held since 1925 by a Yellowstone bull killed by S. Woodring. The skull, exhibited at the Fishing Bridge Museum in Yellowstone National Park, has a tip-to-tip horn spread of 27 inches. Its outside spread is 35⅜ inches. The horns are over 21 inches long and have a basal circumference of about 16 inches. In recent years, trophies high in the listings have come from the Northwest Territories, Alaska's Copper River, and Gillette, Wyoming.

Whereas the wood bison is very dark, sometimes quite black, the plains bison is usually a rich chocolate, shading to blackish brown or black where the hair is long. The horns are wide, black crescents. On a young calf they are mere nubs, but they continue to grow throughout life—more slowly with the passing years.

The coat is so short from the chest rearward that in summer a bison occasionally looks almost hairless except for the cloak

Author stalking nervous herd of plains bison.

on its forequarters and over its head. The hair on the hump, chest, upper forelegs, neck, and forehead grows long, dark, and woolly. Beneath the chin there is a snow-sweeping beard up to a foot long on some specimens. Bison seldom paw through snow to reach grass; they swing their heads slowly from side to side as they inch forward, plowing through with their insulated foreheads and chins. They do not turn from a blizzard as other grazers must, but face into the storm, their densely coated heads and high forequarters shielding their bodies from cold and wind. The head padding also furnishes protection during the rut, a time of butting lunges when the low, massive head, the wide, high-humped shoulders, and the trim but powerful hindquarters combine to transform a bull into a live battering ram.

When French voyageurs described *"les boeufs"* (whence the misnomer "buffalo"), the herds were incredible. As late as the middle of the 19th century, 15 or 20 miles of tall-grass prairie might be dotted with loosely connected herds—perhaps half a million animals visible at once from some high elevation. The wood bison lived chiefly in mountainous and forested regions, from the eastern foothills of the Rockies almost to the Pacific. The far more numerous plains bison were primarily concentrated on the Great Plains, but their range extended to the Atlantic Ocean and from Mexico and Florida into Canada.

Man devastated the European bison—the wisent, or aurochs. The separate but related American species had long before crossed the Bering land bridge to a sprawling continent where Indians stampeded thousands of them over cliffs but, without guns or horses, could not deplete the population upon which they were dependent for food, clothing, rope, robes, glue, tools, shelter, and other needs. General Phil Sheridan equated dead bison with "discouraged Indians." President Grant's Secretary of the Interior advocated the extermination of buffalo as a means of subjugating hostile tribes. In 1871 a single St. Louis firm shipped 250,000 hides; 10,000 market shooters swarmed over the plains, some taking only the tongues of their kills; railroads shipped millions of pounds of bones for fertilizer, sugar refining, and the manufacture of bone china; and the railroad construction crews subsisted for months at a time on buffalo meat, as did some Army posts.

Some authorities claim there were 30 million bison (estimated on the basis of grazing capacity). Others believe there were over twice as many. By 1900 there were fewer than a thousand. A campaign of rescue and refuge was initiated by several organizations—the New York Zoological Society, the Smithsonian Institution, the American Bison Society, the National Audubon Societies, the American Museum of Natural History—and individual heroes—William T. Hornaday, Martin Garretson, Theodore Roosevelt, C. J. "Buffalo" Jones of Wyoming, Michel Pablo of Montana, Colonel Charles Goodnight of Texas. The buffalo nickel is no longer being minted; the thirty-cent buffalo postage stamp and the ten-dollar buffalo bill, a Federal bank note, are no longer being printed, but more than 30,000 buffalo still graze.

GAME BEHAVIOR & HUNTING HABITAT: In November, 1952, Grancel Fitz assisted John Connors, superintendent of the Fort Niobrara National Wildlife Refuge in Nebraska, in removing surplus bison from the range. Scouting the plains in a hunting car followed by a winch-equipped abattoir truck, the two men were able to get very close to the herds. This manner of hunting plains buffalo, though common on ranches, is more commendable as game management than as sport. Yet unexpected difficulties can arise. Fitz, one of the finest game shots of his time, missed a barren cow at 40 yards. He aimed a hand's breadth behind the ear but fired high, deceived by the thick wool in the dip of the neck. Even if his 220-grain .30-06 had struck but penetrated above the spine, the gigantic beast might have been insufficiently shocked to fall. Fitz also reported difficulty stalking on snow-covered ground to get a clear, reasonably close shot at the trophy bull he wanted. Bulls tend to be much more watchful and suspicious than cows. The eventual kill required more than one shot at a range of 100 yards or so, because the animal's spinal cord was located deceptively low in his huge neck. (It is best to aim a trifle low, perhaps severing jugular or windpipe if the spine is missed.)

The bull, which ranked sixteenth in the records at that time, probably weighed 2,200 pounds, as the weight of the dressed meat was 1,078 pounds. Dressing and skinning cuts the weight by about half.

Sometimes a buffalo herd detects a man silhouetted 2

miles away on a prairie horizon, but the animals have relatively poor vision and are stupid by comparison with other game. Relying chiefly on good hearing and scenting powers, they turn into the wind when they suspect but cannot locate danger. Market shooters used to sit or lie prone on a slope above a herd and, without moving from the spot, pick off every bison in sight. The animals fail to associate danger with the report or smoke of a rifle. If the shooter is much more than a hundred yards off, they may continue to graze while companions drop around them. The modern plains hunter may enhance his sport by limiting himself to difficult shots at only the finest bulls or by stalking close on foot.

Hunting bison in the Northwest Territories is more sporting. Their favored terrain near Wood Buffalo National Park is a mixture of open meadows, plains, marshes, muskegs, and rocky hills interspersed with sparse stands of pine and dense thickets of spruce, aspen, willow, and the like. A man can glass the open spaces with a 7x35mm binocular and a spotting scope until he finds a good trophy and then, on the way to it, experience a head-on encounter with a better (and sometimes more belligerent) bull in surprisingly thick timber. If bullet placement is difficult on the plains it is much more so in the woods.

A .30-06 has plenty of power if the bullet is placed within a couple of inches of the ideal spot rather than in the vaguely perceived center of the immense chest area. However, many trophy hunters prefer the .338, .350, or .375 Magnum, the .405, or the various calibers traditionally used for large African game. A .45-90 or a .50 Sharps in safe shooting condition is equally efficient, and the .45-70 has been revived effectively in modern rifles. An aperture sight will do for close stalking, but a 2½-power scope is recommended for precise bullet placement. The zeroing distance may be a hundred yards or twice that, depending on the hunting country.

A bison can gallop at more than 30 miles an hour, yet it is relatively easy game because its tremendous size and power are the only defenses it has had to evolve. In a hostile encounter with a very large grizzly a buffalo might possibly be defeated, and there was a time when wolves followed the herds. (In the North, wolves still cull the aged and a small percentage of calves.) But wolves, bears, and cougars rarely cause trouble for a full-

grown, healthy bison. The species is afflicted with most of the internal parasites common to ruminants and other grazers, and may contract brucellosis, tuberculosis, anthrax, or other bovine diseases. Still, bison have an average life span of fifteen or twenty years, and a few live much longer.

In late April or May, after a pregnancy of nine months or so, a typical cow bears a single orange or reddish-yellow, almost humpless calf that may weigh 30 pounds or as much as 70. Brown hair replaces the infant coat by autumn. (Albinos, the white buffalo sacred to the Plains Indians, have always been rare.) Though weaning is completed during the summer, a calf stays near its mother for protection until she calves again the following spring. Brief ramming, hooking battles erupt in summer between prime bulls—chiefly those from four to eight years of

age—but fatalities are uncommon and most injuries are minor. A herd bull collects as many cows as possible (sometimes several score of them). After breeding season, males and females tend to separate into loose groups. A few bulls may graze together, and nearby a dozen cows or seventy may convoy their calves. They spend most of the night standing or lying about at rest. They feed slowly but constantly from first light until late morning, then rest, chew their cud, perhaps go to water, and resume feeding in late afternoon. Forage, depending on region, includes bluestem and blue gramagrass, buffalograss, dropseed, saltbush, Indian grass, needlegrass, wheatgrass, broomsedge, vetch. They wallow in the dust of prairie-dog towns and, like pronghorns, graze on forbs that spring up where the dogs cut down less desirable vegetation.

Rutting bulls fighting for cows.

TRACKS & SIGN: Dry bison droppings, the buffalo chips that fueled the fires of Indians and pioneers where wood was scarce, look like the manure of domestic cattle. The tracks, too, look like those of cattle, though a mature bull leaves a somewhat larger, rounder hoofprint, measuring about 5 inches in diameter. Usually the cleft is visible, but sometimes on hard ground a print resembles that of an unshod horse.

In wooded habitat, some of the trees may be ringed with light-colored horn rubs where bark has been worn away. The ground beneath is likely to be trampled. If trees are lacking, trampled spots may show around boulders, but wallows are a more common sign on the plains. Near water, a wallow may be muddy (and sometimes a bull urinates on a dry wallow, then cakes himself with mud to fend off insects). Usually, however, a wallow is a dusty saucer, rubbed bare of grass, 8 or 10 feet wide and a foot or so deep near the center.

VOICE: The most common bison sounds are low, piggish grunts uttered to maintain herd contact or contact between cow and calf. A sharper grunt is a threat. Sometimes a charge is preceded by a guttural, growling bellow with the head extended, mouth open, tongue showing, but a bull may switch up his tail, lower his head, and charge without vocal warning.

Wild Boar (Sus scrofa)
COMMON & REGIONAL NAMES: *Russian or Prussian boar, European wild hog (or boar), tusker.*

DESCRIPTION & DISTRIBUTION: Through almost impenetrable laurel hells, across creek bottoms, over the wooded ridges of the Great Smokies, a boar can run 20 miles. The hounds are fortunate if they quit or lose the trail, because a bayed hog—or a hog that suddenly turns on the pack—can inflict terrible damage unless someone gets there fast with a gun. A reasonably short chase is more common. It ends when the boar decides to fight. A hunter runs up, gasping for breath, to find a black swirl of tusked fury lunging and slashing at a ring of frenzied hounds. A bayed hog is one of the most ferocious of beasts and one of the most intelligent. It often breaks off a fight with the dogs to turn on the more dangerous foe, the hunter. Head lowered, teeth clicking, sometimes frothing, a 300-pound boar, top-heavy as a bison on its stubby legs, can run 30 miles an hour, and a hunter may not have a clear shot until he comes within 10 yards.

Charging or fleeing, a wild boar can move as fast as a deer and can scramble through tangles that defeat dogs as well as hunters. Pure-blooded European boars sometimes weigh 600 pounds, but those in America are smaller, more agile. There has been much crossbreeding with small feral hogs and stray stock from the hill farms. Even boars of fairly pure lineage are apt to weigh between 200 and 350 pounds at maturity, probably because so many deer and squirrels compete for mast. A hog of either sex stands about 30 inches high and measures 4 to 5 feet long. The upper tusks—evolved from canine teeth—usually curl out and up on the sides of the disk-ended snout, while a straighter lower pair turns slightly out and back. The snout and tusks are a perfect adaptation for rooting, and one slash of the tusks can disembowel a dog or rip a man's leg to the bone.

Tusk length is normally about 3 to 5 inches, but there are head mounts with almost 9-inch ivory fangs. Males tend to have larger tusks than females, with more upward curl, yet the sexes are indistinguishable in a hunting situation and sows are legal game.

A hog with little or no domestic blood is sometimes dark brown or gray, usually black, often with frost-tipped guard hairs. Some of the hybrids are spotted tan and black. The long, bristly outer hairs thicken into an erect mane or ruff on the neck and shoulders, upper spine, and sometimes on the jaw.

The species is native to Europe and Asia. In 1893 a sportsman named Austin Corbin imported fifty head from Germany's Black Forest to stock a hunting preserve in the Blue Mountains of New Hampshire. Preserve hogs still exist there, and hunters in the locality have come across occasional wild boars in woods near the preserve—escapees or descendants of escapees from the fenced lands. In 1910 and 1912 another sportsman, George Gordon Moore, released Russian boars on a large hunting preserve in North Carolina's Snowbird Range, near the Tennessee line. The first hunt there took place in about 1920. Legend insists it was conducted in European style, with horses and spears; a more credible story notes only that the hogs killed a dozen hounds, treed as many hunters, and escaped into the Smokies.

In 1925 Moore also released wild boars on the San Francisquito Ranch, near Monterey, California, and there have been more recent introductions on Santa Cruz Island, off the California coast. European boars have spread into the Santa Lucia Mountains in Monterey County and crossed with feral hogs to the south in San Luis Obispo County. They may also begin to surprise deer hunters in the Pennsylvania mountains and other regions where they have become a preserve attraction.

Hybrids or feral hogs scuffle and root in a number of additional states—Arkansas, Florida, Georgia, Missouri, Oregon, and Texas. When a hunter speaks of shooting wild pigs today he may mean European boars, hybrids, feral Berkshire hogs as large and surly as true tuskers, or the mean little razorbacks that scurry across back roads in the lower Southeast. All are regarded as pests in most states—with no limit or closed season on them—because they occasionally damage crops or kill a domestic lamb or kid.

Though hybrids and feral hogs are not usually as large, fast, or savage as pure European boars, they are wild and unpredictable. The hunting for them has been best in Florida (where conservation authorities have had the foresight to classify them as game, with an open season usually running from early or mid-November to the year's end) and in south-central Texas, around Kerrville.

Still, the finest hog hunting is for the pure or nearly pure European boars in western North Carolina. Just over the line in Tennessee the hogs are less plentiful if equally large. Probably a couple of thousand wild boars plow through the thickets of the Nantahala and Cherokee national forests. Local hunters provide good hound packs and work as guides. State-managed hunts on Public Wildlife Management Areas are also conducted through the auspices of the North Carolina Wildlife Resources Commission in Raleigh and the Tennessee Game and Fish Commission in Nashville. The North Carolina season has recently lasted from mid-October through mid-November and again through the last half of December; in Tennessee it is generally during the last half of November.

GAME BEHAVIOR & HUNTING HABITAT: Horses follow the hounds in parts of California, Texas, and Florida (and hunting vehicles are also used in Florida), but in the Smokies a man has to go on foot, climbing razorback ridges, slogging through swamps, bulling through whip-tangles and thickets. The densely forested, mountainous habitat is more congenial to boars than to a hunter trying to overtake a hound pack.

The boars have plenty of cover and a wide variety of foods. In addition to digging up roots and tubers they eat grasses, fruits, berries, crawfish, frogs, salamanders, mice, snakes, the eggs and young of ground-nesting birds, the young of rabbits, even an occasional fawn. But autumn modifies their omnivorous habits sufficiently for a hunter to have a strong opinion about where to cast his hounds. Acorns become a staple, with beechnuts, hickory nuts, or pecans next in preference. Later, when the mast is nearly gone, the hogs take to rooting in swamps and marshes. In hot weather a boar seeks out cool spots or scoops a muddy wallow near a seep or stream—effective relief from heat and insects. In cold weather the animal is likely to scrape a shallow bed in a thicket, then heap branches and grass about it for insulation. Sometimes several hogs doze in a heap for the sake of warmth. Pure European boars are seminocturnal, whereas feral pigs are more active in the daytime, but both types move around to feed before sunup—a good time to start hounds—and late in the afternoon.

Hogs usually trot from one foraging spot to another but then slow to a walk. If the mast crop is good, their constant shifts will probably cover a range of less than 10 square miles, but in a poor year they may abandon a formerly good hunting area and show up 50 miles away. Sows and shoats usually wander in family groups or slightly larger herds; fifty have been seen together, half a dozen is a more common number. Mature males tend to separate into their own small bands or become hermits until they begin to look for females in December. Breeding peaks then but is rather irregular. If a sow encounters no boar during oestrus she comes into heat again at intervals of several weeks. Gestation requires sixteen or seventeen weeks, producing most of the young in April; only spring or early summer litters have much chance of surviving their first winter.

The sow heaps branches and grass in a thicket or under

a ledge, cliff, bush, or tree, digs a little hollow in the pile, lines it with grass, and there bears her litter, usually four or five piglets 6 or 8 inches long, brown and marked with nine or ten pale longitudinal body stripes that disappear during the first six months. After their first week they can follow the sow about and she may rejoin a herd. Though weaned at three months or so, they are likely to remain grouped for at least the first winter.

Predation is light. A bear, bobcat, or pack of wild dogs may kill a shoat—unless the attacker is eviscerated by the sow. Ticks, lice, and other external parasites are seldom more than an annoyance. The animals are subject to the common diseases and internal parasites that attack livestock and many wild animals. Though none of these is a severe problem, boar meat should be as well cooked as domestic pork to ensure against trichinosis. (No domestic pork can compare with a young wild hog well fed on acorns; meat from a tough old boar may call

for parboiling with a little baking soda before roasting or frying.)
A wild hog is hardy enough to live ten to twelve years.

Its toughness, in fact, is a problem to the hunter. The
shoulders of a pure European boar are shielded by a half-inch
plate of cartilage beneath a thick hide and bristly mane. Even
at the very short range that is normal, an angry boar seems
to ignore a light or badly placed bullet and can kill several dogs
or a man after being hit. The surest targets are the throat, the
heart (very low in the chest just behind the leg), or the spine.
A spine shot can be difficult from the ground but may be best
from the elevated stands that are used once in a while despite
a hog's unpredictable choice of escape routes.

Owing to the short range, bow hunting has become popular;
a broadhead arrow and a bow with a heavy pull will suffice if
supported by a high degree of skill, a comparable degree of
coolness, and a guide with a rifle. A typical guide in the Smokies

Hound pack circling large boar in water.

carries an old .30-30 lever-action. He shrugs at the probable need for several fast shots, or perhaps he gambles on each client's speed and marksmanship with a more powerful rifle. A friend in eastern Texas rides to hounds with a .38 Special revolver, but the animals he hunts are relatively small feral hogs. The .357, .41, and .44 Magnums are more appropriate handgun cartridges. The average hunter should probably use nothing lighter than 180-grain loads in a .30-06 rifle. Where the law requires shotguns, a 12-gauge rifled slug should be used in a repeater with a receiver sight. A scope can be a frightening impediment at 10 or 15 yards in thick brush, so a rifle should be fitted with an open sight or an aperture with the disk removed.

The same arms can be used for bear hunting; in parts of the Smokies the guides train and use their packs as boar or bear dogs. Plott hounds, Airedales, and nondescript crosses probably outnumber other hounds. Local packs have been bred through many generations for scenting ability, stamina, good voice, pugnacity, strength, and the nimbleness to hold a hog against rocks, a hummock or dry creek bank, or a wall of rhododendron without being gored before the shot is made. The larger the pack, the safer and more consistently successful it is. Some guides dislike using fewer than a dozen dogs except where regulations limit the number to eight.

A dogless hunter does not often come on a boar while scouring the woods for deer or bear, because a hog's vision is its only weak sense. A species that can sniff for underground tubers will usually smell a man before he comes into view, and a wild boar's erect ears detect slight sounds far off. With the wind blowing right, a silent stand in a hardwood grove or swamp is excellent for hunting game of more fixed habits, but a boar has no set trails. Therefore the hounds are cast where hogs have been glimpsed in the past, where sign abounds, or in a feeding area known to the guide. In some locales, natural crossings might tempt any animal, or there might be an old boar that has eluded the dogs before and will probably try the same route again. The guide might then gamble and put a couple of hunters on stands at high spots or over relatively clear crossings. The best hunt involves four or five men in condition for jogging and climbing; numbers increase the chance that someone will reach the dogs while they still hold a boar.

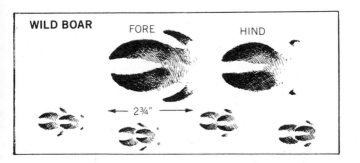

WILD BOAR FORE HIND

← 2¾" →

TRACKS & SIGN: A wild boar's trail is narrower than a domestic pig's, almost a single line, with a stride of perhaps 18 inches and the hind prints often placed about halfway over the foreprints. A good-sized boar's tracks are about 2½ inches long, rounder than a deer's, cloven, and splayed. Each foot has a pair of long, low, pointed dewclaws; those of the forefeet almost always print in soft earth, those of the hind feet sometimes do. They make roughly triangular marks behind and outside the main print.

   Scat can be sausagelike or massed pellets or segments, usually found where other sign appears: tracks, rooted earth, sometimes tree rubs. A wild boar can rub a tree to a height of 3 feet, leaving mud and hairs clinging to the bark. Rooting spots look plowed, and wallows are muddy depressions with tracks about them. A shallow, dry saucer heaped with twigs or grass may be a bed, another promising spot to start the dogs.

VOICE: The grunts are like those of domestic swine. A boar's easily triggered anger is expressed by loud squeals, but the animal can be frighteningly quiet when battling. While the hound voices grow frantic, a boar can maintain a businesslike silence.

Caribou *(Rangifer tarandus)*
COMMON & REGIONAL NAMES: *American reindeer.*

DESCRIPTION & DISTRIBUTION: Between the Tanana River and the slopes of the Wrangell Mountains, a hunter can sit atop a rounded bluff the color of rawhide and watch hundreds of Alaskan caribou drift across a wide, shallow pass in late summer or early fall. Though they are still in velvet, he can spot several prime bulls. One sweeping rack looks almost as high above the animal's head as its shoulders are from the spongy ground. A vertically palmated brown beam juts out over its forehead almost to the muzzle. There may be two brow palms—a double shovel—so closely spaced that the points mesh. The hunter cannot be sure yet, even with his 20-power spotting scope, but the two low branches above the shovel also look well palmated and pronged. The bull is in the clear and coming closer as the hunter tightens the rifle sling around his arm.

The smaller herds of northern Quebec are on the move at the same time. There, too, a hunter on a lookout can watch the high, rolling barren grounds for a white-necked bull with antlers that will tape more than 4 feet around the curve and show a comparable spread between the beams. The woodland caribou of Newfoundland are darker, with heavy-palmed but shorter, narrower racks that permit free movement through brush or timber. A hunter there might pack a fine moose out of the swamps and then move cautiously across the relatively open muskeg in search of a prancing 300-pound bull caribou that is feeling the first tug of the rut. In the Cassiars of British Columbia, a hunter who stops his horse to glass the high plateaus for Stone sheep or grizzlies is just as likely to spot a mountain caribou bedded on a snow patch or nibbling lichen. It may be as big as an elk, with antlers rivaling those of an Alaskan barren-ground caribou. Cover is sparse and the wind keeps shifting, but perhaps the bull has never encountered man. Even if the animal spooks too soon, it may run only a couple of hundred yards and then stop or trot back like a pacing horse, either curious or forgetful of what startled it.

Though caribou take poorly to domestication they belong to the same species as the reindeer of Scandinavia, Russia, and parts of Asia. At least twelve subspecies inhabit the North American continent, the islands above Canada, and the Greenland coast. They are of three primary types: the barren-ground caribou (usually classified as *Rangifer tarandus,* sometimes as *R. arcticus,* with either designation followed by a subspecial name such as *granti* or *groenlandicus*); the woodland caribou (classified as *R. caribou* or *R. t. caribou*); and the mountain caribou (grouped by some naturalists with barren-ground caribou, by others with the woodland group, by still others as a separate category, *R. montanus*). Because crossbreeding is common where ranges overlap, the Boone and Crockett Club has established a fourth trophy classification by separating the Quebec-Labrador caribou from more westerly barren-ground races. The animals of this region represent a series of crosses between barren-ground types to the north and west and a couple of woodland varieties to the south and east.

Subtle differences can be important to a trophy hunter. The scoring of antlers depends on the length, spread, and circumference of the beams; length of brow tines; extent of palmation; symmetry—though caribou antlers are never very symmetrical—and total number of tines. To qualify for the record book a barren-ground caribou must score 400 or better; the minimum is 375 for a Quebec-Labrador caribou, 390 for a mountain caribou, 295 for a woodland caribou. Most of the barren-ground records come from the Alaskan Peninsula and the area between Mount McKinley and the Yukon. Northwestern British Columbia is best for hunting big mountain caribou; northeastern Quebec is best for Quebec-Labrador caribou; and the island of Newfoundland is best for woodland trophies.

An outstanding woodland rack may have more than forty tines and any other type may have more than fifty, but it may also have less than two dozen. Moreover, no one can count caribou tines accurately at shooting range, so a hunter judges a potential trophy by other criteria. Caribou cows are the only female deer that normally grow antlers, but their racks are too short and spindly to cause confusion. Good main beams sweep back, sometimes almost over the shoulder, then curve up and forward in a bow shape. They spread substantially wider than a bull's body and are usually but not always somewhat palmated at the top, where they branch into several tines or occasionally a great many. One of the brow beams, sweeping out over the upper muzzle, usually forms a vertical palm, or shovel, while the other is most often just a spike. The very finest heads are apt to have the rare double shovels. A little higher on the main beams, two secondary beams sweep forward; called the bez formation, they are usually palmated and multitined. About halfway up on each main beam there is usually one more, relatively small tine, pointing rearward. The features are variable, but a hunter can decide about stalking or shooting on the basis of general conformation, size, sweep, and the massive look that goes with heavy beams and some palmation. There are excellent racks with a long, low sweep, but trophy antlers more often have a height equal to about two-thirds of the bull's shoulder height.

The barren-ground caribou, though majestically crowned, is relatively small-bodied. A prime bull may be about 6½ to 7½ feet long and 4 to 5 feet high at the shoulder. A mature cow is seldom quite as large. Weight ranges from about 150 to 400 pounds. The woodland caribou is comparable, but a mountain bull of the Osborn strain *(R. a. osborni)* in upper British Columbia can be more than 8 feet long and 5 feet high, and may weigh more than 600 pounds.

Some of the caribou on the arctic islands are virtually all white. Generally, however, the body color is light tan, grayish tan, or brown, the woodland species being darkest. In fall the animals grow a thick, curly undercoat and a long, air-filled, gray-brown and white guard hairs. Even the nose is haired. The squarish, horsey face is brown or tan with pale or white eye rings and muzzle. The underside of the stubby tail, a small rump patch, and a ring above each tremendous hoof are also white. If a caribou is sufficiently dark, a white stripe usually shows up along the lower flank, separating belly from side. On most caribou the hair on the neck grows long enough to form a frontal mane.

The neck is usually light, ranging from grayish to white and contrasting clearly with the body unless a caribou is very pale. Against far tundra hills, mountain slopes, or the heaving rises of a high plateau, caribou might be invisible were it not for the moving dots of their necks. As a bull matures, his neck grows whiter, and the white spreads, sometimes all the way back over the shoulders. If a caribou is spotted so far away that antler dimensions are impossible to judge even from a spotting scope, daylight hours can be lost irretrievably in closing the distance to a disappointment. A bull that shows plenty of white is worth a gamble, though he may not await the hunter's arrival, or he may be past his prime. A bull seldom develops a better annual crown than the rack grown in his fourth or fifth summer, when the neck has turned quite white. In old age the mane is unchanged, but each season's antlers may be less massively

palmated, less generously tined.

Barren-ground caribou keep to the tundra and taiga, from northern Labrador across upper Canada and through most of Alaska. Woodland caribou range farther south. They are now abundant in Newfoundland, parts of Labrador, Saskatchewan, and upper Alberta, less so in Manitoba, scarce in Nova Scotia and New Brunswick. They seem to be maintaining their numbers in British Columbia, the stronghold of the mountain caribou. Alaska's estimated 600,000 barren-ground caribou are the state's most plentiful big game. The Yukon, Northwest Territories, and the provinces probably have another 200,000, plus smaller numbers of the other races. At this writing the Alaskan season runs from early August through March south of the Yukon River, where the hunting is best. There is no closed season north of the river—a short-sighted policy despite sparse settlement and abundant caribou. (Furthermore, since the bulls drop their antlers in December or January, a later hunt must be for meat alone.) The open season varies among the territories and provinces, but generally opens in late summer or very early fall and lasts into mid-fall or, in a few locales, almost until the onset of winter.

GAME BEHAVIOR & HUNTING HABITAT: The hunting is good just before the rut and during its early phase, from late August or the beginning of September through the first few days of

Trophy caribou in velvet during early part of season.

618/Big Game

Sample trophy chart and complete scoring instructions.

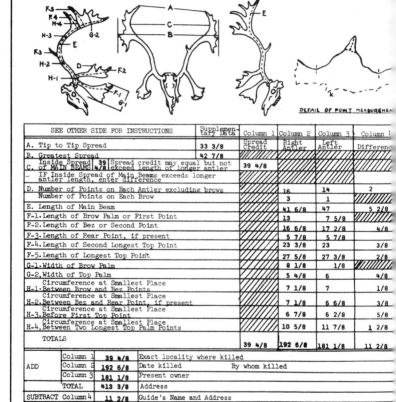

OFFICIAL SCORING SYSTEM FOR NORTH AMERICAN BIG GAME TROPHIES

RECORDS OF NORTH AMERICAN BIG GAME COMMITTEE

BOONE AND CROCKETT CLUB

Boone and Crockett Club
Records of North American Big Game Commit
c o Carnegie Museum
4400 Forbes Ave. Pittsburgh, Pa. 15213

MINIMUM SCORE: Barren Ground - 400
Mountain - 390
Quebec-Labrador - 375
Woodland - 295

CARIBOU

KIND OF CARIBOU   Mountain

DETAIL OF POINT MEASUREMEN

SEE OTHER SIDE FOR INSTRUCTIONS		Supplementary Data	Column 1	Column 2	Column 3	Column !
A. Tip to Tip Spread		33 3/8	Spread Credit	Right Antler	Left Antler	Difference
B. Greatest Spread		42 7/8				
C. Inside Spread	39	Spread credit may equal but not exceed length of longer antler	39 4/8			
of MAIN BEAMS	4/8					
IF Inside Spread of Main Beams exceeds longer antler length, enter difference						
D. Number of Points on Each Antler excluding brows				16	14	2
Number of Points on Each Brow				3	1	
E. Length of Main Beam				41 6/8	47	5 2/8
F-1.Length of Brow Palm or First Point				13	7 5/8	
F-2.Length of Bez or Second Point				16 6/8	17 2/8	4/8
F-3.Length of Rear Point, if present				5 7/8	5 7/8	
F-4.Length of Second Longest Top Point				23 3/8	23	3/8
F-5.Length of Longest Top Point				27 5/8	27 3/8	2/8
G-1.Width of Brow Palm				8 1/8	1/8	
G-2.Width of Top Palm				5 4/8	6	4/8
H-1.Circumference at Smallest Place Between Brow and Bez Points				7 1/8	7	1/8
H-2.Circumference at Smallest Place Between Bez and Rear Point, if present				7 1/8	6 6/8	3/8
H-3.Circumference at Smallest Place Before First Top Point				6 7/8	6 2/8	5/8
H-4.Circumference at Smallest Place Between Two Longest Top Palm Points				10 5/8	11 7/8	1 2/8
TOTALS				39 4/8	192 6/8	181 1/8	11 2/8

ADD	Column 1	39 4/8	Exact locality where killed
	Column 2	192 6/8	Date killed By whom killed
	Column 3	181 1/8	Present owner
	TOTAL	413 3/8	Address
SUBTRACT Column 4		11 2/8	Guide's Name and Address
FINAL SCORE		402 1/8	Remarks: (Mention any abnormalities)

I certify that I have measured the above trophy on _____ 19_____
at (address) _____ City _____ State _____
and that these measurements and data are, to the best of my knowledge and belief, made in
accordance with the instructions given.

Witness: _____   Signature: _____

Boone & Crockett Official Measurer

Instructions

All measurements must be made with a flexible steel tape to the nearest one-eighth of an inch. Wherever it is necessary to change direction of measurement, mark a control point and swing tape at this point. To simplify addition, please enter fractional figures in **eighths.**

Official measurements cannot be taken for at least sixty days after the animal was killed. **Please submit photographs.**

Supplementary Data measurements indicate conformation of the trophy. None of the figures in Lines A and B is to be included in the score. Evaluation of conformation is a matter of personal preference.

A. Tip to Tip Spread measured between tips of Main Beams.

B. Greatest Spread measured between perpendiculars at right angles to the center line of the skull at widest part whether across main beams or points.

C. Inside Spread of Main Beams measured at right angles to the center line of the skull at widest point between main beams. Enter this measurement again in "Spread Credit" column if it is less than or equal to the length of longer antler.

D. Number of points on each antler. To be counted a point, a projection must be at least one-half inch long and this length must exceed the breadth of the point's base. The breadth need not be computed from the deepest adjacent dips in the palmation. The length

may be measured to any location—at least one-half inch from the tip—at which the length of the point exceeds its breadth. Beam tip is counted as a point but not measured as a point.

E. Length of Main Beam measured from lowest outside edge of burr over outer curve to the most distant point of what is, or appears to be, the main beam. The point of beginning is that point on the burr where the center line along the outer curve of the beam intersects the burr.

F-1-2-3. Length of Points. They are measured from nearest edge of beam on the shortest line over outer curve to tip. To determine nearest edge (top edge) of beam, lay the tape along the outer curve of the beam so that the top edge of the tape coincides with the top edge of the beam on both sides of the point. Draw line along top edge of tape. This line will be base line from which point is measured.

F-4-5. Measure from the tip of the point to the top of the beam, then at right angles to the lower edge of beam.

G-1. Width of Brow measured in a straight line from top edge to lower edge.

G-2. Width of Top Palm measured from rear edge of main beam to the dip between points at widest part of palm.

H-1-2-3-4. Circumference. If rear point is missing, take H-2 and H-3 measurements at smallest place between bez and first top point.

Trophies Obtained Only by Fair Chase May Be Entered in Any Boone and Crockett Club Big Game Competition

To make use of the following methods shall be deemed **Unfair Chase** and unsportsmanlike, and any trophy obtained by use of such means is disqualified from entry in any Boone and Crockett Club big game competition:

1. Spotting or herding game from the air, followed by landing in its vicinity for pursuit;
2. Herding or pursuing game with motor-powered vehicles;
3. Use of electronic communications for attracting, locating, or observing game, or guiding the hunter to such game.

I certify that the trophy scored on this chart was not taken in **Unfair Chase** as defined above by the Boone and Crockett Club.

I certify that it was not spotted or herded by guide or hunter from the air followed by landing in its vicinity for pursuit, nor herded or pursued on the ground by motor-powered vehicles.

I further certify that no electronic communications were used to attract, locate, observe, or guide the hunter to such game; and that it was taken in full compliance with the local game laws or regulations of the state, province or territory.

Date _____ Signature of Hunter _____

October. Until September is well along, the bulls in many areas carry velvet, intact or hanging in streamers. Their antlers are fully developed and hardened, however, and the animals are in excellent condition. The bulls are well larded, not for winter but for the rut. During about six weeks of breeding, peaking in October and waning before the month ends in most regions, prime bulls do little feeding. They gather and defend harems of ten to twelve cows. Breeding and battling soon turns a herd master from sleek and fat to gaunt, scarred, and sometimes bleeding. Caribou venison, at other times as good as any beef, is rank, overly lean, and tough when taken from a bull that has been rutting for a while.

Food is the reason for caribou migrations. In spring and summer the tundra is no barren ground but a rumpled carpet of grasses, berry bushes, herbs, dwarf willow and birch, fungi, and thick lichens. The caribou's staple over much of the range is the whitish lichen known as caribou moss or reindeer moss, sometimes growing more than 2 feet thick. Woodland caribou browse more than the mountain and barren-ground races, consuming more birch and heath shrubs, but all caribou supplement the lichen with such plants. In a tundra region frequented by caribou but lacking obvious sign, the kind of land to scout is rich with lichen and patched with vegetation that might include blueberry, bearberry, cranberry, horsetail, willow, Labrador tea.

Hunter lining up on trophy Ungava caribou.

If frost comes, the animals look for bog growth. Later they will scrape through a couple of feet of snow to feed, each animal plowing a forefoot so fast that it blurs.

The very round cloven hoofs are often larger than the feet of a moose weighing three times as much. As a caribou's winter coat sloughs off in spring, the center portions of its hoofs soften into spongy pads that easily negotiate boggy tundra where other species might be mired. The pads harden and shrink by winter, and sprout short insulating hair in the concavity. The hard rims then bite firmly on crusted snow or ice.

Caribou do eventually overgraze some of their choice feeding spots and shift to new pastures. For many years they use the same general calving grounds, summering areas, wide migratory routes, and wintering places. A guide learns where to ride or go on lookout with his hunter—and then one year the herds shift and he has to work harder until he learns their new haunts.

The woodland caribou in Newfoundland move toward the southern part of the island in fall; elsewhere, woodland caribou and some of the mountain caribou shift locally, seeking lowland vegetation, but some of the huge barren-ground herds migrate 800 miles. There are arctic caribou that move north to reach adequate winter fodder. In most hunting regions they head south in August (or sometimes July) to the lower reaches of the tundra, they slow up and travel sporadically to the forest edges. In September they tend to move into the open again to rut, and hunting is therefore good on the lower barren grounds and in the taiga.

The northward shift lasts from April through June. En route, the cows tarry at calving grounds, generally returning to the same meadows year after year. A woodland cow often bears twins, while a single drab brown calf is normal among the other subspecies. It weighs only 10 or 12 pounds but can walk almost as soon as it is dry and can outrun a man when it is a couple of days old. By late August it weighs 50 pounds, and though suckling may continue for some time, it has begun grazing and browsing.

Any defective calf is almost certain to be captured by tundra wolves, which also cull the aged, sick, or injured. The bear, lynx, and wolverine take a few newborn calves, and the Eskimos and northern Indians kill a good many caribou for meat and hides. Just as the snowshoe rabbit is called "the bread of the woods" in its primary habitat, the caribou is known as "the beef of the North."

Caribou are resistant to disease and seldom infested with parasites that afflict more southerly deer. But in the summer they are plagued by mosquitoes, blackflies, other biting insects, and sometimes noseflies and warbles. Early in the hunting season, when insects are still a nuisance, good places to glass are windy rises, ridges, or saddles, where caribou can feed in peace, and snow patches (often appropriated by good bulls), where they can bed without fidgeting at clouds of flies.

Most caribou probably have a life span of seven to ten years. Beset by the normal attrition of age, they ultimately fail to outmaneuver the wolves, though caribou that have not yet lost their vigor and speed often watch calmly as a wolf approaches within 50 yards. They seldom let a man come that close if they catch his scent, but they can be fooled. Their hearing is not outstanding and their eyesight is strangely weak for an open-country species. More than one bull has tried to add a pack horse to his harem. Just before the rut, when they dot the rolling uplands, a good way to hunt is to ride along or sit on a high knoll and glass the country, then concentrate more on wind than on perfect cover while stalking. Once in a while a hunter can find no real cover at all, not even tundra gullies or hummocks. He may soak himself, slithering over a bog, only to be seen before getting quite close enough. He stops and waits. A bull, almost invariably more curious than bright, may trot closer, or resume feeding after a few moments, or gallop away and then trot right back again. If the shot remains impossible, the hunter can try a last-resort gamble, rising to his hands and knees and slowly moving forward like a wolf. Once in Alaska, a hunting acquaintance kept a bull pinned to the spot by walking forward with his arms raised to resemble antlers, at the same time bobbing from the waist like a challenging bull.

Yet it is often difficult to find and stalk a good trophy. As caribou walk along with their heads down to graze, a hunter can work his way forward, but if they spook, they can gallop off at more than 30 miles an hour. A bull often rears up and wheels to one side, then makes a couple of bounds before smoothing out in a run or trot, legs rising high, head stretched horizontal, antlers laid back so they will not catch any obstacle or interfere with balance. If the range is reasonable and the animal is moving at an easy, high-stepping trot, there is a chance of hitting the heart-lung area, but walking or stationary bulls are felled more often. Moving caribou cannot be overtaken, but sometimes they can be intercepted. A look at the terrain and likely feeding or bedding spots, plus the general direction of travel, will give some indication of where to head them off.

They are daylight feeders, usually spreading out to pasture before the sun is high. Late in the morning they rest and ruminate. The places to scan then are hilltops, high slopes, gravel ridges, and snow patches, where they bed at random. On warm days, rivers and ponds should be checked in the late afternoon. Caribou swim very well and they like water. Barren-ground bulls can be hunted to the open conifers edging the tundra, and they may be well into the timber if they are rubbing off their velvet. Woodland caribou prefer muskegs and relatively open forest, while mountain caribou are most often taken above the timber.

Regardless of region, 7- or 8-power field glasses and a 20-power spotting scope are recommended, but the choice of rifle is influenced by terrain and local game. On a tundra hunt a 6.5mm Magnum, .264 Magnum, .270, .284, or similar caliber will serve well, and the .30-06 is popular. A caribou is less resistant to shock than most big game, so high power and heavy bullet weights are not essential. But in parts of Alaska, the Yukon, the Northwest Territories, British Columbia, and Alberta, a hunter glassing the high slopes may spot a caribou, sheep, or grizzly. In some of the same general areas and from Quebec to Newfoundland, he may want to hunt moose as well as caribou. A caribou rifle is fine for sheep, but if there is a chance of taking bigger game the cartridge should be at least a 7mm Magnum or .30-06; one of the .300 Magnums or a .338 would also be a good selection. In eastern moose country, a 2½-power rifle scope zeroed at 100 yards is fine, whereas a 4-power scope should be zeroed at twice that range for more open terrain.

TRACKS & SIGN: Where caribou cross the tundra in migration or where they feed in large numbers, the fragile ground cover is seamed with their long black trails. In soft surfaces the tracks, rounder than those of other deer, are sometimes splayed wider than they are long. A caribou track can easily measure 5 inches

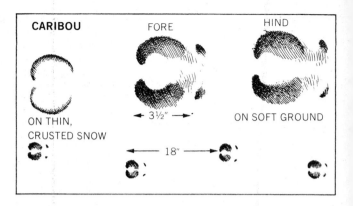

CARIBOU
FORE
HIND
ON THIN, CRUSTED SNOW
← 3½" →
ON SOFT GROUND
← 18" →

across. The widely separated lobes print acute crescents, and the long, low dewclaws, which add to hoof support on bog or snow, clearly print behind the lobes. On thin, crusted snow, however, the hoofs sometimes cut only the round outlines of their rims. Usually the hind prints partially overlap the front ones, leaving a double impression perhaps 8 inches long.

Because of its odd foot structure, a caribou can sometimes be heard walking on soft ground at 50 yards or so, and a grazing file or larger herd might be detected on the far side of a rise that hides them. Long tendons in the ankles slide over the small bones with each step, producing a click. Occasionally, in cold weather, a hidden group is also revealed by rising vapor.

The scat is sometimes massed like that of other high-country or pasturing game after grazing on succulent feed, but it usually takes the form of small, bell-shaped pellets, one end tapered, the other blunt or concave, much like whitetail droppings.

VOICE: Caribou grunt and snort like other deer but are generally spotted at distances too great for the sound to carry.

Elk *(Cervus canadensis)*
COMMON & REGIONAL NAMES: *wapiti*

DESCRIPTION & DISTRIBUTION: Early one fall in the Wind River

Range in Wyoming, the first elk we saw was an average, healthy bull the size of the guide's saddle horse, almost 15 hands high. The horse—snorting, ears pricked up, head cocked—had alerted us as we rode toward a white, black, and gold aspen thicket. The guide raised his hand, but there was no time to dismount and unscabbard a rifle before the elk crashed out across a little burn into lodgepoles as tight as palisades.

In a meadow above the timber a couple of hours later we dressed out a bull that had given away its location with a single whistling bugle call. It was probably the same animal. We had been puzzled to see gray strands hanging like spruce moss from the antlers of the bull we jumped at the aspens. Dried velvet seemed unlikely; an elk rubs the tatters away in August and this was September. The bull we shot had willow wands drooping from its rack. Ordinarily a bull elk can move through thickets too dense for a man without entangling antlers that may easily reach more than 4 feet in height and spread, as these did. But rutting bulls wage sham battles with small trees and shrubs. Ours was a typical Wyoming elk, dark brown along the spine and on the head, nearly black on the legs and thick neck mane, but as pale as a faded tarpaulin on the sides and flanks. Those light tan slabs on a horse-sized animal made it clear why guides are reluctant to bring palominos into mountains frequented by riflemen.

During the season elk are slightly grayish—in the blue, as deer hunters say—but old bulls tend to be a distinctively light beige, and the long guard hair over their woolly undercoats bleaches even lighter before shedding in big patches with the onset of spring. A popular and better name for elk is wapiti, the Shawnee word for white deer. Early settlers first called the species elk, their term for the European moose (which closely resembles the American moose) and for various other large deer. Wapiti look much like Scotland's red deer and even more like the Persian maral; all are very closely related.

American elk turn reddish brown in summer. They have a pale chin patch and eye rings, and a stubby tail that blends with the tawny or sometimes almost white rump patch. A few elk can erect their rump hair, but it is a vestigial ability that has lost its warning function. Occasionally a hunter gets his elk after spotting a pale rump on a far slope. Of all the world's deer,

Sample trophy chart and Boone and Crockett scoring procedure.

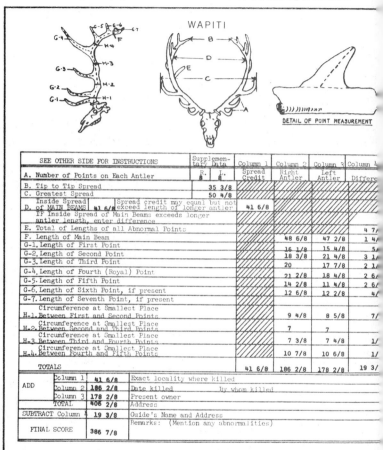

WAPITI

DETAIL OF POINT MEASUREMENT

SEE OTHER SIDE FOR INSTRUCTIONS	Supplementary Data		Column 1	Column 2	Column 3	Column 4
	R.	L.	Spread Credit	Right Antler	Left Antler	Difference
A. Number of Points on Each Antler	8	8				
B. Tip to Tip Spread		35 3/8				
C. Greatest Spread		50 4/8				
D. Inside Spread of MAIN BEAMS 41 6/8 — Spread credit may equal but not exceed length of longer antler			41 6/8			
IF Inside Spread of Main Beams exceeds longer antler length, enter difference						
E. Total of Lengths of all Abnormal Points						4 7/8
F. Length of Main Beam				48 6/8	47 2/8	1 4/8
G-1. Length of First Point				16 1/8	15 4/8	5/8
G-2. Length of Second Point				18 3/8	21 4/8	3 1/8
G-3. Length of Third Point				20	17 7/8	2 1/8
G-4. Length of Fourth (Royal) Point				21 2/8	18 4/8	2 6/8
G-5. Length of Fifth Point				14 2/8	11 4/8	2 6/8
G-6. Length of Sixth Point, if present				12 6/8	12 2/8	4/8
G-7. Length of Seventh Point, if present						
H-1. Circumference at Smallest Place Between First and Second Points				9 4/8	8 5/8	7/8
H-2. Circumference at Smallest Place Between Second and Third Points				7	7	
H-3. Circumference at Smallest Place Between Third and Fourth Points				7 3/8	7 4/8	1/8
H-4. Circumference at Smallest Place Between Fourth and Fifth Points				10 7/8	10 6/8	1/8
TOTALS			41 6/8	186 2/8	178 2/8	19 3/8

ADD	Column 1	41 6/8	Exact locality where killed	
	Column 2	186 2/8	Date killed	By whom killed
	Column 3	178 2/8	Present owner	
	TOTAL	406 2/8	Address	
SUBTRACT Column 4		19 3/8	Guide's Name and Address	
FINAL SCORE		386 7/8	Remarks: (Mention any abnormalities)	

only moose are larger. A summer-fattened bull may weigh only 500 pounds, but 700 is more likely, and 1,000 is possible in some parts of the range. Shoulder height is usually 4½ or 5 feet, length 7½ to 9½ feet. Mature cows are a bit smaller, generally weighing between 400 and 700 pounds.

Instructions

All measurements must be made with a flexible steel tape to the nearest one-eighth of an inch. Wherever it is necessary to change direction of measurements, mark a control point and swing tape at this point. To simplify addition, please enter fractional figures in eighths.

Official measurements cannot be taken for at least sixty days after the animal was killed. **Please submit photographs.**

Supplementary Data measurements indicate conformation of the trophy, and none of the figures in Lines A, B and C is to be included in the score. Evaluation of conformation is a matter of personal preference.

A. Number of Points on Each Antler. To be counted a point, a projection must be at least one inch long *and* its length must exceed the length of its base. All points are measured from tip of point to nearest edge of beam as illustrated. **Beam tip is counted as a point but not measured as a point.**

B. Tip to Tip Spread measured between tips of Main Beams.

C. Greatest Spread measured between perpendiculars at right angles to the center line of the skull at widest part whether across main beams or points.

D. Inside Spread of Main Beams measured at right angles to the center line of the skull at widest point between main beams. Enter this measurement again in "Spread Credit" column if it is less than or equal to the length of longer antler.

E. Total of Lengths of all Abnormal Points. Abnormal points are generally considered to be those nontypical in shape or location.

F. Length of Main Beam measured from lowest outside edge of burr over outer curve to the most distant point of what is, or appears to be, the main beam. The point of beginning is that point on the burr where the center line along the outer curve of the beam intersects the burr.

G-1-2-3-4-5-6-7. Length of Normal Points. Normal points project from main beam. They are measured from nearest edge of main beam over outer curve to tip. To determine nearest edge (top edge) of beam, lay the tape along the outer curve of the beam so that the top edge of the tape coincides with the top edge of the beam on both sides of the point. Draw line along top edge of tape. This line will be base line from which point is measured.

H-1-2-3-4. Circumferences. Self explanatory.

Bulls drop their enormous antlers in March and begin to develop new ones within a month. By July or early August, the fully developed, velvet-sheathed crown of a 7-year-old bull may weigh 50 pounds. As a rule, long yearlings develop sizable spikes; two- and three-year-olds display four or five tines on each beam.

The next year's antlers have six long, sharp tines on each massive beam, the normal complement for a mature bull. Apart from uncommon deformities, only a relatively few great record heads display more than half a dozen tines on either side, and symmetry counts in scoring trophies. It is not so much the number of tines as their length, and the length, spread, and girth of the beams, that sets apart a magnificent bull elk.

The main beams sweep out, up, and back, usually curving inward again near the tips. Almost all of those in the record book are more than 4 feet long and some are more than 5 feet. The traditional descriptive terms are a mixture of western vernacular and European nomenclature with a flavor of heraldry. Close to the head a long brow tine juts forward and slightly upward from each beam. A little above it is a bez tine of about equal length. The brow and bez tines together are known as lifters, dog killers, or war tines. About midway up on the beam is a tres (or tray) tine, usually a little shorter than the lifters. Higher up is a fourth, called a royal or dagger point, that may be over 20 inches long. Finally, the beam tip divides into two or occasionally three tines called sur-royals, for a total of six or seven on each side. A normal 6-point elk is called a royal bull or a royal stag; one with 7 is an imperial. Fully pointed at four years, annual racks grow longer and thicker through a bull's sixth, seventh, or eighth year, after which they may diminish.

A good rack is hard to judge at typical hunting distances because of the characteristic rearward sweep. If a bull holds his head low, tilting the antlers up, their length ought to be almost as great as the animal's height. If the rack is held almost horizontal, it should be about as long as the distance from brisket to ham. From front or rear it may not look very high, but it should look massive and considerably wider than the bull's body.

At one time elk roamed over most of what is now the United States and lower Canada. The Merriam elk of Arizona, New Mexico, and Texas is extinct. According to some authorities, so is the prototype eastern elk *(C. c. canadensis),* though others maintain that it is now common in central and eastern Montana, Wyoming, and Colorado. It would be hard to distinguish from the Rocky Mountain elk *(C. c. nelsoni)* that ranges from British Columbia, Alberta, and Saskatchewan down through the Rockies. Rocky Mountain elk have been reintroduced in South Dakota's Black Hills and Custer State Park (where special annual hunts thin the herds to the habitat's capacity) and in eastern Washington and Oregon. Transplanted or remnant herds also exist in Michigan, Minnesota, Nevada, Oklahoma, Texas, Virginia, Pennsylvania, and New Hampshire. At this writing, Rocky Mountain elk are hunted on public land in eleven western states; the best of them are Colorado, Wyoming, Montana, and Washington.

Invariably, the top records are set by Rocky Mountain antlers, yet Roosevelt elk *(C. c. roosevelti)* are bigger animals. Also called Olympic elk, they inhabit the Cascade and Olympic mountains and the coastal forest from Vancouver through Washington and Oregon—providing fine hunting in both states—and upper California. They are also plentiful on Afognak Island in Alaska, where a herd was established in the 1920s. A hunter there may be able to take a brown bear as well as an elk, and a hunter in Washington or Oregon may find the elk running with blacktail deer. Roosevelt elk have thicker antlers than those of the Rockies, often cusped at the tips and slightly palmated, but neither as long nor as widespreading since Roosevelt elk inhabit denser brush and woods. Some of the bulls weigh 1,000 or even 1,200 pounds. The live weight of a bull elk can be roughly estimated by adding 40 percent to the hog-dressed weight (50 percent for a cow).

A third undisputed race is the Manitoba elk *(C. c. manitobensis)* found in the lower parts of the Prairie Provinces. It has relatively small antlers and, like the Roosevelt strain, is darker than the Rocky Mountain elk. Paler and smaller than any of these is the tule elk *(C. nannodes),* which exists in small protected herds in central California. It is the size of a mule deer and is sometimes classed as a separate species.

In 1919 only about 70,000 remained in the United States. Their migrations to winter range had been impeded by fences, roads, and towns. Their grazing land had been largely appropriated by cattlemen, who shot great numbers of elk to reduce competition with their stock. Farmers also killed thousands to protect their fences, crops, and winter haystacks. Even now there are regions where haystacks are shielded by wooden panels. A great many wapiti were also killed for their excellent meat, their extremely durable hides, and the teeth that once adorned watch fobs and stickpins.

Management programs have been so successful that special hunts must be conducted in parks like Grand Teton and Custer to reduce the herds, and thousands of animals are fed all winter at the National Elk Refuge near Jackson Hole, Wyoming. There are now some 425,000 elk in the United States and Canada.

GAME BEHAVIOR & HUNTING HABITAT: In most states elk hunting begins in September or October, and the season's length depends on the game census. Locality determines where and when hunting is best because some herds are far more migratory than others. There are herds that shift slightly, others that move 60 miles. In the Rockies, generally speaking, conditions are just right early in the season on the high meadows and parks, and again quite late in the season at lower elevations. The weather is milder on the more limited range of the Roosevelt elk, where the season may not open until late October or early November.

In the North a wintering herd may number several hundred animals. Though they can plow through drifts that would yard smaller deer, they gather in large groups as they seek relatively shallow snow and reachable browse or dried grass. Some of the mature bulls keep to their own elite groups of half a dozen or so, a few go it alone, and in the spring migration nearly all of them separate from the juveniles and the cows. The big herds break into bands of a dozen or a score, each led by an old cow. Along the way, in late May or early June, pregnant cows stop to bear their calves on sagebrush flats or benches on broad slopes, usually near open timber, sometimes in dense cover. The gestation period is about eight to eight and a half months, and a typical calf weighs about 30 pounds. A buff rump patch is already visible, but the body is roan with white or light spots that fade before summer wanes. After a couple of weeks the cow and her calf join any migrating herd that comes along. Weaning is usually complete by late summer or fall, at which time the calf probably weighs 150 pounds.

A calf born to a severely winter-weakened cow may soon die. A few calves are stolen by cougars, wolves, bears, coyotes, and bobcats, which can also kill sick or malnourished adults. Winter ticks and mite-transmitted scabies occasionally cause serious debilitation, and elk are attacked by the internal parasites that now and then afflict most deer. Elk swim well but can drown when autumn ice gives way; some become inextricably entangled in barbed wire, or die in fires, slides, and falls. (Forest fires and logging have benefitted them, however, by opening mountain timberlands to low second growth.) It is winter famine, rather than disease or calamity, that controls today's elk populations. In good habitat, they have a life span of ten to fifteen years and occasionally much longer.

Until the snows deepen, they are basically grazers. Before and during the rut, good Rocky Mountain bulls are often shot on open pastures where the herds seek needlegrass, bluegrass, wheatgrass, and sedge. Later, the drifts force them downward to browse on fir needles, Rocky Mountain maple, sagebrush, bog birch, mountain mahogany, pine, aspen, willow, wild rose, berry bushes, and almost anything else within reach. The rut peaks in late September; two or three weeks later, when it has subsided, bulls tend to penetrate such dense woods that hunting becomes very difficult, but it improves again by late October in many regions, as the bulls reach still lower elevations and fan out on relatively open wooded slopes. There are parts of the Rockies and adjacent ranges where early season hunting is done by riding high plateaus and glassing the open stretches, while late-season hunting is on foot through woods on good tracking snow where field glasses may be of no use at all.

Coastal elk eat orchardgrass, redtop, sweet vernalgrass, oatgrass, rye, and so on, but because of the rain forests they browse more than the elk of the Rockies. They feed on salal and other berry bushes, maple, vine maple, devil's-club, ferns, willow, alder, mountain ash, mosses and lichens, decaying logs, and low or fallen conifers.

At summer's end or the beginning of fall, elk begin to drift down, but they are still in high country as the hunting season and the rut commence. At first the bulls travel in small herds or alone. Cows, calves, yearlings, and two-year-olds move along in herds that usually number from about ten to thirty. Soon the bulls disperse; their necks swell and they begin to bugle. A bull does not gather a harem but simply takes charge of a cow herd, driving yearlings and older males out of the group. At first some of the cows break away to rejoin their adolescent offspring, but the bull drives them back with his antlers. Inevitably, rivals appear. Young ones can be scared off by a single charge. A big six-pointer will bugle and stand its ground. The adversaries circle warily, then crash together, pushing, twisting, jabbing. Most often the challenger breaks and runs. Because of rack structure, locked antlers are far less common than among smaller deer, but the long, sharp tines occasionally inflict a fatal injury.

Unattached bulls are the ones that most often answer the call of a hunter or guide, though a herd bull may reply in arrogant

rage to an elk whistle. Bugling for elk works best early in the season, when the most bulls are on the prod for a harem or a fight, and they have not yet become suspicious. No one should try bugling who has not heard elk scream or taken a lesson from an experienced bugler. Novices tend to overuse a whistle and produce too low a pitch (see *Voice*). The challenge should be sounded sparingly, from a high point with a wide view. It seems to be most effective early in the morning and late in the afternoon.

Of several other hunting methods, the simplest is to ride or walk the high country early in the season, scanning the parks and meadows. The horseman watches for sign and dismounts to hunt promising areas. When approaching a crest he also dismounts to glass the slopes, taking care not to spook the elk by skylining. He has to stay high since stalking can be almost

impossible from below. It is also worthwhile to sit on a lookout above pastures, trails, or natural crossings.

In some areas drives are conducted, with or without horses, in canyons or small, fairly steep valleys. The stands overlook clearings or open crossings where animals are likely to spill from the timber. The drivers move through the woods with the wind, as if driving deer, letting their scent push the elk out of cover. At other times an elk's very keen nose can be a problem, especially in mountain country where winds keep shifting. A man has to climb high and hunt down through the rising thermals. Elk also have exquisite hearing; they jump at the click of a camera shutter, or a carelessly worked rifle bolt, at telephoto distances. Their eyes are sensitive to motion, but not to stationary objects, and this characteristic favors the lookout.

Wapiti bulls contesting for harem.

A frequent drawback of drives is that a bull may be sufficiently spooked to gallop out at 35 miles an hour, clearing 6- or 7-foot obstacles. Ordinarily, elk move along at a slow walk or, if mildly suspicious, straighten their muzzles, lay back their antlers, and trot away. At moderate range a trotting elk presents a fair enough neck or heart-lung shot if the cover is not too dense.

Many bulls have been jumped and killed at 30 yards in timber, but most shots are made at ranges of 150 to 300 yards or so. For late-season hunting or where the game keeps to thick cover, a 2½-power rifle scope may be a good choice, whereas a 4-power scope sighted in at 200 yards is usually better in the upper Rockies. Many hunters use the 7mm Magnum, .270, or .284 with 150-grain bullets, but the most popular cartridges are probably the .30-06 and the .300 Magnums with 180-grain bullets. For that matter, a 200-grain weight in the .338 is effective for such large, shock-resistant game.

Much of the habitat is rocky or blanketed with ground cover that makes trail reading difficult, but tracking is good on late-season snow. A large track does not always indicate a bull, but a lone track does, because cows seldom travel alone. Elk move in wide loops, occasionally looking back, and they bed watching their back trails. A tracker wants to parallel the trail or try to circle above and ahead. If he comes to a clearing he looks across and around it before stepping out; a bull may be watching attentively from the far side.

Elk feed actively from before dawn until midmorning, then rest and chew their cud, sometimes feeding sporadically but not moving much until midafternoon. Early in the morning and late in the afternoon promising areas are sunny slopes and meadows near timber. Bedding spots are often high on slopes with a wide view and rising air currents; in glassing such slopes or scouting them while on the move, look closely at unlittered spots around large trees, stumps, logs, or boulders—preferred loafing places. In warm weather the animals sometimes bed on river bars to stay cool and escape insects. In windy weather, lee slopes and timbered ravines become equally attractive. But many bulls also bed in thickets. Open areas are best on rainy or cool, humid days, when elk are most active. In dry, hot weather, midday still-hunting is profitable in heavy timber.

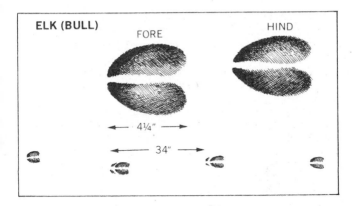

ELK (BULL)   FORE   HIND

4¼″

34″

TRACKS & SIGN: Elk tracks are somewhat smaller and rounder than those of a moose, much larger and rounder than a deer's. The cloven hoofs of a mature elk leave prints averaging 4 to 4½ inches long. At a walk, the hind foot usually comes down slightly ahead of the front print, partly covering it, and the pace is often 60 inches long. The fore and hind feet are more apt to print separately at a gallop, and a big bull's running pace can be as long as 14 feet. The dewclaws usually print in snow or soft ground.

When the hunting season opens, the scat in grassy pastures may be flattened chips, rather like cattle dung. The dried grass and browse of fall will change the droppings to dark pellets like deer scat but larger, sometimes more than an inch long. Rutting bulls horn and thrash saplings or large shrubs, and the mature ones also horn and scuff out muddy wallows where they urinate and defecate copiously. Wallows have a strong, musky odor. They are often smelled before they are seen; occasionally, so are rutting bulls.

Roosevelt elk sometimes gnaw away narrow strips of tree bark, then rub the wood with their lachrymal glands. The purpose of these scent posts is unknown, but newly stripped bark is a sign of elk in the vicinity.

VOICE: Elk snort and grunt, and the young can squeal. Cows neigh to their calves, but the usual warning call is a sharp snort often described as a bark. Cows also bugle, but they do it more in spring than fall and never so imperiously as bulls. A rutting bull emits a bellow that changes immediately to a loud, shrill scream or whistle, terminated by a series of grunts. Only the whistling sound carries over long distances. It is often heard, for elk are America's noisiest deer, and a hunter elicits a response from bulls by imitating only this portion of the call.

Moose *(Alces alces)*
COMMON & REGIONAL NAMES: *l'original.*

DESCRIPTION & DISTRIBUTION: In the Northwest after a couple of heavy frosts a bull moose is sometimes spotted 2 miles away, a white-crowned black splotch standing among newly leafless willow stalks or nibbling at stunted bushes above timber line. His antlers, having shed their dried velvet except for cracked patches in the enormous ladles of the palms, have not yet absorbed an earthy stain. They flash like a beacon, yet a long look through the spotting scope fails to confirm their true size because the animal's body and head are so enormous. The hunter lines up an aspen grove and a rocky bluff to mark the bull's location, then begins the long approach. He may get within 350 yards, close enough for a better appraisal and a shot.

Far to the east, on the Oba River in Ontario, a moose can be a black shadow oozing through dense conifer stands. Sometimes a sudden thirst or the nearness of a cow sends him crashing through the brush, but now he turns his head sideward to ease his rack silently through narrow spaces. The guide has led his client still-hunting along the edges of browse thickets and spongy muskeg, put him on stand at a beaver pond, and followed tantalizing trails. Now he will try the canoe and perhaps the birchbark megaphone he uses to bawl like a lustful cow moose. As he paddles slowly along the shoreline, the hunter kneels near the bow, holding an iron-sighted .35 lever-action. Next to him is a bolt-action 7mm Magnum with a variable-power scope, for at several meanders the view opens and the range will be hardly more predictable than the game. The canoe drifts past a woody point, and there, only belly deep in more than 3 feet of water, a gleaming bull drops a lily stem. A black ravel of velvet still festoons one side of his dripping rack. His great ears twitch as he lifts his head. Catching a sound or scent, he heads up the bank in splashing strides. The hunter, having once helped to quarter a moose in thigh-deep water, forces himself to wait until the bull is well out before claiming his giant trophy.

The moose is North America's biggest game, the world's largest deer. Asia has two subspecies, Europe one, America four. The eastern, or Canadian, moose *(A. a. americana)* ranges from Newfoundland and Nova Scotia across the Maritimes and eastern Ontario; it is also present, but scarce and protected, in the woods of Maine, New Hampshire, and Vermont. The northwestern moose *(A. a. andersoni)* is protected in upper Wisconsin, Michigan, and North Dakota but is plentiful and hunted from western Ontario to central British Columbia, as well as northward through the Northwest Territories and the eastern Yukon. Limited hunting is also permitted in Minnesota, where the moose have increased in recent years. The eastern and northwestern races are so much alike that they are grouped together in the Boone and Crockett record book. A mature bull of either type weighs from 1,000 to 1,400 pounds or so, and a good one may have a 5-foot antler spread. A cow weighs 600 or 800 pounds.

Neighboring them in the Rockies is the smallest and palest, the Wyoming moose *(A. a. shirasi),* also called the Shiras or Yellowstone moose. A Wyoming bull seldom weighs more than about 1,200 pounds or reaches above 6 feet at the withers. A mature cow is apt to be smaller. The animals range through Wyoming, Utah, Montana, Idaho, and southeastern British Columbia, occasionally straying into Washington and Colorado.

Largest and darkest of all is the Alaskan, or Alaska-Yukon, moose *(A. a. gigas),* a slope-shouldered relic of the age of mammoths. A bull may stand 7½ feet high, weigh close to 1,800 pounds, and carry more than 85 pounds of antler. It ranges through all of Alaska except the woodless west and north, and is also hunted in the Yukon, the adjacent part of the Northwest Territories, and northwestern British Columbia. The best hunting for tremendous racks is on the Kenai Peninsula and around Rainy Pass in Alaska, and in the central Yukon.

The current world record is an Alaskan trophy taken by Bert Klineburger in 1961 at Mount Susitna. Its spread is a hair less than 6½ feet. At one time moose were scored on spread

638/Big Game

Sample trophy chart and Boone and Crockett scoring procedure.

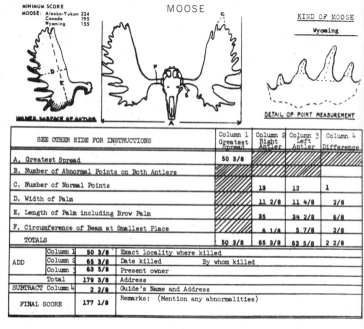

MINIMUM SCORE
MOOSE: Alaska-Yukon 224
Canada 195
Wyoming 155

MOOSE

KIND OF MOOSE

Wyoming

LOWER SURFACE OF ANTLER

DETAIL OF POINT MEASUREMENT

SEE OTHER SIDE FOR INSTRUCTIONS	Column 1 Greatest Spread	Column 2 Right Antler	Column 3 Left Antler	Column 4 Difference
A. Greatest Spread	50 3/8			
B. Number of Abnormal Points on Both Antlers				
C. Number of Normal Points		13	12	1
D. Width of Palm		11 2/8	11 4/8	2/8
E. Length of Palm including Brow Palm		35	34 2/8	6/8
F. Circumference of Beam at Smallest Place		6 1/8	5 7/8	2/8
TOTALS	50 3/8	65 3/8	63 5/8	2 2/8

ADD	Column 1	50 3/8	Exact locality where killed
	Column 2	65 3/8	Date killed By whom killed
	Column 3	63 5/8	Present owner
	Total	179 3/8	Address
SUBTRACT	Column 4	2 2/8	Guide's Name and Address
FINAL SCORE		177 1/8	Remarks: (Mention any abnormalities)

Instructions

All measurements must be made with a flexible steel tape to the nearest one-eighth of an inch. Wherever it is necessary to change direction of measurement, mark a control point and swing tape at this point. To simplify addition, please enter fractional figures in **eighths.**

Official measurements cannot be taken for at least sixty days after the animal was killed. **Please submit photographs.**

A. Greatest Spread measured in a straight line at right angles to the center line of the skull.

B. Number of Abnormal Points on Both Antlers. Abnormal points are generally considered to be those nontypical in shape or location.

C. Number of Normal Points. Normal points are those which project from the outer edge of the antler. To be counted a point, a projection must be at least one inch long and the length must exceed the breadth of

the point's base. The breadth need not be computed from the deepest adjacent dips in the palmation. The length may be measured to any location—at least one inch from the tip—at which the length of the point exceeds its breadth.

D. Width of Palm taken in contact with the surface across the under side of the palm, at right angles to the inside edge of palm, to a dip between points at the greatest width of palm. Measure width of palm from midpoints of edges of palms.

E. Length of Palm including Brow Palm taken in contact with the surface along the under side of the palm, parallel to the inner edge from dips between points at the greatest length of palm. If a deep bay is present in the palm, measure palm length across the open bay if the proper line of measurement crosses the bay.

F. Circumference of Beam at Smallest Place. Needs no explanation.

alone, and the first-place eastern trophy was a 71⅝-inch rack from a Maine moose shot at the turn of the century. Now scoring is determined by spread, palm length and width, girth of beams between skull and palms, number of points, and symmetry. The current first-place holder is 66⅝ inches wide. The record for Wyoming moose is a rack spreading 53 inches.

Most hunters consider moose the toughest antler trophy to judge even when a bull stands in the open. A moose is apt to be 8 to 10 feet long from nose to almost vestigial tail, its shoulder 5½ to 7½ feet high, its rack 8 or 10 feet above its enormous hoofs and looking merely adequate. A front or rear view helps, for a good rack hangs far out, about twice as wide as the chest. The legs, adapted for wading, are often more than 40 inches long, yet a good set of antlers, if upended on the ground, would reach above the legs, perhaps to the middle of the body. If a bull is seen in profile, the antlers ought to shade the eyes and a considerable portion of the short neck. The small points edging the palms will probably be impossible to count.

A moose's body tapers from the high, bulky chest area to relatively slim hindquarters. At a distance it looks coal-black, but actually shades to dark or rusty brown on head, neck, withers, and back. The belly is slightly lighter and the legs fade to gray from the hocks on down. It has a woolly undercoat and long, straight guard hair that bleaches to gray-brown through the winter. After shedding in spring or early summer, an old bull again looks very dark, while a young one or a cow is likely to be cocoa colored. The hair lengthens to a 5- or 6-inch mane on the thick, short neck. A pendulous bearded dewlap called a bell dangles from the throat. Its function remains unproved, but it looks as if it helps to drain off water when a moose raises its head after clipping aquatic plants or drinking. The dark brown eyes are small, but the ears, which move independently and incessantly, are larger than a mule's. The ponderous, mulish face has a very large, haired, flexible, overhanging nose and upper lip that are useful in stripping tough browse.

The range of the species, covering almost the entire North, has shrunk very little in historic times. In the lower Rockies it has expanded, and moose have also fared exceptionally well in Newfoundland, where they were introduced from the mainland in 1904. They have never been as abundant as the smaller deer, but the annual harvest is light because much of the habitat is remote and a moose hunt is often expensive and lengthy. Including about 140,000 moose in Alaska, the United States probably has close to 170,000; estimates for the vast Canadian woodlands run from a comparable number to perhaps twice as many.

Moose are hunted in all Canadian provinces and territories, and currently in six states—Alaska, Idaho, Montana, Utah, Wyoming, and Minnesota. The Alaskan season opens in August. In the Northwest Territories it opens in July. Elsewhere it usually runs from early or mid-September to the end of the month if numbers are low, or into late fall or winter if numbers are high. Special permit systems protect faltering populations, while overcrowding in some areas is alleviated by either-sex hunting. Cows and young bulls have no trophy value but make fine eating. The flesh of old bulls can become tough and rank by the end of September when the rut reaches its peak. At present, the best hunting is in Alaska, the Yukon, the Mackenzie District of the Northwest Territories, eastern Idaho, western Wyoming, northern Alberta, northern Ontario, and Newfoundland.

GAME BEHAVIOR & HUNTING HABITAT: Moose form no herds, but on occasion several will feed together tolerantly or frequent the same small area for extended periods. If the snow gets very deep a small group may yard up in a good browsing spot—a habit more common among eastern moose than in the West—but as soon as the food dwindles the animals disperse.

By mid-August a bull's antlers are hardening, and he soon begins to polish off the withering velvet and thrash the brush in preparation for the rut. Within a month he searches for a cow. For the week or ten days of her oestrus, he stays with her and with her calf if she has one, then searches for another mate. Moose are most unpredictable at this time. Sometimes a bull permits a younger bull to linger nearby in futile hope, though the next one to come along will be chased. Sometimes a bull will also charge a man or, for that matter, a locomotive, though it is safer to approach a bull in autumn than a cow with a calf in spring or early summer. If a genuine rival appears, the bulls start toward each other, stiff-legged, heads lowered, and meet with a rattling of antlers. (A hunter can occasionally attract a bull by rattling sticks or a pair of antlers together, or by thrashing

bushes.) The fight is a shoving and jabbing match. A moose that goes down usually quits. Few of the fights end in death.

In relatively flat, timbered eastern regions where moose cannot often be spotted and stalked from afar, the onset of the rut is the time for calling. Bulls do not bugle, but females attract mates with a moaning trumpet call. Imitation is usually left to the guide, who has listened to moose and practiced for years. Using a birchbark horn or merely cupping his hands, he produces a drawn-out, bawling bovine wail. Unheard by the hunter, any bull in the vicinity is probably grunting in reply. A young one, all lust and no caution, is liable to come crashing into view. An older one comes slowly, not quite convinced, circling for scent. He may decide against the enterprise or take hours to show himself. Calling is most effective in the evening from a canoe, a hiding spot on shore, or a strip of woods that runs into a meadow. The object is to have a good view from concealment in a place where a cow might well be calling. On a calm evening when sound carries far, deception can be heightened by dribbling a hatful of water into a lake or river; the sound of a cow urinating often rouses a bull and dispels his suspicions.

Wyoming bull moose with dry flakes of velvet on palms.

The rut subsides in late October, and most calves are born in May or early June, after a gestation period of about eight months. A two-year-old cow almost invariably bears a single calf; about 15 percent of older cows produce twins. Born in a thicket of trees or bush, a new calf is a wobbly reddish-brown creature weighing between 20 and 35 pounds.

A two-week-old calf swims well, can outrun a man, and is tended by a very protective mother, yet mortality is high. The prospect is poor for a calf born to a winter-starved cow, and weak ones die in cold, wet weather. A few die in accidents or are killed by wolves, bears, or wolverines. They also suffer from a variety of parasites and diseases, the most deadly of which is a roundworm disease called "moose sickness." The average life span is ten to fifteen years or possibly longer.

Where cows can be hunted, those with calves should be passed up because an orphan seldom survives the winter. A calf remains with its mother for almost a year.

A long-yearling bull develops spikes, forks, or a small, flat rack. The second set is a wider, pronged formation called a bootjack, the third shows real palmation, and the fourth has the basins of maturity but is still small. A bull's finest antlers develop between his fifth and tenth year, then deteriorate, and most of the big trophies are probably seven or eight years old.

Both heredity and habitat influence the abundance of great racks. A moose seeks dense coniferous forest for rest and escape cover, but needs second-growth spaces for browsing. "Moose" is an Algonquian word for "twig-eater," and the twigs must be within reach. In spring and summer the animals graze on sedges, grasses, lichens, ground birch, and the like, and feed heavily on marsh and aquatic plants—horsetail, waterlily, pondlily, watershield, wild celery, wild rice, pondweed. Autumn gradually forces the moose back to browsing. From Alaska to Newfoundland, hunters who know the ways of moose look for game near willow, aspen, and birch. Other important food sources are maple, dogwood, alder, serviceberry, mountain ash, fir, balsam poplar, and saplings, bushes, or low-branched trees.

Considering their tremendous size, moose are not hard to kill. Trophy bulls have fallen to 130-grain, .270 loads. A more sensible minimum, however, is a 175-grain bullet in a 7mm Magnum. In eastern woods where brush penetration is more crucial than long-range possibilities, efficient calibers include the .30-06, .35, .338, .348, .358, .350 Magnum, and .444. Even in that fairly flat country a 7x35mm binocular and 20-power spotting scope are recommended for scanning far slopes and sizing up trophies. If two rifles are packed, one may be aperture-sighted, the other equipped for longer range with a scope of medium or variable magnification. If a single rifle is packed, a 2½-power scope is an effective compromise.

In some of the mountainous western range, moose shift with the seasons, but the movement may come late in a mild fall or may cover only 5 or 10 miles to willowed creek bottoms. As the snow begins to deepen, hunting improves at low elevations. Nonetheless, a binocular and spotting scope remain essential in most regions. In the Rockies, western Canada, and Alaska, where shots are usually made at more than 200 yards, a 4-power or variable-power scope can be mounted over a 7mm Magnum or one of the .300 Magnums.

Mountain hunting is mostly riding from one ridge or wide meadow to the next, glassing each opening before moving out of the timber. A moose has rather weak vision but is quick to notice movement and has extraordinary hearing and scenting ability. Good scouting spots are knolls above waters, meadows, or edges of browse thickets. Though a bull is addicted to salt licks while his antlers are growing, he seldom goes looking for them in the fall. He may leave a good feeding spot only to drink —most often late in the day—and may stay in a single large willow clump for a fortnight. Perhaps he will bed right there or climb a little way into taller timber during the warm hours. A bed is nothing more than an oval depression in snow, brush, or tall grass, a hidden spot with a quick escape route.

When a distant moose is spotted, it is stalked like an elk, preferably from above. Unless the wind shifts the target is apt to be standing still or moving slowly, and a rifleman should try to avoid hitting the shoulder blade, as the heavy bone can deflect a bullet. The best zone of aim is the lung area, behind the shoulder. Springing moose have been clocked at more than 40 miles an hour, and their normal running speed, like that of most deer, is between 30 and 35. However a moose almost invariably stops and looks back after running a short distance or entering a fringe of cover. In some situations a good marksman can be confident

of hitting a trotting moose cleanly, but unless the range is fairly short he is well advised to wait for a fast-running bull to pause.

In addition to riding and glassing in mountain country, or canoeing and calling in the lowlands, still-hunting can be productive, especially at daybreak and dusk. A strong wind tends to keep moose in hiding, but they become most active right after a cool, windy period. A hunter can work upwind along shorelines or moose trails, watching nearby water and thickets, or he can move along any elevations where he has found beds. He goes very slowly, stopping every 40 or 50 yards to listen and look. He crouches to peer beneath low branches, and watches for black swatches of hide or pale antlers. He parallels a moose trail, aware that a suspicious bull will circle to get scent or sound, and if the trail begins to zigzag or leads into a dense thicket, he listens again, ready to jump a bedded moose.

TRACKS & SIGN: Larger and more pointed than an elk track, a moose print is usually over 5 inches long, and a prime bull is apt to sink a track 6 inches long, 4½ inches wide. The lobes are close together but splay somewhat in snow or mud or when running. It is also on a soft surface or at a run that the high dewclaws sometimes print behind the cloven hoof, lengthening the overall print to as much as 10 inches. The stride ranges

Bull moose bugling during peak of rut.

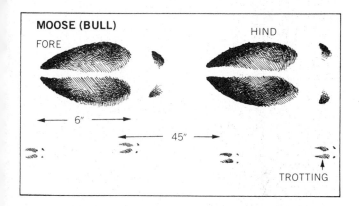

MOOSE (BULL)

FORE

HIND

6"

45"

TROTTING

from 3½ to nearly 6 feet and may lengthen to more than 8 feet at a fast trot. The trail is wider and deeper than that of smaller deer, and more apt to skirt obstructions.

Dung may form chips and splatters where moose are feeding on aquatic plants and grass. Browse produces pellets, occasionally round but usually oblong and larger than deer droppings. A length of 1½ or 1¾ inches is typical. Dry, woody, late-season browse gives pellets a distinctive appearance, like compressed sawdust, and the quantity is large enough to make a hunter suspect moose rather than elk scat.

A bedding depression is identified by tracks and droppings. The rutting wallow is more distinctive. A bull stimulates his mate by pawing and horning a shallow, ragged patch of ground, perhaps 4 feet long, 3 feet wide, several inches deep, then urinating copiously and wallowing in the muddied saucer. The cow rolls in it, too, and unattached moose are drawn to recently used wallows. These are torn, muddy, odorous.

VOICE: Cows grunt to their calves, and calves grunt and bleat. Adults are mostly silent except in the rut. A guide who "talks to the bulls" imitates a cow's loud, bawling mating call— *uuh-wuaugha.* He may repeat it several times, then wait. The bull's reply is a repeated grunt—*ng-uh!* But if the hunter hears any signal of the bull's arrival, it is more apt to be the smashing of brush.

Index

Picture references are in italics